KILLING THE TRUTH

KILLING THE TRUTH
Deceit and Deception in the JFK Case

Harrison Edward Livingstone

Carroll & Graf Publishers, Inc.
New York

Copyright © 1993 by Harrison Edward Livingstone

First Carroll & Graf edition 1993

Carroll & Graf Publishers, Inc.
260 Fifth Avenue
New York, NY 10001

Library of Congress Cataloging-in-Publication Data

Livingstone, Harrison Edward.
  Killing the truth : deceit and deception in the JFK case /
Harrison Edward Livingstone.—1st Carroll & Graf ed.
      p.   cm.
  Includes bibliographical references and index.
  ISBN 0-88184-428-4 : $27.95
  1. Kennedy, John F. (John Fitzgerald), 1917–1963—Assassination.
I. Title.
E842.9.L59   1993
364.1'524'0973—dc20   93-27037
                                                           CIP

Manufactured in the United States of America

This book is dedicated to the *army* of people who came to my assistance after I took a stand against the excesses, abuses, and virulent attacks of the "research community." I say **thank you** from the bottom of my heart.

I also dedicate this book to Herman Graf, Kent Carroll, Laura Langlie, and everybody else at Carroll & Graf.

And also to
Penn Jones, Jr., and his wife, Elaine

They have never lost their faithfulness to the truth and doing what is right in this life. Neither has ever ceased to be fearless and courageous in stating the truth as they know it, and remaining faithful to friends.

During a visit in early 1993, I tested Penn's mind and made numbers of statements to him on certain key aspects of the evidence. On those, and especially with comments about key researchers, he repeatedly responded with this command: *"Print it!"* About some of the leading researchers, Penn has said, "These people are pretty terrible people." With regard to one of the best known, he said, "I have always believed he was an agent."

Whatever is hidden away will be brought
out into the open, and whatever is
covered up
will be found and brought to light.

Luke 8:17

CONTENTS

ACKNOWLEDGMENTS

As usual, there are so many people I would like to thank for helping me along the way. Some give invaluable moral support, and others a great deal of work and research.

First of all, I want to thank Kathlee Fitzgerald, who throughout the tragic sickness and loss of her mother, helped me enormously. And her husband, "Fitz" D. C. Fitzgerald, and her sons, Jesse and Nathan, for loaning her to me repeatedly. And their good friends in Houston, Chip and Clare Pickard.

Special thanks are owed to the Assassination Information Center in Dallas and those who devote so much of their time to it: Robert Johnson, the director of archives; Coke Buchanan; Belita Nelson; John Nagel; Melissa Johnson; and Larry Howard.

Martin Shackelford, although we disagree on some points, is one of the most valuable of all researchers into the assassination of John Kennedy. Jerry Rose, who has put so much effort into publishing *The Third Decade,* has been a wellspring of strength to so many. I'd also like to thank Bob Campbell for his kind words, telling me that we have to "stay at it," as JFK said to his brother, and Pat Dumais, for her constant information. And thanks to Amanda Talbott for her wonderful ability to take my mind off my work, except when I'm broadcasting.

Kevin Brennan for his brilliant legal work and enjoyable company in various Irish taverns on St. Patty's Day in New York at the old port.

I would like to thank Paul Henwood for his great contribution to my research.

And Constance Wagner in Dallas for her devoted friendship, support, and faithful transcriptions of audio- and videotape.

Thanks to Kevin McCarthy in Dallas for his tapes of the Dallas doctors, and for invaluable assistance.

Also thanks to Jim Ewell. I'd also like to thank Al Maddox and Tony Ingargiola for their interviews.

There are numerous folks who keep me updated by sending clippings and other material I need to know about. I owe a debt of gratitude to Cindy McNeill, an attorney in Houston, for keeping me well informed. Cindy also researches the case, and her ideas are stimulating and worthwhile.

Especially do I care about Penn Jones and his wife, Elaine, for many kindnesses and much information and sources.

While a student at Texas A&M, Angela Parker has been one of my many faithful researchers. She has started "Aggies for Truth," a student group devoted to finding the truth in John Kennedy's murder, and training researchers, and is the president. We wish her well.

I'm also indebted to Vince Palamara, Chris Sharrett, Josiah Thompson, William Turner, Teresa Amato, Steve Schassler, Tim McReynolds, Stephanie C., Fred Newcomb, Perry Adams, Larry Haapanen, Dr. Joseph Lee Thimes, Evan Marshall, Dr. Robert B. Livingston, Dr. Donald Siple, Karen Wright, Stan Szerszen, Todd Vaughan, Ray Carroll, Gary Rowell, Steve Barber, Ken Degazio, Craig Ciccone, Roger Feinman, Bill Poulte, Dr. Gary Aguilar, Dr. Randy Robertson, Richard Tobias, Patrick Boyles, Bob Goodman, Jim Lesar, John Judge, John Jones, Seth Kerker, Nancy Wertz, Peggy down in Dallas, Dave Perry, Steve Foster, Peter McKenna, Tony Marsh, Emory Brown, Doug Mizzer, Kathy Cunningham, Paul Hoch, John Jones, Jack Brazil, Paul Rothermel, Madeleine Brown, Earl Golz, Jack White, Buck Revell, Farris Rookstool, Marco Miranda, Joe Butka, and Rick Waybright for his constant assistance and the risks he takes. Rick has been the greatest of friends over the past year and has produced much valuable work.

Sheriff Jim Bowles has been untiring in his assistance over the years, always available for questions at the drop of a hat, and I thank him for the personal attention he gave to my acoustics manuscript.

I also thank Diana Bowron for granting me the exclusive interview in this book, and for all of her time. I am sworn never to reveal her whereabouts.

I'd also like to thank Monte Evans for the great review he wrote of *High Treason 2*.

Richard Gallen, who is an attorney for Carroll & Graf, has also extended good advice and help.

In particular, I'd like to thank the sculptor Judy Schwabacher, of Lancaster, California, for giving me a priceless bronze bust of John Kennedy she made. For a time it was displayed in the city hall of Lancaster, and she wrote me to say that she wanted me to have it because, she said, my writing conveyed more caring for Kennedy than so many others that she had read.

This may be the place to make some corrections for the last book, *High Treason 2,* whose index confused Lawrence Howard with Larry Howard, and somewhere along the line before the first book, typists and computers dropped Larry Harris's name as coauthor of *Cover-up* with Gary Shaw, and dropped Christopher Sharrett's name and the relevant citation for "The Assassination of Dr. Martin Luther King and the 'Raoul' Mystery: Are We Being Sidetracked?" by Richard E. Sprague and Christopher Sharrett, published in *People and the Pursuit of Truth,* June 1977.

There are many other personal friends who continue to stand by me and support the huge efforts and intense work I often do. Their support is emotional support and can be held responsible for what success I have had. The warmth and affection I have in the City of Baltimore from perhaps a thousand friends, and the beauty and love of the city itself is my sustaining strength.

Thank You.

Harrison E. Livingstone

PREFACE

In my last book, *High Treason 2,* I said that I would not write another book on the assassination of John F. Kennedy.

But I never finished this work, and too many letters came along with questions, and expressing the need for me to go on. Besides, I knew I wasn't done. I certainly hope I can go back to my life somewhere along the line.

It must be admitted that the former leadership of the "critical community" so angered me that I responded to the anguished outcries of hundreds of researchers expressing their criticism of the critics, who were the media darlings. So I took a stand against the Old Guard, or the Establishment among the critics, and as many people know, this has cost me heavily, with terrible slanders and smears.

But it was *The Journal of the American Medical Association's* press conference and articles in May 1992, shortly after *High Treason 2* was published, which pushed me over the edge. Within days I was writing again, never dreaming that there was so much still in me that ultimately became this book. I was pushed along day and night without rest or the joy of life for another year.

The Old Guard has misled us all these years. People such as Mark Lane, Robert Groden, David Lifton, Gary Shaw, Mary Ferrell, Gary Mack, Cyril Wecht, and Harold Weisberg have nothing new to add to this case but have obstructed new research, new discoveries, and new evidence, obstructed anything at all that threatens their control.

I am not above criticism, and am certainly fallible as human beings go. I make mistakes—sometimes too many of them—and I have been suckered and misled by some or all of the above leaders. I think now that they have misled all of us and that the real evidence of conspiracy does not lie in criticisms of the magic-bullet theory or most if not all of what they have put forward. And, too often, they pretend to have discovered what others have in fact discovered or developed.

Well, We the People protest, and We the People have raised a rebellion against them. I am not saying this lightly, because I know how many people have come over to my standard. I may not be allowed to speak at any of the meetings run by the above cabal, but I can safely say that I speak for the large majority of active researchers today.

I don't want or need this kind of a war in my life, but I am doing it because I am a patriot, and I feel that these people are not that at all, but are engaging in political warfare against their fellows.

For John Kennedy's murder was a political murder, and certain political and economic victories for one side flowed out of it.

I want to quote from a letter written on February 10, 1993, from Steve Barber to me. "Harry, I deeply appreciate all the kind things you said in here about me, and I like you too, *very* much. As I told Kathlee Fitzgerald during our phone conversation, *you* are the *one and only* person whom I think is really out to find the true facts in this case— rather than boost your ego like I've seen so many of them do, and I'm so proud of you for having the guts to do the work you're doing. Your work is along the lines of Penn Jones'. He was honest and caring too—and I'm just really glad the world has you in it."

I printed this because as a lot of people know, Barber bitterly attacked me in a pamphlet after my first book came out. I listened to what he had to say and realized that he was right and that I was wrong. I was wrong because I listened to a so-called expert in our community who had moved in really close to me, and I was misled. I let him take me over, and I was wrong. I was a fool.

It would seem that this entire operation, until I and some others got into it, was some sort of a police or FBI operation. An intelligence operation, definitely run by those who want to cover up the murder. They put forward actors as witnesses in Dallas, false and doctored evidence, and constantly embellish, change, and distort whatever new evidence appears in the case. I know for a fact that the Dallas FBI office seeks to control this case and keep down any important evidence. Some of their actions flow from the contempt the above heirarchy engenders, which is understandable. The FBI's actions in trying to bury real evidence is not understandable, except that they have to cover their ass. Soon it is easier to scrutinize the bearers of the message rather than the message or evidence, and reject it if the messenger can be discredited.

Discrediting the messenger or researcher becomes of primary importance. When I personally experience such intense slander from people who had been close to me, stories so false they almost killed me, then

I knew that they are dangerous, because no normal person would undertake to ruin another's life simply because they don't like that person.

I am free in this country to criticize their work, but their retaliation is in the form of character assassination, and that is very, very wrong. And there is damn little that can be done about it after the damage is done.

An enormous problem in the evidence was overlooked when the House Assassinations Committee found in 1978 that the first shots were at about frame 157 of the Zapruder film. Since the Warren Commission said that it was impossible to fire until the car came out from beneath the tree at frame 210, how could this be? The House Committee indicated that there must have been a hole in the leaves and branches that the sniper could see through at that point. Surely such a gap would have been observed by the police and federal agents who studied the line of fire from the alleged sniper's window.

But we know from the trajectories that some of those shots came from low down.

Enough credit cannot be shown to some of the earliest researchers, such as Dick Sprague (Richard E. Sprague, not Richard A. Sprague, the first chief counsel of the House Assassinations Committee), who did the earliest and most comprehensive studies of the photographic evidence, later co-opted by various photo technicians and publicists for the case, without their giving due credit (a common disease in academic and assassination research circles). Sprague's landmark articles appeared in *Computers and Automation*[1] and later *Computers and People*. At the time, computers and anything connected with them were very exotic science and technology. Sylvia Meagher expresses her gratitude to Sprague in her book *Accessories After the Fact,* in a footnote stating that Sprague found the photographs and films of some twenty people overlooked by the Warren Commission in their sloppy handling of the evidence.[2]

Christopher Sharrett says that Sprague "was the founding father of the photographic evidence." I might add that Harold Weisberg did a certain amount of work with the visuals as well in those early years of inquiry into the assassination. It is worthwhile to note another article to which many researchers owe a lot: "The Framing of Lee Harvey Oswald."[3]

It is unfortunate that Sprague, like so many other researchers, as Christopher Sharrett relates, was asked by Robert Blakey to go home, after being invited to come to Washington, and the research and evidence was ignored. Those who remained as consultants to the Committee were those who could validate the Committee's needs, such as the wrong motorcycle policeman in the wrong place. Such treatment had a bad effect on the minds of many, and Sprague lashed out at any handy target. From that moment on, paranoia and its results were far more endemic in the "critical community." Sprague began accusing a number of handy targets as being CIA agents.

Sharrett writes, "The November 24, 1967, issue of *Life* is all the more evidence of Dick's tireless work. All the photos in that famous issue were discovered in Dallas by Dick Sprague; he gave them to *Life* on the assumption that they would do a follow-up to their 1966 'A Matter of Reasonable Doubt' issue, calling for a new investigation. The 1967 issue was merely a memoir by Connally and said nothing at all about the question of conspiracy. Dick never received credit for finding these photos."[4] They just used him.

We need to go back to our origins in this case and who did what, because there are too many usurpers and opportunists who have made a name for themselves fooling the public as to who they really are. Some people, for instance, are known to have a storehouse of evidence, but it does not get out to the public except in small doses, and then only for money.

Chris Sharrett writes me that "I hope you can make a pitch to get all of those news films the media owns (unless they were trashed by now) free from the media organizations. The Couch, Weigman, Sanderson, Rickerby, and Alyea films are very important—almost *all* of the films and stills taken by the guys in the press cars have evidentiary value and the media shows them, if at all, only in tiny snippets."[5]

Sheldon Inkol sent along the following from an essay by James Shelby Downard in an anthology called *Apocalypse Culture:* "Something died in the American people on November 22, 1963—call it idealism, innocence or the quest for moral excellence. It is the transformation of human beings which is the authentic reason and motive for the Kennedy murder and until so-called conspiracy theorists can accept this very real element, they will be reduced to so many eccentrics amusing a tiny remnant of dilettantes and hobbyists."[6]

Writing this book and dealing with much that is within it was very painful. First, because I am dealing with the tragedy of John Kennedy's murder, which, after thirty years, is as painful as it was when it happened; and second, because I have felt forced to discuss personalities as well as my own personal experience. Self-exposure is one of the most difficult things in life, and it is not for any self-aggrandizement that I do it, but because of feeling beset by monsters, far beyond what is right and proper in this life.

Not to speak of the immense amount of effort in research, interviews, and writing in a book of this scope. I have written two back-to-back monsters that all but ruined my health in the space of fewer than three years. There has been an enormous achievement in this work that should have won national attention, but I have no doubt but that they will look the other way, just for the same reasons that the Kennedy case has always been covered up. Nobody dares give any real credit to any of us doing this work.

In a way, this book is a tale of human failings, of the easy corruptibility of humanity. The truth is that it's very easy for many writers, witnesses, experts, and investigators to invent things and declare facts which aren't easy to expose as false. The bigger the lie, the easier it is to tell it or to be believed. Such invention is very common in our academic and political lives, and this is why we're shortchanged on the truth so often.

Stuart rose from the ditch, climbed into his car, and started up the road that led toward the north. The sun was just coming up over the hills on his right. As he peered ahead into the great land that stretched before him, the way seemed long. But the sky was bright, and he somehow felt he was headed in the right direction.[7]

INTRODUCTION

After the Warren Commission's report was issued in 1964, in time for Lyndon Johnson to be absolved of any complicity in the crime of murdering President John F. Kennedy and be elected president, a new phenomenon—soon to be an industry—arose on the American scene. The FBI, the Dallas police, the Texas Department of Public Safety, and the Warren Commission had closed up shop regarding the assassination before the election of 1964. Lyndon Johnson had appointed the Warren Commission—mostly friends of his—and had ordered the Justice Department and the FBI to seize all the evidence from the Dallas police and take it to Washington, D.C., something they had no jurisdiction to do. This dictatorial act killed any further chance of getting the truth out. Thus the whole investigation was turned over to amateurs, and from that moment on we became a target.

In the beginning, the phenomenon seemed innocent enough, masked in the guise of criticism of the Warren Report, but soon this undisciplined and unsupervised (or was it?) business would become a circle of a special sort, attracting flimflam artists, con men, small-time hustlers, inspired amateurs, big-time writers, government agents, agents of the conspiracy, and some of the major hoaxers of our time. It was open season on the truth and Americans. Certainly honest, well-intentioned, genuine folks have been attracted to this research. But self-aggrandizement dominated. This is especially true in the rondo of gossip that consumes those for whom the lack of a social life was one of the attractions in the assassination research cult.

Gossips have a tendency to believe what they hear, and the members of the assassination research cult are especially susceptible to this vice. Like so many of their assumptions in this case, the cultists and sensationalists assume to be true whatever one of them says, and don't ask the right questions.

We are vulnerable to persuasion. There were so many things wrong with the Warren Report—which found that a single lone assassin killed the president—it seemed easy to find a conspiracy in the case. Very quickly, the public was duped. The real case remained hidden from us.

Harold Weisberg first began his series of books on the Warren Report, its documents, and the medical evidence, beginning with his self-published *Whitewash* in 1965. He also wrote about Martin Luther King, Jr.'s, assassination and claimed that James Earl Ray was innocent.* Weisberg had been a political warfare specialist for the OSS (Office of Strategic Services) in World War II, and after the war worked for the Department of State's intelligence division. He was eventually fired for alleged leftist connections. Weisberg says that he was able to provide H. L. Hunt with extensive information on a number of right-wing extremists, not long after John Kennedy died. Hunt financially supported every right-wing extremist who came along. They were all welcome in his office. See the chapter "Treason and the Smoke Screen" for further information on this subject and other leaders of the "critical community."

But Weisberg was never able to make clear what he believed about a conspiracy in the murder of JFK, and seems more to function as a "watcher" of others in the case. His interference with others and protection of his turf are legendary.

The first major book was Thomas G. Buchanan's *Who Killed Kennedy*, published in 1964 by Putnum. Buchanan's powerful book began to make waves. A Ph.D. graduate student, Edward Jay Epstein, published *Inquest* in 1966. This volume created something of a sensation in its analysis of how the Warren Commission operated. Epstein's focus in general was the functioning of governmental institutions when faced with a major crisis and the necessity to calm the public. The book— because it was critical of the Warren Commission—became a rallying point for many of those who thought there were major flaws in the conclusions of the Commission. It "raised monumental doubts," as Richard Goodwin was quoted as saying on the cover of the book. Goodwin was a special assistant to Presidents Kennedy and Johnson. Goodwin said, "The investigation should be reopened."

But nobody knew what Epstein thought about what really happened. In fact, he represented what was to become the fallback position of those who said, "Well, if the Warren Report's findings of a single

---

*See Harold Weisberg, *Frame-Up*, published by Outerbridge & Dienstfrey in 1971, and reissued by Carroll & Graf in 1993 as *Martin Luther King: The Assassination*, with a postscript in both editions by James Earl Ray.

assassin can't be perfectly defended, we have to prepare an alternative explanation for the murder of President Kennedy.''

Shortly after Epstein's first book appeared in 1966, Mark Lane, a lawyer, published *Rush to Judgment,* which rocketed to the top of the best-seller lists. This book began the laborious process of establishing that the CIA killed Kennedy, which though seemingly rational in terms of the footprints of intelligence traipsing through the evidence, was *prima facie* preposterous since Kennedy had appointed his own man head of the CIA, and since the Agency as a whole could not possibly have been involved in such a crime.

It is a reasonable explanation only if we are talking about renegade agents. It is not reasonable insofar as there has never been any credible evidence implicating any CIA agent in the murder. In addition, such an explanation runs counter to other more powerful and persuasive evidence that other factions were involved, and the CIA was the designated fall guy.

So why did Lane propose this theory? The CIA is not the main intelligence operation in America, and serves more as a front for the Defense Intelligence Agency and the National Security Agency. Off-the-shelf operations hidden from the public's eye, funded with what is known as the ''Black Budget,'' are the biggest secret scandal in Washington. It was safe accusing the CIA because they wouldn't do anything about it. The Agency was the perfect decoy.

Another reason why this theory was proposed is that various territories were being staked out early on: The CIA did it; Castro did it; the Soviets did it; the Mafia did it; and all of this had a purpose—if it was not planned that way. Nobody was saying that the Texans and their allies did it. Sure there were rumors to that effect, but until recently, nobody put forward any credible evidence. An early book, published in Europe in 1968 with the support of President DeGaulle of France and French intelligence, known as *Farewell America,* was the only work to outline cogently what really might have happened in the plot. Sources close to the Kennedys and private intelligence services were utilized by DeGaulle, a great admirer of Kennedy, in writing this book. Even then, the book was almost unknown and barely distributed in the United States.

Suddenly Weisberg roared off his Maryland ranch and onto the national scene of assassination research, flying to New Orleans, to Dallas repeatedly—paid for by H. L. Hunt's men—intent on denouncing and destroying *Farwell America* before it influenced anyone, especially Jim Garrison.

But why were Lane and Weisberg doing this? To control the evidence, developments, critics, and researchers? Most of all, they wanted to give the impression that there were investigators out there doing the job, and the great amateur extralegal investigation was under way.

The company that first published Mark Lane, the second major critic of the Warren Commission, was partly owned by Clint Murchison, one of the wealthiest Texas oilmen. Lane was the lawyer for the Reverend Jim Jones and was at the Jones Town infamy, where almost a thousand people were murdered. He also represented the Liberty Lobby—a demented right-wing group—in a later suit involving the JFK case. Lane became such a powerful figure in the case that others with far more to offer never reached the public's ear. Lane continues as general council for the Liberty Lobby and has represented them in a number of suits.

Smoke and the Smoke Screen

Unfortunately, doublespeak exists throughout the JFK case, from the Warren Commission and the House Assassination Committee to the "critical community," with its stage props and phony researchers. They are the *smoke screen*. Leading critics are like the machines on destroyer escorts blowing smoke to hide the battleships: the conspirators.

There is an "establishment" of "critics" that has co-opted the investigation into the assassination of President Kennedy and other political leaders. Some of these "critics'" in the "establishment" are bought and paid for. Some are outright spooks. Some can be blackmailed because of their sexual proclivities or past crimes. Some are opportunists who are easily duped and used. But the fact is, part of the research community of which I am technically a member is an intelligence operation from top to bottom. We obtained some of the truth from the best-known names, but we received a lot more misinformation. The assassination of John Kennedy has long been cheapened and trivialized.

The terrible truth is that this tragic case could have been solved long ago if we could have penetrated the smoke screen put up by the FBI, commissions, committees, and researchers, and brought out the real witnesses in the case, as this book seeks to do, before they're all dead.

It will be up to others to explore the leads I present, and to try to flesh out more of the story with facts before it is too late for history.

We have the illusion of freedom because of public criticism and discussion of historical, political, environmental, or economic affairs. Often little will ever be done about many of these affairs. It suits our controllers to keep us occupied with puzzles, games, and entertainment.

Issues are often raised by the Establishment just to get things out in the open, see what comes out of the woodwork, and then bury it. It was always that way. This is not to say that some matters of a very pressing nature will not change, but more often than not, the status quo is maintained.

I deal in hard medical evidence. *At the very moment* I was undertaking to get that out in the open, a massive public propaganda effort moved into the case and took it over, led by Oliver Stone and Time, Inc., owner of Time/Warner films. For half a century Time, Inc., an Establishment propaganda organ that had gone to great lengths over the years to ridicule any conspiracy theory, now exploited the case with a multiplicity of books and films. The media were overwhelmed with the onslaught.

Every sort of phony theory came out of the wordwork. Secret Service men rose up in the car behind the President and accidentally shot him, or the driver of the fatal car turned around and shot the President. The crucial new work was partially buried. Few readers knew what to believe, faced with so many books in the stores. Those who steal evidence, cook evidence, or create a dishonest circus atmosphere have done far more to kill the case than to help it.

The disinformation specialists had a field day in 1991–92.

JAMA

Finally, the ultimate in doublespeak came forward to bury this case in the memory hole. The whole power of the American Medical Association surfaced in 1992 like a pocket battleship to blast away evidence of conspiracy. The way it sounded to the public was that the two autopsy doctors disproved at a stroke all conspiracy "theory." To quote writer Dale Hawkins-Elliott, "When Humes and Boswell had their press conference the reporters' coverage was like a shrug and 'so that's that.' Can you imagine?! How can people still believe the bill of goods they've been trying to sell us all these years?"[1]

This is how clever propaganda works: The public really thought that the two autopsy doctors were at *The Journal of the American Medical Association*'s press conference on May 19, 1992, and they thought that the statements issued by the editor of *JAMA,* Dr. George Lundberg, at that press conference were in fact statements made by the doctors themselves.

* * *

It is time that the intellectual community, the media, and the authorities in the United States face the medical evidence in the assassination of John Kennedy. For too long, officially, those who ought to know better have turned their heads as though the evidence demonstrating a major domestic conspiracy doesn't exist.

Nearly every person who participated in the autopsy has either declared that the photographs and X-rays of the President's body are forged, or has repeated statements about them that throw into question the authenticity of the alleged autopsy materials. In addition, the key fact in the autopsy report—that of an exit wound in the throat—is an admitted fabrication or presumption not scientifically demonstrated. There are more outright lies in the autopsy report. It was directed, bought, and paid for by the Texans.

The week following *JAMA*'s press conference, on May 29, 1992, the Associated Press and Reuters quoted participants at the autopsy who declared at a press conference that the photographs and X-rays are forged. This story was not published in most major cities such as Baltimore, Washington, D.C., New York, Boston, San Francisco, Los Angeles, Pittsburgh, San Jose, Fort Worth, and Dallas.

During the same week, *The Journal of the American Medical Association* published their article quoting two of the autopsy doctors as saying that the entry wound was in a place on the President's head some four inches from where it is in the pictures and X-rays.[2] The doctors told this to the House Select Committee on Assassinations,[3] and placed the entry where they said it was in their autopsy report in 1963. Interestingly, the focus of the press conference announcing *JAMA*'s article was a claim that the doctors confirmed the Warren Commission findings of a lone assassin, something that is nowhere stated by the doctors either in the article or in their autopsy report. It was all propaganda.

Dr. James J. Humes spoke in public hearings before the House Assassinations Committee, and so the famous *JAMA* article in 1992 was not the first time he and the others broke their alleged silence, as *JAMA* claimed in their commercialized and slick hype. Finck has testified in court,[4] and Humes[5] and Boswell[6] have given interviews.

One of the Parkland doctors, Marion Jenkins, confirmed at a forum in Dallas shortly after the *JAMA* article that the entry hole was precisely where the autopsy doctors had placed it,† and not where it is in the forged photographs and X-rays.[7] But it could have been an exit for a fragment.

In addition, the autopsy doctors are quoted by *JAMA* as saying that

†See the chapter on the Dallas "Autopsy Forum."

the President's face was "intact" and "normal" when they unwrapped the head. This is a proof that the X-rays are forged. The X-rays show that the entire upper right front of the face is missing, something that was not reported by any witness. The face would have been blown away or have fallen in without the bone that is missing in the X-rays.

The conspirators, operating at a high level of government, used these materials to trick Chief Justice Earl Warren into believing that there were *only* shots from behind the President. The X-rays and photographs show no missing bone on the *back* of the head. These X-rays are not entirely of John Kennedy.

The Plan

Indications are that the conspirators may have paid or directed police groupies and people familiar to them to stand in Dealey Plaza or to film and photograph the scene so the conspirators would have immediate access to information on how the assassination played out. In that way they could have the visual evidence altered, if need be, and know just what their cover story should be.

As a leading Dallas city councilman said to me, "Mayor Cabell *hated* John Kennedy!" Earle Cabell was at the head of the motorcade, safely out of the line of fire. His brother, General Charles Cabell, was an Air Force general and former Deputy Director of the CIA, and very well connected in Washington, D.C., where he lived. Charles Cabell was fired by JFK for deliberately sabotaging the Bay of Pigs operation. Charles Cabell controlled the autopsy results at Bethesda.

All of the leading figures of Dallas political life—Judge Lew Sterrett, Sheriff Bill Decker, Mayor Earle Cabell, W. O. Bankston, and Morris Jaffe—were close to H. L. Hunt and Clint Murchison, who were the wealthiest men in town. Eugene Locke helped plan the motorcade. Hunt, Murchison, J. Edgar Hoover, and Vice President Lyndon Johnson all wanted Kennedy dead. Some of the planning sessions were held at one of the leading law firms in Dallas, with extensive CIA experience among their partners.

After the assassination, the conspirators created a private security operation to deal with problems and spy on people. In addition, the plotters set up a trust fund to take care of contingencies, hire operatives, and pay off snoopers. The lawyer who acted as paymaster, captured, created, or otherwise obtained provocateurs and "critics" to co-opt and control the case. By setting up (though often unwittingly) critics and researchers in the case, they could crowd out those they didn't want, and control the flow of information to the public. A certain amount of legitimate criticism would be taken over by their operators who, in turn, used it for credibility with that part of the public that doubted the Warren Report.

High-ranking military officers simply ordered military doctors at the autopsy at Bethesda Naval Hospital to lie and to fabricate reports, pictures, and X-rays, killing those who didn't play along, just as they ordered many soldiers to sit in gas chambers while they experimented on them with mustard gas, and just as they ordered half a million courageous young men to walk through ground zero moments after atomic weapons were tested, exposing them to lethal radiation.

The investigating commissions and committees simply ordered their experts and panels and staff to give them the result they wanted. The goal was not truth, not the public interest, surely, but satisfying their masters: powerful people with the money and clout to enforce their will. Most people know what is good for them and aren't going to offend those who have the power. Nobody is going to get the truth out of the authorities in this case. It is only going to come from those once-powerful individuals who have retrogressed to being just folks.

We are be lied to. There is no point in an illegitimate government telling the public the truth of how a loved leader was overthrown.

All manner of frauds and fakers are running about, lecturing and publishing books that perpetrate hoaxes on the public in an effort to confuse or "explain away" the facts. I have no doubt that some of them will claim that the bones fell away as the autopsy proceeded, or that the X-rays we now have were taken at the end of the autopsy after a reconstruction of the head. If so, how come we have no X-rays that show the real damage as described in the autopsy report or in Dallas?

Dr. John Lattimer tries to explain why the bone is missing from the face by saying the X-rays published by the House are of poor quality or cropped.[8] But numerous papers on image enhancement studies published by the House document that the area of missing bone is precisely accurate. "It's really hard to be sure, square this with the X-ray which shows so much bone lost in this right frontal area"—Dr. Angel to Drs. Humes and Boswell.[9]

The original *theory* in this case was that of the Warren Commission, which ignored the actual medical evidence and did not investigate the photographs and X-rays. Apologists for the Warren Commission have ever since made up explanations, and the media have struggled to cope with a situation they were locked into in 1964, when they were forced to accept the official government line. Honest criticism was maligned and the most serious questioners kept silent.

Our society, groaning under the weight of the second-oldest significant government in the world, has become Byzantine with doublespeak and a bureaucracy so dense it has become all but impossible either to see or to speak the plain truth. Official stories are for public consumption.

Our public officials and quasi-governmental propaganda agencies in the media mouth a string of lies, statements that only a few knowing people can see through, and have it reported as fact, unquestioned. As so many have noted, it insults the intelligence of the American people and erodes our political process. Allen Dulles told us not to worry about the facts because "Nobody reads. Don't believe people read in this country. There will be a few professors that will read the record . . . the public will read very little."[10] The truth is, not many in public life dare question official hype for fear of their jobs, pensions, and future. The advent of one-newspaper towns has put enough newsmen out of work to spread fear throughout the Fourth Estate. Many of those who remain do a quick, amateur job, and then go on to other stories.

In the case of John Kennedy's murder, the evidence is so intricate that few have the time to study and understand it. Anything that contradicts the official story comes across as wild fantasy and conspiracy paranoia. We forget that the original *theory* came from the Warren Commission, based on many presumptions and few facts.

America

We live in two countries and therefore two realities. There is the one most of us *think* we live in: the country we read about in the media. The other one is the shadow country known to only the privileged few. That is the one with the real power.

We have all been set against one another. Artificial wars of many kinds are created to keep the population addled, and a warlike nation was built—militaristic in its organization and subtle authoritarianism, greatly brainwashed, diverted with entertainment, bread, circuses, sports, mass communications, subliminal media messages, and pop culture. It is a modern-day Rome respecting no national sovereignty but its own and whose long arm extends to any nation, across any border, to accomplish any goal. National sovereignty—existent for two hundred years—began to recede into the past.

Guerrilla wars, major crime problems, and environmental crisis were manufactured. For example, if the government did not want drugs in this nation, we would not have that problem. The "war on drugs" is a farce, as even a recent government drug czar stated before resigning. Drugs and the crime that goes with them desensitize and destabilize society. But it took an all-out effort by the media to reprogram people, to desensitize people to violence—making random street violence and death from stray bullets a fact of national life.

It certainly might appear that Kennedy's administration was being framed with an authoritarian and Olympian attitude after the fact. This is part of an overall smear campaign set in place over the years to cause the public not to care what happened to JFK.

Doublespeak, identified so well by George Orwell as Newspeak in his novel *1984,* is a fact of our national life. Reporters at the top of the heap are too often fact-totems, afraid or unable to tell things as they really are. If they do, their stories are not published, or they lose their jobs and are unable to work. The result are news reports regurgitated from press conferences that are blatant exercises in propaganda. Respected organs of public or professional opinion engage in outright propaganda to pay their dues to the government and the Establishment.

Our Constitution has been subverted and circumvented by powerful people and forces in our country.

The Founding Fathers were for the most part wealthy elitists who created a country for themselves that protected their interests. One could vote only if he was a freeman, male, and owned property in excess of a certain amount. In addition, realizing that the rise of the middle class would displace their political power in time, they created an electoral college that insulated the voting process from the voting public. That buffer is still in place and, to this day, America does not have direct presidential elections.

In addition, both political parties are co-opted by the same power controllers, and puppet regimes are installed. Finding unemployed actors and other ambitious front men interested in politics and amenable to the office of president is just the cup of tea the Establishment wants. The end result is that the majority of the electorate has been alienated from the political process, finding nobody real enough in whom they can believe. That process of alienation began with the assassination of John Kennedy. One massive government lie after another—from the Warren Report, the Gulf of Tonkin incident, the *Pueblo* Affair, Watergate, the Iran-contra scandal, and the October Surprise to Saddam Hussein—have turned the public off to the political process and participatory democracy. The result is a general malaise in the country and loss of faith in the government.[11]

And that is what the power controllers want: the public out of politics. Politics is a rich man's game. Elections are useful but a bother and just barely tolerated.

Various papers were written by Henry Kissinger and Zbigniew Brzezinski and others on the failure of democracy and the need for an alternative form of government by committees of experts. Democracy was seen as an inconvenience. It was thought that the hired manager was the best way to run a national government. Hire a president. At the time that the Rockefeller study groups were preparing this material, David Rockefeller influenced both political parties, installing the Jimmy Carter presidency and cabinet from the Democratic Party, and his own brother as vice president under the alleged Republican Party. Party labels have become meaningless. The public no longer believes in either party, seeing through the mask of platform beliefs to the emptiness and lack of conviction beyond.

And, of course, lying, as the central fact of political life, is merely a symbol of a much deeper human failing. Lying as a process and social method makes possible so many crimes of history.

We have a problem in our national life intertwined with the concept of doublespeak and deceit and cover-up. That is factionalism and unfairness.

In 1908 Dr. Frederick Cook dogsledded to the North Pole, the first ever to get there. Then for one year he struggled to return to civilization, and nobody knew during that time that he had reached the pole, except for Robert Peary. Peary got wind that Cook had left for the Pole, when Peary was in Greenland preparing to do the same himself the following year. Peary needed to cover up that information.

Dr. Cook traveled to Copenhagen to present his evidence at the Royal Academy. The Academy accepted his calculations and evidence and he was awarded the discovery of the North Pole. But it was not to be. This was a man alone, with little money. A little man who soon found all the power of the United States Navy, the National Geographic Society, and the Explorers' Club of New York arrayed against him, for they had financed and backed Rear Admiral Robert E. Peary's attempt to find the Pole.

Peary claimed to have gone 270 miles on foot and by sled in the final four days, and claimed to have gotten to the Pole, though he never produced his instruments or his complete records. Interestingly, Professor Ross Marvin, Peary's chief scientist and navigator, was murdered during the expedition.

Peary returned from the Arctic and went to New York, where he presented his evidence, which was promptly accepted by the National Geographic Society. From that moment on, Cook was a marked man and made out to be a fraud.

Hugh Eames wrote a seminal book on this major part of our history, called *Winner Lose All,* a book that all Americans should read if they want to know how one's discovery can be taken away, how people can be ruined by the Establishment, by big money and power, and how history is rewritten.[12] Eames's book about Dr. Cook and Admiral Peary is even more instructive on that level—of society and how it treats history.‡

In 1991 the U.S. Naval Institute held its annual meeting and presented the question of who really got to the North Pole first.[13] Extensive evidence demonstrated that Peary faked his data and perpetrated a hoax.[14] However, more than a hundred photographs taken at the "North Pole camp" have disappeared; many key records and documents are missing; and diaries have vanished, along with the field notebook of murdered Professor Ross Marvin. Virtually all of the documentary evidence that could confirm or refute Peary's North Pole claim is missing from the files.

"The murder of Professor Marvin has kept a cloud over the expedition for eighty years. The popular professor served as Peary's private secretary and third-in-command. Marvin led the scientific work and was the expedition's expert in navigation. . . ."[15]

Does any of the above sound familiar?

The issue is that photographs and X-rays were faked to trick Earl Warren and his commission. Humes and Boswell have questioned them in the past and continue to do so in an oblique fashion. That is the issue that *JAMA,* Oliver Stone, and everyone else ignored. That is the core of my research and what nobody in an official capacity can face, and that is why *JAMA* published their article and inflicted it on the rest of us.

The assassination of President Kennedy remains vitally important to us, the survivors, and to historians. We care because from that tragic moment on, our political organization began to deteriorate. The murder was an awful symbol of the real political facts. Assassination as a political instrument took over our country and redirected it.

Harold Weisberg, in his first book on the subject, *Whitewash,* wrote at the beginning of his introduction, "Assassination is a political crime.

‡Hugh Eames, *Winner Lose All,* (Boston: Little, Brown, 1974).

Even in the rare, remote cases where the assassin had no comprehensible political objectives, the crimes had political consequences. Whether it is the head of a state or a lesser official, the assassination has immediate political effects. With the head of state murdered, the changes in the political structure and situation are more immediate and far-reaching. A policy change by the head of state has national and international implications. Even when his successor follows the same basic policies, there nonetheless are changes in the implementation of these policies. No two men work, think, or act in exactly the same way."[16]

For the first couple of years after the assassination, the press was relatively open on the issue of what might have happened. Certainly in Dallas, everyone spoke of "the conspiracy" as though the Warren Commission never happened. There was no monolithic press structure aligned against conspiracy theories, but a wall formed later as a result of Jim Garrison's circus. Richard E. Sprague writes, "A categorical statement can be made that management and editorial policy, measured by what is printed and broadcast in all major American news media organizations, supports the findings of the Warren Commission. This has been true since 1969, but it was not true between 1964 and 1969."[17] "Immediately following the assassination, the media reported nearly everything that had obviously happened. . . . For one year the major media reported everything, from probable Communist conspiracies to the lone-assassin theory. The media waited for the Warren Report, and when it was issued in October of 1964 many of the major media fell into line and editorially backed the Commission's findings. Some questioned the findings and continued to question them until 1968 or 1969. *The New York Times* and *Life* magazine fell into this category. But by the time the Shaw trial ended in March 1969, every one of the fifteen major news media organizations was backing the Warren Commission and they have continued to maintain this editorial position since."[18]

Jim Garrison changed all of that. Sprague speaks for many of us with this comment: "For many of them the Shaw trial became the turning point in the changing of editorial policy toward the assassination. For a few, the Garrison investigation and the Shaw trial took on an aspect of waving a red flag in front of a bull."[19]

I will restate an opinion that I first heard from former high-ranking CIA officers who told me that when people who were connected to the agency came out against it publicly, it was because the Agency wanted them to. They were taking the heat. The *real* intelligence operations were elsewhere, funded by the Black Budget. The CIA is a cover, and a good one. *Nobody* comes out against the Agency without its permission.

Farther along this line of reasoning is the fact that various people oriented toward the military, including Jim Garrison, Mark Lane, Fletcher Prouty, and others, have too easily directed attention at the CIA and away from the military, the obvious power in the United States after the Texas oil people and the FBI.

We have to face the fact that there are patterns to the events in this case that are not just coincidence. It is not just a coincidence that there was such a meeting at Clint Murchison's house the night before to which Richard Nixon, Lyndon Johnson, John J. McCloy, J. Edgar Hoover, H. L. Hunt, and other prominent people came.

Sometimes someone sneaks through the cracks of the cover-up, as did fourteen-year-old Amanda Rowell, the daughter of Gary Rowell, a longtime researcher. With her father's help, she wrote David Slawson, former Warren Commission staffer, and wanted to know if he listened to the tape of Lee Harvey Oswald in Mexico City.§ He wrote her back and admitted hearing it, and his reply is in the appendix of this book. "I did not feel that the voice sounded any different from what I expected his would sound like," Slawson said. Slawson then claims in the letter that there were no recordings of Oswald to compare it with, either in the past, or, "since Oswald was killed only two days after the assassination, of course he was not around, still talking. No one, therefore, can honestly claim to have compared his voice on this tape or any place else with what he actually sounded like." There were plenty of videos and films of Oswald under arrest talking to reporters, and there was his New Orleans appearance in the broadcast media, with which to compare his voice.

The residue of the assassination remained. That is, the cover-up had to continue to protect those who had perpetrated that terrible crime. Covering it up meant to head off at the pass those who snooped around long after the official story closed the books. Researchers and critics had to be co-opted and controlled, and those of us who were fools and trusted the big-name critics among us got suckered. Far too many of the researchers with hidden agendas snookered the public with their dramatic presentations. It never occurred to us that they may have been pointed at us and paid by people in Texas. The CIA and the FBI became the whipping boys, along with the Mob.

There are layers of control in the structure of our country, the least

§Kristi, Amanda, and G. J. Rowell, "The Mysterious Mexico City CIA Tapes II," *The Investigator* (February–March 1993).

of which is the elected government. At the top is big money and the oligarchy that runs things. Below that is the military, which is in the hands of that big money and works with it. But everybody with money can have their own thugs. "Dallas was a wide-open city," Madeleine Duncan Brown told Dick Russell. "H. L. Hunt, because of his oil operations, you know, trained assassins in Mexico. If he wanted something and they wouldn't let him buy it with a dollar, he took it. After Kennedy was elected, I remember him saying, 'We may have lost a battle—but here's a war to win.' "[20]

Madeleine Brown is one person of wealthy background in Dallas who ought to know. She told me, "Don't you know that Washington is controlled by the Texas oil money? It always has been!"[21] It wasn't so long after the assassination when the political establishment of Dallas, which had been headed by the Cabells—for a long time sheriffs and mayors of Dallas—was overthrown by more ordinary citizens fed up with the monolithic power structure. From that moment on, the city began to change and become more human and less of a Wild West town. It became a city. But soon the old power structure reasserted itself and, instead of being "The City of Hate," as it was called in the early 1960s, today it is The City of Fear.

Courage is the virtue that President
Kennedy most admired. He sought
out those people who had
demonstrated in some way
whether it was on a battlefield or a
baseball diamond, in a speech or
fighting for a cause, that they had
courage, that they would stand up,
that they could be counted on.

—Robert F. Kennedy,
December 18, 1963

CHAPTER 1
AN OVERVIEW

So much of the trouble in understanding the evidence in the assassination of President John F. Kennedy—both for the Warren Commission
and for the critics of the Commission—is rooted in language problems,
semantics, and the interpretation of evidence. People from different cul-
tural, educational, and professional backgrounds ascribe different mean-
ings to words and evidence.

The fact that our judicial and political systems are adversarial in
nature makes interpretation of evidence and events that much more
difficult because a certain amount of valid evidence is excluded from
consideration for traditional legal reasons. Too much weight, in addition, can be given to scientific or expert testimony, which can eclipse
valid eyewitness accounts. We also have to allow for the deliberate
fabrication of scientific evidence in political cases.

There is a tendency among some to expect science to be able to deal
with all questions in a murder investigation. This is sometimes impossible and indeed often preposterous at times. Merely because we have
entered an age when science tries to reinterpret the rules of life, it does
not follow that such things as character, ethics, memory, behavior, and
observation are within the rules that test scientific hypothesis.

The fact is that there was very little that was scientific about the
autopsy conducted on President Kennedy.[1] It was an attempted rational
investigation of a body, and terribly flawed at that. The House of Representatives went to a lot of trouble to point out the many flaws of the
autopsy and the alleged autopsy photographs that they admitted would
not even be admissible in court.[2]

37

Rules are often imposed that preclude an overview of a case. We bog down in minutiae. We are too easily swayed by naked propaganda. Opinion and conclusions become fact.

It doesn't help us to be overwhelmed with misrepresentation and sensationalism from every corner in this case. People of goodwill and good intent find themselves discredited by political or intelligence operatives from all sides. Research and publication in the JFK case are unsupervised and undisciplined. In any other professional arena there are boards of overseers to keep things straight.

But there are answers, and I will try to clarify them in this book in such a way that perhaps we can settle most of the issues for all time. Trying to make clear the interpretations I have and make them stick are the purposes of this book.

There is certain evidence that is definitive which has been ignored, misunderstood, or buried. The fact that the autopsy photographs contradict the X-rays, and that some of the photos contradict each other or contain intrinsic evidence of forgery is sufficient on both scientific and rational grounds to overturn the cover-up. The fact that none of the photos shows the wounds described in the autopsy report is definitive. The fact that so much of the evidence is incompatible or conflicts with other evidence proves a cover-up, a faked case, and faked evidence. All of this was outlined in my previous books but went right by the authorities. It did not go by Ralph Nader, whose Public Citizen has filed suit against the government to force the release of the autopsy pictures.*

In addition, the *pattern* of apparently planted evidence, fake evidence, and stolen evidence demonstrates that there is an ongoing conspiracy.

These are some of the questions that, if they can be answered, point in the direction of what really happened in the assassination.

Questions

There came to be a dispute about where the large hole in the President's head was, and whether there was a flap of scalp covering the hole.

There is a dispute as to where an entry hole was in the back of the head. Was there an entry hole in the front of the throat? Was the bullet

*See the chapter on law suits in this book.

wound in the back or at the base of the neck, and precisely where? Was there an exit wound in the back?

Was there any damage to the face and underlying bone? Was there a large segment of bullet found on the outer table of the skull at the autopsy?

Was there a brain in the head? Did the body get switched from one coffin to another? Was the body in a body bag?

Was the throat wound altered?

Was the body altered?

Was John Connally hit with the same bullet that hit John Kennedy? If so, what difference does it make? How big were the fragments found in John Connally? Can a military jacketed bullet break ribs and wrist-bones and not be damaged? Could the bullet, or its trajectory from the assassin's window, go through both men? Could a military jacketed bullet strike a man in the head and break up completely?

Did Oswald shoot John Kennedy?

Was there more than one shooter?

Was the acoustics evidence disproved?

Did the autopsy pathologists and *JAMA* controvert any of this or disprove a conspiracy?

Did the autopsy doctors lie?

Where was the large hole on the President's head? Was there a flap of scalp covering the hole?

The autopsy report placed the large hole in the President's head as covering the right rear quadrant, about a quarter of the skull. The autopsy report reads, ". . . on the right involving chiefly the parietal bone but extending somewhat into the temporal and occipital regions. In this region there is an actual absence of scalp and bone producing a defect which measures approximately 13 cm. in greatest diameter."[3]

This is precisely where the doctors and nurses in Dallas placed it. That fact can be gleaned from their medical reports, but more especially their description of it as described in my books. The dispute really is: Was there more scalp that might have covered some of the missing bone? The Dallas doctors are insistent that bone was missing from the back of the head, including much of the occipital bone.

The photos and X-rays show no missing bone in any of the areas mentioned by the Dallas witnesses or by the autopsy doctors in their report. The X-rays also show all of the bone missing on the right side of the face, including the frontal bone, or forehead. There is no testimony by anyone concerning any significant amount of bone missing on

the face. In fact, all persons who saw the body said that the President's
face was "intact" and "normal." The autopsy report does not mention
missing frontal bone.

Where was the entry hole in the back of the head?

The autopsy report placed it "2.5 cm. laterally to the right and
slightly above the external occipital protuberance."[4] The autopsy pathologists said to the Assassinations Committee panel of doctors that it was
slightly *below* the protuberance,[5] thereby inadvertently indicating that
their report might have been changed. They insisted that what was later
called a piece of brain tissue on the hair just above the hairline in the
photograph of the back of the head was, in fact, where the entrance
was.

This is where Dr. Marion Jenkins in Dallas said he found it,[6] not
four to five inches higher, *as it has been placed since the photography
and X-rays surfaced.* The entry could *not* be where it seems to appear
in the cowlick in some photographs because all that bone was *missing.*

The issue then arises: Can the doctors be so very wrong, or must we
assume forgery of the photographs and X-rays from these disparities
alone?

There is evidence of an entry hole in the face, which can be seen in
the retouched Stare-Of-Death picture at the juncture of the hairline, with
the laceration extending into the forehead over the right eye. There is
evidence of these wounds in the Groden right superior profile picture
as well as what might be the entry hole of a .45 slug in the right temple
area in the hairline.[7]

Was there an entry hole in the front of the throat?

Three times on the day of the assassination, Dr. Malcolm Perry stated
that the President had an entry hole in his throat. Dr. Perry had performed the tracheostomy. Several other doctors saw the hole before it
was obliterated, including Charles Carrico, Ronald Jones, and Charles
Crenshaw, and all of these doctors have continued to insist that it was
a wound of entrance. Nurse Diana Bowron saw an entry there.

The wound was *not seen,* photographed, or measured at the Bethesda
autopsy. It was not officially known at the autopsy. Could the Dallas
doctors have been wrong? Highly unlikely. They had seen many gunshot wounds. Their medical testimony is that far more damage would

have been done to the organs of the throat had there been a bullet exiting there instead of entering.[8]

The fact that the wound was not seen at Bethesda leaves the testimony of the Dallas doctors as the legal and historical finding. Therefore, in front of the limousine there was an additional gunman who shot the President in the throat and probably in the head.

Was the bullet wound in the back or at the base of the neck, and where?

There was no wound in the base of the neck. The autopsy report places it "in the upper right posterior thorax just above the upper border of the scapula there is a 7 x 4 millimeter oval wound. This wound is measured to be 14 cm. from the tip of the right acromion process and 14 cm. below the tip of the right mastoid process."[9] This is not in the base of the neck but well down on the back.

The Warren Report *lied* when it stated that the wound was "observed near the base of the back of President Kennedy's neck slightly to the right of his spine. . . . The hole was located approximately 5 and ½ inches (14 centimeters) from the top of the right shoulder joint and *approximately the same distance below the top of the right mastoid process,* the bony point immediately behind the ear."[10] (The italics are mine.) The wound was 5½ inches *below the shoulder,* not below the ear. This represents a deliberate falsification of the facts. We also know this from the FBI and Secret Service reenactment on May 24, 1964, and from photographs showing a bullet hole circled in chalk about 5½ inches down on the back of the agent sitting in the President's position.

Dr. Marion Jenkins of Parkland stated on June 4, 1992, in Dallas that he felt this wound and that it was not in the base of the neck but a few inches down on the back.

Did this wound penetrate the back?

No. There is evidence both from the testimony of Dr. Pierre Finck and the men who were at the autopsy, and which is detailed in my other books, that the bullet did not penetrate the back or pass through the body. The probe was visible from the inside of the chest and did not come through the tissue. The autopsy report says that it "cannot be easily probed."[11] The doctors did not know that there had been a wound in the throat, and they simply made up the explanation that the bullet passed through the body and exited the throat. This was the major fabrication of the autopsy report and was the theory the Warren

Commission needed to cover up the fact that the President had been killed by multiple gunmen.

Was there an exit wound in the back?

Studies of wound entry holes and photographs of them published in Spitz and Fisher's *Medicolegal Investigation of Death* show that the horizontal ovoid hole in the back 4 x 7 mm. is, in fact, an exit wound. It is called a pitting edema. Diana Bowron told me that the official photograph showing the back wound "is not the President's back." (See her caption on the picture reproduced in this book, and my interviews of her.)

Was there any damage to the face and underlying bone?

According to all those who saw the face, there was no damage at all, contrary to what we see in the Zapruder film and the X-rays. The photographs show no damage at all. There is no witness who has described at any time any damage to the face, or any bone missing. Dr. Humes himself told the *Journal of the American Medical Association* that the face was intact and normal when he unwrapped the head.[12]

Was there a large segment of bullet on the outer table of the skull at the autopsy?

No. It is unlikely that the very large fragment seen on the A/P X-ray of the skull in 1968 was present at the autopsy. The entire point of the autopsy was to find bullet fragments and their paths, and was performed for no other purpose. Normally the head and hair are felt carefully, and the hair combed to find fragments. X-rays of the skull were repeatedly examined during the autopsy, and such a fragment was never reported. Much smaller fragments were seen and removed.

In addition, Diana Bowron washed the President's hair, and it is unlikely that such a large fragment would have escaped her notice. (See the chapter in this book on Diana Bowron.)

The implication is that this fragment was added to a piece of bone after the autopsy and a composite made to try to demonstrate a higher trajectory and entrance hole for the shot that killed the President. X-ray tech Jerrol Custer, described to me having been made to tape bullet fragments to bone fragments the next day and X-ray them.[13]

Was there a brain in the head?

Yes. But much of the brain had been blown out, as Diana Bowron and other Parkland witnesses have described. The *only* persons at the autopsy who indicated that the brain might not have been in the head or that much of it was blown out, Paul O'Connor and Jerrol Custer, told me that they did not see it before it had been removed by Jim Jenkins and Dr. Boswell. He meant that an awful lot of the brain appeared to be missing when they first viewed the skull.[14] Jenkins thought that it had been out of the head prior to the autopsy. There are indications that it slipped from the head in Dallas and was returned to the head along with the cerebellum.

I believe that when the Dallas doctors told us the cerebellum was "on the table," they were saying that couldn't happen unless there was little or no brain left. It is not possible for the brain recorded in the supplemental autopsy report to have been 1500 grams.[15] That is the weight of a normal, intact brain.

Did the body get switched from one coffin to another, and was the body in a body bag?

No. From the available evidence, there was not any period of time when the body might have been stolen, and there is no credible evidence that it had been stolen. Attempts by other authors to find circumstantial evidence indicating that it had been stolen are not credible, since they rely on apparently differing descriptions of the coffin and a possible but not probable arrival in a body bag. The latter two are simple semantic problems, since the coffin was described in wildly varying ways in Dallas, and even the Warren Commission described it as basically a shipping casket.

The body bag issue is a simple confusion over the wrappings. Paul O'Connor actually told the House committee that the body was only "wrapped" in a body bag, which was in fact a zippered mattress cover, or the sheet of plastic material as described by many witnesses.[16]

Was the throat wound altered?

No. Five of the Dallas doctors were quoted in the *JAMA* article as verifying the appearance in the photographs as being what they saw after the tracheostomy. They all had previously told me the same thing. Dr. Crenshaw did not originally maintain that the wound had been altered, as his interview with me shows,[17] but the facts were stretched

by his coauthors, as Crenshaw has stated,[18] to indicate a possible alteration of the wound whose photographic appearance can be explained
in other ways.

The fact remains that all of the other Dallas medical witnesses do
not question the size of the wound as it appears in the stare-of-death
picture.[19] But there is possible airbrushing of the wound in the picture
to make it look jagged. That picture is contradicted by the left profile
picture, which shows clean, even lines of incision and a small, gaping
wound of the same configuration.

Was the body altered?

No. It is impossible to fake or alter wounds.

The body was not altered, and not altered to fool the camera, for the
simple reason that everybody at the autopsy has found fault with the
photographs and X-rays, stating that they do not show the wounds those
people saw. The idea of body alteration to fool the camera and the
autopsists is wrong. It is a hoax because one first has to claim that the
photos and X-rays showed the wounds as they really were, which is
false, and that the altered and reconstructed body therefore fooled the
camera—that the camera recorded a reconstruction. This was unnecessary when simple retouching of the photos would do the job.

The men who took both the photos and the X-rays at the autopsy
have called them forgeries and have pointed out evidence of retouching
and forgery.[20]

Was John Connally hit with the same bullet that hit John Ken-
nedy? If so, what difference does it make?

Possibly but unlikely. Connally is seen in the films reacting to a hit
a bit later than Kennedy. Connally is turned the wrong way to receive
a bullet that just passed through Kennedy. Connally always insisted that
he was hit with a separate bullet. Although it is conceivable that a
victim does not instantaneously feel a bullet strike him, it is irrelevant
in this case. In addition, there is no evidence that any bullet hit Kennedy
from behind where it might have gone through Connally. The fragments
in Connally's body exceeded the amount lost from the bullet found at
Parkland that was connected to the alleged murder weapon. And it is
my opinion that the trajectory from the alleged sixth-floor "sniper's
nest" was down through the floor of the car and could not hit both
men. This question will always be in dispute, however.

How big were the fragments found in John Connally?

According to the medical witnesses, some of the fragments were considerably larger than what are on record today. Drawings made for the author and others show much larger pieces of metal. Backing this up is the statement by the scientist charged with conducting neutron activation analysis of the metal, Dr. Guinn, who said that the weights that he tested did not correspond to those recorded by the Warren Commission.[21] Even those would have to have been smaller than what we know to have been removed from Connally and what remained in his leg.

Can a military jacketed bullet break bone and not be damaged?

Some veterans claim that such a bullet will not be damaged, but this is unscientific. Tests performed by the Warren Commission itself showed that such a bullet is badly damaged but essentially does not break up when it hits bones.[22] John Connally's rib was shattered by a bullet, as were his wristbones.

Could the bullet, on its trajectory from the assassin's window, go through both men?

In some models created by the FBI, *Nova,* and the House Assassinations Committee, yes. But there are serious questions as to what sort of architectural drawings they used. The trajectories look long and flat in the drawings, with little inclination, but we are talking about the second shot at frame 225, not the first available shot from the window at frame 157 of the Zapruder film and which the Warren Commission said missed. I believe the truth lies in the reversal of the complementary angles of the quadrant, and we were lied to on this key issue. Instead of the bullet leaving the window at roughly a 22-degree angle downward, it was much steeper, and came down at the converse angle, or 68 degrees. They simply tricked us by reversing the angle.

Having spent some time looking down from the alleged assassin's window to the street, I believe that the shot could not go through both men, since it actually is firing at roughly a 68-degree angle down through the floorboards of the car and could not have hit both men. If both were hit no later than frames 224–26, this is roughly 15 frames later in the film and therefore less than one second after the first available shot could have been fired from that window at frame 210 after the car had cleared the trees, which is far too soon for the rifle to be reloaded, reaimed, and fired. Therefore this is proof positive that the first, missed, shot came earlier. If it had been fired a lot earlier, such as at frame 160 or so, before the car began to pass beneath the tree, this shot was through the floorboards of the car and might have ricocheted down the street.

The FBI report of Kennedy's autopsy, by agents Francis X. O'Neill, Jr., and James W. Sibert, said that the autopsy doctors found that "the trajectory of the missile entering at this point had entered at a downward position of 45 to 60 degrees. Further probing determined that the distance traveled by this missile was short, inasmuch as the end of the opening could be felt with the finger." The President was sitting straight up during this first shot. Either of the two angles above is far steeper than the Warren Commission dares to admit.

The trajectory arrived at by the Warren Commission was completely unscientific. It was arrived at by a surveyor who "then placed his sighting equipment at the precise point of entry on the back of the President's neck, assuming that the President was struck at frame 210, and measured the angle to the end of the muzzle of the rifle positioned where it was believed to have been held by the assassin. That angle measured 21 degrees 34'."[23]

"Allowing for a downward street grade of 3 degrees 9', the probable angle through the President's body was calculated at 17 degrees 43'30", assuming that he was sitting in a vertical position. That angle was consistent with the trajectory of a bullet passing through the President's neck and then striking Governor Connally's back." This is how they got the angle: "Shortly after that angle was ascertained, the open car and the stand-ins were taken by the agents to a nearby garage, where a photograph was taken to determine through closer study whether the angle of that shot could have accounted for the wounds in the President's neck and the Governor's back. A rod was placed at an angle of 17 degrees 43'30" next to the stand-ins for the President and the Governor, who were seated in the same relative position. The wounds of entry and exit on the President were approximately based on information gained from the autopsy reports and photographs." They found that the trajectory went through both men, but "the alignment of the points of entry was only indicative and not conclusive that one bullet hit both men. The exact positions of the men could not be recreated; thus, the angle could only be approximated."[24]

One problem was that they used a Cadillac limousine rather than the Lincoln that Kennedy and Connally rode in, and the placement of the seats and the distances between them might not have been the same.

Another was that the autopsy information they were given was grossly inaccurate.

Put another way, the distance from the sniper's window to the ground is about 55½ feet, and the distance to the first available shot over the top of the tree is about three times that distance. If you make a scale drawing showing the shot that supposedly went through both men as 3 inches in length and 1 inch high for the window's height above the ground, and draw a trajectory from the window to the point 3 inches away, then measure the angle from the window down.

The angle from the window to the horizon is 18 degrees, and the window to the ground is therefore 72 degrees for the complementary angle, making up the 90 degrees of a circle's quarter; 72 degrees minus 3 degrees for the slope or grade of the street is 69 degrees, which is almost exactly the complementary angle the Warren Commission gives us.

The mistake in the Warren Commission's calculations may be that the angle of entry into the President's back had to be about 68 degrees downward, not 22 degrees, and a bullet traveling at such an angle could not hit a man sitting in front of him, but would go to the floor of the car.

Sixty-eight degrees roughly coincides with the higher figure the FBI recorded at the autopsy for the entry into the back, also reported to me by the men who were at the autopsy and recorded in my last book.

Obviously, once more, some of the problems in this case can be traced to language and semantics, only in this case the impression is one of deliberate reversal of the figures and fabrication.

Could a military jacketed bullet strike a man in the head and break up completely?

No. This does not happen. A military jacketed bullet is designed not to break up (unless altered), even if it hits bone. The bullet that exploded Kennedy's head had to be frangible, and therefore a different bullet from the one that was alleged by the government.[25]

Did Oswald shoot John Kennedy?

No. He was seen a few moments before the shooting in the lunchroom on the second floor, between 12:15 and 12:25 P.M., at the time the motorcade was originally scheduled to pass the Book Depository.[26] The motorcade was five minutes late.[27] If he had shot Kennedy, he would not have been in the lunchroom, where he was seen by a police officer less than ninety seconds after the murder.[28] Oswald did not appear in any way suspicious to the policeman, who talked to him and went on.[29]

He had no nitrate on his face,[30] and although this is not conclusive,[31] in most cases such a rifle would have left deposits. It doesn't wash off.

There were no fingerprints or palmprints on the weapon when they were found. There was no indication that the weapon had even been fired.

No gunman would have attempted what was done that day with less than a full clip of ammunition, let alone just four bullets, as was the case here.[32]

Nobody who had been a U.S. Marine would have used such a poor weapon or scope for any purpose.

The Chief of Police said that they could not even have placed him at the window that day[33] and would have had difficulty going to trial in the case.[34]

Was there more than one shooter?

Alongside the car, on the sidewalk, there was a long bullet scar that pointed directly to the storm drain on the bridge facing the car to the left.[35] It would seem clear that at least one of the two frontal shots that hit Kennedy came from the other storm drain at the juncture of the overpass and the stockade fence.

The medical evidence shows that President Kennedy was hit at least three and possibly four times. The film and trajectory of head matter indicate that there was a second head hit, from in front.

The most compelling argument that Connally was not hit with the same bullet is not that the trajectory would have required so many zigs and zags from one man to the next, but that the bullet that entered Connally's back was not tumbling.[36] This fact has been fudged by numerous apologists for the Warren Report, such as Dr. John Lattimer and Dr. Robert Artwohl, but was reaffirmed by Dr. Robert Shaw, Connally's surgeon, in 1992.[37]

A third victim, James Tague, was hit by debris from a wide miss and that could not have been a fragment due to the fact that it was too far away and out of line with the car.

In addition, the ''magic'' bullet was found on the stretcher of a little boy at Parkland,[38] not Connally's stretcher, showing that it was clearly planted, as so much evidence in the case appears to be.

Was the acoustics evidence in fact disproved?

Apparently, yes. See the chapter in this book on the acoustics.

Did the autopsy pathologists controvert any of this or disprove a conspiracy?

No. The doctors have not, at any time, claimed that their findings *proved* a single or lone gunman either in their autopsy report or in the 1992 *JAMA* "report." Their autopsy report said that the President was killed by "a person or persons unknown."[39] Their findings do not controvert the probability that there were gunmen facing or alongside the car, or preclude this. But the doctors are used by many others who talk or write about them for whatever purpose and result they want.

Did the autopsy doctors lie?

Yes. They lied about the weight of the brain and the liver, about the wound in the throat, about a bullet transiting the body, about the placement of the wound on the back, perhaps about there being any entry wound at all in the back of the head. They had evidence of an entering hole in the right temple and did not report it. They knew that the Dallas doctors had described an entry wound in the throat before they began the autopsy, and they lied and said they didn't know that.

What Does All of This Mean?

A very large wound or hole was seen at Dallas in the right rear quadrant of the President's head. It happens to coincide precisely with where it is placed in the autopsy report and is so described by the autopsy doctors in testimony, and by the other witnesses to me, and is not a matter of semantics or subjective interpretation. It is neither in the position where Dr. John Lattimer has drawn it on a skull after seeing the autopsy X-rays,[40] nor where the X-rays show it on the right front of the face. The large defect is in the back and right side of the head behind the ear, and only there. There was less scalp missing, and that has caused problems in understanding. Some people examining this case fail to distinguish between laceration and incision, between alteration and tampering. Semantics plays a big role in understanding or misinforming.

Slides made from the Zapruder film in the National Archives appear to show the exact large defect just as described in the autopsy report.

Dr. Humes did try to say something about the real nature of his findings to the Warren Commission when he said the bullet had to have exited from behind.[41] The implication for students of the evidence is that perhaps the President was shot twice in the head—once from in front, and once from behind. The autopsy report describes a small wound of entry in the occiput, not in the cowlick, as in the photographs and X-rays.

There has always been strong evidence for an additional shot from in front that tore off the back of the President's head, the trajectory of material that hit the motorcycle policeman just to the left rear of the car, the backward motion of the head, and the fact that the back of the head was blown off.

No, a bullet did not enter the throat and come out the back of his head, because the floor of the skull was not damaged. But where did the throat shot go? The large hole in the shoulder looks like an exit wound to me.

The large skull defect was in the back of the head, extending around to the right side behind the ear, and covered with a flap of scalp there. It is now more than clear that the doctors may have lied and invented a rear-head entry.

CHAPTER 2

SUMMARY OF THE EVIDENCE

My previous books offer in-depth expositions of the principal evidence in the case, with extensive supporting data. This is intended only as a recap of the case for conspiracy.

There are certain givens in the evidence that would seem irrefutable. Unfortunately, they are so overlaid with complications and intricacies that it is easy to lose sight of what is real and solid, and what is a fog deliberately meant to obscure the truth.

It is worth bearing in mind that the Warren Commission was not sure about their main points, knowing they were based on assumptions. They said that there was no way of knowing if the two bullet fragments found in the front of the limousine were from the same bullet,[1] or that Connally and Kennedy were hit with the same bullet (there was only "persuasive" evidence that it happened).[2] They *presumed* that three shots were fired[3] and that only two of them probably caused all the wounds.[4] None of this was certain, even to the President's commission.

It's easy to forget these uncertainties when either criticizing the Warren Commission or holding up their suppositions as actual fact scientifically proven. The truth is that they wrote their Report both ways: They qualified their statements as above, then stated them as facts. Therefore, *it was an exercise in propaganda,* as is much else having to do with this case.

We have also to deal with common legal problems; guilt by association, and circumstantial evidence.

Too often, commentators from the "critical community"—the Establishment composed of those well-known people and opportunists who have made a name for themselves in this research—are like sponges. They are people who absorb whatever obscure researchers come up with of value—and sell it or publish it, often without attribution, making a name for themselves. Popularization of some of the ideas and keeping the case alive are the justifications for any sort of theory, right or wrong.

It is unfortunate that both the autopsy report and the Warren Report either fudged, ignored, or simply lied about certain key facts. Therefore, some intelligent commentators, such as Paul Hoch, tend to give up on key issues because there is always an argument or some other alleged fact to counter what seems established. When dealing with eyewitness testimony, this is particularly true. Therefore, everyone hunts for some scientific answer that never seems to be forthcoming. The truth is that there are answers; solid facts can be established from eyewitness testimony. We just need a guide through the swamp of confusion.

Sophistry can waylay us because it ignores the legal process that must find admissible certain classes of evidence.

Specifically, *eyewitness* evidence is admissible, and controls the issue if there is nothing of substance to refute it. The court weighs that testimony and, if it is credible, must find on the basis of it if there is nothing to offset it.[5] For instance, if a group of doctors all say that they saw a certain type of wound, and there is no credible evidence to controvert it, giving credence to a suspect photograph is a mistake. A contradictory photograph should be suspicious rather than the statements. Their observation becomes a fact. To ignore that evidence is a grave error.

The conspirators did not have to be too careful because, even if there were inconsistencies in the evidence they planted, the government had to lie about whatever else might have happened as a matter of public policy—to keep the general peace. This latter statement is really the controlling political factor in this political killing.

Let us start with hard medical and ballistics evidence that cannot be refuted.

Ballistics

The ballistics studies of Dr. John Nichols have generally been ignored, but those of Dr. John Lattimer, a urologist, have been greatly listened to. Nichols is a board-certified pathologist and professor.[6]

Dr. Roger McCarthy, an engineer who studies wounds and accidents, testified at the American Bar Association mock trial of Lee Harvey Oswald in the summer of 1992 at San Francisco that shots at a simulated head or water bottle with soft-nosed or frangible bullets caused a large explosion.* This contradicts the experiments of Nobel Prize-

*See the chapter on firearms and ballistics for this testimony.

winning physicist Dr. Louis Alvarez, and those of Dr. John Lattimer that showed that a military jacketed bullet seemed to thrust a simulated head back toward the shooter.

In addition, McCarthy also insisted that it would have been irrational for a sniper to shoot at the target going away from him at that elevation, when he could have shot at the car as it approached him as it came down Houston Street.

McCarthy concluded that there had to have been a shooter in front of the car, since one bullet broke up and appeared to be from a different rifle, along with other indications of a trajectory from that direction.

Jack Anderson also announced on his show in the fall of 1988 that studies he commissioned from a photoanalysis company showed the splatter pattern captured in the Zapruder film as having been caused by a shot from in front, not from behind.[7]

The Weapons

There was no evidence that either of the two weapons attributed to Oswald had been fired on November 22, 1963.

There were no fingerprints or palmprint (which showed up days later) on the weapons.[8] Mr. Paul Groody, Oswald's undertaker, described men fingerprinting Oswald as he was being prepared for burial,[9] and it is possible that the palmprint came from there.[10]

"I think this explains the unsigned fingerprint card, but not the palmprint on the rifle," Martin Shackelford wrote me. "There was ink all over the hands of Oswald's body: Ink wouldn't have been used to transfer a palmprint onto the rifle; I believe the palmprint would have been created by perspiration, not ink. Groody probably is credible, but I don't think that has anything to do with the palmprint."

The Rifle

The alleged assassination weapon could only eject a shell and be loaded, aimed, and fired within 2.3 seconds. This is apart from the care needed to aim and shoot. Robert Blakey proved that he could work the bolt action of the rifle and fire off a round in 1.6 seconds, firing from the hip, but he did not aim and hit a target.[11] Unfortunately, his feat then became part of one more Big Lie that implied that a sniper could have gotten accurate shots off in the allotted time.

There is no ballistics evidence that refutes the possibility of another rifle having been used. In addition, one whole bullet was lost entirely.[12]

Metal Traces

FBI studies showed there were no metal traces on the front of the shirt or the tie.[13]

All four wounds were supposed to have shown residual lead or copper.

The Bullets

The bullets allegedly used were military jacketed: a lead core with a copper shell over it and designed to pass cleanly through more than one person but not necessarily to kill. They are unlikely to strike bones and not bruise or distort the tip. There is no credible evidence that the contrary can happen. At the same time, such a bullet will not break up on striking skull, as did the one that struck President Kennedy.

It is not reasonable that a military jacketed bullet was the one that struck the President in the head. The bullet that struck the head was clearly frangible and broke up into small pieces so that none could be identified. It is not reasonable for an assassin or anyone to load a rifle with several different types of bullets.

There might not be a separate exit wound with use of a frangible bullet. Frangible bullets are designed to disintegrate and lose velocity. Therefore there may be insufficient force left in the fragments to penetrate a skull.

Certainly no former Marine bent on killing someone would use a military jacketed bullet designed not to kill so much as wound.

The Fragments

This is one of the key lies and initial point of cover-up in the case. (1) Certain weights of fragments recovered from John Connally and from the limousine were recorded by the Warren Commission and placed in the National Archives.[14] (2) Dr. Vincent Guinn stated that the fragments he was given to conduct Neutron Activation analysis (NAA) tests did not correspond to those recorded by the Warren Commission.[15] (3) Neither can they possibly correspond to those seen and handled at

Parkland Hospital by medical personnel who drew pictures and described them as much larger than those whose photographs the Warren Commission published.[16] (4) The photographs of those published by the Warren Commission show fragments that could not possibly come from CE 399, the "magic bullet."[17]

Mr. Fithian asked Dr. Guinn: "Now, then, did you test exactly the same particles that the FBI tested in 1964?"

"Well, it turns out I did not, for reasons I don't know, because as they did the analysis, they did not destroy the samples."

"So?"

"The particular little pieces that they analyzed, I could just as well have analyzed over again, but the pieces that were brought out from the Archives—which reportedly, according to Mr. Gear, were the only bullet-lead fragments from this case still present in the Archives—did not include any of the specific little pieces that the FBI had analyzed. Presumably, those are in existence somewhere, I am sure nobody threw them out, but where they are, I have no idea."[18]

A very large fragment was found by the Clark Panel to be on the outer table of the skull near the alleged entry wound in the cowlick of the President, which was not noted at the autopsy. Jerrol Custer has described to me taping bullet fragments to pieces of bone the day after the autopsy and taking X-rays of them.[19] The head in the X-rays appears to be a reconstruction *AND NOT ENTIRELY THAT OF KENNEDY.* Yet, all the head X-rays are claimed to have been taken before the autopsy began.[20]

The FBI report of the autopsy (November 26, 1963) described the "snowstorm" of fragments through the brain. "The largest section of this missile as portrayed by X-ray appeared to be behind the right frontal sinus. The next largest fragment appeared to be at the rear of the skull at the juncture of the skull bone."

The second large fragment was seen at the autopsy and surgically removed from the right supraorbital region in the brain against the skull.[21] Commander James J. Humes told the Warren Commission, "In further evaluating this head wound, I will refer back to the X-rays which we had previously prepared. These had disclosed to us multiple minute fragments of radio opaque material traversing a line from the wound in the occiput to just above the right eye, with a rather sizable fragment visible by X-ray just above the right eye."[22] The large right eye fragment is claimed or assumed to be in the X-rays by Wecht[23] and Lattimer,[24] but was *not* noted by the Clark Panel. Are there two sets of X-rays? Lattimer describes the large piece thusly: "The second largest metal fragment of all, measuring about 7mm. in length by 3 mm. in width and roughly crescentic in shape, had come to rest at the front margin of the brain, just above the superior margin of the right frontal sinus.''[25]

Surely the large fragment on the outer table of the back of the skull would have been noted in the autopsy report itself. The noted two fragments, the largest being 2mm. x 7mm. and the smaller being 3mm. x 1mm., are described in the autopsy report as being on the surface of the right cerebral cortex. There is no indication in the autopsy report as to where on the brain these were, front or back, though Humes told the Warren Commission that one of them was just behind the right eye. Francis X. O'Neill said in a 1992 interview that both fragments removed from the brain came from the right front area of the brain.[26] He indicated with his hands that the fragments were just below the eye socket to the middle part of the forehead. But in his FBI report of the autopsy, he indicated that the second largest fragment (on the brain) was in the rear. Why was that fragment not submitted for analysis? We have no record of its removal. They submitted two fragments (the two "missiles") for which we have receipts, but these were evidently the two fragments found on the front of the brain. Humes mentions only one of these. None of this has anything to do with the X-ray showing a large part of a bullet found on the outer table of the skull by the Clark Panel several years later.

The trouble is that the "cortex and much of the white matter of the anterior parietal lobe and central convolutions and *the entire frontal lobe are missing*" (italics mine), according to Dr. Richard Lindenberg.[27] It would seem most difficult for a large piece of bullet to be lodged where there was no brain. Where did Dr. Lindenberg get his information? From photographs and X-rays of the brain that he presumably saw in 1975, or from what he surmises from the X-rays of the skull? (See the section that follows on the brain, for Lindenberg's full report.)

It would have to be assumed that the autopsy report's statement that there are "multiple minute metallic fragments along a line corresponding with a line joining the above described small occipital wound and the right supra-orbital ridge"[28] must mean that the fragments are to a large extent imbedded on the interior skull bone, since there was no brain left in much of the area described.

Humes' observation of the fragment behind the right eyebrow is on the brain, but *there is no bone in that area* in either of the two head X-rays that survive.[29] There couldn't have been much brain, either, in that particular case, because the front of the head is missing, and it may not even be Kennedy's skull we're seeing. Humes has left us another clue as to the truth that was taken from him and distorted.

Lattimer ignores the severe conflict between the placement of the large hole in the first drawing he made (the right lateral) and the next drawing he has of the anterior view,[30] both made from the X-rays. The anterior view drawing accurately portrays the corresponding X-ray and shows the entire right eye and front of the head missing. Both misrepresent what the reality was, though Lattimer was merely reporting what he saw. His first drawing is not according to its corresponding X-ray, and has the hole more centrally placed on the right side of the head, more toward the rear, but, of course, not far enough back.

No fragments or metallic dust were seen upon close study of the neck X-rays during the autopsy or reported by the Warren Commission, but later turned up on those X-rays seen by the Clark Panel.[31] Interestingly, the Clark Panel of doctors who examined this material said the following: "Any path other than one between the two cutaneous wounds would almost surely have been intercepted by bone and the X-ray films show no bony damage in the thorax or neck."[32] Yet, everybody now claims that a transverse process in the neck might be cracked, as two radiologists who viewed the alleged X-rays told the House Committee.[33]

The two large fragments found in the front seat of the limousine weighed as follows: 21 grains entirely of a copper shell, and 44.6 grains of copper shell and lead core. This is less than half the weight of a whole bullet of about 160 grains.

No whole bullet was found in the car or in Connally's leg.

"Assassinations Committee staff were horrified to discover the slipshod way in which the material evidence—including the bullet fragments—had been handled over the years. Some feel this taints any objective analytical conclusions about the evidence. Others have objected that because several tiny fragments have disappeared since 1963 and because Guinn was unable to test one copper fragment, his identification of only two bullets is meaningless. The Committee, however, found nothing sinister about the fragments vanishing and accepted Guinn's findings."[34]

It is not possible that "the fully jacketed 6.5 mm. Carcano bullet would have left the 'lead snowstorm' that is apparent in the X-rays, as described by Humes and Boswell," writes Detective Shaun Roach, an Australian forensics expert, in a letter to Dr. Gary Aguilar.[35] "Secondly, due to the inherent strength of the 6.5 mm. Carcano jacket, I also believe that it would not shear off a fragment upon entering the head, then deposit that fragment on the outer table of the skull, either above or below the wound. The 6.5 Carcano bullet, as I'm sure you are aware, is of particularly robust construction and, coupled with relatively tame velocities, tends to maintain its integrity and penetrate deeply into and through most targets.

"If the entire body was X-rayed, as they say, then no radiopaque fragments were noted in or around the wound track in the upper back. This also raises the question of X-rays (if any) that may have been taken of Governor Connally. One would expect that there would also be no radiopaque fragments visible in any of these X-rays, as the 'pristine' bullet that is put forward as the one that shot both JFK and Connally obviously lost little to no material on passing through both bodies. If fragments were visible on X-ray then this would cast serious doubt on the chance of the 'pristine bullet' being authentic. . . . the Carcano bullet was more than capable of penetrating both JFK and Connally, causing all their associated injuries, then being found intact on a gurney."

Roach says that it is not likely for such a 6.5 mm. Carcano to have left a "lead snowstorm" in the head. "I doubt that quite sincerely."[36]

"The strength of the projectile is the same reason I doubt sincerely the probability of it shearing off a piece upon entry and depositing this on the outer table of the skull. As you (Dr. Gary Aguilar) quite rightly point out, the handling of the President after death should be taken into account in an open-minded assessment of all the facts. It is possible that a bullet fragment may have migrated outside the skull in brain matter during handling, thus finding its way into position for the X-rays. However, if it is possible to interpret the X-ray to confirm that this fragment is *firmly* embedded in the outer table of the skull, then this would preclude fragment migration." (Roach is addressing the fact that the Clark Panel found a large part of a bullet imbedded in the outer table of the skull on the back of the head about an inch from a defect. It is this piece of evidence that we believe was manufactured—as Jerrol Custer says—when he was asked to tape a bullet fragment to a piece of skull and X-ray it the day after the autopsy, evidently as part of the composite X-ray that was being made to fake the evidence in the case.)

"Unless full metal jacketed bullets strike an intermediate object in flight, prompting premature expansion and/or fragmentation, the depositing of fragments outside the entry wound is foreign to my experience. It is not common sense and would only be proposed by a person totally out of touch with the mechanisms of bullet penetration through the human body."[37]

Vincent DiMaio, M.D., a forensics expert, writes that "Military bullets, by virtue of their full metal jackets, tend to pass through the body intact, thus producing less extensive injuries than hunting ammunition. Military bullets usually do not fragment in the body or shed fragments of lead in their paths. Because of the high velocity of such military rounds as well as their tough construction, it is possible for such bullets to pass through more than one individual before coming to rest. These bullets may be almost virginal in appearance after recovery from the body."[38]

One bullet, DiMaio notes, is an exception, and will break up: the 5.56 mm. M-16 cartridge.[39] Roach says that the head wound gives the appearance of such a fragmentation bullet: "The head wound has all the hallmarks of 5.56 mm. bullet performance. I would expect that if JFK were struck in the head from above and behind by a 6.5 Carcano bullet, the bullet would have crashed into the skull, out the other side, intact, and continued on till it hit something else. Unless I am missing something, no one else in the Presidential limousine was struck by this bullet after it passed through his head."[40]

DiMaio writes that "X-rays of individuals shot with hunting ammunition usually show a characteristic radiologic picture that is seen almost exclusively with this form of rifle ammunition. This is the so-called lead snowstorm. As the expanding bullet moves through the body, fragments of lead break off the lead core and are hurled out into the surrounding tissues. Thus an X-ray shows scores of small radiopaque bullet fragments scattered along the wound track (the lead snowstorm). Such a picture is not seen with pistol bullets, nor with one exception, with full metal-jacketed rifle bullets. The exception is the 5.56 mm. cartridge, whose propensity to fragment has been previously discussed."[41] Further, he says, "Full metal-jacketed rifle bullets with rare exceptions invariably exit if the deceased is the primary target and is within a few hundred yards of the muzzle of the weapon. The 5.56 mm. round is the only full metal-jacketed round that has a tendency to stay in the body...."[42]

What about the possibility for one bullet having passed through Kennedy undamaged, and the second, allegedly the same type of bullet, to have broken up? Roach says, "I did not believe that that occurred. I believe that the bullet that struck the deceased in the head was of a different caliber and manufacture to the bullet that struck the deceased in the upper back."[43]

It is worth noting that the whole world is watching what is going on in the United States at this time with regard to the Kennedy case. This is an Australian law enforcement officer's view of the *JAMA* distortions of 1992–93: "I can only say that Doctors Lundberg and Breo seem remarkably swift in their acceptance of the 'irrefutable proof' offered by Humes and Boswell. I am honestly at a loss to describe my disappointment at the sight of learned scientists who seemingly accept at face value, a series of statements that provide far more questions than answers!"[44]

The "Magic Bullet"

The bullet that struck John Connally is known as the "Magic Bullet" because the government claims it passed through both Kennedy and Connally and was almost perfect when found. The bullet did not appear to have lost any of its mass. A certain amount was cut away from its nose by the FBI to conduct NAA and spectrographic tests,[45] and this amount is often not accounted for when the weight of the bullet is given. The weight of the bullet (158.6 grains) is confused with its weight after the portion for tests was removed. Whole bullets of this type weighed 159 to 161 grains, but we don't know what the excised portion of the nose weighed.

The bullet was probably found on the stretcher of a little boy at Parkland Hospital[46] and not that of John Connally. This fact constitutes another outright lie by the Warren Commission. The bullet was clean, devoid of blood or other matter, which seems unlikely. Raymond Marcus obtained opinions from several coroners, pathologists, and criminologists and concluded the following: "1) They had never seen a case involving 'fall-out' through the entrance wound by a bullet that had completely penetrated *the skin,* let alone two or three inches of tissue; 2) They had never heard, through their colleagues or professional journals, of such an occurrence; 3) That the only cases of 'fall-out' they could conceive of—and had occasionally dealt with—were those in which the bullet had come to rest *partially protruding from the skin;* either as a result of failing to completely *enter* the body; or, after almost piercing it entirely, failing to completely *exit.* The reason given by all six experts as precluding 'fallout' was that the missile, upon striking the body, forces its way through skin and tissues, which immediately contract behind it; thereby leaving a free passage smaller than the diameter of the bullet. In reply to the specific question as to whether such 'fallout' was a reasonable possibility if chest massage had been applied in an effort at revival, the unanimous answer was no."[47]

As for the bullet being perfectly clean as it appeared before government investigators, devoid of blood or other matter, Marcus asked the above-cited authorities about it, and "opinions received from experts referred to in footnote on page 74 reveal that such complete lack of adhering blood or tissue would be unusual for a bullet that had pierced a body."[48] FBI expert Robert A. Frazier testified to the Warren Commission, "The bullet was clean and it was not necessary to change it in any way."[49]

This bullet had no defects to its copper jacket and lost only a small amount from its base. One fragment found in the Governor's wrist weighed 0.5 grain, and the total weights of fragments claimed by the Warren Commission to have been found in Connally weighed slightly less than the 1 to 2.5 grains the bullet is supposed to have lost. The trouble with this is the fact that large hunks of metal were found in the car, and they could have come from the bullet that struck Connally. The medical witnesses describe much larger fragments removed from Connally.

Apologists for the Warren Commission, such as Wesley Liebeler, claim that tests they know about show that such a bullet could strike bone and not be deformed.[50]

Tests conducted by the Warren Commission of similar bullets, even fired into cotton, showed more deformity.[51]

Spectrographic Analysis

On November 23, 1963, spectrographic tests were conducted on some of the bullet fragments to measure the presence of eleven chemical elements usually in bullets. The purpose was to see if the fragments could be related to the found bullets in the Book Depository and at Parkland Hospital. On the same day, a five-page report was prepared by the FBI and signed by J. Edgar Hoover.[52] It concluded that the metal smear on the car's windshield, the bullet fragments from President Kennedy, Governor Connally, and the fragments found under Mrs. Connally's jump seat were only "similar" in composition. This would appear to be conclusive proof "that they did not all come from the same type of ammunition. . . . None of the assassination specimens (the bullet that was found in General Walker's house as well) could be matched spectrographically with the comparison samples used by the FBI laboratory personnel," as Emory Brown wrote.[53]

Neutron Activation Analysis (NAA)

Emory Brown wrote, "Even if no one else caught the possible implications of the Spectro results, Hoover certainly did and requested the Atomic Energy Commission to perform additional tests."[54] This is a much more sophisticated method of measuring the elements present in metal, which requires the bombardment of the specimen with neutrons, which causes the specimen to give off gamma rays. Each element has its own radiation level, which can be measured. Brown wrote that "the findings presented in two of the papers he (Dr. Vincent Guinn) had worked on, soon gave me to understand that the NAA results were even more damaging to the Government's case than those of the Spectrographic analysis."[55]

Dr. Guinn either helped do the tests for the Warren Commission, or had access to the papers and results, and having then tested fragments for the House Committee years later, his statements that the fragments were not the same and not of the same weight was of that much more importance. This indicates substitution after the original material was stolen, as is true of so much of the other evidence from the National Archives.

Dr. Guinn had determined that "the usual standard deviation of the Antimony concentration within a single bullet or box of bullets was about plus or minus 3 percent and that the Antimony concentrations [which were the focus of his work] are very uniform within a single bullet and box of bullets." He concluded that "if the percentage of variation is greater, then the bullets or fragments would have different origins."[56] The conclusion of the test was that "the bullet which had killed the President wasn't even remotely related to the fragment from the Governor's wrist. The NAA report had demonstrated that two different types of bullets were involved and since only one type could be associated with those loaded in the ammo which was found with the Depository Carcano, the physical necessity of at least a second weapon was obvious."[57]

Winchester-Western wrote Emory Brown in September 1975 to say that they used the same metal alloys in the production of many different types of bullets. Metal from any one of the other caliber and types of bullets would have matched in both spectrographic and NAA tests. Brown writes, "This bit of information completely invalidates the Government's test results." In addition, other manufacturers may have used the same metal for their bullets.

NAA tests were never applied to the smears from the windshield of the fatal car, to the bullet portions found in the front seat, or to the smears on the curb from which fragments hit James Tague.

Trajectories

The only way roughly two thirds of a bullet could end up in the front seat of the car was for a bullet fired from behind to have struck the framework over the front windshield and broken up. This had to be either an additional shot with a wide miss from a high window, or a shot from low down through JFK's head which then hit the windshield. There was the clear impression in photographs of a bullet or large fragment having struck the framework over the windshield.

Depending on which wounds you accept as valid in the two victims, we get different results as to the trajectories. It would appear that Governor Connally was struck from a high floor or roof but that Kennedy was struck from behind and low down. The same is true if we accept the autopsy report's placement of the entry wound on the back of his head, near the base of the skull or the occipital protuberance. But, as we all know, both of these wounds moved. The latter wound had moved four inches when the autopsy photos and X-rays surfaced and were observed by the Clark Panel. The back wound six inches down on his back is at a very steep, downward angle. The autopsy photos of the back do not show a wound in the back of the neck or high enough on the shoulder to pass through and strike Connally. So they finessed it by *telling* us that the posterior wound was at the base of the neck and exited the throat, without ever proving it.

There is a clear trajectory backward through Kennedy to one of the four motorcycle policemen behind him who was splattered with matter from Kennedy's head. This shows that the shot came from ahead of the car and to the right—from the storm drain at the end of the Triple Overpass balustrade where it meets the stockade fence.

Jack Anderson's analysis of the splatter pattern in the Zapruder film had a similar result.[58]

The Limousine

The question is why the car was taken away to Detroit after the assassination and rebuilt.[59] The next day, Secret Service agents were still going over it and fragments were found on the floor, but the real issue was why the windshield was replaced and why they bought several windshields, as though somebody were experimenting on them and producing evidence of different shots from different directions. There was adequate evidence that a bullet or a fragment had passed through the windshield (see below).

Other questions are why only one brake light (the left-hand one) is showing lighted at the time of the fatal head shot, and whether the brake lights were part of the alternate flashing red light system we see in the films as the car approaches the cameras. As likely, there was sunshine in the south (left) taillight and not in the right-hand or north-side taillight.

Evidence of Other Bullets

"Another unexplained circumstance is a small hole in the windshield of the presidential limousine," reporter Richard Dudman wrote. "This correspondent and one other man saw the hole, which resembled a bullet hole, as the automobile stood at the hospital emergency entrance while the President was being treated inside the building. The Secret Service kept possession of the automobile and flew it back to Washington. A spokesman for the agency rejected a request to inspect the vehicle here [in Washington]. He declined to discuss any hole that might be in the windshield." Frank Cormier of the AP also saw the hole.[60]

"On the day the President was shot I happened to learn of a possible fifth (bullet). A group of police officers were examining the area at the side of the street where the President was hit, and a police inspector told me they just found another bullet in the grass."[61] The photographs taken of Deputy Sheriff Buddy Walters and an unidentified FBI agent, apparently Robert Barrett, bending over to examine and pocket the bullet have been published widely.

There was a long apparent bullet scar on the sidewalk just to the north of the car, which I traced years ago before Earl Golz had the section removed from the sidewalk. It would have been alongside the car before the head shot and would have represented a wide miss from the sixth-floor window, but it pointed directly at the storm drain on the south end of the triple underpass just before the Commerce Street tunnel. I sighted this myself, and it is across the street and halfway up it from the Buddy Walters/Robert Barrett bullet found in the grass.

Medical Evidence

The Throat Wound

The Warren Report's main theory—that one bullet struck both Kennedy and Connally—hinged on one idea: a bullet struck JFK in the back, exited his throat, and entered John Connally's back. They said this because they felt that if the men were hit with two separate shots, the shots could not have been fired from the same weapon, as they were too close together.

There was *no scientific evidence* of a throat exit wound seen at the autopsy. This entire theory—the main peg of the Warren Report—was a *fabrication* in the autopsy report. It hinges on a *supposition* that a bullet exited his throat. Nobody at the autopsy saw any bullet wound in the throat, seeing only a tracheostomy. Was it deliberate? Did some-one order it, or steer Humes to this conclusion?

Admiral George Burkley, President Kennedy's personal physician, had to know about the characterization of the throat wound in Dallas as a wound of entry, since he was both in the emergency room in Dallas and at the autopsy. Burkley had the death certificate from Dallas saying that there had been a gunshot wound to the neck, and the Dallas doctors were not aware of any wound to the back of the neck.

Numerous doctors in Dallas saw what they described as an entry wound in the throat, where Dr. Perry performed a tracheostomy. Could they be wrong in their perception? It is 99 percent unlikely because too many described it as an entry hole, and because they all had seen many entry holes before and could easily distinguish them from an exit hole. Sophistry—attempts by apologists for the Warren Report claim that some exit holes are identical to some entry holes—is specious and fraudulent.

The possibility of a throat entry hole is buttressed by all the evidence that tends to show that the President was also shot in the head from in front and that there were gunmen ahead of the car on the bridge and in storm drains.

Therefore, the evidence of a frontal shot in the throat is legally admissible and, in this instance, must be the definitive conclusion, since there is no hard evidence of any kind to controvert it.

It is greatly unfortunate that *The Journal of the American Medical Association* and others continue to fabricate an exit wound at the throat and pretend that it was measured and photographed at the autopsy when it was not.

Data Supporting a Frontal Shot to the Throat

Parkland doctors testified that considerably more damage would have been done to the trachea if a bullet had exited in that area,[62] and there was no evidence of any other damage that would have occurred from an exiting bullet. Dr. James Carrico stated that it was "unlikely that there was any significant tumbling action because that would usually result in a larger wound, if that were in fact an exit. . . . There was some injury to the trachea behind it, so the thing must have been going front to back, rather than right to left."[63]

Those at Parkland Hospital who saw the wound include Dr. Jones,[64] Dr. Carrico,[65] Dr. Perry,[66] Dr. Baxter,[67] Dr. McClelland,[68] Dr. Crenshaw,[69] Dr. Gene Akin,[70] and Nurse Henchcliff[71] and Nurse Bowron.[72] All stated that it was a wound of entrance.[73]

Dr. Humes's claim that he did not know about the throat wound is possibly another deliberate fabrication, if Dr. Robert Livingston's statement is accurate. He called Humes as the body was being flown to Bethesda and told him that Dr. Perry had said on television that there was an entry hole in the throat.[74]

The Tracheostomy

This appears to be 1.5 cm. wide at its widest and 6.5 cm. (2.5 in.) long, according to the autopsy report. I have shown the photo of this wound to all those Dallas doctors and nurses who saw it, and *none* dispute its length or width, with the possible exception of Dr. Crenshaw, who notes that it is not quite right.[75] Paul O'Connor, one of those at the autopsy, told me that one of the photos showing the wound is retouched along the edges to make it look like a jagged exit wound,[76] and this is what I feel is bothering Dr. Crenshaw, who told me (prior to publishing his own book) that it looked wrong, but not cut with a knife.[77] He said it was distended from someone digging in there with their fingers. Of course, Perry did conduct something of an exploratory operation there, and the head is hanging back on the autopsy table in the pictures, opening and distending the wound.

There is a notch at the center of the bottom rim of the wound that could either be from an entering bullet or from the endotracheal tube. Dr. Perry said that it was "quite likely" that it was the rim of the bullet entry hole that he observed, but that it might also be caused by the weight of the tracheal tube pressing there.[78]

Perry: "I thought it looked like an entrance wound because it was so small."[79]

The Large Head Defect

It seems to me that there is a semantic problem with the placement of this wound. My interviews show no real difference between where Humes and Boswell placed it in the autopsy report and where it was seen in Dallas.

The autopsy report states that a large amount of bone and scalp was missing from the right rear quadrant of the head.[80] *There is no missing bone or scalp showing at all in this location in the X-rays or photo-*

graphs. The same wound was described in Dallas by all witnesses, with shredded scalp overlying part of it, and scalp missing from the rest, more toward the right rear of the head.

The exact position of the large defect was confirmed to me by witnesses from both hospitals by drawing on mannequin heads and human heads, and it was in the identical place on the head. There was no alteration of the body to fool the camera because many persons at the autopsy dispute the autopsy photographs and X-rays, which don't show the wounds the people saw. They state that the wounds are either not in the right place or that the photos and X-rays of the head are fake. The X-ray tech and the photographer have stated that the pictures are not the ones they took.[81] The FBI's Francis X. O'Neill placed the large defect in the same area at the back of the head. He put his hand on his head in that position in a video when asked where the large wound was.[82]

There was a large amount of scalp missing in the back and right rear of the head, as the autopsy report and all witnesses have said. This does not show in the photographs or anywhere else. The large hole—it seems to me—can be seen clearly in the Zapruder film in certain frames in the identical position noted in the autopsy report, depending on *which* copy one is viewing.

"Although the fractures of the calvarium extend to the left of the midline and into the anterior and middle fossae of the skull, no bony defect, such as one created by a projectile either entering or leaving the head, is seen in the calvarium to the left of the midline or in the base of the skull. Hence it is not reasonable to postulate that a projectile passed through the head in a direction other than that described above," says the Clark Panel on reviewing the alleged X-rays.[83] That is, it could not have come from the Grassy Knoll, but from in front or from behind. It is also crucially important from the standpoint of those who claimed the large defect was all across the head from right to left in the back or top.†

There is no doubt that the back of the President's head was missing

†Chapter 2 of my first book on the case, *High Treason,* "The President's Head Wounds and the New Evidence of Forgery," contains an extensive treatment of the head wounds and a comprehensive listing of all evidence, witness testimony, and conflicts with regard to the placement and size of the large defect and the alleged entry wounds. My second book, *High Treason 2,* contains considerable new information I developed on the subject through interviews with the autopsy witnesses, and this book contains information on the head wounds in the Diana Bowron, *JAMA,* Dallas "Autopsy Forum," and autopsy X-ray and photographic chapters.

on the right. There was something of a flap of scalp over the posterior defect, but it was too badly shredded and holed to appear so perfect, as it does in the present photographs alleged by the government. That large defect extended from the occipital bone itself on the very lower back of the head nearly to the top of the head on the right and as far forward as the ear. There probably was a flap of scalp and bone above the ear where a bullet entered and which flap was closed by Jacqueline Kennedy. A small bone between that flap and that of the large defect behind the right ear may have fallen in on the way to Bethesda, making the defect larger.

The point is that the known large exit wound observed by all witnesses and reported in the autopsy report was in almost precisely the same place, and this concretely refutes its position in the X-rays.

The Back Wound

The wound was in fact probed.[84] It was described by Dr. Finck in the trial of Clay Shaw, in the FBI autopsy report, and by numerous witnesses to the author, and the aforementioned state that it did not penetrate the body. The location in the autopsy report is given with improper reference points: the acromion process and the mastoid process.[85] The spine and the top of the head should have been used.

When the autopsy was over, the doctors believed that a bullet had fallen out of the back wound during external cardiac massage in Dallas.[86] This is further confirmation that the autopsy doctors felt this was a shallow, nonpenetrating wound. Yet there is evidence that a bullet actually fell out of the wrappings as the autopsy began.[87]

The FBI report states that the wound in the back was "below the shoulders" and "45 to 60 degrees downward," stating that it had *no point of exit*. The wound is roughly 4 to 4.5 cm. from the midline of the back, and the top of the wound is about 5.7 cm. below the first crease (bottom) of the neck. It looks to be about 5 x 7 mm. in size in the photo.

This wound was not traced by dissection.

The FBI agents who were present were clearly given a different impression of the autopsy report and findings, as the Bureau continued for two months to state that different bullets hit the two victims. The undated autopsy report may have been written much later than claimed, and, of course, the FBI report was suppressed for a long time.

The wound is higher in the autopsy report than it is on the President's clothes and on Dr. Boswell's autopsy drawing. Paul O'Connor is adamant to me that the higher, larger wound shown in the photograph of the back is in fact the back wound, and this would correspond to where Dr. Marion Jenkins said he felt it, during a conference in Dallas on June 3, 1992. Nevertheless, this wound cannot be described as at the base of the neck. It is 3 to 4 inches down on the shoulder. I personally don't think we're looking at Kennedy's back in the death photograph, which mirrors Diana Bowron's surprising comment in this book on the alleged autopsy photo: "THIS IS NOT THE BACK I SAW!"

Measurements made from the ruler alongside the wound indicate that this hole is considerably larger than that recorded in the autopsy report but that a small spot, perhaps 2 inches lower and closer to the spine, corresponds to the 4 x 7 mm. measurement recorded at the autopsy. Some researchers, therefore, assume that is the bullet entry.

The bullet hole appears to be about 6 inches down on Kennedy's back on the drawing made by Dr. Boswell at the autopsy, and this corresponds perfectly to the holes in the clothing, but there is no corresponding hole shown in the photographs. Here again, language such as "base of the neck" is used to obfuscate the issues. Boswell was gotten to cast doubt on the accuracy of his own drawing in a newspaper story years ago.[88]

The Rear Head Entry

There was no small rear entry hole in the head seen in Dallas or when the body was first examined at autopsy. Not until midnight, when some pieces of bone arrived—ostensibly from Dallas—was a partial small hole of entrance seen.[89] At least this is the official story. There is no chain of evidence to prove where the bone came from, which also applies to the bullet fragments found in the car the next day.

In addition, the pieces of bone did not fit perfectly together.[90] This indicates that either additional bone was missing, or that they were from a different head.

The alleged entry hole in the head is 4 inches higher in the photographs than it is in the autopsy report.[91] The autopsists strongly disputed the location in the photos and X-rays,[92] and none of the corpsmen at the autopsy recall any entry hole in the back of the head. After making it clear to the panel of doctors examining them for the House Committee, Dr. Petty said this to the autopsy doctors: "I'm showing you now photograph No. 15, and here, to put it in the record, is the posterior hairline or margin of the hair of the late President, and there, near the midline, and just a centimeter or two above the hairline, is an area that you refer to as the inshoot wound.''

Dr. Humes: ''Yes, sir.''

''. . . And what we're trying to do is satisfy ourselves that the bullet actually came in near the margin of the hair and not near the tip of the ruler as is shown in photograph No. 16.''

Dr. Humes: ''I can assure you that as we reflected the scalp to get to this point, there was no defect corresponding to this in the skull at any point. I don't know what that is. It could be to me clotted blood. I don't, I just don't know what it is, but it certainly was not any wound of entrance.''[93] Humes was referring to the alleged wound in the cowlick area.

In addition, Dr. Marion Jenkins from Parkland stated that he felt both of the rear entry holes as he held the President's head before he died and that the rear head entry was near the hairline.[94]

I have repeatedly stated in my writings and made an issue of this almost single-handedly: There is a 4-inch difference (noted by the House Committee) between the alleged wound in the cowlick and the placement of the entry wound in the autopsy report near the hairline.

Beveling

With regard to the alleged bevelling of the skull surrounding the entry hole, described by Dr. Finck and the autopsists, the photograph clearly shows that the bevelling is on the *outer* table of the skull in the photograph taken, which shows the interior of the skull through the large hole. Close cross-examination of Dr. Michael Baden of the HSCA Forensic Panel by Mark Flannigan, an attorney who was formerly a staff member of the House Assassinations Committee, before the Bar Association of the District of Columbia's mock trial of Oswald in the summer of 1992, showed that it was probably an invention to say that anyone could have examined the alleged interior bevelling from an exterior shot when there was no photograph taken from inside the head. Baden answered lamely that he had used spectrographic analysis. This point was not pursued, as part of the gentlemanly agreement among the parties not to press any issue to the point of demolition of someone's reputation or stability. It was left up to us to guess that maybe that evidence had been made up, too.

Right Front Head Entry

Some men from the autopsy describe metal smears in the right temple area on the skull, indicating a bullet's entrance or exit, but one of the men (James Jenkins) thought it was an entrance.[95] The 1963 statement that there was a hole in the left temple from an entering bullet has never been confirmed or substantiated, and the witnesses have retracted this statement. Tom Robinson, the cosmetics person from the funeral home, described to the author perforations of the skull—evidently from fragments—one of which was in the temple area, but he could not recall which temple.[96]

There was a large metal slug just above the right orbit inside the skull reported by Humes, who removed it.[97] It is reported by Wecht, who saw the X-rays in 1972.[98] But this seems to conflict with the X-rays that show no skull bone in that area, and with the failure of the Clark Panel to report it upon examining the X-rays.

Objective analysis of all the data indicates that a bullet entered the right front temple and blew off the back of the head, driving the President backward and to the left.

The Brain

The brain was not sectioned,[99] and sectioning is normally how bullet trajectories are traced. Its weight was recorded at the time of the supplemental report, and not at the time of the autopsy two weeks earlier, at 1500 grams. This is roughly the exact weight of a normal male brain (some authorities say the average weight of a male brain is 1380 grams—see *High Treason 2* for references), in spite of the fact that at least one fourth to one half of it was described as missing.

The supplemental autopsy report has a description of an examination of the brain, which would not seem possible without sectioning it.[100] It would seem that this part of the report was fabricated as well.

There was an examination of the autopsy photographs and X-rays in 1975 by a group of doctors for the "Rockefeller Commission," which was the Commission on CIA Activities Within the United States. Dr. Richard Lindenberg, the Director of Neuropathology and Legal Medicine for the State of Maryland's Department of Health and Mental Hygiene, was one of those who entered the Archives to study the material. With respect to the brain, he wrote, "Instead of leaving a distinct wound canal through the brain, the bullet produced a severe injury in the right cerebral hemisphere commencing in the posterior parietal region near the border of the occipital lobe, becoming larger anteriorly. Cortex and much of the white matter of the anterior parietal lobe and central convolutions *and the entire frontal lobe are missing.* (Emphasis added.) Walls and floor of the large defect, essentially formed by deep

white matter, show no hemorrhage and no unusual defects except anteriorly and laterally where a small, parallelogram-shaped opening exposes
the anterior portion of the sylvian fissure in which two branches of the
middle cerebral artery can be seen. This defect was noticed by the 1968
Review Panel and by Wecht (1972), but not identified. Still present are
orbital, temporal and occipital lobes, the operculum, and most convolutions which faced the falx. Deprived of support by white matter, the
latter lean over towards the defect. Except for small superficial and
non-hemorrhagic lacerations opposite fractured bones of the base, the
convolutions of these preserved portions of the hemisphere show no
defects. The corpus callosum seen between the hemispheres is grossly
intact. Some fresh subarachnoid hemorrhage is present in the open,
anterior sylvian fissure.

"The entire left cerebral hemisphere is preserved except for superficial nonhemorrhagic lacerations of some convolutions opposite fractured
bones. At the convexity the convolutions are somewhat flat. The leptomeninges are transparent and intact. Over the lateral aspect of the frontal
and temporo-parietal areas there is local, fresh, thin subarachnoid hemorrhage over intact convolutions. Also, the convolutions of the medial
aspect of the hemisphere, which faced the falx, are fully preserved.

"At the base of the brain there are small defects in the tuber cinereum
and nonhemorrhagic tears in both peduncles of the midbrain. These
alterations are probably postmortem artifacts. There is no subarachnoid
hemorrhage. The brainstem and the cerebellum show no signs of injury."[101] With regard to this latter, one wonders about the stories that
the cerebellum was out of the head in Dallas. Clearly this was not the
same brain.

In addition, one cannot have the frontal lobe missing, as he says, and
still have bullet fragments seen in it on an X-ray of the skull that has
no bone in that area either.

The photographs of the base of the canal cut in the brain by the bullet
on the right side show a "gray-brown, rectangular structure measuring
approximately 13 x 20 mm." on the right side.[102] It would seem to be
some sort of growth or other foreign material. There is no corresponding
object in the X-rays in that position. It was first noticed by the Clark
Panel years after the autopsy. Why then? Because it was unlikely that
this structure, along with the big fragment on the outer table of the
skull in the back, was on the X-rays seen during the autopsy.

The alleged brain is missing from the Archives. Robert Tannenbaum,
former chief counsel to the HSCA, reported at the 1993 Chicago Conference that Frank Mankiewicz told him that Robert Kennedy placed
the brain in the casket with JFK when the body was reinterred.

The Autopsy Report

The autopsy report does not give information that would preclude shots from in front and more than one gunman. The doctors were not officially aware of the reports of shots from in front or of a frontal throat wound described in Dallas, and the missing portion of the head could just as easily have been taken off by a tangential shot from the front. The autopsy has been criticized on many counts by the House panel of doctors[103] and many others, including Wilber.[104] It was not competent and fabricated various key matters of evidence, such as the throat wound as exit wound and the brain's weight, and covered up the fact that the President had no adrenals. The weight of the brain and the liver appear to be fabricated. An average adult male brain weighs 1400 grams and average livers weigh 1650 grams.[105] Kennedy's brain weighed 1500 grams, after losing much of its mass due to the gunshot, and his liver was 650 grams, insufficient for any adult human being to survive upon.

The fact that there was an autopsy at all was kept secret from the nation for some days afterward. The Associated Press dispatched an article, "No Report of Autopsy Given on Kennedy." The first sentence read, "The White House has so far declined to say whether an autopsy was performed on the body of slain President John F. Kennedy."[106] Bethesda, likewise, kept mum and revealed nothing, not even that there had been an autopsy. But word leaked out.

Lyndon Johnson, then in the White House and Commander In Chief of the military, was quite clearly afraid of whatever might flow from any premature release of information, until they had gotten everything faked and their stories just right.

The Autopsists

Dr. Humes had only one course in forensics and, in fact, had almost no experience with gunshots.[107] He was a hospital pathologist. Dr. Pierre Finck was trained but had little actual experience with gunshots. Dr. J. Thornton Boswell, also a hospital pathologist, had almost no experience with gunshots.[108]

Critique of the Autopsy Photographs and X-rays

The Clark Panel stated that there was a "lack of clarity and detail" in the photographs.[109] The House Assassinations Committee published a long critque pointing out many problems with the photos[110] and that they would not be admissible in court.[111]

Forgery

The Autopsy Photographs

A panel of experts who examined and claimed to have authenticated the alleged autopsy photographs[112] overlooked various matters and was seriously flawed in its work. There was nothing "scientific" about their examination. They did not know what to look for in the photographs.

The quality of the photos is very poor, and the House panel publicly criticized them.[113]

The key pictures of the back of the head are out of focus in the area between the hairline and the hair on the back of the head, behind the ear all the way down to the center of the head, above the neck, where it appears to be retouched to cover up the fact that the scalp was torn loose all along that area by exiting bone. I no longer agree that this is a composite photo and that is a matte line. My original position in 1979 was that it is simply retouched. All the rest of the hair and scalp in the area where it should be missing is retouched. In addition, numerous of the other pictures show evidence of retouching.

As far as the integrity of stereo views being maintained, we are expected to take this on faith. Researchers have not been granted access to the relevant photographs to evaluate such pairs; for the rear head photos in particular, this is crucial evidence. The two photographs published in *High Treason 2,* however, can produce a steroscopic view.

It is fallacious for anyone to ignore the major attempts by all the medical witnesses to point out serious problems with the pictures, or to ignore their outright denunciations of the photos and X-rays.

The Skull X-Rays

These show all the bone missing from the midline of the frontal bone forward of one coronal suture down as far as the maxillary area in the lateral view. They apparently show an entry in the cowlick but clearly no bone missing anywhere from the right side to rear in the area the autopsy report described as missing. Other medical people insist the X-rays show an entry at the external occipital protuberance.

There is a severe conflict between the AP view and the lateral view, because there is much more bone missing on the lateral than the AP on the right face. Both have a massive amount of bone missing on the face.

The missing frontal bone is documented by several reports in Volume 7 of the appendix to the Report of the House Assassinations Committee,[114] and commented upon by the doctors themselves during their interview with Humes.[115] Humes and Boswell are strangely silent in the transcript more than once while discussions are occurring about the missing frontal bone.

Dr. Humes stated to the Warren Commission that the photos and X-rays were not developed at the time of the autopsy.[116] He mispoke himself and was only referring to the photographs, which were developed later. The X-rays were needed to look for bullets, and there is ample testimony indicating that they were, in fact, developed during the course of the autopsy and studied.[117]

Enhancement of copies of the X-rays are not the reason bone appears to be missing. The bone is missing in the unenhanced copies as well and is commented on by others.[118] (Please see the chapter on X-rays.)

X-Rays Showing the Cervical Vertebra and Neck

According to some, there was slight damage to the transverse process of one vertebra, which was *not seen at the time of the autopsy,* and a metal fragment or artifact—definitely not bone[119] in the neck, *which was also not seen at the time of the autopsy,* during which these films were closely studied, looking for just that. Dr. Carrico said that had a bullet struck the transverse process, it would have lost much more energy than CE 399 apparently did, if it went through two men.[120]

The Clark Panel said that "there was no evidence of fracture of either scapula or of the clavicles, or of the ribs or of any of the cervical and thoracic vertebra. . . . The X-rays show no bony damage in the thorax or the neck." They also said that "Several small metallic fragments are present in this region."[121]

It is unfortunate that Dr. John Lattimer's 1972 lone speculation— never verified by anyone scientifically—that "a 'graze' of the tip of the transverse process of the seventh cervical vertebra could not be excluded,"[122] was converted by him in his lectures and other writings (and as a result, by others) over the years into a statement of fact that Kennedy had assumed the Thorburn position as a result of an actual strike on that piece of bone.

From this came the wild argument that Kennedy would have died from the neck wound, or certainly would have been a quadriplegic. Kennedy actually had raised his hands in response to the pain of having been shot in the throat, as we see in the film of the assassination. Lattimer's exaggeration is based on what he thinks he sees in the Zapruder film, but he never saw any such evidence of an actual strike of the vertebra on the X-rays, and neither has anyone else. Certainly the hands in Thorburn's original article of 1887[123] are not remotely in a position similar to that which Lattimer attempts to ascribe to Kennedy's hands after he has been shot in the throat. Thorburn has the forearms and hands well above the shoulders and outside the torso, not grasping at the neck, as Kennedy was doing. It would seem that Lattimer might have found more recent sources to back his ideas if they had any real substance, since there has been a vast amount of new data acquired on spinal injuries in the succeeding century.

Lattimer begins to convert his possible "graze" of the vertebra in 1972 to "We believe that this upward movement resulted from a stimulation of C6, some time between frames 220 and 224, with the greatest probability that the spinal cord was injured at about frame 222," in 1977.[124] Time works strange things on the minds of men. His theory remains speculation passed off as fact.

Transfer to the Archives of the Photos and X-Rays

The official transfer of the autopsy materials from the Kennedy family to the National Archives was on October 29, 1966. This is the day that Lieutenant Commander William Bruce Pitzer was found shot to death at Bethesda Naval Hospital.[125] Pitzer was said to have filmed the autopsy, and one of the men who assisted there insists to me that he helped edit the film.[126]

Humes, Finck, and Boswell viewed the photos and X-rays for the first time on November 1, 1966,[127] and inventoried and categorized them. They saw them again on January 27, 1967, during which time they summarized their findings, and were reported to have said that the pictures confirmed their autopsy report. However, during their meeting with a panel of doctors for the HSCA, they strongly questioned the location of the wounds on the head, a subject I treated exhaustively in my other books.

The materials were reviewed by Ramsey Clark's panel of four doctors in early 1968, and a number of startling observations were made that conflicted with the autopsy report itself. This was the time of the Jim Garrison prosecution of Clay Shaw. One of the conflicts involved the placement of the rear head entry four inches from where it was at the autopsy, and another the discovery of metal fragments in the neck. Another is the appearance of a large fragment on the outside of the back of the head, and the near total loss of frontal bone on the right front face, though the front and side X-ray views show a different amount of bone missing.

In 1972, Dr. John Lattimer reviewed the materials,[128] and Dr. Cyril Wecht reviewed them on August 23–24, 1972,[129] among a few other doctors who saw them.

The Films

The Zapruder Film

The film shows the upper right side of the President's face blowing out—a large, balloon-shaped object. Some speculate that brain or a flap of skull is hanging over the eye, which I call the Blob. No such damage was seen minutes later at the hospital or at any time. The face was completely intact. There is no medical or physical way to explain what is seen in the film other than to postulate that the Blob is drawn onto the film to make it appear that a shot from behind has removed part of his face. The Blob corresponds with or corroborates the X-rays that show the upper right front of the face missing. Both are fake.

The back of the head following the head shot at Z 313 is either in shadow or it has been blacked out to cover up the missing portion of skull. Shadow in that position is highly unlikely at midday, with bright reflections close by on the film, so it appears to have been tampered with.

The Nix Film

Doug Mizzer reports evidence of forgery with this film, with a frame having been removed following the headshot.[130] His theory is that the first frame shows the vapor from the brain shot at the moment of impact on the front of the head, and the following frame shows a large piece of skull fragment in the air coming from the back of the head. This would be conclusive proof that the shot came from the front. The original film was lost during the HSCA investigations, and the only copies available are the ones upon which Groden worked.

Martin Shackelford comments that "It seems like a skull fragment flying through the air would appear in more than one frame, suggesting that this may be an artifact on the film; also, there seems to be no indication of a missing frame in the film. A missing frame is not that easy to disguise, and impossible to disguise in a frame-by-frame viewing.''[131]

The Bronson Film

There is evidence that this film is not at all the same film that was described by FBI agents Newsom and Horton in 1963[132] and by Charles Bronson to me in 1992.[133] (See the chapter on films.)

Aberrations

The Clark Panel first pointed out that there was a large slug 6.5 mm. in diameter embedded in the *outer table of the skull* close to the alleged entry wound on the back of the head, which they found to be 100 mm. (4 in.) above the occipital protuberance.

1. The slug was not noted on examining the X-rays and head at the autopsy. This seems impossible.

2. There was no bone in that region of the head because it had all been blown away.

3. The entrance wound was found to be only "slightly above" the occipital protuberance at the autopsy, and there are statements by the doctors that it was "slightly below" it[134] but that the language was changed later. There was no bone in that region of the head at the time of the autopsy. The alleged entrance hole was claimed to be discovered by assembling pieces of bone that came in at the close of the autopsy, and for which there was no chain of evidence established, and these pieces of bone have vanished from the evidence.

A large part of a bullet was removed from the forwardmost part of the right brain, behind the right eye's supraorbital ridge. This fragment does not appear in the preautopsy X-rays examined by the Clark Panel in 1968, yet was described by Dr. Humes to the Warren Commission as being "visible by X-ray just above the right eye."[135] Dr. Wecht's drawing, after he first saw the autopsy materials, has marked the position of this fragment in what he calls their "approximate position."[136] The indication is that Wecht did not actually see this fragment on the X-ray but may be repeating what he was told, because he notes that "the exit point of the bullet or its larger fragments cannot be determined because of the large loss of skull bone in the right parietal and frontal regions."[137] Why did not Wecht start screaming in 1973 that there was a massive conflict in the evidence? The frontal bone was gone, and nothing was missing on the posterior part of the skull. Think about that. He merely mentions that it is gone. "The bullet trajectory therefore cannot be determined, although it is clear that the bullet entered from the rear of the President."[138] This is just invention.

Lattimer also notes that "The second-largest metallic fragment (7mm. x 3mm. but crescentic) had come to rest in the front margin of the brain just above the top of the frontal sinus on the right."[139] The conflict with this is again that there does not appear to be any bone in that area, though it might have been possible for the brain still to have been there, uncovered, holding the bullet fragment, something nobody has said happened. And the fact that the fragment does not seem to appear on the X-rays observed by the Clark Panel, or surely they would have noted it.

The FBI report of the autopsy has conflicting statements on several matters—missile receipt, surgery to the top of the head, and so on, and this has caused a great deal of confusion.

Conflicts in the Photographic and Radiographic Materials

The photos show an intact face. *All* witnesses have repeatedly testified that the face was undamaged. At no place does the documentation state that the bones of the face or forehead were removed during the autopsy. Dr. Humes reaffirmed that the face was "intact" and "normal" in his statements to *The Journal of the American Medical Association.*[140] This means that the X-rays are fake. The entire right front of the face as far as the mandible area is missing in the lateral X-ray, and as far down as the eye orbit in the AP view.

The Clark Panel noted that "with respect to the right frontoparietal region of the skull, the traumatic damage is particularly severe with extensive fragmentation of the bony structures from the midline of the frontal bone anteriorly to the vicinity of the posterior margin of the parietal bone behind. Above, the fragmentation extends approximately 25 mm. across the midline to involve adjacent portions of the left parietal bone: below, the changes extend into the right temporal bone. Throughout this region, many of the bony pieces have been displaced outward; several pieces are missing."[141] The last phrase is the key one. They meant that what is missing is all of the bone throughout that area of the face is missing, according to the phony X-rays.

The photos and X-rays show no missing bone and only fractures to the back or right rear of the head. *They conflict with the autopsy report itself,* which describes bone missing in the back of the head, as well as the descriptions given by *most* witnesses who saw the body.

Some photos conflict with each other. The Left Profile shows a side view of the tracheostomy incision, which shows clean, neat edges of an incision. This conflicts with the tracheostomy incision shown in the Stare-Of-Death photo, which shows the left side of the incision with irregular, gaping edges. Several autopsy witnesses who saw it say that the photo is doctored by photo retouching on the incision.

Connally's Wounds

Back Wound

Dr. Robert Shaw restated on June 4, 1992,[142] that the wound he saw in Connally's back was not that of a tumbling bullet or of a bullet that had struck anything else before striking Connally. He insisted that it was a clean, round wound of entry—very small. He said this in the face of Dr. John Lattimer, who had just claimed before a large audience that it was "butterfly," "keyhole," or figure-eight-shaped—that of a bullet that had just been through someone else.

The forensic pathology panel report of the House Assassination Committee found that the configuration of the wound indicated tumbling. But the elongation of the wound on Connally's back was horizontal. Clearly, nobody went back to the source: the Dallas doctors who saw it, such as Shaw.

Dr. Shaw had cut away the edges of the wound, and so the scar did not reflect its original appearance, enlarging it from 1.5 cm. to 3 cm.[143]

Leg

There is a controversy as to whether a whole bullet entered Connally's leg and then fell out, due to Dr. Robert Shaw's statement at the Parkland Hospital press conference that day that a bullet had entered his leg.[144] Shaw had merely mispoken himself, and meant that only a small fragment entered. There has never been any hard evidence to indicate that any bullet had actually entered the leg. It is likely that the rest of the bullet grazed the leg and is one of the large fragments that were found on the floor under his seat in the limousine. A tiny fragment would be driven into the Governor's femur (as it was), and the whole bullet would not drive deeply into the leg or even make a superficial wound and then fall out. Normally bullets do not fall out, even if stopped in a fairly shallow wound.

Dr. Robert Shaw restated on June 4, 1992, that only a fragment entered Connally's thigh, and not a whole bullet.† Bill Stinson, Connally's press secretary, told the press at 4:00 P.M. the day of the assassination that a fragment had entered the Governor's thigh.

Two different bullets may have actually struck Connally: one in the wrist and leg, and one through his torso.

Clothing

Connally's clothes were cleaned and pressed before any tests could be conducted for metal tracings. It is very hard to believe that the investigating bodies allowed this to happen. But it was Lyndon Johnson's aide who took Connally's clothes and cleaned and pressed them, and they ended up in the possession of Congressman Henry Gonzalez.

Fragments

The size of the fragments removed from Governor Connally, as described and illustrated by the medical witnesses,[145] does not correspond at all to the small fragments recorded by the Warren Commission,[146] and those recorded by the Warren Commission—according to Dr. Guinn—do not correspond to that which he was given by the National Archives to test with Neutron Activation Analysis.[147]

Conflicts in the Evidence Generally

On the day of the assassination, the AP published a story that a Secret Service man had been shot. There was a pool of blood seen on a sidewalk and reported by others.[148]

There was no evidence that either of the weapons attributed to Oswald had been fired. If they had been fired, that evidence would be in the record.

†See the chapter on the Dallas "Autopsy Forum" in this book

There were no fingerprints or palmprints reported on the weapons for three days.

Many people reported shots and gun smoke from the Grassy Knoll area.[149]

Some Secret Service men reported that some of the shots sounded like pistol shots at close range.[150]

The storm sewer alongside the car had an escape route leading out from a tunnel at its base, which was traced in 1992 by Jack Brazil, and years before by Penn Jones, Jr.[151]

The Dallas papers reported six shots fired.[152]

Men flashed Secret Service identification to Dallas policemen and others who ran up on the Grassy Knoll.[153] It was later determined that no Secret Service agents were there.[154]

Men were seen with rifles and running from the knoll after the shooting.[155]

Films and cameras were seized from witnesses and never returned.[156]

Transcripts of testimony were altered.[157]

Witnesses who had been or who were in Dallas soon died.[158] But there are questions about some of those alleged "deaths," some of which are more likely to have been accidental, and some of the people may not in fact be dead, but are in witness protection programs or otherwise underground.

Two different types of bullets struck JFK: one frangible, and one not.

It is illogical not to fire at the limousine if there was only one shooter, when there was a clear shot as the car approached.

There were two different types of shell casings found at the site of the Tippit shooting.[159]

The FBI interviewed the Secret Service men closest to Kennedy, and the following is an interesting comment on the state of affairs. Keep in mind that if J. Edgar Hoover was involved in the conspiracy, his men could not know that—though some suspected it. If any information came to their attention that was dangerous, Hoover simply buried it and made sure everybody kept their mouths shut. "The Specter memorandum suggests that the FBI was maintaining close surveillance on the Secret Service in the days immediately following the assassination. In fact, according to one veritable report, there was discernable suspicion between the two organizations that led to both of them being represented at the Presidential autopsy conducted at Bethesda Naval Hospital."[160]

Lee Harvey Oswald

Oswald, it is now known, thought very highly of Kennedy.[161]

Oswald was seen moments before the shooting on the second floor.[162]

There were no powder burns or residue of nitrate on Oswald's face, a seeming impossibility after firing such a rifle.

The Warren Commission put much store on the link between Oswald ordering by mail an Italian rifle from a sporting store advertisement that said it was 36 inches long—a carbine. The rifle claimed by the Warren Commission to have killed President Kennedy is 40 inches long and a Model 91/38.[163] The model advertised was probably a Model 41. The National Archives will not let anyone measure the rifle they have. We are only allowed to see a movie of the rifle now at the Archives.

I find it hard to believe that *any* former Marine would use a $13 rifle to shoot a President. The Marines instill pride, and I am sure that Oswald would have taken pride in his weapon and what he did with it.

Oswald could not have gotten from his house to the scene of the Tippit shooting in the allotted time before Tippit was reported dead.[164]

Oswald was reported to be in several different places at the same time prior to the assassinations. For example, reports place him in Mexico City when he was also supposed to have been with Sylvia Odio in Texas.[165]

Oswald clearly had an intelligence background.[166]

Oswald was so fluent in Russian that his wife thought he was Russian when she met him,[167] and Count DeMohrenschildt thought that he was totally fluent, literate, and highly intelligent—not a lone nut redneck.[168]

The Russian nationals who translated the tapes of someone alleged to be Lee Harvey Oswald calling the Soviet Embassy in Mexico City shortly before the assassination listened to tape recordings of Oswald provided by House Committee investigators and said that it could not possibly be the same person. They said that the person they heard had a very broken accent and could barely speak Russian.[169]

There are conflicts about the height and appearance of Oswald in various records and photos.[170]

Marina Oswald insists to me and others that she was not standing where the camera is in the "Backyard Pictures," but was standing *under the stairs* in the background when she took pictures of her husband.[171]

Tippit Shooting

There is nothing that links the slaying of John Kennedy and that of Officer Tippit less than an hour later. This was strictly guilt by association. The Warren Commission junior counsel David Belin claimed that the Tippit shooting was the "Rosetta stone of the assassination of President Kennedy," meaning that they felt they could prove the later slaying was perpetrated by Oswald but not the former. It also meant in their minds that only a guilty person fleeing the assassination would have shot a policeman, despite evidence that a jealous husband might also have had a motive.

They knew that all they had in the JFK case was circumstantial evidence. They had little or no evidence that could stand up to prove that Oswald killed Tippit. This case relied upon eyewitness identifications from lineups, which are notoriously poor gauges.[172] Respected Dallas researcher Greg Lowrey has done an exhaustive study on Tippit's moment-to-moment movements the day he died.

Ruby

Ruby called a police officer, Billy Grammer, the night before he shot Oswald, asking them to change the transfer route for Oswald.[173] Ruby probably hoped that if they had changed the transfer route, he would not have known where Oswald was and would not have been able to shoot him.[174]

Ruby, just after his arrest, expressed vast relief at the news that Oswald was dead, even though he was told it meant the death sentence for him. His jailer, Don Ray Archer, was sure that Ruby was glad Oswald was dead because Ruby had been ordered to kill him, and it would go badly for Ruby's family if Oswald survived.[175]

Jack Ruby gave a note to his jailer, Al Maddox, just before he died, seeming to say that he shot Oswald to silence him.[176] Al Maddox told Baltimore City police officer Marco Miranda, "Sure there was a conspiracy in the case. It was local, too!"[177]

In a later interview with Officer Marco Miranda and myself, Al Maddox indicated that Ruby was killed because he was trying to talk, and because he had won a new trial. Ruby was writing too many letters, or trying to.[178]

Medical

The Dallas doctors reported that the cerebellum was out of the head and on the table. This came into some dispute by the autopsy report.

The cerebellum was evidently put back in the head in Dallas, as the autopsy witnesses do not report this information.

Too many witnesses have reported that a major portion of the brain was missing at Parkland. Diana Bowron told me that there was almost no brain left on the right.[179]

There is a question as to whether the incisions for the chest tubes actually penetrated the chest.

There are a number of instances where dissembling by the doctors at Bethesda Naval Hospital seems to be the only way to explain some of the conflicts.

We uncovered Navy doctors and others who felt that Kennedy had Potts disease (a disease of the spine that atrophies the adrenals) and not Addison's, which also atrophies the adrenals.[180]

I was told by Dr. Karnei that there were no adrenals left.[181] Dr. John Lattimer reported that he could "well visualize" the "adrenal gland areas" on the X-rays and that there were "no abnormal calcifications seen in these areas to suggest tuberculosis or hemorrhage of the adrenals. It is the author's firm belief that the President suffered from bilateral adrenal atrophy."[182] This would seem to be the opposite of what Lattimer shows on slides of calcified and shriveled adrenals in his lectures. Adrenals cannot be seen on an X-ray without dye, and this is not done to a corpse.

Dr. Boswell told me that they did not remove the spinal cord,[183] and Dr. Karnei does not recall it being removed.[184] Boswell's assistant James Curtis Jenkins said that he removed it with a Stryker saw.[185] There are various reports from the men and the officers at the autopsy that a whole or nearly whole bullet fell out of the wrappings when they were preparing the body for autopsy.[186]

Dr. Humes claims that he did not know about the wound in the throat, which Dr. Perry said three times on TV the day of the assassination was a frontal entry wound, until he called Perry the next day.[187] Dr. Robert Livingston wrote me that he in fact told Humes as the body was being flown to Bethesda that Perry had said this. If this is true, then Humes knew. Dr. Burkley, who was in Dallas, should have told or possibly did tell Humes they saw a frontal wound in the throat. Burkley carried with him the death certificate from Dallas saying there was a wound in the throat.

The main conflict here is that the autopsy report claimed that there was a wound of exit in the throat when there was no observed evidence of that. Officially they did not know at autopsy that there was anything but a tracheostomy there, and did not scientifically study it. This lie or fabrication became the principal premise on which the entire Warren

Commission "single Bullet" theory hangs—that is, one bullet passed through Kennedy and struck Connally.

These are the principal conflicts in the evidence. They do not include the many crazy theories that further confuse the evidence. These include the claim that the body was stolen, based on confusion over what the casket looked like; whether the body was in a body bag; whether there was a brain in the head; whether a Secret Service man shot JFK, and so on. I have discussed all of this in my books and resolved many of the issues.

One example of confusion is the clear-cut conflict between the appearance of the throat wound in the left profile portrait and the way the tracheostomy incisions look in the Stare-Of-Death photograph, due to retouching of the edges of the wound.

The body was not altered because there was no change in the wounds from Dallas to Bethesda. The men who took the photos and X-rays say that *they don't show what they saw at the autopsy*. Therefore, there was no change in the *wounds* to fool the camera, but rather a change in the *photos and X-rays*. They described wounds identical to those seen in Dallas.

So far there is nothing of substance to prove the body was stolen. There is nothing substantial to back any premise in the hypothesis of body theft. When and how could they have done it?

Moving Medical Evidence

The location of the entry hole on the rear of the head has moved four inches above where it was in the autopsy report, upon surfacing of the autopsy photographs and X-rays at the time of the Clark Panel.

The location of the large defect on the head has approximately four positions, all wildly at variance with each other, according to one official report, photograph, X-ray, or another.

The location of the entry hole in the back has moved around several inches from where it is in the clothing, the Warren Commission drawings, the photographs, and the descriptions.

The "Shipping Casket" Story

A document discovered by Patrick Boyles surfaced that originated at Gawler's funeral home in Washington and was passed around at the 1992 Dallas A.S.K. conference. The document had a handwritten notation on it that read, "Body removed from metal shipping *Casket* at USNH at Bethesda." Joe Hagan, the president of Gawler's, wrote this himself.[188] Hagan explained that the confusion is over semantics. He told me that the use of the term "Casket" cannot be confused with what bodies are normally shipped in, such as a Zigler case, an air tray, a combination casket, or a "shipping *container*," which, he said, is what the military normally ships a body in. He stated that it would always be called a "container" in that case, and is not considered a casket, nor would it be called a casket.

Hagan went on to say that "The only reason we used that phrase was to identify the casket as a casket and as metal." He said that no one at Gawler's saw the body come out of any casket, nor was anyone from the funeral home there when the body arrived, but came much later, so they had no knowledge of it. He wrote the notation about a shipping casket because this is what he was told the body came in from Dallas. He said that no one would have called it a casket if it had been a shipping container or anything else, and that a casket is only called a casket if it is for viewing. (See "Encyclopedia of Medical Events and Witnesses Testimony" at the back of this book for witnesses and events regarding the shipping casket.)

Planted Evidence

The Alleged Palmprint

There were no fingerprints or palmprints on either of the weapons ascribed to Lee Harvey Oswald at the time of his arrest. After his death, a palmprint arrived at the FBI lab in Washington, supposedly taken from the alleged murder rifle, and was linked to Oswald.

The Hidell Identification Found on LHO

Oswald, when interrogated, admitted having the Alek Hidell ID, but told police it was their job to figure out what it meant, and wouldn't discuss it further. The fact that the Hidell name goes back to the New Orleans events, and is mentioned from that period by Marina, further suggests it was probably in Oswald's possession. Nevertheless, the clear impression is that it was planted by the police on Oswald after his arrest, as it was not listed in the initial inventory.

The Alleged Assassination Rifle

We have reports of more than one rifle found on the day of the assassination. There is nothing to prove absolutely beyond doubt that the alleged murder weapon actually fired bullets at the victims. In fact, there is nothing to prove that the rifle had been fired at all.

The "Magic Bullet" CE 399

This bullet was found on the stretcher of a little boy, as is well known by now, and could not, therefore, have come from John Connally or President Kennedy, even if it could have fallen out of one of their bodies, which is highly unlikely.

Missing Evidence

The National Archives

The President's brain, color photographs of the interior of the chest, numerous X-rays and other photographic views, and the pathological slides taken from the margins of the wounds are missing. The bone fragments are missing.

The bullet fragments recorded by the Warren Commission are missing.

Many documents are missing. In 1976, hearings were held detailing such losses (National Archives, "Security Classification Problems Involving Warren Commission Files and Other Records," Hearings Before the House Subcommittee on Government Information). There is no reasonable way for this material to have been stolen other than by someone with great power, such as Vice President Nelson Rockefeller, Vice President Gerald Ford, or President Lyndon Johnson, to be able to enter the NA and remove them, or authorize their removal, or through burglaries organized by the conspirators themselves.

It is possible that employees of the agencies (FBI, CIA, Secret Service, etc.) might have "borrowed" or removed the materials from the Archives. Martin Schakelford told me that he thinks "the rules governing access by executive branch employees to the records are considerably less restrictive than those governing public access."

In addition, there is an indication that the rifle and other materials, including the fragments, are stage props and not the real evidence and are there only for public consumption. This material is generally inaccessible except by video, so that their authenticity cannot be determined.

The Archives seems to be more of a politically controlled bureaucracy rather than a historic institution, and has no real interest in educating the public or otherwise helping with evidence in John Kennedy's murder. In addition, they claimed in 1993 to the author to have no money allocated for the Kennedy assassination collection and would offer no assistance in obtaining or showing documents and evidence. They are overwhelmed with their tasks and unable to process or even catalog materials. It's a dead end for access to these materials.

The National Archives has no mandated priority for the JFK assassination materials and therefore could care less. During our lifetime they have presided over the loss and mismanagement of all this material, which should have been on permanent public display.[189]

Dallas Fires

I personally noted a pattern of house burnings in Dallas of people who had important evidence stored in those houses. These people did not know one another but, in each case, the evidence has apparently been lost.

Other Evidence

The Zapruder Film

The Z film shows Connally reacting to a shot at about frame 228, less than a second after Kennedy is visibly hit.

Kennedy may be hit earlier than frame 210, which is when the Warren Commission said he could first be shot from the window after the car passed from beneath the tree. The first shot is at about frame 160, or 188–90. Perhaps this was the back shot. The shot at about Z 161 is more likely the one that hit the street, as observed by several witnesses.

There is an abnormal structure appearing on Kennedy's face shortly after he is struck in the head. I call this the Blob, and it is completely at variance with every eyewitness description of the President's face, which has been universally described as "normal" and "intact." We have *The Journal of the American Medical Association* and the autopsy doctors (Humes and Boswell) to thank for proving that this was true, and therefore for demonstrating that both the autopsy photographs and the X-rays are fake.[190] (See the chapter on film.)

The Storm Drains

Alongside the car as it approached was a storm drain on the right side of the street, under the sidewalk. A man could stand inside and shoot the President with a pistol, a much more logical weapon at the close ranges in the plaza. Penn Jones, Jr., who first suggested it, Jack Brazil, and others over the years have gotten inside and traced out an escape route through tunnels at its base. The Secret Service men said they thought they heard pistol shots.

There were two storm drains on the bridge facing the car on each side: one on the bridge to the left, and one at its juncture with the wooden fence to its right. The first has been paved over, but the bullet scar on the sidewalk pointed precisely at it. Both were on the edges of parking lots, and cars could park over these storm drains. Someone could stand beneath a car, fire at the limousine, and never be spotted. It is more logical to fire from there, as the car approached straight on, than from a high building.

A shot from the stockade fence on the Grassy Knoll is illogical because it would strike the President from the side and could have led to irreconcilable conflicts in the conspirators' cover story. Conflict would arise because a shot from the side would, normally, violently push the President to the left side of the car. Debris from his body might be photographed or filmed going in that direction. As it is, the motorcycle police officer to the left rear was splattered, but not the man to the officer's left, which demonstrates a trajectory to the right front storm drain.

Oswald's Exhumation

The undertaker who buried Oswald was at his autopsy and his exhumation. Mr. Groody noted the craniotmy, which was well documented at the autopsy—that is, the top of the skull was sawed off to remove the brain. He has stated repeatedly that Oswald's grave had been previously opened, that the body that was later exhumed had its head severed from it, and that the severed head found in the coffin did not have a craniotomy.[191] This was kept from the public, and the videotapes and photographs were kept from the widow in spite of agreements to the contrary.

Marina Oswald has described to me as recently as July 3, 1992, her struggles with both her lawyer, John Collins, and with the photographer, Hampton Hall, the son of Congressman Ralph Hall of Texas. Hampton Hall took the photographs at the exhumation, and they are quite clearly being suppressed.

Evidence of Advance Planning and Knowledge

Researcher Martin Shackelford suggests the following as hard evidence of conspiracy in the assassination of John Kennedy:

1. Remarks by Jack Ruby to his tax lawyer on November 19, 1963, indicating he expected to be receiving money soon to cover his debts[192] and his first use of a safe in November.[193]
2. The Mexico City attempts to link Oswald with the Soviet and Cuban embassies, claimed by the CIA to be documented with recordings and surveillance photos, which turned out not to be of Oswald. Testimony of the Cuban Embassy personnel was that Oswald wasn't the person with whom they dealt.[194]
3. "Second Oswald" appearance in which "Oswald" talks about coming into money soon, as related by car dealer Albert Bogard.[195]
4. The old Oswald palmprint on the Texas School Book Depository rifle,[196] a rifle which otherwise cannot be shown to have been owned or possessed by Oswald.[197]
5. The presence of Joseph Milteer in Dallas on November 22, after he predicted JFK's death by a rifle from a tall building. He told Willie Somersett that day that he was calling from Dallas.[198] Hurt tells us that the House Committee was unable to prove that Milteer was in Dallas then.
6. The well-documented prediction of Rose Cheramie on November 20 that JFK would be killed in Dallas on November 22.[199]
7. The clearly retouched "Backyard" photos of Oswald. Various magazines and news organizations doctored the photos at the time, but that does not explain (as yet) all that is wrong with the pictures.

Evidence in Dallas on November 22

1. The presence of an unidentified man in the Texas School Book Depository sixth-floor southwest corner window moments after the shots

were fired, a man almost certainly on the sixth floor at the time the shots were fired.[200]

2. The presence, attested to by several witnesses, of other men on the sixth floor prior to and at the time of the shooting.[201]

3. All witnesses who saw the "sniper's nest" gunman, including Howard Brennan, described him as wearing a light-colored shirt. Officer Marion Baker, seeing Oswald after his arrest, thought he was wearing the same shirt or a darker one than he wore at their Depository encounter 90 seconds after the shots; Brennan made a point of saying Oswald must have changed shirts before the lineup, though Oswald was wearing the same shirt as when he was arrested.[202]

4. The presence on the Texas School Book Depository sixth floor of a rifle with the same serial number as that ordered and received by Oswald in March, but a model four inches longer than Oswald's rifle, indicating substitution.[203]

5. The paper bag and ammunition clip offered into evidence, neither of which appear in any of the photos taken of the southeast corner locations in which they were allegedly found, though other evidence reportedly found at the same time by the same people does appear in the photos; also, no evidence that the paper bag ever contained the rifle.[204]

6. The presence on one of the boxes inside the "shield of cartons" by the window of a palmprint that the FBI determined did not match that of Oswald or any other School Book Depository employee[205]

7. The presence of fradulent Secret Service agents, verified by Dallas police and other witnesses, just after the shots, both on the Grassy Knoll and behind the School Book Depository; the Secret Service has made it clear that none of their agents was anywhere near those locations at that time.[206]

8. The evidence of the Grassy Knoll witnesses who saw smoke (Jean Hill, S. M. Holland), commotion (Lee Bowers), and a man with a gun (Ed Hoffman, Gordon Arnold, and Jean Hill), smelled gunpowder on the Knoll (Officers Joe Smith and Earle Brown, Mrs. Donald Baker), and saw a fresh mass of footprints and fresh cigarette butts behind the Knoll fence in the newly wet ground (S. M. Holland and others);[207] acoustic corroboration; "Badgeman" photograph by Mary Moorman.

9. Response to the Texas Theatre from the downtown headquarters rather than from the neighboring police station, and the makeup of those responding (including FBI agents, Assistant D.A. Bill Alexander, Hugh Aynesworth) given the nature of the police call (suspicious, entering theater without a ticket!).

10. Identification of Oswald as the President's killer by a Dallas police

officer at the Texas Theatre prior to any identification of Oswald there.[208]

11. The location of bullet CE 399, unrelated to the assassination, on a Parkland stretcher.[209]

12. Santos Trafficante's FBI surveillance tape made after the death of Sam Giancana: "Now only two people are alive who know who killed Kennedy. And they aren't talking."[210]

Professor Jerry Rose

Professor Jerry Rose of the State University of New York at Fredonia, the editor and publisher of *The Third Decade,* which I admire, attempted to summarize what we know about the assassination in an article by that title, which he distributed at his conference in the summer of 1991. He begins with the statement, "We know almost beyond any reasonable doubt that Lee Harvey Oswald, operating alone, did *not* kill President Kennedy and officer Tippit and wound Governor Connally." Rose bases this on the following: "The timing and trajectory of the bullets that entered the presidential limousine are totally inconsistent with a single shooter from the sixth floor of the Texas School Book Depository."

I respect Rose, but I have to argue with many of his assumptions in what he then wrote after that first statement. In fact, I think that many of the assumptions about the evidence that we made for many years, listening to the reasoning of those who became famous in this research, have been wrong. The fact is that we know little about the timing of the shots, other than what we can assume from the Zapruder film. So far, the acoustical recordings are not solid evidence of the timing and number of the shots until further work can be done on them. It may be a case of their fabrication by other researchers, or those covering up the crime. Neither is the Zapruder film a clear-cut record of when both men were hit. Not much, so far, is definitive.

As for trajectories, I have never set any store by them. I don't think we can prove much of anything. Theoretically, the shots could have come from several places, including the sixth-floor window. Jerry Rose has no idea what those trajectories really are. I think Rose's statement that we can assume that something else happened other than the official story is correct, but I don't think we can assume much of anything about his second statement. We haven't got hard evidence of either the timing or the trajectory. What we have is evidence of other shots. Rose's approach in this regard is, therefore, wrong, from the investigatory point of view.

Rose's next major presumption is totally wrong: "The President's body was in a different condition when it arrived at Bethesda than when it left Parkland." I went to a great deal of trouble either to prove or to disprove that, keeping an open mind, and my second book, *High Treason 2,* decisively destroys that theory.

He then says that both the bullet found at Parkland and the fragments found in the limousine were planted so they could be linked to the alleged murder weapon. I agree that the bullet was planted, but there is no hard evidence to support the planting of the fragments. We don't need them to be planted because the NAA tests were in fact inconclusive in linking the found rifle bullets, limousine fragments, and the fragments removed from the victims.

Rose next argues that the fingerprints on the boxes at the assassin's window were arranged by the police to point at the kill scene. Rose does not *know* this is true, though he says it is a matter of common sense, since the boxes had already been moved before the photographs had been taken.§

Rose thinks that the rifle was carried to the morgue where the dead Oswald lay, and his palmprint placed on the stock. He cites an author's mere speculation as an authority.

The undertaker, Paul Groody,[211] says that the police came and fingerprinted the corpse; that is a more likely way to obtain the palmprint that showed up at the FBI lab later.

Rose has done considerable research into the handwriting problems and the probable forgery of much of Oswald's documentation. He says, "The original fingerprint card for Oswald made at police headquarters contains an 'Oswald' signature in a handwriting of someone other than the person who wrote most of the 'Oswald' documents.[212] Oswald apparently refused to sign the first fingerprint card, so someone signed his name for him, and then it was erased."[213]

I agree with Rose's empirical contention that ("for reasons too numerous to mention here") "physical evidence was planted and fingerprints were placed in ways that would generate a false connection between Oswald and the instruments of the President's death."

Rose contends that the Dallas police "had foreknowledge of the impending assassinations and the role of Oswald as the 'designated patsy' for the crime. I have shown that the Dallas police, and specifically homicide captain Will Fritz, singled out Oswald as an assassination

§Richard E. Sprague, "The Framing of Lee Harvey Oswald," *Computers and Automation—and People,* 10–73. Some of the photos also appear in Shaw and Harris, *Cover-up,* pp. 68–69.

suspect because he was 'missing' from an employee roll call at the Depository. This roll call never occurred; and if it had, there would have been 17 *other* suspects: employees who did not re-enter the building between the assassination and the supposed 1:30 'roll call.' "[214] Rose also says that "a massive mobilization of police effort to arrest at the Texas Theatre a 'suspect' in the Tippit killing was based on police movements that strongly indicate a pre-knowledge of Oswald as the suspect to be.[215]

"Once arrested, the police displayed an uncanny certainty that they 'had their man' on both the Kennedy and Tippit killings without any real evidence of his guilt in either crime."[216] Finally, Rose says with regard to this aspect of his article that "the descending police officers for searches of Oswald residences in Irving and at the Beckley Street address in Dallas long preceded any innocent knowledge of the police of the location of these residences, especially the 'O. H. Lee' on Beckley. Members of the Dallas police seemed aware of Oswald's assassination role even before the crime was committed."[217]

The presence of Officer Tippit in Ruby's and Oswald's neighborhood shortly after the assassination never made any sense. Why was he dispatched there when most other police officers were downtown? Sheriff Bowles told me that Tippit was there because that was his post.[218]

Rose points out that the FBI issued its first report on December 9 naming Oswald as the lone assassin, "though the Bureau had hardly *begun* the extensive investigative work necessary before *any* conclusion of fact could have been reached." He also makes something of the statement by J. Edgar Hoover on November 24 that "The thing I am concerned about, and so is Mr. Katzenbach, is having something issued so we can convince the public that Oswald is the real assassin."[219] Although I put the same spin on it that Rose does, it does not necessarily carry a sinister connotation, in spite of what we now think we know about J. Edgar Hoover and the assassination.

Rose points out that the Dallas police may have felt some heat from the intense FBI investigation by January 1964 and that they then engaged in operations to put the FBI on the defensive.[220] Hoover soon rearranged the efforts of his men, and the FBI accepted the Lone-Gunman Theory. For many years thereafter, the Bureau seemed to stymie any serious investigation. Nobody, as Rose again points out, dealt with the chain of possession of the acoustical recordings. We have suggested that the recordings may have been tampered with if not faked in 1963, later, leaving the crosstalk on the tapes like a ticking time bomb.

Although Rose says, "We know that the FBI with amazing consistency, from the day of the assassination to this very day has avoided like the plague any searching analysis in the direction of investigating the conspiracy that murdered John F. Kennedy,'' I have reason to believe that both the Justice Department and the FBI do, in fact, work on this case. There is a three-man team at the Department of Justice in Washington that monitors all the work being done in this case by independent investigators, and the FBI men I have talked with seem to be investigating the case actively. Those men are specialists in the case. They fail to see what is real that has been developed. Even with pretty good evidence on the forgery of the autopsy evidence, they indicate they do not have enough to act. At this stage, the case is of such a highly political nature that it is all but impossible for an individual either suing in court, or individual agents, to bring a prosecution. It is not enough to develop evidence of conspiracy. One must have someone to prosecute, and we saw what a nightmare that can be in the Jim Garrison case.

In my opinion, what is needed at this point is a real trial of the evidence, and very close questioning of some of those who had custody of the evidence. We need a task force to take up residence in Dallas.

Misled by appearances, Rose writes, ''We know (and I must say this with a lesser degree of certainty) the identity of the assassination conspirators—not their names, necessarily, but the identity of the causes and viewpoints which they represented. We know as well the motives of the crime: what the conspirators hoped to gain from their actions. . . . I would say the crime was committed by people representing the Mafia, the CIA, and more.'' Rose goes on to elucidate his primary but superficial and simplistic theory: ''The assassination of President Kennedy was, to put it simply, an anti-Castro 'provocation,' an act designed to be blamed upon Castro to justify a punitive American invasion of the Island. Such action would most clearly benefit the Mafia chieftains who had lost their gambling holdings in Havana because of Castro, and CIA agents who had lost their credibility in clandestine warfare through their connection with the Cuban freedom fighters from the ill-fated Bay of Pigs invasion.'' This is partly true, but not the whole story.

It is unfortunate that with so much microanalysis of the physical and other evidence in the case, many of the researchers are reduced to the above type of speculation because they lack any confessions from participants as to who did it. Harold Weisberg has carefully avoided this sort of speculation and theorizing throughout the years, but his forbearance is unwarranted. He ought to spell out what he thinks.

Rose feels that Guy Banister in New Orleans may have been ''the catalyst who may have 'put together' the various elements of the assassination conspiracy."[221] Rose gives us a list of those he implies were involved, including General Edwin Walker. Rose included "key operatives within both the Dallas police department and the Secret Service." I agree with that, and Vince Palamara's focus on the Secret Service's complicity in his unpublished manuscript tells this story. History, including the shooting of Indira Gandhi, is replete with the murders of leaders by palace guards. Rose details the failures and acts of both of the above agencies that indicate complicity in the murder, as I have in my chapter on the Secret Service in my first book on this case, *High Treason.* Somebody there betrayed Kennedy.

So a lot of these people were going to know each other. So what? A plot like this, revealed in its complexity by the nature of planted, forged, stolen, and faked evidence, was created and directed by very-high-level former or active-duty military intelligence operatives. The CIA was completely incapable of pulling off such an operation, in spite of some of their proud little victories in the past. This was too big for them. Don't get the idea that I am protecting the CIA. The CIA deserves a lot of praise for what they have done to protect this nation and the world, but it is simply unreasonable to imagine that as an institution they got together and killed JFK. There were too many people at the Agency who argued against the Vietnam War, for one thing. Too many liberals at the Agency believed that détente had everything to gain for us and the world and that Kennedy's program was a winner.

In addition, some of those who accuse the CIA as an institution of complicity in the assassination have highly suspicious motives *prima facie* for saying this.

Rose goes on to say that his other proof of conspiracy, after the associations of some of the people involved in the case, "lies in examination of a pattern of behavior of supposed conspirators which serves to further the suspicion of the assassination as an anti-Castro provocation. I refer here to the striking pattern of associating Oswald with pro-Castro sympathies and actions that began at least by the summer of 1963 and continued long after the assassination."

Again, this is guilt by association. This was just to explain Oswald to the public. Identifying him with a discredited individual such as Castro helped convict Oswald without a trial.

"The strong likelihood that Oswald's pro-Castro and more broadly 'leftist' sympathies were a charade sponsored or manipulated by right-wing agents like Banister in New Orleans has been well established by assassination research."[222] Of course, numerous instances of this are demonstrated by the alleged Mexico City trip to the Soviet and Cuban embassies by an alleged Oswald. Rose says the FBI lab in Washington fabricated the records of the Mexico City trip.[223] Yet the lawyers who conducted the Mexico City investigation of the Oswald trip believe he did, in fact, go there.[224] They just don't think it was he at the embassies.[225]

Of course, the indications are very persuasive that the anti-Castro element helped frame Oswald in the press to try to get another invasion of Cuba going.

That isn't how the plot worked. People were simply used in all of those groups, from the radical right wing to the police to the CIA, to force those groups to cover up the murder. One hand didn't know at first what the other was doing. There was a mastermind who hired each person, unknown to the next.

Cover-up

Gary Shaw and Larry Harris wrote a chapter at the end of their book *(Cover-up)* discounting the possibility that various other groups had anything to do with President Kennedy's death. Not the least among them were the Dallas oilmen and their flunkies, aligned with Lyndon Johnson. What these folks from Dallas and Fort Worth came up with was a plot by the Military-Industrial Complex and the Joints Chiefs of Staff. They wrote:

"Only the Military-Industrial complex with its intelligence apparatus, in our opinion, was able to persuade certain government officials to lie in the interests of national security. For instance, it would have been easy to convince these officials, by the use of false documents, photographs or other evidence, that John Kennedy had communist ties or tendencies; the officials could be told that rather than expose that shocking, ominous information to the public, it had been decided that murder was the only alternative—'for the good of the country.' Only the Military-Industrial complex, we believe, could *command,* where necessary, certain Federal officials to help perpetrate the cover-up. What one individual would dare refuse that awesome cartel?''

Shaw and Harris conclude: "We believe his death was ordained and carried out by a force far greater than can be imagined by the average citizen: a super-power comprised of the Military-Industrial complex. Within this sphere is an elite body of men who make the decisions which govern this nation's destiny. . . . It is a sobering thought when one finds that the murder of a President has been planned and executed by a force within the government which is more powerful than the government itself.''[226]

Presentations like this fail to focus on specifics. These writers and researches lived in Texas right in the middle of a great many witnesses who had personal knowledge of pieces of the conspiracy. Those witnesses and their information were there for thirty years, and the principal investigators, so-called, did nothing. They never asked questions of the right people, the powerful people, who might know the truth. Why? What we have is possible disinformation: We obtained some of the truth, but not all. Like the Giancana book, we get everything stated as a conclusion but not a shred of corroborating hard evidence.

I think their conclusion is preposterous for the very reason that I think it is ridiculous to say that either the Mafia or the CIA or the FBI killed Kennedy alone. Certain people were used all down the line from each group or agency—that way, they all had to cover up as accessories after the fact. To this day, the FBI in Dallas is covering its ass.

The conspiracy theorists who believe that there was a governmental cover-up don't really believe what they say because if they truly believed it, they would automatically suspect every piece of evidence put forward in this case that has the appearance of legitimacy. They cannot accept the fact that each and every piece of evidence they're presented with has a high degree of probability of being fake. So they never see the totality of the fraud perpetrated on us by everyone—the Warren Commission, the HSCA, and some of the *researchers*.

Conclusion

I have tried in this chapter to present what there is of hard evidence, along with the circumstantial evidence that can establish that there was a conspiracy in this case. I realized, when I cut myself loose from some of the more famous people in this case and ended my reliance and belief on them, that perhaps the real evidence was of an entirely different nature from what we had been told through the years. The terrible realization that we had been duped dawned on me. Then I began to progress in my investigation along entirely different lines.

For good, early discussions of some of the evidence, see *Accessories After the Fact* by Sylvia Meagher.

The author maintains that President Kennedy was a victim of an ambush with gunmen in front of and behind his car and that numerous shots were fired. The administration was overthrown by a military-style ambush conducted by intelligence operatives. They were in a position to fake, plant, or steal evidence, and flash fake autopsy photographs and X-rays at the Chief Justice to convince him that there were shots from behind and only from behind from one lone nut assassin.

The only thing that was necessary to cover it up, no matter what the evidence was, was control at the top. President Lyndon Johnson had that control.

Johnson had the will to impose a Big Lie explanation to the public. Powerful people think nothing of lying to the public. They allow a certain amount of truth to seep through so that those smart enough to recognize it and what it means will keep their mouths shut.

I pursue this because we need to set or history straight before all the witnesses are dead. We have to educate our youth in how things work.

The truth would reveal something very terrible in our political system that our leadership doesn't want us to face: The system is meant to fail for us when they want to cover something up, and the system is there to protect the real truth that democracy is a charade. Our institutions will fail us when there is something in the Big Picture that they don't want us to know. And that is how it really works, not to speak of covering up various crimes committed by those who are above the laws the rest of us have to live by.

The policies of the United States changed shortly after November 22, 1963, and certain domestic political and economic matters were settled in favor of the oilmen, bankers, and defense industry investors who supported the coup. Financial interests in the short term greatly benefited, to all of our loss. And we all lost John Kennedy.

CHAPTER 3

THE JOURNAL OF THE AMERICAN
MEDICAL ASSOCIATION

One of the most respected institutions in America attempted to try to "close" the JFK case and end criticism of the President's autopsy. Repeatedly, the American Medical Association, through its magazine, announced that it was closing the case: in May 1992, in October of that year, and then again in March 1993. There was no outside peer review of the in-house articles, written by Dennis Breo, prior to publication, and no counter articles were allowed for publication, though a handful of letters in protest were printed. (See Appendix.) The 1993 articles claimed peer review, but "it was so poor as to be a scientific embarrassment," writes Gary Aguilar, M.D.[1]

The Journal of the American Medical Association began its first article, prepared by a journalist with no experience in the case, with "There are two and only two physicians who know exactly what happened—and didn't happen—during their autopsy of President John F. Kennedy on the night of November 22, 1963, at the National Naval Medical Center in Bethesda, Md."[2] This was the first sentence and their first mistake, showing the inattention to detail, carelessness, and foolishness the journal was capable of. Before the first paragraph was done, there would be another mistake ("It is the only time Humes and Boswell have publicly discussed their famous case...."), and still another falsehood in the first sentence of the following paragraph ("The scientific evidence they documented during their autopsy provides irrefutable proof that President Kennedy was struck by only two bullets that came from above and behind from a high velocity weapon that caused the fatal wounds."). *This was nothing but naked propaganda.*

There were quite a few doctors observing or participating in the autopsy during the terrible night of November 22, 1963. Months after the articles mentioned above appeared, the *Journal* tacitly admitted it messed up, and journalist Breo flew to Switzerland to interview Dr. Pierre Finck, after a letter in New York's *Daily News* castigated them: "While *JAMA* spoke with Drs. Humes and Boswell from Bethesda, it interviewed none of the other members (of the autopsy team). Conspicuously absent was Dr. Pierre Finck, the only trained forensic pathologist at the autopsy."[3] They forgot Dr. John H. Ebersole as well, but so did the Warren Commission.

A forensic pathologist, of course, is trained in the medical-legal study of violent death. The *Journal* had neglected to interview the only person theoretically qualified to conduct the autopsy: Dr. Pierre Finck. A number of other doctors, such as the President's physician, Admiral George Burkley, and Dr. Robert Frederick Karnei and numerous others from Bethesda Naval Hospital observed the proceedings as well.

The advent of big Texas oil money in the Kennedy case from the moment of the assassination, and the resurrection of radical right conservatism and militarism were the primary factors in the propaganda onslaught that covered up the medical truth of the President's wounds. The oilmen had the money to fund clinics and hospitals and have names put on buildings at universities. They could influence mere physicians' bosses to do their will. Since they also killed John Kennedy, the picture becomes devastatingly clear in terms of understanding the claims of the autopsy doctors such as the supposed 1,500-gram brain, the lack of passage from front to back of any bullet that could have been traced in the body, foreknowledge that Kennedy had been shot in the throat, and their failure to be candid about the fake autopsy pictures and X-rays, about which they could only obliquely indicate did not show the wounds they observed.

In May and June of 1992, the case of the assassination of President John F. Kennedy reached a seminal point. Two books rocketed to the top of the best-seller lists: that of Dr. Charles Crenshaw and my own book *High Treason 2*. These two books severely threatened the cover-up, and prompt action on the part of the Establishment trying to keep a lid on things was undertaken.

Crenshaw's book, *Conspiracy of Silence*,[4] was the first extensive account released publicly by one of the Dallas doctors who treated Kennedy as he died. Crenshaw insisted that the back of the President's head was missing and that there was a bullet entry hole in the President's throat. Almost every single point made by Dr. Crenshaw was to be found in a comprehensive interview with him in my own book *High*

Treason 2,[5] along with the interviews of almost every other known medical witness in the case. There was firm backing for nearly all of the doctor's major observations from his colleagues in my book.

Crenshaw's opening appearance on his first television broadcast was a good one; however, the following broadcasts saw a steady decline in his ability to project the important ideas and observations he had. Soon, strong charges surfaced and he came under stiff criticism. It appeared that his colleagues were denouncing him, when in fact their statements had been responses to specific questions. One dealt with Crenshaw's statement that President Johnson had called Parkland Hospital at the time they were operating on Lee Harvey Oswald and trying to save his life. Few could imagine that this was true.

This statement was distorted in the press to sound as though Johnson called *him*, Charles Crenshaw—a mere resident in surgery—when in fact Johnson had asked to be connected with anyone in the operating suite. Even that was instantly doubted, as it would sound peculiar that the President would be calling at all.

Of course, we know that Johnson had called Will Fritz and Chief of Police Jesse Curry[6] after Oswald's arrest,[7] and had otherwise involved himself closely in the case. I, also, discovered doctors who corroborated the call from Johnson to Parkland. They were near the phone when Crenshaw, quite through happenstance, picked up the receiver.

Johnson wanted a deathbed confession from Oswald, if possible, and Drs. Phillip Williams and Robert McClelland[8] volunteered to me that they knew that Johnson had called and spoken with Crenshaw. The day after *The Journal of the American Medical Association*'s press conference, I so informed Lawrence Altman of *The New York Times,* along with other information refuting some of the false statements in *JAMA*'s article. But before *The New York Times* corroborated the Johnson call in Larry Altman's article,[9] the attempt was made by *JAMA* to discredit Crenshaw on the basis of the skepticism about the call. Never mind that he was talking about two shots from in front striking the President. That was not discussed, in *JAMA*'s zeal to discredit Dr. Crenshaw with the implication that he had invented Johnson's call to the hospital.

The fact that what he was saying, in almost every respect, was no different from what any of the other Parkland doctors said was overlooked because the media did not know the evidence.

The American Medical Association launched their attack with a press conference on May 19, 1992. The day before, I received word that *The Journal of the American Medical Association* was having this affair. I left for New York within the hour and stayed overnight, anticipating the worst from these people.

The following morning I went to the place where the press conference was being held and was briefed by *JAMA* officials before going in. I was told when I could talk and when not to talk. To this day I wonder if they knew what was going to happen. Somebody must have had a personality profile on me because, after the presentation and some questions, it became *my* press conference (they should have known this was going to happen, as I was the *enfant terrible* of the assassination critics!), though the following week I had my own press conference, which in every respect was most extraordinary.

Twelve television cameras were set up in a bank along the back wall at *JAMA* press conference, representing every national network. The AP, Reuters, *Der Spiegel, The New York Times,* and the press from all over were there. This was an *event*! But who needed one more exercise in sensationalism? All I knew was that I wasn't getting out the findings in my new book and research, and everyone else was all over the news. This was guerrilla/gonzo journalism.

Dr. George Lundberg, the editor of *JAMA* and a former military pathologist and friend of Drs. Humes and Boswell, appeared with his Dennis Breo, who wrote the article they were so hot to tell the world about. Lundberg had the following military background: His internship was served at Tripler Army Hospital, 1957–58; Residency in Pathology at Brooke General Army Hospital, 1958–62; Staff Pathologist at Letterman Army Hospital, 1962–64; Chief Pathologist at Beaumont Army Hospital, 1964–67. He became the editor of *JAMA* in 1982.

A lot of us wondered why the AMA would go to such effort to publicize an article dealing with matters far from their normal realm. Why were they doing this—interfering in our investigation of the assassination of President Kennedy?

Lundberg smoothly began by expounding upon the "findings" of their "investigation." I had to laugh, though I was a little scared that all of this would have some real and telling truth. Instead, what I heard were distortion after distortion, omissions and misrepresentations.

Lundberg claimed that the autopsy doctors proved that the Single-Bullet Theory was correct and that one lone assassin shot the President from behind.[10] Almost every phrase he uttered was wrong, or just plain mistaken, to put the best face on it. I was stunned. I could not believe my ears. One journalist turned to me and said, "I feel like I am in Berlin in 1938."

Lundberg, after perfunctorily introducing Dennis Breo, spun rapidly into the second of the two articles *JAMA* was publishing, in their May 27 number,[11] which dealt with five of the Dallas doctors and presented them as being in opposition to Crenshaw, the public target of the two pieces. For want of a better way to describe them, these were among the worst examples of yellow journalism since the profession began.

What we got were quotes from the Dallas doctors indicating that Crenshaw was some kind of a fraud: "They emphasize they believe Crenshaw is wrong."[12] About what? This is not stated. "His claims are ridiculous,"[13] Dr. Charles Baxter is quoted as saying about Crenshaw. But Baxter was referring to only one statement. Baxter fundamentally agreed with Crenshaw on the main points as to the appearance of the throat wound looking like an entrance wound, and other matters. Baxter shortly thereafter reaffirmed that it was an entrance wound in Dallas.[14]

"Crenshaw's conclusions are dead wrong,"[15] Dr. Jenkins is quoted a saying. Yet, at the same Dallas forum two weeks later, Dr. Jenkins not only reaffirmed his statements in his reports after the assassination and to the Warren Commission, but also described having his fingers in the holes in both the President's head and in his *back,* and said that one could not see the massive hole in Kennedy's head without lifting it.

JAMA's article claimed that Dr. Malcolm Perry said that "When I first heard about Crenshaw's claims, I was considering a lawsuit."[16] The article forgot to mention that Perry had been misinformed about what Crenshaw had said, and that Perry and Dr. Crenshaw were in fundamental agreement on other important points. There is nothing that Crenshaw said about Perry that is damaging, derogatory, or actionable.

But the doctors were being set against each other, just as some assassination critics were starting to accuse these same doctors of lying. The same critics who had once relied on these doctors were now discrediting their own witnesses for the sake of a point.

"Nothing we observed contradicts the autopsy findings that the bullets were fired from above and behind by a high-velocity rifle."[17] Yes, but nothing they saw contradicts shots from in front, nor do their observations of shots from behind *preclude* shots from in front, something most of the doctors have discussed or believe in, and the fact that the autopsy report indicated shots from behind in no way conflicts with or precludes shots from in front. Once again semantics raises its hoary head.

Breo, the author of this piece, was asked a couple of questions. One of them was, "How could John Connally have been hit with the bullet when more lead was found in his body than was missing from the magic bullet?"

Lundberg replied, "I cannot get into any other people or questions here other than what happened to John Kennedy." He avoided the key point on which the Warren Report hung.

The reporters wanted to know from Lundberg why the doctors weren't there. How come, indeed, were there no witnesses at all there? After all, *I* had been producing them.

The roomful of reporters seemed tense to me. I became more insistent and tried to get in more questions. Finally, Lundberg threatened me. "Mr. Livingstone, you were warned before you came in here. Now I must ask you to leave if you will not be quiet." So I was silent for a time and soon Lundberg and Breo quit their exercise in propaganda, and it was over. That is when I stood up and began denouncing the whole deal.

"This is cooked!" I shouted. "The whole report is cooked!" That's when the television cameras came down from their tripods and made a circle around me. Nobody was going to drag me out of there then. All the reporters closed in, writing furiously.

I knew then that I had to keep writing, had to keep trying and write another book, if I was really to get this case and the facts out in the open and keep them alive. Everybody from Oliver Stone to the AMA was trying to cover up the real facts. This book sprang out of that press conference.

For an hour and a half I talked to reporters, answered questions, and delivered an impromptu lecture on the case. Reporters were hungry for information. Or were they merely after the bizarre? They already had what they wanted. I was their resident madman.

Then the strangest thing happened. Throughout all of this, when I was surrounded by many reporters and television cameras, I glanced over at Lundberg, who had one or two people to talk to, boring them some more. He seemed a bit forlorn. But was it planned this way? I didn't realize at that moment—because there had not been time to read the long articles thoroughly during such a meeting—that the autopsy pathologists had actually said enough to corroborate the central, focal point of my research—that the autopsy photographs and X-rays *were forged.*

It came time to leave the room, and the last of the reporters preceded us through the doorway. I didn't want to be alone, so some of them said they would go outside with me. But as we left the room, photographers asked me to pose for more pictures, and just then Lundberg put his arm around me, and there we were, the two antagonists, arm in arm. Perhaps *JAMA* had an ulterior motive and was trying to help us, but the *power* in this nation is so great that they have to operate in a convoluted fashion.

The reporters regurgitated exactly what they had been told during this propaganda briefing. It was like the Iraq War, Desert Storm. They were like trained seals and printed what the government wanted them to print, as I was later told at a private dinner given for me at the National Press Club in Washington. Long experience with whistle blowers and people like me told them to keep their mouths and pens silent. The next week I would have much better luck with the AP and Reuters.

My research was the real target of all of this, but they chose an oblique attack to deny that all these doctors had been interviewed by me, and that I published faithfully what they had to say. They were trying to make it look like anybody else who wrote about the medical evidence in the case had to be wrong because they, *The Journal of the American Medical Association,* had investigated the whole business and found it false. I don't think they dared attack me directly because the integrity of my reporting was too well known by them. In fact, a few months later *JAMA* was forced to credit me with a major finding.[18] Six months after that, Lundberg claimed it for himself, as we'll get to.

Let us review some plain facts in the evidence, and then take apart the *JAMA* article piece by piece.

During the May 19, 1992, *JAMA* press conference, Lundberg lamely disassociated himself from the American Medical Association itself. Clearly, he inflicted his propaganda on the nation under the protection of the AMA, but without their sanction. This should give some idea of the ethics, which we will discuss.

Some facts: On the day of the assassination the doctor (Malcolm Perry) who performed a tracheostomy on President Kennedy announced at a news conference on three occasions that there was an entry hole in the President's throat from a shot from in front. That doctor obliterated the evidence of the entry hole, so *it was not seen or known about at the autopsy.* It was not "scientifically measured or photographed," as *JAMA*'s article implied all of the wounds had been. Those who saw the wound include Dr. Jones,[19] Dr. Carrico,[20] Dr. Perry,[21] Dr. Baxter,[22], Dr. McClelland,[23] Dr. Crenshaw,[24] Dr. Gene Akin,[25] and nurses Henchcliff[26] and Bowron.[27] All stated that it was a wound of entrance.[28]

X-rays of the neck were closely examined at the autopsy, and no damage to the cervical vertebra was noted, as well as no metal dust or fragments from any bullet striking any part of the neck. Anything like this would have been noted in the autopsy report, since such findings would support the theory the government wished to state as fact—that a bullet had traversed the neck back to front and gone through John Connally. Four years later the drastically moved rear head entry wound, the missing part of the face, and a big hunk of lead turned up on the outside of the skull.[29]

The primary assumption, therefore, in the autopsy report that a bullet had exited the neck and gone through John Connally was fabricated upon no evidence at all, insofar as Humes had not actually seen the bullet hole in the throat. Numerous Dallas doctors who saw the wound before the trach incision was made through it have never retreated from their position that the throat wound was an entry from in front.[30] They repeated it to this author, and three of the same doctors quoted by *JAMA* on other matters (the attempt generally to discredit Dr. Crenshaw—another of the Dallas doctors) were present and repeated their observation of an entry hole in the throat at a major forum two weeks after *JAMA*'s news conference.

JAMA's article proclaims that it is their ''attempt to confront the defamers of the truth.''[31] It is *JAMA* that is actually defaming the truth, since they have ignored many crucial points of evidence, such as Dr. Humes' (and that of everybody at Parkland) insistence to Arlen Specter before the Warren Commission that the bullet found at Parkland Hospital could not have been the one that deposited significant fragments in the body of John Connally.

Some of the falsifications in *JAMA*'s article include innuendo and implications that Dr. Crenshaw could not have been present when Kennedy was at Parkland Hospital. *JAMA* says that Crenshaw is not mentioned in the ''summary Warren Report.'' Neither are most of the other witnesses who are in the appendices. In Volume 6 of the Appendices, Crenshaw is mentioned by no fewer than five other medical witnesses as being on the scene.[32] Somebody didn't do homework. But accuracy didn't matter to *JAMA*'s élite. All they were after was a restatement of the official story, based on flimsy evidence.

JAMA, claiming to have interviewed the autopsy doctors, quoted them as ridiculing the idea that generals and admirals were present at the autopsy. In fact, the Assassinations Committee published a list of numerous flag officers present,[33] and some of the men who assisted at the autopsy told the story at my press conference a week after *JAMA*'s that General Curtis Lemay and ''the entire Joint Chiefs were there.'' In fact, that is the most reasonable assumption, because enlisted men certainly would not have filled up the large gallery viewing the autopsy.

Herein we have the sort of problem that occurs when inexperienced journalists attempt to pontificate on the evidence in this case with inadequate preparation, and who put their own spin on what they think they are being told by a witness. It takes years to study this case. The headlines emblazoned over America the following day proclaimed "Autopsy Doctors Sure JFK Shot by 1 Gunman." Nowhere in *JAMA*'s article, which focuses on this statement, do the doctors say anything of the kind, and nowhere in their autopsy report or in any of their other testimony do they say it. The autopsy report says that the President was shot by "a person or persons unknown." The whole point of *JAMA*'s propaganda perpetrated on the world is to get across the lone-gunman thesis, which the House Assassinations Committee disproved. The lone-gunman conclusion is not related in any way to any statement of evidence in *JAMA*'s article or anywhere else.

As for the shots from behind, I'll accept that the President was shot from behind, but there is clear evidence that he was also shot from in front. As for the same shot going through both Kennedy and John Connally, Dr. Robert Shaw said it well enough when he ridiculed the idea at the Dallas forum on June 4, 1992: "Did you notice the 'figure eight' configuration of the wound on his back as you were operating on him, which Dr. Lattimer had alluded to? From a tumbling bullet rather than one going straight as a missile would go that had not encountered any obstruction?" "No," Dr. Shaw said. "The wound that I saw in the back, which was just to the side of the scapula, and ripped out the long portion, 10 percent of the center of his sixth rib, that wound was a rather typical entrance wound. It was not a large wound. Of course, then, the bullet went on through, struck his wrist, where it did a lot of bone damage, and nicked his thigh. But the wound in his thigh was just a nick. It was just a little superficial wound. It was nothing."[34]

When *JAMA* quotes Dr. Carrico as saying, "Nothing we observed contradicts the autopsy findings that the bullets were fired from above and behind by a high-velocity rifle," this is a *non sequitur* and meaningless. Most of the Dallas doctors believe that, but also believe the President was shot from in front, and that is the reason why some of the key doctors who saw the throat wound are not quoted in this article. They told (or tried to tell) Arlen Specter that the throat wound was an entry wound, and they certainly insisted on it to me in 1991, which is one reason why *JAMA* has put forward their attempt to cover up.

Certainly the President was shot from behind, but he was also shot from in front, and the wire story claiming that the autopsy doctors said that these shots were fired "by a single gunman" was nothing that the autopsists have ever said. Even if they had said it, it would be beyond their competence. Many people in Dallas know there was an ambush that tragic day, with gunmen all around the car.[35]

The *JAMA* article makes a major point of quoting the autopsy doctors as stating that the beveling made it quite clear where the bullets entered and exited the head. Nothing could be farther from the truth. The photographs showing the edges of the large defect show outward beveling around the edges of a small semicircular hole at the edge of the large defect, which would mean that a bullet or fragment *exited* there, though it is about in the position of the entry in Humes' autopsy report. The semicircle is too large for an entry, since living skull bone actually closes up slightly smaller than the diameter of the bullet traversing it. It is doubtful that the photograph is entirely of Kennedy's skull.

According to Dr. Humes, in fact, they had no entry or exit during the autopsy until bone fragments, allegedly from Kennedy's head, arrived hours after they began work. These seemed to show the entry hole in the back of the head, closer to the hairline, at or "slightly above the occipital protuberance." They didn't have it until then because there was a significant portion of bone missing from the back of the head. Dr. Gary Aguilar commented on this issue: "The beveling was determined on late arriving fragments whose proper orientation was always in doubt, before and after the HSCA. If the bone fragments had been oriented differently, the directionality of wounding might have been reversed."[36]

How, then, do we have an X-ray with an intact back of the head? And how do we have a large 6.5 mm-in-diameter bullet fragment on the *outer table of the skull* 0.5 in. below that alleged entry hole in the cowlick? Clearly we are talking about two different small holes in the back of the head. Unfortunately, there is no proper chain of evidence on these bone fragments.

In addition, the issue is *where* is the large defect? It is not placed in the article, so the statement is meaningless.

We have chains of evidence on the smallest metal fragments found on the floor of the limousine the next day, but not on these bone fragments, which clearly did not perfectly fit the edges of the skull's defect. They could have come from some other corpse. Not all of the bone was buried with the body. Who made that decision? Why? Dr. David Mantik told Dr. Gary Aguilar that it is impossible to authenticate the Back-Of-The-Head autopsy photographs.

As for the position of the entry hole in the back of the head as allegedly documented in the photos and X-rays, what we really appear to have is a serious conflict between the position in the X-ray versus the position in the photographs. The entry holes don't match. As neuro-anatomist Joseph Riley has written, "Unfortunately, other than asserting that the photographs show the wound in the 'cowlick' area and relying on visual impressions from the photographs, the Panel [HSCA subpanel of forensic pathologists who had not previously reviewed the autopsy materials] fails to present any objective evidence that the scalp wound corresponds to where the Panel locates the wound on the X-rays. The question remains: Based on the location of the scalp wound, where is the entrance wound on the skull? Two lines of evidence indicate that the entrance wound is not where the Panel places it.

"First, the Panel asserts that the scalp wound is located in the 'cowlick' area. Apparently the Panel believes that the visual impression of the combed hair established the location of the wound. However, it is standard forensic procedure to comb the hair around a scalp wound in order to better display it. . . . In addition, even a cursory look at a picture of John Kennedy shows that his cowlick is inches above the top of the ear. The scalp wound cannot be in the cowlick area.

"Rather than relying upon visual impressions, the Panel should have used objective reference points to establish the location of the scalp wound. For example, the top of the ear may be used as a reference point. In figure 1A [the Ida Dox drawing of the photo of the back of the President's head, JFK Exhibit F-48], a line is drawn from the top of the ear perpendicular to the ruler. This line passes through the wound. Figure 1B [I can't find the exhibit number, but it's the posterior view of Exhibit JFK F-58], from the HSCA Report, is a representation of the back of John Kennedy's head. A line drawn from the top of one ear to the other approximates the level of the wound in Figure 1A [JFK Exhibit F-48]. This line falls inches below the point of entry described by Humes et al. and illustrated by Boswell on the autopsy [face] sheet. In the sole objective measurement the Panel makes, it notes that the scalp wound is 13 cm. above the neck crease in the photograph [JFK Exhibit F-48]. As shown in Figure 1C [JFK Exhibit F-58], 13 cm. above the neck crease is consistent with the description of Humes et al. but incompatible with the Panel's location of the entrance wound.

"The second line of evidence presented by the Panel to support a 'high' entrance wound is visual analysis of photographs and X-rays. . . . Baden stated in his testimony [1 HSCA 301]: 'We, as panel members, do feel after close examination of the negatives and photographs under magnification of that higher perforation, that it is unquestionably a per-foration of entrance; and we feel very strongly, and this is unanimous, all nine members, that X-rays clearly show the entrance perforation in the skull to be immediately beneath this perforation in the upper scalp skin.'

"There is little doubt that the scalp wound is an entrance wound; the evidence is clear and convincing. However, the assertion that the scalp wound corresponds in location to the 'high' skull entrance wound is not established. The Panel presents no objective evidence that the scalp wound is located near the 'high' skull wound. The evidence, in fact, *indicates that the scalp wound cannot correspond to the area determined by the panel to be an entrance wound*. Since the scalp wound cannot correspond to the 'high' skull wound, the most probable alternatives are: (1) the photographs and X-rays were misinterpreted, or (2) there was a second entrance wound."[37] Riley believes that there were two entrance wounds, since he does not question the authenticity of the fake photos and X-rays.

"Humane learning leaves an aura like a ray of bright light shining on those who come after," Abdul Lateef wrote.

JAMA wrote, "In truth, though, there were no examinations, measurements, or photographs performed in Parkland's Trauma Room 1 that in any way, shape, or form allowed any of the physicians attending the President to make any meaningful evaluation of the entry and exit gunshot wounds and the forensic circumstance [sic] of death."[38] This shows the intellectual poverty, élitism, and fundamental dishonesty of a magazine purporting to represent the medical community of the United States. So, too, there were no examinations, measurements, or photographs made at the autopsy of the entry bullet hole in the President's throat, because they did not know that the President was shot in the throat until the next day. The autopsy report was blatantly fudged on this point, since as Humes admits, he did not known about the wound until he called Perry, who told him it was an entry hole. Further doubt is cast on Humes' account, as Dr. Burkley was apprised of the wounds at Parkland, and he accompanied the body and was present at the autopsy. Would he not have mentioned the throat wound to the autopsists?

When doctors as experienced as those at Parkland were with thousands of gunshot wounds said, at the time, that the throat wound was an entry wound,[39] it has to be so, and there is no evidence from the autopsy to controvert it. When those same witnesses in Dallas describe large hunks of metal having come from the body of John Connally,[40] they could not have come from Specter and Ford's "magic bullet."

I am disturbed by the leadoff statement in the article that "it is the only time that Humes and Boswell have publicly discussed their famous case. . . .'' I don't call this a public discussion, and I have had extensive discussions with both of them, as have others, and have a chapter on our interviews with Dr. Boswell in *High Treason 2*. Dr. Humes was on national television at the hearings of the House Assassinations Committee in 1978, and previously gave interviews,[41] and Dr. Boswell was extensively interviewed years ago by the *Baltimore Sun*.[42]

There was a lot that was unscientific in that autopsy. We have an opinion based on the beveling of skull and its placement. This opinion is soundly in question due to Boswell's own claim that his drawings were highly inaccurate.[43] In fact, there is nothing to refute the clear indication that the President was shot twice in the head—once from in front, and once from behind. Certainly, the large hole in the head was behind the right ear and not forward of it. The actual physical ballistics show that a shot came from in front.[44] And nobody else at the autopsy remembers any entry hole at all in the back of the head. And the alleged entry hole on the back of the head is beveled outward and not in.

The *JAMA* article claimed that ''Humes had performed several autopsies on military personnel killed by gunshot wounds. . . . [Boswell], too, had previously autopsied several gunshot wounds. . . .'' Neither man was a forensic pathologist, and it is doubtful that they had ever worked with victims of gunshots at that time. The House Committee stated that ''The pathologists charged with performing the autopsy had insufficient training and experience to evaluate a death from gunshot wounds,'' and ''he [Humes] had not performed autopsies in deaths due to shooting previously—neither had the other autopsy pathologists.''[45] While the House was at it, on the same page, they wrote, ''Proper photographs were not taken.''

When Humes was asked by the Warren Commission what experience he had with *gunshot wounds,* he simply avoided answering.[46]

Finally, there is more distortion when Humes, in continuing to fudge certain evidence, continually repeats that there was an entry hole ''at the base of the neck.'' No one saw it there. It is not in the photographs. There are three things in the photographs on the back that might be a bullet hole, and Dr. Finck and all others at the autopsy have stated that that hole—wherever it was—did not penetrate the wall of the chest or the body in any way.[47] It simply could not have been the ''magic bullet'' that then transited the neck. X-rays never show pathways or soft tissue. The alleged entry hole actually has the shape of an exit. It's too big for an entry.

Humes told *JAMA* that ''dissecting the neck was totally unnecessary and would have been criminal.'' These people were removing the President's brain, cutting open his chest, cutting up his organs, and otherwise grossly violating the sanctity of his body, and by making this statement Humes has the audacity to excuse the fact that he did not do his job. Dr. Finck testified that they were ordered not to dissect the throat.[48] Dissecting the track of the alleged bullet wound would have been in accordance with the Armed Forces Institute of Pathology protocol and necessary to prove bullet path.

Dr. Robert Livingston wrote me that he told Humes over the phone before the autopsy began that the Dallas doctors had publicly stated that the President had been shot in the throat from in front.[49] That is something to cover up for sure, because it proved a conspiracy. "Humes' claim that he was ignorant of the neck wound until the day after the autopsy suggests that he was changing history to fit," comments Gary Aguilar, M.D.[50] Dr. Robert Livingston wrote me the following: "Inasmuch as I was Scientific Director of two of the institutes at the NIH—and both institutes were pertinent to the matter of the President's assassination and brain injury—the Navy Hospital operator and the Officer on Duty put me through to speak directly with Dr. Humes, who was waiting to perform the autopsy. After introductions, we began a pleasant conversation. He told me that he had not heard much about the reporting from Dallas and from Parkland Hospital. I told him that the reason for my making such an importuning call was to stress that the Parkland Hospital physicians' examination of President Kennedy revealed what they reported to be a small wound in the neck, closely adjacent to and to the right of the trachea. I explained that I had knowledge from the literature on high-velocity wound ballistics research, in addition to considerable personal combat experience examining and repairing bullet and shrapnel wounds. I was confident that a small wound of that sort had to be a wound of entrance and that if it were a wound of exit, it would almost certainly be widely blown out, with cruciate or otherwise wide, tearing outward ruptures of the underlying tissues and skin. I stressed to Dr. Humes how important it was that the autopsy pathologists carefully examine the President's neck to characterize that particular wound and to distinguish it from the neighboring tracheostomy wound. . . .

"I said, carefully, *if that wound were confirmed as a wound of entry*, it would prove beyond peradventure of doubt that that shot had been fired from in front—hence *that if there were shots from behind, there had to have been more than one gunman*. Just at that moment, there was an interruption in our conversation. Dr. Humes returned after a pause of a few seconds to say that 'the FBI will not let me talk any further.' I wished him good luck, and the conversation was ended. My wife can be a good witness to that conversation, because we shared our mutual distress over the terrible events. . . . I exclaimed to her my dismay over the abrupt termination of my conversation with Dr. Humes, through the intervention of the FBI. I wondered aloud why they would want to interfere with a discussion between physicians relative to the problem of how best to investigate and interpret the autopsy.

"Now, with knowledge of the apparently prompt and massive control of information that was imposed on assignment of responsibility for the assassination of President Kennedy, I can appreciate that the interruption may have been far more pointed than I had presumed at that time. I conclude, therefore, on the basis of personal experience, that Dr. Humes did have his attention drawn to the specifics and significance of President Kennedy's neck wound prior to him beginning the autopsy. His testimony that he only learned about the neck wound *on the day after* completion of the autopsy, after he had communicated with Doctor Perry in Dallas by telephone, means . . . that the autopsy was already under explicit nonmedical control," writes Dr. Robert B. Livingston, Professor Emeritus of Neuroscience at the University of California, San Diego.[51].

The military autopsy protocol requires that the organs of the neck be examined.

I defy anyone to show me photographs showing the President's shirt and coat bunched up to explain why the bullet holes are so far down on them. One more misconception is that Robert Kennedy buried the President's brain with the body.[52] There is a lot more than the brain missing from the National Archives, and an investigation by the House Select Committee on Assassinations concluded that the brain was not buried with the body. Or are we being lied to about this since the brain they examined was of normal weight, as though it had lost none of its mass in the shooting?

As for the alleged linking of the bullet fragments to the murder weapon, the neutron activation analysis has always been a joke because Dr. Guinn stated that the weight of the fragments he tested for the HSCA bore no relation to those recorded by the Warren Commission, AND WERE NOT THE SAME AS THOSE TESTED BY THE FBI IN 1964.[53] "The particular little pieces that they analyzed, I could just as well have analyzed over again, but the pieces that were brought out from the Archives—which reportedly, according to Mr. Gear, were the only bullet-lead fragments from this case still present in the Archives—did not include any of the specific little pieces that the FBI had analyzed. Presumably those are in existence somewhere, I am sure nobody threw them out, but where they are, I have no idea." And Guinn adds that "the FBI did not appear to be able to draw any conclusions from the numbers."[54]

In addition, the findings were, in fact, not conclusive, since there were variations in the molecular structure among the fragments and bullet. *Any* variation at all in the molecular structure indicates that different batches of metal are involved. Thus "essentially similar" is not good enough.

Such pseudoscientific expertise is preposterous because many bullets can be made from one lot of lead and fired from several identical guns, though the barrels might show different land and groove marks. Many Manlicher-Carcanos had the same serial number as that of the gun attributed to Lee Harvey Oswald.[55] Mere circumstantial evidence that a gun can be traced to a particular individual doesn't mean that the subject fired that gun at the victim. The fine bullet found at Parkland on the stretcher of a little boy might certainly be linked to the gun alleged to belong to Oswald, but it certainly could not have left any of the fragments found in John Connally. No fragments as such could be linked to the gun itself or to the bullet. If there is any variation in the molecular structure, as there was between the fragments found and that of the bullet found at the hospital, it could not have come from the same lot of lead. Of course, two different bullets can be made from two different lots of lead having *different* amounts of antimony and so on in them. The metallurgy in the bullet is not homogenous.

It is also clear from the descriptions of the Dallas witnesses that along with the other stage props at the National Archives, the bullet fragments cannot be the same ones removed from Connally's body. They held in their hands in Dallas fairly large chunks of metal that could not have come from the "magic bullet," as Dr. Humes tried to tell Arlen Specter, who covered up what the Dallas doctors had to say.

As for the credibility of the National Archives, years ago the Archives published a long list of the missing documents stolen from there,[56] and we all know that the brain and numerous other physical specimens and photographs are missing.

What we have is a compartmentalized case. The evidence and testimony from Dallas were kept in the far compartment, separate from that supposed evidence concocted at Bethesda and in Washington.

What we have from *JAMA* is the stating of fact and evidence that are actually suppositions or tortured distortions of the evidence. There was no "exhaustive investigation" by *JAMA*. *JAMA* and Dennis Breo actually talked to only a tiny percentage of the medical witnesses, and they are selectively reporting only thimblefuls of information when compared to what their witnesses have to say. There have been lots of writers like Breo in this case who think they have made a big breakthrough or settled something just because they were lucky enough to have a couple of hard-to-find witnesses be polite to them or pose for photographs. Some aspects of *JAMA*'s article are so low so as to appall civilized people. The second of the two *JAMA* articles starts off with the bald implication that anything the Dallas doctors have to say about the wounds is not only to be discounted but also will not be seen in the article because "There were no examinations, measurements, or photographs performed in Parkland's Trauma Room 1 that in any way, shape, or form allowed any of the physicians attending the president to make any meaningful evaluation of the entry and exit gunshot wounds and the forensic circumstances of death. That assignment was left to the autopsy pathologists at the Naval Medical Center, and their comments in the preceding story stand as the definitive version that Kennedy was struck by only two bullets fired from behind and above from a high-velocity rifle."

JAMA's article, of course, was published in such a way that most people won't have access to it, and so we have presented to us the predigested pronouncements about the alleged contents from its author and editor presented to the media.

Certainly Breo and his editor, Dr. George Lundberg, never *dared* take a close look at the evidence. It is clear that they were running scared and opted for sensationalism as a way of setting back serious research that threatens to tear the lid off the entire cover-up of the same medical evidence they are trying to bury. Some people in this country are evidently quite frightened at what is written in the books of Dr. Crenshaw and myself, so they directed an oblique attack by never discussing the main evidence of the autopsy and what was seen at Dallas.

Let us point out that one of the autopsy doctors, Dr. Pierre Finck, whom *JAMA* alleges would not be interviewed by them at the time of their first article, testified in a court of law under oath that the bullet that struck Kennedy in the back never penetrated his body,[57] let alone his neck. In addition, I have this independently from the men who saw the probing.[58]

Only days after Breo's article appeared, three of the four he claims to have spoken to completely controverted the statement he attributes to one of them that "Crenshaw's conclusions are dead wrong." What conclusions? That is what we aren't being told by *JAMA,* since Dr. Marion Jenkins more than confirmed almost every statement Crenshaw has made about the wounds. The fourth doctor was not present.

Something in Crenshaw's book was distorted. In discussing the appearance of the throat wound, his comments are in conformity with what the other Dallas doctors have said about the throat wound being of the same size in the photographs as what they saw. Crenshaw thought it had been tampered with, as we all suspect, but not enlarged. There is evidence of retouching along the edge of the wound to make it appear as an exit wound. Originally all we had was the imperfect Ida Dox drawing of it made by the HSCA, which exaggerated not only that wound but also the alleged entry in the back of the head at the cowlick, which Humes "defied" the other doctors to show him in the other photographs,[59] meaning it was never there in the first place. It was the exaggerated Dox drawing of the throat wound that gave everyone a bum steer and got the doctors saying things that weren't true. Publication of the pictures would have prevented all of this.

As for the other doctor mentioned in *JAMA*'s article, Dr. Malcolm Perry, who performed the tracheostomy right through the bullet hole in the neck, I am sure he will repeat what the other doctors said at the forum in Dallas—that he saw an entry wound. He has told me often enough that what he said in 1963 stands.[60] Also, there was a fifth Dallas doctor written about in *JAMA*'s article, Dr. Robert McClelland. He has spoken out so strongly—ridiculing the X-rays and some of the other aspects of the evidence—that *JAMA* did not dare attack this man.[61].

It is a shame that *JAMA* tried to divide the "experts" in Dallas—those who performed what they call the "primary care" from all those other medical witnesses who were standing there, including the President's wife and widow, and the very many other doctors and nurses who at one time or another came in and viewed closely the President's body, including the nurses who washed and wrapped the body. Their word is the final word. The Dallas doctors had vast experience with gunshot wounds, and the autopsy doctors had almost no experience with gunshot wounds.

Four of the Dallas doctors—Carrico, Baxter, Peters, and Jenkins—repeated on June 4, 1992, that they saw an entry wound on the President's throat. Those four, who said that they would let stand in all respects the observations they made in 1963, are not all who stated at one time or another that there was an entry wound there. Add to them: Jones, Perry, and Crenshaw. None of them has ever changed his mind.

The *JAMA* articles contain statements attributed to the autopsy doctors denying that they had received any orders or directions from high-ranking officers—generals or admirals—in the autopsy room. But isn't it safer to believe what they told us when under oath rather than that reported by the author of this article, Dennis Breo, as when Dr. Pierre Finck testified in New Orleans that he was ordered not to dissect the track of the wound through the back, and that there were generals there who told them what to do?

To end this section, I note that Lundberg advised, "It is the reader's responsibility, no matter whether an investigator, a physician, a medical reporter, or any member of the public, to read all with a skeptical eye."[62] He further said that we should "Sift these data, challenge the hypotheses, results, and interpretations. And let us hear from you."[63]

The Criticism

A legion of doctors wrote in and criticized *JAMA*'s first article, and the editors only noted that it had been pointed out that Dr. Finck had not been included in the interview. "Is Lundberg seriously suggesting, via his surrogate, Breo, that these guidelines are to be ignored for the peer review discussion of Kennedy's autopsy? To be sure, there are 'cogent questions' that are still unanswered despite Breo's flip dismissive," write Doctors Gary Aguilar, David Mantik, Patricia James, Anthony White, and Wayne Smith, Ph.d.[64]

"For example, if *JAMA* would be, in Lundberg's words, '. . . as correct as it is humanly possible to be . . .',[65] it might have requested that the autopsists discuss their claims in reference to the extensive work of the panel of forensic pathologists of the House Select Committee on Assassinations. Their findings contradict the claims of the autopsists regarding the location of the fatal skull wound by 10 to 12 cm.![66] Furthermore, the photographs and radiographs also contradict the claims of Humes, Boswell, and Finck. We cannot imagine how Lundberg and Breo could have failed to ask the autopsists such fundamental questions, or how any peer review analysis of the data in the case could have neglected them. These contradictions were the source of the greatest and unresolved medical controversies considered by the HSCA."[67]

The doctors then point out in this joint letter some of those conflicts, which I had listed in my book: How can there be a normal-size brain in the autopsy report if, as Humes says in the *JAMA* article, two thirds of the right hemisphere is missing? How could a bullet strike the head, which was slightly anteflexed, at the occipital protuberance and come out at the vertex in the HSCA diagram? Could the large fragment seen on the X-rays in 1968, "a fragment so large and so easily retrievable, and so important evidentially, have been ignored by three pathologists? Would the radiologist who was present, Dr. Ebersole, have failed to bring so important an object to the attention of the pathologists for retrieval if it had been overlooked by them? It was not mentioned by any of the pathologists in their Warren Commission testimony. In fact, after reviewing the autopsy radiographs for five hours on 1-26-67, all three autopsists signed a statement declaring that '. . . careful examination at the autopsy, and the photographs and X-rays taken during the autopsy, revealed no evidence of a bullet or of a major portion of a bullet in the body of the President. . . .' "[68]

They want to know if the autopsy doctors recalled seeing the fragment on the outside of the skull the night of the autopsy. "If they did, why did they not retrieve it while exploring this precise area, given Burkley's request?[69] Why did Dr. Ebersole, the radiologist, not recall seeing this fragment when questioned about it twice by Dr. Mantik?"[70] The doctors point out in this letter to *JAMA* (which *JAMA* declined to publish), how could the autopsy doctors have made such an enormous (4-in.) mistake in the placement of the entry hole in the back of the head? This is an issue I made a big effort to bring out in my first book.

The doctors point out that "Boswell, with Humes at his side, twice asserted that a fragment of bone brought late to the autopsy fit a defect in the occipital bone surrounding the fatal entrance wound.[71] In fact, Boswell stated that it was the beveling on the inner aspect of precisely this fragment that allowed them to determine that the 'inshoot' had occured so low in the occipital bone.[72] . . . Significantly, no defect in the occipital bone is seen on the current lateral radiograph. The radiographs were taken before the autopsy had begun and, presumably, at a time when the defect in the occipital bone was present, according to Boswell and Humes' testimony.[73] Was there a single, large 'temporo-parietal-occipital' defect as described by Finck?"[74] or two defects, one the entrance in the occipital bone reconstructed when the rest of the bone came in, and the second large hole, or one large hole?

The doctors ask in their letter (as I previously had pointed out) how they can reconcile the autopsy report's description of a large, irregular defect of the scalp and skull on the right involving chiefly the parietal bone but extending somewhat into the temporal and occipital regions, "with the photographs which show no defect even remotely close to the occipital region." This question is very important, since the photographer who took the photographs, Floyd Reibe, claims the photographs currently available are forgeries.

"The evidence Humes, Boswell, and Finck have given to *JAMA*, the Warren Commission, and the House Select Committee on Assassinations appear to support Reibe's stunning allegations of forgery and to undermine the conclusions of the panel of forensic pathologists of the House Select Committee which accepted the photographs as valid.[75] Is that their intent? Humes himself categorically denied the legitimacy of the higher skull wound, whose existence is 'proven' by the photographs and radiographs. Reviewing a photograph of the back of the skull showing a high wound of entrance before the HSCA, Humes protested, 'I can assure you that as we reflected the scalp to get to this point there was no defect corresponding to this in the skull at any point. I don't know what this is (referring to the higher wound seen on the photos). It could be clotted blood. I don't, I just don't know what it is, but it certainly was not any wound of entrance.'[76] ... How do the autopsists reconcile the striking discrepancy between their localization of the fatal wound and contradictory photographic evidence?'' And they want to know why Humes reversed himself twice on the issue of placement of the rear head entry high or low.[77]

Dr. Finck had told the House Committee that he "believed strongly that the observations of the autopsy pathologists were more valid than those of individuals who might subsequently examine photographs."[78]

"Why was the designation '14 cm.' on Dr. Boswell's diagram in dark blue ink, while the remainder of the diagram was entirely in pencil? When was the '14 cm.' notation inserted?"[79]

The doctors then discuss the statement by J. Lee Rankin of the Warren Commission that the bullet entered below the shoulder blade. Of course, there is extensive evidence to support this. The location of this wound is essential to the confirmation or refutation of the single-bullet theory. They suggest that the abrasion collar at the inferior border of the back wound mean a rising bullet, as the HSCA pointed out. "How did it then reverse course, without striking bone (as everyone agrees), and enter Connally going downward?" The doctors point out that the autopsy physicians strongly disagreed with the single-bullet theory (passing through both Kennedy and Connally) in their testimony to the Warren Commission.[80].

The doctors' letter goes on to discuss the cerebellum issue, the order to Finck *not* to dissect the track of the back wound, the missing chest photographs, the fact that the doctors were not shown the photograph of the back of the head for their comment, the conflicts in size of the large defect in the head, and why Humes did not in fact coronally section the brain (the truth was that there was very little brain left with which to work). "Why are there no photographs of the brain in the skull? Were any photographs taken before manipulations had been performed? Were the skull radiographs taken before or after the brain was removed, or both? Do the extant radiographs purport to contain brain?" They also point out that the trail of bullet fragments in the head was much lower when Ebersole saw it in 1963 than it is today in the X-ray.

"Why does the autopsy report describe Kennedy as falling forward (by implication from a rear fatal head shot) . . . who told the pathologists that Kennedy fell forward with the fatal head shot?"

The following statement by Drs. Aguilar, Mantik, James, Smith, and White in their *Third Decade* joint letter bares full quoting: "The *JAMA* interview makes frequent use of phrases rarely found in scientific papers: 'irrefutable proof,' 'foolproof,' 'blatantly obvious.' (The authors challenge the reader to find similar terminology in any contemporary *JAMA* articles.) The autopsy report, however, makes liberal use of the word 'presumably,' even when describing such critical items as wounds." "The wound, presumably of exit . . .".[81]

This historic letter ends with the following final question to Lundberg: "Were outside consultants used by *JAMA* to analyze the data given by Humes, Boswell, and Finck, *JAMA*'s standard peer review process?"[82]

I call this a historic letter because it seems to me that it is the first time in thirty years that a group of doctors came together as a team to fight the lies in this case.

Another View

Philosophy professor Dr. James Fetzer, with a strong background in scientific reasoning, wrote: "I was extremely disillusioned to read the articles on this subject that have been published in *JAMA,* including interviews with Humes and Boswell and subsequently with Finck. In my opinion, these pieces should never have been published, especially in a journal as prestigious as *JAMA,* because they display the application of improper and unwarranted methods of investigation and procedures of inquiry that lead to unjustifiable conclusions and create the impression that the AMA has engaged in a cover-up in JFK's assassination. . . . Subsequently I discussed the matter with Dr. Lundberg and the substance of our conversation convinced me that I was correct in thinking that the articles were based on improper methods of research and inquiry, which had led to faulty conclusions presented as facts in a biased and unjustifiable presentation in *JAMA.* Because the issues involved here are so important and because the editor's behavior is so blatant, I wrote a series of letters to the members of the Board of Trustees of the AMA, which outlined these concerns. . . . The more we talked the more apparent it became to me that he was operating on the basis of what might be called the principle of selection and elimination, selecting the evidence that agreed with a predetermined conclusion and eliminating the rest. This approach violates a basic principle of scientific reasoning, which is known as *the requirement of total evidence*. According to the total evidence requirement, scientific conclusions must be based upon all of the relevant evidence that is available, where evidence is relevant when its truth or falsity makes a difference to the truth or falsity of the conclusion. In the case of JFK's assassination, any evidence about the number of shots fired obviously qualifies as relevant. . . . I was struck by Lundberg's reliance upon a double standard. Evidence that upheld the Warren Commission's findings was included (even in cases where it could properly qualify as no more than 'heresay'), while evidence that undermined those findings was excluded (even in cases where it properly qualified as relevant photographic evidence that has gone unchallenged). . . . Indeed, it is striking how blatantly those articles are biased in favor of the recollections of Humes and Boswell, as though there were no other or more reliable evidence available. Photographs and X-rays might provide more accurate and dependable information than fallible and limited memories, especially nearly thirty years after the event. Yet none of the autopsy photographs or X-rays appear here, much less any photographs or diagrams of Dealey Plaza. . . . The tone in which these articles are written, moreover, ought to give pause to anyone who imagines that they are objective reports of the testimony of these physicians. From its first sentence to its last, these stories are clearly intended to present the case in support of the predetermined conclusions that the Warren Commission's findings were correct. Indeed, the language in which it is written seems to be altogether antithetical to a scientific or medical journal.

"Instead of qualified characterizations of the evidence and the conclusions that it might render 'probable' or perhaps make 'likely,' many definitive declarations are advanced in a case where it should be painfully apparent that conclusive findings are not available. Thus, consider the second paragraph found on page 2794 of *JAMA*: '*The scientific evidence* they documented during their autopsy provides *irrefutable proof* that President Kennedy was struck by only two bullets that came from above and behind from a high-velocity weapon that caused the fatal wounds. This *autopsy proof,* combined with the bullet and rifle evidence found at the scene of the crime, and the subsequent detailed documentation of a six-month investigation involving the enormous resources of the local, state, and federal law enforcement agencies, *proves* the 1964 Warren Commission conclusion that Kennedy was killed by a lone assassin, Lee Harvey Oswald.' (Italics added for emphasis.)

"This passage, which reads like a promotion for the Warren Commission, not only grossly exaggerates the kind of evidential support that is possible here but ignores the controversial character of the Commission's most important conjectures, including, for example, the single-bullet theory. This emphasis upon 'scientific evidence,' 'irrefutable proof,' and so forth ought to be taken as a sign that what is being presented here consists of opinions masquerading as facts. If we know anything about this case at all, it is that 'irrefutable proofs' are out of the question. I cannot imagine, moreover, how anyone could take seriously the suggestion that the Warren Commission had 'proven' that Oswald killed Kennedy, given everything that is known about the case today. Lundberg's own bias is evident when he extends his personal endorsement on page 2803. His attitude, like those Humes and Dennis Breo express in the last few paragraphs on this page, is that any other evidence simply does not matter.[83]

"For reasons such as these and others conveyed in my correspondence with the AMA Trustees, I believe the editor of *JAMA* has abused his position by the publication and promotion of these articles on the assassination of JFK. I believe that his conduct has been unprofessional and improper. I therefore suggest that his behavior in this case be subjected to formal review. In my view, the AMA could make an important contribution by clarifying the attitude of the association about the conduct of its journal editor. Whether or not all of the facts in this case will ever be brought to light, it would be unfortunate for the AMA to be even remotely associated with a cover-up in the assassination of President John Fitzgerald Kennedy. . . . There is a disproportionate percentage of opinion and quotation provided in lieu of evidence. The complete absence of documentation undermines the purpose that these 'reports' were allegedly intended to fulfill. It reads more like tabloid journalism than scholarly research." Thus ends Professor Fetzer's cogent comments from the University of Minnesota at Duluth.

JAMA, Second Try, October 1992

On October 7, 1992, *JAMA* came out with their second set of articles, which they called "JFK's death, part III—Dr. Finck speaks out: 'Two bullets from the rear.'"

This was also written by Dennis Breo, and he began by changing the language of the autopsy report in the third paragraph: "Humes and Boswell concluded that Kennedy was 'struck by two bullets from the rear, with the fatal wound entering at the back of the head, slightly to the right and above the external occipital protuberance. . . ." I would imagine that Breo—rather than consulting the autopsy report itself—used as his source the book put out by Howard Donahue and Bonar Menninger, who also changed the language of the autopsy report in this same vital respect, by not saying how near or how far above the entry was from the external occipital protuberance.[84]

Ignoring the major criticisms leveled at the first set of *JAMA*'s articles, Breo tries to lump all criticism as follows: "So, the conspiracy theorists tried to discredit the *JAMA* reports by implying that the absence of Dr. Finck is evidence that either he or *JAMA* must be hiding something." I find this kind of journalistic answer to criticism—rather than a reasoned academic response—disgusting. "The conspiracy crowd can now forget the possibility that there was disagreement among the three autopsy pathologists. For the benefit of doubters in the news media, and for the real historians, Dr. Finck is again making it unanimous—two bullets, from the rear."

If I had less reason to believe their story that Finck was unavailable for personal reasons for the May article, I would say they planned it this way so they could give us the old one-two punch. But Finck wouldn't talk to them the first time around, when they wrote and published their poorly prepared exercises in propaganda, so they tried to pretend he wasn't there. Or they didn't want to know about Finck, and they underestimated how many physicians were knowledgeable about the case. Or were these articles intended to probe just that—if the case was alive, well, and hostile to the official story among the nation's medical doctors? If so, they sure found out quickly, and had to revise their game plan.

Once again we have the same sort of distortions we had in the May 1992 *JAMA* articles, and they contribute nothing to the medical history and evidence in this case, other than the most important point: Finck had been very clear about the entrance wound in the back of the head. "The opening of the large head wound, in the right front fronto-parietal-occipital, is 130 mm. in diameter. I also noticed another scalp wound, possibly of entrance, in the right occipital region, lacerated and transversal, 15 x 6 mm. Corresponding to that wound, the skull shows the portion of a crater, the beveling of which is obvious on the internal aspect of the bone: On that basis, I told the prosecutors and Adm. C. B. Galloway (commander of the U.S. Naval Medical Center) that this occipital wound is a wound of ENTRANCE. No EXIT wound is identifiable at this time in the skull, but close to midnight portions of the cranial vault are received from Dallas. . . . Two of the bone specimens, 50 mm. in diameter, reveal beveling when reviewed from the external aspect, thus indicating a wound of EXIT. Most probably these bone specimens are part of the very large right skull wound, 130 mm. in diameter and mentioned above. This right fronto-parietal-occipital wound is therefore an EXIT.'' This was from a letter obtained by Breo through FOIA that Finck wrote to General Blumberg of the Armed Forces Institute of Pathology,[85] and cited in the *JAMA* article herein.

Finck also repeated his testimony to the Warren Commission: ''Another bullet struck Kennedy in the back of the head at 25 mm. to the right of the external occipital protuberance and slightly above.'' *Slightly!*

So once again, and repeated more often throughout the article, Finck is actually proving my thesis of forgery of both the X-rays and the photographs, because he places the entrance hole in the back of the head four inches below where it is in the fake X-rays and photographs. He has not budged from where it was placed in the autopsy report. The attempt by the House Committee's medical evidence lawyers to change the position of the entrance wound so that it is in the same place as it appears in the photos and X-rays has ultimately failed.

But then, how can the entrance wound be in the cowlick when the head had to be reassembled to see where the small hole was? How can they see it? They see it because it isn't Kennedy's skull, at least in the posterior part of the X-rays. We know that it isn't his skull in the front part either, so the only part of the X-rays that can belong to Kennedy might be the maxillary sinuses and the jaw. And that is in doubt.

But there are problems with Finck's statements. He wrote a summary to General Blumberg on February 14, 1965, printed in the *JAMA* article we are discussing, ''. . . I found a through-and-through wound of the occipital bone, with a crater visible from the inside of the cranial cavity. This bone wound showed no crater when viewed from outside the skull. On the basis of this pattern of the occipital bone perforation, I stated that the wound in the back of the head was an entrance.'' The problem is, the photographs of this crater, only in a semicircle, is beveled *outward*, if we have it correctly orientated, which is disputed.

Therefore, Finck has the large exit wound in one of the four positions in which it has been placed. Boswell had it in an entirely different place: the top of the head. Certainly, if the President's forehead was blown out as it appears in the Zapruder film, and if the skull X-rays are accurate, then they certainly did have some other body that they unwrapped and worked on, and played ''let's pretend it's Kennedy.'' The autopsy photos showing an intact face were faked for some other reason, and *all* of the many witnesses who saw his face after death are lying about it. That is if, and only if, the X-rays are accurate.

The bottom line of this is that all three autopsy doctors and the radiologist appear to be wrong on some key points. I have pointed out some of those fabrications, such as the exit wound in the throat. They are claiming to see beveling on the inside of the alleged entrance wound on the back of the head when it is on the outside in the photographs. There was, in fact, evidence of entrance wounds more forward on the head, and the bone that was brought to them had no chain of evidence. The bones simply did not fit together. What happened to the cup of skull and scalp (the back of the head) that Clint Hill said was lying in the backseat of the limousine?[86] It is assumed that this is the large 10 x 6.5-cm piece brought into Bethesda at the end of the autopsy.

Finck is quoted as saying, "The generals did NOT interfere with the autopsy." Yes, but some admirals did. Here again, we have word games.

Probably the most important aspect of the second *JAMA* effort, in October 1992, is its publication of numerous letters, some four pages of them, from medical doctors who had clearly read my books and other assassination literature closely. Later I met some of them, and they were indeed familiar with my work. Those letters were often composed of the synthesis of the medical evidence I had performed, and I was gratified to know that my work had gotten out to that extent. They quoted the original sources I had put together.

Furthermore, *JAMA, The New York Times,* and Dr. Lundberg credited me with a major discovery in that they were able to get the autopsy doctors to admit that Kennedy had no adrenals at all. I had published this in my book *High Treason 2* only months previously.

For thirty years it seemed that the question that was foremost in every physician's mind in the country was not the medical evidence of the assassination at the autopsy, but *what were the state of Kennedy's adrenals?*!

As an example of the sort of extreme distortion involved is a statement in Dr. George Lundberg's article in the same issue of *JAMA* as follows with regard to Dr. Cyril Wecht: "Yet even he stated agreement in 1966 and wrote in 1973 that all shots were fired from the rear." This does not reflect the strong arguments put forward in the article by Wecht that "Medical and photographic data, including measurements of wound angles and calculations of bullet trajectories, strongly suggest there were two rifles used. The indicated locations are in the same building concluded by the Warren Commission to be the site of a lone assassin, but at points further West in this building and on two different floors."[87] Yes, that is the rear, all right, but much more. Was Dr.

Wecht's statement not fully disclosed because it was in conflict with *JAMA*'s dictum of one lone assassin?

Not that I don't think that this conclusion and type of trajectory analysis are questionable, but nevertheless, it is one more example of misrepresentation by *The Journal of the American Medical Association.*

JAMA, Third Try, March 1993

I would have liked to be able to end this chapter with the preceding *JAMA* distortions. But I can't because, since writing the above, *JAMA* struck again in their never-ending battle to close the case, an obsession that has drawn many people to the light like moths, and perhaps to their ultimate woe. After saying on two or three different occasions that they were closing the case, *JAMA* gave up and joined the growing cottage industry in the assassination business, now fast becoming big stuff.

In March 1993 the AMA tabloid published yet another set of articles and comments. No doubt this latest confabulation was in reaction to the tremendously negative responses of so many doctors and AMA members to *JAMA*'s previous try. They had to try to answer the storm of criticism. Meanwhile, the critical doctors who wrote the *Journal* called for the resignation of *JAMA*'s editors.

Now comes the heir apparent as chief apologist for the Warren Report theory. Dr. Robert Artwohl apparently hoped to fill the shoes of Dr. John Lattimer. The two physicians wrote the 1993 articles.

Artwohl throws down the gauntlet by calling (presumably) those of us who dare to criticize the spin put on the President's autopsy report by the Warren Commission, *conspirati,* which is a Latin term from the verb *conspiro,* meaning to breathe or sing, and with the prefix *con* means that they breathe or sing together, or in the bad sense, to conspire, if they have sworn an oath. The word *conspirati,* never came into general use in the English language, and as such, for those without a Latin dictionary, implies that those of us who criticize the Warren Report are somehow conspiring together with those who killed the President, or at least conspiring together to overturn the Warren Report, if not with the killers, to perpetuate this case on false premises. "He's trying to talk high-toned, kind of like the Kingfish in *Amos 'n' Andy,*" William Alfred, Robert Lowell professor of English at Harvard University, told me when I read him Artwohl's piece over the phone.[88]

Knowing that Artwohl has a semantic and linguistic problem right at the start of our inquiry into his credibility is helpful in trying to interpret

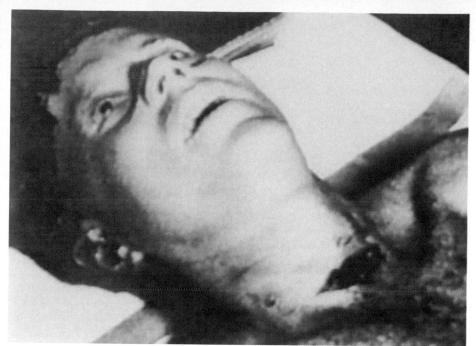

The new and mysterious color "Stare of Death" photograph which surfaced on Wavelength Video's "Assassinations of the 20th Century." They don't know where they got it.

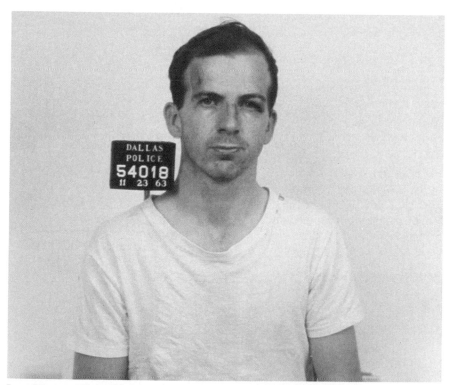

Lee Harvey Oswald, November 23, 1963. This is the only extant color photo of Oswald under arrest following the assassination.

The perfect view up Houston Street as the car approached the fatal window.

The view from the TSBD "Assassin's window" of the meeting of Houston and Elm streets. A shooter would have shot long before the car reached the corner.

The view through the trees.

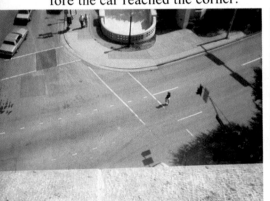

Note the steep angle of fire.

The view from the TSBD's sixth floor. This is a very bad place to shoot from, when the same window afforded a completely clear view of the car as it slowly approached the building.

The perfect shot down the center lane of Elm Street from the third floor window of the Dal Tex Building.

some of his wilder scientific ideas. "This guy is nuts!" one doctor told me while reading Artwohl's flight of fancy in my presence.

Having worked the propagandistic trick of mind warp by playing games with language, Artwohl gets into his arguments. He discusses the fact that Dr. Gary Aguilar, in his letter to *JAMA*[89] in response to their May 1992 article, said that the autopsy doctors should have noticed the big slug on the back of the head that was not noticed until the Clark Panel looked at the materials five years later. "He states that these physicians would not have failed to mention such an obvious radiographic finding if it was there. Thus, he implies the published roentgenograms that show this fragment must be forgeries. Aguilar's attempts to use a negative to prove a positive is pure conjecture and, in fact, proves nothing. There are several large fragments of metal evident on the roentgenograms, none of which was specifically mentioned in the [autopsy] report."[90] I regret that Artwohl fails to cite what he says with regard to specifics, and is incorrect: "From the surface of the disrupted right cerebral cortex two small irregularly shaped fragments of metal are recovered. These measure 7 x 2 mm. and 3 x 1 mm. These are placed in the custody of Agents Francis X. O'Neil, Jr., and James W. Sibert, of the Federal Bureau of Investigation, who executed a receipt therefore."[91]

Dr. Aguilar asked to insert his response here:

Artwohl claims that Boswell's drawing refutes a low entry point (near the external occipital protuberance—EOP). He states that Boswell depicted two 10 cm. fractured but attached segments of bone extending down from the posterior edge of the large skull defect, and that there is not enough room below the EOP for two 10-cm. fragments to lie. Thus, he argues, the wound must be higher, presumably where the photos and X-rays show it, and where current Warren Commission "loyalists" insist the rear skull entry wound is. Even a casual reading of Boswell's remarks in his HSCA testimony uncovers that Boswell referred to a "10-cm. fragment," not "fragments" (House Select Committee Voc. 7:253)—Artwohl's own reference, of course). There are two fragments depicted in the area to which he refers. The 10-cm. fragment Boswell is referring to is easily seen, and is marked "10 cm." very clearly and is to the left of the large 10 x 17-cm. defect depicted in the diagram and which is labeled "missing." So Artwohl has mistaken the fragment, but there is much, much more he's "missed."

Please look at the diagram yourself and compare the fragments pictured at the bottom of the skull. What is indicated is two 6-cm.

fragments extending down from the lowest edge of the skull defect. In Chicago I showed a huge blowup of Boswell's diagram and there is no question that what he read as "10" is really a "6," although one can understand, given the penmanship, that it might have been confused with a "10 cm." Moreover, I showed that all of Boswell's "6's" look exactly the same as the "6" at the bottom of the diagram. I showed "6's" from his face sheet and from his signature and dating of the cataloging of the photos in 1966, etc.

More importantly, if one measures from the lowest point of the skull, the foramen magnum, upward 6 cm., one finds that you are spot, on the EOP-the verbal location given for the wound by Humes, Boswell, and Finck!! Furthermore, if one measures from the most anterior location in the skull possible for the exit wound to have been, 4cm. above the supraorbital ridge, and measure backward 17 cm. (Boswell's "17 cm." labeled "missing"), you are, again, spot-on the EOP. Thus Boswell claimed that the skull defect was 17 cm. long and this measurement corresponds exactly with Humes, Boswell, and Finck's placement of the wound at the EOP! Furthermore the 6 cm. fragment also corresponds with the EOP as 6 cm. below the EOP is the foramen magnum. For the lowest portion of the wound to have been anywhere but the EOP, if Artwohl's apparent faith in the diagram is justified, would mean that Boswell erred both in the anterior-posterior measurement as well as the vertical measurement! Boswell in effect "triangulated" the wound beautifully to the EOP. Any other placement makes no sense, especially in view of the defiant defense of that location by Humes, Boswell, and Finck to the Warren Commission, the HSCA, and again to *JAMA*. (I am ignoring, of course, Humes's second interview before the HSCA, where he changed his mind to agree with the 10-cm. higher location in parietal bone. He seems in *JAMA* to have reverted to his original location—a wound in occipital bone "just above the EOP.")

Artwohl denies that the wound was in the occipital bone and endorses the higher, parietal location selected by the HSCA's forensic panel, and "confirmed" by photos and X-rays. The photos and X-rays, as you know, show the skull entrance wound 10 cm. higher than Humes, Boswell, and Finck claim it is in *JAMA,* and that is the rub. Humes, Boswell, and Finck refused to answer my letter in *JAMA* regarding this discrepancy to explain how their localization could differ so from the "official" location that is currently accepted by Warren Commission loyalists. [The irony could not be sweeter. Current Warren Commission "loyalists," including Lundberg's allies in the debate, Artwohl and Lattimer, insist that the autopsists missed the fatal skull wound by 10 to 12 cm. After such an error, if it was an error, how can Lundberg have confidence in anything the autopsists say, let alone state publicly that their *JAMA* revelations provide "irrefutable evidence"?!]

To graphically prove the point in Chicago, I showed a slide of a halved skull with centimeter rulers demonstrating precisely these points. Such precisely measured correspondence from two directions that confirmed Humes, Boswell, and Finck's placement of a rear skull defect as low as the EOP, and which refuted Dr. Artwohl's unresearched claim that the diagram proved a higher location for the wound must have been difficult for Artwohl. Artwohl was, well, incapable of response other than to graciously admit that he had erred. *JAMA*s "peer reviewers" must have "missed" this one.

A second issue raised by Artwohl was the failure of the autopsists to mention or seek the largest fragment currently seen in the X-rays. I raised this issue in a letter to the editor published by *JAMA* in the 10-7-92. I asked the autopsists to explain why they had not mentioned, or apparently sought, the largest fragment seen on current radiographs, a 6.5-mm. fragment seen unmistakably in the rear of the skull. It is simply the largest fragment seen on the X-rays in the entire body.

Artwohl argued that their failure to mention it was no indication that they had not seen it or that it was not present in the X-rays reviewed the night of the autopsy. The issue has relevance as the X-ray technician who took the X-rays, Jerrol Custer, claims that current X-rays are forgeries. Artwohl argued that the failure of the autopsists to mention the largest fragment meant nothing as "... There are several large fragments of metal evident on the roentgenograms, none of which was specifically mentioned in the (autopsy) report. One large 7 x 2-mm. fragment, not commented on in description of the roentgenograms, was removed from the brain and given to the FBI. ...''

Artwohl is right that the fragments are not mentioned in the "autopsy report." As a summary report, however, it would not discuss matters in detail such as small fragments on an X-ray. Humes's 1964 Warren Commission testimony, however, makes very clear that seeking the largest recoverable fragments was an important concern the night of the autopsy. And it is clear that this largest fragment was not pursued. Reading Humes's testimony before the Warren Commission (Vol. 2:353–54) is quite revealing on this specific point: He describes the X-rays revealing "30 or 40 tiny dustlike particle fragments of radio opaque material, *with the exception of this one I previously mentioned* which was seen to be above and very slightly behind the right orbit. ..." This anterior fragment measured 7 x 2 mm. and is approximately ½ the size of the fragment that is now seen, and which was unmentioned by Humes, at the rear of the skull—the famous 6.5-mm. round fragment.

Artwohl argues that this large fragment in the rear might have been missed as, "... Their (the autopsists) immediate concern was finding a bullet they thought was still in the body, not identifying and locating each bullet fragment...." Humes, however, recalled the situation rather differently before the Warren Commission: They performed "... a careful inspection of this large defect in the scalp and skull ... *seeking for fragments* of missile ...." (WC, Vol. 2:353); and, we tried to "... *seek specifically this fragment* (the 7 x 2-mm. anterior fragment) which was *the one* we felt to be a size which would permit us to recover it. (sic)" (WC, Vol. 2:354). [The rear fragment, you recall, was embedded in the outer table of the skull. It would have been far easier to retrieve than the 7 x 2-mm. fragment they pursued—finding a fragment embedded in bone is usually far easier than fishing one out of brain substance.] If Humes is to be believed, and Lundberg has more confidence in him than I do, the autopsists did seek the largest fragment they could find. Humes's testimony is unequivocal on this point.

Moreover, Humes's recollection of the search for fragments was corroborated by Secret Service Agent Roy Kellerman who was present at the autopsy. He testified to the Warren Commission, "... The reason for it (the taking of numerous skull X-rays) was that through all the probing which these gentlemen were trying to pick up little pieces of evidence in the form of shell fragments, they were unable to locate any ... (except the one) that was above the right eye ..." (Warren Commission Vol. 2, pg. 100). The evidence is therefore overwhelming that a dedicated search was conducted for bullet fragments in the skull. The controversial, and now unavoidably obvious, largest rear fragment was not noted by the four physicians in attendance, leaving many constrained to conclude that it was not then present in the X-rays. Artwohl just didn't do his homework, and neither did his *JAMA* "soft-ball" peer reviewers who can only be viewed as Artwohl's "peer" in that they share his ignorance of the data. They are certainly not the peers of other physicians who are familiar with the record. *JAMA,* however, has a clear bias against better informed physicians than Artwohl as they cannot be counted upon to abandon scientific truth to parrot *JAMA*'s "political truth."

As a final example of Artwohl's poor science is his description of John Connally's "5-mm." exit wound on the volar surface of the wrist.... Artwohl uses the measurement "5-mm." as the "*size of the documented* wrist exit wound" (Artwohl, *JAMA*

Vol.269:1542) to bolster the claim of loyalists, like him, that Kennedy's throat wound, also described as 5-mm., was not unusual for an exit wound. Artwohl fails to mention that the surgeon who operated on Connally's wrist, Charles Gregory, M.D., gave *three* measurements for the size of this wound, 5-mm., 1-cm., and 1.5-cm. For Artwohl to claim that 5-mm. is *the* size of the wound violates the *total evidence* rule: he selects only the evidence that supports his argument, the smallest size given, and ignores the contrary evidence. He doesn't even acknowledge the larger descriptions! [Of course he is comfortable insisting that the dorsal entrance wound dimension was *2-cm., 4 times the size of the 5-mm. volar exit wound*—a seeming contradiction to common sense. He makes it surprisingly easy for conspiracists.] Even if Artwohl is right about the wound dimensions—an entrance wound 4 times the size of an exit wound, failing to present, or address, the contrary evidence is "unscientific." I suspect that if a Warren Commission critic committed a similar "total-evidence-rule" violation Artwohl and other "loyalists" would be the first to cry, "Foul!" This again raises the question of how carefully *JAMA* "peer-reviewed" Artwohl's piece. As Lundberg has admitted he is quite unfamiliar with the Kennedy case (Chicago debate, 4-3-93), he would be the last to know how flawed Artwohl's work is.

As I mentioned there are many more flaws in Artwohl's *JAMA* piece. For the purpose of your book, however, the above examples, and *JAMA*'s "untruths" about Crenshaw, should do rather nicely to embarrass Artwohl, Lundberg, and the pretensions of "peer review" in the AMA's journal. It is an embarrassment to me as a physician. My biggest disappointment in this whole thing is that Lundberg's uninformed, biased handling has made *JAMA* and the AMA very inviting targets for those who will argue that the AMA has joined the cover-up of Kennedy's death. Kennedy's death deserves better in a major medical journal. With any luck it might get it in the future.

More Artwohl

"For many physicians the only contact they will have with arguments for and against conspiracy will be through THE JOURNAL," Artwohl writes. "Second, judging from the letters, it is apparent that many physicians need education in the pertinent forensic and ballistic sciences that pertain to the assassination. Finally, *JAMA* should not perpetuate speculation based on medical misinformation or misunderstanding by physicians.''[92] Watch out. We should *not* get our education in the case from either this man or *JAMA*.

"Their [the autopsy doctors,] immediate concern was finding a bullet they thought was still in the body, not identifying and locating each bullet fragment." So, tell me, is this what autopsy protocol says? Not at all. Interestingly, Artwohl makes his first citation here, and whom does he cite? Certainly not an autopsy manual, but Dennis Breo, a writer by trade who wrote the initial articles for *JAMA* some months previously. From this point on, in the space of two paragraphs there is so much wrong with the reasoning it would take another chapter to detail all of it. One statement that stands out says, "Aguilar has discounted the possibility that three pathologists could have been wrong about the location of the wound and, instead, implies this is further evidence the roentgenograms and photos were forged or altered."[93] So here we have this prestigious journal, which has descended to the level of a tabloid, saying subtextually, "Well, reader, the autopsy doctors were wrong by four inches on the placement of that wound. Ignore it, because we are going to go with their integrity and credibility on everything else, which we need badly to save our case." For *JAMA,* the autopsy doctors are great heroes and can do no wrong (except, maybe, a four-inch mistake), even when they are obviously in trouble and caught making things up. *JAMA* originally ignored the statements of the autopsy doctors related early in this chapter and published in their original articles indicating that the photographs and X-rays had to be fakes. Breo and Lundberg were too ignorant of the overall evidence to know what the doctors were talking about. Even the doctors don't want to admit what it means because it's so scary. "If the pathologists cannot be relied upon to accurately localize the fatal skull wound within 10 cm., what reliability can anyone, especially pathologist Lundberg, accord their other observations?" Dr. Gary Aguilar asks.[94]

We are finally joining the issue of the authenticity (or lack of it) of these materials with that autopsy report. It is finally coming to a head after thirty terrible years. But some hear only what they want to hear.

Artwohl asks what advantage there was in taping a slug to a piece of bone, as the man who asked to do it has described.[95] The advantage is so that someone could then come along and say, look, here is where the bullet went in, but part of it just scooted along the bone and lodged itself on the outer table of the skull and didn't penetrate. Artwohl explains that he sees a bullet hole with "intercranial bullet fragments coning out from it, soft tissue swelling in the area of the wound, and small, inwardly depressed bone fragments from the inner table of the skull where the bullet entered. Surely that would have been enough to indicate an entrance wound at that level."[96] It's magic! The last comment indicates that he knows there is quite a problem with this new bullet hole high up on the back of the head, thus answering his own question, since it shows in the pictures and X-rays, according to the Clark Panel report. He can't very well attribute these observations to the autopsy doctors who say the wound was four or more inches lower on the head.

Artwohl then makes a specious argument to explain "why it is unlikely that the bullet entered near the level just above the EOP (external occipital protuberance). First, given the position of the President's head in frame 312 of the Zapruder film (the moment just before the head burst), for a bullet to enter just above the EOP and exit the right fronto-temporoparietal area, it would have had to travel in an upward direction, fired from inside the limousine's trunk." I'm glad he said that, as it saves us some time. Not even the most radical or imaginative of the *conspirati* has supposed a sniper to have been in this location. Of course, nobody thought to look there, that day long ago.

"Furthermore, Boswell's testimony and autopsy drawing refutes such a low entry point." This is an example of one doctor who didn't see the wound telling another who did see the wound what he saw when he didn't. Boswell's drawing shows an apparent wound on the back of the head low down, near the neck, and he repeatedly testified that the hole was there, not higher, and insisted that the House pictures are wrong (as I have many times pointed out and sourced in my previous books), and as Boswell and Humes told *JAMA* in their first article.

Artwohl struggles blindly on, "Boswell depicted two fractured but attached segments of bone 10-cm. long that extended posteriorly, beyond the edge of the large defect." The area that Boswell has marked "missing" on his drawing, though not perfectly clear, refers to that area described in the autopsy report and at Bethesda. Boswell's placement of two triangular pieces of bone are drawn on the back of the head—this is what Artwohl is referring to—and they are the pieces that were put back into place during the reconstruction when they arrived later that night. That is where bone was missing. Not from the top of the head. The photographs claimed to be the top of the head with a long, narrow strip missing front to back are not of Kennedy. Artwohl admitted in Chicago in 1993 that he misread "10 cm." for "6 cm." on Boswell's drawing, "Thus shooting down the entire premise of his *JAMA* article," notes Kathy Cunningham.[97] And Kathlee Fitzgerald says, "His 'misreading' of this crucial measurement of wound location, in itself, has basically destroyed most of his theorizing."[98]

Artwohl then says, "a review of the lateral X-ray taken before the completing fragment was brought into the autopsy room, confirms the

accuracy of Boswell's drawing.''[99] Of course, there is no connection
whatsoever between the drawing and the X-ray as they are in conflict
with one another.

I don't believe there is a doctor on the face of this earth who could
follow Artwohl's proof presented above (presented a bit more fully in
JAMA's article). It is an example of the wildest allegations ever to appear
in a scientific journal. Artwohl, like so many, takes the easy way.

Believing him on that point raises the question of how can we then
say the doctors are wrong or lying on other scores? Perhaps there never
was an *entry* hole in the back of the head. None of the other men at
the autopsy saw it, even when they reconstructed the head. The only
real evidence we have is of a shot or fragment through the skull that
is beveled *outward*. If we have that large defect photograph oriented
correctly, then we have a missile exiting the back of the head, rather
than entering there, and nobody has addressed that question. This photo
shows a large defect with the scalp reflected back, and the empty interior of the skull.

Artwohl attempts to deal with the problem of the missing frontal
skull bone by attacking the credibility of the man who took the X-rays
at the autopsy and who has ridiculed the present official versions by
saying they are fake. ''Is the roentgenogram fake, or was it misinterpreted by the technician who took it?'' Artwohl just prior to this question tries to say that Jerrol Custer in 1988 was not pointing at the part
of the skull he thought he was, and therefore was all wrong. ''The
technician, holding up the lateral skull view, pointed to a large triangular skull fragment at the superior aspect of the skull and stated that this
fragment should not be there since that area of the skull was missing.
Thus, he declared, the roentgenograms are fake. However, the technician actually pointed to a fragment of the extensively fractured left
parietal bone. In fact, the roentgenograms do show bone to be missing
on the right side of the skull in the parietal area indicated by the
technician, just as he claimed.''[100]

Can you follow this? Artwohl has Custer pointing at something at
which he is not pointing; then has him pointing at it; then says that it
is the left side of the head and not the right. He claims bone to be
missing where it is not and says that is the right place for it to be
missing, and falsely says that the X-ray shows it missing there when it
isn't. Got it?!

The key statement Artwohl makes in the above is that he admits that
bone is missing on the X-ray: ''On the right side of the skull . . . the
bone of the right frontoparietal area of the skull is missing. . . .'' He
then tries to completely tie us in knots with semantic tricks by telling

us in the next part of the same sentence that "the right frontal sinus, the fractured (but entirely present) right orbit, the right nasal bones, and the frontal bone" can be brought out, using a spotlight. He doesn't say that he actually did this. Dr. David Mantik, a qualified radiation oncologist, had this to say about Artwohl, an emergency room surgeon: "He just can't read an X-ray!"[101]

To set the record straight once again, the lateral X-rays do not show any bone missing in the right occipital-parietal area, which is—along with some part of the posterior temporal right bone—the area described as missing in the autopsy report and at Parkland. Instead, they show bone missing almost entirely in the frontal area. Artwohl ignores how strongly Humes and Boswell protested these pictures in their interview with the panel of doctors at the House Committee.

Artwohl presses on and tells us that the X-ray tech who took the roentgenograms of Kennedy, and Dr. Robert McClelland, one of the Parkland doctors who saw them in the National Archives and who treated Kennedy as he lay dying, are wrong when they say these X-rays are not of Kennedy. Artwohl is going against probably every single medical witness who *saw* the body. He says that their interpretation is wrong because "the 'anterior-posterior' skull film taken during the autopsy is not a true anterior-posterior projection, but a modified Waters' view in which the roentgen beams project upward through the face, through the frontoparietal area of the skull, and then onto the X-ray film. Since the bone of the right frontoparietal area of the skull is missing, much more irradiation has reached the area of the film depicting the right upper third of the face, causing this area to be overpenetrated. Using a spotlight (or enhancing it by computer) one can 'bring out' the right frontal sinus, the fractured (but entirely present) right orbit, the right nasal bones, and the frontal bone. The swollen and ecchymotic right orbit seen in the autopsy pictures and Humes' description of the instability of the face in this area correspond precisely to the extensive right orbital fracture and frontal bone fractures seen on the available roentgenograms."[102]

I have trouble with the way this starts out: "Since the bone of the right frontoparietal area of the skull is missing . . ." He admits that its gone, then tries to put it back. I admit that I'm not a scientist, but this is too much! Here is a man who refuses to back up almost a single statement of fact with citations or sources. The face itself was not unstable. The bones of the face, except for the floor of the right orbit, were not fractured, nor was the forehead. There was one fracture through the back of the right eyeball (orbit), which lent some instability to the underlying bones in that small area.[103] The eyes are quite clear in the photographs, and there is only a little swelling over the right eye. The A/P view shows quite clearly that much of the right frontal bone at the forehead is missing, and we can see the edge of the defect there halfway down the right orbit (which did not exist on Kennedy's body) quite clearly. The right frontal sinus is missing and could not possibly be brought out as he says because the bone itself is missing in the X-ray. But too many people felt Kennedy's face and know that there was no damage there. I have collected this evidence in great detail and presented it in my last book, as well as in the interview with Diana Bowron in this book.

Don't lose sight of the fact that plenty of people complained about the frontal bone being missing in these pictures among the House Committee's specialists. There are lots of professionals around who can be found to say there is or is not a sinus there, there is or is not frontal bone there, there is or is not a brain weighing 1500 grams. Plenty of people don't even need money, but just assurances that they'll never lose their pension, that they won't be prosecuted for income tax evasion, that they'll get promoted. People were afraid of getting killed in November 1963 or losing their jobs. Lots of people were afraid of the sometimes naked power Robert Blakey exercised. Sometimes it was more subtle, but too many people feeding at the government's troughs.

Press on. "What sort of technology existed in the 1960s to produce or alter a photographic negative so exact, so precise, and so consistent in its subtle anatomic, radiographic, photographic, and pathological details that it could fool every forensic pathologist, anthropologist, and dentist who studied them? People are fooled when they don't know what to look for. "There are many ways to make fake X-rays. One way is to make composites," Dr. Donald Siple, a chief of radiology, told me.[104] "And they'll fool just about anyone." The technology for making composites did exist in the 1960s but was not generally available. As for his statement as to what technology existed to fake X-rays then, the government, especially, obtains advanced technology long before the public ever hears of it. The U.S. Patent Office is a good way for the government to keep up with the inventions.

The late Smithsonian anthropologist Dr. Lawrence Angel pointed out the missing frontal bone.[105] Bethesda technician Jerrol Custer described how they had him tape bullet fragments to bone fragments (obviously not buried with Kennedy or documented to be a part of his body but claimed to him to be so) and take X-rays of them. You can't get around the very odd place for a large bullet fragment not noticed by any medical witness in 1963, including the nurse who combed his hair as well as the cosmetician who put his head back together and combed his hair for the coffin in Bethesda. Plenty of people have found fault with the X-rays who have studied them, not to mention autopsy personnel who viewed the X-rays at the scene on the very night of the autopsy who were assiduously looking for large fragments. Dr. McClelland studied them and questioned them, as did other of the Parkland people.

You can't get around the fact that both the undertakers in Maryland and everybody in Dallas said they could see no defect in his head as long as it was lying on the table or on a pillow.[106] Yet we are being asked to believe that fully half the skull was missing front to back on the right![107] In direct conflict with the missing frontal bone on the X-rays are descriptions of the right orbital ridge in the autopsy report,[108] and statements to me by the undertakers,[109] by Dr. Boswell to me that the frontal bone "was intact,"[110] and numerous other witnesses in Dallas[111] who state that the bones of the face were not damaged.

Artwohl's second question as to why the X-rays might be faked is why were two A/P views made from slightly different angles? The answer is to make things appear to be authentic for just the reason he asks the question. Both are fake. Both are not of Kennedy. Neither is the lateral view of Kennedy. It would seem strange that *JAMA* would print back-to-back authors contradicting each other on such a key point. Artwohl claims that the frontal bone was actually there if we "bring it out with a spotlight" (something he did not do), and Lattimer traced the X-ray in 1972 showing that the frontal bone in that region was completely gone.

Speaking to the question of the missing right forehead or frontal bone, including part of the right orbit, radiologist Dr. Donald Siple wrote me the following—and came to see me on the same day that he sent the letter—to explain with illustrations why Artwohl cannot read an X-ray and had not read the X-rays correctly.

Dr. Siple wrote that "so called temporal thinning refers to the fact that the temporal area of the skull is thinner (usually) than the other areas, i.e., occipital, parietal, and therefore appears less dense, or more grey than the dense, compact bone which appears white (dense). On a normal skull X-ray, this so-called temporal thinning is a *gradual* change, with a long transitional zone, rather than an abrupt transition from compact bone to black (i.e., air). Secondly, the cortex remains intact on all normal skull views.

"On the lateral view of President Kennedy's skull, the temporal bone near the skull base appears beveled as if a chisel had been applied, but not normal thinning, which is gradual. Finally, more than one view(s) (i.e., A/P and Lateral) are used to localize abnormalities. A large defect in front on lateral view has to be in front on A/P view, either right, left, or midline—not shine through from occipital defects."[112]

Artwohl touches briefly on other analysis and criticism of the evidence and then attacks it as follows. He discusses the "head burst and backward movement of the President" by dismissing it. He explains pressure cavities (which seem to me to be a vacuum) and sudden bursts, and then states that the head has not started to move backward until frame 315 of the Zapruder film. "Clearly, the impact of the bullet had nothing to do with the subsequent backward head movement. The complex backward movement of the President, probably due to several interacting causes, is beyond the scope of this discussion. Alvarez and Lattimer et al. provide further analysis. A reflexive pushing off of the president by Mrs. Kennedy should also be a contributing factor."[113] I note that after Alvarez and Lattimer's name above, he cites their work, but does not bother to cite each medical or scientific issue he has raised earlier in his article. Dr. Gary Aguilar notes here that "Jackie's hand is nowhere near the head," and so could not push him backward.

Artwohl, trying desperately to be worthy of the urologist Lattimer's mantle, a man *manqué,* then claims to have mapped out where all the debris and blood from the head went, and "If one takes a pair of calipers to the entire circle of blood in 313, one finds it radiates from a point fairly well centered in the right frontotemporoparietal opening. . . . However, it is not the exiting bullet fragments, but the symmetrically enlarging pressure cavity that was responsible for the head burst and the dramatic ejection of material."[114] (See the cited quotes by Massad Ayoob in this chapter a little later with regard to the head burst.) Interesting theorist, this man. I'd love to know what sort of controls he used. Artwohl is trying to explain why Hargis and Martin, the two motorcycle officers on the left rear of the car, got clobbered with debris. He is saying that "after the head burst, blood was pushed out from the head as an expanding sphere and hit several people within a certain radius." Certainly some of the material went in several directions, but a large proportion of it hit only one person, and that was Billy Hargis, who received quite a bit more than that which hit Officer Martin alongside of him. That establishes a direct trajectory to the storm drain in front of the car, which is where Sheriff Decker always believed the shooter was.

What happened when the bullet struck the head from in front was a splash of blood and debris, just what happens when a missile, stone, or rock strikes water. Liquid fans out, coming back in the direction of the shot. Fluid squirts back through the small entry hole. The entering bullet has imparted a certain amount of its forward force to the object it strikes, and the exiting bullet imparts its directional force to the skull it strikes at an angle, breaking away a large part of it, and driving it back with the shot.

"If you have ever seen films of men getting hit in battle," Dr. Siple told me, "the part of their body that gets hit with a rifle bullet or a .45-caliber slug will always go back with the direction of the shot."[115]

Artwohl writes some more nonsense with this line: "The sketch of the wound as drawn by the Dallas physicians, which depicts a low, right posterior wound, is also cited as evidence that a shot fired from the front blew out the back of the President's head. The theory that there was a wound in this location has several problems. . . ." Artwohl is saying that the **observations** of some twenty-five witnesses, including many doctors, is a **theory**. Without exception, everyone who was with the body in Dallas described a large defect lacking in scalp and bone in the right posterior part of the head, basically in the autopsy report's placement without change.

Artwohl relies on the Zapruder film for proof, saying the posterior head wound as they described it "is not visible on the Zapruder or Nix films." The Nix film is too far away for it to be seen, and the back of the head is blacked out or in shadow on the Zapruder film. He is trying to prove something with a negative against all the positive testimony of such a wound.

His other proof that there was no such large wound in the back of the head is: "For this wound to have been created from a shot fired from anywhere behind the picket fence, the bullet would have had to enter the right front of the head at a sharp angle, then veer sharply to the President's right when inside the cranium to exit from the right occipital area." I agree with most of that. The storm drain in front was a long way from where everyone was led to believe another shooter was to the side on the knoll.

The picket fence is about a hundred feet long, and I do not believe that the shot came from the part of it directly behind Zapruder. People such as Gordon Arnold felt the bullet come by them from behind, but it was coming along the fence, across the length of the Knoll, in my opinion, from its juncture with the overpass. It is unfortunate that the trajectory from the storm drain that I had drawn in the diagram of Dealey Plaza in my first book was removed by someone, but a shot from there, which is where the Sheriff and other officers believed there was a shooter, would satisfy the ballistics of the wound. The trajectory from the storm drain perfectly satisfies Artwohl's requirements.

Artwohl then tries to dispute the large rear defect seen in Dallas by everyone, especially the Secret Service men and the President's wife, by giving us some hot scientific gobbledygook: "This wound would have caused much of the right lambdoidal suture to be missing. This suture is complete in the autopsy roentgenograms, and forensic anthropologists have verified its authenticity by comparison with skull films taken of President Kennedy during life." He cites no source for saying the suture is present. His mistake is in assuming that the authentication of the X-rays was on the up and up, when the whole point here is that they are not of Kennedy at autopsy, only alleged to be. Don't you get a little tired of people coming along and saying that twenty-five witnesses made a mistake? Or fifty witnesses? Who is he to tell the President's widow and those closest to them that they are either lying or mistaken?

"I have not been able to find one Dealey Plaza eyewitness describing a low right occipital wound." We have just seen him discount eyewitness testimony in general, and now he tries to prove his case by saying there is nobody on the *street* ("Dealey Plaza") to support the opposite view of the evidence. In addition, this is the worst kind of dishonesty, as with what follows, when Artwohl tries to quote Secret Service man Glenn Bennett by taking his testimony out of context: ". . . described it as a shot that 'hit the right rear *high* of the President's head (emphasis added)' " and then gives us a completely wrong citation for this so we can't find it.

Clint Hill, who climbed up on the trunk, actually said, "The right rear portion of his head was missing. It was lying in the rear seat of the car. His brain was exposed . . . the one large gaping wound in the right rear portion of his head."[116] Artwohl names only two people, Glen Bennett and Bill Newman, to support his thesis, and quotes Newman saying that "he was hit in the side of the head" (true: he was hit in the right temple, so what has this place of entry—the hit—got to do with discounting a large rear exit wound?). Then he goes on to say, "Not one of these witnesses described a wound in the low right posterior portion of the skull." Marilyn Sitzman, who was seventy-five feet away looking down in the car and holding Abraham's Zapruder's legs to steady him as he filmed the motorcade, said that "the next thing I remember clearly was the shot that hit . . . him on the side of his face . . . above the ear and to the front . . . between the eye and the ear."[117] "Secret Service agents Kinney and Roberts[118] support Newman and Sitzman in their assertion that JFK was struck on the side of the head," writes Doug Mizzer.[119] It was a tangential shot striking the temple.

Artwohl engages in misrepresentation when he attempts to dismiss the massive research I have done with the Parkland doctors when he wrote Dr. Douglas DeSalles that "ALL DALLAS DOCTORS, every single, Dallas doctor who has studied ALL the autopsy photos and X-rays agree, unequivocally, without a shadow of a doubt, that they show the wounds as they were in Dallas."[120] What are his sources? In fact the opposite of what he says is true. Not one doctor accepts the photographs or X-rays as showing the wounds that they saw, and many have come out publicly against them. This man either cannot read or is unaware of the major works I have published on this issue. This is one more count for his certification as mentally defective, since the pictures and X-rays can't very well show what the Dallas doctors saw if the pictures don't represent anything they recorded as being a wound that day.

Another claim is in a posting on Prodigy to Martin Shackelford: "Your claim that the X-rays show the upper right face missing is undeniably, irrefutably, absolutely wrong. The entire right orbit, the right frontal sinus, the right frontal bone, and the right nasal bones, are present. Any claim to the contrary is wrong. Period. I am disappointed in your promulgation of this obviously erroneous *conspirati* mythology."[121] This matter has been dealt with elsewhere in this chapter. Artwohl evidently sees things on X-rays that do not and cannot exist. He ignores even his own partner, Lattimer, who shows that all those bone structures are missing from the upper right front of the face, not to speak of the documentation by the House of Representative's scientists.

Another error Artwohl makes is in assuming that the rifle was a high-velocity weapon, when the rifle had only medium power. The much slower bullet has a different effect from a high-powered missile.

Frankly, for *JAMA* to print such scholarship is incomprehensible. Here is a man who spent a vast amount of time maligning solid, documented research on a national computer network before anyone ever even heard of him or his remote interest in the assassination, and either he never bothered to read or disregarded the compendium of many witnesses describing the right rear large defect in the autopsy report, which I gathered and published in my first book on the case, as well as having been documented by numerous other researchers.

Artwohl discusses the liquefaction of the congealed blood on the way to Bethesda, and "it probably was absorbed by the towels and sheets surrounding the head, rendering the true nature and extent of the wound more apparent." What evidence does he have that there were towels on the head? Did he get that from Livingstone's writing? The only place where he could have gotten towels was from my chapter on Jim Jenkins in *High Treason 2*. Where does he get liquefaction? The blood was cleaned up and the hair washed before the body left Dallas, and everybody knows that. In fact, it was one of the complaints that evidence might have been washed away. He's saying that the clots then disappear. Artwohl evidently thinks the wound looked different between Dallas and Bethesda, which it basically did not, and which I think I conclusively demonstrated in my last book.

Artwohl maintains that there was a huge flap (this is what I call "the Blob") that opened up "which is so evident in the Zapruder film, which was closed over and was held in place by clot. Other adherent skin flaps, bone fragments, tissue, and coagulated blood no doubt concealed the true nature of the wound from the Dallas physicians. . . ." Artwohl again ignores many other factors. No such flap existed, although apparent in the film, which I believe is animated. The small flap—if it existed—may have opened up on the side of the head above the ear, which flap was then closed by Jackie, but Artwohl seems to blend this into the overall major structure we see on the right front of the face in the film. Kennedy's face, as seen at Bethesda, was intact and normal, and he has no face on the right in the Zapruder film or in the X-rays. Or at least a major part of his face on the right is gone. His face is not a flap hanging down, either. There was no laceration seen extending forward on the head that might have allowed his face to fall forward, even if it could have been blown free of the underlying skull bone, which was completely intact. The front-to-back laceration on the scalp seen in some photos is not present on others and was not seen when the body was unwrapped. Nor was it seen in Dallas. Possibly they made it up to explain "the Blob." Granted, the laceration was described by Boswell and Karnei to me.[122]

The Neck Wound

Artwohl then attempts to refute the observations of all those doctors in Dallas who observed the neck wound prior to it being obliterated with a tracheostomy. He insists that it was an exit wound, for which there is no scientific evidence or autopsy observation whatsoever, and he attempts to ignore the vast experience with gunshot wounds of all those doctors in Dallas who saw it.

I say that neither Artwohl nor anyone else can lightly dismiss the observations of the Dallas doctors that what they saw was an entry wound. The size of the wound is not so important as how it looked, its appearance; they unanimously judged it to be an entry hole, which was common in their experience. Artwohl is again indulging is specious generalizations and selective inattention to detail and facts as well as a total disregard for the credibility of the Dallas physicians, whom he is quick to support when he thinks they support him. As we saw above, he completely changed the force and effect of their observations with regard to the autopsy pictures. They have all said at one time or another that the pictures do not remotely show what they saw. They attempted to say publicly that the pictures we published are what they saw in the National Archives, and this was twisted to say something else: that they did not show the wounds.

The rest of what Artwohl has to say in that paragraph is completely off the wall and disconnected to the issues. His broad connection of Kennedy's neck wound to the size and characterization of Connally's wrist wound as a means of proving that the neck wound was one of exit is the wildest kind of speculation. Lattimer admits in the following article that the neck wound was only 5 mm. across. Artwohl writes that a wound of 5 mm. can be an exit wound for a 6.5-mm. bullet. The manner in which he tries to prove that it is an exit wound is a contradiction in terms. He writes that "a heavy metal-jacket, high-velocity bullet that loses very little velocity and does not deform or tumble as it passes through the body will often produce a small exit wound." He then describes the 3-mm. wound on the dorsum of Connally's wrist, and a 5-mm. wound on the volar surface. "The size of the documented wrist exit wound is the same size as Kennedy's anterior neck wound. Thus based on size alone, the anterior neck wound is compatible with an exit." Is Artwohl now discrediting Lattimer's statements regarding the much larger wounds on Connally's torso from a "tumbling bullet" before it ever got to the wrist, making such small holes? Connally's surgeon, Dr. Shaw, denies that bullet was tumbling and said that the back wound was small. He enlarged it.

Doug Mizzer, a Baltimore researcher, comments on his fellow city dweller's speculation. "This is a direct contradiction of Artwohl's own statements. In Artwohl's scenario, when the bullet passed through the neck it still had most of its velocity. By the time this same bullet has entered the Governor's back, exited his chest, then enters the wrist and exits the wrist and only leaves an exit wound of 5 mm., its velocity has been seriously dissipated. The neck and wrist wound would therefore not have the same exit wounds because of the severity of the differences in velocity."[123]

Artwohl's Conclusions

"The autopsy findings and all photographic and available assassination films support the fact that there were two shots from the rear.

Although the preponderance of nonmedical evidence indicates that Lee Harvey Oswald acted alone as a maladjusted individual, killing President Kennedy with a Mannlicher-Carcano rifle, it cannot totally disprove his acting with (or being duped by) a small private group of conspirators in a plot to assassinate President Kennedy."[124] I don't dispute the latter statement, but his first conclusion is preposterous.

The autopsy findings support one shot from the rear—in the back and only in the back, not near the neck, and that he was struck somewhere in the head, but from which direction is not scientifically clear. The placement of the entry hole in the back of the head in the autopsy report, if it in fact existed, was low down and could not have come from a high window so near the car. Artwohl fails to distinguish between the autopsy findings and the photographic evidence.

Artwohl then plunges wildly on, saying that it would have taken "several years" to set up Oswald as the patsy, rather than a few weeks. Then he implies that it is unbelievable that they would have gone to the trouble to get Oswald a job at the School Book Depository, and plant evidence to frame him.

The surgeon then thinks that it is incredible that someone would go to the trouble to "arrange to have the President fired upon from several different directions using at least three teams of marksmen. (Why would it take several teams of marksmen, not one, not two, but, by *conspirati* count, three to six volleys of gunfire to hit a slow-moving target at close range with the fatal head shot?)" Well, when they ambushed De Gaulle, the car was surrounded with gunmen. Ambushes are as old as time. Artwohl assumes the car would always have been a slow-moving target. The killers didn't know for sure that the car might not speed away before they got their target. The doctor is going at this the wrong way. We know there was an ambush because we know there were shots from more than one side. (Note what Dr. Roger McCarthy has to say about ambush tactics in the chapter in this book on the American Bar Association's mock trial in 1992.)

Artwohl then indulges in sarcasm: "After the President is hit with multiple bullets from multiple directions, the military and numerous government agencies, beginning right at Parkland Hospital, move quickly to conceal multiple bullet holes from civilian physicians (or coerce them all into silence), whisk away bullets, alter the President's body, forge roentgenograms and photographs, and alter every home movie and photograph of the assassination to conceal the true nature of the injuries and the number of accomplices involved." Nobody concealed anything from the Parkland doctors. It wasn't necessary. The doctors reported what they saw and later were told that they were all wrong and made a mistake, since it conflicted with the result the conspirators wanted. It took only a few people to do all this. It took only a couple of high-ranking officers in attendance at Bethesda to order the forgeries of the photographs and X-rays and tell the autopsy doctors what to write and what they saw and didn't see.

Bullets may have been whisked away. Lots of people there saw a bullet hole clean through the windshield of the limousine parked at the hospital, and some stuck their pens and pencils through it, which just fit nicely.[125] That hole could not be reported because it evidently came from a missed head shot low down to the car from somewhere behind it, and probably hit the cement in front of James Tague, who was struck with debris while standing in front of the overpass. The Secret Service than ordered a number of identical windshields, and we can speculate as to their purpose.

It stands to reason that if there was a conspiracy to replace Kennedy's administration, they would certainly have the ability and capacity to alter all of the evidence necessary, steal and destroy evidence, and plant what they needed, such as the Hidell identification on Oswald, giving him that legend. But Artwohl seems to think this is unreasonable: "The most astonishing feature of this plan is that the plotters would have to have been confident in advance they would be able to recover every bullet, find every witness, control the movements of hundreds of witnesses, and destroy every photograph and home movie that had incriminating evidence and leave behind those that did not." He calls this a Rube Goldberg scenario.

Well, this is pretty much the end of his article, which finishes with "As the years pass, one thing becomes abundantly clear: For the *conspirati,* it is conspiracy above all else, including forensic science, and common sense."

Anybody who doesn't think that the awesome power of this nation is not sometimes up for grabs, that control of that power is disputed and fought for, that there are often disgruntled losers out there who represent large factions vying for control of the reins of power in Washington is naive.

My opinion is that the evidence is absolutely clear that there was more than one gunman on November 22, 1963. The only question is: What kind of conspiracy was it? The evidence in this case was faked to hide the fact that there was more than one gunman. The evidence is very clear that Oswald was set up long in advance, and frankly for any professional person in this nation to come forward now in the face of such evidence as I have just mentioned, and which is well documented in my previous work, elsewhere in this book, and by numerous other authors, is to make that person suspect as being paid or otherwise politically motivated.

Yes, Artwohl is entitled to his opinions, which, in almost all cases, are a rehashing of those of urologist John Lattimer, and Vincent Di-Maio, a doctor trained in Dallas by Dr. Earl Rose.

End Lines

To end this tawdry affair, the reader should be treated to some of Artwohl's tag lines from his notes on Prodigy.

Yes, he distorts lots of things, such as "The head wound was not touched at Parkland, and when they put the body in the coffin, they avoided washing the head."[126] The doctor makes wild assumptions with no evidence whatsoever to support them, and much evidence to the contrary.

We find Artwohl playing expert on acoustics, ballistics, radiology, criminology, and the philosophy of the streets, and signing off with countless slams such as this: "Really Ron, this is all basic ballistics. I am surprised a man like yourself can form such solid opinions with so little knowledge. Wait a minute, no I'm not."[127]

Another public letter to Ron Carmichael has Artwohl saying the following: "When people refer to the back or rear of the head, they can just as easily be talking about the upper rear of the head, i.e., the parietal area." (Now you see it, now you don't!) "The Dallas staff made some errors [that day]. . . . It is not until a deliberate effort is made to stop the bleeding, clean off the wound, can an accurate assessment be made, and none of this was done in Dallas."[128] (Wrong again. They examined the head several times, making sure a number of witnesses saw it. Kathlee Fitzgerald commented on this manuscript with regard to the throat wound as follows: "It seems logical that they would have cleaned the area of the throat wound with at least an antiseptic solution before doing the trach, and with that done, the 'accurate assessment' of the wound was that it was an *entrance* wound.") "But you must believe in a totally unprovable and so far undocumented uberconspiracy that involves uncounted numbers of doctors, anatomists, osteologist, photograph experts, darkroom technicians, etc., and that you know more or are more honest than all the forensic experts who have examined the evidence."

To another person he writes, "But if you want to believe that the Harper fragment is occipital, just because someone says it is, and just because you want to believe it is, and despite that the claim is demonstrably erroneous, that is your right and duty as a member of the *conspirati*."[129] Kathlee Fitzgerald wrote here that "Artwohl is forgetting or is ignorant of the fact that two fellow physicians originally identified this fragment as occipital. Does he now claim to know more than doctors who actually held the fragment in their hands and examined it? An invective he hurls at others?" Once again we have modern "experts" claiming to know more because of questionable photographs and X-rays and therefore have superior knowledge to eyewitnesses. Eyewitness testimony, of course, has to be weighed and tested, and not all is equally valid.

"Boy, if Nagell was making claims that LHO was the lone assassination [sic], the *conspirati* would be having a feeding frenzy with him."[130]

Another night on Prodigy everybody was treated to the following when Artwohl began his daily tirade, this time directed at Robert Wagstaff: "Before I rip you to shreds . . ."[131]

A point I am making by publishing this material is that within these letters purports to be some scientific fact or opinion masquerading as fact. One can lose sight of this when it is presented in the middle of a sort of street fight by a bully who beats people up with his righteousness. Either accept what he says or be abused. "Sorry, Dave, your half-baked, wrongheaded, unscientific and unsupported speculations must yield to well-documented, well-known, experimentally and autopsy-proven behaviour of military weapons." This was to David Lifton.[132] Believe me, these two guys deserve each other.

Dr. Gary Aguilar wrote a general letter that he addressed to Artwohl concerning Boswell's recorded 17-cm. measurement from behind the coronal suture to the back of the head and which Aguilar tested on a skull he had for anatomy lectures. Artwohl responded, "Instead of relying on measurement, why don't you measure a few of your patient's heads. Just tell them you [sic] taking an 'coronoparietal screening test' to check for 'early signs' of 'macroorbitosis.'

"Just kidding, you should never tell your patients anything that isn't true. But I am sure your patients won't mind you taking a few measurements. Maybe your skull was from a pinhead pigmy [sic]."[133] Come now, Doctor. You are writing to another physician (the one who dismantled the base upon which many of Artwohl's theoretical house of cards rested at the conference in Chicago in 1993).

He accused Dr. Gary Aguilar of being irresponsible in one public letter on the national computer network, but then signed it, "the kinder, gentler, medical curmudgeon."[134]

Most of Artwohl's letters had for their subject heading "Misinformation." I guess he assumed that he was striking a blow for truth by implying that only he had the truth and that somebody else was spreading misinformation, which is often true in this case.

He has one tag line I liked. He wrote Thomas Belfiore, "What Lifton describes and what is reality, is not usually the same." If Belfiore could find one forensic pathologist who after reading Lifton's book, "and who has studied the medical evidence for himself, and then still agrees with his thesis, then I will ship you a case of your favorite beer!"[135]

Artwohl tries to deal with the picture published in my last book showing the large defect in somebody's head. He claims that I have published it upside down.[136] We could be wrong about the orientation of it, I admit, but I doubt it. "If he (the reader) inverts the book, he will be able to correctly interpret the photograph. Shot from above and in front, the photograph actually depicts part of the large right frontotemporoparietal defect." I have since shown this picture to numerous doctors, and *nobody* can say that this hole is in the front of any skull. The picture was oriented for me in my last book by the men from the autopsy as being in the back of the head. More work needs to be done, and if we could identify some of the bones, we might have a better idea. Certainly, the bone in the picture is far too thick to be in the frontal area, which is so thin it doesn't show on the X-rays, he says.

John Lattimer, M.D.

There was one last spasm from the contrarians. It was an article back to back with that of Artwohl in the same issue of *The Journal of the American Medical Association,* March 24–31, 1993.[137] Dr. John Lattimer has made himself such an expert in the Kennedy tragedy. Let me jump around a bit in dealing with his rehash of old work, as some of what he says really should start this hatchet job off.

"President Kennedy, having seen Governor Connally make the exaggerated movement to try to look back at him, may have been leaning forward to ask Connally what he wanted when the bullet struck him on the back of the neck. . . ."

This man has spent years maligning those of us who question the findings of the Warren Commission, President Johnson's handpicked cover-up implementers of the Kennedy tragedy. He makes a statement here that is unsupported by any evidence on the face of this earth: that Kennedy was struck in the back of the neck. He has even stated elsewhere that we can't see the bullet wound in the back of the neck in the photographs because it is hidden in the fatty folds of the neck. How come nobody ever saw any wound there at either hospital? And why docs he say Kennedy "may have been leaning forward"? Why does he *need* Kennedy to be leaning forward?

"Because the back of Kennedy's neck was the site of a large fat pad from the steroids he was taking, the bullet strike would have passed more downward than in a normal person's neck." ("More downward?") This is one more wild *assumption*. He assumes that Kennedy had a fat pad, but doesn't know that. What are his sources? "The fat pad, plus any leaning forward, would have accounted for the course of the bullet through the right side of the base of Kennedy's neck. . . . The wound of exit in the front of Kennedy's neck was unexpectedly small because the skin was supported by the double layer of his overlapping collar band at this point. This prevented the skin from bulging ahead of the exiting bullet and bursting open widely, as it might otherwise have done. . . . The smallness of this neck exit wound led, at first, to some speculation that it might have been a wound of entry rather than the usually large wound of exit. The reason for its smallness clearly was the restraint of the collar band, as our repeated experiments demonstrated. . . ."[138] This work can really get wild!

Well, if skin is compressed, and a bullet passes through, when the skin is released from its compression, the hole will be a hell of a lot larger than the diameter of the bullet that just passed through. He ignores the other signs seen in Dallas indicating an entrance wound, such as the appearance of the edges of the wound. In addition, the bullet hole was just above the necktie knot (according to Dr. Charles Carrico) and the shirt collar. But at least he admits that the combined observations of the Dallas doctors that the bullet hole was only 3 to 5 mm. wide is a fact. The bullet that was supposed to have passed through was 6.5 mm. If a bullet that size had exited there, it would have made a larger hole than 6.5 mm. in normal circumstances.

But Lattimer and DiMaio[139] are going to tell us about buttressing or shoring of the wound edges. Fine. Lattimer has always brought us new ideas, and this is *new*!

*Reader, **watch out! Here it comes:*** "Other factors causing the head and torso to jerk backward were reflex contractures of the erector spinae muscles, some of the strongest muscles in the body. These tend to jerk the body upright and backward when all the muscles of the body are violently stimulated by the downward rush of impulses following a massive brain wound. Another factor was the contraction of the muscles of the back of the neck, as part of the 'righting' mechanism that makes us jerk our heads upright if our heads are bent sharply forward. These muscles were already partly in contraction as a result of the bullet strike on the neck."[140] The rearward movement of JFK's head occurs in a single frame, which is about 5 milliseconds—far faster than the 50 milliseconds required for any neuromuscular reaction, says Dr. Aguilar. Aguilar adds that for a "jet effect to occur, something has to be jettisoned. Alvarez calculated that 10 percent of the mass of the melons he shot was required to explain the jet effect motion he observed while firing at them. For a 5-kilogram skull, a reasonable estimate, this would require the loss of 500 grams. Of course that includes skull fragments, but one sees, if one believes in the authenticity of the Z film, that the fragments do not all go forward, thus those fragments wouldn't contribute to the 'jet effect.' So the brain must be missing material that it is not if the jet effect is to be used to explain head motion. What about 'neuromuscular reaction?' explaining the motion of the head? There is forward motion at 312. There is an abrupt change in direction between 313–314, $\frac{1}{18}$ of a second later—far, far faster than could occur by any neuromuscular reaction, but within a reasonable range if there had been a momentum transfer from a bullet traveling rearward and imparting some of its momentum to the skull. Besides, the 'neuromuscular reaction' was theorized on the reaction of goats shot in the head. Goats have an inhibitory interneuron to release its inhibition on the nerves of the back muscles. Without the inhibition, the back muscles contract and you have a neuromuscular reaction. Humans, however, have no inhibitory interneuron. A bullet 'decerebrating' a cortex leads to flaccidity. (Please recall that 'decorticate' is different and the rigidity associated with 'decortication' takes a very long time—i.e., seconds to minutes, not 5 milliseconds, the time between 313–314."[141] Humes told *JAMA* that roughly "⅔'s of the right cerebrum" had been blown away, and this should be about 250 grams.

Lattimer starts off his article telling us that part of Humes' and Boswell's problem with their terribly flawed autopsy report was because they did not have access to the photographs and X-rays taken during the autopsy, which with regard to the X-rays was grossly untrue. He then says: "The photographs had been confiscated by the Attorney General (the President's brother) without being developed, and they were turned over to the National Archives." It is well documented that the Secret Service took the rolls of film and kept them for several days before taking them over to the Navy labs to develop. The Kennedy family did not have actual possession of the photos and X-rays at any time, though officially the material was under their control later.

Lattimer then makes another even more wild claim in his article that "Having examined these full-color photographs, I can say that they are far more shocking than the contrived latex dummies and allegedly genuine illustrations that are now appearing in certain 'entertainment' features." [142]

It would appear from this that Lattimer is saying that what we published is not what is in the Archives. Although it is possible that some slight alterations have been made to the later generations, I quote Dr. Artwohl, Lattimer's cohort, as follows: "The pictures in *High Treason 2* and in *Best Evidence* are undoubtedly the autopsy photos. They match the Dox tracings (which came out before any of the photos were published in these books); they match the conversations between Humes, Boswell, and the HSCA forensics panel; I believe one or two of the Dallas doctors have stated the published photos are the same, and even Humes and Boswell said as much in their October 7, 1992, letter in *JAMA*: 'We continue to believe that no useful purpose would be served by widespread publication of the very unsightly head wounds and we lament the fact that this has already, to some extent, occurred.' " [143] If the pictures were not what is in the Archives, the autopsy doctors would have said so at that moment in their letter to *JAMA*.

In addition, Dr. Wecht confirmed to me that what I had published was precisely what he had seen in the National Archives. So did Dr. Dulany, Dr. McClelland, Dr. Peters, and Dr. Jenkins from Parkland.

A more important point is the fact that he indicates that what we have published are presented with more taste and are less shocking than what is in the National Archives. I did not agree with publication in tabloids such as the *Globe,* and I personally never would have done that. The fact is that the *Globe* story was generally accurate and served to inform that part of the public that does not normally have the time, interest, or money to read scholarly books on the subject of John Kennedy's murder. In addition, I have on several occasions had the opportunity to check the work of both the *Globe* and the *National Enquirer,* and I found that they can be occasionally a lot more accurate and honest than either *The New York Times* or *Journal of the American Medical Association.* It just wasn't a good place to publish them with dignity.

Lattimer implies in the above statement about the "allegedly genuine" photographs that they are not basically the same as those in the National Archives. I put them out there to find that out. We are trying to force the issue and get this whole thing out in the open because the stuff in the National Archives is fake.

Lattimer in the next paragraphs says, "The autopsy surgeons had only a brief time to look at them and little chance to make precise measurements on the films (for example), to pinpoint the wound of entry on the skull." They didn't need the pictures for that, since they had the skull itself to examine, and since they couldn't very well find the entry if it wasn't there until some bone was brought in several hours later.

Lattimer's intellectual arrogance shows through his statement that "The large number of letters to the editor commenting on the articles in *Journal* demonstrates physicians' concern about the issues the contrarian community and the entertainment industry have pressed on us and about our forensic questions such as, 'Did a single bullet wound both men?' and 'Why did President Kennedy's head move back toward the gun after it was struck?' I present information about each of these points," he says with heavy portents, reading the entrails. Sadly, Lattimer ignores questions about the real issues, and he raises straw issues as above that have nothing to do with that which is listed, for instance, in the joint letter a group of doctors published in *The Third Decade* in March 1993.

I have to give credit to Lattimer for one thing: "The contrarian community of critics insists that the backward movement of the President's head indicates that he was shot from the front and the right. Careful examinations of the roentgenograms of the head showed no sign of a bullet exiting the head on the left side. This would have been necessary if he had been shot from the front or the right." He is right that if he had been shot from the right side or the Grassy Knoll proper, that it would most likely have exited on the left side of his skull and shown up on the X-rays. From the front, no, because it can still be a tangential shot. I don't think anybody was firing from the Knoll itself. Those researchers who sold that bill of goods misled us. The shots came from the storm drain.

Lattimer agrees with the establishment of Connally's wound at frame 224, which is a little before where most researchers think it happened, but then he says, "The bullet went on through his right wrist, and, traveling backward, buried itself in his left thigh."[144] The trouble with that is that a whole bullet couldn't end up there and still be on a stretcher sometime later in the hallway, where CE 399 was allegedly found. Granted there has always been some dispute as to just how much of the bullet managed to get to Connally's leg, which seems rather a strange destination if it had gone through John Kennedy sitting some distance behind Connally, unless it deflected off his wrist. A little bit later in the article, Lattimer tells us that "a fourth fragment, in his thigh, was not recovered because it was of no importance."[145] So what was it that Lattimer had in his thigh, a fragment or a whole bullet? I don't think he knows or dares answer.

Another major discrepancy lies in his statement that "The right arms of both President Kennedy and Governor Connally started their upward jerks in frame 225 immediately after the bullet went through both men."[146] Kennedy is actually behind a sign completely obscuring him from view when he is evidently hit. When he emerges, John Connally, clearly not hit, is turning around twice to look at him and see what has happened, and Kennedy has his arms raised, with both hands clutching at his throat. The point is, Lattimer cannot see Kennedy raise his arms as he claims, since he can't be seen.

Still another problem with Lattimer's thinking arises in the same long paragraph when he relies on one Kenneth J. Strully for "Also pointing out that the bullet that hit President Kennedy in the neck traumatized both vagus nerve and the phrenic nerves (bilaterally) resulting in respiratory paralysis, cardiac rate disturbances, and quadriplegia caused by the trauma to his lower cervical spinal cord from the shock wave. Strully's interpretation reinforces my belief that the neck wound was undoubtedly a fatal injury that was largely overshadowed because the brain wound was so much more obviously fatal."[147] It is a shame that none of this was seen at the autopsy. It is even more of a shame that Kennedy's X-rays demonstrated no such damage as Lattimer originally speculated had occurred to a tranverse process. Now we hear that it was a shock wave that hit his spinal cord and killed him.

The core of Lattimer's most famous assertion over the past decades is contained in the following: "The first movement of President Kennedy's head was forward (away from the gun) for the first two frames after being struck in frame 313. The blast of heavy, wet brain substance, the everting scalp, and three skull fragments all went forward. This forward motion of heavy, wet brain substance through the large exit wound on the front right side of the head acted like a jet engine and helped drive the head backward (toward the gun), after its initial forward movement. Because the point of exit was on the right side of the head, the heavy brain substance also drove the head toward the left, so that the President fell down where Mrs. Kennedy had been sitting."[148]

I admit that I haven't got a scientific answer to his assertion that a human head attached to a body becomes a jet engine when struck with a bullet. In the previous article Dr. Artwohl wrote that the backward movement was caused by a pressure cavity forming behind the exploding bullet. Not that anybody can explain to me how this excessively tough bullet such as those attributed to the case can explode. I have an answer, but it isn't scientific. It is that the head is basically inert and muscle reactions don't enter into it when it or any part of the body is struck with an antipersonnel bullet designed to kill or maim. That part of the body will simply go with the bullet. There will be a splash where the bullet hits, and there will be an ejection of material following the bullet out. The bullet imparts forward motion to the body part, and if it is a head, the skull is being struck twice and driven with the bullet. I cannot conceive of the incredible neuromuscular reactions described by the apologists to explain the backward movement, when the brain is instantly dead and devoid of any electrical capacity. Lattimer's ultimate flight into the stratosphere of logic is this statement, which bears repeating: "Other factors causing the head and torso to jerk backward were reflex contractures of the erector spinae muscles, some of the strongest muscles in the body. These tend to jerk the body upright and backward when all the muscles of the body are violently stimulated by the downward rush of impulses following a massive brain wound. . . ."[149] The impulses—if any—might be going downward, but so what? That doesn't of necessity send the body backward or forward.

With regard to whatever hit John Kennedy in the head, a police trainer and firearms journalist, Massad Ayoob, who has taught programs on the effects of bullets on human bodies in formats that range from police instructor schools to medical school, says that the head wound "is far more consistent with an explosive wound of entry with a small-bore, hypervelocity rifle bullet traveling between 3,000 and 4,000 fps . . . an explosive wound of entry occurs when a highly liquid area of the body, such as brain, is struck by a high-velocity round. The tissue swells violently during the microseconds of the bullet's passing, and seeks the line of least resistance. . . .

"That least resistance is the portal of the entry wound that appeared a microsecond before, and the bullet will not bore an exit hole to relieve the pressure for another microsecond or two—perhaps not at all, if the bullet fragments itself inside the brain. Therefore, the force is directed backward and outward, creating an explosion effect and massive wound at point of entry. If the cataclysmic cranial injury inflicted on JFK was indeed an explosive wound of entry, the source of the shot would have had to be forward of JFK's limo, to its right, and slightly above . . . the area of the Grassy Knoll."[150] In other words, not the Grassy Knoll, but down at the end of it in front of the car, where it joins the bridge and where there was a foxhole (the storm drain) for the shooter.

Lattimer ends his rather strange and perhaps last desperate exercise in those pages, hopefully writing *finis* to *JAMA*'s failed effort to stop the groundswell in the growth of real understanding among the medical community of the medical evidence. Lattimer's swan song is the final statement in his essay that "President Kennedy's neck wound would have been fatal [a longtime theory of his, which, of course, depends upon a bullet ruining his spinal cord, which it did not]; that the backward recoil of President Kennedy's head resulted from a bullet from the rear; that the small size of the exit wound on the front of the neck was due to the buttressing of the skin by his shirt collar; and that there is no difficulty in accurately firing every 5 seconds with the 6.5-mm, Mannlicher-Carcano firearm." Of the final statement here, nobody ever disputed. The question was whether, it could be loaded, aimed, and fired faster than 2.3 seconds, which it could not.

Conclusion

I often marvel at how much of a fool I was throughout much of my life. We are all being taken for suckers. This world is filled with innocent, trusting people on the one side, and predators on the other. Predators who will do anything to have their way or to cover up their crimes. Some people will do anything or say anything to defeat competition or bury rightness or goodness. Not to say that I'm perfect, but I am not a predator.

The one shining thing that comes through the whole sordid *JAMA* business is the fact that the autopsy doctors have stood fast on the undamaged appearance of the President's face and on their 1963 placement of the entrance wound in the back of the head, both of which conflict wildly with the X-rays. The skull in the X-rays is simply not entirely that of Kennedy.

They have proved my case for forgery, so I can't rail too loudly. The possibility exists that *JAMA* was helping us in the most indirect fashion imaginable. After all, one cannot openly say the Emperor is wearing no clothes. Why are we so arrogant to suppose that what is true for so many countries in the world is not true here? We cannot openly state the bottom line of the truth of certain issues when it exposes to the public the horror of just how true it is. There are those up-front scandals that it's okay to talk about for the sake of appearances, but they cover up for the real criminality, which is much worse. Where it deals with those we trusted and who were or are our leaders, the truth can never be told. That is taboo.

It is like incest and rape in the family. There is just too much power out there that would be offended if the truth were known. Somebody has weighed the costs and thinks that if the truth comes out in a straightforward fashion, too many people will be hurt, and they don't mean the public. Certain persons and families.

JAMA got us to third base with the issues of forgery I have raised.

I'm up at bat again and have to try to hit a home run. Maybe somebody else can do it if I fail.

JAMA hired some apologists and threw them at us. It is the last-ditch stand of the cover-up artists. After this they have nothing left between them and the truth.

"Don't pay any attention to that fool!" a prominent Baltimore doctor said of Artwohl. "He doesn't know what he is talking about, and nobody reads *The Journal of the American Medical Association* anyway. Nobody I know is even a member of the AMA anymore. I subscribe to the *New England Journal of Medicine. JAMA* is just trying to hype up their circulation to keep their advertisers. It's only a drug advertiser, anyway."

Dr. George Lundberg

Lundberg basked in the glow of the stink he raised for all of the remainder of 1992. The new year saw him digging in for the long battle. Here is a man who said in Chicago at Carlson's conference, "I wasn't in Dallas or Bethesda those days. I am really not much of an expert at this thing at all. It has never been all that interesting to me until the last year or so. My role in that and in this whole thing is that of a journalist along with Mr. Dennis Breo of our own *JAMA* staff. I have essentially no primary source of information to share with you nor do I plan to achieve any. It's really not my main interest. I am a journalist."[151] So what brought him into the case all of a sudden? He sure came into it with a lot of power, but why did he wait thirty years?

Who is this man and why did he do it? "Whom do I trust?" as he asks. "I have known Dr. James Humes, the principal autopsy pathologist, personally since 1957. To paraphrase Ronald Reagan, who was paraphrasing Lloyd Bentsen, 'I know Jim Humes. He is a friend of mine. I would trust him with my life.' Dr. Humes is an outstanding general pathologist before and after 1963 acclaimed by his peers thirty years, forty years perhaps; but never was before, during or after an equally trained forensic pathologist and never claimed to be. Moving from 1963 to 1968, the U.S. Attorney General appointed a four person blue ribbon panel to study and re-evaluate the JFK autopsy. The reason that was appointed was a request by the second autopsy pathologist, Dr. Jay Boswell, that there be such an independent investigation. This four member panel had developed unanimous support for the autopsy work, results and interpretation. A team member of that panel was the late Dr. Russel Fisher, Chief Medical Examiner for the state of Maryland and probably the world's top ranking pathologist of his time. I knew Russell Fisher. He is a friend of mine. I would trust him with my life. He concurred—two bullets from the rear. A simple story," Lundberg says. Lundberg, *a former military doctor,* does not tell you that Dr. Russell Fisher was closely tied with the Armed Forces Institute of Pathology, which Dr. Humes had been slated to head until the President's autopsy.

These people are protecting their own, at our expense, and at the expense of our history.

"I have known Dr. Rose since 1973. He is a friend of mine. I would trust him with my life. He concurs—two bullets from the rear. Another member of that 1979 subcommittee was Dr. Charles Petty. . . . I have known Chuck Petty since 1968. He is a friend of mine. I would trust him with my life. These are the keys to trust: Jim Humes in 1963, Russell Fisher in 1968, Earl Rose in 1979 and again in *JAMA* in 1992, Chuck Petty in 1979, and again in *JAMA* in 1993 and then there is me." This is why we should base trust on these people? Because *he* says *he* knows them and would trust his life to them? I'd bet he'd get a second opinion! "To imagine or state that somehow these people say we have been duped, misled or are somehow part of the conspiracy to deny the truth on this issue for all ages, strains the vocabulary to find strong enough words to describe such absurdity. Such charges are somewhere among the descriptors wild and crazy, off the wall, out in left field in Cubs Park, incredible, insulting or worse."

But what does this tell us about that conference in Chicago on the assassination that let Dr. Lundberg create the medical panel, closing out the principal researchers in that area, as well as others?

I quote Dr. Lundberg, "I stated at the press conference in New York that based upon solid, in my opinion, unequivocal forensic evidence as reported in the May 27th, *JAMA,* I can state without concern or question my agreement with Drs. Humes and Boswell that President Kennedy was struck and killed by two bullets and only two bullets fired from one rifle. The first bullet entered the back near the neck and exited the front of the throat. The abrasion, pallor and bruising of the skin surrounding this wound is diagnostic of the wound of entrance. The second bullet entered the back of the head and exploded in the right side of the head destroying the brain. *Now whether it entered here or here is irrelevant and meaningless. It does not matter.* [Lundberg first pointed to the top rear of his head and then to the bottom rear of his head.] It exploded on the right side of the head and he was dead. The ordinary bullet path you don't get because of the explosion inside the skull, so don't look for simple arthimetic and geometry to be relevant. It went in there and came out here and exploded in the head, period. . . . As both bullets struck from behind, no other bullets struck the President. Or putting it another way, the forensic evidence along with the findings gives us a single assassin with a single firearm." As he said in May that year, he wasn't going to discuss John Connally's wounds. They didn't matter, either.

One must ask how Lundberg could "trust with his life" Humes, whose claims regarding the evidence had been discredited by the Clark Panel, the HSCA, Lattimer, and even Artwohl. Lundberg, who dashes about the country promoting his views, psychoanalyzes the rest of us by saying those who believe there was a conspiracy in the assassination are motivated by profit, paranoia, personal recognition, and public visibility, a diagnosis for which he is presumably certified.

Why am I indulging in this sort of vituperation? Because you are about to see just how he plays ball.

"Now with and after that press conference in New York on May 19, 1992, came a world-wide media hullabaloo, huge shouts of acclaim from many, shrieks of anger and pain from many others and a plethora of media appearances, newspaper and magazine columns, letters to the editor, telephone calls and even death threats. . . . We had published a bunch of letters almost all critical of our position at that time and a few responses mostly to an editorial which some thought and which also said that Humes had been on Dan Rather."

Watch what is coming. The speech we are quoting from was in April 1993, a year after I published my last book: "The rest I take no credit at all except for the journalism. *I do take credit on the adrenal glands* [emphasis author's] because that has been very quiet, almost totally, since the autopsy. It was not in the autopsy report. The autopsy itself, as a general pathologist, I say was not well done. Lots of problems with it. I identify those problems in the editorial, list them one by one. I am not happy with that autopsy but I am happy to say the findings regarding the bullets, and *I discovered with the original journalism on my part a whole bunch of stuff about the adrenals that I know to be true and we reported that for history in that editorial as well. . . .* [emphasis author's] I think we are clearly winning this thing in general and that brings us to last week's *JAMA,* too soon to know how many protests we will get on that one and today's program."[152] This is *Winner Lose All,* as Hugh Eames wrote, when the doctor who first reached the North Pole had the discovery robbed from him by the U.S. Navy. I can only say that the military has a long reach, because here they are at it again almost a century later, doing the same thing. He thinks he is winning this thing because thugs like this are used to beating up on people since they were in grade school and walking off with their lunch and pocket knife. Well, think again, if he thinks myself and others are already nonpersons, our work to be erased from the face of the earth.

Dear reader, this has got to be the end-all. I have watched repeated examples where the original research of others is co-opted and taken over by interlopers. Now we have an example of the editor in chief of *The Journal of the American Medical Association* calling himself a "journalist," a longtime military pathologist, appropriating right in front of the world the discovery of his chief critic: me.

I quote you from Lundberg's *own* editorial in *JAMA* for October 1992: "Any description of the adrenal glands was strangely missing from the autopsy report of the Warren Commission. . . . Drs. Humes and Boswell and now Dr. Finck had, since 1963, consistently declined to describe the adrenals, never explaining why. *The claim in a recent book that at autopsy the pathologists could not find the adrenals grossly, despite careful serial sections of the perirenal fat, has been independently corroborated* [emphasis author's] on the record, by Robert F. Karnei, M.D., of Maryland. . . . On August 31, 1992, Dr. Boswell confirmed, on the record, that serial sections of the perirenal fat pads demonstrated no gross evidence of adrenal cortex or medulla. . . ."[153] Guess whose book he speaks of? My book, *High Treason 2,* but Dr. Lundberg could not recall six months later that he had written the above quote.

Dr. Larry Altman of *The New York Times* recognized my little discovery of such vast importance to the political and medical world, and wrote: "In his book *High Treason 2* (Carroll & Graf, 1992), Harrison Edward Livingstone wrote that no adrenal tissue could be found at Kennedy's autopsy and that his body showed the effects of long-term hormonal replacement therapy. The source was Dr. Robert F. Karnei, a pathologist who witnessed the Kennedy autopsy.

"Although the pathologists had vowed to remain silent about Kennedy's autopsy, they spoke in an interview with CBS in 1967 and again with Dr. Lundberg's journal last May. But in May, they declined to discuss Kennedy's adrenals. Dr. Lundberg said Dr. Boswell agreed to discuss Kennedy's adrenal glands after he was told that Dr. Karnei had disclosed they were missing and after Dr. James J. Humes, the other principal, released Dr. Boswell from the vow of silence.

"The impact of full disclosure about Kennedy's adrenal condition on the 1960 Presidential election, which was decided by fewer than 115,000 voters, has not been discussed as fully as have many other what-ifs involved in that campaign.

"Dr. Lundberg's editorial raised the question of whether Kennedy would have been elected President if the public knew he had 'suffered for 13 years from an incurable, potentially fatal, although fully treatable disease and that there were potential serious adverse effects of treatment.

"Journalists who covered Kennedy now say such a disclosure probably would have swung the election to Mr. Nixon. 'A statement like that would have been fatal to his campaign,' Russell Baker, a columnist for *The New York Times,* said.''[154] It is unfortunate that this article then deteriorated into a general attack on the question of physical fitness for the presidency, which had nothing to do with how good a president the man was.

President Kennedy's adrenals have been used as a political football in this case by the medical Establishment in the United States for forty years, dating before he was dead. I resolved the question when I got the doctors to talk to me about it.[155] Most if not all of the medical witnesses talk to me. *JAMA* was embarrassed that they could get so little out of them. The editor tried to pretend that this was the first time the doctors had talked at all. Then it was pointed out to the editors that my book had this information and was filled with medical interviews with nearly everybody. I can see them now going back to the doctors and begging to find out about those adrenals, which certainly detracts from the main issues of just *where* the bullets entered the body.

Ultimately, the issues we are faced with are of the same order we have above. This man, Dr. Lundberg, thinks—like so many others—that he can say or do anything he wants, and as George Orwell tried to tell us, he is evidently so confident of the power he has that he can change his story from one day to the next and never dream that he will get caught.

That has been the way this case has gone for thirty years. It started with massive lies by the autopsy doctors, and it continues thirty years later with one of their friends printing still more misrepresentations by them, and lying himself to steal the thunder of myself and others who dare to criticize. And *JAMA* completely failed to close the case.

It is regrettable but true: The three sets of *JAMA* articles at issue in this chapter are blatant misrepresentation and cover-ups, and if there ever was a reason to reinvestigate this case, this is it.

New York (AP) Photographs and X-rays from President Kennedy's autopsy were doctored, probably to conceal the fact that he was shot from the front as well as from behind, three former Navy technicians said.

—Richard Pyle, May 19, 1992

CHAPTER 4

THE AUTHOR'S PRESS CONFERENCES

JFK X-Rays Called Fake (Reuters)

"Two Navy medical technicians who witnessed the autopsy of President John F. Kennedy said yesterday that published autopsy photographs and X-rays have been tampered with and falsified.

". . . Photographer Floyd Riebe, who took pictures of the body during the autopsy, said the photographs released by the government are 'phony and not the photographs we took.' He said the Secret Service agents prevented him and others from leaving the autopsy and that as he took out the film from his camera, it was quickly taken by the agents. 'These films are doctored one way or another,' he said."[1]

This chapter centers around me. I apologize to the reader. It's not my nature, but it is the only way I can tell the story.

I had or attempted to have two press conferences that bracketed that of *The Journal of the American Medical Association*'s press conference in the spring of 1992. For thirteen years I had been trying to bring out the testimony and statements of witnesses indicating that the autopsy materials were falsified. Attempting to get any part of my findings in the national media was all but impossible. Certainly no fair presentation was allowed, let alone discussion, even though I had published two successful books. I was now to learn that national stories often carried with them the seeds of their own destruction.

The powers-that-be did not take what I was trying to present seriously. How could they, after so many hoaxes in the case? The leading

163

researchers in the area of the medical evidence tried to stifle my findings and integrity because my work competed with and threatened theirs.

Shortly before the AMA unleashed their big guns, my first attempt to have a new press conference was a dud. I held it in Dallas on April 30, when *High Treason 2* and I succeeded in bringing together several of the men from the autopsy with some of the witnesses from Parkland Hospital at the JFK Assassination Information Center. I had no idea what the AMA was about to do.

Unfortunately, this was the day after the Rodney King verdict was handed down in Los Angeles, and that city exploded in riots during the night. I was due to appear on the morning TV news in Dallas that day, and arrived to find myself shoved off the air.

"Kennedy Evidence Phony, author says" was the title of David Real's article in the *Dallas Morning News.*[2] "He says Warren panel was deceived. . . . The accusations came as Mr. Livingstone assembled a cast of supporting medical witnesses Thursday at the JFK Assassination Information Center in downtown Dallas. He was there to promote his new book. . . ." The story did not get national play. I had brought Jim Metzler, Paul O'Connor, and Jim Jenkins, along with Audrey Bell, Dr. Richard B. Dulany, and others together, though I had succeeded in doing much the same for television filming two years before, in Dallas.[3] That was never produced, either.

The *Dallas Morning News* article made it sound as though I were accusing Arlen Specter of showing the phony autopsy pictures to Earl Warren, though I have no idea who showed them to Warren.

Because the riots in L.A. crowded this story off the news wire, this conference basically failed, though Paul O'Connor was quoted as saying that the photographs of the body were tampered with. His statement was promptly defused in the article by the statement that O'Connor had previously claimed that the body had been "secretly switched from a heavy, bronze coffin and arrived in a body bag inside a shipping casket. . . ."

I must once again repeat that so much of the problem in this case is language. This reporter, an otherwise nice guy who a month later did better with another story when five of the Dallas doctors gathered at the Stauffer Hotel, decided that the casket was a "heavy, bronze" casket and that O'Connor said it was a "shipping casket." The Warren Commission had stated that it was a "bronze colored plastic casket."[4] Here we have an example of the unproven theory of one author infecting the perception of the media. A slippery undertaker, trying to charge the government all he could get, had put a high price on his coffin, causing it to be described as something more than it was.

Secondly, the young reporter who wrote this used previous statements by Paul O'Connor to discredit what he might have to say now by making him sound confused. To arrive "in a body bag" does not answer the questions, Was he *wrapped* in a body bag? Or was he *inside* a body bag? O'Connor had told the House Assassinations Committee that he was *wrapped* in a body bag and not *in* it.[5]

The problem is always in interpreting statements from witnesses. Too often it's too easy to take a statement literally. And what was meant by "body bag"?

"But Mr. Livingstone, in his book, dismisses the theory. Mr. O'Connor said he is not bothered by the criticism. 'I think that's good, healthy trashing,' Mr. O'Connor said. 'I'll be the first person to admit I'm not the perfect expert on this thing. I could be wrong.' " This is how the article ends, inconclusively, with whatever of value O'Connor had to say being obscured by indicating that he is only expressing opinion and could be wrong.

If this book has another purpose equal to trying to illuminate the evidence in this case, it is to teach readers to examine language and evidence more carefully, to ask many more questions, because those who write the news are not infallible and often make thoughtless mistakes. That happens in the books I write, regrettably.

There is a truth in what the medical witnesses say with regard to each medical-forensic issue, and I believe I have been able to sort that out in a definitive fashion. The problem has always been to dig through the massive pile of confusion.

I was to get another chance. This chance was provided by the American Medical Association's publication of their articles on May 27, 1992, and their press conference that preceded it. On May 29 I held my own press conference in New York, at the Berkshire Hotel. All the same reporters came, to my great surprise, and all the same TV cameras came that were at *JAMA*'s press conference.

The American Medical Association actually proved my most central contention, that the autopsy photographs and X-rays were forged. They published quotations from two of the autopsy physicians which cast serious doubt on these materials (see the chapter on *JAMA*). But no other critics understood this.

My second press conference with the autopsy witnesses succeeded because both Jean King at Reuters and Richard Pyle of the Associated Press wrote straight stories that were among the best and the most significant ever done in the case. These were experienced journalists. Mr. Pyle tested me and the witnesses to the hilt. He found that we couldn't be budged from our stories, and ran with it on the AP.

Even then, Pyle did not get all the main points right. This story was just too big and too startling for journalists unfamiliar with the vast amount of supporting documentation. Almost nobody dared treat it in an absolutely straightforward manner, so most put their own twist on it or selectively failed to report key points.

Although I did not succeed one twentieth as well as *JAMA* did, I achieved most of my goals, got on the wires with two very good stories, and film clips of my witnesses denouncing the autopsy evidence were shown all across the United States on the late-night news. Since the whole affair was so extraordinary, let me tell the way it was from my personal viewpoint as its creator.

I had returned from *JAMA*'s news conference May 19, 1992, greatly disheartened. I had made a bit of a splash there with my guerrilla tactics, getting onto the prime-time news. The reporters were hungry for news and a big story.

Because the two *JAMA* articles were only made public the day of their news conference, it was not until returning home that, in combing through them, I found not only extensive misrepresentation but also a vital key to the case. This was the infamous *Nova* show all over again—things taken out of context and misrepresented. With all the other reporters on deadline that afternoon, with no time for close study and analysis of the *JAMA* articles and presentations, they were forced to report with what they were told by *JAMA*. That's the way it works, and it is planned by those who give press conferences. Nobody is going to wait until the next day to study the material and print a story, for fear of being scooped.

Among the false picture of the facts given in the *JAMA* article were two vital pieces of information that corroborated my findings that the autopsy photographs and X-rays were forged. The two autopsy pathologists, James Humes and James Boswell, were getting back to me and signaling that I was right. The vast effort I had poured into this research was paying off inch by inch.

Perhaps the doctors couldn't come right out and say that the stuff was forged, but they certainly stood fast on the fact that the entrance hole in the back of the head was where they had placed it in 1963,[6] and that the face was undamaged, "normal," and "intact" when they unwrapped the head.[7] By insisting on the entry hole being at or near the occipital protuberance, Humes and Boswell repudiated their public testimony in 1978, and reaffirmed what they told the House Committee's panel of doctors off-camera. (This is intensively detailed in my previous books.) It took a couple of days for the idea to jell in my mind that perhaps I could do the same thing and have my own press conference.

But undertaking to have a major news conference alone was quite a task. My editor and publisher was in Los Angeles at the American Book Association booksellers' fair, and it was Memorial Day weekend. The first task was to call the autopsy witnesses I hoped to produce. I had no idea if they would put up with me and trust me with yet one more demand on their time and good will.

To my surprise, each one I called was hopping mad over the stories that came out about the *JAMA* conference and some of what the autopsy doctors had allegedly said. This worked to our advantage because the first men I called said they would be glad to come. I was excited. This time, for the first time, Jerry Custer, the X-ray technologist who had told me so much and to whom I had devoted a chapter in *High Treason 2,* would come. He had perhaps the most startling evidence of all.

Then it was up to me to book flights and hotel reservations for everyone, find a room in which to hold the press conference, prepare press releases and a press kit, send out press releases, and go to New York myself. I had the idea on a Friday morning, and within a few hours it was all settled. At first everything went like clockwork. Dr. Charles Crenshaw agreed to come, as well as Dr. Cyril Wecht, the doyen of the assassination community. Cyril had gone to my first press conference at the National Press Club in Washington the day the gun on the *Iowa* blew up three years before. He had thundered at the few reporters who were there, about my first book on the assassination of John Kennedy: "This is hard stuff. This is not speculation; this is not fanciful, subjective rumination; this is concrete, tangible, hard, physical, medical evidence!"

I spent the weekend writing the materials to be handed out, and had some help from friends. We sent out a barrage of press releases, and we Faxed news organizations with the notice.

I was very glad that Dr. Crenshaw was coming to the conference because it would afford him an opportunity to answer the massive attack launched on him that week by *The Journal of the American Medical Association.* Or so I hoped.

I came to New York a day in advance and still had no idea that things would go wrong. Everything seemed to be going smoothly. Too smoothly. My experience had led me to suspect that if something could go wrong, it might. My nature was to expect the worst and hope for the best. I didn't used to be that way. These lessons come hard, especially to lunkheads like me.

At 10:00 A.M. the room was set up, and the press came flooding into it. I recognized many of the same people from *JAMA*'s conference the week before: the woman from *Der Speigel; Newsday;* Jean King from Reuters; Richard Pyle from the AP; Dr. Lawrence Altman from *The New York Times,* standing on a chair in the back of the room and straining to hear; and the network cameramen.

But there was a saboteur in the room whom I didn't spot until the conference was over. This man made a major effort to slander and libel me at the very moment I was making this great effort. He passed out mug shots of me and told reporters I was an ex-con (which is completely false).

As Mark Crouch would later say during an investigation of the perpetrator, identified as Robert Groden, "Why would he try to destroy the very evidence and witnesses he needs to prove the case?" Good question. I would begin to understand the answers only when I understood Dallas better, and the treatment of evidence by leading researchers with a Dallas connection for so many years.

With regard to the actions of those in the research community who seemed to sabotage important evidence in the case, you have to study the patterns and actions and their consistent results to grasp what the intent is.

"Where is Dr. Crenshaw?" Paul O'Connor repeatedly asked me. "I called the desk, and they said he hasn't come in yet."

"I don't know," I said.

"Dr. Wecht isn't here, either."

A sickening lump gathered in my throat. I was deeply embarrassed, and feeling the effects of the past days of effort to put all this together. Floyd Riebe, Paul O'Connor, and Jerry Custer had flown in to make their statements about the *JAMA* "investigation." None of them had anything good to say about the autopsy doctors.

When I began to speak, I was immediately interrupted by reporters: *"Where is Dr. Crenshaw?"* That became the refrain I could not escape for the next two hours. They ate me alive, and Richard Pyle was one of those who never let up: *"Where is Dr. Crenshaw?"* It was all I could do to go on, as I tried to explain why we were there and what we were going to do. *"Where is Dr. Wecht?"*

I had to deal directly with the fact that Crenshaw and Wecht were not there. I said, "Look, I don't know why they aren't here, other than I was told that Crenshaw's publisher (Viking Penguin) didn't want Crenshaw here and may have prevented it. The last word I had from Mrs. Crenshaw was that he was coming. That is the truth. I have some integrity, and I would not lie about this or falsely pretend that I had advertised him coming here in order to get you to come to this conference.''

It took an hour to get down to business. The press conference was tumultuous. The reporters waited for the worst to happen to me. (I don't blame them in a way: I had been systematically kept off the national television shows, off the news in spite of two major bestsellers on the case that year, and they didn't know who I was.) They thought I would fold up or get trapped in some lie. They had seen me interfering and more or less take over a major national press conference just the prior week, and now it was my turn to be a target, to be out in the open and vulnerable. What did I bring them? What was so new about the Kennedy case that I was breaking into their lives this way?

I managed to introduce one of the witnesses. Floyd Riebe got up, and the room grew quiet.

''See these here pictures?'' he said in his thick Oklahoma accent. ''They're wrong. I don't know what this is, but that ain't the way it was. He didn't have a back of the head.''

Floyd Riebe said that he didn't think the pictures were taken in the autopsy room at Bethesda because there was a small wooden table in the background. The reporter translated this as follows: ''Riebe . . . contended they were doctored because they show Kennedy lying on what appears to be a wooden table, with a dark background and odd shadows. 'We had no such structure, all we had was white tile and stainless steel,' Riebe said.''[8] The color autopsy pictures are remarkable for their lack of background and their shadows, which make them different from the black-and-white pictures.

In his statement, ''They're wrong. I don't know what this is . . .'' Riebe was referring to a small wooden table in the picture that was used to hold an instrument tray and that could be wheeled around. He was not referring to the autopsy table itself. But so much of what we had to offer was discredited because the AP said this, even though it is clear in the photographs that the large autopsy table is made of steel.

'' 'The pictures I've seen resemble the pictures that I'd taken. That's all I can say. The quality of these prints is very poor. I'd have been in deep trouble if I'd turned in work like this,' Riebe said.''

Inch by inch, we were getting out the story, warts and all.

Jerrol Custer came forward and said, ''These are not the X-rays I took. These are fake. I don't know what these are.'' Custer demonstrated that the upper right front of the face and underlying bone were missing in the X-rays. ''His face was not damaged. There was no bone missing, I can tell you that.

"In these X-rays, all this bone is missing [he demonstrated], and I can tell you that this X-ray is not of President Kennedy. That's how I remember it. To my recollection, there was no frontal damage at all."

Custer went on to describe the way in which he was made to tape bullet fragments to pieces of skull and X-ray them, the day after the assassination, being told it was somehow connected to the making of a bust of Kennedy.

Both O'Connor and Custer said that a bullet from the wound in the back fell out when the body was lifted from the coffin. Both men reaffirmed that the probing of the hole in the back did not reveal an exit wound. They said it was probed to a depth of about two inches.

Dr. Crenshaw told me some months later that his publisher did not want him to come to our press conference, even though he had agreed to come and then no-showed. The truth of that is somewhat revealed in the seeming contradiction related in the AP story of that day (May 29, 1992):

"However, he (Livingstone) said Crenshaw's publisher, Viking Penguin, had prevented him from making the trip. Leonida Karpik, a spokeswoman for Viking Penguin, said Crenshaw had just 'returned exhausted' to Dallas from a twenty-city book promotion tour and had never consented to go to New York. 'We didn't see any reason why he should,' she said. 'It wasn't his news conference.' "

For many years there has been a strange pattern affecting my research into the JFK case. Others whom I respect have had the same experience when they cease to be low-profile. Every step of the way I have met with major opposition—at the Capital in 1976–77, in Dallas, in my home city of Baltimore, and in trying to publish. There has been deliberate obstruction by other "researchers." There has been so much slander that it often almost broke my health and spirit. Let's be careful to define slander and libel (libel is slander in print), since far too many people slide over the meaning of slander, confusing it with criticism. One of the necessary elements of slander of a public person is the making of knowingly false statements. The public has a right to know, and the journalist's privilege of writing the truth about people is protected by the First Amendment. Those who are of reprehensible character due to gross moral turpitude and who are in the public eye are rightfully the subject of the media, and are not defamed by the truth. They did it to themselves. Some people of this type use assassination research as a cover, and the media have the right to alert the public as to whom they are giving their support. This is a far cry from trying to destroy someone with false stories for illegal or other reasons. It is greatly unfortunate that there is a pattern of behavior among some leaders in this case of deliberately defaming their competitors for one reason or another, and of then inventing a new definition of the tort of malice for their critics.

None of this is in the natural course of business. The only way it can happen is if there are paid provocateurs and saboteurs to knock out people like me who try to objectify evidence. Most often it comes from those who are visibly members of the "research community" or the "critical community." Normal, ordinary citizens don't act that way. To try to explain their actions in terms of territorial disputes, ego, and the like, is too easy. There are far more compelling reasons to know for sure that the attacks mounted by the Old Guard among the researchers have only one purpose: to destroy the *real* evidence of conspiracy in the case, and their messengers. For that you need only to look at the pattern of who and what are attacked. This is not just fair criticism of someone else's research, but attempts to destroy major evidence that should be beyond dispute. In its place was erected a false structure of alleged evidence of conspiracy, and the case was co-opted by those who put such evidence forward.

I was fighting an uphill battle. At the very moment of the press conference other "researchers" were right there in the room sabotaging me and the very witnesses we needed to prove a conspiracy at the autopsy. There was something even more infamous in all of this: *Many of the so-called leading researchers or critics in the case had never really contributed any original research.* These actors created the appearance of scholarship, activity, and original research, but what they had really done was steal other people's work, claiming it for their own, and muck up the evidence. They were charlatans deluding the public and the press. It was easy when trading on such an emotionally charged issue as John Kennedy's murder.

This case has been rigged by the conspirators in Dallas for a long time. Their vast financial resources have been able to buy almost everything they needed: silence, the media, and even people.

The wound that I saw on the
back, just to the side of the
scapula, that wound was a rather
typical entrance wound.

—Dr. Robert Shaw

CHAPTER 5

THE DALLAS AUTOPSY FORUM AND THE PARKLAND DOCTORS

On June 4, 1992, Kevin McCarthy, one of the top radio news journalists and talk show hosts in Dallas, asked General Will Lathem, the moderator of the meeting, to begin questions for five of the November 22, 1963, Dallas doctors. He asked the following question: "Are you aware of all the inconsistencies between what the doctors at Bethesda reported in their autopsy and what has been described in the official record for the doctors at Parkland and their experience? Isn't it a shame that we finally get them here after twenty-nine years and no one asked them about their inconsistencies?" *It was the first time the doctors had been publicly gathered:* Drs. Marion Jenkins, James Carrico, Charles Baxter, Paul Peters, and Dr. Robert Shaw. Among them they had pulled a bait and switch on their hosts, substituting Dr. Shaw for Dr. Robert McClelland. "Dr. Shaw just happened to be here," Lathem explained lamely. "Dr. McClelland was invited and said that he would come, but one of his children had an accident in San Francisco." So how come some of the other dynamite witnesses in the audience, such as Nurse Margaret Henchcliff Hood, were not allowed to speak?!

"Well, we thought we had some questions about it, but you can see we ran out of time. We're going up for another off-the-record discussion with these doctors at dinner and I've got the questions in my pocket, so we'll be asking them up there."

"Who is going to attend that?"

"It's for the members and officers and the Board of Directors of the Council."

There you have it. One more example of propaganda exercises for public consumption, and the real stuff is private, behind closed doors.

*   *   *

For ninety long and terrible minutes, a packed audience suffered through the long-winded exposition of the government's case by Dr. John Lattimer, an urologist who has become a chief spokesman and apologist for the Warren Report. Lattimer insisted that the bullet that he says exited Kennedy's neck was tumbling and had made a "butterfly" or "figure eight" entry on Connally's back. When asked, Dr. Robert Shaw, who operated on Connally, laughed at this and said it was a small, neat, round hole of entry. "The wound that I saw on the back, just to the side of the scapula, that wound was a rather typical entrance wound."[1] Shaw also ridiculed the idea that both men were shot by the same bullet, since they removed from Connally large pieces of metal that could not have come from the "magic" bullet. Dr. Humes himself had tried to tell this to Arlen Specter in 1964.[2]

There was another major abortion at this meeting, and that was the failure to invite Dr. Charles Crenshaw. It is important to record here that the Dallas doctors repeated at the meeting on June 4, 1992, shortly after the *JAMA* article, extensive corroboration for almost every assertion Crenshaw had made, including that there was an entry hole in the President's throat. Dr. James Carrico stated it once again.[3] Dr. Ronald Jones, whom *JAMA* dared not speak to, has always insisted the throat wound was a frontal entry wound.[4] The Dallas doctors reaffirmed that what they saw was a "neat, round, hole of entrance" in the throat. This is the legally binding testimony, since the wound was never seen at the autopsy. Of course, none of this important meeting—which fundamentally overturned the *JAMA* article days after it was printed—was reported nationally. The name of the game was to give all of the national press coverage to *JAMA*, and no real reporting for the opposition, even if they were the only real medical witnesses on that issue.

I did not grasp how deep authoritarianism and militarism were at this meeting, what a series of setups there were in Dallas and the role the local assassination research community played in being the handy tools of the local establishment. The researchers wanted to think that the failure to criticize the appearance of the tracheostomy incision in the autopsy pictures meant that the doctors were all lying, *thus discrediting the very witnesses these same researchers needed to prove a conspiracy.*

Perhaps one of the most important questions dealt with the appearance of the tracheostomy wound in the autopsy photographs. Each doctor indicated that what was in the picture was quite accurate. This statement corroborated the research I had just published in *High Treason 2,* but their answer invited the wrath of Gary Shaw and others who had bought the body-theft and body-alteration fantasies hook, line, and sinker. As the meeting broke up, Shaw promptly accused the doctors of changing their story, and implied that they were lying, as some of the other former leading researchers perpetrating the theory of alteration had blatantly and publicly stated. In other words, some critics were discrediting the very witnesses they needed the most. The doctors had hammered home the forgery of some of the pictures and retouching of the throat wound in the Stare-Of-Death picture.

As part of the regular program, Dr. Peters asked a question of Dr. Marion Jenkins about physically feeling and knowing about the entry holes on the back of the head and in the back. Many researchers were previously unaware of this. "Pepper [Marion Jenkins] said that he felt a wound down in the neck. I remember that from twenty or thirty years ago. You did say that, didn't you?"

"A few moments ago I said I felt first the one in the *occiput* when I tilted the head."

"Right. That's what you just said a minute ago, but twenty-five years ago—"

"Then I said I felt the other one lower down on his *back*."

General Lathem asked a question: "If you're called to testify again under oath about the nature and location of the president's wounds, will your description be consistent with your original written statements, your Warren Commission testimony, and your House Select Committee on Assassinations testimony?" Each doctor was then polled:

"If I had to testify again today, I would have no substantially different observations. I would correct or at least be far less definite about seeing cerebellum. We saw significantly destroyed brain and we thought it was cerebrum and cerebellum. I'm not at all sure that we saw cerebellum," Dr. Carrico said.

Dr. Baxter said: "I wouldn't extend what I saw, and I think that all of my testimony and written stuff would stand up today. I don't know of anything that I would change."

Dr. Peters: "Dr. Shaw, you've taken a stand different than the popular one by siding with Governor Connally on his wounds. Do you feel the same today? Has anything appeared over the years to cause you to modify your initial impression about the wounds?"

"No. I have the Warren Commission Report at home. I read the portions that had to do with the Governor's wound, and the care of the Governor."

"Did you notice the 'figure eight' configuration of the wound on his back as you were operating on him which Dr. Lattimer has alluded to?

From a tumbling bullet rather than one going straight as a missile would go that had not encountered any obstruction?''

"No. The wound that I saw in the back which was just to the side of the scapula, and ripped out the long portion, 10 percent of the center of his sixth rib. That wound was a rather typical entrance wound (loud applause from the audience!). It was not a large wound. Of course, then, the bullet went on through, struck his wrist, where it did a lot of bone damage, and nicked his thigh. But the wound in his thigh was just a nick. It was just a little superficial wound. It was nothing."[5] Groden and others have claimed that there had been a whole bullet in the thigh. "That bullet had to go to the bottom of the limousine. It *couldn't* have been on his stretcher and so forth." This was one of the most important observations in the case, but poor Dr. Shaw was about to die.

Peters gave his own testimony: "I had thought originally, twenty-five years ago, that the cerebellum was damaged, but when I went later to the National Archives, the cerebellum was indeed shoved down, compared to its mate, it didn't have any tear in it. I attributed that to the terrific pressure in his head from the bullet on that side. This was only a 7-cm. hole in the occipital parietal area, which I saw. Pepper, have you changed your mind about anything that you testified to?" He turned it over to Dr. Jenkins.

"I wrote this up extensively from my own notes at the time. And also the Oswald resuscitation attempt. I reread them this afternoon. No, I haven't changed my views of it from that time. We all mentioned cerebellum here. In my official report, I said the cerebellum was hanging out, and I thought it over after I turned it in. Well, I confused my three lums at times. I'd call one by the other one's name. I'd call cerebrum cerebellum. When I looked at the photographs again [!], I can see why we did that, because this coming out of the temporal-parietal area, brain was so convoluted right there, that the cerebrum had a cerebellum look. But it wasn't cerebellum. That's the only thing I'd change, but I'd change it today after I'd written it. I knew I was wrong."

Dr. Baxter said, "Everyone concerned was asked never to talk about the case because, with the different interpretations of the different words the press puts in your mouth, many stories could evolve. Consequently, this was confidentiality of the management of the case. The government took the records and the testimony of several people in the case and that became the public record. The FBI asked us if they had all our notes and so on." There it is again: the public versus an implied private record.

As for the cerebellum hanging out of the wound, not only can the brain that was examined at the supplemental autopsy not be the President's brain for the reason that it has the weight of a normal brain having lost none of its mass, but also the autopsy photographs these doctors saw with the help of a television program made for government-sponsored television are fake. As far as we can determine, no weight of the brain was recorded at the autopsy.

Someone asked from the audience, "Could each physician who saw the President in the hospital put his hand on the part of his head where he saw the President's brain?"

They did this, and their placement was identical with what they demonstrated to me in 1979 and on *Nova* in 1988. (Note the photographs from *Nova* in this book.)

This was the end of the regular program, and we were all supposed to get out right then. But some of us dashed up to the stage and surrounded the six doctors before they could leave and began peppering them with questions about the wounds.

Kevin McCarthy asked Dr. Jenkins about the large wound and if it was consistent with being an entrance or an exit wound: "Large holes are exit wounds, and small holes are entrance wounds," Jenkins responded.

McCarthy: "And you gestured in the middle of the collarbone."

Jenkins: "In your back near the base of the neck."

McCarthy: "And you're pressing me in the collarbone. There seems to be an inconsistency in what you are saying with what the other Parkland doctors have said."

Dr. Peters explained, "They just pulled his hair over here to cover up. You could peel that back there and see that large hole."

"But it was described by the doctors as being shredded with a large hole here," I said.

"Yeah, that's right. I *saw* that. I *know* that," Peters said. "They probably pulled it back over to make this picture or something—it was right there—his holes!"

"Was that above his right ear or behind his right ear?"

"It was both. It really went behind and was also a bit forward of the ear. It could be either. I thought it was an exit wound at the time. I still think that."

"Where did it come from?"

"I think it had to come from lower on the occiput. Maybe an inch below."

"Below the exit wound?"

"That's correct."

"Behind or below? To the left and below?"

"Behind the patient and could be to the right of him."

"But you're gesturing to an area below the wound."

"What I'm saying is that if you pulled his hair back right here, you'd see a big hole right here."

"Point to me on this picture and show me where you think the bullet that caused this wound could have entered the President's head. . . . The entrance point you are showing me is below and to the left of where you show me the exit—the larger wound was."

"No, that's not right, to say it's to the left." Peters asked for some paper to draw the exit wound. He placed it fairly high on the back of the head.

Peters went on, "I never felt the hole. Nor did I see the supposed entrance hole in the skull."

Peters also said that he never saw the back/neck wound. "The things that I *know* I saw was the wound in the [anterior] neck and the large one on the head. Now, the thing that annoyed me when I first saw the X-rays was how extensive the fracturing of the skull was. But I've learned over the twenty or thirty years that that was fairly typical for that caliber of missile with that impact hitting the skull." Except that the wound is in the wrong place on the X-rays.

I asked him, "Was there any damage to his face, or was there any outward sign of the skull fractures in the frontal area?"

"Gosh no!" Peters exclaimed. "All it looked like when you looked at President Kennedy was that he might have been frowning a little. I thought about that over the years. It's where the scalp was so torn that it was pushed forward and down just a little bit."

McCarthy asked him, "The photo we saw of the tracheostomy we saw described and photographed—the jagged wound—is that what the President's neck looked like when you saw it at Parkland?"

"No, because I saw it before Dr. Perry and Dr. Baxter made the incision. but that's what it looked like just when they finished to put the tracheal tube in. It looks like they just pulled it out."

"Was it that jagged?" he asked Peters.

"Oh, *that wasn't bad.* I mean, the part they incised looked very nice. The jagged part was probably where the bullet had gone through. They wouldn't have cut that irregularly with the knife."

Peters put on the screen a picture of the throat wound as seen in the autopsy photographs. He then asked Dr. Baxter to comment on it.

Baxter: "The hole was only the size of a pencil eraser, about 2 or 2½ mm. across, and air was bubbling out of it, and a little blood. . . . My immediate thought was that this was an entry wound because it was *so small.* And we knew nothing about what had happened downtown. We had about seven minutes to do everything that was done. . . . We went right through it. You obviously would go through where the hole was if you are going to try to control what the hole is doing. It happened to be at exactly the level that we do tracheostomy. That much incision is just the size that you have to have to get down to get the muscles spread to get the tracheostomy tube in. So there is nothing about that that is not routine.''

Peters: ''Some of us had seen a huge hole in the back of his head. At first we thought that the bullet had come in the [front of the] neck, hit the cervical spine, and come out the back of his head.''

Dr. Peters then turned to Dr. Jenkins and tried again. ''Now, Pepper, you have been quoted as saying that you actually felt the hole back there with your finger. Isn't that what you said? You knew it was there when the rest of us didn't know. Isn't that what the truth is?''

''Yes,'' Jenkins said. ''But that was a secondary finding, though. When I tilted the head back to put the neck in a better position for the tracheostomy, I put my thumb first in the hole in the back of the occiput where the bullet had entered. And then, while doing that and adjusting the head, I found what I later decided was the other wound: a wound of entrance. I didn't know what it was then because I was watching too much what was going on in the front.''

The whole program of the ''Forum,'' filled with so much promise, was terribly handled and a crushing disappointment. Some worthwhile points of evidence were a little farther buttressed, but all in all, this was a great opportunity lost, and that is what was so sad about the whole evening.

But then, powerful people in Dallas organized it and wanted things just this way: to fail. More was to come—more staged meetings in Dallas covering up their murder of John Kennedy. In October, Ray Hunt, H. L. Hunt's son, would host the ''Assassination Symposium''—a farcical affair—at his hotel, charging the suckers a hundred bucks a head per night—all the traffic would bear.

CHAPTER 6

DIANA BOWRON

Diana Bowron was a twenty-two-year-old British nurse employed at Parkland Hospital in 1963, and she was on the loading dock behind the hospital, the first person to arrive with a cart, after President Kennedy's limousine pulled in. She had been in the United States only three months, and as she told me, "It was a hell of an introduction to America!"

I was fortunate to gain interviews with her after she had dropped out of sight for twenty-seven years. Many people sought to find her, but all failed. What she had kept in her head all that time was in a way the most important of the medical evidence. I had a number of very specific questions for her that might resolve some of the major conflicts in the evidence.

Bowron is the vital chain of evidence from the time the car arrived to the time the body departed in its coffin. Except for one brief departure from the Emergency Room to get blood ten minutes after the President arrived, she was with the body until all life ceased and every moment after that.

"I was away only two to three minutes (to go to the blood bank), and on my return I continued to assist where needed until the President was declared dead."[1]

This testimony established that no one had access to the body to remove a bullet or otherwise tamper with the body.

I wish to start this historic interview with the story as her mother told it to a British newspaper forty-eight hours after the tragedy. The British newspaper stories at the time made it sound as though the reporters had actually talked with Bowron, but they got it secondhand from her mother and didn't care to say that. The Warren Commission published the British newspaper articles as is, and no questions were asked as to whom they actually interviewed.

"All I noticed at first was the big official car. Then I spotted Mrs. Kennedy. President Kennedy was lying with his head slumped in her lap. She was cradling his head. There was blood pouring from his wounds down her legs . . . there was blood all over his neck and shoulders. There was a gaping wound in the back of his head.

"The doctors tried everything. They performed a tracheostomy to help his breathing. They tried massaging his heart manually."

On Mrs. Kennedy: "At the beginning Mrs. Kennedy just sat on a chair at the side of the room, not saying anything—just staring into space. All she asked for was a glass of water. When the room became crowded, someone led her outside. She didn't come back until the doctors finally decided President Kennedy was dead. Then she stood by the table, lifted his hand, and kissed it. She took off her wedding ring and slipped it on his finger."[2]

As Bowron told her mother and me, "It was the most terrible and shocking experience in my life." She said in 1963, "I realized who the man in the car was as soon as I saw Jackie Kennedy. Mr. Kennedy was slumped forward in his seat—and so was Mr. Connally. We had to bring in Mr. Connally first before we could get the President."

Diana told me that she got into the backseat of the car while they were attempting to move Connally out of the way and took Kennedy's pulse.[3]

She told Sidney Brennan, "His jacket was covered with petals from Mrs. Kennedy's bouquet. I helped to cut away Mr. Kennedy's clothing and to administer intravenous injections. Ten doctors and several nurses—including myself—assisted in giving blood transfusions. Then I handed instruments to the doctors who performed a tracheostomy operation to assist his breathing.

"But there was no hope for him. Mrs. Kennedy was there nearly all the time. She went out for a short while. But, in spite of what the doctors said, she came back in just as Mr. Kennedy died. When he had died, Mrs. Kennedy kissed his hand. Then she took off her wedding ring and slipped it on his wedding finger. But the ring only reached the first knuckle.

"We all wept with Mrs. Kennedy. It was the most moving thing I have ever seen," added Diana.[4]

Her mother explained to reporters the day after the assassination, "Diana always wanted to go to America, and when she noticed the advertisement for jobs in Dallas in a nursing journal she jumped at the chance."[5]

Bowron wrote in her hospital report of the events, "Miss Henchliffe and myself prepared the body by removing the remaining clothes . . . we then washed the blood from the President's face and body and covered him with a sheet. During this time, we were assisted by David Sanders, the orderly."[6]

One of the key issues was how much brain was left in the President's head after such an explosive shot. Diana told me, "There was *very* little brain left. I had my hands inside his head, trying to clean it up so there wouldn't be more of a mess in the coffin. I put cloth inside, and then removed it. The brain was almost gone."[7]

Diana was put in touch with me and I obtained answers for all my questions. This came at the same time as a letter from Dr. Thornton Boswell.

Diana sent a drawing of the head wound (reproduced herein), captioned, "this is where I remember the wound," and she returned a copy of an autopsy photograph of the President's back with the comment "THIS IS NOT THE BACK I SAW" written in capital letters.

Her drawing of the large head wound showed it in the right rear of the head, starting at the hairline. Along with these illustrations, she sent a typed statement, which follows. With regard to the head wound, Bowron wrote, "I first saw the large wound in the back of the head in the car. When we were preparing the body for the coffin I had the opportunity to examine it more closely. It was about five inches in diameter and there was no flap of skin covering it, just a fraction of skin along part of the edges of bone. There was, however, some hair hanging down from the top of the head, which was caked with blood, and most of the brain was missing. The wound was so large I could almost put my whole left fist inside."

Written Statement

She went on to answer questions I had sent her as follows:

"Being new to the establishment, I was assigned to Minor Medicine and Surgery, which was across the hall from the Triage desk and the major sections of the Emergency Room. It being very quiet, there were only two or three patients waiting for the results of tests. I was talking to the Triage nurse when the call went up for gurneys. I grabbed a gurney in the hall and together with an orderly ran to the entrance. I saw that the person in the back of the car was injured, so I climbed in to render what assistance I could until such time as we could move him to a trolley, then to the trauma room (others were assisting the Governor in the front seat). I saw that there was a massive amount of blood on the backseat, and in order to find the cause I lifted his head and my fingers went into a large wound in the back of his head. I turned his head, and seeing the entry wound in the front of the throat, I could feel no pulse at the jugular.

"Having seen the extent of the injury to the back of the head, I assumed that he was dead (not my job, only a doctor can certify death). When we got the President to the Trauma room, word had reached the Trauma team, and they were ready with IVs, etc. I worked with the team, assisting where needed for about ten minutes (time is difficult to judge in these circumstances), when I was told to go to the Blood Bank. I was away two to three minutes, and on my return, I continued to assist where needed until the President was declared dead.

"When the President expired, everyone left the room apart from Miss Henchliffe, a male orderly, and myself. We tidied the room and changed the linen on the gurney and washed the body as best we could. Miss Henchliffe and the orderly left the room, but I was told to remain with the body until the casket arrived. I was told that I had to stay because I had been one of the people who had taken the body from the car. I remained in the room while the widow paid her respects. After she had left I was asked, by a man I assumed was Secret Service, to collect all pieces of skull and brain I could find and place them in a plastic bag, which he gave me. This I did, and returned the bag to him (there were only a few fragments of bone that had stuck to the dressings and towels that we had used to pack the hole in the back of the head). I remained in the room until the people from the funeral home arrived. After we had placed the body in the casket and it had been closed, I was allowed to leave. During the time I was with the body only the widow and the priest came into the room. Any dealings I had with the Secret Service were done in the doorway; no one else entered the room and no photographs were taken.

"Apart from two to three minutes, when I left the trauma room to collect blood from the Blood Bank, I was with the body from the car until it was placed in the casket.

"Miss Margaret Henchliffe and an African-American orderly and I prepared the body for the coffin. I observed no strange activity of any kind and saw no bullets.

"As explained above, I thought after examination in the car that he was dead. There was no damage to the front of his face, only the gaping wound in the back of his head, and the entry wound in his throat.

"When we prepared the body for the coffin, we washed the face and closed the eyes: There was no damage to the face, there was no flap of scalp on the right, neither was there a laceration pointing toward the right eyebrow from the scalp.

"When we were preparing the body for the coffin, we rolled it over in order to remove the blood-stained sheet from underneath and to wipe way the blood from the back of the body. I saw another entry wound in the upper back (the other entry wound being in front of the throat). With reference to the photograph, "The Back" (F 5), I only saw one wound, and not the number of wounds in the photograph: I do not think that the photo (F 5) is of the President. I have marked for you on the photostat that you sent me where I think the entry wound was.*

"When we prepared the body, I washed as much blood as I could from the hair; while doing this, I did not see any other wound either in the temples or in other parts of the head.

"I did not see anything suspicious about any of the doctors, though there were far more doctors there than there should have been. Perhaps because it was the President, they all wanted to get in on the act. You must remember that I had only been there a short time and I did not know all the doctors. Some I never saw again, but they were all known to each other. With regard to a post (inquiry): In this context, I think it would refer to a gathering of the doctors, after the event, to discuss the case. This was standard practice when more than one or two doctors were involved.

"When the body was placed in the coffin, the wound at the back of the head was packed with gauze squares and wrapped in a small white sheet. There was no terry cloth or other type of towel used.

"The coffin or casket was bronze with plain fittings, as in the enclosed photograph.

"I don't think the body was removed from the coffin. After I left the Trauma room, I was in a position to see if anyone entered or left the room. No one entered or left until they removed the coffin.

"A clear plastic sheet was placed in the bottom of the coffin, which may have been a mattress cover. The body was wrapped in—at the most—two sheets plus the one around the head. All the sheets were white and none had zips. There was no 'body bag.'

"As soon as the coffin left the trauma room, I went back to Minor Medicine and Surgery to resume my work; I don't know anything about the fight with Earl Rose, which happened at that time. (Earl Rose was the medical examiner who tried to stop the removal of the body from Dallas.)

---

*Diana Bowron drew a circle around the arrow (see photo section).

"Perhaps the following will be of interest to you. When I arrived in Minor Medicine, I found the patients had been moved elsewhere, and the department had been taken over by the Vice President and his staff. They were getting ready to leave when I got there, as they passed me, I heard the Vice President say to his wife, 'Make a note of what everyone says and does.' "Did Johnson say so that he would know what their cover story had to be later on? (See Chapter 15.)

Phone Interview

This is a transcript of our first telephone interview, verbatim, except that one mistake is corrected (by her), and identifying (as to address) information is removed.[8]

DB: Hello?

HL: Diana, it's Harry.

DB: Yes . . . but everybody calls me Di.

HL: All right, well, can I ask you some of these questions and then if you want to go ahead and write them out at a later time that would be very important.

DB: Oh, right, okay.

HL: Let me ask you: Were you ever out of the Emergency Room—were you there when the body came in? When President Kennedy came in?

DB: Yes, I got him out of the car, and I basically stayed with him the whole time until I put him in the coffin, apart from about two minutes when everybody was in there when I went to get blood. But I was with him when I got him out of the car, and I put him in the coffin.

HL: So the longest that you were separated from the body was two minutes?

DB: Well, say four or five minutes at the most.

HL: Okay, four to five minutes. Was Doris Nelson there when you went to get the blood?

DB: Margaret Henchliff was.

HL: Okay.

DB: And all the doctors were still there because he hadn't been declared dead by then. He was still alive—they were still working on him.

HL: Okay.

DB: Everybody was there. You know, all the chiefs who were getting in the way and shouldn't have been.

HL: Okay. So, after he died you never left him?

DB: No.

HL: Would anybody have had access to the body to remove a bullet or anything like that?

DB: No.

HL: You're absolutely sure?

DB: Positive.

HL: Okay. Did anybody look like they were—

DB: There was a black American—a black American orderly with me, too, you know?

HL: Yeah. David?

DB: He was helping me clean up. He was there for a while. But apart from that, he went out, and I was going to go out, and there was a guy standing outside who I assume was Secret Service—I don't know—who told me to stay in there because somebody—somebody has to be with the body the whole time.

HL: So in your opinion, I'm sorry to keep going over this ground, but in your opinion nobody—well, let me ask you, do you have the impression that any doctor that you didn't know or anybody else might have come to the body to remove a bullet from the throat or do anything like that?

DB: The thing was, you've got to remember, I hadn't been there very long.

HL: Yeah.

DB: Okay. And I didn't know a lot of the doctors, and a lot of them evidently were, you know, heads of services and that sort of thing, who really were getting in the way, if you know what I mean. So, apart from the actual emergency doctors who I knew, you know, sort of, there were a lot of them just to look at, you know, to recognize. There were a lot of doctors there, but I can't say that there was one that nobody talked to, if you know what I mean, that nobody knew. Everybody knew each other, everybody was talking to each other. After everybody had gone out, after they decided to declare him dead—nobody came in again.

HL: Yes.

DB: But . . .

HL: Go ahead . . .

DB: I know what you're trying to get at.

HL: I'm just trying to verify it—when he was still alive and they performed the trach, which I presume you saw that operation . . .

DB: Yes.

HL: You didn't see anything funny or anything that didn't ring right with you as far as tampering with the body or anything like that— anybody that might have taken a bullet from it?

DB: No.

HL: Okay. Do you remember any bullets or bullet fragments?

DB: No.

HL: You didn't see anything come from the body when they—

DB: No.

HL: Did you see the tracheostomy performed?

DB: I wasn't standing over it, no. I was working on one of his arms.

HL: Yeah. Did you know Dr. Perry?

DB: Well, I didn't know him that well then, but I knew Dr. Perry reasonably well afterwards.

HL: Okay. So—but you knew who was operating on the throat, right?

DB: Yes.

HL: And did you think that was Perry, or somebody else?

DB: It was Perry. You see, as I say, I'd not been there very long and I just sort of walked into the whole situation, because I was nearest to the front door.

HL: Yeah, okay, and who helped you prepare the body for the coffin? That was Henchliffe?

DB: Yeah, Margaret and myself and the African American all did— well, he was sort of in cleaning up and everything.

HL: And how about Doris Nelson?

DB: Well, Doris tucked her head in.

HL: Okay.

DB: Well, let's put it that way. I don't want to sound nasty or anything, but it's a case of when something like this happens, all the chiefs have to say they were there, you know?

HL: That's the thing. A lot of them testified to things that I'm sure that they didn't see, that they were repeating what they were told by the others. And so then, trying to find—well—who's actually a witness and who actually saw this or saw that, you know, that's a big problem. Do you think there were any X-rays taken of the body that day?

DB: No.

HL: And any photographs? Do you remember any cameras?

DB: No.

HL: You're saying that you're sure that none were taken.

DB: Yes, I'm positive. Not while I was there.

HL: Do you remember when the body was wrapped up to go into the coffin, was a towel put around the head before the sheets were wrapped around it?

DB: A towel?

HL: Yes.

DB: No.

HL: No towel?

DB: No towel, because I washed his hair. This is what I was going to write to you about all these autopsy photographs with all the blood clots and everything on the back. . . .

HL: Is there anything peculiar about those pictures?

DB: Very peculiar, very peculiar. (Very long pause as she awaits a question.)

HL: Well, I think they're fake as hell.

DB: Definitely. Definitely. On those pages that you told me, there's three together, top of the F 6 and F 7, and something that—all are fake completely because I washed all the clots out of his hair before I wrapped it up.

HL: Yeah.

DB: And also somebody, which I don't know whether you know anything about—I haven't seen it written anywhere—we wrapped him up, and Margaret had gone, and somebody came in and flashed a badge or this thing at me and just gave me a plastic bag, and said I was to collect all the bits of brain and any bits of skull that was floating about. So I had to unwrap everything again, and collect all these bits and give them to him.

HL: And you don't know who he was?

DB: No. You know the situation, you sort of—I was new to the States, and you're sort of only a lowly nurse and these guys come flashing things at you, you're never quite sure, you can't stand up and say, "Yeah, who are you, who's authority?"

HL: Do you think he was connected to the hospital or to the Secret Service?

DB: I don't think he was connected to the hospital, no.

HL: Would you say that Kennedy was alive when you first saw him?

DB: No, he was dead. Sure he was.

HL: And that was in the car?

DB: In the car, yes.

HL: So you saw him in the car?

DB: I had to—I got into the back of the car because we couldn't get him out, because we had to get the Governor out first. So then I was with him in the back, sort of trying to do first aid. And I couldn't get a pulse at all, from anywhere, and I mean the damage that was done to his head, when you've worked in things like that your first impulse is, "Oh God," you know, "Forget it," but of course, being the President, you can't.

HL: So, in order to do the last rites, you think they sort of faked it a little bit?

DB: Yes.

HL: And what was the status of his head? Did you see any other wounds besides the head wound?

DB: There was the wound in the back.

HL: You saw that?

DB: In the, lower down on his back, the entry wound for the bullet.

HL: How far down was it?

DB: Oh, no, wait a minute, I'll send back your photograph, and mark with an arrow where I think it was. But, I mean, it's lower than the top one.

HL: Did you turn over the body?

DB: Yes.

HL: Did anybody tell you to wash the body? I mean, tell the nurses to clean up the body?

DB: No. I think it was just sort of a general consensus that—I think it was Doris, actually, who said clean him up and get him ready. But, I mean, we would have done it anyway, sort of as a courtesy. I mean, you don't sort of leave the President, you know, to go to his—

HL: But you definitely saw—did it look like an entry or an exit wound in his back?

DB: Entry wound.

HL: Okay. What size was it?

DB: Oh, it was small.

HL: Were the edges turned in?

DB: Yes.

HL: You remember that?

DB: Yes. The thing is, when you work in emergency rooms and you get to know what looks like an entry wound and what looks like an exit, you know.

HL: Sure, yeah. There's like an abrasive collar or whatever.

DB: Mmm, yeah.

HL: Could you tell how far that hole went in to his back—or—did you probe it or . . .

DB: No, no.

HL: And, so did you see the wound in the throat before? When he was in the car?

DB: Yes.

HL: Okay. And what did that look like?

DB: Well, that looked like an entry wound. It was larger than the one in the back, and from what I can remember, I mean, I didn't see them in a close space of time so I could actually say it was twice as big, but I got the impression it was bigger than the one that was in the back.

HL: Just by a bit? Or a whole lot?

DB: Quite a bit. Yeah, a whole lot, I'd say.

HL: But you still think it was an entry wound?

DB: Yes.

HL: Okay. Now, on the head wound, did you see anything that looked like holes or perforations in the skull and the temple areas, or the forehead?

DB: No.

HL: No?

DB: No.

HL: You haven't read my second book, have you? *High Treason 2*?

DB: No.

HL: Okay. I'm going to send it to you, if you like. The reason is that if you had read it, it might influence what you're telling me now . . .

DB: Uh-huh.

HL: Because I have, I have reports from the morticians in Washington. So, since you haven't read it—that's good. Because, what you're telling me is not influenced by what I wrote already. But do you remember any perforations in the head or did you see any holes or anything like a bullet hole anywhere on his skull or in the back of the skull?

DB: At the back of the skull, an enormous hole.

HL: And would you—is that in the general area where that drawing— those drawings—I'm sure you've seen them—where they've got a big piece of skull missing in the very back of the head?

DB: Yes.

HL: Would you say that the hole's extended as far around as to be just behind the right ear?

DB: Yes. It was more towards the right ear, definitely, then the left. But it was, it was big. I mean, I could—and for when I did the thing, I had to pack, you know, linens into there.

HL: And did you mean when you prepared the body for the coffin?

DB: Well, before that.

HL: Oh, to stanch the flow?

DB: Yes, to stanch the flow.

HL: Do you remember anything about the cerebellum?

DB: There wasn't much there.

HL: Not much brain?

DB: No.

HL: On the back of the head, did it extend around as far as the top of the head? How much of the top of the head was missing? Was top of, was bone missing as far as the sagittal suture—is that the one that goes across the head?

DB: Hang on, you're getting terribly technical. I haven't nursed for years. I'll have to go back to the textbooks.

HL: How much skull was missing on the top of the head, would you say, that extended into that back of the head region?

DB: Oh, a reasonable amount.

HL: So part of the top of the head was missing in the back?

DB: Just trying to think how to put it to you. The hole was basically almost the size of a saucer, and sort of from the occiput. So there was quite a reasonable amount missing from the top as well.

HL: Was the occiput missing itself?

DB: I would say—

HL: I mean the protuberance.

DB: Part of it, yes.

HL: Okay. And how about the face, his face, how did that look?

DB: Well, it was—it looked like a face, let's put it that way. When he left us, his eyes were closed, which they weren't in these photographs.

HL: His eyes were closed, not open?

DB: Yes.

HL: Would they, would they normally open after death after they'd already been closed?

DB: Not usually, no.

HL: Or could they have opened on the emergency table?

DB: Well, no. When we put him in the coffin, you know, before we wrapped him up and everything and then they were closed and when we wrapped his head up in the sheets, they were closed then. So, with the pressure of the material on them . . .

HL: You think they would have stayed closed?

DB: I would think so. I mean, I'm not a mortician.

HL: Okay. But when you saw him in the car, were his eyes open or closed?

DB: Open, sort of half open.

HL: And how about in the—on the ER table, do you remember?

DB: They were open.

HL: Okay. If you can try to remember anybody taking pictures in there, photographs, it's very important because there's a reason to think that some of these autopsy pictures—I published a lot more of them in my last book—that they're not taken at Bethesda, you know. Now, do you think that any part of his face—like the right eye and the right forehead above it—did that sag in or was there any bone missing in that area? Did his face look so perfectly normal? Did you feel his face?

DB: Um . . .

HL: You washed his face?

DB: I can't remember whether I washed it or Margaret washed it. I know I washed his hair.

HL: Well, you would have noticed if a large piece of bone—see, the X-rays, if you look at the X-rays in my book, they show the whole right front of the face is gone from the eye area. And the lateral view X-ray is not the same as the AP view. There's a lot more bone missing in the lateral view. But most of the—most of them have the whole right eye area, from the top of the orbit, at least, plus the forehead and the temporal bone is gone.

DB: No, no. I mean, I would have noticed something like that. You know, to say his face looked like a dead body's face. You know, there was no injury to the face.

HL: Yeah.

DB: It was just to his—the back of his head. And the one in his, in his throat. But and by then it was the tracheostomy opening. But his face itself, no.

HL: Okay. One more question about that. Do you remember any laceration across the scalp from front to back where it comes on to the forehead, where the scalp would have been lacerated and it goes straight back from that area? Picture the right eyebrow. A laceration about a half an inch into his forehead, and then going straight back, where the scalp was torn. Do you remember anything like that?

DB: No.

HL: You would have because you washed the hair, right?

DB: Yes. When I say washed it, I just took cotton swabs and washed all the clotting blood off. I mean, I didn't shampoo it or anything.

HL: So, in this massive hole, was there a flap of scalp there, or was scalp actually gone?

DB: It was gone. Gone. There was nothing there. Just a big, gaping hole.

HL: We're talking about scalp first, and then bone, right?

DB: Yeah. There might have been little lumps of scalp, but most of the bone over the hole, there was no bone there.

HL: Was there any part of a flap of scalp over that big defect in the bone missing?

DB: What I'm saying is that the hole where the bone had gone, perhaps the skin was a little bit smaller, if you know what I mean, but only fractionally, just over the edge . . .

HL: So the scalp was blown out, too?

DB: Yes.

HL: I don't know if I should ask you this question—but did you have enough experience either before or after to think that that was either an exit or an entry hole?

DB: Well, to me it was an exit hole.

HL: Yeah.

DB: I mean, I've never seen one as big as that, but—

HL: Okay. Listen, you're going to draw me a picture, aren't you, to show just where that hole is?

DB: Yeah.

HL: Okay. Great. Let's see, and you don't remember any towel at all being wrapped around the head when it got to uh—

DB: What do you mean by towel? Sort of like a bath towel?

HL: Yeah, but the little ones, like—I forgot what they're called—service towels, or toilet towels.

DB: No.

HL: Any, you know, smaller towels, any kind of towel at all?

DB: Terry cloth, you mean?

HL: Yeah.

DB: I'm just trying to think of the American word—terry cloth. No, there was no terry cloth towel.

HL: And no—nothing that you would call towel? They were just sheets and linens?

DB: Yes. Just sheets.

HL: Okay. Do you remember the coffin? Now, I want to tell you how some of the others described it, in Parkland, but do you remember what it looked like? Could it have been anything like plastic or a shipping casket?

DB: No. I was going to write to you, I've got a copy of an old *Illustrated London News* of the unloading—when it was taken from the plane at Andrews Air Force Base. That's the same coffin that he was put in.

HL: The coffin that you see coming off the plane at Andrews Air Force Base?

DB: Yes.

HL: It's the same coffin?

DB: Yes. If you like, I'll send you photostats of the photograph. If it would be of any help.

HL: Yes, please. Oh, yes. It's very important because one of the things

I'm doing, Diana, is exposing a lot of fraud among the people that write on this case. You know, there's a tremendous amount hokum in this, and so the evidence that you give is very important. But the same coffin at Andrews?

DB: Yes. It was bronze. Bronze color.

HL: Bronze . . .

DB: And I can't remember what the funeral home was called, but I do know—

HL: "Oneal's."

DB: That's it, "Oneal's," Yes. I knew vaguely two of the guys who brought the coffin because they used to run the ambulance.

HL: "Peanuts" and "Al," ah, Aubrey Rike.

DB: Aubrey rings a bell. You know how these people who bring in off road accidents and things like this, you sort of get to know them. You don't know them well, but you know—

HL: Okay. So you knew the men who brought the coffin?

DB: Yes. I'd seen them before, a couple of times. When they brought it in they said it was the best that the home had at the time—if that's of any help.

HL: Yeah. And so, it looked expensive to you?

DB: Well, I didn't really know terribly much about American coffins. You know, all I knew was that American funerals were very expensive. But they did say that they'd brought the best that they've got because it was for the President.

HL: Okay. Did you have any reason to think that there was any sort of a post exam that went on after he died, you know, like the beginning of an autopsy, or was there any inspection of the body by any medical people or anybody else after they, after the doctors began disconnecting their tubes and all that, before you started to clean it up?

DB: No. No.

HL: Okay. And no inspection, nothing organized?

DB: Nothing organized, no.

HL: Did you hear any rumors, or have any reason to think that the body was removed from the coffin because they had to fight with Dr. Rose, who wanted to have the autopsy there—do you remember that there was a battle with the medical examiner out in the hall, and he didn't—

DB: No. Evidently all that took place outside in the hall. I have nothing to do with that.

HL: Okay, but you were—

DB: I only heard it vaguely afterwards.

HL: Okay. Well, was the coffin in the room with you closed while—

DB: When we'd put him in the coffin, and the coffin was locked—sealed, then I was told I could go. So I left, and I went across to the nurses' station, and in the time it took someone to go and get me a cup of coffee and get about half of the coffee down, then the coffin came out of the room. There's no way that they could have got—because I faced it. I couldn't see the actual door, but the angle was such that anybody coming out of there I would have been able to see.

HL: There's no way they could have got the body out of there?

DB: No.

HL: Were there any other doors to the emergency room? Was it just one door?

DB: No. There are other doors. But to get out of the building, it would have to come past where I was, with a lot of the other staff. There was a connection between—there was an alleyway between—sort of towards the back of the emergency, not the trauma room where he was. He'd have to come out of there, go down, there was an alleyway. But it wasn't wide enough for a trolley, so he couldn't, he couldn't have taken it out there and any other way would have to come out past the nurses' station.

HL: Do you remember whatever was used to line the coffin or wrap the body?

DB: It was a plastic sheet.

HL: And was it, was it—

DB: It wasn't a mattress cover, it was clear plastic. . . .

HL: Clear?

DB: Yes.

HL: Not a mattress cover?

DB: No.

HL: And do you remember anything like a body bag?

DB: No.

HL: Sheets and then the mattress cover outside the cloth?

DB: Yes.

HL; And that was it?

DB: Yes.

HL: Okay. I hope you'll still write me as quickly as you can—and draw the picture and just make the mark on the back, you know, to show the entry wound. That's very important.

DB: Yes.

HL: If you remember anything else that might be important, I sure hope you'll tell me.

DB: Oh, yes, I will. If I remember anything else. The thing is, you forget about all this and if you start thinking about it, you remember other bits and pieces.

HL: Well, it must have been a very traumatic day.

DB: Oh, well, it was. Yes.

HL: How long did you stay in the country after that, in the States?

DB: Oh, I stayed for another, oh, what? Another two years at Parkland, and then I spent a year in New York.

HL: Were you pursued at all much by the press, or researchers, or anything?

DB: No.

HL: Oh, because I know they published stories in your hometown in England.

DB: Oh, God. That was my mother.

HL: She did all that?

DB: She did all that. I mean all these, all my quotes and things that have nothing to do with me. I was furious.

HL: I still can't get over the fact of finding you where I found you right now.

DB: Yes, yes. I've been in rather a lot of places.

We ended the interview with one more recap of what the head wound looked like:

HL: Did you see any entry hole in the back of the head?

DB: I assumed and I still do that that was an exit wound.

The only people who actually claim to have seen an entry hole in the back of the head were the autopsy doctors, and only after assembling part of the skull from the pieces that were brought in hours after the interview.

Months later I spoke again with Diana Bowron. I had sent her a few additional clarification questions. I wanted to know exactly how much brain was left in the head, but of course there could be no exact answer. "There wasn't a normal brain at all. There was a lot of it on the seat. There was very little brain left. Very little."[9] I asked her for a percent estimate, and she said that it was "far less than 50 percent on the right. A lot of the left side was gone, too," she said. And she promised to write me with a more exact opinion. "Most of the right side was gone."

I asked Diana to give long and careful thought to the amount of brain left in the head, and a month later I got back to her. Di said that only about one third remained on the right and that about a quarter of the brain was missing on the left.[10]

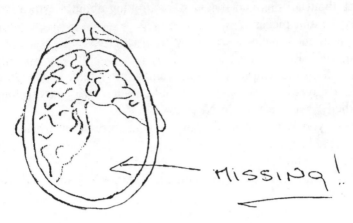

In the same conversation in response to my question, she told me that no one had ordered her to clean up the body. She had done it on her own. It is highly doubtful that any evidence could have been destroyed by the nurse's actions. "We normally cleaned up a body after a violent death." If there had been some mystery about how Kennedy died, then obviously they would not have washed away potential evidence.

I believe this nurse, because I think she is honest and her recollections are precise and accurate, even thirty years later. I know that she is telling the truth about the brain. There could not have been a 1500-gram brain (the weight of a normal brain), because every single witness has described substantial amounts of brain missing. I believe the autopsy doctors left that figure (1500 grams) as a clue as to what was going on. They spoke in code

There was a failure on all of our parts to understand what added up from the pieces each witness brings to the puzzle. In 1979 one of the Parkland doctors described shining a flashlight around in Kennedy's head after he died, and the impression then was that there was little or no brain left. The statement of other doctors that the brain was lying on the table, and that Jackie came in with a large hunk of it, and knowing of many pieces that were blown onto other people and the street and grass, one cannot believe that there was much brain remaining in the head.

Bowron explained that she had her hands inside Kennedy's head and packed it with gauze swabs. She left them inside. It was "quite a few." Some cerebellum was still in the head, she told me. She did not see the flap of bone and scalp sticking out of the side of the head, as we see in the photographs.

It is unfortunate that Bowron had been unavailable for so long, and that some of the other witnesses had been less candid. She reaffirmed seeing the back wound, which means that it was not manufactured, as some inventors in this case think. She said "it was a good six inches down on the back." She said that the trajectory could not possibly have connected up with the throat wound and gone out to hit John Connally. "It was too far down on the back." She saw no wound in the back of the neck.

She described the tracheostomy operation itself, and doesn't think the wound was retouched in the photograph. "Its the right length and width in the photographs," she told me. "That's what I saw in the Trauma Room. Dr. Perry had to perform an operation there. Normally it would be quite small, but he had to probe and examine for the damage caused by the bullet."

"In answer to your question about the trach wound," she later wrote me, "it appears in the photos much the same size as I remember it. As you will recall from our last phone conversation, I think that the doctor made the incision larger than normal due to the fact that it was a bullet entry wound, and he wanted to check on local damage before inserting the tube. That is just a guess."[11]

Bowron again made it clear that there was no bone or scalp missing from the top of the head.

"With regard to how much brain was left, I have enclosed a tracing of a drawing in your book and indicated on it the amount of cerebellum that was missing. It was not, of course, an empty space, there was blood and pieces of brain tissue within the wound. How the autopsy could record a brain of 1500 grams is beyond me, but then so are so many other things about the whole affair."[12]

With regard to Arlen Specter's questioning of her, which seems to give an erroneous impression as to how many wounds she saw, she says: "My answer, 'I just saw one large hole,' was in response to a series of questions about what I saw and did in the car and the condition of his head. As I understand it at the time Specter was taking things sequentially and one large hole in the back of his head was what I first saw in the car. He never asked me about any other wounds, and by the time we got to the end of the interview, I was probably so nervous that I had put the back wound out of my mind.[13]

"You asked me about the news stories in the British press. As I told you in one of our previous conversations, I did not give any interviews with any members of the press, British or American. Their information was, I suspect, obtained from my mother, whom I had rung the night of the assassination, and then elaborated upon. None of the quotes are direct, as I did not give any interviews."[14]

Another letter had this to say in response to my calls and additional questions, and request that she put her answers in writing: "You asked me yesterday about the packing of the head wound. I packed it with 4-inch gauze squares to prevent any seepage of fluid and loss of remaining brain tissue. I don't know the number of squares I used but it must have been a fair amount. Nobody told me to do this. I thought it was the right thing to do at the time.

"You also asked about broken bones of the face. When we wiped the face prior to the last visit by Mrs. Kennedy, there was no indication at all of any damage to the underlying bone structure. All the damage was confined to the back of the head."[15]

Thus ends a historic firsthand account from the nurse who was with the body of President Kennedy almost every moment from the time he was rushed to the hospital, to the time his body was wheeled away.

For twenty-seven years she has been out of sight, married, and living under another name in another nation, free of so much turmoil that engulfed the other Parkland witnesses, often buffeted about by many conflicting forces, warping and manipulating the vital evidence these witnesses live with.

Diana Bowron has told us that the large head wound is in the back of the head, near the hairline, and extending upward to the top of the head and toward the area behind the right ear. She said that little brain was left in the head, the reason for the cerebellum being able to exit. She has insisted that the throat wound is an entry wound, making the accounts of the Parkland witnesses unanimous to this day.

She saw the back wound and its placement and finds that it was far below where it is in the photographs.

This lady, like so many others from Parkland Memorial Hospital, demonstrates that persons who participated at the President's autopsy lied about one or more important points. These lies are easily demonstrable. In addition, she is not in a position to be paid off, intimidated, or otherwise bought with donations from the "Big Texans," as Dr. John Lattimer calls them, to their medical centers, hospitals, and other fronts.

Members of the Warren Commission staff can no longer change the testimony of the Dallas medical witnesses, nor can FBI and Secret Service agents convince them that the autopsy scientifically found results in conflict with their own observations on November 22, 1963, which agents did in fact do after that date and before the witnesses testified to the Warren Commission, thus coaching, coloring, and leading the witnesses to a false position. Many television shows and "researchers" have done the same thing over the years.

We are indeed grateful to the British authorities who assisted me in finding Diana Bowron.

Johnson has ruined morally all
who deal with him at home and
he will ruin all who deal with
him abroad.

—I. F. Stone
July 16, 1993

CHAPTER 7

FIREARMS AND BALLISTICS

The key things to keep in mind when discussing the weapons used to kill John F. Kennedy is that, in Dallas at the time, anyone could walk into a store and purchase a gun without a permit or any record of the purchase being made. In other words, why buy by mail? One might answer that it was possibly cheaper, but postage and handling added to the cost. It was more complicated to order by mail. The same guns that Oswald allegedly acquired were available at most corner gun shops. Ordering a weapon by mail laid a paper trail to the buyer, which seemed to be the point. The next questions are: Did he do this himself? Were the signatures forged?

An example of being set up as the patsy is his discussions with Adrian Alba, the operator of a garage filled with FBI and Secret Service cars in New Orleans.[1] Oswald wanted to know how to order guns, and he perused gun and sporting magazines there. Oswald already possessed the Mannlicher-Carcano, and Alba helped him fix the sling for it.

The Handgun

The weapon taken from Lee Harvey Oswald at his arrest was a .38 Smith & Wesson Victory Model six-shot revolver. It bore the serial number V510210.

It had been rechambered to hold .38 Special bullets, which are longer and narrower than a normal .38 bullet.[2] This means that the chambers were bored deeper to accommodate the longer bullets. But the cylinder was not replaced because the frame would not accommodate it. That means that the chambers were .005 inch too large for the smaller .38 Special bullets. The revolver was not rebarreled. The whole point of

200

using smaller bullets in a gun not made to accommodate them is that the bullet will not be sufficiently marked by the lands and grooves of the barrel as it travels through to identify them as having come from that particular gun.

When Oswald was arrested, it was said that he had five live bullets in his pocket, and the revolver was fully loaded with six cartridges.[3] Four expended .38 Special cartridge cases were found about one hundred feet from the place where Tippit was killed. Two were Remington-Peters, and two were Western. According to the Warren Report,[4] the four expended shells were found to have been fired from the above gun, which does not mean that they were fired that day. They could have been planted. Shells are not bullets.

Oswald would have had to take time during his flight to reload the revolver. "All four bullets could have been fired from the V510210 revolver, but none could be positively identified to the revolver—that is, in his [FBI expert Cortlandt Cunningham's] opinion the bullets bore the revolver's rifling characteristics, but no conclusion could be drawn on the basis of microscopic characteristics. Cunningham did not conclude that the bullets had not been fired from the revolver, since he found that consecutive bullets fired in the revolver by the FBI could not even be identified with each other under the microscope."[5]

There is, of course, something missing from this report. There is no mention of the expansion of the shells or of a split shell. Tests conducted by the FBI for the Warren Commission and the tests by the HSCA[6] firing Oswald's gun found that one of the chambers had a characteristic that caused the shell to split. Also, the smaller shells of a .38 Special would normally expand much more noticeably when fired in the larger diameter of the .38 revolver's chamber. There is no indication that the shells found at the scene of the Tippit slaying had this normal expansion, and any thorough police report would have mentioned the fact.

Evan Marshall, a retired Detroit homicide sergeant with a long list of credentials in such matters, wrote me to say, "Oswald's revolver was a S & W [Smith & Wesson] Victory Model that had originally been chambered for .38 S & W [Smith & Wesson] and then converted to .38 Special [a more powerful round]. Because the .38 chambers are a bigger diameter than the .38 Special round, .38 Special cases fired in such converted weapons tend to split or bulge when fired. The pictures I've seen of the casings supposedly recovered at the Tippit scene fail to show any such bulges or splits.

"The Tippit shooting has always been to me a red herring of the first order. As someone who spent twenty years as a big-city cop, I can assure you that nothing affects a cop like the murder of a brother officer. Perhaps the hope was that the officers who responded to the theatre would kill him there."[7]

Of the four bullets recovered from Tippit's body, three were made by Western-Winchester and one by Remington-Peters. In the opinion of expert Joseph D. Nicol, who was the superintendent of the Bureau of Criminal Identification and Investigation of Illinois, "one of the four bullets could be positively identified with test bullets fired from V510210 revolver, and the other three could have been fired from that revolver."[8]

The Rifle

Evan Marshall wrote me that "while Oswald was a poor shot, he belonged to the Marine Corp at a time when they prided themselves on turning out riflemen. Oswald could not have missed the point that his issue rifle was capable of performing such a task, while the piece of junk he had would have been ill-suited. I can't believe that someone who supposedly was bent on murdering JFK would balk at stealing an adequate rifle."[9]

The Warren Report says that the rifle was 40.2 inches long and weighed 8 pounds, and that it was a Model 91/38.[10] The advertisement in the *American Rifleman* that Oswald (posing as Hidell, if Oswald in fact did order the rifle himself) is supposed to have answered was for a Model 41 carbine, 36 inches overall, weighing only 5.5 pounds.

But the Warren Report actually referred to an ad that was published in the November 1963 issue of *Field and Stream*.[11] Richard Waybright writes, "the basic difference between the two ads is the length of the barrel." It's this sort of make-do attitude on the part of a government investigatory agency that gives rise to vast confusion, suspicion, and paranoia!

In any event, the story is that Klein's gun mail order house did not have any more of the carbines available and therefore sent him the longer rifle. The trouble with that story is that, even broken down, the longest piece could not be supported in the hand and the other end fit beneath the armpit, which is what we heard with the "curtain rod story" from two people who told the Warren Commission they saw Oswald carry the package with the one end cupped in his hand and the other end lodged in his armpit.[12] The Commission said that they were mistaken about the length.[13]

*   *   *

The Warren Report also states that the serial number of the rifle found at the Depository is C2766.[14] The Commission said that Klein's Sporting Goods Co. of Chicago had an order filled out in handwriting by an A. Hidell, using post office box no. 2915 in Dallas, on a coupon[15] cut from *American Rifleman* magazine. Hidell (Oswald) paid $21.45 for the rifle, including the scope. Referring to the handwriting on the coupon, the Warren Report says, "These words were also in the handwriting of Lee Harvey Oswald."[16] The money order for the rifle was purchased in Dallas on March 13, 1963. Klein's placed an internal control number, VC836, on the rifle when they received one lot of them in February 1963. The rifle was sent to "Hidell" on March 20, 1963.

"The post office box to which the rifle was shipped was rented to 'Lee H. Oswald' from October 9, 1962, to May 14, 1963. Experts on handwriting identification from the Treasury Department and the FBI testified that the signature and other writing on the application for that box were in the handwriting of Lee Harvey Oswald. . . ."[17] The Warren Report reproduced photocopies of all of these documents on the pages with the last quoted statement.[18]

But there is trouble with this serial number. "Information received from the Italian Armed Forces Intelligence Service has established that this particular rifle was the only one of its type bearing serial number C2766."[19] However, J. Edgar Hoover told the Warren Commission that "The Mannlicher-Carcano rifle was manufactured in Italy from 1891 until 1941; however, in the 1930s Mussolini ordered all arms factories to manufacture the Mannlicher-Carcano rifle. Since many concerns were manufacturing the same weapon, the same serial number appears on weapons manufactured by more than one concern."[20] Therefore, the serial number cannot be used to link the rifle found to the one that is imputed to Oswald/Hidell.

As for the coupons, two were found that had been torn from magazines. One of them fitted the edges of a magazine found at Adrian Alba's Crescent City Garage, which Oswald frequented in New Orleans.[21] Strange that he passed time there, since it was a parking lot for FBI and Secret Service cars.[22]

The coupon whose edges fit so perfectly was found among Oswald's possessions shortly after the assassination. The coupon could have been a plant. There was a stranger who came to Alba's garage in the early morning the day after the assassination, and he could have torn out the coupon and planted it with the Dallas police.[23] This may be a point of further investigation with regard to the time the stranger appeared at the garage the day after the assassination and the appearance of the coupon in the Dallas evidence.

*   *   *

One unfired round was found in the rifle and the Warren Commission claimed that only three shots were fired. As stated in my first book, it is simply unlikely that the gunman would have had only four bullets, one of which, as we know, was not used. There is no evidence of any other bullet imputed to the alleged assassin. It seems to me and everyone else that he would have had at least a full clip and possibly some in his pockets. The alleged murder weapon was advertised for sale as a six-shot, clip-fed rifle. The ammunition had to be especially manufactured in this country for his rifle, and it was not easy to obtain.

The National Archives will not let anyone actually examine the rifle. They wrote Patricia Dumais, who was suspicious that it was a stage prop and wanted to see the "internal control" number supposedly placed on it by Klein's, "We cannot disassemble Lee Harvey Oswald's rifle because this action might be destructive to the object."[24]

Dumais kept at it. Sue McDonough of the Archives wrote her to say that they had examined the rifle "but did not locate the identification 'VC836.' Commission Exhibit 1977 is an FBI memorandum dated March 17, 1964, which describes the rifle in great detail. There was no mention of 'VC836' in this document. Mitchell J. Scibor, the General Operating Manager of Klein's Sporting Goods, testified on May 20, 1964,[25] that it was company policy to engrave an inventory control number on all firearms in stock. Mr. Scibor states that 'VC836' was the inventory control number for the rifle purchased by Oswald. It is possible that this inventory control number is not visible when the rifle is assembled."[26]

Paraffin Test

The Warren Commission admitted that the paraffin (dermal nitrate, or paraffin gauntlet test) was negative with regard to Oswald's face.[27] This would tend to indicate that he had not fired a rifle. Generally there would have to be nitrate on his face if he fired such a weapon. They found that he had nitrate, a primary substance in the explosion of gunpowder, on his hands and felt that this indicated that he had fired some weapon that day.

There are problems with paraffin tests. "There are several scientific objections to the test in its simplest form," write O'Hara and O'Hara in their treatise on criminal investigation.[28] "The role of the nitrate on the hand is that of an oxidizing agent. Other strong oxidizing agents can produce the same effect. Hence, launderers, chemists, pharmacists, and other persons handling bleaches or other oxidizing compounds may have materials on their hands which would yield a positive reaction. Thus the test does not necessarily indicate the presence of nitrates, but established merely that an oxidizing substance is present on the hand. In brief, the test is non-specific.

"Another objection is concerned with the fact that there are many non-incriminating sources of nitrates such as fertilizers, explosives, tobacco, urine, and cosmetics. Certain foods also contain nitrates. Finally, some experimenters have found that it is possible to obtain a negative reaction from the hand of a person who has recently fired many rounds of ammunition. Conversely, a positive reaction can be obtained from the hand of a person who has never discharged a firearm.

"Thus, in the hands of the uninformed, the test may be not only unreliable, but also misleading." So much for simplistic answers.

O'Hara and O'Hara quote the Interpol Seminar on Scientific Aspects of Police Work: "The seminar did not consider the traditional paraffin test to be of any value, neither as evidence to put before courts, not even as a sure indication for the police officer. The participants were of the opinion that this test should no longer be used."[29]

This deals with the claim that the "physical appearance of nitrates from gunpowder is distinguishable from nitrates from other sources when found on the hands because of the fact that the discharge of the gun tends to imbed particles in the intradermic layers of the skin ... opponents of the test consider only the chemical aspect, and ignore the physical appearance, which constitute the most important part of the test. Some of the proponents place great emphasis on the topographical distribution of the blue specks in the case, which is a characteristic configuration of gunfire and not merely the result of random contact with various materials."[30]

Dr. John Nichols describes the best way, in his opinion, to run the test. The hands are first washed and scrubbed with cold water. Paraffin is painted on and a reagent is used on the cast. Within a couple of minutes, dark blue specks appear on the cast if gunpowder is present. "On the basis of these phenomena and also the distribution of the specks, a positive reaction is interpreted as proof that the hand was used in the discharge of a gun."[31]

Not all police departments were skilled in the use of this test. Certainly, the important thing in our case is the distribution or pattern of the powder residue on the skin of the alleged assassin's hands, and the police lab report indicated that "nitrate patterns consistent with the subject having discharged a firearm were present on Exhibits #2 and 3. The pattern on Exhibit #3 is typical of the pattern produced in firing a revolver."[32] Exhibit #3 was a paraffin cast of the right hand. Number

2 was of the left hand. Note that the above statement again does not mention the firing of a rifle, which might leave different nitrate patterns on a hand.

Either the evidence of a firearm—and more likely a pistol, not a rifle—having been discharged is mistaken, the nitrate tests faked with regard to the Tippit slaying, or Oswald fired a gun that day.

Concerning the lack of nitrate on his cheek,[33] if Oswald had washed his face, this would not have removed the gunpowder. It takes hot wax or paraffin to draw it out of the pores. The report says that they performed the test on the right cheek.[34] Had he been left-handed, the police would have tested the wrong cheek. The sight for the gun was set up for a left-handed person. Oswald was right-handed, though some dispute it.

The supplementary offense report cited above states that hair samples from his head, chest, arms, armpits, legs, and pubic areas, along with fingernail scrapings of Oswald, were taken and given to the FBI.

Muzzle Flashes

Patricia Dumais, who worked many years for an arms manufacturer, writes that the term "muzzle flash" is a misnomer. "I don't understand why the term 'muzzle flash' is used when, as you no doubt know, the flare comes out of the barrel-breech area."[35] Dumais brings up the issue because she feels that someone had to have seen a "muzzle flash" from the sixth-floor window of the Texas School Book Depository, had a weapon been fired there—unless the weapon was equipped with a flash suppressor, as she points out in her letter to me.

"No such flare—which should have been highly visible against the darkened background of the TSBD sixth floor—apparently did not 'catch the eye' of any witness. And when Roy Truly and Officer Baker, minutes after the shooting, went from the bottom floor to the roof, it appears that they did not detect the odor of gunfire on the sixth floor.

"This might be significant; it might indicate that no discharge of a firearm took place there during the preceding few minutes."[36]

Bar Association Mock Trials

The following is the testimony of three experts who appeared at the American Bar Association Mock Trial in San Francisco in the summer of 1992 and testified on ballistics. It was televised by Court TV.

TESTIMONY—Dr. Martin Fackler
John Keker, Prosecuting Attorney

JK: Do you expect in President—in Governor Connally's back—would it be a nice little round hole or would it be an oblong hole?

MF: No, it would have to be an oblong hole.

JK: Alright, and what happened to the bullet after it entered Governor Connally in your opinion?

MF: After it entered Gov. Connally it passed through some subcutaneous tissue and muscle, and then it impacted a rib and destroyed about ten centimeters, that's about four inches, of rib. Now, in order to destroy that much rib, in my opinion, it would almost certainly have to be going practically sideways because the bullet going point forward presents such a small diameter it would be unlikely to hit the rib. But the bullet is a very long bullet. It's a bullet that was an inch and a quarter long. And, going sideways—I have the bullet here in my pocket—going sideways, as you can see, impacting a rib, it could sweep a rib—sweep right by a rib—and easily take out four inches.

JK: And that's the—taking out that much rib—what damage would you expect to the Mannlicher Carcano bullet?

MF: I would expect it to be flattened somewhat on the side because its going sideways and impacting something from the side. So, therefore, it would be squeezed from the side, much like if you would squeeze it in a vice.

JK: When the—after striking the rib, where did the bullet go?

MF: The bullet then passed through the subcutaneous—the muscle—and subcutaneous tissue and came out the skin of the front of Governor Connally just below the nipple.

JK: Was the wound below Governor Connally's nipple consistent with the bullet that was falling—that was flying—sideways?

MF: Yes it was because it was a large [Unintelligible—u.i.] type wound—a blown out type wound—and when a bullet is going sideways through tissue, it flings the tissue aside and causes a large wound as described.

JK: How fast was the bullet going, in your opinion, when it came out of Governor Connally having struck the rib?

MF: I would estimate that it was probably traveling about 900 ft./sec.

JK: Alright, and the bullet traveling 900 ft./sec., was it still tumbling?

MF: Yes it was.

JK: What did it strike next?

MF: It struck the wrist of Governor Connally.

JK: What sort of hole would you expect it to make—a little round hole, as if it were going straight, or an oblong hole?

MF: No. Again you'd have to have it make an oblong hole if its going sideways.

JK: Could a bullet going 900 ft./sec., entering on its side, making an oblong hole, fracture Governor Connally's wrist?

MF: Most certainly.

JK: Have you done any experiments to indicate what would happen to the bullet going at approximately that speed; a similar bullet, at approximately that speed, going through a wrist?

MF: Yes, we have. Several weeks ago we shot the carcano bullet at a lower velocity by experimenting with powder charges, and determined the powder charge with which we could get the lowered velocity, and shot this directly into a cadaver wrist.

JK: Do we have an X-ray of the cadaver wrist that this bullet, at this lower velocity, went through?

MF: Its on the screen right now.

JK: And that shows the hole that was made—is that more or less damage than the actual bullet made in Governor Connally's wrist, based on other X-rays that you have seen?

MF: That's somewhat more damage because we—our bullet was going 200 ft./sec. faster. It was about 1100 ft./sec., the one we shot.

JK: Could we see what happened to your bullet making this much damage going at 1100 ft./sec. smashing through that wrist? First of all, tell the truth, did anything happen to the bullet.

MF: The bullet was non-deformed, not at all, not—not flattened in the least. And here's the bullet on longitudinal view and I think there's the end viewing. You can see, there's not the amount of flattening that the so-called pristine bullet shows.

JK: Dr. Fackler, very briefly because we're running out of time, what speed was it coming when it came out of the wrist, in your opinion?

MF: Probably about 400 ft./sec.

JK: At that speed would there be enough power to go in and break bone in the leg?

MF: No, there would not.

JK: And is the wound to Governor Connally consistent with a bullet going at that low speed—400 ft.?

MF: Entirely consistent.

JK: Would it cause any damage to the bullet to go in at that speed?

MF: Unlikely to cause any damage to the bullet.

JK: Have you had an opportunity to examine photographs of exhibit 399 to the Warren Commission which is this bullet that was found on Governor Connally's stretcher that went through President Kennedy and Governor Connally?

MF: Yes, I have.

JK: And did you observe the damage to that bullet—the flattening that is apparent?

MF: The flattening—I did observe that.

JK: Well, was the damage to exhibit 399 consistent with what you would expect to happen to a bullet that goes through President Kennedy's back and through Governor Connally as you've described?

MF: It was entirely consistent.

JK: Alright. Couple of other questions—as an expert in the field of wound ballistics, do you know who the other experts in that field are?

MF: Yes, pretty much. My last ten years of my military career was spent as an expert in the field running a laboratory unit so I'm very familiar with the world literature.

JK: Is Dr. Cyril Wecht, an expert in the field of wound ballistics?

MF: Well, the only yardstick that's objective that I could have to judge this is the contribution of articles to world literature on wound ballistics, and I have none—I have seen none.

JK: OK. Dr. Wecht and, possibly another expert for the defense have opined that President Kennedy's head wound could have been caused by something called a "frangible bullet" fired from the front. Do you have an opinion about that opinion—about that as a possibility in this case?

MF: Yes I do. In view of the very solid physical evidence in this case, I find that absurd.

JK: OK. Finally there is a question in this case about the fact that there were 4 cartridges of one manufacturer which were identified as coming from Oswald's gun having been fired from the Smith & Wesson that killed Officer Tippit. And then there are 4 bullets, one of which doesn't match up in terms of the same manufacturer with one of the cartridges. Is there anything unusual about that?

MF: Not at all. The explanation, is that these were what we call "reloads." The most expensive part of a cartridge is the brass casing. And, therefore, to save money, you can take this brass casing and re-use it. You must resize it, clean it, put a new "primer" in it and use it again. If you go down to any major gun store and ask for 38 special bullets—a box of bullets—they will give you a box of Winchester or Remingtons and they'll be rather expensive. Now, if you know weapons well, you will ask them, "Do you have any reloads?", and they say, "Well, but we do," and they cost you less than half as much. So the reason for reloads is that they're much more economical and someone who understands weapons would naturally use reloads.

JK: Nothing further, thank you Dr. Fackler.

CROSS EXAMINATION—Dr. Martin Fackler
Evan Chesler, Defense Attorney

EC: Dr. Fackler, I want to be sure that I heard you correctly. The bullet that you say went through the President's back, out his throat—you say began to tumble, hit the Governor in his back, went through his chest, fractured his rib, came out below the right nipple, then went into his wrist, fractured his wrist, and then landed in his left thigh. That, in your words, is an absolutely typical trajectory for that bullet—is that your testimony, sir?

MF: It certainly is.

EC: Alright. Now, you say that that bullet, in your view, was tumbling when it left the President's neck—throat—on its way to the Governor's back. Is that correct?

MF: It had just begun to tumble. I would guess the degree would be off, probably within no more than 5 to 10 degrees.

EC: But you characterize that as "tumbling," is that right?

MF: Well, it's the beginning of tumbling, certainly.

EC: Would you characterize the wound in the back of Governor Connally—which, by the way, you never saw that wound, did you?

MF: I only—no, I've never seen the wound.

EC: Alright. Would you characterize the wound—based on your "after the fact" examination of evidence concerning the wound—as a puncture type wound?

MF: No.

EC: Now, you're aware, are you not, Connally was attended on November 22, 1963 by the Chief Thoracic Surgeon at Parkland Hospital—his name was Dr. Robert Shaw?

MF: Yes. I read the operation report by Dr. Shaw.

EC: And you're aware, aren't you, that Dr. has told the House Select Committee investigating the assassination of the president that the wound was not caused by a tumbling bullet—that is, the wound to the back of the Governor. Isn't that so?

MF: The operation report of Dr. Shaw indicates a wound that was 3 centimeters long, which is entirely consistent with this bullet traveling sideways.

EC: Well, let me read to you from the report, Dr., because your recollection may be flawed. It says the wound was actually approximately 1 and ½ centimeters long. The ragged edges of the wound were surgically cut away, effectively enlarging it to approximately 3 centimeters. Isn't that what he told the commission, sir?

MF: I recognize that later on he changed his recollection to 1 and ½ centimeters.

EC: Is that what he told the House Select Committee, Dr.?

MF: I'm not aware—I don't think I read the particular document you have in your hand.

EC: Alright. Let me show you this. This is the report of the interview of Dr. Robert Shaw for the House Select Committee on the Assassination—1977.

EC: Did Dr. Shaw tell the House Select Committee investigators that the wound was a puncture type wound, and I'm referring to the bottom of the first page?

MF: He says it was a puncture type wound.

EC: Did he say that it was 1 and ½ centimeters and that he increased it to approximately 3 centimeters by surgically cutting it, at the top of the next page?

MF: He says the bullet had struck the body at a slight declination and the wound was actually approximately 1 and ½ centimeters.

EC: Thank you. Does he say, further down the next page, and I quote, "It is Dr. Shaw's opinion that the wound was not caused by a tumbling bullet, an inference drawn explicitly from his belief that a tumbling bullet would not have had sufficient force to cause the remainder of the Governor's wounds." Did he say that?

MF: Yes, he says that.

EC: Did he also say that he believes that the bullet which hit the Governor had not struck any other objects? Does he say that as well?

MF: He says that.

EC: Thank you. I have no further questions, your honor.

TESTIMONY—Dr. Robert Luis Piziali
John Keker, Prosecuting Attorney

[Testimony begins with John Keker referencing Dr. Piziali's schooling and value to the case.]

RP: I have a Ph.D. from the University of California, at Berkeley.

JK: It doesn't mean you have to talk as fast as I talk. Make sure they understand.

RP: (Laughs) OK. And then I was in the faculty at Stanford University for 14 years where I taught Mechanical engineering and did research work in how people are injured. And since that time I have done—have—numerous publications and experience in the area of recreating events and analyzing injuries.

JK: Were you asked by the Government of the United States for this trial to determine the number of shots and the location of the shooter of those shots for President Kennedy's assassination on Nov. 22, 1963?

RP: Yes.

JK: Would you tell the jury very briefly what methods you used in order to carry out that task?

RP: I studied the Zapruder film very thoroughly, looked at all the physical evidence that was available, read the witness testimony, reviewed the work of Dr. Locum and Fackler, conducted several tests and analyses, and then prepared for my testimony today various exhibit and animation material to help explain to the jury how those conclusions were reached.

JK: What are your conclusions as to the number of shots and the location of the shooters that day? Mr. Piziali, first—in general.

RP: It's my belief that there were 3 shots that day and that they all came from the southeast corner window on the 6th floor of the Texas School Book Depository (to be referred to, from this point on, as TSBD).

JK: Would you show the jury what you did? Simply, if its all right with the court, narrate for them what you did and move through the exhibits to show them your analysis of each one of these 3 shots.

RP: Yes. Here first is the Zapruder film (shows film). Now, that film as it was somewhat difficult to analyze. So what we did was to do it in slow motion and to zoom in some on the cars so we could see things a little bit more clearly.

JK: You might slow down just a little bit and perhaps keep your voice up.

RP: OK. Here you can see the President waving, and he and Governor Connally heading behind the sign. The little flash here is [because] there are a few frames missing, but they have been accounted for. Now they're emerging from the sign. There's evidence that they have been shot at this point. The car will continue down the road. You can see them reacting to their wounds. And then, very quickly, we'll have the fatal shot to the President's head.

The next thing that we did was to look for other physical evidence. The other physical evidence consisted of the scene on the 6th floor of the TSBD. (Jury is shown video of the "sniper's nest.") This is generally referred to as the "sniper's nest." You can see that boxes have been lined up so somebody could be on the other side of those without being observed by someone in the room. And behind that sniper's nest there were found 3 cartridges that were identified as being fired from the Mannlicher Carcano rifle owned by Lee Harvey Oswald. From that, then, we're able to look at what Lee Harvey Oswald would have seen from that position as the car moved down through Dealey Plaza. This was done by the FBI, where they mounted a camera on to the scope of the gun.

And you can see (shows video) there's about where the 2nd shot would have been fired and this area somewhere the third shot would be fired. So you could see the advantage that the vantage point that he had.

Then what I did was to analyze each individual shot. The first shot—there's very little evidence for the first shot. Governor Connally said that he heard a shot and turned to the right. Here at frame about 166 we see the Governor sort of starting to turn to the right and if we continue on just a little further you can see he turns just a little more to the right.

He's kind of high in the overhead structure on the presidential limousine. But anyway, before he goes to (behind) the sign he's turned to the right and later we'll see that even after out (from behind) of the sign he's still turned to the right. So his reaction to the sound that he thought was a rifle shot was somewhere in that time frame. Now, unfortunately there's no physical evidence of that— where that bullet was. The question is, what happened to it? First there's several people (who) thought it sounded like a fire cracker or a misfire to a rifle. In addition, if you look at the view from the scope produced by the FBI in this area, there are things that the bullet could have been deflected off of. This (more video pictures from frames of the Z film) is actually a structure that supports a stop light. And a little further in, you'll see that the President goes behind trees. So we don't know exactly what happened with that bullet. But there is a funny sound and there is the opportunity for deflection.

The second shot—I believe—that a single bullet created the wounds the President and the Governor. In order for that to be true, we have to number one: show that, obviously, they were hit at the same time. Secondly we have to show that the trajectory that a bullet would travel is consistent with passing through the wounds on the President and the Governor.

Third, we have to show that the injuries are consistent with how a bullet would react to going through two people, and lastly we have to show that the damage to the bullet is consistent with having produced the injuries. OK, those are the 4 things that we'll be discussing.

JK: You might—you might again slow down a bit.

RP: OK. First of all lets take a look at the Zapruder film.

JK: This is—now what we're talking about is the 2nd shot?

RP: Now we're gonna go towards the second shot. The first shot was fired sometime up to 166. Now, the second shot occurs about 3 seconds later and I'll show you the basis for that. If we look at the Governor right here, you can see his tie and you can see that his lapel is open widely. If we go to the next frame here, what I'll do is outline that lapel. Now watch the sudden motion in one frame. There's tremendous motion of his right lapel. Remember the bullet goes through his right chest, enters under his right nipple. You can see the effect of the bullet going through his jacket.

So there's definitive evidence at frame 224 that's when the bullet passed through the body of Governor Connally.

Now, if we take a look at President Kennedy, the question is when did he receive his wound. I'm sorry, here we'll just look at the Governor reacting to that wound (jury watches on the video). You can see that there's continuing evidence of him being shot. If we now look at President Kennedy from before the sign. Notice the arm. Notice that he's waving to the crowd. His hand is up around his face, his elbow slightly elevated off the side of the car. You can see it right there as he continues behind the sign. You'll see his hand is still up by his face. As he emerges from the sign, you'll see that his hand is in a down position. As he was waving, he's now bringing it down. You can see that's his right hand right there.

If we go to the next frame you will actually notice that the hand drops slightly. If we go back and forth, see the—the shiny part of the back seat of the car? You'll see his hand is still coming down from the wave. He has not yet reacted to the bullet that's gone through his body. If we now move on, what we'll see is that in the next frame, there's his arm at the frame I was just talking about. Now watch it again. The elbow still hasn't jerked. Now the elbow jerks up. Okay, so it's a few frames later when you actually watch the elbow pop up. That is the President's first sign of reaction to being shot.

Now, if we move forward to look at where his arms and hands finally end up, OK now, so that's about 200 milliseconds after the Governor's shot. Now look where his hands are. Look where his elbows are. He's not reaching for his throat, as has been commonly said. If you look, he has his left fist against his chin, excuse me, his right fist against his chin, his left fist against that, and his elbows up in the air. That's not grabbing for his chest. What it is—its a known reflex reaction to spinal cord shock at the base of the neck. The bullet has just passed near the base of his neck.

The shock from this bullet causes spinal cord shock and forces this reflexive reaction of the President. That reflexive reaction takes approximately 200 milliseconds which is exactly the time from when the bullet passes through Governor Connally's lapel and we see the first motion of the President's elbow. Therefore, both men were shot at the same time.

Now the next question is, were they shot by the same bullet? And in order for that to be true, we have to have the path of the bullet being consistent.

Now, the way we did this is we had to develop the geometry associated with the shooting. We did this by creating a computer animation of Dealey Plaza. What you saw first there was an aerial photo. By using 2 aerial photos, we developed the complete 3 dimensional geometry of Dealey Plaza. We then created an engineering animation of Dealey Plaza, which is geometrically exact within a couple of feet. We can then take photos of the buildings and do what's called "texture mapping" so the facades of the building look as they do in Dealey Plaza.

So, consequently, through our engineering animation, we have a physically correct and a visually correct representation of Dealey Plaza. The next thing we did is we made a model of the car. The model of this car was based on dimensions that appear in the literature, plus we sent one of our staff to actually look at the limousine. We re-created the limousine, and now we can actually move the limousine through Dealey Plaza. But the only really important part of where this limousine is and where the people are is at the time the shots are fired and the way we do that is by using reverse projection. And this is a technique that allows us to place the President and the Governor where they are at the time they were shot. We made a physical model of the car which is to scale for all the seats. We then put a camera up at the position where Mr. Zapruder was. And by using the same focal length, we can actually now look down at the car and have the same view that Mr. Zapruder had. There it is through the lens. Now we take the actual piece of film from Mr. Zapruder. We sketch the President and the Governor. We take people the same size and weight and put them in the car, and once they're properly located, we now know where the President and Governor were. By using a 3 dimensional digitizing scheme called a "sonic digitizer,'' we were actually able to measure where their bodies are in 3-D space.

We can now put these bodies into our animation. And if you watch the next scene, what you'll see is a fade. That's the Zapruder film. Watch the Governor and the President. What you'll see is the animation has put the Governor and the President in the exact same position they were on—in—Dealey Plaza in 1963. What we did then is accurately went back and measured the location of the wounds on the President and the Governor. You can see here where we're taking these measurements. These then get entered into the animation and what we can do then is say, ''Well, given those wounds, where does the shooter have to be. Where is the sniper that makes the shot?'' We drew a straight line through the President's back wound and the Governor's chest wound.

What we found is—given the slight inaccuracies of wound location and car positions—that in fact, this says that the sniper has to be somewhere within that cone. And you can see that that cone is almost centered on the 6th floor TSBD southeast window.

JK: OK. Let me stop you. And that cone is where—if a bullet came from within that cone—the wounds could have been made to the President and Governor Connally by the same bullet. Is that what you're saying?

RP: That's absolutely correct. The cone is because, as you know, the President wasn't visible when Connally's coat moved. So we had to do one frame later, which is only 50 milliseconds, but that makes small errors, and there are other errors, so we can't point exactly where it is. But you can see that the cone—error cone—is relatively small and the 6th floor window is the most reasonable place for it. Now, in order to see what that actually looks like, what the bullet would look like going through 2 people I have a piece of footage here that shows that. What happens is we have the 2 people placed as you see them in the car. The bullet now starts to tumble. We do know it's tumbling because the entrance wound is too large for a non-tumbling bullet. It deflects through the chest, comes out, goes through the wrist and enters the thigh. And that gives you—you can see the straight line trajectory through both men, before the impact with the ribs where there is a deflection. Now I think we also have an overhead of that, just to show you that its essentially a straight line in this plane.

JK: This [is] looking down the same position . . . ?

RP: This is looking down. The President is on the left, the Governor is on the right. This is the same line you saw before, only now you're looking straight down and you can see it comes through the President, through the Governor's chest, wrist and you can't see it enter his leg because his hand blocks it. So, it's clear that the trajectory analysis is consistent.

JK: Dr., excuse me just a second. These models have been placed, as I understand it, based on the techniques that you just explained to the jury; taking the Zapruder film and making sure that the models are in exactly the relationship of President Kennedy to Governor Connally at the time of the shot, is that right?

RP: That's right.

JK: And you've shown us from the side and from the top what that would look like?

RP: Yes I have.

JK: OK, go ahead please.

RP: So, therefore, we know that not only were they shot at the same time, they were shot with the same bullet. And, in order to make sure that we address all the issues with that one of the things we looked at was the question of how much mass was in the bullet. The bullet was not severely deformed. And there were some fragments left in Governor Connally. If you look at the weight of the bullet after it was found and its original weight and the mass left in Governor Connally, there's actually still 1.3 grains left unaccounted for. So the amount of mass lost is consistent with the mass deposited in Governor Connally. Okay.

JK: Dr., a question was asked in Cross Examination about whether or not—I think of Dr. Loquvam, the pathologist—was there any evidence that the wound to Governor Connally's wrist was caused by the bullet that's known as exhibit 399? Do you know of any such evidence?

RP: Yes I do.

JK: What is it?

RP: In the late 1970's, Dr. Guinn from the University of California in Irvine did a "Neutron Activation" study and . . .

JK: Slow, slow—a little bit more slowly, this is important.

RP: He did a "Neuron Activation" study and determined from that study that the fragments found in the Governor's wrist were consistent with the lead in Exhibit 399. So, therefore, the bullet found at Parkland Hospital is the same bullet as left the fragments in Governor Connally's wrist.

JK: Anything else on the 2nd bullet—on your opinion of the second bullet?

RP: Only that if you combine what we've just talked about plus the evidence that Dr. Fackler put in that I think that the evidence is absolutely conclusive that a single bullet went through both the President and the Governor at frame 224 on the Zapruder film.

JK: Alright. That's the 2nd shot. First one missed. 2nd shot went through the back and the neck and into Governor Connally. Tell us about the 3rd shot which all the jury has seen.

RP: OK. Let's go back to the Zapruder film, and watch it. Now this again is the slow motion close up. You can see that the head wound occurs at frame 313. It's approximately 5 seconds after frame 224. Therefore, there's 5 seconds for a sniper to make that shot which is more than enough time for that to occur. So what we then did was use the same reverse projection techniques, located the models in the car, located the President in the car, located the head wounds on the President, located the sniper cone and then looked at where the individual would be to shoot the President and hit him in the back of the head. And again, when you look at the cone, it heads right back up to the 6th floor, south—or northeast—corner of TSBD. OK. So now, again, what we've found is that this wound is completely consistent with Lee Harvey Oswald shooting from that window.

JK: Were there any—you've told us about the bullet that was found on the stretcher and the analysis of that—were there any fragments found from the bullet that caused this wound that killed the President?

RP: Yes.

JK: And where were the fragments found?

RP: There were 2 fragments found in the car and there were fragments taken from the President's brain. And again, Dr. Guinn's Neutron Activation analysis determined that they came from the same bullet.

JK. OK—Dr. Guinn tested the fragments in the car and the fragments that were taken out of the President's head?

RP: That is correct.

JK: OK. Go ahead please.

RP: OK. Then the other thing that's been mentioned several times is what happens to the President after the shot. And there's always been statements to say that the President moves off to the left, and if the President was hit from behind, he should not move off to the left. Also at this point I think its important to note where that skull fragment is. You can see the President's ear, you can see the back of his head.

It's clear that the fracture pattern is at the front of the head. Now your intuition would sometimes tell you that if something gets shot from the back it should move forward, and to a certain degree that's true. But you have to understand that with a head filled with brain it's more complicated than that. So what we did is we ran an experiment in which we took an empty skull and we shot at the same position that the President was shot, and you can see where the point of entry is and you can see what happens is that the skull in fact does go in the same direction as the bullet. An empty skull, shot from the back goes forward.

JK: And that bullet came from the left side of the screen that the jurors are watching from the back of the skull and hit in the back and caused that movement right?

RP: Right. We're at about a 45 degree angle with the camera to the direction of the bullet and you can see the skull rolls forward. We then took another skull and we filled it with beef brain and we put a skin-like substance substitute on it, and we did the same experiment.

JK: Excuse me, where are you aiming? Are you attempting to hit the entry wound?

RP: We are attempting to hit the exact entry wound of the President. We laid that geometrically on the skull. What you can see is that it goes to the left. If we could start that over again (the video). Now watch what happens. The reason it does is because the brain matter exits the right—its almost like an explosion—and part of the material can escape to the right. The other part of the material pushes the head to the left. So what we've shown here is that the President's head motion to the left is exactly consistent with a shot that entered where the bullet entered the President's head and where it exited his head.

JK: What was your conclusion then about where the, the killing shot— the 3rd bullet—came from and where it entered and left President Kennedy's skull?

RP: Well, both the wound location and the head motion shows that the shot was fired from the 6th floor of the TSBD.

JK: OK. In your opinion, did Oswald have the ability to make these shots from the TSBD, that you've just described?

RP: I believe he did, yes.

JK: Would you explain to the jury why you believe he did?

RP: OK. Well, first of all, if you look here—we also have a blow-up somewhere but it might be a little bit easier for the jury to see . . . [he is referring to an evaluation form re: Oswald's shooting capabilities while in the Marines]

JK: Let me get it.

RP: OK. First of all let me just describe what this is. These are, these are the results of Oswald firing as a Marine. This is called a "rapid fire" drill. He was in a seated position, he had open sights. He was at 200 yd's., more than twice the distance of the head shot. And he was required to shoot 10 shots in one minute. That also includes a magazine change, ok, because they'll have 5 shots, change the magazine out, fire another 5 shots in one minute. His two scores were 49 and 48. Therefore, he did demonstrate at this point in time the ability to have sufficient skills to make these shots. In addition, Marina Oswald has testified that when they were in New Orleans he used to work the mechanism of the gun. He used to keep it oiled and cleaned so he did have practice in opening and closing the chamber relatively rapidly.

JK: OK. Is there any evidence that Oswald had any other rifle?

RP: Not that I know of, no.

JK: You said that he was shooting 10 shots a minute with a magazine change in the Marines. How far were these shots from Texas Book Depository?

RP: The shots that we fired were, let's see, I believe it's about 88 yd's—it's two hundred and ninety feet.

JK: 88 yd's. was the head shot?

RP: Head shot.

JK: The ones to the back and the throat, how far was that?

RP: That's 64 yd's. I believe and these shots that we see here are 200.

JK: OK. Now there has been, Dr. Piziali—there has been wide spread speculation and no little money made over the possibility that somebody else did the shooting here. Do you have an opinion, based on the physical evidence, about whether or not President Kennedy could have been shot from the grassy knoll?

RP: Yes, I do.

JK: Or placed in front of him or to his side?

RP: I do have an opinion.

JK: Would you please explain to the jury what that opinion is.

RP: There is absolutely no physical evidence to support that theory. None whatsoever.

JK: Would you explain to the jury what the—maybe show them what the view looks like from the grassy knoll and explain some of the problems with the theory.

RP: Sure. I think I can. First of all, as it comes up [the video] what you'll see is the view from the grassy knoll. You're looking very much at the right side of the presidential limousine. It's a little bit above you so may—maybe you're looking over the front just a little bit. You can see it there, [video is now on], so you can see there is a very small figure of the President there.

And if you look at that, there's absolutely no evidence of an entrance wound on the right side of the head. All of the fragments on X-rays were noted along a path from the entrance to exit hole as described by Dr. Locum. There's no other material found in the brain at autopsy, so consequently there is simply no physical evidence to support a shot from any other position than from above and behind.

JK: Could I ask you to quickly sum up the conclusions in this fairly rapid testimony?

RP: Yes. I believe the evidence shows that there were 3 shots fired from the southeast corner, 6th floor window of the TSBD. The first bullet is not accurately accounted for, we simply have an approximation of when it was fired. The second bullet was fired more than 3 seconds after the first bullet. It wounded both the President and the Governor. The third bullet was fired 5 seconds later, hit the President in the head and killed him. The bullets found were fired from the same gun, the Mannlicher Carcano owned by Lee Harvey Oswald.

JK: Thank you very much, Dr. No further questions.

JUDGE: All right, Cross Examination.

CROSS EXAMINATION—Dr. Robert Piziali
Evan Chesler, Defense Attorney

EC: Thank you, your Honor. Dr., you say that there were 3 shots fired from the depository. One missed, one is the so called "magic bullet," and one hit the President in the head. Is that correct?

RP: That, sir, I believe to be true, yes. The first shot, as I said, there's not a lot of strong evidence for except the cartridge, empty casing in the window—and the bulk of the witnesses in Dealey Plaza at the time believe that they heard 3 shots, as well as it being very consistent with Governor Connally's body motions.

EC: I appreciate the explanation Dr., but we're a little short on time. If you could just try to confine yourself to answering my questions. Were any other shots fired at the Presidential limousine that day, sir?

RP: I don't believe so.

EC: Do you know?

RP: There's no evidence for any.

EC: Do you know?

RP: Well, if you have to have evidence to have an opinion, I guess you could say that I would know what is—what the evidence says— and the evidence says there were only 3 shots.

EC: So then you reject the finding of the Select Committee of the U.S. House of Representatives in 1978 that a 4th shot was fired from the grassy knoll. Is that correct?

RP: I believe they said there was a possibility that there was a shot fired from the grassy knoll.

EC: Do you . . .

RP: And yes, I do.

EC: You reject that?

RP: Yes.

EC: Now, you talked about the timing of the shots between the excuse me, the shots that you say hit the President and also hit the Governor, and you say that from your examination of the film, you believe it was the same bullet. Is that correct?

RP: Correct.

EC: Now I'd like to before I go to a frame of the film, I just want to be sure that I understand something. You said that the fact of placing the shot at frame 224 of the film, in your view, is based upon the Governor's lapel flap, flying forward. That's your testimony, correct?

RP: That's my testimony, yes.

EC: So the—the fact which causes you to place the impact on the Governor at that precise moment in time is what you perceive to be the movement of his lapel forward—that way—obscuring his shirt, correct?

RP: That's precise. His other body activities would also place it at that point, but in order to get within a frame, that's what I would use for the frame. But in fact they're—all his other body motions are exactly consistent with him being shot at that very moment also.

EC: Sir, so you assign significance to your theory that his lapel moved and that was the bullet passing through him?

RP: That's one of the things that I based it on, yes it is.

EC: Did you examine the evidence from the Warren Commission of the Governor's clothing—the clothing he was wearing that day—in reaching your conclusion about the lapel flap?

RP: I did not have a chance to examine the actual clothing, no.

EC: Did you examine the photographs of the clothing which are part of the Commission's report?

RP: Yes.

EC: I'd like you to look, if you would, at page 340 and at page 343. 340 of the report is the Governor's suit coat, and page 343 is the Governor's shirt. Would you look at those please—if I may approach the witness stand?

J: Yes.

EC: This is the jacket . . .

J: Why don't you step behind him?

EC: Yes sir. Do you notice the lapels, Dr.?

RP: Yes.

EC: They're very small, the fashion of the early 1960's. Very small skinny lapels sort of all the way up here near his neck, aren't they?

RP: Correct.

EC: And would you look at the shirt. You see the circle on the shirt where the wound is?

RP: Correct.

EC: That was all the way down here. It blew out part of his rib below his right nipple. Is that correct, sir?

RP: About right there [gestures on himself].

EC: Right there, right there, correct?

RP: Correct.

EC: May I show these pictures to the jury, your Honor?

J: You can walk in front of them and hold the pictures up.

EC: Suit coat . . .

J: Without discussing them.

EC: I'm sorry, excuse me. Got carried away.

J: Now, ladies and gentlemen, have you all had an opportunity to see that? Who hasn't? Hold it up high for them so they can see it. OK, thank you very much.

EC: Thank you. Now, Dr., I'd like to turn to frame 225 of the film. The President is visible. This is the first frame in which you can see the President emerging from the rear of that road sign, is that correct?

RP: That's where you can see his face. You can see his hand in the previous frame.

EC: Yes. Now, Dr., if it is the case—and I understand that on direct testimony you disagree with this—but if it is the case that on frame 225 the President was moving his arm up toward his neck, if that's so, would you agree, sir, that that would mean that the bullet must have entered the President's body no later than approximately 4 frames earlier, about 200 milliseconds—as you testified?

RP: No. I think that if it was happening, his hand would simply still be in the waving motion, because his hand was up at the time he left the sign. It was now moving down—and he has been waving throughout this video—so there's no evidence he was reaching for his throat. And since his hand never went to his throat, then I think it's very clear that in fact he would not be reaching for his throat.

EC: Dr., if the President was moving his hand up towards his throat, is it the case, sir, if he had a throat wound, with respect to which he was reacting by his hand moving up to his throat—a movement which begins, I ask you to assume, at frame 225—would you agree

with me that that would mean that the President had not been hit
with the bullet any later than frame 221?

RP: Well, the reason . . .

EC: Yes or no, sir?

RP: The way you phrase the question can't be answered because it has
some inconsistencies in it. So if you can ask a consistent question,
I'd be happy to answer. [Audience laughs] You said that if the hand
was moving up . . .

J: Alright, ladies and gentlemen. [Quieting laughter]

RP: . . . he had to be grabbing for his throat and I said "No, that's not
the case." If what you're asking is, if you make the assumption that
his hand is reacting to a bullet wound, then I would say, "Yes, it
would be 4 frames before that," but that wasn't your question.

J: Thank you, Dr. Alright, ladies and gentlemen, if you will please [ref.
to laughing]

EC: Dr., you're aware, are you not, that the Warren Commission found
that the bullet that hit the President may have hit him as early as
frame 210 of the Zapruder film?

RP: The Warren Commission was non-scientific. I read all of that and
I believe that they did not bring any—even at that time—modern
science to bear on their analysis of this film. And I believe they did
say that, but I would not rest any of my professional opinion based
on the Warren Commission study.

EC: I think somewhere in that answer you said, "I believe they did
say that." Is that correct?

RP: Yes.

EC: Alright. Are you also aware that the House Select Committee in
1978 said that they believe that the President had been hit somewhere
between frames 188 and 191, some 40 frames earlier than you
placed? Isn't that so?

RP: They had it earlier than I did, yes.

EC: Yes. So the Warren Commission is at 210, the House Select Committee is at 188 to 191, and you say because the Governor's flap
moved at 224 you're certain that the bullet hit him at 224. Isn't that
so? Isn't that your testimony?

RP: You are mixing up the President and the Governor there, I—so . . .

EC: Don't you think they were both hit in the same frame, sir?

RP: I do, yes.

EC: Alright, thank you.

RP: Yes, that's fine.

EC: Thank you. Now let's talk about the path of the bullet. You put
up those cones on your trajectory that you say tell us that the path

of that "magic bullet"—so called—was back to the TSBD. Do you recall that testimony?

RP: I didn't call it the magic bullet. I did call it 399, yeah.

EC: Right, right. Now, do you agree with me, sir, that in order to plan—to plot—the trajectory or the path of the bullet, you need to understand at least 3 absolutely clear facts: The placement of the wounds in the body; the position of the body in the car; and the placement of the car on the road in Dealey Plaza. Don't you need those 3 things?

RP: Yes.

EC: And for the wound part of that you accepted the wound placement of the, of the pathologist who testified earlier before the House Select Committee in 1978, isn't that so?

RP: Yes.

EC: And that pathologist found that the doctors who saw the President's head wound in 1963, doing the autopsy of the President, placed the wound four inches too low on his head. They were wrong by 4 inches, isn't that so?

RP: Yes.

EC: Isn't that what she said?

RP: It is about 4 inches, but you have to remember that that autopsy report did not give a dimension. It just said it was slightly above something . . .

EC: Don't you think, sir . . .

RP: . . . But it's about 4 inches.

EC: It's about 4 inches?

RP: It's about 4 inches.

EC: Thank you. And also you accept a placement of a wound which is critical to your trajectory analysis which said that the back wound that the autopsy doctors found was 2 inches misplaced, isn't that so?

RP: I don't know that the Warren Commission—I don't remember their exact placement of it, but I did rely on the Select Committee placement of that wound, yes.

EC: Alright, and the Select Committee placement was different from the autopsy placement of not only the head wound but the back wound, isn't that so?

RP: It would not surprise me since there were very poor dimensions on the autopsy report, sure.

EC: Now, with respect to the placement of the car in Dealey Plaza—one of the other elements you need for your trajectory—you placed the car in frame 224, because that's when you say the Governor's lapel flap moved, isn't that so?

RP: No. What I said was—is because we couldn't see the President in 224 we had to move him 1 frame further. So that moves the car, I guess it's about a foot or so further. But what we found is, that's why the cone, the yellow cone, is a little bit bigger—because we had to move the car one frame.

EC: Alright.

RP: So I've located the car at 225.

EC: You've located the car at 225. Now, isn't it so, sir, that the House Select Committee in 1978 brought NASA in—the space agency—and they did an analysis to place the car in the plaza, and they said the car should be located according to frame 190 on the Zapruder film—34 frames earlier, isn't that so?

RP: No. What happened is NASA was brought in by the Select Committee and NASA was told by the Select Committee to please locate the car at frame 190.

EC: Thank you. So they put the car at 190, you put the car at 224. They put the head wound up here, the autopsy puts it down here. Isn't that right?

RP: Those are all correct statements, sure.

EC: Those are all correct statements. Thank you. Now let's go to the head wound.

J: Just ask the question. There is no need to repeat the answer, we're all getting the point.

EC: Yes, I'm sorry. Let's go to the head wound. You and your colleagues performed certain skull firing tests in preparation for your testimony, isn't that so?

RP: Yes.

EC: And you fired Mannlicher Carcano full metal jacketed bullets through human skulls, isn't that so?

RP: Well, at that time, we actually used some bullets that were obtained by Dr. McCarthy and they were nickel chrome coated because nobody at that point could find the copper jacketed until later.

EC: Is it true that they were full metal jacketed bullets?

RP: Right, but they weren't the same jackets as the Mannlicher Carcano copper.

EC: Not one of those bullets broke up into fragments, did they?

RP: No, it's, it's also a different kind of skull material, so there are a lot of things that were different. The purpose of that experiment was simply to show the mechanics of head motion to the left as brain comes to the right.

EC: Excuse me, Dr. I appreciate your explaining all of that to us, but my question was whether any of those bullets fragmented and broke up into pieces.

RP: No. You wouldn't necessarily expect them to. It's a different skull material and its a different bullet material.

EC: Is it or is it not a fact, Dr., that a full metal jacket bullet is a standard form of military ammunition which is specifically designed not to break up, to remain intact, and to wound rather than kill. Is that the purpose of full metal jacket bullets?

RP: Yes, that is, but . . .

EC: Thank you.

RP: . . . the FBI used that material—those same bullets—to hit a skull and they, in fact, broke up the Mannlicher Carcano full metal jacket bullets by an impact with the cadaver's skull.

EC: Dr., we could continue this debate for a long time, but, you see . . .

J: This is not a debate, it's question and answer. The question did not call for that wide an answer, but there is no re-direct, so I'm gonna exercise some . . . Cross Examiner . . . ?

EC: Thank you. Dr., I'd like to ask you one other thing. I'm gonna switch—move to the film—and I've just moved the film to the, uh, wrong place, so let me move it back. I guess I don't have that frame. Sorry. Dr., while they're bringing the film up, what was the approximate distance from the group of trees on the grassy knoll where Mr. Arnold is positioned on this chart up here, to the position of the President's car at the time of the fatal head wound? Do you know approximately the distance?

RP: No.

EC: Excuse me?

RP: No.

EC: Alright, do you know the relative distance between those—that location and the car, and the 6th floor of the SBD and the car? Which one was closer and which one was further away?

RP: Well I never measured it, but I think it's pretty obvious the grassy knoll is closer.

EC: Grassy knoll is closer.

RP: Right.

EC: Now, sir, let me ask you this. I understand you disagree with this—so I'm asking you as an expert to assume with me that there was someone—a shooter—located on the knoll that day, in that clump of trees, at the stockade fence as the President's car moved to the position at which the Zapruder film shows unequivocally he was struck in the head. Do you understand that assumption?

RP: Yes, I do.

EC: Alright. My question is this, sir: If there had been such a shooter at that location, could such a shooter have had a shot at the right side of the President's head? Yes or No?

RP: Oh, . . . sure.

EC: Thank you. I have no further questions.

J: Alright, thank you very much. You may step down, Dr. You may call your next witness.

TESTIMONY—Dr. Roger McCarthy
Evan Chesler, Defense Attorney

RM: My name is Roger Lee McCarthy.

EC: . . . Failure Analysis Incorporated . . .

RM: Yes.

EC: And among the things that Failure Analysis does, does it conduct engineering and scientific analysis concerning questions relating to ballistics?

RM: Yes. Up to 37 millimeter canon.

EC: Are you also an expert in the field of sniper weapons and sniper tactics?

RM: Yes, I was trained as an ordinance officer and honed and proficient with most of the great sniper weapons that have been developed over military history, at least in the 20th century.

EC: And are you also a qualified marksman yourself, sir?

RM: Yes.

EC: Now, sir, have you conducted a review of the ballistics related evidence compiled in connection with the assassination of President Kennedy?

RM: Yes, I have.

EC: Have you also conducted your own ballistics analysis in connection with your testimony here?

RM: Yes.

EC: And have you reached any conclusions?

RM: Yes, I have.

EC: I wonder if we can put up the board which has several conclusions on it? Dr., I'm just gonna hand you a copy 'cause you're at an awkward angle for that board. Could you state please for the jury in your own words, very briefly, the conclusions you have reached as a result of the analyses you performed?

RM: Yes. As a result of reviewing the records of the various government investigations of this crime, I have learned and come to 4 conclusions which I've attempted to summarize briefly here, the first being that the evidence shows that the best shots from the TSBD were passed up in favor of difficult shots from that location, which were easy shots from the grassy knoll. The 2nd the evidence shows that the alleged weapon that was used for the assassination and the bullets used in it are frankly wrong and unlikely choices for an assassination. Third is the prosecution's evidence I believe shows clearly that President Kennedy and Governor Connally were shot by different bullets under their scenario; and then, finally, that the evidence that we have in front of us is consistent with the conclusion that the fatal shot was fired from the grassy knoll which would have been a far easier and more believable shot to me.

EC: Dr., I'd like to turn to your first conclusion and I'd like if I do this to put an animation up on the screen. Would you describe for the jury what this animation shows?

RM: Yes. Dr. Piziali described the technique earlier and we are now going to fly around Dealey Plaza and into the fully open 6th floor window. Now remember on the day, November 23, the window was—excuse me—was not open all the way, as it was shown there, it was only open a 3rd of the way. And we're looking now down Houston Street and this is the view from the 6th floor window as it would have seemed to someone sitting in that window, because the computer computes not only scale, but perspective—the tendency of railroad rails to come together in the distance—all of that is computed by the computer and this is a true image of what you would have seen.

EC: I would like to move to another animation and I wonder if you would explain to the jury what we're seeing here, sir?

RM: This is the ride of the President down Houston Street, turning on to Elm Street, as would have been seen through the rather inferior 4 power scope that was mounted on the Carcano, that was alleged to be the murder weapon.

EC: Now, where has the car stopped in this animation with respect to the TSBD?

RM: It has just turned the corner off of Houston Street and has started to come down Elm Street. It's turned, he's almost completed his left turn. In fact, because he's gonna go down Elm Street, he's got to make a hard left. He's got to turn more than 90 degrees.

EC: Now, I'd like to show that same animation again and I want to ask you please to explain what, if anything, is shown in this animation which leads to your conclusion that the best shots from that location in the Depository were, in fact, passed up if someone was there.

RM: Well, there's 2 reasons. First of all, this is an assassination attempt and an ambush. And you can see that now every vital organ of the President is exposed to the shooter in the Depository and at the closest point in that shot he's got a shot of 86 ft. That's not even the length of this room. With a high powered rifle and a 4 power scope! Now, that is a high probability shot. And if you're in the business of committing a heinous crime, like an assassination, you would shoot the target as it was coming towards you because, first of all, if you miss, every subsequent shot gets better if it is coming your direction, unless he can turn and escape. One of the big draw-backs of a President and presidential motorcade is there's no escape to the rear. There's other cars, there's vans, and there's people along the side. It is easy to figure out the path of the motorcade, there's people along the route the whole line. The car cannot veer off the path of the motorcade unless it wishes to run down people.

Therefore, if you take your shot when he's coming towards you down the street, first of all you get a closer shot than the ones that were ultimately taken. Secondly, the quarry to escape the target of the ambush—that is the person you're shooting at—if they wish to escape they have to come over you and that's the ideal ambush target 'cause every shot becomes a higher probability in the attempt to escape.

EC: Let me continue the animation if I may. Would you describe what the car is doing now?

RM: Now the presidential motorcade is continuing its route. You can see some obscuration—obscuring the screen by the oak trees. And now, we're going to stop at the point of the head shot—at least as being seen from the 4 power scope in the repository.

EC: So let me just make sure we're clear. What exactly is the location of the car in terms of the alleged event of that day in the scope view that we're looking at right now.

RM: This is the alleged moment and car position of the head shot. If that shot were taken through the 4 power scope mounted on the subject rifle, this is what would be seen.

EC: Now, Dr., do you have an opinion, based upon your analysis of why a shooter located in the 6th floor window of that building would pass up what you believe are the best shots coming down Houston Street in favor of shots as the President is moving away down Elm Street.

RM: Well, the only rational reason that I can think of for giving away those shots which are much much easier to make, would be the same argument I advanced before about the ambush dynamics. Only this time you would have to have an assistant who was going to gain better shots as a result of the target escaping if you missed. And, of course, the assistant wouldn't have to take shots if you hit.

So you would be in a situation where you would start the shooting sequence at the earliest that your second—your assistant—could acquire the target; start your shooting sequence from the 6th floor, then you would drive the target into the 2nd shooter who would get progressively better shots as yours got progressively worse.

EC: Alright. Let me show you this animation and will you describe for the jury now what this shows?

RM: This is the killing zone from the 6th floor Depository window.

EC: What do you mean by the "killing zone," sir?

RM: This whole area in white is the area of Dealey Plaza where you could see and acquire a target if you were a shooter from the 6th floor. You've got elevation and you've got range. Now, of course, out here the shots become very, very difficult.

EC: Now can we move to the animation which shows the zone from the knoll please? And what is this, sir?

RM: If a shooter were located at the corner of the stockade fence here, this would be the zone of the Plaza they can command. You see, they don't have a shot at the turn onto Elm Street, and indeed they only have a shot almost identically with the moment when the next shot is going to strike the President according to the prosecution's version of this accident—of this assassination.

EC: Now, can we go to the next please? What is this?

RM: This is an overlap, where we've just overlapped the zones from the stockade fence with the over—with the shooter at the 6th floor. And you can see that the 2 zones overlap in this area and indeed start their overlap just at the location of the head shot—excuse me— the neck shot.

EC: Thank you. Now, Dr., I'd like to ask you some questions about the weapon. First, can you identify this for the jury please?

RM: This is a peculiar member of the 9138 Carcano family. It's an Italian military weapon. This is a carbine. There is one version of this longer, that's a rifle. It's bolt action. And the reason that it's bolt action is that it's based on a design that was essentially formulated in 1891. It's a pre-WW1 technology. When it was manufactured at arsenal in 1940 and these types of weapons chambered in 6.5 in this version were made because of ammunition shortages of the 765 that this weapon was originally barreled at. It was made in 1940 and it is an unfortunate weapon. It is not well made; it was obsolete the day it was produced. It is a rough working weapon; the bolt works rough, the trigger is not even in pull. They were not intended to be well made, they were cheap when they were made, they're cheap today.

EC: Let me ask you if you can quickly open this package which we've seen before during one of the earlier witnesses. Tell us what's inside there, sir.

RM: Well, there's some hardware. This is a broken down Carcano stock and barrel—there's a broken down stock and barrel combination.

EC: Now, Dr., if you were to—are you able to put together and disassemble this weapon?

RM: With some time, yes.

EC: If you were to disassemble it, sir, what is the length of the longest piece once the weapon is disassembled, and what is that piece?

RM: It's the stock. You can see the wood extends up past the steel.

EC: And how long, approximately, is just the stock of the weapon?

RM: 35 inches.

EC: And is it possible if you disassemble this Carcano to get it shorter, that is to get the longest piece of it shorter than about 35 inches?

RM: No. This weapon, to my knowledge, was never made in a folding stock configuration.

EC: If you were to assemble it from the pieces I've handed you, could—what tool, if any, would you need to do so?

RM: You would need at least a screwdriver.

EC: Can you do it with a dime or some coin if you didn't have a screwdriver?

RM: No. The screws on this weapon have slots that are too small for any American minted coin.

EC: Would you—could you do it without putting fingerprints all over the stock and other parts of the weapon in the course of assembling it from the pieces you have in front of you?

RM: No. It has an—what I would call an aggravating assembly sequence whereby the front grip—fore grip—retaining rate won't slip over the front barrel retainer with the screws in it. So this has to be put on without the screws while the forward grip retainer is put on and the sling attachment. It is not an elegant assembly.

EC: You talked about the rifle a little while ago. I wanted to ask you if there was any defect that was—in which the scope was mounted on the actual Carcano allegedly used in the assassination according to the record of the ...

RM: The assassination—the alleged assassination weapon has a scope that is improperly zeroed and shoots high and to the right.

EC: Does that defect have any relevance, sir, in the context of shooting a target moving away from the shooter across his field of fire to the right as alleged by the prosecution?

RM: Well, yes. The bullet doesn't go where the cross hairs on the subject weapon— where the cross hairs point.

EC: That's because of this defect you mentioned?

RM: Yes, that's right, and it's a defect you can cure if the scope is, is reasonably well mounted, you can adjust the cross hairs. But on the subject weapon—on the day it is found—it shoots high in the right, 3 to 5 inches at 100 yd's. If you are shooting a moving target and you understand that your scope is not properly zeroed, you have 2 compensations to make. First, when you shoot a moving target you have to aim ahead of the target because the target will not be where it is when you pull the trigger. The target will be where the bullet arrives. So you have to move the scope ahead and that's called "lead" and that's a common activity in shooters. Some scopes actually have lead calibrations on them to help you along. Secondly, if you know your scope is misadjusted, you get to simultaneously factor in how much your scope is out of adjustment and that's 2 things that a shooter would have to correct in his aiming sequence every time he aimed.

EC: And according to the prosecution, sir, how long, how much time elapsed to account for the 3 shots allegedly fired from the Carcano that day?

RM: I believe we saw in a previous graphic display by Dr. Piziali it's a shade over 8 seconds.

EC: Your Honor, may the jury examine the assembled version of the Carcano—with your Honor's permission?

J: You can walk in front of them with it and they can have it in the jury room with the bolt out.

EC: They may ... I'm sorry your Honor, they may have it in the jury room?

J: With the bolt out.

EC: With the bolt out? Your Honor, may they attempt to operate the bolt?

J: In the jury room we'll allow it to be brought in with the clerk so they can demonstrate—they can use it at that time.

EC: Thank you, your Honor.

J: Then it will be taken out.

EC: Thank you your Honor. Now, Dr., I believe you also said that the—your second conclusion that you think the ammunition is unlikely—that is the ammunition allegedly used. Is that correct?

RM: Yes.

EC: Would you tell us what this photo is that's coming up on the screen?

RM: This is a photo of Bullet 399, which has variously been called the magic bullet or the pristine bullet so far in the testimony. This bullet—it's not apparent from this photograph, although if—you may remember in some other photographs shown by Dr. Piziali you notice that there was a gray center and a copper outline on the bullet. That's because this is what is called a full metal jacket bullet. Around the lead core is about a 26 thousandths—that's about 30 secondths of an inch thick—layer of copper covering the whole front—everything but the rear. That layer of copper is there for only one purpose—it's demanded by the Geneva Convention. This is the same Geneva Convention that tells you that P.O.W. only have to give you their name, rank, and serial number; the same signatories—those nations that have signed it have agreed they will not make war with lead bullets because lead bullets make too vicious a wound and are more likely to kill.

Signatories will fight their wars with jacketed bullets which are more likely to wound and less likely to kill. That is the only reason the metal jacket is on there, in a full metal jacket configuration; to make this a wounding bullet and not a killing bullet. By definition, an assassination is a heinous crime where you are setting out to kill the target, and it is precisely the wrong bullet.

EC: Have you examined the evidence with respect to Mr. Oswald's record that is his record as a marksman in the military?

RM: Yes.

EC: And what did you find in your review of that record, sir?

RM: Well, when he was in basic training he barley shot sharpshooter. By the time he had to requalify, he barely shot adequately to stay an active duty marine. He was 191 over the minimum of 190 that would be called a marksman. He shot those patterns with a far superior weapon than the bolt action Carcano and perhaps most importantly he shot those with a semi-automatic weapon.

EC: And what is there about it being a semi-automatic weapon—if anything—which in your mind is a significance of difference from the Carcano?

RM: If you're trying to shoot a rapid fire sequence of well aimed bullets, it's night and day. With a semi-automatic weapon on your shoulder, you squeeze the trigger and a round goes off. Nothing else moves. The way we teach our soldiers to wrap their forearm, they don't take the weapon down. They don't move. If they practice they will not even lose the site picture and the next bullet can be fired as fast as you can squeeze the trigger.

BREAK

[Commercial interrupts the proceedings]

J: Except that not when it's being offered as a basis for the defendant.

EC: But, your Honor, as I understand it, once the prosecution puts that issue into controversy, our expert has, in fact—as he testified much earlier in his testimony—has examined the entire records and formed his conclusions. He has a conclusion concerning the use of reloads here.

J: Ladies and gentlemen, I'm going to allow this testimony is as to what Mr. Cunningham may have done or said, not on the basis that it was done or said, but on the basis that this individual relied upon is an expert to render his opinion. I also am reversing my ruling with reference to the testimony that I struck about Mrs. Oswald and about what was in the record with reference to her and it also is offered and admitted into evidence for that very limited purpose. Alright?

EC: Thank you, your Honor. Let us go to the 3rd conclusion, Dr. This has to do with the wound to the President's neck and the wounds to Governor Connally.

RM: Yes.

EC: I'd like to go to a frame of the Zapruder film. Now, this is frame— for the record—frame 224. The frame about which you heard Dr. Piziali testify earlier, sir?

RM: That is correct.

EC: Now, what I'd like to do is, is move to the very next frame, 225. How much time elapsed on that day between the time frame 224 was filmed and time that frame 225 was filmed?

RM: About 56 milliseconds. This camera is running at a shade more than 18 frames/second, so between any 2 frames there's about an 18th of a second or 56 thousandth of a second.

EC: Now I'd like to go to frame 226 if we can. Now we're at 226. This is another 18th of a second?

RM: That is correct.

EC: Now, would you tell me, Dr., what—if anything—you have observed and what conclusion you have reached about the movement of the President here—frames 224 through 226—2/18ths of a second?

RM: Yes. I would submit that review of the photograph we're gonna now look at the gap between the President's chin and his cuff is showing, and you can see the cuff, that piece of white showing below his suit coat. Let's run back 224, 225, and 226 and watch that cuff.

EC: Here's 225. now let's go to 226?

RM: Yup. I submit it's very clear and this is only an interval of 56 milliseconds. I submit not only is it moving, but it's moved a lot. It's moved several inches in a very short period of time. There is . . .

EC: Can we do this one more time?

RM: I submit there's 4 inches of white. There's five—it's literally even with the chin—it has moved 4 inches in a 20th of a second. This arm is moving up extremely rapidly to move that far in this short of a time. Now, is that a wave to the crowd? I think it unlikely—I can't imagine seeing anyone in the crowd he would want to wave to with that kind of energy. I think a more likely explanation for the timing of the arm would be that this is a reaction.

It's that you've energized the muscle, the muscles have got the news that you're gonna move. I mean to get the arm up 4 inches in the next frame it isn't that you start here.

EC: Now, Dr., based upon that, do you have a conclusion or an opinion as to when the President was in fact hit with the bullet—how much before this point?

RM: Yes, and I think, as Dr. Piziali accurately indicated, there a latency or a delay of about 200 milliseconds between the time that a message is delivered by either traumatic shock to the spine or by your mind to a muscle before you can get movement. You've experienced that all, every time you've ever grabbed something hot. You've known it was hot and were burned because of the delay, because you couldn't get—let go or move fast enough to avoid the damage. You knew it, and you just couldn't make your body move fast enough. There's nothing wrong with you; it takes about a fifth of a second to get all the hardware up to full power—the muscles to move.

EC: Now, Dr., if, then, the President was hit 200 milliseconds before the movement on 225, how many frames back in the film would that be?

RM: That would be at 221 at a minimum.

EC: And at 221 he's behind the sign, is that correct?

RM: Yes.

EC: Alright. If he was hit at 221 and the Governor was hit at 224 according to the prosecution, then could they have been hit by the same bullet?

RM: No.

EC: Alright. Let me go to another question, we have to move on for time. If the President was hit earlier, what is the earliest time that the record indicates the President was hit—any body's estimate— what frame?

RM: I think an earlier government investigation put the impact at frame 188.

EC: Alright. If he was hit at 188 and the Governor was hit at 224, could they have been hit by 2 consecutive bullets fired from the Mannlicher Carcano from the TSBD?

RM: No. I think it would be impossible.

EC: How much time would elapse between those 2 points in time, sir?

RM: It would be a 2 point—a shade over 2 seconds—2.1 seconds.

EC: Alright. Let me go to your 4th conclusion. Let me ask this; do you have a conclusion, sir, as to where the shot came from consistent with the evidence in this case?

RM: Yes I do. The fatal shot, the, the one that's being called the head shot . . .

EC: Could that shot, sir, have been fired—by the way, what is the opinion? Let's get that out first.

RM: I think it is far more likely and consistent with what physical evidence still remains that the fatal shot was taken from the grassy knoll as opposed to almost 100 yd. shot made from the book depository.

EC: Could such a shot have caused the explosive wounds to the right side of the President's head shown on the Zapruder film?

RM: Not only could caused it, but if the proper type of ammunition was being used for the assassination instead of the wrong type as I've talked about earlier, that is precisely what would happen.

EC: Could it have driven the President's head back and to the left as shown on the film?

RM: It—again, if it was the correct ammunition, it would be predicted and should drive the President's head violently back and to the left. There would not be the genteel movement you saw in the skull shooting photograph, it would be a violent reaction.

EC: What kind of ammunition are you talking about, sir? What would do that?

RM: You would—it is not new technology or anything—that's been discovered in the last 100 years. But if you have a bullet that disintegrates—frangible bullet—sometimes you hear the term "explosive bullet," that's what a dum dum bullet is a bullet that disintegrates. That type of bullet imparts all of its energy into the target. The worst thing that can happen to a bullet if you're trying to kill the target is to have it enter—as the testimony has precisely indicated—at 2000 ft./sec. and have it exit at 1700. Most of the energy is still in the bullet going down range and you haven't imparted energy to your target. If you're trying to kill somebody, that is exactly the wrong thing to do. You want all of that energy in the target and no exit wound. If you have an exit, you've got the wrong bullet.

EC: Can we show the film that was taken? Have you done a test of such a frangible bullet from the distance between the grassy knoll and what was the President's car that day, sir?

RM: Yes I have.

EC: Can we show that film very quickly?

RM: This is a setup of a water bottle in my basement, and I have just shot that with a glycerin bullet.

EC: A glycerin bullet?

RM: Yes.

EC: And is that a type of frangible bullet such as you talked about?

RM: Yes.

EC: Can you identify this exhibit?

RM: Yes. This is the water bottle that I shot. I was aiming for the center, and this is without a scope. This is a very easy shot to make 'cause this is 30 yd's.

EC: The bullet went in on the side that's blown open, is that correct?

RM: That is correct.

EC: The water came out toward you, is that correct?

RM: That is correct.

EC: Was there any exit wound on this plastic bottle, sir?

RM: No.

EC: No exit.

RM: There's no exiting damage.

EC: No exit damage. One last point. Have you—you said you fired the skull shots, is that correct?

RM: Yes.

EC: You heard the pathology testimony about the beveling on the inside of the skull?

RM: Yes.

EC: Can you just take out one of the skulls very quickly, Dr., and show the jury? This is a skull that you fired at, sir?

RM: Yes.

EC: And did you shoot it from approximately the distance at which the President was from the TSBD that day?

RM: We shot these skulls somewhat closer.

J: You have to turn around.

RM: I'm sorry. We shot these skulls somewhere closer than the TSBD distance, but the difference in terms of the test would be very marginal. The bullet wouldn't slow down much.

EC: Alright. Last question: Can you explain to the jury what the skull shows at the points of entry and exit from the bullet?

RM: Yes. Basically this is a skull where I know the entry and exit wound because I shot it. This is—this is, by the way, real human skull. And you can see an entry wound, there is the sharp circle. And there is some beveling on the inside. Here's the exit. If you hold it up, down the line of access you can see the entry and exit very clearly.

And you can see more pronounced beveling on the inside of the skull at the point of bullet exit than there was at the point of bullet entry. Skulls are very inhomogeneous—by that I mean they've got different layers and they've got different form and they are not a homogenous material that is all the same, that always responds to the same impact. In fact, some of the skulls we shot—and this is another one that I shot—actually developed a beveled wound, with a knockout, and it wasn't anywhere near the bullet.

EC: That is it was not caused by a bullet piercing the skull?

RM: That is correct. So by nature, it being human tissue have all sorts of defects in them, there are areas of this skull where it barely closes. There are other areas where it is full thickness. Areas where it is not fully thick are internally beveled.

EC: Thank you. I have no further questions, your honor.

J: Alright. Thank you. Cross Examination.

CROSS EXAMINATION—Dr. Roger McCarthy
John Keker, Prosecuting Attorney

JK: Could I, your honor, have the water bottle used to simulate President Kennedy's head? When did you shoot this, Dr. McCarthy; this Arrowhead water bottle in your basement, meant to simulate President Kennedy's head?

RM: I don't think I testified I meant this to simulate a head, but it does simulate the ballistic reaction that a head would have, I believe, and I shot these yesterday.

JK: Yesterday.

RM: That is correct.

JK: How long have you been working on this case?

RM: Couple weeks.

JK: OK. Where—if we continue to use this as an example—President Kennedy's skull, as seen by many independent pathologists, had an entry wound into it. Where's the entry wound in your Arrowhead bottle, and where'd the entry wound go—in President Kennedy's skull? What is your opinion about that, sir?

RM: Well, if you play back the high speed of my shot you'll see I had a cap on this bottle and it shoots off with a lot of hydraulic force as a result of the hit here. All you have to have is a skull with all sorts of what I'm going to call "frangible disks" on it; you've got beveled areas all over. In past government investigations there's been at least 2 locations identified as entry wounds 4 inches apart. Frankly, when you have a skull and you pressurize it hydraulically—and that's what a glycerin bullet does—one or more blown out beveled areas would not surprise me.

RM: I bought the glycerin at Walgreens for $2.69 and I drilled out a Glacier safety slug and filled it with glycerin.

JK: You made up something and you call it "glycerin bullet" and you shot it into this water bottle yesterday?

RM: That is correct.

JK: OK. There were no such thing as "glycerin bullets"—unjacketed glycerin bullets—in 1963, was there?

RM: There's no—they're not commercially sold today. You have to make them, they're just very easy to make.

JK: OK. And a professional assassin, you believe, would have used some ammunition that Oswald didn't use?

RM: Well, if Oswald used . . .

JK: Just—because the time is so short—what is your opinion?

RM: A professional would have used an explosive ammunition.

JK: And, and a professional would have used a different rifle than the Mannlicher, right?

RM: Unquestionably.

JK: And a professional would have had a way to get away from there instead of kind of wandering around and shooting a police officer, right?

RM: Undoubtedly.

JK: And a professional wouldn't have had a wife who 3 hours after the event said, "Yes, that's my husband's rifle," right?

RM: I wouldn't assume so.

JK: And a professional wouldn't have a wife who said, "Yes, as a matter of fact, he would sit on your porch practicing that bolt to get it right." You wouldn't have that kind of wife if you were a professional, would you?

RM: Not that you'd be currently married to, I don't think.

JK: And if . . .

[Laughter]

J: Alright, ladies and gentlemen.

JK: And a professional, a professional would not have, uh, tried to shoot another public figure 6 months earlier, would he?

RM: It would depend . . .

[Objection from the defense over JK's question]

J: Overruled.

RM: It would depend what line of business you were in.

J: Now, if you missed the earlier statement today, that says there's only going to be one humorous person in the courtroom and I nominated myself.

RM: I'm sorry.

J: OK.

JK: OK. You don't believe that President Kennedy was shot from in front then, do you? You're not one of the conspiracy theorists who think that the shot came from the front.

RM: I believe the only thing consistent with the reaction of the—if you just play the tape on the glycerin bullet, you see it drives the head straight back. So I believe he had to be shot toward the front to get the reaction and to see the explosion in the head.

JK: Was Mr. Oswald's rifle used that day to shoot President Kennedy, in your opinion, Dr. McCarthy?

RM: It certainly is consistent—the ballistics evidence is certainly consistent with a bullet coming from that rifle striking Kennedy or Connally because they were shot at different times, I can't tell you which.

JK: Are, are you aware sir that Neutron Activation tests have shown that the, that the bullet fired from Oswald's rifle left a residue in Governor Connally's wrist?

RM: I have looked over the neutron activation counts of the wrist fragments versus the bullets, yes.

JK: And are—and the answer is "Yes, I am aware that is what the neutron activation test shows"?

RM: I would concur in the analysis of the wrist fragments and the bullet.

JK: OK. And are you aware that same Dr. Guinn of the University of California doing the neutron activation test on fragments of a bullet—found fragments taken from President Kennedy's skull and fragments that are found in the car, that those all were fired from Oswald's rifle? Are you aware of that?

RM: That is a misstatement of the record. The two pieces found, as you just asked, in the skull, were in fact found in his scalp. And the record is very clear on that. They certainly match the other fragments in the car, and there undoubtedly were a number of loose fragments that matches. But none were in the President's skull, they were in his scalp.

JK: Could I have a picture of the paper bag with the rifle broken down below it, to ask Dr. McCarthy about? And while we're getting that up on the screen, let me ask you about fingerprints. The, somebody could easily wipe this rifle off and get the fingerprints off it, right?

RM: Not if—if they did not assemble it with gloves, no.

JK: OK. If they assembled it with gloves, then, there wouldn't be any fingerprints on it?

RM: That is correct.

JK: You're aware that in its broken down condition the FBI did find a palm print in a place where a person assembling the rifle would have left a palm print, and that that palm print was identified as Lee Harvey Oswald's. You're aware of that aren't you?

RM: I'm aware there was a palm print found and identified as you indicated. I would disagree you would put a palm there if you assembled the weapon normally.

JK: OK. It was part of the plot that day—in addition to killing Mr. Kennedy—to kill police officer Tippet?

RM: I'm sorry, I don't understand the question.

JK: Well, was—in your view; you've given opinions, you're an expert in assassinations, you've told what a smart assassin would do—I'm asking, was part of the plot to kill officer Tippet?

RM: It would certainly, I would predict, not be part of the plot of whatever person delivered the shot from the grassy knoll and it would seem to me that person was using professional grade ammunition. To my knowledge, that person has not been apprehended, either.

JK: And you're aware that the 4 cartridges found at the scene of the Tippet killing were fired from the pistol that Oswald had on him when he was arrested?

RM: I would have agreed to that without hesitation 30 minutes ago. If those bullets were reloaded, then all of the face imprints that were relied upon by the FBI are not—it's not a valid technique—because reloaded ammunition will have the imprint of a number of weapons.

JK: There's a stipulation in the case that those casings that were found were fired from Oswald's weapon. You agree—you're aware of that?

RM: And what—as long as we agree they weren't reloaded, there's no question that is correct.

JK: OK. How many autopsies have you performed?

RM: I'm not a doctor.

JK: OK. That's all, I don't have any further questions. Thank you very much, Dr.

J: Alright, Dr., thank you very much. You may step down.*

*This testimony, reprinted with permission, is taken from a mock trial, entitled "Trial of the Century: United States v. Lee Harvey Oswald." Copyright © 1992, American Bar Association. The opinions expressed by participants in the mock trial do not necessarily represent those of the American Bar Association or of the speakers in the mock presentation. The individuals quoted here are the following: Hon. Carol Corrigan, Alameda County Superior Court, Hayward, California; John W. Keker, Keker & Brockett, San Francisco, California; Martin Fackler, Ph.D., Failure Analysis Associates, Inc., Menlo Park, California; Evan R. Chesler, Cravath Swaine & Moore, New York, New York; Robert L. Piziali, Ph.D., Failure Analysis Associates, Inc., Menlo Park, California; Roger McCarthy, Ph.D., Failure Analysis Associates, Inc., Menlo Park, California.

All statecraft is founded on the
indifference of most of those
concerned. Otherwise, no
statecraft is possible.

—Disraeli

CHAPTER 8

LAWSUITS

The year 1992 saw a series of lawsuits, including suits among the researchers. Of most interest to me was that of Ralph Nader and Public Citizen, but I feared that all of these lawsuits, of such great potential importance, and straw cases were intended to eat away further at the monumental evidence some of us developed in the preceding years, and forever cover up the murder of John Kennedy. Worse was the fear that they would be decided politically, and the people who brought the suits could not know how they played into the hands of the cover-up artists.

Public Citizen's Lawsuit and the Autopsy Pictures

The bill that was passed into law in 1992 mandating the release of the files held by the National Archives for the Warren Commission, and other files of the House Assassinations Committee, the Rockefeller Commission, and Senator Church's Intelligence Committee, had some problems. First there was the review board set up and controlled by the Administration, second, material was excluded from the bill. The keys to the assassination were excluded from the law. Those keys were President Kennedy's autopsy photographs and X-rays.

This exclusion made futile the enormous effort of many well-meaning people who were led by so many pied pipers. No thinking person expected much of real value to turn up in the files. After all, most was held secret merely to protect living sources.

The problem of the autopsy pictures remained. A suit was almost filed in Federal District Court in Baltimore against the National Archives by two Baltimore City police officers and the wife of one, an attorney. This suit was similar to one finally filed by Ralph Nader's

Public Citizen in 1992 against the Archives on behalf of Mark Katz, whose Freedom of Information Act request for the pictures had failed. Katz was a former Los Angeles cop, free-lance book writer, and authority on Civil War photography. Theresa Amato, the lawyer for Public Citizen, was the attorney for the plaintiff.

The government's position always had been that the autopsy pictures and X-rays never belonged to or were in anything other than constructive possession of the government and were therefore subject to the Presidential Libraries Act governing deeds of gifts, and not subject to the Freedom of Information Act. The situation was contractual in nature, and the government respected those agreements.

The trouble was, that evidence thus became unavailable. Although Kennedy family lawyer Burke Marshall would occasionally allow outsiders to view the autopsy photographs, this was inconclusive, since studies could not be made of them. Prior to the establishment of the House Select Committee on Assassinations in the autumn of 1976, some five doctors had been allowed to see the pictures. When the Committee was set up, the pictures were taken to the Committee's offices and studied by a photographic panel, as well as by a panel of doctors interviewing Drs. Humes and Boswell, Some staffers saw this material, and some leaked out through staff to Robert Groden, who immediately sought to sell them to Jerry Hunt of the supermarket tabloid *National Enquirer,*[1] and another researcher who immediately upon receiving the pictures tried again to sell them to tabloids,[2] and Groden later did sell them to the *Globe.*[3] Legitimate attempts to point out inconsistencies and forgery in the pictures to the public failed until the publication of my first book on the subject.

Nevertheless, to this day there has been no adequate professional outside study made of the pictures due to the unavailability of good-copy prints.

History

The Kennedy family transferred the photographs, X-rays, and all other autopsy material in their possession to the National Archives by deed of gift dated October 29, 1966. That was the day Lieutenant Commander William Pitzer was found shot to death at the National Naval Medical Center in Bethesda, Maryland, the place where the President's autopsy was conducted.

The letter of transmittal for the deed of gift was written by Burke

Marshall for the Kennedy family to the administrator of General Services, Lawson B. Knott, Jr.

The deed of gift contained restrictions and stipulations, which included the right of the Kennedy family lawyer to allow outsiders to view the autopsy pictures and X-rays. None of those who saw the materials in the past thirty years cast into question their authenticity, but merely reported on what they saw.

Dr. Cyril Wecht did not question this material until many years after he saw it, and only when I involved him with my first book. Until that time, he remained unconvinced of forgery and did his best to dissuade me of it. In 1991 he changed course and allied himself with Tom Wilson, who claims forgery can be shown through computer studies. Wecht has helped Wilson file suit in Dallas in 1992 on this issue against Robert Blakey and David Belin.

The question that the two Baltimore City police officers and Mark Katz raised was whether the Kennedy family ever had ownership of these autopsy materials in the first place. Was all of this an incredibly intricate subterfuge to put access to the pictures by the public and researchers out of reach forever? Granted, there is a legitimate interest in protecting the feelings of the Kennedy family, but not at the expense of solving this crime.

Unfortunately, the intent of those who leaked or stole some of the autopsy pictures from the House Committee and the Archives was never to amplify inconsistencies and forgery. After the fact, I have been privy to the first attempts to sell the pictures through Jerry Hunt to the *National Enquirer* in 1978. This was strictly for commercial purposes. My attempt a year later to print them along with explanatory articles pointing out the forgery and the observations of the medical witnesses was frustrated, and false trails in the chain of possession were laid to me.[4] I pulled out of the situation for ten years while I prepared my first book on the case.

Marshall put it like this: "the family of the late President John F. Kennedy shares the concern of the government of the United States that the personal effects of the late President which were gathered as Evidence by the President's Commission on the Assassination of President Kennedy, as well as certain other materials relating to the assassination, should be deposited, safeguarded and preserved in the Archives of the United States as materials of historical importance. The family desires to prevent the undignified or sensational use of these materials (such as public display) or any other use which would tend in any way to dishonor the memory of the late President or cause unnecessary grief or suffering to the members of his family and those closely associated with him. We know the government respects these desires."[5]

The Suit

The complaint by Public Citizen on Katz's behalf was filed April 29, 1992. The suit was based on the concept that the autopsy photographs and X-rays were created by government personnel at the National Naval Medical Center at Bethesda, utilizing government property to create same, such as government film and cameras, and developed in a U.S. Navy film lab. Constructive possession of the film was maintained by the U.S. Secret Service for several years.

The argument was that this material could not be treated as presidential papers and documents normally are, but was part of a governmental criminal investigation and therefore was not private property to be deeded to the government by the family of the deceased president.

Government has a franchise on criminal investigation, and in consideration of the traditional and widespread use of medical examiners' offices to cover up illegal police murders, political and economic crimes, and other matters, it would seem that this is an issue that ought to be faced by legislatures. The *de facto* franchise on the criminal investigation business is intended to keep the public and the press out and, in the case of the murder of President Kennedy, has worked to cover up the case.

The defendant National Archives moved to dismiss the complaint. They based their motion on the simple argument that the government did not own the materials requested under the Freedom of Information Act and the suit at issue, and were therefore immune from any request to produce these materials by terms other than those in the deed of gift. They further maintained that the defendant's argument that the materials were created by the government and at the autopsy and were never the property of the Kennedy family was of no worth.

The tragedy here is that the key evidence we all need, such as the many films, photos, and the autopsy evidence, is out of reach. Even if we could legally get it, a lot is known to have been missing or stolen a long time ago.

The complaint maintains that "most if not all of the autopsy records are photographs taken by a U.S. Navy photographer and/or other federal agency personnel as part of their official duties at the autopsy of President Kennedy on November 22, 1963."[6] The lawyers argue that the autopsy records then were transferred to the FBI by the Navy. Actually, the Secret Service had them in between. "At some time thereafter, the autopsy records came into the possession of the Kennedy Estate. The transfer of possession of the autopsy records to the Kennedy Estate was in contravention of the statutory obligation of federal agencies to preserve and maintain federal records and of the procedures governing the disposal and alienation of agency records. . . . The autopsy records are and always have been 'agency records' subject to the Federal Records Acts, and have been since July 4, 1967, the effective date of the FOIA, subject to the FOIA. The autopsy records are not exempt from FOIA, and the Archives has not asserted any FOIA exemptions with respect to them. The National Archives has improperly withheld the autopsy records from plaintiff, and he is entitled to have access to them in accordance with the Freedom of Information Act."

The government tried to brush this off with a motion to dismiss the complaint. The motion was based on three claims by the government: (1) that the autopsy records are the personal records of the dead President; (2) that the autopsy records are presidential records of the Kennedy administration; and (3) that the autopsy records are not being improperly withheld because the records are the subject of a 1966 deed of gift allegedly transferring all right, title, and interest in the records from the Kennedy estate to the defendant.

The plaintiff argued against the motion to dismiss, saying the defendant failed to refute the only legally relevant point: "These records were created by agency personnel. Therefore, in no sense can these records be defined as personal records of a dead president, let alone the presidential records of his administration."[7]

The plaintiff's memorandum further states, "The defendant is improperly withholding these records because, to the extent that the Deed purports to 'donate' and thereby control access to these records, it is invalid and cannot supersede the government's title to them. Hence, plaintiff has a valid claim to access the autopsy records under the FOIA." This paper also states that there was no statute or other valid authority that would allow agency records, such as these, to have been transferred to private party in these circumstances.

Ralph Nader's Theresa Amato argued law. "Under the relevant Supreme Court test, the autopsy records are 'agency records.' " The Supreme Court set forth a two-part test to determine if autopsy records are "agency records." "First, an agency must 'either create or obtain' the requested materials 'as a prerequisite to its becoming an 'agency record' within the meaning of the FOIA."[8] "Second, the Agency must be in control of the requested materials at the time the FOIA request is made. By control we mean that the materials have come into the agency's possession in the legitimate conduct of its official duties."[9] The Court also said in that case that this was to mean that it included personal materials in an employee's possession.

Theresa Amato further pointed out that the deed purporting to transfer the autopsy records was not executed until more than a year after the Navy transferred these records to the National Archives, which already had "possession and control" of the materials. "At no time did these documents ever leave the possession and control of the defendant."[10] This was hotly disputed by the Archives, who insisted that the autopsy materials had been under the control of Evelyn Lincoln, President Kennedy's secretary, and of Robert Kennedy. Forget, in this tangled dispute, that he was the Attorney General of the United States at the time.

The government contended that the photographs are of a "personal nature" because they were taken during an "invasive medical examination." Plaintiff says, "The records were created for law enforcement purposes; they were government-generated medical evidence of a crime. The logical extension of the government's claim that these are 'personal' records is that any FBI photographs of any victim of any crime would be a personal record of the victim. Moreover, if defendant's attempt to characterize these materials as 'personal' rather than 'agency' records were plausible, then Exemption 6 in the FOIA would be completely superfluous because it creates an exemption for certain medical files which, under defendant's view, would be personal records anyway, and therefore not subject to the FOIA."[11] A footnote in the pleading says, "Because these records were created for law enforcement, not medical treatment, purposes, they are very different from the President's routine medical evaluations, conducted by agency personnel, which may be 'presidential' rather than 'agency' records."

The lawyers point out that the FBI sells color autopsy photos of Lee Harvey Oswald for $41.50, that they are agency records and subject to the FOIA.[12]

The government claimed that there was an understanding between it and the Kennedy family: Admiral Burkley's acceptance of the transfer of the records from the Navy to the Secret Service, the fact that the "photographs were turned over to the Kennedy family in 1965," and Senator Kennedy's authorization stated that the material was not to be released to anyone without the senator's written permission and approval. Of course, the plaintiff countered this with the following: "None of these 'events,' however, alters the original or continued agency status of the photographs. First, the government certainly knows that its records do not lose their agency record status on the basis of 'understandings' between it and private citizens. Federal law prohibits agencies from donating or destroying their records unless agency personnel comply with specific procedure. . . . The existence of one letter from a relative of the subject of the records, who had no legal authority to control the disposition of these records, does not convert them into personal records.''[13]

In addition, ''There is no support in the record . . . for its claim that the records were 'turned over' to the Kennedy family.''[14]

Claims that the autopsy records are presidential are easily dismissed with this definition in the law: ''Presidential records'' are ''documentary materials . . . created or received by the President . . . in the course of conducting activities which relate to or have an effect upon the carrying out of the constitutional, statutory, or other official or ceremonial duties of the President.''[15] And the FOIA applies to all agency records, whether they were created before or after the effective date of the FOIA.[16]

The defendant U.S. government then took the position in their reply that ''the test for determining whether materials are agency records subject to the FOIA, enunciated by the Supreme Court[17] that an agency must have either created or obtained the materials sought, 494 U.S. at 144, and the agency must be in control of the requested materials at the time the FOIA request is made. . . . However, while the autopsy photographs were created by Navy personnel during the autopsy of the President, *see* Def.'s Mem. at 8, the subsequent custody of these photographs demonstrates that they were appropriately treated as personal records of President Kennedy, and donated as historical materials to the United States. The donation was made pursuant to a Deed of Gift executed by the executors of President Kennedy's estate and accepted by the Administrator of General Services, acting on behalf of the United States. . . . Therefore, the Archives is not in 'control' of these personal records within the meaning of *Tax Analysts* and the autopsy photographs are not 'agency records' subject to the FOIA. . . . While Mrs. Lincoln was occupying a courtesy office at the National Archives at that time, she was not a government employee. *Id.* Thus, at this point, the Archives was not in 'control' of the autopsy photographs; Mrs. Lincoln (or more precisely, the estate of President Kennedy) was.''[18] They go on to argue that an example of their lack of control over the autopsy materials was the fact that they were stored in a trunk for which they did not have the key. The materials were inspected following their donation to the archives on October 31, 1966. ''The footlocker was locked, no key was delivered with it, and its contents were not divulged to officials of the National Archives and Records Service.''[19] Robert Kennedy's secretary, Angel Novello, delivered the key.

The basic argument put forward by the government is that "the Archives obtained these records through the Deed of Gift, and is bound to enforce the restrictions contained in the Deed, and the Archives does not 'control' the autopsy photographs within the meaning of the FOIA."[20]

How neatly things turned around to protect the conspirators, utilizing the dead President's brother and family as the unwitting participants in the cover-up.

The government maintained that the use of FOIA by the plaintiff was an effort to circumvent the Presidential Libraries Act "and the protections offered by it to prospective donors of historical material to the United States...."[21]

The defendant government of the United States argued—in a declaration attached to the motion to dismiss, written by Claudine Weiher, that "The photographs taken in connection with the autopsy of President Kennedy were treated as personal Presidential papers of the late President. A letter from Dr. George G. Burkley to Dr. John Nichols, dated September 1, 1966, states that the medical files of President Kennedy are being held in the same condition as his private papers. Records dealing with the private affairs of the President, as opposed to records dealing with the official constitutional or statutory duties, have always been treated as personal to the President by the Government. This is so even when the records have been created by government personnel as part of their official duties.

"Medical records of the Presidents have always been treated as personal Presidential papers, regardless of the fact that the creator of the record may have been a government doctor or the facility used may have been a government hospital. When President Johnson had gall bladder surgery at Bethesda Naval Hospital, his medical records were transferred to and retained by him as personal Presidential papers. The transfer of the autopsy photographs by the Navy doctors at Bethesda Naval Hospital to the Secret Service, as recounted in Exhibit 6, was consistent with the manner in which medical records and other personal papers of Presidents have traditionally been treated."

The government also maintains that nothing would be safe in the Archives. "The National Archives and Records Administration performs a valuable service for important figures and others who donate their papers and other historical materials to the United States, and for scholars who will eventually use these materials as basic sources for research. . . . The authority of the Archivist to accept such donations on behalf of the United States subject to conditions of limited access requested by the donor, and with which he concurs, ensures that during the period when a degree of sensitivity attaches to the historical materials, the rights of privacy of the donor and others are fully protected. . . . to violate these restrictions would destroy public confidence in the ability of the Federal government to honor its commitments to donors of papers, oral histories and other historical materials. If this confidence is destroyed, the validity of the whole concept of accepting donations of historical materials and the Presidential Library system will be placed in question and the future development of these and similar institutions will be imperiled. If public figures no longer feel assured that their interests will be protected when their papers and historical materials are deposited in public institutions, they will cease to place important and sensitive materials in such institutions such as the National Archives. The result will be the drying up of basic research resources, damaging the cause of education, culture and public enlightenment.''

The plaintiff replied with a memorandum of points and authorities in opposition to the defendant's motion for summary judgment.

So the battle was joined. Are the autopsy photographic records "agency records" as defined by the FOIA, or are they not, and merely personal records subject to a deed of gift or private contract with the government? The plaintiff maintains that "they are agency records—because they were created and obtained by a federal agency [and], which have never been properly disposed of by a federal agency.'' If so, Mr. Katz and the public must be given access to these records.

A hearing was held in Federal District Court for the District of Columbia on December 16, 1992, in Judge George H. Revercomb's court. The hearing seemed to me to be the sort of farce that telegraphed to all parties that the Judge intended to dismiss the case. He brought up the matter of the "President John F. Kennedy Assassinations Records Collection Act of 1992," and suggested that the newly passed law's exclusion to the autopsy records, on the basis of the deed of gift, was a new law that applied to the case, and they quite clearly did not intend to consider the legal issues as raised by Public Citizen in their briefs.

Revercomb said that since Congress had passed it and the President had signed it into law, it therefore applied to the case, period.

This judge seemed to me out of those wonderful Daumier lithographs in *Punch* from so long ago that lampooned lawyers and judges for the buffoons they too often can be. He was there to serve the government's position right or wrong, or at least he gave that impression by his manner. The tragedy of this case was that the *real* issues were not being discussed: Both sides stipulated that there were no issues of material fact, when it seemed to my untutored legal mind that they should have insisted on the issue of forgery. If it was not pertinent, make it pertinent.

But they weren't going to because the plaintiff, Mark Katz, seemed to have a frivolous motive. He wanted the autopsy pictures for a picture book showing the President's fatal trip to Texas from start to terrible finish.[22] Katz was the author of two previous books of photography: *Custer in Photographs*,[23] and *Witness to an Era: The Life and Photographs of Alexander Gardner*.[24]

Later, his Declaration filed with a number of other affidavits from several of us, explained his motives better: "I seek access to the autopsy records, both the X-rays and optical photographs, for a photoanalysis of, and in furtherance of my research and writing on, the assassination of President John F. Kennedy. Photoanalysis depends upon being able to locate the photographers or eyewitnesses to an event and to have them explain in great detail what transpired at the moment the photographs were taken. . . . without accurate copies of the X-rays and optical photographs at issue in this case, the photoanalysis would not be complete, and therefore the story could not be told. It is critically important to the integrity of the photoanalysis that I seek to publish that I am able to verify the authenticity of the photographs used in the Photoanalysis."[25] Katz hoped to obtain the negatives. Good luck!

Mark Katz believes there was a conspiracy in the assassination, but he apparently did not care a jot whether the pictures were forged, until we had our little talk after the first hearing. There are times when I believe that my constant effort with regard to making an issue of the forgeries bears fruit, for I gave them the powerful argument that began to seep into this suit through many holes, pressing it upon Katz and the lawyers of the Public Citizen Litigation Group.

The judge asked for the defendant United States to prepare a motion to convert their motion to dismiss into a motion for summary judgment. I was absolutely certain that was going to happen.

This was a straw case, I feared, establishing more case law that helped prevent the one big clue to the cover-up of the assassination from ever coming out. Katz said Public Citizen would take it to the U.S. Supreme Court, though. Public Citizen was not bringing this case on the real issues that needed to be heard, but instead promoting a picture history. Or so at seemed at first. Truth was, Amato was for real.

New Focus

In February 1993, Public Citizen's lawyer Theresa Amato collected affidavits from some of the principal players in the autopsy pictures drama, and filed a cross-motion for summary judgment. It seemed to me that the case was shifting in focus and had become far more fascinating, intense, and filled with hope. It was clear that the focus had shifted from the relatively simple issues outlined above as to whether a private family could control governmental agency records and whether the autopsy materials were in fact governmental records, to whether *criminal evidence* made by the government of any kind could be alienated by the government to a private family and denied the public (a suggestion I had made to the attorneys), to the issue of authenticity of the autopsy photographs and X-rays. When I first suggested to Amato that this should be part of her suit, it was rejected, but then became a new and major facet in the evolution of the case and her next pleading that was to be filed.

I wondered at what was going on, and saw so much of my research into the forgeries coming to fruition. Here, in a federal district court in Washington, D.C., were statement after statement suggesting that the pictures and X-rays might not be authentic. My affidavit and those whom I named for Public Citizen were taken and filed on February 16. Here a federal judge was repeatedly told that there might be something seriously wrong with the photographs and X-rays that the government claimed were those of President Kennedy. How would the law treat that? Was the Court bound by narrow interpretations of what issues it might entertain in a given lawsuit, or if other matters came of sufficient legal or constitutional importance, was the Court either at liberty or bound to look at them?

The plaintiff's memorandum of points and authorities in support of his cross-motion for summary judgment and in opposition to defendant's motion for summary judgment went in, and that is where the case began to turn. "Access to the government's medical evidence will permit the public to assess the authenticity of the autopsy records that have already been widely published, as well as those that are in the possession of the Archives."[26]

Amato, who is from Illinois and a graduate of Harvard, argued that the Assassinations Records Collection Act (ARCA) could not affect the outcome of the case. She said that the ARCA had "no bearing on this case because it does not purport to repeal any of the rights plaintiff had when this lawsuit was filed. The ARCA, passed by Congress in the wake of public outcry over the movie *JFK,* and signed into law on October 26, 1992, provides for the public disclosure of many of the records associated with the assassination. However, the ARCA specifically excludes the records at issue in this case by exempting them from the definition of the 'assassination record' subject to the provisions of the act. The language which exempts the autopsy records from the definition of 'Assassination record' reads as follows: 'Autopsy records donated by the Kennedy family to the National Archives pursuant to a deed of gift regulating access to those records, or copies and reproductions made from such records.' Thus the plain language of the ARCA says nothing about whether the records are agency records, personal records, or Presidential records."

Thus Amato argues that the language of the new disclosure act was not prescriptive and therefore descriptive—that is, meaning the new law did not implicitly repeal the FOIA with respect to the autopsy records.

The Archives and the U.S. Attorneys arguing for them claimed that the courts are "reluctant to permit access to records under the FOIA where the Congress has established an administrative procedure for processing and releasing records to the public. . . ."[27] This argument certainly seems to upset the whole purpose of the Freedom of Information Act.

At every step of the way in this case, the issues are underscored with philosophical questions going to the core of our society, political organization, and legal system. This is why I present so much of the technical argument in the case, in hopes the reader appreciates the issues and the brilliance of the plaintiff's attorney and her legal argument.

Amato explores several other tests that, as she argues, show that the intent of exclusion of the autopsy materials in the ARCA of 1992 was not an implicit repeal of the Freedom of Information Act authority to disclose records to the public. "When there are two acts [laws] upon the same subject, the rule is to give effect to both if possible. . . . The intention of the legislature to repeal 'must be clear and manifest.' "[28] "The language actually enacted by Congress demonstrates that Congress did not endorse the claim that the Deed supersedes any rights under the FOIA. . . . Rather, the ARCA explicitly provides the right of judicial review of the Archives claims under FOIA is preserved—without purporting to prejudge or dictate the outcome of such review."[29]

Amato then points out that the rule against construing statutes to effect an implied repeal has particular force with respect to the FOIA because Congress has provided that the exemptions stated in the act are "explicitly exclusive."[30]

The next part of this important pleading states, "These agency records must be disclosed because the public interest in disclosure outweighs any privacy interest at stake. When promulgating the FOIA, Congress established 'a general philosophy of full agency disclosure unless information is exempted under clearly delineated statutory language,' " and the whole issue of privacy in the suit comes up once again. "Plaintiff does not dispute that the records at issue here are 'similar files' or that the Kennedy family has a privacy interest in those files. The privacy interest of the family, however, is narrow in that it is limited to the interest in preventing public disclosure that would cause clearly unwarranted anguish or grief to family members. . . ."[31]

"There is no explanation of how disclosure of forensic X-rays would cause anguish, and no evidence offered to support such a claim." What we had here was a case of the designers of the cover-up leaving the Justice Department and the National Archives holding the bag thirty years later, trying to explain why they don't want to give up the X-rays and photographs when there is no good explanation they can give.

Undiscouraged, Amato then launched into a new set of arguments designed to undercut what remains of the intricate arguments for nondisclosure of the autopsy records: "Some of the X-rays have already been published *by the government,* apparently without any objection by the Kennedy family. . . ."[32] Dr. David W. Mantik, a radiologist, was asked to submit a declaration with this pleading, and he maintained that if he could have access, he would construct a three-dimensional computer model of the wounds and the metal shown in the X-rays, which might give us a lot more answers as to the trajectories of the shots. "These records are clinical in nature and do not reveal anything that could lead to an invasion of privacy,"[33] she says, referring to Dr. Mantik's attached declaration.

Amato argues that the X-rays cannot possibly cause anguish "Because these X-rays reveal no more than an osseous structure. With respect to the optical photographs, the privacy interests have been diminished by the passage of thirty years since the photographs were taken, the widespread exposure of these records through access already granted to government and nongovernmental investigators, and the worldwide publication of the records. Conversely, as the attached six affidavits set forth, there is an overwhelming public interest in the disclosure of these records. The records reflect the government's medical evidence of what has been called 'the crime of the century.' Access to the records will (1) allow the public to assess the government's conduct of the autopsy, (2) allow the public to examine the validity of the conclusions reached by the Warren Commission, and by the HSCA, (3) allow the public to attempt new and different analyses on the records that have never been performed by government-sponsored investigations, and (4) may, as more than one assassination scholar concludes, shed light on whether the government's medical evidence has been altered or forged."[34]

This was the turn in the case that I had hoped for, even though it might never become a serious issue in this particular suit, just as such suits almost never went to trial, but were decided as matters of law.

We turn to the issue of disclosure of the photographs. "Plaintiffs acknowledge that different considerations apply to the optical photographs. But there, the privacy interests have been diminished by prior publication and dissemination of the photographs. Moreover, there is no doubt that millions of people have already seen autopsy photographs in broadcasts or movies shown worldwide."[35] "Given that two different sets of these records have already been shown to mass audiences, published in tabloid journals, and made into comics and trading cards, the Archives' assertion that it is withholding the records under the FOIA to prevent 'sensational use' is unpersuasive. The Archives obviously cannot prevent such use because copies of the photographs are in the public domain. . . . 'Public nature of information may be a reason to conclude under all the circumstances of a given case, that the release of such information would not constitute a 'clearly unwarranted invasion of personal privacy.' The only purpose served by denying access is to prevent authentication and serious analysis that requires access to better copies of the records. Preventing the disclosure of these records only fosters the perception of governmental wrongdoing, 'cover-up' and scandal . . . the autopsy photographs are among the most significant and controversial records created by agency personnel in this century. Nonetheless, the Archives incredibly claims that there is only a 'minimal public interest' because 'whatever public interest might exist in overseeing agency action . . . through photoanalysis or other use of the autopsy photographs has already been adequately addressed through existing access provisions and access already provided to numerous panels and individuals under terms of the 1966 Deed of Gift. . . . In other words, the Archives is replacing its judgment for the judgment of the Congress, which passed FOIA in order to provide access to the public at large, not just a few handpicked individuals or government-endorsed commissions. The Archives' behavior is, of course, precisely the type of agency behavior the FOIA is designed to combat. ('Purpose of FOIA is to permit the public to decide *for itself* whether government action is proper . . .'; 'public oversight of government operations provides a public benefit' even if the requester's efforts 'overlap the government's in full or in part.') Thus, it is not for the Archives to tell the public whether information may be significant or to limit access because the Archives does not believe information to have any further purpose. Public interest is not limited to the analysis the government chooses to conduct, but extends to any form of analysis (including photoanalysis or three-dimensional reconstruction, *infra*) that will inform public understanding of governmental actions.

"Indeed, despite the passage of thirty years, the public interest in the assassination of President Kennedy remains intense and fuels on-going controversy and public speculation over the conduct of the government during the event and its investigation, including the conclusions of the Warren Commission and the House Select Committee on Assassinations. Contrary to the Archives' unsubstantiated assertion that access to the records by several governmental panels and other private researchers has adequately addressed legitimate public interest in these records, the Archives' effort to limit access to the records has instead fomented controversy and reinforced the perceptions that secrets are being kept from public scrutiny."[36]

The pleading notes that the Archives' position is refuted by two doctors who saw the autopsy photographs and X-rays, Dr. Cyril Wecht and Dr. Louis Kartsonis, who submitted declarations with the pleading that conclude that the public interest outweighs any privacy concerns and favors disclosure. "The records shed light on the validity of the autopsy report and the findings of the autopsy doctors."[37]

This pleading continues with a new and reinvigorated discussion of authenticity, which was not an issue in the case: "The records will shed light on the authenticity of the photographs that have been published to date and the condition of the Archives' set of photographs. Two sets of photographs of the autopsy are in the public domain (the 'Fox' and 'Groden' sets). The photographs differ in material respects, and there is an active debate concerning their authenticity."

And paraphrasing my own declaration filed with her pleading, Amato writes, "Dozens of doctors, nurses and autopsy assistants, including the medical photographer and the X-ray technician, have 'denounced' the publicly available autopsy records. (*See also* Livingstone Dec. Paragraph 11: 'Various assassination scholars, including myself, have raised serious questions about the authenticity of the publicly available autopsy materials.')[38]

"Moreover, the authenticity of the Archives' photographs—on which the conclusions in the HSCA report is in part based—is also a matter of public debate that may be further developed by permitting access to the records."

The pleading concludes with a long quote and exposition from my main research that revealed some of the problems with the pictures and X-rays and the wounds, and then points out that "The Department of Justice routinely releases under FOIA records of the autopsy of Lee Harvey Oswald, despite the fact that these records, like the autopsy records at issue here, include photocopies depicting twenty-seven photographs and two post-autopsy photographs of the body of the deceased. (They charge $41.50 for a set of autopsy slides of Oswald.) Thus the Department of Justice has concluded that the public interest in this autopsy (which is less controversial than the Kennedy autopsy) outweighs any privacy interest under exemption 6. The same conclusion must follow for the records at issue here. Indeed, the Archives' argument to the contrary represents an arbitrary distinction suggesting preferential treatment of the privacy interests of one family over another.''

For the foregoing reasons, Amato writes at the end of her pleading that ''summary judgment should be granted to the plaintiff because the autopsy records at issue are 'agency records' and the public interest in disclosure clearly outweighs the privacy interests at stake.''[39]

The other aspects of law and the issues argued in this pleading make it a quite brilliant piece of work, but it remains to be seen how well it will fare in the court, which has too often been stacked against justice.

The Body Exhumation Suit

A lawsuit that illuminates some of the dark corners in the research community was filed in 1992 by Joe West in Dallas to exhume Kennedy's body.[40] Joe West is the one time preacher and sometime private investigator who, along with Gary Shaw, had Charles Nicoletti and John Roselli on the Grassy Knoll firing at John F. Kennedy.

''The new information came mostly from an unidentified source, who provided Shaw and West with his direct conversations with persons whom he determined had taken an active role in the planning and the murder of President Kennedy. The source said that while incarcerated in an Arizona prison, he saved the life of a person he later found out was the son of Jake Guzik, a well-known mobster (often referred to as 'greasy-thumb Guzik'). After his release he was contacted by Guzik and went to work for him as an enforcer—that is, a strong-arm type and hit man. This was followed by similar employment for the Bonnano crime family. His work was so respected he was retained by 'the commission'—that is, the highest power clique in the Mafia.

''In the midseventies when the possibility of Mafia involvement in JFK's murder was being discussed, 'the commission' directed the source to find out who the participants in Kennedy's murder were, and to interrogate them. This led them to John Roselli, and eventually, Sam Giancana and Charles Nicoletti, an enforcer for Giancana. Roselli had to be tortured before he revealed the involvement of the other two, and additional information concerning JFK's assassination. . . . There came a point in time when CIA personnel, distraught over the gangsters' lack of success with the Castro death plots, and angry at JFK, told their hired murderers that they could keep the money for the Castro job if they would murder the president. . . . The gun which fired the head shot that snuffed out the life of the President . . . was fired by Nicoletti from a hiding place behind the picket fence, located on the 'grassy knoll.' Roselli told the source he patrolled the parking lot while Nicoletti did the shooting. Roselli then took the rifle and got away in a car. The other two shooters supposedly fired from buildings located behind the President. They were not named, but the source claims to know who they were. They are still alive.''[41]

This press release followed a presentation by West at the annual meeting of the National Association of Certified Legal Investigators held in Galveston, Texas. I put this forward before discussing West's suit because I find certain elements of this preposterous. It is plausible insofar as the conspirators needed the cooperation of highly placed people in Washington to control the autopsy and the cover-up. Theoretically, the CIA as an organization was in a position to do this, but certainly as an institution it did not do it. Certainly, low-level or even middle-level functionaries in the CIA could not have done all of that either, and they would not have done it without tremendous backing. The clue to the nature of the plot is in the policy changes that followed the assassination. Those were financial and in foreign policy. Kennedy could not have known—and if he did, agreed with—the plan to run up the national debt deliberately to put this nation into hock with banks. A war was needed to start the ball rolling for such a debt, and that was the Vietnam War. Kennedy was trying to free us from that.

The Mob did not kill Kennedy within this framework. The House actually found—after long study—that the Mob was not in a position to do all this, and it would not have been their nature.[42] To suppose that two such important people as Roselli and Giancana were participants in the killing and near the riflemen when it happened is preposterous. The fact that both men were killed shortly before testifying to the House Committee may be significant because they may have known something, but the significance of any information that comes from the Texas assassination research community is that it might be coming from a police operation (as with this Houston private detective, Joe West) connected to those implicated in aspects of the assassination. Certainly no Dallas police officer in or out of uniform would have been one of the shooters for fear of being recognized, but, unfortunately, the Dallas police were used—drafted into the plot after the fact, though some had foreknowledge.

There were plenty of boys around who sometimes killed someone for money. The big boys knew who to go to when they wanted someone killed. What we have here is one more fatiguing attempt to frame the Mafia for the assassination.

Joe West tried to relaunch his story in 1992, and the papers made this reference to him: "He has found a Mafia hit man who can shed new light on the assassination. . . . West and noted lawyer Don Ervin believe the president's murder was ordered by renegade elements of the CIA and executed by CIA operatives and members of the Chicago Mafia. . . . The assassination was executed by members of the Sam Giancana Mafia organization in Chicago and by two CIA operatives who worked for the spy agency after leaving the Naval Intelligence service, West says. A pivotal figure in explaining how the murder conspiracy unfolded is the former Mafia hit man that West and Ervin call 'Hugh.' They declined to reveal his full identity. If he is granted immunity, Hugh is willing to tell authorities that Jack Ruby, the Dallas nightclub owner who killed Oswald, ordered him to steal three rifles in Crane, Texas, that Ruby gave to Kennedy's assassins."[43] Previously we heard from Robert Morrow, another specialist in this field of information who claims he has First Hand Knowledge of the plot and who says he had been ordered to acquire several Mannlicher-Carcanos that were used in the assassination.[44]

Attorney Don Ervin—Joe West's partner—interestingly enough, represented convicted hit man Charles Harrelson, who was previously quoted as saying that he had been involved in the assassination of John Kennedy. Ervin also represented televangelist Jim Bakker, who was put away, too. Is Harrelson, who repudiated his confession, one of the above-mentioned hit men? He just might be. Harrelson certainly resembles one of the "tramps" arrested that day.

West believes that the story put forth by Geneva and Ricky White that Roscoe White was one of the gunmen on the Grassy Knoll. However, West played a role in exposing what he feels was fabrication of some of the evidence in the case with regard to one of Roscoe's alleged diaries, and three alleged CIA cables ordering him to kill Kennedy. Those are *prima facie* fabricated.

A big problem in dealing with anything coming out of Texas is credibility. It's all press releases and publicity; the law and criminal cases are just show biz. "West also says he interviewed the third surviving assassin in a meeting attended by Ricky White."[45] The *Houston Post* article goes on to say that West is keeping the name confidential but that "in her affidavit and tape-recorded statement, Geneva White Galle names the third gunman, a lifelong friend of her late husband's. Her husband and a Mafia hit man, she says, fired shots at Kennedy from behind a stockade fence atop the so-called Grassy Knoll while the third gunman fired from the County Records building adjacent to the Texas School Book Depository."

As we have seen, the third gunman is being confused with the second gunman, who was supposed to be Charles Nicoletti. We know from Harold Norman[46] that somebody was definitely firing on the floor over his head from the corresponding window in the Texas School Book Depository, so we have four gunmen, not counting the gunman who had to be firing from the manhole facing the car on the bridge to the right where Sheriff Bill Decker always believed there was a gunman. "The shots fired from the Texas School Book Depository were merely signals for the other gunmen to open fire, West says."[47] There may be some truth to that, since I now know from my December 1992 survey of Dealey Plaza that it was impossible to hit the car from the window during the time the first shots were fired. The shots would have gone through the floor of the car when it became possible to see the car from the window, and not through both victims.

West wrapped himself in the flag after hearing a speech by J. Gary Shaw, who said that the case may never be solved. (I wonder if Shaw has some foreknowledge of this, busy as he was representing the film rights of Ricky White.) West remarked, "I said if no one else has done it, I'm going to do it myself. I came straight back to Houston that night and put everything aside. . . . I was never in the service of this country. I've always felt I needed to give something back to the country. I know it may sound corny, but this is my way of saluting the flag."[48]

West said this shortly after telling the reporter that they had talked to associates of filmmaker Oliver Stone about using Hugh's story as part of the script for the movie *JFK*.[49] This is what it almost always gets down to in dealing with the Texans involved in this "research": film and book rights. In Dallas, they hype that business pretty well.

Quixotic to say the least, West entered court without a lawyer, but had some legal advice from a mysterious character in Houston. The medical issues seemed solid enough to argue that there was adequate reason for an exhumation. But West was shortly to die.

A little-known federal statute allows any local or state court or medical examiner to order the exhumation of a body from a national cemetery.[50] Just as the local authorities have criminal jurisdiction over any open federal base, so do local authorities have jurisdiction over bodies buried on federal land. This was the basis of West's suit, though his first attempt was thrown out of court in Houston. To get back into court, West had to state in his petition that "he is a Texas resident, and a credible person."

"This is an action to compel defendant [the Medical Examiner of Dallas County] to conduct an inquest into the death of President John F. Kennedy," the suit began. After some preliminary material, West listed witnesses who indicated that shots came from some other direction than the government cared to admit, and he listed some of the medical observations of the doctors at Parkland Hospital that indicated wounds that showed such shots came from in front.

West quoted a comment by the panel of medical experts for the House Assassinations Committee: "As noted earlier, the panel unanimously concludes that the autopsy was faulty for a number of important reasons, some of which contributed to the speculations and controversy concerning the medical evidence."[51]

West wrote in his petition, "Plaintiff insists that it is imperative that the one thing that can be done to settle the controversy about whether or not there was a conspiracy to kill the President—that is, exhumation and examination of the President's body—be done forthwith. If it is determined that a single gunman could have fired the shot or shots that killed the President, then the long-existing controversy that has divided this country and undermined the integrity of our government's institutions will be put to rest. If, on the other hand, exhumation and examination show that the President was shot and killed by more than one gunman, then adherence to the Warren Commission's conclusion can no longer excuse failure on the part of law enforcement, Federal and State, to identify by relentless investigation, and to punish, where possible, those responsible for this outrageous crime."[52]

The defendant, Medical Examiner Dr. Jeffrey Barnard, had a quick, single-sentence answer to that: "Denies each and every, all and singular, the allegations of Plaintiff's Original Petition, says that the same are not true in whole or in part, and demands strict proof thereof."[53]

On October 15, 1992, the defendant, the Dallas County Medical Examiner, filed a motion for summary judgment as a matter of law because "The office of Dallas County Medical Examiner was not created or effective until November 1, 1969, six (6) years after the death of President John F. Kennedy. There was, therefore, no duty imposed nor authority granted by statute to a Dallas County Medical Examiner to conduct inquests or order disinterments on November 22, 1963, since such office did not exist on that date." The defendant also claimed laches, or failure to act sooner on the part of the plaintiff Joe West, and that mandamus "will not issue to compel a public official to perform a discretionary act or an act involving the exercise of independent judgment such as the decision of a medical examiner to order disinterment of a body.

"Plaintiff Joe H. West does not have a justifiable interest in the subject matter of this litigation and may not maintain a petition for writ of mandamus." I'll let you have your own thoughts about that.

I could not but hope that this suit somehow succeeded, but I was sure all along that it would fail because of West's erratic track record and because the issue was really too germane. Exhuming the body might expose some awful truth that certain people would never want to surface.

Sad to say, Joe West, tilting at windmills, having done his best to expose the sort of fraud and fabricated evidence coming from the visible leaders of the research community in Dallas regarding Kennedy's death, died on February 12, 1993, of apparent heart trouble and difficulty during surgery.

But Texas law allowed his heirs to continue a lawsuit already in court, and his widow decided to go forward with it.

Thus his suit to exhume President Kennedy's body almost died with him. We can only hope that somebody didn't plan it that way, and give him his final rest.

The Tom Wilson Suit

Days after Tom Wilson's electric announcement at the 1991 convention of assassination researchers in Dallas that he was able to detect specific elements of forgery in the autopsy photographs he had seen in screened versions published in books, and see things with computer image processing of videotapes of the Zapruder film, I met with Wilson in Pittsburgh for a series of extended discussions.

I found Wilson to be a personable gentleman but somehow eccentric. We met in hotel lounges, airports, motel rooms, and at the home of Kathlee Fitzgerald. I thought there was something passing strange about the manner in which he was presenting his startling findings to the world. He was an engineer and former executive of maintenance with U.S. Steel who told us he held a number of patents for some cutting edge technologies.

"You are looking right now into the eye of the assassin of President Kennedy," he says. "You are looking at a mole on his cheek. I can tell you right now, his eyes are brown."[54]

He sees a bullet in the President's back, and metal in his head. He says he can see right inside Kennedy's head after the fatal shot. "Basic," he says. "Basic." He got all this from poor television video-copies of the film.

Robert Blakey called it garbage when questioned by a newspaper reporter. "You know the saying among computer people, 'garbage in, garbage out'? This is garbage."[55] Belin took the bait as well, saying, "It's a series of massive lies. The man is basically making an outrageous claim."[56]

The newspaper explained his process: "What he does, he said, is measure frequencies of light that bounce off a photograph or film strip. The light is measured on 250,000 solid-state charge-coupled devices using a 256 shade gray scale; the human eye can perceive only 30 shades of gray. Then his computer program develops a kind of layered picture, sometimes adding lifelike colors." It sure does. "Nothing is theory. Nothing is speculation," Wilson said.

Mark Potok, who wrote the article, talked to Professor Michael Bove of the Massachusetts Institute of Technology. He said, "Yes, some of these things can be done. But the point at which it starts getting to be a little bit less certain technology is when someone shows you a [blurry] picture and says I can identify all the cars, and worse, all the Fords. Fundamentally, all you've got to go with is what's on the film. Anything else you pull out of there, you're making assumptions about." Actually, what Wilson had to go on was what some of us previously described.

Potok writes that watching Wilson's video is like watching the movie *Fantastic Voyage,* where a miniaturized submarine crew enters the human body. Except in Wilson's case, zooming in on an autopsy photo of the President, you enter the hole in his throat where a tracheostomy was performed. "As you go down, Wilson points out what he says is the bullet hole and its configuration—a pattern he says proves the shot came from the front, meaning it could not have been fired by Oswald, who is supposed to have fired from above and behind.

"Looking at the president's brain by examining one spot in the Zapruder film shows that the shot also was fired from in front. Wilson also claimed to be able to pick out pieces of scalp and brain matter as it flies through the air in a backward arc. He says that part of the Zapruder film has been altered.

"Probing several autopsy photographs shows a shot in the lower left back and also shows that a picture of the rear of the president's head has been altered." Wilson claimed that he could prove that the face of Oswald on the backyard photos has been superimposed and that the white puff of smoke in the Moorman photo is just that. He says his computer program takes us through the halo of smoke "to show the gunman's eye, a mole on his cheek and a rifle's scope; a camera to the gunman's right, operated by another conspirator; and an adjacent puff of smoke, marking where another sniper fired a fifth of a second earlier, but missed. Wilson also claimed he can see the killer's eagle-shaped badge—indicating the assassin wore the uniform of a federal official— and the outline of his nameplate." Dear reader, do you believe this malarkey? Gary Mack (a.k.a. Larry Dunkel), taken to exploding the theories and embellishments of his peers, said all this was "like ink blot tests. Magic is a polite term." Not that Mark hadn't put forth plenty of his own magic, with the Moorman photograph, the Bronson film, and the alleged police acoustical tapes with alleged shots on them.

One big problem is Wilson's claim to have found the bullet exit wound in the back of the President's neck in some pictures. But there wasn't any exit there. The nurses who washed the body saw nothing there when they turned the body over.

The trouble with the Moorman photograph and the police officer/gunman that has been emerging over the years in the work of Gary Mack and others is that the man and those beside him would all have to be standing on the bumpers of cars for so much of their bodies to show over the top of the stockade fence in any photograph. There is no reason to stand on a bumper, since the fence is neck high and there is plenty of room for the average man to see over the top of it.

Unless there was a little boy in a cop outfit, and he had to stand on a bumper, maybe with his toy rifle, to see over the fence.

I found that Wilson was reluctant to be videotaped, although he allowed us to audiotape him. He didn't want any record made of the pretty pictures he had in his looseleaf binder.

I remonstrated with him about all this, and he told me that their plan was to sue someone and prove his case in court. Great plan, eh? Here's a couple of guys who set a trap for some unwitting victims and subject them to all the horrors of a lawsuit just to prove their point, if that be their true intent. This should never happen, one would think, but soon the likely couple of fools presented themselves in the persons of David Belin and Robert Blakey telephoned by a reporter from *The Dallas Times Herald* and who, opening their mouth and putting their foot in it—as they were wont to do—blurted out that Wilson was a fraud.[57]

It took Wilson another year to launch his suit,[58] and to my amazement, his lawyer asked *me* to prove his case. After our initial face-to-face discussions in early December 1992, Brad Kizzia wrote me to say, "I realize from what you told me that you have some concerns about

Mr. Wilson's technology, and what you perceive to be its lack of verification. However, because your efforts and those of Mr. Wilson's have reached the same results, that is, proving a conspiracy to assassinate JFK, and particularly the same conclusion regarding the fake autopsy photographs, I urge you to set aside your concerns for the time being and focus on assisting in proof of the fabrication of the autopsy and X-ray photographs. Thus, the evidence that you have developed, or otherwise are aware of, confirms Mr. Wilson's findings concerning the autopsy photographs and/or vice-versa.''[59]

So I was drafted. I did not want this, because I thought the whole thing, like the rest of these straw suits, was rigged, and no one was answering my questions as to just who was financing this monstrosity. I questioned Brad closely about it, and he wouldn't admit to it being either pro bono or on contingency. I was sure his Dallas law firm of some 170 lawyers (Strasburger & Price) would never agree to contingency or *pro bono* on such a case, and surely Wilson wasn't paying to take on David Belin and Robert Blakey and the whole Law School of Notre Dame.

Robert Blakey, with whom I have a tense relationship, told me that the suit was "frivolous."[60] Yeah. He doesn't believe the phony autopsy materials are phony, either. Everybody is at everybody else's throat in this business.

Scott Van Wynsberghe wrote that he has two words for the "inventor Tom Wilson of that image-processing system: peer review. If the system is so good, please, *please* have it judged by a competent laboratory or journal devoted to optical and/or photographic science. It is not good enough to place articles in books on forensic pathology edited by your collaborator, Cyril Wecht, who is no more a photographic specialist than he is a ballistics one. My fear is that this, too, is a balloon waiting to burst. I still cringe over the humiliation inflicted on our field when Jack White testified before the HSCA and uttered the immortal words 'What is "photogrammetically"?'[61] Don't say you haven't been warned.''[62]

Dr. Charles Crenshaw

On May 17, 1993, Dr. Charles Crenshaw filed suit for libel and slander against the American Medical Association for *The Journal of the American Medical Association* for defamation.[63] The suit alleged that the defendants published defamatory statements about the plaintiffs that were false. Additionally named as defendants in the suit were Dr.

George Lundberg, the editor of *JAMA; JAMA*'s writer David Breo; David Belin, the former Chief Counsel of the Warren Commission; *The Dallas Morning News;* and Lawrence Sutherland.

"Plaintiffs also maintain that the defamatory comments were done intentionally, maliciously and/or recklessly with conscious indifference to the rights of Plaintiffs, and with the knowledge and intent that the area of the damaging impact of their defamation would include Texas, Johnson County."

Attorney Bradley Kizzia, of Strasburger & Price, who filed this suit, also planned to show that the defendant *Dallas Morning News* "agreed to publish a rebuttal article tendered by or on behalf of Plaintiffs, which agreement was supported by valuable consideration, but that said Defendant breached that agreement. Such breach of contract also resulted in damages to Plaintiffs, for which Plaintiffs seek actual damages, plus attorney's fees."[64]

Kizzia and Strasburger & Price, a very large Texas law firm, also had filed suit against David Belin and Robert Blakey for allegedly libeling Tom Wilson.

Dr. Crenshaw deserved a lot better than what he got from the AMA for his courage.

CHAPTER 9

THE AUTOPSY PHOTOGRAPHS

The historicity of President Kennedy's autopsy pictures that leaked out to the public may be of vital importance in determining whether possible alteration by those who obtained these pictures is significant. As I played a role in publishing some of these materials in my previous books, I will try to tell the whole story here as best I can, based on the information at hand. Unfortunately, we don't know all the facts, and may never know them. I will start by saying that possession of these pictures is like holding a secret treasure from a tomb with a curse on it. The possibility exists that those who took this material came too close to the sacred fire and perhaps will be consumed. Whether those who obtained them performed a public service may be far outweighed by their abrogation of responsibility in that trust that devolved on them. Possessing and managing such a treasure trove—potentially of vast historical import—requires more than the personality and character of a simple thief or con man, though well versed in the case as such a pirate might be. History is full of thieves who stole from tombs and then set themselves up in front of the place and did business as an authority on the antiquities looted from within.

Mark Crouch and the Fox Pictures

Mark Crouch got in touch with me in 1990, attempting to get me to credit him for the use of "his" autopsy pictures (the "Fox set") in my first book on the case, *High Treason*. Crouch said that he had a copyright, and gave me the name of his lawyer, Richard Cooper, as the man having all the documents. Crouch, as he says in his "affidavit,"[1]

269

had received a number of the black-and-white autopsy photographs from James K. Fox in 1981.

In 1990, Crouch lived in New Castle, Delaware, and was part owner of a radio station in West Chester, Pennsylvania. This is close to Robert Groden's house in Boothwyn, Pennsylvania after Groden moved there from Hopelawn, New Jersey, where Groden lived during the House Assassinations Committee period. Crouch claims not to have met Groden or known where he lived until 1989, and Crouch told Richard Waybright that he did not want me to know that he knew Groden. Groden told Waybright not to tell me that he knew Crouch.

Previously, Crouch lived in Chestertown, on Maryland's Eastern Shore of the Delmarva Peninsula. He says that James K. Fox, a former Secret Service man who specialized in photography for that agency, had retired to Chestertown and ran a small convenience store known as Phil's Farm Market, near where Crouch managed a Radio Shack store. From 1979 to May 1980, Crouch often dropped in the convenience store to buy cigarettes and other items, and got to know Fox. "I seem to recall that I met Mr. Fox during that period but it was a very casual sort of thing."[2] Fox collected Hitler memorabilia and showed some of this to Crouch.

March 30, 1981, was the day John Hinckley shot President Ronald Reagan. Crouch had stopped in Fox's store and bakery, and they discussed the shooting, which led to Fox telling Crouch that he had been in the Secret Service, and he showed Crouch his autopsy photos. Crouch said that Fox showed him nine pictures.[3] But in his letter to Oliver Stone of March 27, 1991, Crouch wrote, "Mr. Fox revealed to me *ten* black-and-white photos." He also indicates that he was shown the photographs within a month of meeting Fox, but triggered by the attempted assassination of President Reagan at the end of that month.

Crouch said on the same page of his affidavit describing his obtaining possession of the autopsy pictures that Fox told him that Robert Bouck, his "boss," handed him a stack of negatives and said, "here . . . make a set of these for me and a set for yourself. They'll be history someday."[4] Bouck denied this story to Richard Waybright.[5] If it was true, he would have good reason to deny it. But David Lifton writes that Fox told him the same thing, except that it was Secret Service agent Roy Kellerman who told Fox to make the copies, not Bouck: "On three occasions, he (Fox) supervised their processing. According to Fox, shortly after the assassination, he was told by Secret Service agent Roy Kellerman: 'Here, make a set of these for yourself. They'll be history someday.' Fox showed me the pictures he had, and later I was able to obtain a set."[6] Crouch says he thinks he's right and Lifton is wrong because "I am sure I spoke to Jim Fox at least a hundred times about this, and Lifton spoke to him once."[7] Crouch adds, "Since Lifton was recording the conversation when he spoke to Fox, I guess that's what Fox said on the tape but it was simply because Lifton was talking to him late in the afternoon when he was more likely to get things mixed up which in fact he did that day when I introduced him to Lifton." Crouch makes the point that Fox was past seventy, unwell, and exhausted. Crouch has stated that he has tried many times to get Lifton to correct this historical inaccuracy, published in *Best Evidence,* but "he (Lifton) just shrugs."

Roy Kellerman, the Secret Service man who rode in the front seat of the fatal limousine, received the X-rays and photographs from the hospital at Bethesda after the autopsy was over, and took them to Secret Service headquarters.[8]

Crouch writes that Fox told him that "the pictures validated the Warren Commission 100 percent and how they would be history someday and prove all the conspiracy theorists wrong."[9] Crouch said that a few days later (no later than April 6, 1981) he was in Fox's store and his morning radio announcer, James Jones, came in and Fox "replayed the same routine for Jimmy." He saw the autopsy pictures. One wonders why Fox never showed this material to his son.[10]

Crouch writes that he then contacted David Lifton in April or May 1981 to tell him that the "pictures were outside the [National] Archives." Lifton soon traveled to see Crouch, and from then on the story becomes a bit murkier. Lifton had already published *Best Evidence,* maintaining that the body had been stolen and altered and, of course, would want to have a look at such photographs, which ultimately disproved his theory of body alteration. Lifton had already seen Robert Groden's color and black-and-white autopsy pictures in 1979, as he says in his book, without naming Groden. The pictures had been passed around Washington in 1963.

"When did Lifton first contact you?" "I'm pretty certain it was in May because it was only a few weeks at most before he came down to Chestertown to meet Mr. Fox."[11] He brought Lifton to Chestertown to look at the Fox material, and Lifton used the name "David Samuels." His cover story was that he had come to look at the Hitler memorabilia. "It was around the twenty-seventh of May 1981 when Lifton came." They went to Fox's store and "it was always the same little presentation, Hitler will, marriage certificate, limo pictures, then autopsy pictures."[12]

Crouch writes, "Now, remember, we were playing a ruse on this poor old man. He was simply talking to my friend David Samuels, the

World War II history buff and everything's flowing right along. Then Fox brings out the autopsy pictures and hands them, envelope and all, to Lifton. Lifton takes the pictures out of the envelope, flips them one-by-one onto the bakery table face up, reaches into his jacket and pulls out this microcasette recorder and begins dictating a running narrative description of each picture."[13] Lifton didn't seem real interested in the pictures. I remember him saying that there was really nothing new, that they basically resembled what was in the [National] Archives. There was some discussion about trying to talk Mr. Fox into sharing the pictures with us for history's sake. Lifton's position was that the pictures were important and if Fox could be persuaded to share them for history's sake, that would be good."[14] But "Lifton had been nonchalant about the pictures having any value. . . ."

But another conflict in this story appears with the statement that Fox "consented, in May of 1981, to let Lifton see the photos, he was hoping David could help put the spin on them that would help make them saleable."[15] This makes it sound like Fox *did* know who Lifton was— that he was an author capable of obtaining money for Fox.

Crouch explained that shortly thereafter, at the beginning of June, "Lifton began calling me and he seemed to become more interested in the pictures. At the same time, Mr. Fox's situation gets more desperate. . . . Fox is literally working himself to death. Somewhere in this period Fox decided to sell his store and take his losses. I recall telling this to Lifton and as I remember he started to worry that Fox would move back to Florida and the pictures would never become public. By the way, he was right about this because if Fox hadn't let me copy the pictures this is exactly what would have happened. . . . If Fox hadn't been able to sell the store in late 1981 [in Crouch's February 27, 1991, letter to Stone, Crouch states that Fox sold his store in 1983, not 1981], I'm certain he would have died within months. In fact it was a near disaster that sort of set the whole process in motion which allowed me to copy the pictures. . . . he's not totally against selling the pictures provided his identity can be protected and provided he's paid enough to bail him out of this situation with the store." There was then a gas explosion at the store and Fox was slightly injured and Lifton called Crouch shortly afterward. "When I told him what had just happened, he became very anxious and that's when I agreed that I would try to do whatever I could do to get Fox to release the pictures."[16] ". . . Lifton and I both figured the only way to get Fox any amount of money for the pictures was to sell them to a tabloid and at that time tabloids and tabloid journalism was still considered very, very seedy. Lifton made the point, though, that in this case, due to the situation with Fox likely to die or blow himself and the pictures up, that the ends would justify the means."[17]

"Did Lifton help you in your efforts to try and sell them to a tabloid?"

"He was real concerned that his name not come up in any of my discussions and this sort of pissed me off. He was pressing me with all these noble historic reasons why I should push Mr. Fox to sell the pictures to some rag paper but he didn't want his name dragged into it. To answer your questions, all David Lifton did was give me one contact name at *The National Enquirer*."[18] Did his family know about the pictures? "His wife, Edith, hadn't said much about the prospect of selling the pictures but after that incident with the ovens, she was 100 percent in favor of doing anything to get out of this situation with the store. Her and I had talked about it. . . . anyway, he agreed to let me broker his pictures, provided his identity was totally protected."[19] Crouch goes on to tell us that he wanted nothing for the pictures at that time, and was doing it as a favor. He would, of course, have to protect Fox, and take responsibility if there was any repercussion over publication of the pictures. Crouch went to see his lawyer in Chestertown, Dick Cooper, who told him that he could set up a legal transfer where Crouch would absorb the tax liability when the pictures were sold. "I was never to receive one penny more than the amount needed to pay taxes and cover the legal bill."[20]

They tried Larry Flint at *Hustler, The Washington Post,* and Dave Sussman at *The National Enquirer,* asking $55,000. The effort to show the pictures to the *Enquirer* ultimately fell through, but it was necessary for Crouch to make copies of the pictures to take them to the tabloid's people, and this is how copies began to metastasize. "This is when Mr. Fox and I decided we've got to make copies of the pictures to protect ourselves."[21] They shot the pictures on Crouch's dining room table, and a priest, Gary Fry, came over and saw the pictures, according to Crouch. I knew Gary Fry in Baltimore years before.

Crouch writes that the man from the *Enquirer,* Peter Judd, came to see the pictures at his radio station at 11:00 P.M. Crouch showed him the originals that Fox had given him for the evening, and then returned them to Fox the next day and drove to Denton, Maryland, to pick up the negatives and a set of prints his brother-in-law, Paul Fountain, had made of the pictures. Crouch kept the negatives and pictures at the radio station in case any other deals came up.

The interrogator in Crouch's affidavit then asks, "David Lifton has stated in recent months that you stole the pictures from Mr. Fox. He claims that you copied them without his consent when you had them. Why would he say this?''

"Well, David says that because he has a very selective memory. He says it because I once told him I'd done just that, that I'd copied the pictures without Mr. Fox's knowledge."[22]

"Why'd you lie ... or I guess why are you lying now? What's the story?"

"It'll all make a lot more sense if you let me talk about the *Enquirer* event first, then I'll explain. ... Several weeks go by and I don't hear anything from Sussman, when one day he calls and wants me to fly to Lantana, Florida, with the pictures. They make all the arrangements. It was toward the end of July. I flew down on a Thursday afternoon. There's a lot to this story which I'll come back to, but to make it short and sweet, they met with me for about fifteen minutes on Friday morning, then sent me packing. They didn't want the pictures at any price, and I'll come back to that. Mr. Fox wanted me to take the originals so I gave him the combination to the safe at WCTR in case something happened to me and the pictures. ..." Crouch describes his return to Chestertown and, "I was very paranoid about all this. I wanted to be done with it but when I met with the Foxes that night they encouraged me to keep trying. There were two things I did that I guess Mr. Fox didn't know. The first one was that I never made any more contacts to sell the pictures after the episode with the *Enquirer,* and the second was that I shared a set of the pictures with Lifton."[23] Crouch says that he returned the originals to Fox.

All this was, according to Crouch, in the summer of 1981. The *Enquirer* had already seen Groden's color pictures, something Crouch and Lifton did not know. Jerry Hunt, one of the tabloid's writers, had tried hard to place a story.[24] Why they shied away from the pictures at that time is not clear.

Picking up the story, Crouch writes, "He let me keep them because he figured I'd need them to show other prospects. Not long after this, in the fall, I believe, maybe winter, Mr. Fox sells the store and moves back to Florida. He came to see me at WCTR before he left. I asked him if he wanted the pictures back and he said no. He still held out some hope that I might make a deal for him with them. He gave me his address and phone number in Florida and I remember him saying he trusted me to do right by him if I sold the pictures. Jim Fox said to me, 'if nothing's happened with these things, then after I'm dead, you do what you think is right.' That was the last time I saw or spoke with Jim Fox."[25]

But what about Fox knowing that he copied the pictures? "Okay, in late 1981, Fox is back in Florida and I'm still talking to Lifton. I tell him I have a set of the pictures, but I'm honor bound not to share them until after Fox is dead. That's when Lifton starts in on me that I 'must' share them with him. His logic, and I couldn't argue with it, was that every day that went by more people who might be able to shed some light on this thing, die. He wanted a set of pictures so he could 'quietly' show them to the autopsy witnesses and the Dallas doctors."[26] (Author's note: I had already done this in 1979.)

"So you broke your word to Fox and sent Lifton a set?"

"That's right."

"This is when?"

"Late '81." Some of these dates are in conflict with prior statements made by Crouch. In his letter to Oliver Stone of February 27, 1991, Crouch says, ". . . in 1982, I shared a set of photos with him [Lifton]." Lifton, however, has stated that he received the Fox photos in 1983.[27] Then Lifton said he received them in 1982.[28]

"So why did you tell Lifton you'd copy the pictures without Mr. Fox's approval?"

"Let me sidetrack for just a minute to give you an example of how Lifton works. In December of 1992 he sent a really scurrilous fax to the president of Emerson College complaining about the lecture I gave there in November of 1992. In that fax he calls me a 'former Radio Shack salesman.' Now, this is true, I did work two years for Radio Shack, but I've been either a broadcast newsman or a manager of news people for twenty-one years. Lifton never mentions that. He uses one single fact, which although true, is not representative of the whole story. In our early conversations, Lifton was fully aware that Fox had allowed me to copy the pictures. There was never any secret between me and Lifton on that point."

"I'm waiting for the answer here." Crouch then digresses and tells the story of Lifton losing all that he made on his first book in bad investments. "There's this phone call and he starts out real depressed about his situation but then he gets mad at the situation and he says, 'I don't know why I don't just walk into *The Star* tomorrow and sell 'em the pictures.' This is when I panicked because Fox was a very serious man. He'd been ripped off once by a guy who stole from his store and there were many, many times he discussed how he could kill or have that guy killed. Now I had Lifton on the phone telling me he was going to do this and all I can see is Fox coming up the road from Florida to nail me. I tried telling David that it wasn't the right thing to do but he kept saying it was. I have to point out that I was also in pretty bad financial shape at this time, and David knew it. I had even turned down an offer of $10,000 for the pictures. So David and I go 'round and 'round on this and finally I say to him, 'you can't do that because Fox doesn't know I have the pictures and he'll kill both of us if you do!' "

"Did you ever correct this with Lifton?"

"Yes. In 1988, when we discussed the impending release of the photographs. It's another case where he's gone back and taken the exception, pulled it out of context, and made it the rule."

"Let me see if I've got this right. You told Lifton you'd stolen the pictures to prevent him from selling them to *The Star* and having Fox find out you'd shared a set with him while he was still alive?"

"Exactly."

"Well, it worked!"

"No, it did not!"

"What do you mean?"

"For seven years, I thought it had worked. In early 1991, David and I had a parting of the ways. During a very heated phone call he confesses that he did indeed try to sell the pictures to *The Star* in 1984."[29] In a letter of March 26, 1991, Lifton confessed to Crouch that he continued to attempt to sell the photos to *The Star* from 1985 to 1988.

Another point comes up in the Crouch affidavit: "Are there any other witnesses to the fact that Fox knew you had a set of the pictures?"

"No. As far as a clear and direct witness . . . someone who was privy to the conversations between me and Mr. Fox, no, there isn't. I mean, my wife knows and of course Dick Cooper knew and the people around the station knew, but no, there was never anyone aside from Mrs. Fox around when these things were discussed."

"So it's your word against Lifton's?"

"No, I think my word is supported by some rather clear and simple logic. Do you honestly believe this man would let me take the only set and fly off to Florida with them? He was old and sometimes a little senile, but he was not stupid."[30]

Crouch said that he turned down an offer of $10,000 for the pictures[31] and he himself got into serious financial trouble at the same time. He said that he had met with Jim Metenger of the *Enquirer,* who offered him the $10,000 in late July 1981, when they flew him down to Florida.[32] Crouch met with Dan Swartz as well, and says that the publisher, Gionoresso Pope, turned down the pictures.[33]

"What was Lifton's reaction to your adventure with the *Enquirer?*"

"Well, this is when I first find out that there's another set of photographs outside of the [National] Archives."

"The Groden set?"

"That's right. Now David never mentioned Groden. What he told me in July of 1981 was that there were some pictures 'stolen' from the House Select Committee on Assassinations in 1978 and the *Enquirer* must have thought I was trying to sell them the stolen HSCA photos. David referred to the other set as 'the jewels' as in the 'family jewels.' He meant that the Groden pictures were regarded in the assassination research community as the most prized possession. Looking back on what I know now, if Groden had the family jewels, I had the Hope Diamond."[34]

Crouch explains that Fox justified having the pictures when he says that Fox told him, "Look, what difference would it make if I had stolen them? . . . We burned a safe full of that shit."[35] Crouch implies on the same page that Metenger of the *Enquirer* indicated to him that the reason they did not buy them was a suspicion that they were stolen. "Metenger said that Pope [the publisher] had called someone in Washington and was told that 'if he published those pictures he'd lose every friend in Washington and somebody would go to jail.'"[36] Crouch says that his lawyer, Dick Cooper, told him that it was legal for him to try to sell the photos.

"Fox was saying that he didn't steal the pictures, but even if he had, he would have been taking something that the government was going to destroy. All he ever said about the burn party was that it occurred several days after he was allowed to copy the black-and-white pictures (around December 6, 1963). His 'boss' called him into the office where the Secret Service safe was located. Fox stated that they got two wastepaper baskets and filled them up with autopsy pictures and possibly X-rays from the safe." Was Fox telling the truth: Crouch says, "Yes, absolutely. Jim Fox may have confused people at times but he never made up anything that I can determine. I asked him why he remembered the burn party and his answer was so logical. He remembered the burn party because the very next day he was told to take some negatives of the autopsy pictures back to the Naval Photo Lab at Anacostia and make additional prints. . . . The boss comes to him one night and they burn a bunch of photos and the very next day he has to make more. I think the burn party was a cover-up. When you look at Robert Bouck's testimony to the House Select Committee it coincides almost perfectly with Fox's recollections.

"There's the first trip to Anacostia a week after the assassination to process the undeveloped film from the autopsy, there's the printing of black-and-whites by Fox in the Secret Service lab, then there's the second trip to Anacostia."[37]

As previously stated, Bouck denies that any material was ever burned.

But why would Mark Crouch make up this story—if it is false? "If the episode where Fox is sent to his lab to make those prints was not for him and his boss, then who? The Secret Service has the color pictures and negatives. Are these prints for the FBI? Then why give them black-and-whites? And what or who prompts the second processing run to Anacostia? Fox did indicate that the second processing run to Anacostia was for enlargements of the head."[38]

According to Crouch, Fox also told him that they had a Secret Service agent killed that day, but Fox knew nothing more about it.[39] In fact, there were Associated Press wire stories on the day of the assassination saying that a Secret Service man had been killed.

Crouch tells us that Fox's widow died not long after he died, and "apparently everything in that little brown folder just got lost in the shuffle," speaking of Fox's original autopsy photos, as well as copies of Hitler's marriage license and will, and a personally inscribed commemorative booklet to Fox from President Truman.[40] So cheaply is history treated. If such a packet existed, it ought to be with Fox's son.

Crouch thought that Fox did not have any major or inside knowledge of what might really have happened in the assassination.

Crouch, along with others, believes that the autopsy pictures have been altered. "Do you believe Jim Fox, the man who is on the record as processing these pictures, was involved in their alteration? In other words, was Jim Fox part of the cover-up?"

"I believe with all my heart, he was not. It just wouldn't make any sense."[41] Crouch's theory is that the pictures were altered during the week they ostensibly sat in the Secret Service safe in Washington, when it was "off the record." I'm inclined to agree.

Alternately, it is possible additional alterations were made in the succeeding two years or so, but some pictures had to be fabricated quickly to trick Earl Warren and the few others who had this material flashed at them in order to substantiate the single-assassin theory.

But first, Crouch: "When I talk about the soul searching that I went through before I allowed the pictures to be released I'm not talking about the actual release because I obviously couldn't have stopped David from releasing them after I'd given him a set in 1981. The issue was whether I wanted to marry myself to these photographs, which meant I'd forever be known as the man who released the JFK autopsy pictures. With Fox dead, I'd be the one who'd take the heat as much as David."[42]

Crouch states an issue of justice as his rationale: "My convictions told me that I couldn't honor the memory of what John Kennedy stood for when I believed that our own government deliberately lied about the truth concerning his murder. It was the same sort of hypocrisy. How could I say I respected and admired what Kennedy stood for in life which was truth and justice, but deny history the truth and justice of the autopsy pictures?"[43]

Crouch then tells the story in his affidavit of trying to retrieve his negatives from Lifton for a long period of time. It is this fact that he uses to indicate that Lifton could not have gone back to Fox and gotten a set directly, or he would not have given Crouch so much grief. Lifton also had access to Groden's pictures, but Groden would have held them on pain of death unless there was money involved.

Crouch closes with a statement on the amount of money the pictures brought him, which was about $7,000. He says, "I never wanted to establish myself in this case as an authority." He says that his book on the affair is mostly written but "I do not intend for it to ever be published . . . if I combined the story of the pictures with theory then it would give them an out. They like to find one mistake in a person's writings and use that to discredit the entire effort."[44] "If these pictures are lies, they're government lies," he says at the end of his statement, referring to the apparent effort of Dr. John Lattimer to discredit the autopsy pictures as we have published them.

There is a bit of a flaw in Crouch's story when he says in a newspaper account that Fox stipulated to him that he "could release them [the photos] to the critics for their research."[45] Researcher Kathlee Fitzgerald writes that this is different from Fox saying Crouch could *publish* the photos to the general public as he has done with Stone's *JFK,* and Lifton's *Best Evidence.* She also notes that "Crouch's directive from Fox concluded '. . . with the understanding that they would remain with me,'[46] which was something Crouch didn't do since he gave Lifton a set in 1982, "and until both his death and that of his wife . . . I followed this instruction to the letter."[47] Mark Crouch did not honor his agreement with a sick old man. He did not tell Fox the truth about who David Lifton really was. He chose to lie to Fox. Crouch has stated conflicting dates in his story about the Fox photos. Why?

David Lifton

The history of how David Lifton obtained the photographs is partially revealed in a letter that attempts to write someone else's book review for him: "Crouch is the person who provided David Lifton with prints of the autopsy photographs, which he had obtained from Secret Service official James Fox. Lifton later published these in the Carroll & Graf edition of *Best Evidence.*"[48] But in Lifton's letter to me on March 17, 1990, he says, "I came into possession of certain black-and-white prints of the autopsy photographs from Secret Service agent James K. Fox." Lifton has also publicly maintained this story at the Assassination Symposium (ASK) in Dallas.[49]

Lifton goes on in that letter to me to say that "Sometime in 1982, I showed these prints to Robert Groden, but did not want to provide him copies—one reason being that I wanted there to be a clear distinction between the 'Groden' collection (which apparently were obtained by a method which incurred legal liability), and the pictures I obtained, which pictures are protected under the Constitutional privilege relating to an author and his source." There is no such Constitutional amendment or privilege. Reporters go to jail for not revealing their sources, and Shield Laws in a few states protect information only.

The *Dallas Times Herald* reported that Lifton said he got the Fox set from Fox in 1983, which is a year later than we are led to believe in other documents.[50]

". . . In view of the possibility of a subsequent legal investigation which encompasses the JFK autopsy, and who got what pictures from where—it is absolutely *imperative* that there be a clear distinction between the autopsy photographs which I published and which were obtained directly from a Secret Service official with whom I met in 1981, and the autopsy photographs published in *High Treason;* photographs that are in the possession of Robert Groden, and which I saw at his home in the spring of 1979 *before* my book was even published. I will not stand idly by and watch the distinction blurred, as printing after printing appears which contains certain photographs which I provided, and which were legitimately obtained from a Secret Service official, in a context that implies that all autopsy photographs published in *High Treason* came from 'the Robert Groden collection.' Some did. But some did not. You know that, and I know that. . . ." I didn't know that at the time. It was the first I heard of it, and there were just too many conflicts in other aspects of all this to know whom to believe about anything. Groden had switched pictures on me.

Lifton endeavored to obtain the pictures from Crouch, and stated in the reprint of his book in 1988, "Fox showed me the pictures he had, and later I was able to obtain a set."[51] Crouch admits that he gave them to Lifton for study, and Lifton then tried to sell them to *The Star.*[52] I tell this story because in 1979 Lifton planted a story in the newspapers saying that I was trying to sell the autopsy photographs. Lifton thereby attempted to discredit me by linking me to a commercialization of the pictures. Then he turned around and tried to do the same thing himself. And according to Crouch, Lifton did this without the knowledge of the rightful owner.

Interestingly enough, at the same moment that Crouch was trying to hit me for the use of what he claimed were his photographs, David Lifton was trying to hit Robert Groden[53] for the use of *his* photographs (identical), which he had taken from Mark Crouch. Lifton wrote Groden, "You have consistently maintained that Harry did the actual writing . . . and, from what you say, he seems to have editorial control and final say regarding what goes into the book. Moreover, from what you have said, Harry is not only the actual writer (although I realize you are coauthor) he is in fact the publisher—which makes him very definitely responsible for what is in this book, as well as very legally liable.

"I assume that you do understand how important it is that the proper photo credit be given regarding these pictures," Lifton writes. "In fact, I'm sure you do understand that. Also, this is not a psychological problem, this is a legal problem. If proper credit is not given, there could be legal consequences. . . .

"I cannot stand idly by and watch photos published which were either obtained by photographing my book, *Best Evidence,* or which were handed directly to you by me, without any mention—when they are published—of where they came from."

Groden sued me three years later for the use of *his* photographs in my succeeding book, one of which (the Right-Superior-Profile) I did use. He admitted during the depositions in the suit that he used the Fox pictures in *High Treason,* implying that I knew that, which I certainly didn't. Once he said, "Harry, you know I could never allow those pictures to be used." He did allow the right superior profile to be used, while saving the rest to sell to the *Globe* for $50,000. Meanwhile, Crouch was trying to hit me for using his pictures. And why didn't Groden publish his color pictures in the book I gave him, *High Treason*? The two regularly back-doored each other—that is, one would sell the other's pictures to the *Globe,* to Gamma Liaison, to Ron Laytner, to this one and that one, or (as in my case) make me think that he was giving me the right to publish some of his pictures in exchange for hiring him as "coauthor" and then the other of the two in the team would come around. Meanwhile, they are both partners in the deal. Same thing with the Zapruder film: Groden acted as advertiser for the film, sold for money the use of his "enhancements," and then Henry Zapruder's lawyer would come around to collect for the same use.

Buyers and publisher beware: This is a flimflam. Both of my publishers were shaken down for payments, paying twice to two different people for the same material, in spite of the Fair Use doctrine.

One of the counts in the Groden suit was an accusation that I had libeled him by writing in my last book that he had switched the pictures. He then admitted that he had used Crouch's Fox pictures in my book during his court depositions, which he then asked to seal.[54] He claimed that I knew about it. If I had known about it, I would not have put up such a fight against Lifton and Crouch, who when the book came out, wanted credit. I bitterly resisted for two years the idea that someone else's pictures were in the book, until it was proved to me that he had tricked me and undertaken the contract as "coauthor" in bad faith.

Later we have Lifton telling another researcher that "Mark Crouch did not 'graciously allow' me to publish the pictures. Indeed, his permission was not needed, and therefore you will not see any permission acknowledged in the Carrol & Graf edition. Permission was not needed because Crouch does not own any copyright. No one can because these are public documents—the reason being the pictures were made with a government camera, and for a government purpose. For years, the Kennedy family had sole possession of these public documents. Then, two things became [sic] happened: One set leaked, somehow, to Groden; and another leaked, somehow, to Secret Service agent Fox. But neither of these persons owns a copyright, because of the nature of the under-lying materials."[55]

Again, "I am very sympathetic to the idea that the autopsy photographs in some important areas, may have been photographically altered—my big turning point on this coming in October 1988, and having little to do with Groden, who apparently can't distinguish between hypothesis and fact."[56]

Double standards here? Lifton pursued me trying to get me to acknowledge him as the owner and source of the pictures I used. At the same time, Lifton publicly denounced any remote possibility that the pictures were altered. When he saw that this was a fertile field, he began to change.

And Crouch lied when he told me that he had a copyright. He said that the former Attorney General of Maryland, Steve Sachs, and attorney Richard Cooper had taken care of the problems. But years later, Crouch eventually gave me a copy of a letter from the U.S. Copyright Office denying his request to copyright the pictures. He had not actually applied to register a claim of copyright until July 15, 1991, which was after we met and he had asked me to recognize his copyright. "Under the Copyright Law," the U.S. Copyright Office wrote him, "the person who owns copies of a work does not necessarily own the copyright in the work. When an author creates a work, the author of a work initially has the right to claim copyright in the work. The author may give all copies of the work to others and retain ownership of the copyright.

"With respect to your claim in these photographs, because you did not take the photographs, you are not the author. It is not clear who took the photographs, and apparently you do not have a written assignment of the copyright in the photographs from the author, or from a person who has obtained ownership of the copyright from the author. As a result, you cannot claim ownership of copyright in this work."[57] Crouch and Groden presumed that whoever had copies of the pictures could charge for their use. Unless it was finally determined that they were stolen government goods, they could claim exclusive ownership or copyright. For those who claimed to have "enhanced" the pictures and therefore tried to copyright them on that basis, that doesn't work either, because they have no assignment of copyright or legal right to do so or they don't own the copyright for the underlying material.

The copy of the above letter from the U.S. Copyright Office that Crouch gave me had no date. I note that Crouch applied for a copyright *after* we met in the circumstances of his telling me I had used his copyrighted pictures, and I should credit him. Lifton was, of course, trying for raw sales himself. I got the date.

For history's sake, Lifton documents in a letter to Crouch that he obtained Crouch's autopsy photographs he published and later made wide use of: "I've always said that the good fortune you had in crossing paths with Fox and then in acquiring the autopsy photographs was a very important turning point in this case. I will always remain grateful that you made the material available to me. My offer still stands to help in any way so you may obtain remuneration for journalism connected with the pictures, and not for 'raw' pictures sales."[58]

When did Crouch and Groden meet? In July 1989, according to a letter of David Lifton.[59] Crouch offered to drive Lifton and his film crew to Groden's house, where Lifton was going, after a visit with Crouch. Lifton says in the same letter that he was "both excited and delighted" when Crouch wrote him and told him about having the Fox pictures, and "pleased" that "you made them available in 1982; and pleased when you overnighted the negatives, in 1988, when push came to shove regarding publication." It is worth mentioning that Crouch begged for the return of the negatives. However, Lifton did not see fit to return them for two years.[60]

Groden and Crouch entered into a "mutual licensing arrangement," and Lifton pompously comments, "I was amazed to hear these words come out of your mouth—but held my tongue. What had happened to the Mark Crouch I thought I knew for eight years? As you know, the next thing that happened is that they (the Fox photos) were published all over the world—in a lurid context—and because of Groden's giving the pictures to Laytner.... I find this whole thing disgusting. When Groden next turned to Gamma Liaison and directly sold them a set of prints, too, I am surprised that your reaction was to stick your hand out and say: 'Hey, where's my cut?' How about taking the position that he had no right to do so? I realize that this is water under the bridge, but there's probably going to be many Gamma Liaison sales in the future, and you along with Robert Groden are now going to be in the position of having sold the autopsy photographs of JFK to a photo agency. Not exactly my cup of tea [he tried to sell them to *The Star*[61]]; but then you have to live with this sort of thing becoming a matter of public record. Apparently, Groden has no trouble with that; I thought you [Crouch] did. ... But what disturbs me the most is your readiness to get in bed with him. You can rationalize it all you want (that you wanted access to his color photographs, etc.). The fact is that when push came to shove, 'mutual licensing arrangements' is what was on your mind; that's the phrase I heard on the telephone; and you are now formally associated with the sale of President Kennedy's autopsy photographs to the Gamma Liaison photo agency. That's not the Mark Crouch I met in 1981.''[62]

Meanwhile, Lifton sought to obtain his own copy of the Zapruder film, and disabuse Groden of his exclusive franchise in a subtitle in the above letter: THE MOE WEITZMAN SITUATION: ''Because I thought you were a friend, I confided in you certain details of the operation of duplicating the Zapruder film. I was aghast when, several weeks ago, you telephone me and basically destroyed an entire Friday at the word processor by telling me that you knew things you couldn't tell me, because I'd be upset. Do you know how upsetting *that* is? Do you think a person does that to another person who is a close friend? Finally, after TWO HOURS on the phone, I finally extract information in the form of a dark warning: 'Check your relationship with Weitzman.' Thanks for half a loaf, Mark.'' Lifton checked it and found ''that the key negative had been returned to Groden—and you in fact already knew that, but just didn't bother telling me.

''Is the piecemeal disgorgement of vital information the way one friend treats another? Indeed, there is a more important question I have been asking myself ever since: Did in fact you kept [sic] a Chinese wall between your knowledge of my Zapruder operation, and Groden? Or was it breached, and is that in part responsible for my problems with Weitzman? I'll never know the true answer to this. Only you do.

If, in response to fragmentary information, you told all, that would be very serious.''[63]

Lifton ignores the fact that the Zapruder film had a rightful owner, Henry Zapruder, Abraham's son and heir.

Moe Weitzman is the alleged source of Robert Groden's original copy of the Zapruder film, purloined from *Life*, which provided Groden with a living for so many years.

"Let's turn to 'Livingstone,' " Lifton writes, "which has a number of subcategories. . . ." I won't burden you with the ferocious and false attack made here and in many other letters of Lifton to many people about me. He maintained this attack from 1979 to the present time. It has to do with competing ideas and research, and his response to an intellectual threat was character assassination. I hope in my presentation of the activities of others in this book I have at no time been guilty of the same serious mistake.

Lifton writes Crouch, "Finally, I suppose the most serious thing I am concerned about—in terms of there being a valid friendship between us—is the extent of your knowledge of Livingstone's calls to the BEST EVIDENCE witnesses." Lifton was furious when he learned that after years of effort, I had located his witnesses. He knew that I was sharing transcripts of them with others, and he was desperate to see them. "If your idea of friendship is to know all about such a destructive strategy, to read the transcripts, to say 'Gee Whiz,' and keep your mouth shut for weeks if not months—that's not mine."

What could Lifton possibly care if I talked to his witnesses years after he dealt with them? Why was he so worried about anyone finding them? I was the only one who did find any of them in an entire decade, and I sure discovered quickly why he didn't want anyone to talk with them.

Groden did not seem to have black-and-white autopsy pictures during most of the 1980s. We saw them in his possession in May 1979. He then reacquired some of them in about 1988 first from David Lifton, who got them from Mark Crouch, and then another set from Crouch. "Regarding Groden," Lifton writes, "he first got some of the autopsy photographs—specifically, the ones showing the back of the head—from me in the fall of 1988, when I was a consultant to KRON; and they were buying footage from him. At that point, both Pat Valentino and I argued with him that the photo of the back of the head showed no wound; whereas the Dox drawing did. To make this point, and so he could compare with the color, I sent him 'the back of the head' pictures. But I never knew what his so-called book was; and the first time I actually saw them published (by him) was when I saw the book (*High*

Treason, spring 1989). At that time, I demanded a proper photo credit—your name included—mainly for historical accuracy. He (Groden) kept stalling; that led to my agent's letter to his publisher . . . just an attempt to force him to honor his agreement with me."[64] Lifton notes in this letter that Groden kept other researchers away from key evidence in his possession, such as the 35 mm. copy of the Zapruder film he had. Lifton's dates on giving Groden the Fox set, not just the back of the head photos, is April 1990.[65] *High Treason* was published in 1989. Where did Groden get the black-and-whites he used? If they weren't the Fox set, what were they? Where did they come from?

This is important from the standpoint of my not realizing that the pictures in my book had been switched, and with one exception, were not Groden's color autopsy pictures in black-and-white.

And then Lifton writes, "Regarding Groden. I never intended to paint a 'saintly' picture of him and I deny that my opinion of him has ever really changed very much. I've always been aware what a mixed bag he is. The problem has always been his access to material he has stolen. . . . I definitely decided, early on, not to tell you about Groden; because as far as I was concerned, he was just someone with a rather superficial understanding of the case, who had apparently stolen certain evidence while on the staff of the House Committee. However, once he managed to get his screwy book published, I have never intended to deceive you about him. I had to work out a deal with him regarding our filmed interview."[66]

Mark Crouch wrote me, "Firstly, let me state that since I did not know you or Robert [Groden] prior to March 1989, and since I was not present during your discussions concerning the set-up and printing of the book, I cannot offer first-person testimony concerning the issue of switched pictures at the printer's. I must also respectfully add that it was you and not I who arrived at the conclusion that Robert must have switched pictures at the printer's. I must confess, though, that I likely drove you to that conclusion when I finally convinced you that all but one of the photographs published in *High Treason* came from the Fox black-and-whites and not from the Groden Color Collection.

"In March of 1989, I obtained a copy of *High Treason* and the autopsy photographs. I immediately obtained a copy of the book and noted that all photographs except for the right superior profile appeared identical to photographs in the Fox collection.

"I subsequently contacted David Lifton, who informed me that he had granted Robert permission to copy the photographs directly from the Carroll & Graf 1988 release of *Best Evidence*. Both David and Robert acknowledged that this was done. It was also clearly stated to me by Lifton that his motivation was to gain Robert's favor in anticipation of a July 1989 filming by Lifton of Groden at Robert's home.

"There is and was no doubt in my mind that all but one of the photographs in *High Treason* came from *Best Evidence.* This fact is based on: (1) Numerous statements from David Lifton and Robert Groden confirming the fact. (2) The Fox photographs as printed in *Best Evidence* contain uniquely identifiable anomalies which are also apparent in *High Treason.* The photographs in *High Treason* have clearly undergone double screening, meaning they are reproductions of reproductions.

"As you recall, when you and I first began communicating in late 1989 and early 1990, the issue at hand revolved around Lifton's insistence on a photo credit in *High Treason.* My recollection and notes of the period indicate a great deal of confusion and conflict surrounding this issue and many discussions between the four of us, you, me, Robert and David. It is also very clear in my mind that everyone except you was in agreement on the photo credit. I was confused as to your motivation until January of 1991, when the issue of Ron Laytner's expurgation and use of the photographs from *High Treason* sparked several heated discussions between you and I. It was during one of those conversations you stated emphatically to me that all but one of the photographs in *High Treason* were from Groden's Color Collection and that the Fox F 1 (Stare of Death) was the only photo that was copied from *Best Evidence.*

"You recounted to me on several occasions your rendezvous with Robert at a restaurant and the ensuing trip to the printer in Hanover. You have stated repeatedly that on this occasion, which was for the purpose of laying out the photographs for the book Robert brought his collection of color pictures.

"At some point in late 1991, we came to a mutual understanding on this issue: You accepted—based on my arguments—that all but one of the pictures in *High Treason* was in fact from the Fox Collection as printed in *Best Evidence,* and I accepted your explanation that Groden had switched pictures at the printer's. My acceptance of the occurrence of a switch was based on the following:

(1) Your strong conviction that neither Lifton nor I had any right or credit to the photographs in *High Treason.* (2) Your statement concerning bizarre 'crescents' which are visible in the hairline in the Groden close-up of the back of the head but not in the corresponding Fox picture. It is my recollection that you claim to have made this observation at the printer's. Therefore the color Back-of-the-Head shot was

present that night. (3) The Right Superior Profile shot which is unique to the Groden collection was present that night.

"As I've stated to you on previous occasions, I cannot challenge your recollections of the events on the night in question, because I was not present. Since you are as firm in your recollections that Groden Color Photographs were brought to the printer's that night as I am that Fox black-and-whites eventually ended up in *High Treason,* then logic dictates the only explanation is the photographs were switched."[67]

New Autopsy Color "Stare of Death" Photograph

In 1993, Wavelength Video, of Burbank, California, issued a video dealing with a number of assassinations in history. The video put on the screen a color autopsy photograph that appears to be almost identical with the Fox "Stare of Death" (F 2) photograph. The origin of this photo is as yet unknown.

The Navy photographers at the autopsy utilized a tripod and could easily switch black-and-white with color film plates in the camera, so the fact that the pictures appear to have an identical point of view could mean nothing. It could also mean that the color picture is a colorized or tinted black-and-white photo, or even vice versa, that the black-and-white picture is made from the color picture.

Martin Shackelford, who spotted this new photo, writes, "The picture isn't taken from the same angle as the 'Fox Stare of Death' photo as it makes an excellent stereo pair with either of them. Examination of the stereo pair makes me even more certain than before that we see about half the circumference of the original bullet hole along the lower margin of the tracheostomy wound."[68]

There are some interesting points to make about this picture. It has no background—that is, the floor and walls are not showing. Kathlee Fitzgerald notes that "A very little of the tile can be seen. If this is a cropped F 2 (Fox 2), it's about right for the tile area to begin to be discernable."

There appears to be a cut on the President's throat on the right about an inch or so before the top.

There is something else that looks to me like a bullet hole about a third of an inch above and just to the right of the center point of the tracheostomy incision. Both of these apparent holes could be spots of blood, but, though smaller, they appear startlingly similar to an apparent bullet hole just visible on the right forehead/temple area of the same photograph.

In addition, the tracheostomy incision seems exaggerated in length along the left of the throat, though the left-hand end of it might be confused with hair and shadows at the base of the neck where it meets the chest. We know from the left profile picture that the incision is neat and clean in that same area, in apparent conflict with what we are looking at in this picture. Fitzgerald thinks that the appearance of the trach in this picture "is just picking up the curve of the trach edge so the real left side isn't hardly visible."

The eyes are not divergent in this photograph, which is true of the others that we have seen. I find that this conflicts with the greatly divergent right eye I saw in a Groden "Stare of Death" picture in 1979, which appears to be missing at this time. The autopsy reported the eyes to be divergent, a fact we see in none of the photographs today.

I note that the above-mentioned apparent bullet holes and cut on the throat are brushed over or otherwise burned out of the Fox pictures, and just barely visible. Fitzgerald notes that the alleged bullet holes "almost are as clear in my 8 × 10 F 2 as the color. . . ." However, she notes, "I'm not very sure that these are bullet holes, especially the one above the trach. . . ." I am not maintaining that these are bullet holes in this new picture, but they sure look that way. In addition, the writing on the towel under his head, at the top of F 1 and which is so visible in that (the Fox picture), is not visible at all in this new color picture, and in fact, the upper corner of the towel is cut off. Fitzgerald says that she cannot see the name of the hospital on her good copy of the F 2 photo, though, whereas it is clear on my F 1, which was given to me by Mark Crouch. Martin Shackelford comments that the color photo and F 2 are both more overexposed, washing out the detail in the towel, whereas F 1 is darker and brings out the lettering.[69]

The color quality is poor in this picture, either because of the print or the manner in which it was shot on video. It is of a predominantly sepia or amber tone.

Shackelford further comments as follows: "The photo isn't colorized black-and-white, but several generations away from the original color photo, possibly made from a print that has faded somewhat. The overexposure of the upper neck/lower face seems true of all the photos from this angle; darker printing from the negative would bring out more detail here.

"A tile pattern is faintly visible in the upper corners of the photo, though not enough to determine whether it is consistent with the pattern in the other photos. The close similarity of the photos in all respects argues strongly for them having been taken at the same place and time.

"The neck 'cut' seems to be a deeper crease in the neck, slightly shadowed, which in this photograph can be traced farther to the right than in the others.

"I don't see the marks on each side as bullet holes. For one thing, I note an apparent swelling around each, or drawing back, which seems more characteristic of a cut than a bullet wound: scalpel cuts? I wonder if these were cuts made by the nurses when they were cutting away the President's clothing in haste? The left side mark looks even less like a bullet hole in the left profile photo. Note also that the possible bullet hole in the temple area, which is farther from the camera, appears larger in size than the two neck marks.

"I think the appearance of the tracheostomy wound is the result of angle, as it is consistent with all the other photos, including the left profile.

"The towel has no lettering because it's very overexposed—looks like it glows. I think locating the Groden 'divergent eye' photo is crucial to helping determine whether there are two sets of autopsy photos in existence," Shackelford concludes.[70]

The new color photo had last been traced to someone in North Carolina. Another story concerning the autopsy pictures is in a letter of Mark Crouch, and this may be a clue to the origin of the new photograph. Crouch spoke to Richard Sullins over the phone from Burnsville, North Carolina: "Mr. Sullins wished to obtain a set of autopsy photos from me . . . when Mr. Sullins offered that he's seen some color autopsy photos a number of years ago. He stated that the photos were in the possession of Mr. Warren Graham of Charlotte." Graham is the author of *Deed of Horror*. Crouch talked to Graham, who told him that in 1979 "he was in communications with Mike Marsh. Marsh reportedly showed Graham two color autopsy photos. One of the pictures was a color version of the Stare of Death, and the other was a left lateral shot. Graham stated that Sullins was present at the meeting and perhaps thought the photos belonged to him. Graham stated that Marsh told him he had obtained the pictures from an unidentified Charlotte doctor who in turn stated that he obtained them from Dr. Cyril Wecht." Crouch checked with Groden, who "disputed the fact that Wecht could have color autopsy pictures. According to Groden, Wecht had no autopsy picture until he obtained a set from Josiah Thompson, who in turn had obtained them from KRON and Lifton."[71]

I am certain that I saw a color "Stare of Death" photo in Groden's possession in 1979. I never saw it again, and he claims never to have had it. "Groden has maintained that he does not have a 'Stare of Death,' first saying he simply didn't have that one.[72] The issue of whether

Groden has a 'Stare of Death' pix is relative to the issue of possible alteration in that one must give weight to such an allegation when taken in the context that if Groden (a) stole the pictures and (b) possibly destroyed the pictures, then would he have had any reservations about (c) altering the pictures? The evidence that Groden. . . . at some point in 1979 has a Stare of Death picture is: Livingstone claims to have seen one, with 'Property of National Archives' stamped on the back. This point is reinforced not only by Livingstone's recollections, but his confusion as to the origin of the autopsy photos published in his own book, *High Treason*. Livingstone is confused as to why Groden needed pictures from Lifton in the first place. He assumed that the Fox photos were used by Groden simply for the sake of clarity and better black-and-white reproduction and until January of this year when I supplied him with a chain of possession flow chart, was still under the impression that Robert had virtually identical pictures . . . in color.'' Crouch then notes that Lifton wrote in the 1981 edition of his book that when he saw the autopsy pictures for the first time (Groden's) he mentions that he saw '' 'Bethesda Naval Hospital' printed on a towel (p. 662). The actual wording is 'U.S. Naval Medical Center—Bethesda Maryland.' '' To Crouch's recollection ''all color photos shown me by Groden, this imprint can only be seen in the Fox 'Stare of Death' shot. Lifton asserts that he must have therefore seen a 'Stare of Death' picture in Groden's collection in 1979.''[73]

Crouch then notes that Lifton told him, upon seeing the Fox photos for the first time, that there was essentially no difference and that they were ''virtually identical'' to what was in the National Archives. ''I recall this as a great letdown, because I had hoped Fox's photos were unique in some way. Therefore it would seem likely that Lifton was not seeing a 'Stare of Death' picture for the first time on May 28, 1981.

''Groden claims he showed Dr. Perry 'A photo' from which Perry comments on the throat wound. The only photo currently in the Groden set which shows the throat wound is his right profile shot. And only a portion of the right side of the wound is visible. Since Perry would have likely been quick to spot the Dox drawing of the throat wound, then Groden must have been showing him a 'Stare of Death' shot.''

''Since one must assume that Groden had control over the event of obtaining the photos . . . in other words, since he most likely either stole or copied the autopsy photos . . . then one would have to assume that he'd make a copy of the color 'Stare of Death' because otherwise he possesses no photograph that clearly shows the throat wound . . . one of the most vital artifacts in the case, and the photo most easily recognizable as JFK.''[74]

But it appears that Groden no longer possessed a "Stare of Death" picture, unless it turns up in his new picture book. He told Crouch and others that he had no such picture, and told me that I had imagined it. "Lifton's recollections of a 1983 meeting when he showed Groden the Fox photos and compared them with the color pictures. Lifton vividly recalls Groden's envy of the 'Stare of Death' picture. According to Lifton, this envy was so pronounced that he (Lifton) was afraid to leave the room for fear that Groden would somehow copy or steal this picture. Groden's zest for collecting evidence coupled with his numerous lamentations about Lifton not making good on a promise of sharing a complete set of the Fox photos, prior to April 1990, would seem to indicate he no longer had a 'Stare of Death' picture and desperately wanted an unscreened copy of same. Therefore one must believe that Groden had a 'Stare of Death' picture in 1979, but no longer had one by 1983.

"Groden might have accidentally destroyed the picture during duplication, lost it, sold it, or had it stolen. Or he has lied all along about not having that particular picture, for some reason."

The Inventory

The inventory indicates that there are five additional black-and-white photographs and two missing color pictures in the National Archives, that were accounted for when the materials were transferred to the Archives.

Obtaining the Autopsy Pictures

Groden told many researchers that he was left alone with the autopsy photographs for a while when he was allowed to examine them by the House Committee. His wife, Christine, brought him his lunch in a brown paper bag, and inside was a Minox camera, which he used to photograph the autopsy pictures.

Jane Downey was in charge of guarding Groden and the pictures while he observed them.[75] Downey, a Washington lawyer, denies that he was ever left alone for a moment with the pictures. In addition, there was supposed to have been an FBI guard present.

Groden told another story to Mark Crouch, saying that he and his wife, Chris, were "Asked by Blakey to do some late night work on the photos. Blakey opens the safe and Robert is to work, under the watchful eye of a guard. This arrangement was made prior to a dinner break, so Robert coordinated the scheme with Chris. Robert goes to Blakey's office with Blakey and guard ... Blakey opens safe and instructs guard to stay with Robert while photo work is being done. ... Blakey leaves. Chris is stationed outside. She waits and watches for Blakey to depart and comes to Blakey's office with brown bag dinner for Robert. She gives Robert the bag, then departs, but returns shortly thereafter with story of 'some strange man watching her in the hallway or lobby.' She leaves her purse in the office while guard accompanies her to see about this mysterious man. In her purse is a small camera. Robert told David [Lifton] the reason the photos's [sic] are a bit fuzzy [is] because 'I'm shaking and I'm about to pee my pants.' Robert makes his snapshots and places camera back in Chris's purse. She returns with guard and casually picks up her purse and departs and Robert now has autopsy photos. Since Robert, according to Lifton, used a similar M.O. to get the Zapruder film, this scenario seems reasonable.''[76] (See the chapter on Robert Groden for his own sworn testimony as to how he obtained the autopsy pictures.)

I find these explanations a problem because I am quite certain that the pictures I saw in his house in 1979 in Hopelawn, New Jersey, along with Steve Parks of the *Baltimore Sun,* had stamped on the back of them, "Property of the National Archives." This to me indicated that someone at the House Committee simply gave him these.

Groden told us in his deposition on March 15–16, 1993, in New York, that he was allowed to copy them by Michael Goldsmith, who was in charge of photographic and film evidence of the House Committee. Goldsmith flatly denies this.[77] It is possible that someone on the staff of the House Committee may have let him copy the photos, "thinking he would make them available to the research community, and unaware that he would keep them to himself for such a long time," Martin Shackelford writes.[78]

Much of what Groden removed was received for the first time by the Committee from other witnesses. "He stole everything we had," numerous staff members of the House Committee told me often. Many there said it. Groden found a publisher for hundreds of his pictures, scheduled for release in the fall of 1993.

In 1979, after Steve Parks and I observed the photographs for the first time, Steve sent me to Dallas to show copies of the Dox tracings of them to the Dallas doctors. This resulted in a stunning series of interviews wherein every doctor said that the pictures showing the back of the head were grossly fake, in that they insisted that there had been no scalp and no bone on the back of the head and that there was no such flap as appears now in the photograph.

The *Sun* would not publish this, as I did not work for them, and the findings were immediately suppressed for the time being by the editors, through no fault of Steve's. I then sought to publish an article with this startling news, but this struck out. Groden suggested that I provide them with the actual pictures, so I offered the pictures to go with an article, not asking money for the article, though Groden, of course, wanted to be paid for "his" pictures. Nobody would even take a chance and look at the pictures. Groden was good at using people and then fingering them.

Groden informed David Lifton of the above and soon there was an article in the news saying I was "trying to sell the autopsy pictures." I was horrified and heartsick. I called the papers and the story was largely retracted the next day.

I sought only to present them in a dignified format and have never arranged for their publication in anything other than my books. Autopsy photographs are normally published everywhere in the world, just as we see photos of dead bodies every night on TV and in many major magazines in the United States. We had the Vietnam War on prime time TV every night for dinner for years.

That is the extent of my involvement with the alleged autopsy pictures of President Kennedy, which I have believed for more than a decade are largely fake.

Conclusion

Few have enough honesty simply to state, "I stole it." But some have the audacity to go for squatter's rights, as has Robert Groden. As I heard Groden say across the table from me during his deposition in his lawsuit for *copyright violation* against my publisher and myself, he asserted "proprietary rights" on the pictures. Some children are taught that possession is nine tenths of the law. It's amazing how many ordinary citizens too often have quaint notions of the law, and their sense of justice is often greatly offended when they find out the law is the opposite of what they'd like it to be. Both he and Crouch now claim a proprietary interest. Crouch claims the alleged James K. Fox set of pictures. Fox's son denies that his father ever had such pictures.[79]

It was not enough for Groden apparently to alter ("enhance") photographic records himself, as he implied in his deposition, but he claimed to own them. He claimed stolen government property, or property in the possession and trust of the government, as his own, and believes that by altering them he can assert a copyright claim regardless of the issue of ownership of the underlying material. This, of course, is ridiculous, and puts us in the position of being shown evidence that was altered.

The questions then become: What did he alter? How much? To my way of thinking, any change at all is serious.

People tend to justify and rationalize their actions after the fact. Good intentions pave the road to hell. The necessity for the possessors to take responsibility and maintain order over usage was contradicted by human nature: greed and need. Once the pictures had leaked out, there was no stopping their replication.

We have to guess at the alteration of the autopsy pictures by Groden. It is observable that his color pictures have no background to speak of. One cannot see the floor or the walls or almost anything other than the body. Simulated (by tinting) bright red blood added on to the pictures he published in the *Globe* to enhance them.[80] I personally observed other changes, which are detailed in my last book.[81] In addition, some of the pictures are simply at wide variance with what we saw in 1979. At that time, he had differing versions of a large defect in the side of the head, one showing the brain inside, the other not, and differing versions of the back of the same head picture. The pictures showing a large hole in the side of the head were with full profile, and a "Stare-Of-Death" picture, showing a widely divergent right eye, simply disappeared from his inventory. At the time, I thought they were paintings.

In general, though, his pictures appear to correspond with what is supposed to be in the National Archives as traced by Ida Dox for the House and as seen by those who studied them in the National Archives. Verification of this is published in the medical chapters in this book. As such, they are all false. The *Globe* denied adding red to the pictures.

Comments

One of my readers whose husband has undergone the major spinal fusion operation that John Kennedy suffered is insistent that "his scar made me very suspicious of the JFK autopsy photos. You very kindly sent along copies of Boswell's autopsy face sheet, which shows that a scar existed. . . . but my problem is with the photo. Even if there are no known photos of the lower back, I still maintain that a scar remaining from his surgery should be apparent, *even on* the back photo we *have* seen!"[82] Some say that the back scar would have been lower on the back than the photo can show, but not according to Dr. Boswell's drawing.

Researcher Scott Van Wynsberghe wrote me to ask how I can so easily dismiss the expert panel authentication of the autopsy photographs relied on so heavily by the House Assassinations Committee. That's easy. The authentication of all this material is ridiculous for the countless reasons outlined in this and my last two books. We cannot simply overlook the observations of the authentic witnesses in the case, and the intrinsic conflicts in the photos themselves. I have gone to vast lengths to prove just this point in answer to Scott's question, and I believe at this point it is conclusive.

Martin Shackelford wrote me, "As far as the integrity of the stereo views being maintained (as reported by the HSCA), we are expected to take this on faith, as to date researchers have not been granted access to the relevant photographs to evaluate such pairs; for the rear head photos in particular, this is crucial evidence."[83]

All the evidence that has gone through Robert Groden's hands appears to be tainted. He has admitted to "enhancing" each film and each photograph that has come to him. He then puts this out to the public without telling us that the picture or film frame has been refocused, eliminating some data from the picture. In the case of his color autopsy pictures, for the sake of asserting copyright or "proprietary rights," as he called it during his deposition in 1993, the background is missing, and what we see is darkness, among other changes.

The problem is, the public has not been told by Groden that what they are seeing has been changed in some way by him. Is the result sinister? Some say that making a film steadier has its good points, but I can't see that steadying the film can do much with this evidence other than detract from its evidentiary value. "A steadied version is invaluable for study purposes."[84] But I think nothing whatsoever should be changed in something so important as the President's death, unless we understand fully that it has been done and just what was done and can compare at all times the two versions. Since we can never know what he has done to each piece of evidence, it becomes confused, and ultimately discredits the very message that the photograph or film frame carried. In the case of the Zapruder film, Groden stated that he was giving his enhancements to Zapruder's lawyer, James Silverberg, and the questions that arise are: What are we seeing when researchers or the public is shown material received directly from Silverberg? Groden's altered pictures?

The problem there is that the version of the Zapruder film that Groden worked with for so many years was a terrible copy that was unclear and grainy. If he had been a serious researcher, he would have bought copies of each slide *Life* made for the National Archives from the individual frames of the film. That would have made up the best copy for study, and those frames cost only two to three dollars each, a cheap price for a much better copy of the evidence.

Lattimer claims in his article that "having examined these full-color photographs, I can say that they are far more shocking than the contrived latex dummies and allegedly genuine illustrations that are now appearing in certain 'entertainment' features."[85]

To repeat what was said in the chapter on *The Journal of the American Medical Association*'s articles (Chapter 3), Dr. Artwohl wrote the following: "The pictures in *High Treason 2* and in *Best Evidence* are undoubtedly the autopsy photos. They match the Dox tracings (which came out before any of the photos were published in these books); they match the conversations between Humes, Boswell, and the HSCA forensics panel; I believe one or two of the Dallas doctors HAVE stated the published photos are the same, and even Humes and Boswell said as much in their October 7, 1992, letter in *JAMA:* 'We continue to believe that no useful purpose would be served by widespread publication of the very unsightly head wounds and we lament the fact that this has already, to some extent, occurred.' "[86] If the published photos were not what is in the National Archives, the autopsy doctors would have said so in their letter to *JAMA*.

In addition, Dr. Wecht confirmed to me that what I had published was precisely what he had seen in the National Archives in 1972. This was confirmed to me by Dr. Dulany, Dr. McClelland, Dr. Peters, and Dr. Jenkins from Parkland. The doctors confirmed this on the television show *Nova* in 1988.

The historiography of the autopsy photos has now become a vital part of Americana and this case. With the possibility that certain people—in the research community—trained in photography, image creation, alteration, and composition, we must consider with great scrutiny not just the possibility that people close to or in the government tampered with the photos to cover up the case. The fact that the autopsy pictures have secretly been a football kicked about in this community with the most vicious fighting at times over their possession is still another story, here told for the first time. It is one more tragedy.

There is no significant bone
missing on the posterior part of
the head in these X-rays.

—Comment of a radiologist
viewing JFK's alleged
autopsy X-rays.

CHAPTER 10

THE X-RAYS

Documentation of Missing Frontal Bone

Counterarguments began to surface after the publication of my second book on the case in 1992 to try to explain away the apparently missing right forehead portion of the frontal bone extending into the face. Frontal bone loss is something that is not described in the autopsy report or by any witness. I made this discovery in 1978 and dealt with the issue in both of my previous books.[1]

Several papers on image enhancement studies that were published by the House Assassinations Committee document that the area on the skull is in fact missing on the X-rays. The problem was discussed by the autopsy pathologists with the panel of doctors who interviewed them in 1978, though it wasn't much of a discussion, and during the interview with Drs. Humes and Boswell, the following comment came up: "It's really hard to be sure, square this with the X-ray which shows so much bone lost in this right frontal area," Dr. Angel said.[2]

Dr. David Mantik reported in 1993 to me that he found significant differences in the AP view versus the lateral X-ray of the skull, and that he believed the two pictures were incompatible with each other.[3] He said that he would prepare a report on this subject. I first published my observations that the two pictures were incompatible in my previous book *High Treason 2*.

Nevertheless, a major effort got under way, beginning with *The Journal of the American Medical Association*'s attempt to overturn the strong challenge to the cover-up of the medical evidence that I and Dr. Charles Crenshaw had mounted. Leading the counterattack were Dr. Robert Artwohl (a part-time emergency-room surgeon), Dr. John Lattimer (an urologist),[4] and Jerry Organ (a researcher and, by profession, a graphic artist).[5] Organ took at face value an unusual interpretation of the X-rays put out by Dr. Artwohl on November 11, 1992, on Prodigy, a national computer network, and later repeated by Artwohl in the *JAMA* articles of March 1993.

Organ repeated some of the same erroneous language regarding the X-rays that Artwohl wrote in his *JAMA* article. Artwohl wrote that "The 'AP' view shot by Jerrol Custer is not a true AP view. The occipital area of the skull is not even visible on the 'AP' view as it was shot. It is obvious that McClelland does not realize the 'AP' film was not really a true front to back film, but it was shot at an upward angle so the TOP of the head that is missing projects through the face. Since bone is missing at the right top of the head the upper right third of the face has been over penetrated, thus it is much darker on the film. McClelland apparently doesn't know this and no one has told him."[6] This statement by a nonradiologist was then picked up by Jerry Organ in an article influencing many researchers. Interestingly, though, Artwohl hung Organ with this statement when Artwohl wrote that "The occipital area of the skull is not even visible on the 'AP' view as it was shot."[7] This is completely false.

Organ states that "of course, the 'missing' frontal bone is nothing more than normal luminosity best seen when the actual X-ray films are back-lit. The President's X-rays were cropped, and may have been purposely printed poorly by the HSCA out of deference to the family. Dr. McDonnel reported the frontal bone present (1 HSCA 205) and Dr. Wecht, who also examined the films, did not report anything so unusual (Jim Moore, *Conspiracy of One,* p. 109)." This statement, of course, like so much of what the apologists for the Warren Report have to say, is false. Wecht reported that "The exit point of the bullet or its larger fragments cannot be determined because of *the large loss of skull bone in the right parietal and frontal regions*"[8] (emphasis mine).

Still one more wild claim ends that section of his writing: "Critics who assert the frontal bone is 'missing' . . . have never published the President's antemortem lateral X-ray (1 HSCA 241). Could the reason be that it also conveys the false impression of 'missing' bone in the frontal region? Even Livingstone's normal X-rays (following p. 432 of *High Treason 2*) show the frontal bone white like the background and would likewise 'disappear' if printed negatively (black background) like the autopsy X-rays."[9]

This is false because, as I related in the chapter on *The Journal of the American Medical Association* in this book, radiologists point out the *chiseled* edge of a large defect in the right temporal-frontal area on the lateral X-ray and state that all that area is missing, and that it coincides with the area of the head that appears to be missing on the AP view. The two different X-rays views have to be read together.

I will repeat what Dr. Donald Siple, a chief radiologist, wrote me. "The so-called temporal thinning refers to the fact that the temporal area of the skull is thinner (usually) than the other areas, i.e., occipital, parietal, and therefore appears less dense, or more grey than the dense, compact bone which appears white. On a normal skull X-ray, this so-called temporal thinning is a *gradual* change, with a long transitional zone, rather than an abrupt transition from compact bone to black (i.e., air). Secondly, the cortex remains intact on all normal skull views.

"On the lateral view of President Kennedy's skull, the temporal bone near the skull base appears beveled as if a chisel had been applied, but not normal thinning, which is gradual. Finally, more than one view(s) (i.e., AP and lateral) are used to localize abnormalities. A large defect in front on lateral view has to be in front on AP view, either right, left, or midline—not shine through from occipital defects."[10]

Siple also felt that bone clippers had been used to remove the bone of the right forehead, evidenced by the line of small connected crescents above the nose in the center of the forehead, with the bulge of the crescent pointed left. He told me that there is no such anatomic structure and bone should not be missing there.

The forehead was not cut with bone clippers at the autopsy, and there is no record indicating any reason to do so. The bullet fragment behind the supraorbital ridge was lodged in the brain and was extracted from it. Indications that the bone was cut with nippers, and the chiseling Siple noted in the right temple area can mean that another skull was used, and the X-rays are fake. Bone could have been cut out of the right front face of another skull and the forward top of the head to make it look like what they were trying to show in the Zapruder film: a bullet from behind blowing out the upper right part of the face. If Kennedy's skull was cut up this way, there is no record of it, but it might explain the authentications of the X-rays at a later date. They would have had to reconstruct the top and rear of the skull to fill in all the bone that was missing on the posterior skull. The trouble with that is, they did not have all of the bone from Kennedy's head, and the X-rays—if a reconstruction of Kennedy's own skull—do not show corresponding vacant areas in the bone between the pieces.

The serious conflicts between the AP and the lateral views both with regard to the extent of the enormous forward exit defect on the right and the rear entry holes as shown in the X-rays and photos (and pointed out by Dr. Joseph Riley[11]) are not explained by the above supposition of a reconstructed head. It seems more likely to be a composite X-ray, as suggested by the man who took the real X-rays, Jerrol Custer.[12] Custer also remembers that the skull "was not damaged in that area. It was all further back."[13] "And there was no frontal damage at all."[14] Dr. John Ebersole, who interpreted the X-rays during the autopsy has stated, with regard to the lateral X-ray, "To me, it [the defect] seems too much forward." He also stated he remembers "seeing an intact forehead."[15]

Organ then takes issue with me about the exasperated Dr. Levine repeatedly telling me to look at the original X-rays, which, of course, nobody is ever going to allow *me*—a nondoctor—to do. It's a sort of cruel joke. I think Organ, if his connections are better than mine, ought to look at the actual X-rays.

Organ makes up everything in his above statement from his article: Dr. McDonnel says no such thing on page 205 of Volume 1 of the House Assassinations Committee books and, in fact, McDonnel writes as his very first finding upon viewing the X-rays that there is "a nearly complete loss of structure of the right frontal and parietal bone."[16]

In addition, the caption beneath a photograph of X-ray No. 1 (anterior-posterior) in the House Committee books reads that it shows "the occipital defect and adjacent missile fragment."[17] So here we have several major conflicts in the evidence joined. What sort of "defect" is meant? The large hole or the small entry? All we can possibly discern from this view (AP) is a large defect either front or back, unless we take it together with the lateral, and then know the defect is in the front. Some dispute that anyone can see a small bullet entry defect there. If it means that we are looking at the large defect in the occiput, then God is in his heaven and all's right with the world. That's where it's supposed to be.

This picture indicates that frontal bone is missing, and we know that for certain when we study it beside the lateral view, which shows no part of the occiput, top, or right rear side of the head missing. This same picture shows us a very large bullet fragment on the back of the head, which the caption points out, evidently hanging in midair, purportedly lodged in bone that the same sentence tells us is missing. They are implying that the missile fragment is *above* the large defect.

Some radiologists insist that there is neither an orbital ridge nor a right frontal sinus in the picture. *Part* of the ridge may be there, but even that is unlikely. A major problem with Organ's reasoning is in the following: "Naturally, where the frontal bone curves to flatten, it presents less density to the X-ray plane and registers luminous on the *film*—when printed on paper, it can seem to 'disappear.' " His error is in the fact that the right side of the face looks far different from the left. If what he says about penetration and density (which radiologists tell me does not apply to the issue we are discussing) is true, then the large defect is in the back of the head in the X-rays. It isn't true because the lateral X-rays show no significant bone loss whatsoever on the rear of the head, let alone anywhere else but in front. Lattimer's drawings corroborate that the frontal bone is in fact missing.[18]

The truth is, Lattimer is hoist by his own petard in this case while trying so desperately to defend the Warren Report and therefore the massive stretching of the autopsy results. Lattimer's drawings, if accurate, show conclusively that the autopsy doctors are mistaken, because the drawings show that there is no bone in the right front, and no bone missing anywhere behind the ears.

Organ doesn't dare have it in the back of the head because that could mean a shot from in front. So he later says it's on top, by changing the angle of projection.

Organ says that "What X-ray No. 1 reveals to me is damage to the upper *rear* of the skull, not the front which is luminous and visible only on film." But why is there no such defect on the rear of the lateral skull film? There is none that large whatsoever. Why can we see the frontal bone and orbit clearly on the left side? Certainly the left side of the head was not damaged or fractured to any extent. Why is there no X-ray of the back of the head? Or of the top? The answer is obvious.

Dr. David O. Davis describes the large defect, which he seems to get from these X-rays,[19] as roughly in the area described by the autopsy report and the Parkland witnesses. "There is an extensive, comminuted, open, explosive calvarial fracture which seems to radiate in various directions . . . from a central point which is located in the right parietal bone, 3 cm. from the midline and about 9 or 10 cm. from the external occipital protuberance. There is an absence of calvarium, beginning near the impact point and extending anteriorly to the coronal suture. . . ." The trouble with that is that it is not actually in the X-ray and, as Dr. Lattimer traced (or very accurately drew), *cannot* be in them because it is much too far back. Where Davis has the large defect ending as it goes toward the front of the head, the defect is only just beginning on the X-rays that Lattimer drew. In addition, the photographs of the body show no such large defect on the head in the area Lattimer describes.

Davis goes on to describe the frontal "fractures": "There is a significant fracture in the frontal region extended into the right orbit and frontal sinus. The fractures also extend, from the posterior impact point, into the occipital bone on both sides."[20] Did Davis intend to be describing the margin of the large defect and the *absence* of bone with his use of the term "fractures"?

Dr. David O. Davis: There seems to be a serious conflict with the X-rays shown to Dr. Davis which appear to show no bone in the back of the head, and nothing about the X-ray which was made public or interpreted by Dr. McDonnel.

Dr. Fred J. Hodges (examined the X-rays for the Rockefeller Commission on April 18, 1975 [President Gerald Ford Library]: "The X-rays ... are diagnostic of a gunshot wound ... producing a small hole of entry largely obscured on the X-ray by the more extensive havoc caused in the brain and anterior skull represented by extensive fractures, missing bone, disrupted soft tissues and gas within the cranial cavity ... finally a bursting forward of bony fragments and brain tissue in the frontal region, apparently adjacent to the coronal suture within the right frontal bone. The main portion of the bullet had thus left the skull." (p. 3)

The House Assassinations Committee reported that, "X-rays 4, 5 and 6 show a large piece of skull vault, clearly frontal bone with an apparent jagged line indicating coronal suture, about 7 to 8 cm long. . . . This large fragment appears to be the upper part of the frontal bone, extending more on the right than on the left, and leaving spaces both in front and to the right. . . . The two big loose fragments of skull vault, from upper frontal and parietal areas, more on the right than the left side, do not articulate with each other and leave three appreciable gaps unfilled." (7 HSCA 230)

As for the authentication offered by the House Committee's experts on these X-rays as being those of John Kennedy, I repeat Organ's characterization of my dismissal of them, which is to say that those alleged authentications are absurd in view of the massive defects already apparent in the conflict of the photographs with the autopsy report itself, as well as the conflict of each X-ray with one another, with the photographs, and the autopsy report, and with the scientific observations of many witnesses. It's absurd.

In other words, we already know that the autopsy doctors fabricated several key aspects of their report. The X-rays cannot be (except perhaps for part of them if they are composites, which seems likely) of John Kennedy for the simple reason that the wounds have all moved drastically from where they were placed in the autopsy report. The doctors didn't make a mistake. They didn't make a mistake on some of these things because they are corroborated by many people, and therefore the X-rays are wrong.

Organ implies that the cropping of the X-rays by the House Committee may explain away what I say is missing, though there is no connection. The jaw is cropped off so that we cannot identify Kennedy's teeth ourselves (in case there is someone out there with his own dental X-rays of Kennedy's mouth), and the very end of the back of the head, which includes the occipital protuberance, is cropped, for obvious reasons. That is where the autopsy doctors claimed Kennedy was hit with an entering bullet.

Organ then speculates that the X-rays "may have been printed poorly" out of deference to the Kennedy family. Many have often commented that the printing was as good as can be done and certainly does not conflict with the reports of those who have seen the actual X-rays. They show the same thing. Lattimer's tracings of the actual extant AP X-rays, published in 1972, demonstrate indisputably that the frontal bone is missing at least as far as midorbit, including all of the right forehead.

Organ then claims that the missing frontal bone is nothing more than "normal luminosity which is best seen when the actual X-ray films are back-lit." I never said a word about this issue until 1979, when I had a chief radiologist and his colleagues, sitting in the radiology office of a major hospital, read photographic copies of the X-rays for me, confirming what I thought I was seeing. Luminosity has nothing to do with it when we already know from Lattimer, Wecht, and all those who reported on the X-rays to the House Committee that the frontal bone is missing.

"HSCA consultants who actually reviewed the original radiographs, confirm the skull wound locations as seen in the autopsy photographs and Zapruder film, and described in the autopsy report,"[21] says Organ. Nonsense. *Some* HSCA consultants seemed to confirm only the alleged authenticity of the X-rays, but nowhere are the locations coincident with what is in the autopsy report, and certainly not with the autopsy photographs (they show no damage to the face). Organ gives no citations for this statement.

Lattimer's drawings make clear the conflict in location of the large defect on the head.[22] His second drawing or tracing of the anterior-posterior skull X-rays places the major loss of frontal bone precisely where we see it in the copies of the House Committee X-rays. In other words, there is no conflict. Lattimer saw what everyone has observed who saw the actual X-rays: a complete loss of frontal bone extending into the face in that area. But in his lateral view, he has the large defect a bit farther back, though extending into the face. His observations in 1972 show that he saw no defect in either the back of the head, the top of the head, or basically where it is placed in the autopsy report.

Finally, Organ claims that the problem might not be the same if the X-rays had not been photographed and printed with a black background.

This claim cannot overturn the previous observations of those who noted the frontal bone missing on the actual X-rays. Such speculation is tiresome. Organ refers us to Jim Moore, who says that Dr. Wecht's failure to report something unusual is a positive piece of knowledge. A negative cannot prove a positive. Wecht has in fact commented on the missing frontal bone.[23]

As for the sinus problem, what is claimed to be right frontal sinus by those who authenticated the pictures may not be there at all.[24]

Organ says, "Livingstone makes much of '. . . that slug on the outer table of the skull on the back of the head.' " Well, Jerrol Custer did not make up his story that he was required by his superiors on November 23, 1963, to tape bullet fragments to skull fragments and X-ray them.[25] The skull in the pictures seems to me to be quite clearly a composite film reconstructing a skull. Organ gives us a speculation: "That fragment, just below the entry wound's lower margin, is the initial strike-point of a bullet from behind. Striking on a tangent, the bullet skidded a bit before digging into the bone, causing massive fracturing which buckled skull plates to allow the bullet to finally penetrate." In my view, this is ridiculous. Why didn't the nurse who washed and combed his hair not find the bullet, and why was it not seen during the intense search for a bullet at the autopsy and in the X-rays that night? How could there have been such a big slug there without it being observed on November 22, 1963? And where is it in the evidence now? We have two halves (almost) of a bullet found on the floor of the front seat of the limousine, which clearly had to have been the head shot, if it came from behind. It wasn't the bullet that allegedly hit Connally, CE 399. The bullet that hit the windshield combing and fell down, broken, either had hit the President's head or was a missed shot.

Organ comments that "Since four Parkland doctors verified the autopsy photographs in the *Nova* documentary, as well as three more for the *JAMA* article, is there really any reason to question the photos?"[26] Yeah, lots. Those four doctors (Peters, Dulany, McClelland, and Jenkins) put their hands on the *back* of their head in the *Nova* show and demonstrated the large wound which is not present in the autopsy photos and X-rays. They have all since disputed *Nova*'s interpretation and distortion of what they said. What they verified is only that the pictures that have been published are what they saw in the National Archives, and *not* the accuracy of the photos in depicting what they actually observed.[27]

The autopsy doctors in the *JAMA* article inadvertently made statements that quite clearly throw into doubt the authenticity of the photos and X-rays when they said his face was intact and normal and that the entry hole in the back of the head was not in the right place. Therefore, Organ is mistaken when he says here: "The Bethesda pathologists and photographer John T. Stringer have also recently endorsed the pictures."[28] What does "endorsed" mean?

Organ gets into more difficulty with this statement: "They [the Parkland doctors] felt the wound was an entry wound from the *front*. By their own admission, *the hole is in top, right side* [emphasis the author's] of the head as recorded in the Zapruder film, and autopsy photographs and X-rays."[29] Here he has taken a half dozen concepts and thrown them together in the soup. The Parkland doctors have never varied from their insistence that the large defect was in the right *rear* quadrant of the skull,[30] where it is in the autopsy report. Nothing about the top of the head. Note that Organ doesn't offer supporting data for his assertion. He then scrambles what we see with his misplaced wound and the altered Zapruder film, which shows the right front of the head blowing off. He seems to be telling us, *yes, the wound* (large defect) *is in fact* on the front, top, right side. You can't have an entry wound from the front if you're Organ and his friends, so you mean that the large *exit* is in front, and that never happened.

Whether it is a flap or "the Blob," as I call it, on the face in the Zapruder film, is not clear, and nobody can yet prove that it is a flap. If it is a flap, it would appear to be the entire right side of the face (at least) and forward scalp hanging down, and I don't believe that was possible. There are too many anatomical details anchoring the face and scalp to the skull, and we are talking of such an explosion as to have no relationship to normal rifle bullets as exist in this case. Organ claims that the X-rays, in the quote above, verify that the hole is in the "top, right side of the head . . ." which seems to mean that he is trying to have his cake and eat it, too, claiming that there is in fact a large hole in the right side frontal area of the X-rays, certainly not in the occipital area, which he had previously used to try to bolster another of his absurd propositions.

An even worse example of this man's reasoning is that "These doctors [at Parkland] originally developed the impression that the President was shot from the front as they only saw the frontal wounds. As they saw just the one gaping opening in the head and thought it was caused by a shot from the front, how could the wound be in the very rear of the head? If it was there, they would have then thought the shot came from the rear. If they thought there was an exit wound on the rear skull, you would think they would have searched for an entry wound to the front of the head." Now you see it, now you don't.

First he starts off saying that "they only saw the frontal wounds."

Nobody testified to it. How can they only see the wounds on the front and then, in the next breath, see "just the one gaping opening in the head and thought it was caused by a shot from the front, how could the wound be in the very rear of the head?"? Organ has somehow moved their unanimous observation of a large right rear quadrant opening to the front of the head. He is talking about a big hole in front. He ignores their death certificate, which mentioned a small wound of entry in the front. Organ is so confused, he forgets that some of them *did* examine the head, and all of them said that they couldn't see the entirety of the large hole unless they lifted the head when it was on the table.[31]

Organ seems to be saying that the *entry* hole was in fact in "the top, right side of the head," which is what several of the doctors believed. In other words, in the right temple area, where we see a small piece of bone and scalp sprung open, but this is not strictly "the top of the head." "Rather, they felt the wound was an entry wound from the front." Obviously, then, the Parkland doctors—if placing an entry hole precisely where others (and perhaps the X-rays) have the exit, there has to be another large wound of exit somewhere. Where is it? On the right rear quadrant of the head, naturally. It was a tangential shot from the storm drain near the overpass in front of the car. "The sprung-open skull flaps are visible in the exact location as shown in the autopsy record, locations now acceptable to nearly all the Parkland doctors"[32] as an *entry* wound.

Then, with regard to my notion that "the Blob" on the Zapruder film was added for special effect, he accuses me of the following: "Livingstone's so-called facial damage is an illusion caused by plane shifts."[33] His problem is that Lattimer and Artwohl both discuss in *JAMA* the authenticity of this huge aberration on Kennedy's face after he is hit, indicating that it is a flap from the head and face hanging down. So what did Organ mean when he said the Zapruder film confirms the large forward defect? Certainly "the Blob" seen so clearly on the Zapruder film is no "illusion," as he calls it, and certainly the plane is not shifting from the right side to the front. "The Blob" covers that entire area around to the front of the face.

Organ quotes this statement from the *JAMA* article: "Nothing we observed contradicts the autopsy finding that the bullets were fired from above and behind." Remember, there were a lot of "presumablys" in the autopsy report, and this statement does nothing to preclude additional shots from the front. Organ is simply confused.

Riley

I discussed briefly Dr. Joseph Riley's article in the *JAMA* chapter. Riley maintains that there are apparently two bullet entries in the X-rays. Riley's article appeared in the March 1993 *Third Decade*. I'd like to quote Kathy Cunningham, R.N., on Riley at this point, in a short letter to me.[34]

"Using the same evidence the HSCA subpanel used, Dr. Joseph Riley determined that they made several gross errors in their assessment, and concludes that if the photos and X-rays are authentic, that they prove that the President was shot twice in the head.

"Dr. Riley observed in this paper that the higher mark to the back of the head in HSCA Exhibit F 48 is not located in the vicinity of the 'cowlick' as the HSCA subpanel concluded, but is really situated just above the external occipital protuberance, as related by the Bethesda pathologists. He also determines that this wound and the entrance wound identified by the Baden panel in the X-rays, do not correspond. After assessing the position of the head and neck in this Ida Dox drawing, he determined that there was little significant tilt present. He then drew a line from the top of the President's ear in the sketch through the higher mark in the drawing. Because there is little or no tilt present, he assumes that this line would be horizontal if the President were standing erect. Then using HSCA Exhibit F 58, the Dox drawing of the right lateral view of the President's head with the features of the skull drawn in, he places a horizontal line across the top of the ear. The line passes right above the EOP. As Exhibit F 58 is drawn to scale, Dr. Riley was able to approximate the distance from the EOP to the fold in the back of the neck at 13 cm. The HSCA subpanel determined that the entrance wound was 13 cm. from the same crease; thus, in error, the panel concluded that this wound would correspond to a wound 100 mm. above this point.

"He next questions their placement of a wound of entrance 100 mm. above the external occipital protuberance. Not having access to copies of the actual X-rays to assess, he falls back on Dr. Baden's formal testimony (1 HSCA 301), in which he states that all nine members of the panel unanimously agreed that there was a wound of entry some four inches above the EOP, and assumes that this is true. He then correlates the information in HSCA Exhibit F 302, the Dox drawing of the damaged brain, and HSCA Exhibits F 53 and F 56, the lateral and AP X-rays of Kennedy's skull. Using the pattern of metal particles in the X-rays, he determines that there is no anatomic continuity between them and all of the damage that is present to the brain. He asserts that although it is probable that they resulted from an entrance 100 mm. above the EOP—even if the missile in question was copper jacketed—that an entry at that point would not explain the subcortical damage that is present. He concludes that if the autopsy materials are genuine, that they prove that two shots struck Kennedy's head, one at the point that the Bethesda pathologists identified, and the second at the higher point identified by the HSCA subpanel (and the Clark Panel). Although Dr. Riley does not attempt to determine the direction of the two shots, he notes that if they were both fired from the rear, the lower shot, with its resultant subcortical damage could not have been fired from the Texas School Book Depository at Zapruder frames 312/313.''

Even the *JAMA* writers (Dr. Artwohl) admit this last fact, saying the shooter might have had to be in the trunk of the car. Or, in my opinion, in the storm drain alongside it in the street.

There are too many things wrong with the X-rays for them to be anything but altered or fake. This is the proof that there has been major tampering with the evidence to cover up the true nature of the conspiracy that killed him.

Jerrol Custer

I asked Jerrol Custer, the X-ray tech who took the films of JFK the night of the assassination, to respond to the *JAMA* article that criticized his work. Custer is the chief radiological technician at Presbyterian Hospital in Pittsburgh, and he runs a large department. He has thirty years of experience in the radiology field. He wrote a statement at my request, which I present here in its entirety:

''As I have stated before, the (government's alleged) anterior/posterior and the lateral views of the skull that were taken of JFK didn't match the X-rays that I took and which were taken that night in the morgue. I will repeat myself as I have done before: In the alleged lateral projection of the skull, a bony prominence called the sella turcica was floating in midair. Any person that knows basic anatomy would realize this is a physical impossibility, since this is part of the sphenoid bone, which holds the bottom of the skull together where the brain lies upon it.

''I was there. I saw things at firsthand. The President's face didn't show the massive damage that is quite evident in the alleged anterior/posterior view of the skull and also on the lateral view. The alleged AP view shows massive destruction of the right orbital rim and also the floor of the orbit. With this much damage, the President's eye most certainly couldn't have remained in its socket. This was not true of the body we had. The eye was firmly in the President's head, but the face was loose and drooped, and it could have been reflected downward. It was pulled back to appear tight as the photos were taken. The bones were somewhat mobile beneath the face on the right. It was like moving around a bag of mush when we took films, and I was afraid I would damage it.

"But in the photos the right eye and the orbit appeared to be intact. There also appears to be massive damage to the forehead and part of the parietal bone on the right side in the X-rays. Again, as I remember, this damage didn't show on the photos also. The anterior-posterior view of the skull wasn't a modified Waters projection, as Dr. Artwohl suggests. I know the head was tilted back a little, but this didn't make that much difference. The massive damage was still evident on the right side in what I saw on the body.

"Let me answer some of the statements made in the *JAMA* article. First, the X-rays weren't of poor quality because each film was checked by a staff radiologist of the National Naval Medical Center. If these films weren't excellent, he would have made me take them over again. These examples that this person is commenting on were photographic copies of the X-rays, which do have a tendency to be dark. But still, the evidence was indisputable. The quality of the copies, and I do mean (enhanced) copies, not X-rays, can be taken in account for what Dr. Artwohl is saying. Processing these copies of X-rays are very critical. There is no latitude in the process. One changed factor will change the copy quality.

"Let me also make a statement to the fact that I described a wound in the lower posterior portion of the President's skull. Another thing I will bring to light: The next day I was placed in a room in the X-ray department with a portable X-ray machine and films, and was told to take X-ray films of bones of the skull with bullet fragments on them. I was ordered by Dr. Ebersole to complete this duty—so that a bust of the President's head could be made. These fragments were brought to me the next day by Dr. Ebersole.

"One must realize the situation that occurred in the morgue when the President's body was brought in. Confusion with people running here and there trying to do a job. With all this confusion we had the doctors who by Naval documentation had never done an autopsy before. Especially one that dealt with forensic evidence.

"And by the way, to the gentleman in the *JAMA* article, I am glad you thought my roentgenograms of the President were of 'superior quality.' These films were taken by me, *not* Dr. Ebersole. Dr. Ebersole examined each film I had taken and *never*, and I do mean *never*, touched the X-ray machine. I know, I was there in the morgue most of the evening. And when I was done, I had taken the X-ray equipment out of the morgue with me back to the towers where the X-ray department was. Dr. Ebersole was a Naval radiologist, not an X-ray technician. A Naval officer wouldn't lower himself to do this job, because it's what an X-ray tech does, not a radiologist. That evening Dr. Ebersole would examine every film that was taken in the morgue by myself, and then he would give his interpretation to the doctors during the autopsy. These films were of the highest quality. Because Dr. Ebersole visited me in the call room along with Captain Brown and said that I should be proud! They said that I had done an excellent job. One must remember that the government can do anything it wants to do when it comes to a cover-up in this situation.

"That night I did a job because of that situation. What I saw that night has been questioned by many and understood by so few. What would I have to gain by muddying up the waters? I took the X-rays of President Kennedy and I told many what I had observed that night. Many believe me, and many believe I don't know what I am talking about. I have been an X-ray technologist for about thirty years and I do feel that I have some expertise in this field. Why is it so hard to believe that a great man can be killed by the government and that that same government can cover it up?

"Even now, after some thirty years, people seem to be afraid to tell the truth. Will we ever know the truth? I doubt it, because I am afraid the people would doubt the system we live in. Can only a few influence and govern the people and tell them only what they want the people to do?" /Signed/ Jerrol Custer, May 1993.

CHAPTER 11

THE BRONSON, ZAPRUDER, AND OTHER FILMS

It is my opinion that there are two sets of evidence in the assassination of John Kennedy, and that evidence has undergone a process of continuing evolution throughout the years. When the House of Representatives established its Select Committee on Assassinations, new evidence had to be created. Autopsy pictures and other materials may have been burned or destroyed in 1963, and materials had to be altered, substituted, or created at once. Some material remained, but the gaps in the record had to be filled. Some call this the "Buffet of the Evidence."

I think that there are two versions of the Bronson film, two Zapruder films, two sets of autopsy pictures, two acoustical tapes, and maybe more. Mistakes might have been made by the forgers, but the overall purpose was as much to confuse the evidence as to falsify it. We know that law enforcement in this case often wrote two sets of documents—affidavits that say exactly opposite things from the same witness. They were prepared for all contingencies.

Deobjectifying the evidence makes it soft, like a puff of smoke through which we poke our fingers. Things are amorphous, vague, and untrue. This is the smoke screen that hides the truth.

That is the goal of some of the leading so-called critics and researchers: to soften everything. Nothing has a hard core. Counterintelligence agents and provocateurs have co-opted this case, and are misleading the unwary and untrusting. The visual evidence in the case proves either nothing or almost nothing, but it's a good meal ticket for its purveyors.

The Bronson Film

The fact that Charles Leslie Bronson had taken a film of the assassination scene came to light for the House Assassinations Committee in the closing days of their investigation on December 2, 1978.[1] The existence of the film was revealed when an FBI list was declassified. This was a little too late for them to do much with the film, but Robert Groden asked to look at it and claimed that some of the frames of the film taken six minutes before the shooting showed movement in the sixth-floor assassin's window of the Texas School Book Depository. Studies were made that denied his claims: "The experts disagree unanimously with Mr. Groden that 'you can actually see one figure walking back and forth hurriedly.' "[2]

C. J. Leontis of The Aerospace Corporation noted also in his letter to the Committee that there were similar phenomena in the Hughes film and that "the apparent motion in the windows seems to be random and therefore it is not likely to be due to human motion behind the window."[3]

Movement in itself, of course, means nothing, since there were plenty of employees in the building who could perhaps be seen (but not identified) from a block away, where Bronson was standing. Yet it was claimed that this movement had to be that of assassins, perhaps constructing the sniper's lair. I submit that this hiding place might just as well have been there a long time for malingering employees to hide in, a common situation in such a warehouse.

Gary Mack and Robert Groden claimed from 1978 on that the film shows the assassination itself. However, Earl Golz and *The Dallas Morning News* studied the film, and after examining ninety-two frames, found nothing that could be printed in their story that showed any part of the actual shooting.[4] The ninety-two frames cover only the first part of the film, which is the Texas School Book Depository/ambulance (an ambulance came there a few minutes before the motorcade to pick up a man who had an epileptic seizure and take him to Parkland Hospital) sequence. The last sequence allegedly shows the shooting, or in Bronson's description of his film to me, not the shooting, but Clint Hill on the trunk of the car.

Nevertheless, claims continue to be made that the film shows the assassination. This is stated in a book by Ron Rosenbaum, *Travels with Dr. Death.*[5] In fact, versions of the film were shown by Gary Mack (a.k.a. Larry Darkel) on KXAS-TV in Fort Worth in November 1991. That version shows the limousine on its trip down Elm Street after the first shot, something Bronson says he did not shoot.[6] It's not clear if the head shot occurs on the film. Bronson was taking still pictures with his Leica at the time of the first shot. He then tried to switch cameras.

In August 1979, Gary Mack and Steve Barber went to the home of Charles Brehm, a witness seen in the Zapruder film who stood near the limousine as President Kennedy received the fatal head shot. He is the man in a white jacket with a small boy near Mary Moorman and Jean Hill, the so-called lady in red.

Brehm became extremely upset the moment he saw this part of the film and all but threw up, Barber told me.[7] Mack, who got the film from Robert Groden, said the film was "intentionally flawed" to get around Bronson's copyright. This is in line with Groden's long history of manufacturing optical enhancements of other people's work, which allows him to claim his own copyright, regardless of the fact that he has not contracted for the use of the property with the owner.

Earl Golz wrote on November 26, 1978, that "FBI agent Newsom viewed the movie with Bronson as soon as it was processed at the Eastman Kodak Co. in Dallas in 1963." Bronson was quoted as saying, "He told me the film was of no value because it didn't show the book depository building. I didn't realize myself that the building was on there until a couple of weeks ago."[8] Did the FBI lie? I don't think so. Why would they lie about this?

There are elements here that just don't add up. Golz writes further that he was "told last week that the film showed the building and two moving images framed in the alleged assassin's window." Newsom asked whether Bronson was "certain that's the film that we looked at" in 1963. "Whether or not we actually saw what you are talking about, of course, [we] have no way of knowing that," Newsom said. "Whatever was reported there in the memo was what we saw."

But what was the point? Was it to create a composite film with portions from some other film? Did they create another hoax? Surely we have had enough fraudulent evidence perpetrated upon us over the years, such as the fake or misinterpreted frame 413 of the Zapruder film, showing an apparent rifle poking out from the bushes almost six seconds after the head shot.[9] Bronson told me that after he switched cameras, all he was able to capture was Jackie on the trunk of the car—after the fatal head shot.[10]

Golz wrote in an article a little later that "The film was discovered last month by *The Dallas Morning News* after a previously classified FBI memo indicated its existence. An FBI agent viewed the film three days after the assassination and said he could not see the depository building on any frames. The 8-mm. film was then returned to Bronson, who lived in Dallas at the time. He kept it for home movie use until the depository window scene was detected at a showing in his home in Ada, Oklahoma, last month."[11] It would certainly appear that the films were switched, or tampered with. What does this do for Bronson's reliability as a witness?

Bronson, formerly an engineer at the Gault Company in Ada, Oklahoma, had taken still photographs of the motorcade as well. *The Dallas Morning News* printed one of those, which was taken as the first shot was fired. "The sound made Bronson jump and blurred the images."

I stood on the pedestal where Bronson stood taking his still pictures. It is a short block up Houston Street from the Texas School Book Depository and Elm Street, and it was clear to me that by the time the car emerged from the trees on Elm, which blocked the view from where Bronson stood, he would have had little time to switch cameras and get his movie camera aimed and started if there were a chance of capturing the remaining sequence. Also, it's doubtful that his lens would have captured Jackie on the trunk, due to the trees.

Martin Shackelford comments on the above: "The position from which the Bronson film was taken is consistent with the position from which the Bronson slide was taken; the fact that the view of Jackie on the trunk would have been obscured by trees may simply be further indication that Bronson's memory on the contents isn't that sharp, or that he has difficulty distinguishing between what HE saw and what THE CAMERA saw."[12] The problem with this is that it would be very difficult to put aside one camera and select a lens, focus, and start a movie camera so quickly.

I asked Bronson's lawyer, John Sigalos, about this.[13] (Sigalos also represented Jack Daniel, who took a film of the assassination.) I asked, "Does the film show the assassination?" He responded, "I won't answer that." I'd like to point out that since January 1992, FBI agents have been attempting to look at the film, but Sigalos, a patent attorney, refuses to allow it. It was stated on Channel 5 (KXAS) in Dallas that in November 1991 Sigalos had agreed to let the FBI study the film. A year later, this has not happened. The whole thing seemed to be a publicity gimmick. Upon learning from Earl Golz that the FBI was being refused access, I discussed it with them, and offered to pay for a look-see for all of us and/or to buy a license to use frames of the film. They refused.

Here are some discrepancies in the sequence of events. The above newspaper story indicates that the FBI (agent Walter Bent) did in fact look at the film shortly after the assassination. "Before the week ended, Bronson was viewing the results at the Eastman processing plant with two FBI agents who studied the pictures." Bronson said he went to see the film for the first time at the end of the following week after the assassination with two FBI agents.[14] But the FBI memo saying the film did not show the building is dated November 25, which is a lot sooner than the end of the week (November 28 or 29).

The UPI and AP wrote stories on November 27, 1978, that claimed that the film "also captured the grisly, fatal shot to Kennedy's head, as the presidential limousine approached the triple underpass at Dealey Plaza. Jacqueline Kennedy can be seen rising from the rear seat after her husband was shot."

Groden claims that the Bronson film shows the assassination sequence and both the limousine and the follow-up car with Secret Service agent George Warren Hickey during the fatal head shot. If true, this film is vital to the claims by Howard Donahue that Hickey accidentally shot Kennedy in the head after the shooting started. Yet experts agree that the film is so grainy that no such fact can be determined.[15] Shackelford writes, "On the other hand, the film viewed at *The Dallas Morning News,* if the original, might be much clearer than the Groden copy, which the reports criticized as a poor copy. The copy shown on TV, if from Gary Mack, is probably similar in quality, or another generation away."

Some Additional Comments

The Aerospace Corporation of Los Angeles was given a copy by Groden. They evaluated the film on December 11, 1978. They were given a 16-mm. copy that "had been generated by Mr. Bob Groden, and a set of 35-mm. slides showing the area around the sixth-floor window of the Texas School Book Depository Building also made by Bob Groden. . . ." A computer scanner and contrast enhancement of a frame of the original 8-mm. film were compared with it. This is what they said:

"1. The Bronson film, although taken from a slightly different angle than the Hughes film, shows about the same area around the sixth-floor window of the Texas School Book Depository Building, but the Bronson film is of superior quality compared to the Hughes film. . . .

2. If the Bronson film had been available earlier, the experts would have recommended that it be analyzed along with the Hughes film.

3. Following careful examination of the Groden 35-mm. slides and 16-mm. movie film, the experts at the meeting couldn't say conclusively whether or not the frame-to-frame changes in the sixth-floor and fifth-floor windows were due to real motion behind the windows. The experts

disagree unanimously with Mr. Groden that 'you can actually see one figure walking back and forth hurriedly' as he was quoted by *The Dallas Morning News* on 26 November 1978. A more definitive conclusion may result through computer processing of selected frames from the 8-mm. Bronson original.

4. In viewing Groden's 16-mm. copy of the Bronson film and recalling from memory the Hughes film and the computer processed frames of the Hughes film, the experts observed similar dynamics in the two films: i.e., the apparent motion in the windows seems to be random and therefore it is not likely to be due to human motion behind the window. Computer analysis of the Bronson film similar to that applied to the Hughes film may clarify this issue especially since the Bronson film is of superior quality to the Hughes film." (Martin Shackelford comments on the last statement as follows: "The statement about the Bronson film being 'of superior quality' to Hughes is another indication that the original film is much clearer than was shown on TV. In addition, the sharpness of the partial frame blowup sequence that was shown on TV in 1978, and the frames printed in *The Dallas Morning News,* had to come from a *very* clear 8-mm. image."[16])

Robert Selzer of the Jet Propulsion Laboratory agreed but added, "To my knowledge, this is the only possible evidence of movement behind the two CLOSED windows adjacent to the half-open window. . . . Every other photo or movie frame that I can remember shows these windows completely opaque . . . the speed of shadow change, if clarified, could easily be distinguished from human movement . . . in either case, the movement should be analyzed.

"The original 8-mm. Bronson film is not only better than Hughes and better than the Groden copy of the Bronson film, but in the latter case, vastly better. To give an example, the lower window framing is so blurred on the Groden copy that it cannot be identified as a structural part of the window. On the digitized version of one Bronson original frame on the Comtol display, this structure was clearly evident and well defined."[17]

Earl Golz wrote, "The FBI had discarded the film four days after the assassination after erroneously reporting the depository building could not be seen in the footage."[18]

The UPI story made these comments:[19] "Bronson said he is satisfied with the Warren Commission finding that Oswald acted alone. He also said that he is uncertain that the film will provide new information on the slaying.

"John L. Sigalos, Bronson's attorney, and Robert J. Groden, a staff consultant for the House Assassinations Committee, viewed the original 8-mm. film and made 35-mm. slides of every fifth frame of the film and then enlarged the slides. Groden said he thought the slides showed activity that indicated the completion of 'a sniper's nest.'

"Bronson said he showed the movies to the FBI shortly after the assassination, 'but they didn't see anything of particular value in the films.' "

Groden claimed that "you can actually see one figure walking back and forth hurriedly."[20] "Bronson's movie camera also captured the grisly fatal shot to Kennedy's head as the presidential limousine approached the triple underpass at Dealey Plaza. Jacqueline Kennedy can be seen rising from the rear seat after her husband was shot." I made every possible check of this statement, and no such head shot is visible in the film. Earl Golz told me that they would have printed such a picture if they had it, and they studied the whole film. Why was this claim made, then?

The FBI report, written by Special Agent Milton L. Newsom, stated, "These films failed to show the building from which the shots were fired. Film did detect the President's car at the precise time shots were fired; however the pictures were not sufficiently clear for identification purposes."[21] The problem with the later part of this statement is that Newsom failed to differentiate between the Leica still pictures and the moving picture film.

Only once has the film been shown to the public. Gary Shaw and Gary Mack have seen it, along with Charles Brehm and Steve Barber. The film was partially shown on Dallas TV in 1978, in the form of a blowup sequence showing the two corner sixth-floor windows. In a three-part series on Fort Worth TV in November 1991, the ambulance/TSBD and Elm Street sequences were shown in their entirety for the first time.

But what we really have is one more of countless examples of embellishment of the evidence, exaggeration. A lot of people think that whatever they have to do to keep the case going, to keep the pot stirred, they will do it—for *the cause,* as Shaw calls it.

Former researcher Chris Sharrett writes, "You will note that in all the images of the sixth-floor 'sniper's lair' window taken at the time of the murder, the window is *half open.* There is a stack of three boxes pressed against the window by larger piles of boxes. This is exactly what Jack Beers saw when he took his famous stills at about 3:00 P.M. that day. There was never any 'wall of boxes' constituting a sniper's lair; there were piles of boxes all along the south wall of that floor as workmen prepared to install a new floor. The Dallas police/FBI photos of the remade lair show a totally different configuration of boxes with the window now wide open. The point is, with the boxes as they originally were as depicted in Hughes/Dillard/Beers, et al., there was *no room* for anyone to move in that window, much less fire a rifle. It would have been very difficult for Howard Brennan, Amos Euins, and others to have seen anyone in that window, since the boxes and the half-closed window provided an impediment, not a 'lair.' The 'lair,' like the paper bag, was created after the assassination.''[22]

A Short History of the Zapruder Film

Abraham Zapruder and his secretary, Marilyn Sitzman, went to Dealey Plaza with a new Bell & Howell camera to film the motorcade of President Kennedy. He captured for all time the assassination. But the film is questionable, and appears to have been altered.

Zapruder was a friend of H. L. Hunt.[23] That might begin to tell the reader something about where this chapter is going.

Zapruder's offices were on the fourth floor of the Dal-Tex Building, across the street from the Texas School Book Depository, at the corner of Elm and Houston. The best possible place for a sniper to shoot at the President as his car moved away from that corner down Elm Street was from a window on the Houston Street side of the building, on the second, third, or fourth floor.

Life magazine bought the film from Zapruder for $150,000,[24] and printed various of its frames over the years. *Life* would not allow the film to be seen. Zapruder gave the first year's installment to the family of slain officer J. D. Tippit. At the time of the Jim Garrison trial of Clay Shaw, Garrison let Mark Lane make and distribute bootleg copies. The film thereupon lost its value to *Life*, and they sold it back to the Zapruder family for $1 in 1975, after Groden showed it on national television. Sometime later, after the film had fallen into the public domain, or so it appeared due to laches, Zapruder's heirs began charging the public and researchers for the use of this vital evidence in the murder of President Kennedy. Under the legal doctrine of fair use in the public interest, it would seem that the manner in which frames of the film are being sold by Zapruder's heirs—after having fallen into the public domain through laches—is reprehensible.

French Intelligence had this film before 1968 and gave a second- or third-generation copy to author, researcher, and former FBI agent William Turner.[25] It had never been shown in public, and not even members of the Warren Commission saw it. The story Turner tells of *Farewell America* that follows this last is fascinating. "I then understood," Turner writes, "why *Life,* which had taken a stand in support of the Warren Report and featured Gerald Ford's rendition of how the no-conspiracy conclusion was arrived at, had kept the film sequestered. In fact an anonymous caption writer at the magazine had described the head-shot frame as a shot from the front, and a number of subscribers received copies with that caption. But the press run was quickly stopped at tremendous expense, and the offending plate broken and replaced by one whose caption was in conformity with the official position.

"An explanation of how the French had pierced *Life*'s tight security over the film was offered by Richard Lubic, at the time a staffer on *Life*'s sister publication *Time.* He told me that very early in 1968 the film was missing for several days from its vault in the *Time-Life* head-quarters in New York. There was quite a stir. The FBI and CIA investigated. Although the obvious conclusion was an inside job, no suspects were ever identified.

"The Zapruder film was offered to the major networks, but perhaps fearful of treading on *Life*'s proprietary rights, all declined to air it. Bootleg copies were a smash hit on college campuses, however, and in time the film became so widely shown that it fell into the public domain. It became a kind of *McGuffey's Reader* of the assassination, a socko illustration that there were at least two shooters."[26]

Richard Stolley, who purchased the film for *Life* in 1963, wrote in *Entertainment Weekly:* "Zapruder's son, a Washington tax laywer, does a brisk business in renting (the film) for one-time use (Oliver Stone, for instance, says he paid $40,000 to use the film in *JFK*)." Stolley suggests we would be better off without it "because of all the controversy it generated over the years."[27]

"The family of the man who made a home movie capturing the assassination of President John F. Kennedy in Dallas nearly twenty-five years ago is selling the film for as much as $30,000 per use," the *Houston Chronicle* reported. "Some people believe that profiteering from the historical film made on November 22, 1963, is wrong, and that the movie should be in the public domain.

"Copyrighting the film is 'immoral, socially speaking,' said David Wrone, a history professor at the University of Wisconsin.

"Zapruder, a tax lawyer who has been negotiating the sale of the film's rights out of his Washington office, would not comment about his financial interests in the film. However, he did say: 'Anybody who is using it for their own use, research, showing it to college students, colleges, can have it free of charge, other than the costs of reprinting the film. But if they're going to be making commercial use of it, then we charge."[28] The loan fee is $75. Granted, there are costs of administering the film, a responsibility that devolved to the heirs. Shackelford comments, "Clearly misleading, on Zapruder's part, due to the hoops one has to go through even to rent the film or slides, and they clearly indicate it is *not* for sale, even under their amazingly restrictive contract."[29]

Some "critics," taking advantage of this, show the film at colleges but charge as much as $5,000 per appearance, and do not pay the Zapruder corporation anything. The film is the main draw, not the disinformation these exhibiters disseminate. Since the film is allegedly fake, one wonders about the motives and activities of the film's publicist.

In the case of Groden's copy of the Zapruder film, he claims to have copyrighted his own version of it and sells or offers use of it for a fee to many people, including Oliver Stone and Berkley Publishing Group, even though his claim, based on what he calls his "optical enhancement," is of dubious legal force and effect. This latter fact has been disregarded by publishers and others, to their horror, who paid Groden, and are now being pursued by the Zapruder family lawyer and forced to pay additional fees for the use of their film. The Zapruder family lawyer, James Silverberg, told Kevin Brennen's law office that Abraham Zapruder sold the copyright to Time/Life in November, 1963, but the copyright was later assigned back as explained herein.

Josiah Thompson, a former Haverford professor and the author of *Six Seconds in Dallas,* told me that the original Zapruder film that *Life* bought was kept in their vault at all times. He said that the copy in the National Archives is poor. Thompson was hired by *Life* in October 1966 and had access to the transparency while working for Ed Kerns and Richard Billings, who later wrote the report of the HSCA and coauthored a Mob-did-it *(The Plot to Kill the President)* book with Robert Blakey. Thompson felt that there was a small forward motion of the head between frames 312 and 313, but this has been disputed by others.

Thompson was the first to publish significant commentary on the film in his book in November 1967. Unfortunately, lawyers came after him for publishing sketches made from frames of the film, and demanded $60,000, which made it impossible for him to pursue the case further. His book remains one of the best ever written in the case. Today Thompson is a private detective in Bolinas, California, and the author of *Gumshoe,* which he wrote about his detective work.

Prior to the transfer of the original back to Zapruder, *Life* made color transparencies or slides from the individual frames of the film and placed these as a gift in the National Archives on May 12, 1975, where researchers have been able to study them, along with two copies of the film. In my opinion, the three sets available to the public are not identical and may have significant differences. The conditions under which study may be maintained are next to impossible. No other pictures can be brought in to compare with what we are shown at the National Archives. Don't try to bring your own pencil or paper, either.

Even the contract that the Zapruder lawyer demands people sign for the study of copies of the film or slides has a fantastic demand never to mention that the film belonged to *Life*. "Borrower shall be prohibited from using or authorizing the use of the name of Time, Inc. or the name of any division, subsidiary, or publication of Time, Inc., [borrower prohibited from] in any manner or format, including but not limited to, any reference in said material that the Zapruder Film was ever owned by Time, Inc., or that Time, Inc., ever published any frames from the Zapruder Film in any publication of Time, Inc." Why?

Meanwhile, bootleg copies of the film, several generations removed from the original and therefore of poor quality, metastasized across the nation and the world, and various copies have been shown on television, especially at the time Oliver Stone's film *JFK* stirred great interest in the case. The film was first shown on national television by Geraldo Rivera on *Good Morning America* in March 1975.

A high-quality copy of the film was made for the PBS program *Nova* from a 35-mm. print of the film, and is known as the Thompson version, from the fact that Josiah Thompson narrated it for Walter Cronkite. The Thompson film can be spotted by the frame numbers in the corner of the picture. It also continually backs up, enlarges, slows down, and speeds up in various segments, and it lasts fourteen minutes. All this from a twenty-two-second film clip.

Martin Shackelford notes in a letter to me[30] that the "Thompson film is not a copy of the Secret Service copy; it was made from the original film, as is clear from the obvious splices not present in the Secret Service copy, made before the original film was damaged."

The origin of the three copies of the Zapruder slides now in the Still Picture Branch of the National Archives is contained in the following comment from Elizabeth Hill of the National Archives: "Time, Inc., turned over 'A color transparency of each frame of the above. ('Motion pictures: First- and second-generation copies of the 8-mm. motion picture film taken by Abraham Zapruder, etc.') Number 164-486.' This set is referred to as the 'original' set. In the place where frame 349 should have been, there was a note dated 8/1975, from J. Thomas (former Still

Picture Branch chief), that this frame was not received at the time of transfer.

"There is no other documentation in the files to indicate what sets of slides were made by whom and from what generation copies the various copies were made. My statement that the other two sets of slides were made by the National Archives is only a guess.

"It is standard procedure to make any copies from the 'reproduction set' where possible. Any missing images, with the exception of frame 349, would be made from the other sets."[31]

The attached *Change of Holdings Report* from the National Archives reported that they had received "First- and second-generation copies of the 8-mm. motion picture film taken by Abraham Zapruder showing the assassination of President John F. Kennedy, November 22, 1963" with a handwritten note "30 feet each." Next the accession report states that they received from Time, Inc., 323 still pictures, which are "a color transparency of each frame above. Number 164-486."[32]

What the Film Shows

"The main thing about the Zapruder film is the brevity of the firing sequence, which impressed me most (rather than the head shot) when I first saw the film in 1969," Chris Sharrett writes.[33] Chris Sharrett teaches a history of journalism course at Seton Hall University and has intensely researched this case. Sharrett is familiar with firearms and, as he says in the same letter to the author, "there is no way in hell that you can operate a bolt action rifle with any accuracy in 5.6 seconds or 7 seconds or whatever. Quibbling about incredibly minute slivers of time won't help the government's case. The Blakey/Cornwell idea that Oswald achieved all this by 'point aiming,' as when a hunter has 'buck fever,' is on a par with Cronkite's idea that Oswald's mechanical skills were improved by the quality of his target. This is disingenuous nonsense for the gullible. I spent afternoons in the early 70s trying to duplicate this feat under optimum conditions: impossible. This is what needs to be emphasized over which bullet went where: The official verdicts (both of them) are patent nonsense that above all violate basic principles of law and even logic."

The National Archives

On September 1, 1992, Martin Shackelford, a fellow researcher whose primary focus has been on photographic evidence in the case, and I went to the National Archives to study the slides made by *Life* from each frame of the Zapruder film.

We also viewed video copies of the films—which is all they would show us—and they were so poor as not to be worth the time and effort to look at them. They look like the bad bootlegs of the early 1970s. Maybe they are.

The following report was prepared with the collaboration of Martin Shackelford.

The National Archives contains, in fact, three sets of slides. The "original set" includes frames 164 through 486, with frames 180, 304, 321, 349, and 372 missing, and apparently was made (at least primarily) directly from the original Zapruder film. The frame numbering is based on this set, as the numbers were written or stamped on the slide mounts by *Life*.

The "reproduction set" includes frames 171 to 343, though a note says "168–190 not copied," and frames 208 through 211 are missing. This was apparently the set viewed by Harold Weisberg and others in the Old Judicial Branch of the Archives in past years. The "reference or viewing set," or what is currently available for the use of researchers, includes frames 164–483 (the President's limousine first appears in the film at frame 133; frames 484–86 are extremely blurred), except for 349 (noted as missing in an August 1975 memo) and 378 (which disappeared sometime after 1976). The Archives has indicated it has no records of when or by whom these sets were made, except that they assume this was done by their own staff.[34]

Most frames are sharp and clear, with supurb color quality, and were copies of the slide made from the original film, including the area of the frames between the sprocket holes. This area is missing in two groups of slides, which were instead made from a copy of the film (also made clear by color shifts): frames 208–11, which were damaged in the original film, and frames 413–36, for which no explanation has yet been forthcoming, despite inquiries at the Archives.

The National Archives' numbering of the frames of the film are identical with the numbering ascribed to the frames by researchers until after frame 313. It is not clear where the numbering changes, but it diverges at least after frame 321 and before frame 413.

It is not clear why the substitution was done, but the sprocket hole area of the frame is the area that contains such off-screen details as the Secret Service follow-up car, the escorting motorcycle officers, a larger portion of the Stemmons Freeway sign, and continuing views of people and objects that appear earlier in the main portion of the frames. The area also includes the usual flaring from reflections and light leaks, and some image overlap, all common to cameras of this type.

But most of the slides had all of the sprocket information, though there was an anomaly, some sort of bleed-over from the picture into the sprocket area just beneath the upper cutout hole for the sprocket. In other words, there is a sort of miniphotograph from just one part of the scene that is out of place in that spot.

We did not see any information of great value in the sprocket areas, although it would take considerably further study to be sure that something important was not missed.

A couple of frames are missing (349 and 378) from the collection. The first 163 frames of the film are not in the collection. The film's slides continue up to frame 483.

The previously noted missing slides at frames 208, 209, 210, and 211 have been replaced.

The "Gunman" in Frame 413

What has heretofore been publicized as frame 413 of the Zapruder film is actually frame 415 of the National Archives set. It has been claimed by Robert Groden that there was a rifle barrel in this frame.[35] Martin Shackelford and I went to the National Archives and studied this frame.

We saw no rifle barrel upon close scrutiny with a large magnifying glass over the blown-up viewing screen of the slide in frame Groden Z 413/415.

Shackelford comments with regard to this, "The 'rifle barrel' image *is* in the frame, it just isn't a rifle barrel. Contrast buildup in copies makes it look *more* like a rifle barrel than in the original, but no one has to add anything to the frame, just misinterpret it."[36] Shackelford and many other critics of Robert Groden state that "Very many times, Groden sees things I don't see." But many people differ on the alleged rifle barrel as to its either being fake or simply a misinterpretation. It is unlikely that a gunman could be in that place at that time.

The photograph made from frame 413 published in *Rolling Stone* by Robert Groden[37] might possibly be a forgery. Certainly the slides at the National Archives do not show the steel rifle barrel that we apparently see in that photograph. In addition, there can be no gunman in the position where the alleged gun is because it is right out in the open where Zapruder and others could see him *in front of* Zapruder. The gunman would have to be standing in the plaza behind the white wall, which is only belt high and some feet in front of the stockade fence. There is only the slightest bush in front of the wall. Shackelford adds: "Never underestimate the human capacity for self-deception and certainty which is used to convince others of the error's truth. The man in 413/415 is standing OUT IN THE OPEN, and NOT behind the concrete wall. The head would be larger if he was behind the wall and that much closer to the camera. As it is, the head is about the same size as the head of the man waving near the Stemmons sign earlier in the film, who we KNOW to be farther from the camera."[38]

Certainly there was no face of an assassin visible over the stockade fence in frame 454.

Chris Sharrett makes a comment about the man whose back of the head we see in frame 413, a man whom Robert Cutler identified as Emmet Hudson: "There *is* a man in frame #413, and it's not Hudson; Hudson is standing below Zapruder's range-finder. The flesh tones on the man's ears and neck are very clear in Dick Sprague's slide of this frame. I don't see a rifle in this frame either, only branches of the shrub through which Zapruder is aiming his camera, although the man is holding something." (Shackelford says, "The head is too small in the frame to be as close as Zapruder's side of the wall. Note also that the man at the wall in the earlier photos seems to be wearing a dark hat, and this head is bare.")[39]

Sharrett says that "Z 413—The man in this frame is also seen in Betzner, Willis 5, Moorman 2, Nix, and Martin.

"He's the same figure squatting (based on the ground level behind the wall at the time) behind the wall in Willis 5 and Betzner. He's also visible in Moorman and the original Nix. He causes the white blob which I must assume is the puff of smoke seen by Holland, Dodd, et al. The puff is in Moorman, Martin, and Nix. When Josiah Thompson asked Holland to pinpoint the smoke for *Six Seconds in Dallas*, Holland drew a circle around the wall area. In Anthony Summers' *Conspiracy*, he notes that Rose Willis stated that she saw a man 'pop up' from behind the retaining wall, and then run.[40] Perhaps the man had ducked down behind the wall when the bullets flew, and Zapruder's camera missed him.

"This is the figure Hargis is chasing in the Bond photos; he runs down along the fence line and hops over the balustrade—he obviously had his escape planned, because he managed to avoid the railroad workers on the overpass."[41]

Bobbie Hargis is the motorcycle policeman who rode inboard to the car, close to the left rear fender, and he was struck so forcefully that in the Nix film, we see him all but stop. He in fact did stop an instant later and run up on the Grassy Knoll toward the overpass, looking for the shooter. All four motorcycle police officers are visible in the Nix film.

To a certain extent, I have allowed my books to perform as a forum for other researchers, and I have presented opposing views. Some of those views are worth hearing. I do not say Chris Sharrett is wrong about the man not being Hudson.

I'll quote what he wrote me: "The man in frame 413 of the Zapruder film absolutely is not Emmet Hudson or the man standing with him on the steps leading up to the pergola. They were below Zapruder's sight-line. This man appears in at least five other pieces of photographic evidence. He runs along the fence line after the shooting. He causes the smoke puff at the corner of the wall. It is true that he was in a very exposed position, but so were the assassins behind the fence and at the pergola. My conclusions and that of Dick Sprague are that they didn't give a damn if they were seen or not. The phony Secret Service agents were there to run interference for them."[42]

I respect the vast amount of work Chris Sharrett has done on this case, and since so many others feel that there must have been a shooter behind that three-foot-high retaining wall, I want to say that my opinion is that this is poppycock. The stockade fence was only a few feet behind the retaining wall and would be a far better place from which to fire, since it offered so much concealment and a much easier escape route through the parking lot and railroad yards. Zapruder and others said they felt a bullet whiz by their head from behind, meaning from the stockade fence behind them.

It is unreasonable that a gunman would position himself in front of a movie camera, even if Zapruder was used unwittingly in the conspiracy. Basically, the alleged gunman's position was completely out in the open on the Knoll in frame 413.

It is unreasonable and fundamentally ridiculous that a gunman would take the chance of running the entire length of the stockade fence to the balustrade from such an exposed position on the Knoll. A large number of people ran to the balustrade where it joined the picket fence for the same reason that Decker ordered his men to get up to the same spot. He thought the gunman was there, by the storm drain at the bridge.

Furthermore, any shot from that retaining wall position to the side of the car where the President was hit in the head would have had a much different trajectory of brain and skull material.

There is a spectator in plain view of the motorcade on the Grassy Knoll steps who is some distance from Zapruder's camera, and a bush that grew a few feet in front of the camera. The "rifle" is closer to the camera than the bush, and the "barrel" portion passes between the camera and the leaves from the bush. The "stock" portion is likely the side of the limousine there as elsewhere through the leaves of the little bush. The "suspicious relationship" of the two supposed objects exists only in the single frame (which is numbered 415 in the National Archives set, suggesting that other sets may be missing a couple of frames after 323, as the numbers match at least until that frame). Due to National Archives and Zapruder family restrictions, a more exact answer has not yet been determined.

Martin further comments that "the 'rifle' image in Z 413 passes in front of leaves of the bush from the perspective of Zapruder's camera, and is therefore between the leaves and the camera; the only straight objects in that location, as we can see in Exhibit C, are branches of the same bush. At least two leaves of the bush are between the head in Z 413 and Zapruder's camera, indicating that the bush is between the head and his camera; the other side of the bush from the 'rifle.' For the object to be a rifle the correct size to be held by the man whose head we see in Z 413, but would have to be far enough from the camera to be completely exposed to everyone present, but the 'rifle' is in front of at least two leaves, or much closer to Zapruder's camera than the head. Judging from the leaves it obscures, the front 'barrel' part of the 'rifle' would be four inches or less in length; for the head to be close to the leaves, the leaves would have to be four inches or more at their longest; the bush does not have leaves of nearly that size. Clearly, the 'barrel' part of the 'rifle' is a branch in the bush; the 'stock' part of the rifle is part of the side of the limousine visible through the leaves of the bush; the head is that of the head of a spectator; the head and the 'rifle' bear no relationship to one another."[43]

Frame 418 shows Jackie still reaching out over the trunk. She is back in the seat by 421. Emmett Hudson (the groundskeeper for Dealey Plaza) and two companions are standing on the steps that ascend the Grassy Knoll. Robert Cutler has theorized that the highest of the three is the man whose head is seen in frame 413–15 and identified that man as Hudson. It's his head Groden is taking for a gunman.

The analysis by the House Committee was accurate in its refutation of Groden's rifle-in-the-bush theory.

The Disappearing Motorcycle

It should be repeated that one of the three lead motorcycle policemen (H. B. Freeman) on the far right does *not* disappear down Houston

Street—as some popularizers have said—but is partly visible in the first Zapruder frames on the right side of the street, making the turn down Elm Street. Of course, the motorcycle is very clearly one of the three motorcycles we see in their proper position ahead of the car in the Bell film. Mel McIntire's photo in *The Dallas Times Herald* showed the limousine rapidly overtaking all three of the cycles as it approached the Stemmons Freeway on-ramp.

As for the limousine's brake lights, the left rear taillight seems to be brightly lit up as soon as it emerges from behind Clint Hill's leg in frame 364 and remains visible until frame 383, but we do not see the right rear taillight lit up. Perhaps there is sunlight lighting the left taillight. This is simply not clear to me, since the right taillight is dark in the film. From the actions of the car up to that point, and the fact that (1) the driver, William Greer, has turned around twice (he first turns around at frame 281 and is looking at the President, who is then shot in the head), and (2) one of the motorcycles on the left rapidly starts to overtake the car and then that cycle and the others clearly slow down and fall back momentarily after the shot (as seen in the Nix film). I observed a similar Lincoln with sunlight fully lighting one brake light and not the other. The taillights protrude out from the rear of the car and are not in sight.

Either the right brake light was burned out—which seems unlikely—or the brakes were not in fact depressed. Studies of the car's movements indicate that the car momentarily appeared to be slowing down during the shooting. It did not actually stop, and shortly picked up great speed.

The Shooting

Kennedy turns very rapidly from left to right at Z 154, Shackelford agrees. The House Committee said that the first shot was at frame 160, missing the limousine.[44] "There is no corresponding rapid turn at Z 189, though a turn from right toward center does begin after that frame."[45] Shackelford thinks that the shot might have happened at about frame 170, in view of the testimony of Bonnie Ray Williams, Harold Norman, and James Jarman.[46]

There is a splice at frames 154 and 157, which deleted frames 155 and 156. Since frame 155 is badly blurred, it would seem that there was a shot there, and the fact that there is a heavy splice line on frame 154 is highly suspicious. Blurs often came from Zapruder shaking the camera in response to a shot, according to the House Committee (see *High Treason*). Robert Morningstar made a presentation at *The Third*

Decade's Midwest Conference in late June 1992, presented studies in Gestalt psychology showing how the splices in the Zapruder film detract attention from other material in the film, and suggested that the splices were deliberately made for that purpose.

Researcher Karen Wright is of the opinion the first shot occurred at frame 155 and says Kennedy is reacting to the noise at frame 157.

The Slides in the Archives

In the early part of the film that occurs after a shot has perhaps been fired, the Kennedys, the Connallys, and the driver (Greer) are looking to the right. The House Committee felt that a shot had been fired at frame 160 and missed. Mrs. Kennedy begins turning her head from left to right at frame 162.[47] "Years later, the HSCA determined the same for Governor John Connally. Both testified that they did this in response to hearing the first shot."[48]

It is a shame that the relevant slides were not made for the National Archives set. Jackie begins looking to the right a second time at about frame 183. Everyone in the car is looking to the right by frame 183, apparently attracted in that direction by gunfire.

Z 187, Rosemary Willis, a young girl who has been running along with the car, slows and pauses at frame 175. This is about the time of a shot, if not the first shot. She walks and comes to a full stop at 188. She is last seen in frame 212. At frame 174 the car begins to be progressively obscured by the Stemmons Freeway sign; the occupants' area of the car remains in view until frame 193; the sprocket information ends at 207, with 208–11 made from a copy, as noted above.

Christopher Sharrett wrote me that Richard E. Sprague's 1967 analysis of the Zapruder film indicates the following, and he says that "all subsequent interpretations are reflections in some way or other of what Dick wrote in 1967":[49]

Z 189—The shot to the throat, based on the sudden backward jolt of JFK and the very rapid sweep of his hand passed his face in the frames just following. Willis 5 and the Betzner photo were both taken, according to their statements, just as they heard a shot fired—the sound of the shot caused them to click their shutters (author's note: This was also true of Bronson's last snapshot). Dick Sprague timed both photos as Z 200. His timing of both photos at 200 was clearly wrong; Bonar Menninger's book *Mortal Error* also makes the mistake of having them taken at the same time.

Allowing time for voluntary and involuntary responses, Z 189 makes good sense. Note that when JFK first appears from behind the sign, his right hand is still moving *down* past his chest. He is already grimacing. He was absolutely hit before the Stemmons sign, so the sign itself is fairly negligible in importance.

Shackelford comments: "The shot had to be before 189 if Betzner, 186 was taken in response to it; allowing a little reaction time, probably in the 170s. Rosemary Willis's halt at 188 may reflect a response to the same shot, also before 189."

Sharrett says, "It is very important to appreciate JFK's very rapid change of position after Z 189. He is suddenly facing dead ahead in less than a half second, his right hand flashing past his face. This is a transfer of momentum followed by involuntary neurological activity. When we see JFK's right hand appear at the edge of the Stemmons sign at Z 224, it is moving *down*. It is moving *down* in the next frame when we see JFK grimacing in pain. Then his elbows suddenly fly upward. This is one shot followed very quickly by another, with two different sets of reactions seen on the film. The Stemmons sign has no real relevance to anything: It conceals the people in the car for only a fraction of a second. Its position allowed Specter and allies room for obfuscation, but let's stop taking the bait."[50] Some of us feel that "*flashing* past his face . . ." is an exaggeration of the speed of the President's hand.

The last clear frame before the car and Kennedy are obscured by the Stemmons Freeway sign is at 208. Everyone is looking to the right, and this is where the House Committee said a shot hit both Kennedy and Connally. But Connally is clearly hit much later. His reactions contradict that supposition.

It seems to me that arguments that Connally's failure to react visibly to being hit before that are ridiculous. Often, people don't immediately know they have been shot, as was true when President Reagan received a bullet. From this point of view, it is quite possible that both Kennedy and Connally were hit with the same bullet, but that cannot have happened for a number of other reasons in the physical evidence.

The frames badly blur at 190–92, which may indicate Zapruder's reaction to a shot. JFK is clearly reacting to a shot by frame 197. All of this is before frame 210, which the Warren Commission said was the first time anyone could have shot Kennedy from the alleged assassin's window. Todd Vaughan thinks that Zapruder jerked the camera at 190 not in reaction to a shot, but "to the decision-making process," when he realized that the car was going to disappear behind the sign. He had to decide whether to keep filming or to stop his camera until the car reappeared.[51]

Frame 225 gives us the first clear view of Kennedy as the car emerges from behind the sign. Frame 225 is where Johann Rush argues that the bullet hit both men. His reasoning is that until 225, JFK's right hand is still coming down, but that just after that frame, both arms begin to come up (Thornburn's position, as argued by Lattimer), JFK's head jerks back, and Connally's right wrist jerks, flipping his hat up in front of his face, then drops limply. This can be viewed in slow motion with any copy of the Zapruder film. Rush made a short video with Dr. Michael West called *Confirmation of the Single-Bullet Theory*.[52]

There is a splice at frames 207–12, indicating that frames 208–11 are deleted. We have been provided with slides from a copy of the film replacing those few frames. Frame 210 is badly blurred.

The sprocket data return at frame 212, where we have a tree cut in half. Connally is clearly not hit. He reappears at 221. Kennedy is already raising his arms, with his right hand moving down, still, and his hands to his throat at 225, clearly shot.

Chris Sharrett writes, "Z 225—the back shot. JFK's position is suddenly reversed in an eighteenth of a second. His elbows fly upward as he is pushed down and forward. He is never *clasping* his throat as people keep saying, although at one instant his forefingers are pressing on the tiny throat wound. In this sequence, his actions seem responses to two different injuries." Connally is forward, then reacts to a shot at 228. Because Kennedy has been hidden by the sign when he is shot, we cannot see his reactions until this point. Others doubt that Kennedy's fingers ever seem to get that close to his throat.

The first indication that Connally has been shot is at about frame 225 as he continues to turn in his seat. By frame 228 Connally is grimacing, faced forward as he said he was when he was hit. He has turned rapidly since frame 226. By frame 233, his hand with his Stetson begins to fall and his body begins to turn to the right as he slips backward into Nellie's lap. "The sudden rise of Governor Connally's right arm in frames 225–30 should be mentioned, as I believe it has relevance to when Connally was hit, Z 223, I believe. Both by Z 228 Connally is grimacing and the right shoulder of Connally is depressed at Z 230 (it is depressed at Z 228). I think it is proof that he had been hit before Z 228, and at 223."[53]

In the next frame, 234, Kennedy's hands are up at his throat level. Connally's face is distorted. JFK's elbows are rising by 235. Connally's mouth is opening in 236. Martin Shackelford writes, "Connally continues to twist to the right as his right shoulder drops; what appears more clearly later as blood on his right wrist first comes into view in this frame. Robert Groden has postulated that the shot which hit Connally did so between 237 and 238, but the reactions we see here clearly begin sooner.''[54] And by frame 239 Connally's cheeks have begun to puff out.

Chris Sharrett confirms Shackelford's observations as follows: ''Z 234—the shot through Connally's chest. This is based in part on what Connally himself told *Life,* but also study of the radical change in his position at this point. Note how Connally's movements correspond exactly with his very detailed and consistent statements about his wounding.''

In frame 243, Connally twisted to the right, and he is crying out. He is observably in pain. Kennedy's hands are covering the lower part of his face.

Frame 255, which is at the same time as the Altgens photo of the shooting,[55] showing Jackie's hand grasping Kennedy's left wrist, as seen through the windshield of the car, and a retouched Greer turned to his right just barely visible in profile. Connally is beginning to say, ''My God, they're going to kill us all.''

The second box of slides at the National Archives starts at Z 244, and Connally looks shot, mouth open, faced right. There is a sort of stasis for a time, with nothing much changing. Then at 280, Greer is looking back to 287.

The driver, Greer, turns his head to the front at 290. At 300 in the National Archives set, he begins a rapid turn of his head toward the rear of the limousine again; we see his right profile in the Altgens photograph through the windshield of the car. Greer turns his head rapidly forward again in frame 316.

The House Committee said that a third shot (of the admitted four) was fired at frame 301 from the Grassy Knoll, and missed.

Z 287—a shot misses the car. Altgens also said he pressed his shutter as a shot was fired. Of course, all this is happening very fast, but we'll take Altgens at his word that he was responding to a shot at this instant rather than an earlier shot. Note that for this shot to be a near miss of the car, striking the sidewalk near Tague down by the center of the overpass, it most likely came from a low floor in the Dal-Tex Building. A shot from high in the TSBD would miss the car by a country mile.

But Shackelford comments, ''This seems to be the source of the idea that Altgens was taken at Z 287 instead of 255; this is clearly wrong. In 255, as in Altgens, JFK's arms are still up, whereas by 287 they are down and he is slumping. Chris may have transcribed this wrong, as a shot at 255 would be wide of the car from TSBD, but not from Dal-Tex.''[56]

Frame 313—the fatal head shot. We did not detect any streak coming in on the car in the surrounding frames. Some claim a bullet is captured by the camera.

There are those who see streaks or what they think are bullets coming in from the front on the film or videotapes. Vince Palamara sees one streak mark coming in at the level of the head from the lower right front,[57] though it does not look to me like it could come from the grassy knoll almost alongside. Others see up to three streaks on the film.

It is probably physically impossible for a bullet to be photographed in those conditions and at that distance. Matter is spraying from JFK's head upward, forward, and toward the camera (per stereo analysis), according to Martin Shackelford. The driver is still looking to the rear and continues to do so for a few frames.

Sharrett suggests, rightfully or wrongfully, the following based on Sprague's notes: "Z 313—obviously the head shot sequence. The sudden whip around by Connally suggests that his wrist and/or leg were hit by other bullets or fragments. The National Archives copy of the film shows the skull fragments striking the car's trunk."

Anthony Marsh has conducted a computer study based on the relationship of each person in the fatal limousine to parts of the car such as door handles and so on. His finding is that the President's head does not move forward at any time at the time of the fatal shot (frame 313 of the film). The head only moves backward, and there is no connection with the later acceleration of the car, when all in the car move backward slightly. Marsh's findings are in contrast with that of Josiah Thompson's mentioned early in this chapter.

The head wound is partially visible in National Archives frames 316 and 317. Frame 316 shows the head much more disrupted in the area of the large defect as in the autopsy report. I find it suspicious that those who popularized this film did not make a point of demonstrating the position of the head wound and instead placed elsewhere from the area where it actually is, and then on top. Greer turns back toward the front at frame 316. There is a very clear picture of Greer turned to his right at 317. There is a large hole in Kennedy's head right above and behind the ear. A very clear hole in the head. In 318 there is a big hole in the head generally in the precise position noted in the autopsy report. *But* it is not visible in each set of slides at the National Archives, and there is no way of knowing which set we are given.

This box of slides ends at 323, and the next box of slides starts at 324.

A close observation of the frames shortly after the fatal head shot shows a black shadow over the back of the head. This shadow appears highly suspicious. Although the head would be somewhat out of the direct sunlight in that position, facing to the northeast, the shadow appears to be drawn on the film, and would mask the large loss of skull and scalp known to have occurred in that area of the President's head.

Martin Shackelford speculates on the shadow as follows: "After the shot frame (313), the hair at the back of the head seems to be thrown upward. This may be what survives on the film of an exit wound in the right rear of the head. It may have been concealed simply by slightly darkening an area already in shadow. The wound may have had bright highlights, requiring such darkening to conceal it. This wouldn't have required any sophisticated technical work, and could have been done quickly, simply by underexposing that portion of the frame. This would have been done after the initial copies of the film were made, so one of the initial copies could contain information exposing this manipulation. Of course, this would include the Secret Service copies of the film, unless manipulated prints were later substituted for those made the afternoon of November 22, 1963.

"The details we saw in the National Archives copies of frames 316 and 317 are also present in the Groden 35-mm. slides. Any manipulation of the frames probably occurred before slides were made for the Warren Commission, and certainly before any publication of the relevant frames."[58]

Frame 337 may show the hole in the back of the head. Much of the front of his head and face is gone from frame 335. What remains appears as a stub and totally contradicts what we know: that there was no damage to the forward part of his head or face. This is where I feel the film has been forged and "the Blob" has been drawn in. (See *High Treason 2* with regard to "the Blob" and photographs.) "The Blob" is a large structure appearing on the right side of the face shortly after the head explodes. It does not correspond to anything seen at Parkland or the autopsy, and is an impossibility, since the face was not damaged. It appears to be the entire brain hanging out of the forehead, corresponding to the loss of bone in the fake X-rays in that area. (See *High Treason 1* and *2* with regard to the frontal bone missing in the X-rays.) It cannot be a flap.

Frame 378 is missing from the slides. The left brake light appears to be lighted until 383.

The color of the film shifts and is redder until 394, with less or no part of the top of the frames showing. The color of the film becomes greener from 395. From here to the end of the film, there are parts of each adjoining frame showing in one frame, top and bottom. This box ends at frame 403, which is blurred, and is darker in the sprocket hole area. Clint Hill is on the car's bumper.

The fourth box of archival slides begins at frame 404, which has a serious blur from 404 to 406.

Frame 412 is the last of the sprocket hole information until 437.

Frame 413 has no sprocket hole information. The color changes radically, is not as clear, and is grainier.

Frame 413 (Groden's numbering) or 415 (the numbering of the National Archives set) is the frame that Groden has claimed shows a rifle poking out from a sprig of leaves in front of the low cement retaining wall close beside Zapruder.

Until frame 436 all sprocket information is gone.

There is sprocket hole information from frame 437 to the end of the frame set at 483.

There is a bleed over the sprocket holes from other parts of the frame (in some frames—e.g., 448—there appears to be a tree standing in the sprocket area). Frame 440 has all sprocket hole information out of order.

Only half of the sprocket hole information shows (vertical) from 439 back.

Frames 461–62 appear to be badly damaged.

The Betzner photograph was taken at Z 186, Willis at Z 202, Bronson at Z 232, Altgens at 255. The Robert Croft photo was taken at frame 161. The Bronson slide was reportedly taken in reaction to the first shot, or to the first shot he heard. Some people thought the first gunshot noise was a firecracker and did not react as much. Of course, the first shot came a lot sooner than frame 210 of the Zapruder film, so these frame numbers provided by Martin Shackelford are tentative at best.

The Nix Film

An important film showing the fatal head shot was taken by Orville Nix from the side of Elm Street opposite from Zapruder. UPI had originally bought this film from Nix, and it was supposed to revert to his estate in 1988. This did not happen, and in 1991 the film was no longer in the possession of UPI. Gayle Nix Jackson was told that the National Archives had the film, but it was *missing* from there also. It was then traced to the House Assassinations Committee, which was set up in 1976. The film was studied there, but *lost*.[59]

Robert Blakey told Gayle Jackson that her grandfather's film was lost. Robert Groden showed this film several times on national television in the fall of 1991, most notably on the Geraldo Rivera show and the Montel Williams show. Each time, sometimes just one day apart, Groden stated, ''now, for the first time on national television, you are going to see an unknown film of the assassination. . . .'' It is hard to believe he would thus describe the Nix film, which he has shown since 1973, and which is in the 1964 Wolper documentary *Four Days in November,* as Martin Shackelford comments.[60]

The Dallas Cinema Associates Film

There is a poor copy of this film, titled *President Kennedy's Final Hour,* in the National Archives. It was made up after the assassination, distributed, and sold commercially in 1964, but it is not well known, and was widely pirated by others. A group of people had gone to see the motorcade to film the President, and remained on the scene, filming what occurred. They saw and filmed a man coming down the fire escape of the Texas School Book Depository and carrying a rifle. It also contains a short snippet of the Johnny Martin film.

Referring to the Mentesana film, ''It shows a rifle being brought down the fire escape,'' Sharrett wrote me, ''of the TSBD by a Dallas cop. The cop is coming from the roof. He holds up a rifle that the DCA (Dallas Cinema Associates) filmmakers caption 'The Assassin's Rifle.' This weapon has a fairly short stock, a heavy barrel, and a different action from the so-called Oswald rifle. It looks to me like a 30-30 Enfield. When Sprague questioned the Dallas authorities in 1967, he was told it was a security man's rifle accidentally left there. What security man? The Dallas cops all carried shotguns. The sheriff's office had rifles, but they were of American manufacture (the Enfield is British). There is no record of any 'security man' being on the roof of TSBD before, during, or after the assassination. The scene taken by the DCA filmmakers occurred at 2:00. Lieutenant Carl Day brought the Oswald rifle outside at 1:30; there are plenty of photos of Day quickly carrying this rifle away, holding it by its strap. In the DCA film, the cop holds the rifle up as a crowd gathers. The same scene is captured in Phil Willis's tenth photo.''[61]

Martin Shackelford has argued that the two Mentesana clips are confused in the above. The first shows two Dallas Police Department officers on the upper outside of the east side of the TSBD on a fire escape; the other shows several officers down at street level examining what is captioned ''The Assassin's Rifle,'' and another photographer also cap-

turing the scene. A still from the second segment appears on p. 129 of
Cover-up by Shaw and Harris.

As for a "security man" being on the roof of the Texas School Book
Depository, that dovetails with Deputy Sheriff Harry Weatherford being
across the street on the roof of the Dallas County Jail (Records Building) with a rifle during the assassination.[62]

"Grodenscoping"

Robert Groden was a hero for getting the Zapruder film out, but "the
question is, did he stumble ethically after that?" Martin Shackelford
asks.[63] It is worth noting that Groden has applied a system of alteration,
which he calls "optical enhancement," to the vast amount of photographs and film frames that have one way or another fallen into his
hands.

So now we come to *"Grodenscoping,"* which, he says, is optical
enhancement. "I perform a variation of a technique called rotoscoping
on the film. The variation is so unique from actual rotoscoping that
certain people [Gary Mack and his wife] have called it Grodenscoping.
What I did was I stablized the film, I blew it up so it was as if Zapruder
had had a longer telephoto lens. I repositioned the crosshairs of the
camera, of the optical camera, the optical printer, on the President and
rephotographed the film frame by frame, enlarging it, eliminating a lot
of the extraneous material in the background. I color corrected it and
I stretched framed it to slow it down, so it created a more coherent
version of the film. Now our eye didn't have to travel all over the
screen to see what was going on. It was now stabilized. . . ."[64]

Shackelford comments: "Grodenscoping is, indeed, optical enhancement, and a particularly useful form of it. If you look at the Thompson
version, you will see concentration on certain things happening in the
film. Because the enlargement is done simply by enlarging a certain
portion of all the frames, it is difficult to focus on what is being emphasized. Grodenscoping focuses on the subject of interest, and removes
the bouncing around which results from the other approach. It is true
that certain portions of the frame are unseen in this process, but to
suggest something sinister in this, you need to show that there is something of significance in the missing portions. If the Grodenscoping centers on JFK, you can clearly follow JFK; if it centers on Connally, you
can clearly follow Connally; ditto Rosemary Willis, Phil Willis, Mary
Moorman, Jean Hill, Jackie, Howard Brennan, Robert Croft, Hugh Betzner, or whoever else is selected as the subject."[65]

"What is rotoscoping?" attorney Kevin Brennan asked him.

"Rotoscoping is taking a visual image and using it as an anchor or a guide to create another visual image. In other words, if you have one piece of film and you need to match another piece of film to action, you use the original piece of film as a guide, and the technique of doing this is called rotoscoping. What I did was take a visual anchor on the film, which in one version was the president's ear, ear and temple, as the visual anchor. In another case it was the handhold that's welded to the trunk of the car, and I used that in the lower left-hand corner as the visual anchor."

"How does Grodenscoping differ from rotoscoping, as you defined it?"

"I basically just answered that. I used—I used a quadrant or a marking within the viewfinder of the optical printer, as opposed to using a piece of film. In other words, I wasn't matching film to film: I was matching image on film to a visual point of reference. That's the difference between the two techniques." Groden explains that an optical printer is a machine with one or more projectors and one camera, specifically for the duplication and enhancement of films.

"If you are doing rotoscoping without the visual anchor technique that you described, how does it differ from the way you did it?"

"Well, as I said, rotoscoping would use a predetermined image on an initial strip of film, an initial piece of film. You'd be matching action to a preshot piece of film as opposed to an arbitrary visual anchor. In one case it's a matching process. Best way I can describe it that way, that rotoscoping is a film matching process, and Grodenscoping, what has become known as Grodenscoping, is simply a stabilization process."

"And what do you mean by 'stabilization'?"

"As I said, the original film is very shaky. What I did is I steadied the image, I stabilized the image by eliminating a lot of the extraneous material around the president, the material that in a study of the actions of the occupants of the car is not relevant. I blew it up, made it larger, so that the grain structure, contrast and color correction are better, and then I rephotographed it frame by frame."

"What is the purpose of rephotographing it frame by frame?"

"If you don't rephotograph it, then you're not making a copy. The idea of making the copy and enhancing it is to stabilize the image so that the eye can follow what's going on, what's happening on film. Otherwise, what happens is what happened previous to that, where the image is just so shaky and so incoherent to the eye and to the mind that you can't really tell what's going on. If the president appears in the upper left, your eye shoots to the upper left to see him, but by the time it gets there, running at eighteen frames per second, all of a sudden he's on the lower left; by the time your eye gets there, he's already gone. And nobody could look at the film and tell what was actually going on.''

"So the focus or the view of the Zapruder film was much broader than simply the president or even the occupants of the car."

"Oh, yes, absolutely."

"So what you are describing as what you did to a certain extent involves a narrowing of the field of vision or the focus."

"What's called the field of view, yes."

"And when you say that you took a visual anchor—say, in the case where you used the ear and temple as the visual anchor—did that become the center of the field of view in each frame?"

"Yes."

"You mentioned two visual anchors that you used, one, the handhold, and the other, the ear and temple. Are they the only two visual anchors that you used for making your optical enhancements?"

"No."

"What other visual anchors have you used?"

"Governor Connally, Mrs. Kennedy, various witnesses in the background, the driver, and Secret Service guard, things like that. Various different focal points for different studies."

Rotoscoping is a useful technical tool, but what is often going on is that we are being told what to think during narratives of the film. The copy of the Zapruder film shown on *Nova* in 1988, which has come to be known as the Thompson Version, is simply a 35-mm. copy made from the 8-mm. copy with no alterations or rotoscoping. This film is of startling clarity, with very fine colors, and infinitely better than anything Groden has ever shown publicly.

There seems to be a subliminal element: When the fatal shot to the head strikes, we are then told by the narrator, "Now, see, Jackie is crawling out on the trunk to retrieve the back of the head." This fixes the moment in our mind and associates it with the fact that we are not seeing the back of his head on the trunk, but we *are* seeing his face blow out toward the front, and nothing is ever said about that by the narrator. If asked, we are told that we are looking at a flap of scalp. But from *where*?

"What does 'stretch frame' mean?"

"Okay, as I mentioned before, the Zapruder film runs 21 seconds. It's very quick. It was shot at 18.3 frames per second. Projecting it back on a normal sound projector or projector for a film chain, it will run at 24 frames, way too fast, almost half again as fast as it was originally shot, and it goes by so fast the mind cannot comprehend what's going on. So some of the versions I stretch framed it, which you shoot—in which you shoot two or in some cases three [Author's note: Presumably he means that he rephotographed the same frame and inserted it so that there is not actually any movement between several frames.], depending on how slow you want it to play back, to compensate for the projector's speed error. That's stretch framing. Or if you just want to slow down the image so the mind can comprehend what's going on quicker.''

"Why would you do that rather than just running the film at slow motion?''

"Not all projectors are capable of running slow motion. In some cases, if you try to force slow motion, the intensity of the light will burn up the film.''

"I would like to know all of the optical enhancements that you have created.''

"I have basically lost track of all that I have done. As I have mentioned before, I not only optically enhanced and rotoscoped or Grodenscoped the president but Mrs. Kennedy, Mr. Connally, Mrs. Connally, the driver, the Secret Service guard; Clint Hill, who had jumped on the back of the president's limousine; many witnesses in the plaza, Howard Brennan, Phil Willis, Linda Willis; areas of the stockade fence behind— the area behind the stockade fence in the Grassy Knoll; a man who has become known as the black dog man, the back of his head; sections of the car itself; other witnesses in the plaza that I can't specifically remember. And these just relate to the Zapruder film, and I did optical enhancements of the other films as well.''

"What were the other frames you did optical enhancements for?''

"I mentioned Zapruder, Nix, Muchmore, Bell, Hughes, Towner, Dorman, Paschall, Bronson, Daniel. I'm sure I'm missing some others, but . . .''

With reference to the slides he has made and distributed through the old Assassination Information Bureau and other sources, he says, "Those slides are one duplicate, one set of duplicates. I had done many different versions of those, and it's difficult to tell which specific one it had come from, or another. But the red slides do have a specific cast, from specific prints rather than Ektachromes.'' (Ektachrome is reversal film.)

He said that he had never had any contact with Zapruder or his lawyer until he was about to show the film for the first time on national television in 1976 on Geraldo Rivera, and he called Zapruder to tell him, and was told it was okay. He in effect became the publicist for the film.

But when he published some of the Zapruder frames in Larry Flynt's (publisher of *Hustler*) magazine on the assassination, for which he was paid $20,000,[66] did he have a copyright? "That's a very grey area, I would think, because the copyright, the common law copyright exists upon publication of the item. The creation of the item generates the copyright. The underlying copyright relates to the unenhanced film, and that, at that particular time in 1978, belonged to the LMH Company. But I did have permission from Henry Zapruder to do this, to do the work on the film, and the copyright office granted me my own copyright on the—which you do have those papers—on the enhanced versions of the film."

"What's shown [in the *L.A. Free Press*] on page 23 represents not just the Zapruder film but your optical enhancements of the Zapruder film, correct?" Kevin Brennan asked.

"That's correct."

"And in 1978, when this periodical was published, did you own the copyright on the optical enhancements that you had made to the Zapruder film?"

"I—in one sense, no, in one sense, no. In the sense that I had created them and the common law copyright existed on them, yes. I had not yet filed an official copyright paper as yet."

Groden failed to understand that in 1986 when he registered a copyright claim on a "motion study" of a number of the films in the case, that mere registration has nothing to do with the actual granting or entitlement of copyright, and that perhaps "this copyright page relates to the motion study," Groden said, "not the specific individual frames. The individual specific frames would have been covered by the common law copyright, as I understand it, of the individual frames. This particular copyright page relates to the publication of the intact elements, the motion elements in a specific form."

There is a doctrine of "fair use" in publishing and the media. Here is someone who is attempting to assert a claim over countless visual films and photographs that often do not belong to him, by refocusing them in some way and reselling them. In most cases he never had any legal agreement to do so.

On a possible conspiracy, the
Sheriff of Dallas told me, "Lets
put it this way: If we could go to
trial now, we couldn't make a
case because of what the
researchers have done to the
evidence."

—Dallas sheriff Jim Bowles

CHAPTER 12

ACOUSTICS

"I believe that there was a deal among the staff of the House Select Committee on Assassinations and the defense contractors they hired . . . to find an extra shot on the Dallas Police Department [DPD] recordings when there was none. In fact, there were no shots at all on the tape." Researcher Steve Barber told me this in the summer of 1991, and it stunned me. Dallas's Sheriff Jim Bowles has given me a somewhat similar concept of distorted evidence.[1] Due to the fact that he is the sheriff and therefore part of Dallas political life, can we be sure that what Bowles says is not biased?

I have come to a simple explanation of the whole acoustical issue, as complicated as it appears. I was wrong in the position I took on the acoustics in my first book. I regret it.

For those not familiar with it, the Dallas Police had two recorders, a Dictaphone and a Gray Audograph, recording all of their radio communications. The Dictaphone recorded Channel 1, and the Gray Audograph recorded Channel 2. During the time of the assassination, a motorcycle police officer had his microphone stuck open on Channel 1. We know from the sound throughout the recording that it was a motorcycle. We also know that it was not in Dealey Plaza but quite some distance away because there are no crowd noises at any time during that recording, whereas on the special events channel (Channel 2) there were loud crowd noises whenever a mike was turned on near a lot of people. And no motorcycle. Researcher Todd Vaughan feels that voices of bystanders can be heard on Open mike sequence 3, of the four open mike episodes, at Parkland Hospital on Channel 1. There were four sequences when there was an open microphone on that recording.

There are no sirens for the first two minutes following the time when

Bolt, Beranek, and Newman said there were shots on the recording of Channel 1, which means that the motorcycle cannot be in the motorcade. Almost every vehicle engaged their sirens as soon as there was trouble. Officer Chaney, on a motorcycle, sped up to the car bearing Chief of Police Curry and Sheriff Bill Decker and told them that the President had been shot. The chief and Decker then began broadcasting directions to their men, and the motorcade sped off to Parkland Hospital, sirens wailing, passing the Trade Mart on the way.

The motorcycle with the stuck microphone on Channel 1 appears to have been at the Trade Mart,[2] in a motor pool some 280 feet east of Stemmons Freeway, and some 75 feet south of Industrial Boulevard, alongside several other city police cars, State Police cars, and two and three wheeled motorcycles—some of which had their radios on. The radio on this idling motorcycle faithfully rebroadcast on Channel 1 what was on Channel 2. So the same transmissions came to be recorded on both recorders during that period of time.

That same stuck mike faithfully picked up the sirens of the motorcade as it passed the Trade Mart on the way to Parkland "at the only and proper time and place," as Bowles noted. I should tell the reader that I often send my chapters to some of the persons most concerned with them, whether witnesses or experts, and ask them to correct my work. This chapter has been corrected by the sheriff of Dallas, among others, and Tony Marsh, Steve Barber, Todd Vaughan, and Kathlee Fitzgerald.

Officer H. B. McLain, whom the House Committee claimed was the officer with the stuck mike, was trailing more than a block behind the fatal limousine.[3] We know his motorcycle did not have its mike on because we do not hear any siren on that entire channel for two full minutes, which is the time it took for the motorcade, sirens screaming, to pass the Trade Mart on its way to Parkland Hospital, a mile farther on. McLain stated that he turned his siren on immediately after he heard a shot.[4]

The House Committee not only lied about this, but they also lied when they said McLain lagged behind the motorcade and stayed a while in Dealey Plaza, then caught up with the motorcade. This is how they explained the lack of sirens on the recording.

Catching up with that motorcade, even if only seconds behind, would have been unlikely, since the motorcade was traveling at more than seventy miles an hour out Stemmons to the Industrial Boulevard exit past Oak Lawn. Officer McLain never left the motorcade, because it was he who helped Mrs. Kennedy get out of the limousine.[5]

McLain was not allowed by the House Committee to listen to the tape or to see the evidence. It was one more example of rigged evidence and rigged testimony. After it was all over, he heard the whole tape and knew it was not he. He appeared on TV in Dallas and told the whole story, of how he came around the corner of Main and Houston and looked through the latticework of the pergola alongside Houston Street, and wondered what Secret Service agent Clint Hill was doing up on the trunk of the car, going down Elm and underneath the Triple Overpass.[6] He turned on his siren and sped off as fast as he could. Sheriff Bowles has added to this last sentence so it reads: "He turned on his siren and sped off as fast as he could in response to Chief Curry's command which McLain heard over his radio, *as it was tuned to Channel 1, not Channel 2, as the HSCA claimed.*"

"Looked like they were trying to pull the wool over my eyes," McLain said.

Steve Barber was the one who determined that the alleged shots on the tape were not there, and he so notified the Committee on Ballistics Acoustics of the National Academy of Sciences (NAS) (the Ramsey Panel), earning him the wrath of some researchers.

"This was at least a year if not two after I had notified the HSCA and the FBI," Bowles wrote on the manuscript here. "The FBI took up my case, then passed this information and my data to the National Academy of Sciences. Then they came to me. The rest is history!"

At every step of the way in this case, there is something wrong with the evidence. Each piece of evidence seems tainted. There seems to be two of everything. In my last book, look at the section "Conflicts in the Evidence" and give that some thought. Barber found conversation at the place on the recordings where shots were supposed to have occurred—because it was crosstalk recorded from another radio channel whose timing was well documented. The National Academy of Sciences backed him up.

As hard as I tried when I wrote a chapter on acoustics in my first book on this case, I made mistakes. Understanding the scientific issues is all but impossible without the equipment to repeat all the experiments and findings claimed by all parties. We have to take the word of many people, and they are very much in conflict. In this new attempt, I will try to explain the issues in as clear language as possible, and let the reader decide. I try to be objective. *The weight of the evidence is that there were no shots on the recordings.* The claim of a microphone being open appears to be fabricated evidence.

I never relied on the acoustical findings for proof that there was a conspiracy in the assassination. How could I? Only a fool would do so, even in this modern age when we are taught to trust all the scientific gobbledygook to which we are exposed. I believed that the proofs of conspiracy were simple and available but were being ignored.

After my first book was published, Steve Barber climbed all over me in his booklet *Double Decker,* published by Robert Cutler.[7] Barber's research paved the way for the NAS. I came to know and like Steve Barber, and my suspicion that he might have the key to one of the biggest puzzles in this case was worth a hearing, even if it disproved some of the very evidence that appeared to prove a conspiracy. On the other hand, maybe his findings are a key to the conspiracy itself.

Dr. James Barger admitted that "Barber discovered a very weak spoken phrase on the DPD Dictabelt recording that is heard at about the time of the sound impulses we concluded were probably caused by the fourth shot. The NAS Committee has shown to our satisfaction that this phrase has the same origin as the same phrase heard also on the Audograph recording."[8] Barger goes on, "The Audograph recording was originally made from the Channel 2 radio. The common phrase is heard on Channel 2 about a minute after the assassination would appear, from context, to have taken place. Therefore, it would seem, and the NAS Committee concludes, that the sounds that we connected with gunfire were made about a minute after the assassination shots were fired."[9]

Things have a habit of leaking out when they have to do with the sensational. For example, the backyard photos of Oswald were copied and distributed to numbers of the Dallas Police for souvenirs, and a police officer provided copies of the recordings to local "researchers."

According to Gary Mack (a.k.a. Larry Darkel, Larry Dunkle), a tape copy of the recording was made by officer Gerald Hill, who passed either that copy or a copy of the copy to Judy Bonner, author of *Investigation of a Homicide.* Bonner's tape was then either given to or copied for Mary Ferrell. A copy of Ferrell's tape was copied and given to Penn Jones, and a copy of that was made for Gary Shaw. Many copies of that tape were then distributed far and wide. Mack heard Jones's copy and decided that there must be shots on it.[10]

With the help of resident critics, the public was to be thrown a bone by the government in 1978 and told that there was a conspiracy in the murder of John Kennedy. That bone would turn out to be a time bomb. The findings of conspiracy on the basis of the acoustical tapes were false. It was, of course, unnecessary to base a finding of conspiracy on the physics of acoustics. There were plenty of other proofs of conspiracy without it.

Trying to sort through information and data in the issue of the recordings made by the Dallas Police during the time of the shooting of President Kennedy is like sorting through somebody else's trunk in the attic and trying to make sense of thousands of bits of strange paper.

Perhaps that is the point. Sheriff Jim Bowles did his own study of the recordings after the House Assassinations Committee concluded that there was a fourth shot in one of them, and stated in a book-length manuscript that he believed there were no shots at all on the recordings.[11] Independently, a committee formed by the National Academy of Sciences also found that there were no shots on the tape.

By timing the replay of the tape and checking against the dispatcher announcing the time, Bolt, Beranek, and Newman (BBN) claimed it could be easily shown when both tapes were running or stopped. It was possible to determine that Channel 1 was playing continuously during minutes surrounding the murder shots, even though it was noise-activated. Sheriff Jim Bowles states that the machines were not strictly voice-activated, but *noise*-activated, "as all sound over the carrier would start the recording." Channel 2 was being used for the motorcade that day. Channel 1 played continuously during the known time of the assassination, at 12:30 P.M. Central Standard Time, due to the stuck microphone.

Although the Dictaphone on Channel 1 was noise-activated, it ran continuously when the mike was stuck open because the mike was picking up the broadcasts from Channel 2 and strong background noise.[12] Tony Marsh adds that the Dictaphone did not run continuously *because of* Channel 2. It ran continuously because the mike was stuck open, and as Bowles tells us above, noise activated the recorders.

During the time the microphone was stuck open, some other officer pressed the button on his microphone and tried to transmit, there was a "heterodyne" or beep. Officers became frantic trying to reach the dispatcher, until a radio officer became furious and ordered his men to find the officer with the stuck mike and turn it off.

"Another type of interference was caused when two radios were side by side and one of them transmitted to the dispatcher or to another unit. This caused feedback audible during the transmission."[13] The recording by a mike side by side with a receiver whose speaker was playing a message on another channel becomes a key factor in the mess in the evidence that followed.

Four major (more than five or ten seconds each) open-mike sequences on Channel 1 were identified during a half-hour period surrounding the assassination. The one we are concerned with is the second, during which time the assassination occurred.

Bolt, Beranek, and Newman studied the original recordings (or what is alleged to be the originals) made by the Dallas Police, as well as tape recordings made by the Dallas Police of the originals. The tapes were more reliable, as time and usage had altered the originals. BBN used the tapes to make a graph on a strip of paper 234 feet long, after running the tapes through an oscilloscope. This yielded the sound waves in graphic form. Thus they were able to study the impulses on the tape and correlate them with identifiable sounds. A motorcycle, for instance, was easy to identify. What might have been shots and their echoes were more difficult, since they were not clearly discernible from other sounds.

BBN tried to filter out the motorcycle noise that predominates the tape but did not succeed very well. "The filtering removed some low-frequency noise and hum on the tape, but the overall effect was not dramatic," Todd Vaughan writes.[14]

They had to pinpoint the moment of the assassination by comments on the tape indicating that the assassination had occurred.

BBN identified four impulse patterns from a total of seven that occurred during the open-mike sequence, which they thought were shots. They recommended tests: Gunshots were fired and recorded by thirty-six microphones spaced along the streets in Dealey Plaza, and some fifty-seven test shots were fired into sandbags from two locations—the TSBD sixth-floor window and the Knoll.[15] Again, graphs on long strips of paper were made from each gunshot recorded from each mike, and these waves were compared to the waves or spikes they had from the 1963 police tapes. "BBN found four test shots that matched the four sounds on the tape within certain possible percentages." One of the four shots was found to have come from the Knoll.

Another pair of scientists, Weiss and Aschkenasy, confirmed these findings.

Todd Vaughan writes with regard to their conclusions: "The acoustical tests were the basis for the HSCA conclusion of conspiracy. Thus, the accuracy of the tests are [sic] very important. In the end, four members of the HSCA dissented from the final conclusions because of the acoustics tests. They felt the tests were not definitive enough and more work was needed.[16] BBN has been criticized for their failure to fully study all of the many sounds on the DPD tape of Channel 1. They did little testing on the tape other than the work with the gunshots. Their lack of interest into the other sounds was a great error on their part, for the failure to fully study the tape led BBN to the wrong conclusions. There are sounds on the DPD tape that make BBN's conclusions almost a physical impossibility."[17]

Channel 2, which was voice-activated, had been recording intermittently, but shortly before 12:30 P.M., it became continuous throughout the period of the shooting.[18]

Researchers Steve Barber and Todd Vaughan independently determined (confirmed by the Committee on Ballistics of the National Academy of Sciences) that during the open-mike sequence at the time of the shots, the first bit of crosstalk heard on Channel 1 (the police channel) is Sheriff Bill Decker on Channel 2 (the motorcade channel) saying *"Hold everything secure until the homicide and other investigators can get there."* (Remember, Decker is talking into Channel 2, but all receivers are playing it, and an open mike somewhere is rebroadcasting Decker onto Channel 1.) Todd Vaughan writes, "This was picked up on Channel 1 at 146 seconds into open-mike sequence 2. This is only 8.3 seconds after BBN's first shot at 137.7 seconds and a mere .39 second after their last shot at 145.61."[19]

The fact that the recording was continuous during this period allows the time at which the assassination occurred to be established accurately, and this can be related to Channel 1 at the point where BBN claims the four shots occur. "This is made possible through the open mike picking up of the Channel 2 transmission at 146 seconds."[20] At about this time, Chief Curry in the lead car radios in on Channel 2 that he is at the Triple Underpass. Eight seconds later, the dispatcher announces the time: "12:30 KKB 364."*

Eighteen seconds later, Curry radios in again and says, "We're going to the hospital, officers." We know from these events that the assassination, therefore, occurred during a twenty-six-second period from 12:29:52 to 12:30:18 P.M. CST.

Sixty-four seconds later, at 12:31:22, Sheriff Decker says, "Hold everything secure until the homicide and other investigators can get there." *This is the crucial piece of crosstalk that throws out the findings of the committee.* Decker said it on Channel 2, and it is picked up by the open mike and recorded on Channel 1. This is the core of the mistakes made by the House Committee scientists.

"Accordingly, since the Channel 2 transmission is made at 12:31:22, the BBN shots occur at about 12:31:13 to 12:31:21 P.M. CST." This is more than one minute after the only possible time the shots could have occurred.

---

*The time announced by the dispatcher is an approximation, as it could vary depending on the angle at which he looked at the clock. "It is an arbitrary benchmark. The real time could have been anywhere from 12:29 to 12:31, depending on which clock was off by how much from the real time," Tony Marsh wrote on this manuscript.

The Decker statement "Hold everything secure ..." occurs at 12:31:22 P.M. CST on both channels, which is 146 seconds into open-mike sequence 2 on Channel 1. BBN's four shot sounds occur between 137.7 and 145.61 seconds into sequence 2, only 8.3 seconds to .39 second before the Channel 2 transmission picked up at 146 seconds into the open-mike sequence.

What this gets down to is that the scientists in 1978 did not hear the statement "Hold everything secure ..." because it was very faint, but Steve Barber's trained percussionist ear did, and Decker's order could be timed precisely. The trouble was that the placement of the four impulses thought to be shots by the government's hired scientists occurs *after* Decker's order to deal with the shooting. "BBN's shots fall 54 to 63 seconds after the latest time that the assassination could have happened, according to the computed times from Channel 2."[21]

Sirens

Another apparent flaw in the findings was the identification of officer H. B. McLain as the one with the open mike.

There are no sirens on the tape until about two minutes after the assassination. We know that most of those who remained in the motorcade with sirens turned them on as soon as the shooting was over. H. B. McLain turned his siren on. We hear sirens in the recording, but they are "sirens passing the open mike and not a siren mounted on the cycle with the open mike, as it would have been had McLain had the open mike." The HSCA said that McLain was simply mistaken and that he probably did have the open mike on Channel 1.[22] A photograph taken outside of Parkland Hospital after the motorcade arrived, shows McLain's cycle parked there.[23]

"The whereabouts of the cycle with the open mike can be located with reasonable certainty by listening to the sounds during each open-mike sequence. Open-mike sequence 1 is the first time the open mike comes on. It lasts for 18 seconds and is almost totally uneventful, with the exception of some faint, unintelligible voices at 2.5 seconds into the sequence. The level of the motorcycle engine noise remains steady throughout the entire interval. Open-mike sequence 2 begins 7.5 seconds after sequence 1 and lasts for 344 seconds. Sequence 2 contains almost all of the sounds indicating the location of the motorcycle.

"At 19 to 27 seconds are the faint sounds that Gary Mack thought were gunshots. These sounds, however, are not shots. They are static and momentary increases in engine noise. Also, by referring to the

Channel 1 time correlation with Channel 2, done earlier, it is seen that these sounds occur 29 to 37 seconds before the assassination took place. They cannot be gunfire.

"BBN's four 'shot' sounds occur shortly after this, at 137.7 to 145.8 seconds. Only one of their 'shots' is audible, the first at 137.7 seconds. It is important to note that this sound does not resemble a gunshot.

". . . Beginning at 262 seconds and lasting until 299 seconds are the sounds of several sirens. These sirens are very important as to determining the location of the cycle with the open mike. The sirens are the sirens mounted on the motorcade vehicles. They were all turned on following the assassination. . . . The sirens on the tape sound as if they are passing a stationary microphone not in the motorcade but on Stemmons Freeway. The sirens rise in intensity, fade, rise again, and fade again. This continues and suggests that several vehicles are passing the open mike. It is clear that the open mike is not in the motorcade but somewhere on Stemmons Freeway."[24] There is also a Doppler effect as the sirens approach the open mike and then pass it by. Sound is compressed in intensity as it comes closer, then changes.

Vaughan presents more technical analysis of the tape in narration, and concludes that "there is no possible way in which this cycle was with the President's motorcade. It's a physical impossibility."[25] Vaughan says that at the time we hear the sirens on Channel 1, he believes that the motorcycle is at or near Parkland Hospital.[26]

The Discs, Copies, and Play Speed

Steve Barber noted that the original Gray Audograph disc has "much missing, plus a lot of skipping/repeating, just as an LP record skips due to a poor stylus. The Audograph disc recorder used by the Dallas Police had a worn 'worm gear,' plus the stylus was in poor shape. When they transferred the disc onto tape, the Dallas Police recorded it the way it was and it skipped and repeated many times. In 1964, when they began making transcripts of the recordings onto paper, they had to back up and play it over and over. The broadcasts weren't easy to understand. This accounts for much of the wear on the disc."[27] The point of this is that the "critics' copy"[28] of the police recording was very poor.

Barber was able to obtain a second-generation high-quality copy of the tape of the original Channel 2 recording. "I had been told by NAS panel member Paul Horowitz that they had made a nonskipping copy of the original Channel 2 disc from 12:03 to 12:48 and that it contained each and every broadcast originally recorded that day."[29]

The next question to be resolved is the one of speed distortion in playback. Does this affect the timing of the statements and crosstalk where they now apparently overlap the gunshots claimed by some to be on the tape?

The Gray Audograph disc is like a phonograph record except that it plays from inside out, and the turntable speeds up as the recording progresses. Regular turntables operate at a constant rpm.

"Thus, when the tapes are played back, there is a speed distortion that causes material at the beginning of the tape (the inside of the record) to be slowed down, and the material at the end of the tape (outside of the record) to be speeded up relative to true speed. 'Speed distortion is no joke,' " Barber writes.[30]

Overdubbing

The NAS investigated the possibility of superimposed recordings. "The Committee studied seriously the possibility that the impulses analyzed by Bolt, Beranek, and Newman, and Weiss and Aschkenasy, were overlaid at a later time onto the 'hold everything' message. Such overrecording could have occurred if the Dictabelt on the recording head was knocked backward by about one minute, in the first minute after the assassination, or if a new Dictabelt copy, made by audio-coupling while a Channel 2 recording was playing in the background, was substituted for the original. The committee concluded this was not the case on the basis of (I) physical examination of the Dictabelt for indications of overrecording a substitution of a copy for the original; (II) the unlikely nature of any of the highly contrived scenarios required to provide such an undetectable overrecording either accidentally or deliberately; (III) the compatibility of the timing implied by the 'hold everything' identification with other firmly established evidence, and (IV) the conclusive acoustic evidence in the Dictabelt itself that the crosstalk recordings were made through a radio receiver with automatic gain control (AGC)."[31]

Sheriff Bowles noted here that "Both machines operated by wire induction. There was no speaker induction possible."

For a close review of item (IV) above, see pages 5 to 8 of Barber's booklet *Double Decker*. In succeeding pages, Barber disposes of Blakey's jumping-needle theory, the leading proponent of which was Gary Mack, for a time. "A widening of the grooves would occur if someone caused the needle to jump back ... it would take 'quite a thump' for the needle to jump back a full minute-plus after the assassination," according to an executive at the Dictaphone company to whom Barber spoke.[32]

Vaughan writes, "There was and has been no addition, subtraction, deletion, overdubbing, or otherwise alterations done in the area of interest (the open-mike sequence) on the Dictabelt described today as the original belt. While the Dictabelt in evidence today containing this area may not in fact be the original Dictabelt recorded on 11/22/63 (but a Dictabelt recording of the original Dictabelt), this would not affect the conclusion of nonalteration. **This can be proven through an objective and accurate linear regression analysis of the dispatcher time annotations on both Channels 1 and 2.** [emphasis in original]."[33] Vaughan goes on to write, "All four major investigating groups of the acoustics, BBN, WA, FBI, and CBA, could have and should have conducted additional study and analysis."

Gary Mack, in the first of many attempts to explain what cannot be explained, said that the tape was overdubbed. "What probably happened to explain the overdub is that it occurred at the Oklahoma [recording studio], or some other, recording studio while the FBI was making copies. Dallas had more, and better equipped studios than any other city in the area, so going to Oklahoma seems very odd, I suspect the FBI removed possibly incriminating or embarrassing sequences without even realizing the portions of one recording bled through onto the other. They must, therefore, have created new Dictabelt and Gray dubs and they are the ones sent to the HSCA."[34]

Mack wrote, "Within days, if not hours, of Kennedy's death, the original recordings were borrowed by either the Secret Service or the FBI. To avoid suspicion on the local level, agents took them to an out-of-state recording studio where the low-quality audio was dubbed from the discs to high-fidelity tape.

"After identifying broadcasts not consistent with a lone gunman and cop killer, those remarks were edited out. Then new 'original' discs were made from the altered tape, and they were what was later returned to the Dallas Police. Who would know or even suspect such a possibility?

"There is strong evidence of substitution with the police recordings. Even then Sergeant J. C. Bowles, who was a supervisor in the radio room and who prepared the second transcript of the Warren Commission, told me two years ago that agents borrowed those recordings a few days after the assassination and took them to a recording studio in Oklahoma."[35] Bowles strongly denied ever having talked to Mack about this or saying that the recordings were taken away to Oklahoma.[36]

"Mack asserts, if the radio recordings really were changed, they could hardly have been altered without the knowledge or assistance of Supervisor Jim Bowles. . . .'' Bowles wrote the following comment: "Wrong. I never listened until they were returned for transcription. None of us gave them a second thought.''

Bowles repeatedly told me, "We did nothing to the tapes" other than copy them and transcribe them after the FBI failed to decode the language used by the Dallas Police.[37] Bowles told me that playback of the noisy recordings over a hundred times during the difficult transcriptions probably altered the recordings due to the stylus plunking up and down on the belt and disc. "It wore them out," he told me. He thinks this caused some of the spikes. Bowles made the two backup copies on reel-to-reel tapes.[38]

Bowles told me, "Also, this is evidence of the fact that the Select Committee, Blakey and his bunch, made the assumption that any spikes [Dictabelt spikes] that fitted their shoot pattern or their desired shoot pattern—the shots that were adjacent to every other place were just 'coincidental.' Now, how could they look at a spike and tell the difference, because the spikes were all the same? They had all the same wave patterns. But they just said, 'Well, those were coincidental, we can't explain their presence,' so they just denied their existence—if you caught anything that superimposed over their desired shot pattern.''[39]

Bowles wrote on the manuscript next to Mack's comments about the substitution and the Oklahoma caper above as follows: "Wrong! The FBI took the first recordings—I presume to D.C.—and tried to transcribe them. When they couldn't, they returned them for me to transcribe. My tapes had already been made. I then made two copies: one unabridged and one filtered. These went to the FBI. I understand (but do not know for a fact) that one copy went to—I think—a lab operated by the Singer Corp., maybe in Oklahoma.''

Bowles told me that the police often recorded gunshots at headquarters from an open mike, and that the shots were distinctly audible and recognizable even though the peaks were squelched. This is why he believes that none was recorded on November 22, 1963. The gunshots would have been lowered and could not exceed 2,400 hz. "You would be able to hear them," he said.[40]

"You see," Bowles told me, "just because Blakey had a suspicion before the fact that organized crime was involved in the assassination, and just because he couldn't possibly sell Lee Harvey Oswald as being the contract hit man for the Mafia, he had to have the window open. However weak the threshold, he had to have the plausible excuse that someone else shot. If it was left to be only Lee Oswald that pulls the trigger, the next question is, who in the Mafia ever came upon the idea of puttin' a contract like that in the hands of someone like Oswald? He would never be able to sell Oswald as an organized crime super contract hit man! It's a self-fulfilling prophecy. You declare that the result is inevitable, and explain how you want it to be and nothing else is possible."[41]

Dr. James Barger found two different hum tones not long after the Committee ended and before the Ramsey Panel completed its work. Two tones can only result from copying, a fact which Barger reported to the Panel.[42] Barger had listed a number of things that needed further study, and the first was the hum tone. "The original Dictabelt could be studied more extensively for possible evidence ... of being a copy. ... Further studies could include a careful search for a second hum ... which would characterize a copy." At that time, Gary Mack was trying to explain the failure of his evidence to show shots, and he wrote, "There is strong evidence of substitution with the police recordings."[43] As with so much that he says and does, Mack fails to demonstrate what his overstatements claim. What is that strong evidence? In addition, although Barger told me that he heard another hum tone, indicating a copy, I can find no documentation from him for this.

But Mack has never explained how he heard such loud and clear shots as he described in 1977, even with the help of equipment, when nobody else on this earth can duplicate his work and hear them.

Dr. James Barger did have some doubts about his work. He found only a 50 percent probability that the third shot was a shot from the Grassy Knoll. This was increased to 95 percent by the next team studying the question for the House Committee. The Committee and Barger wrote, "The high degree of correlation between the impulse and echo sequences does not preclude the possibility that the impulses were not the sounds of a gunshot. It is conceivable that a sequence of impulse sounds, derived from nongunshot sources, was generated with time spacings that, by chance, correspond within one one-thousandth of a second to those of echoes of a gunshot fired from the grassy knoll. However, the probability of such a chance occurrence is about 5 percent."[44] They gave us twenty-to-one odds that the impulses and echoes were of a gunshot from the Grassy Knoll.

Barger, in his February 18, 1983, letter to Blakey, proposed some tests, and he wanted somebody to "look for indications of double recording on both channels, by examining the number of hum signals that have been recorded."

Origins

Mary Ferrell, a Dallas-based researcher who fundamentally despised John Kennedy and all he stood for, told the House Committee about the tapes.[45] Gary Mack was involved with her on the issue from the start and stated on the radio, and in writings in August 1977 in *The Continuing Inquiry*,[46] a research journal, that there were seven shots on the recordings. Mack is a news director at a television station in Fort Worth, and had the equipment to hear or not hear such shots. Was he fooled?[47]

Mack writes in *The Continuing Inquiry* that "Copies of these priceless tapes are readily available and are the only known recording of the gunshots which killed John F. Kennedy."

Mack goes on with his claim, "I contacted two Dallas production-recording studios. . . . Working from an exceptionally clear, second-generation copy of the original belt recording, we were able to eliminate virtually all the sound of the motorcycle engine. Finding the precise location of the gunshots, then, was easy, and without any further processing we heard the first shot: A very loud, sharp crack immediately following some conversation between two policemen ('10-4, three . . . 10-4'). Despite the crude, low-fidelity recording quality, the first shot was frighteningly clear, thus implying the open microphone *was* in Dealey Plaza, not on nearby Stemmons Freeway, and quite possibly six floors below the 'infamous' TSBD window. The remaining shots were not as clear, which meant they were either fired from different locations or the motorcycle had moved. The latter is most unlikely since the engine noise would have changed in pitch as the vehicle traveled; there was no change whatever throughout the entire eight-minute period." Then Mack gives us a lecture on the distinctive signature of a rifle blast, adding weight to his identification of imaginary rifle shots.

BBN said that they tried to filter out the motorcycle noise but were not very successful.[48] Mack's correspondence with other critics indicates that he in fact had no better than a multigeneration copy, probably a seventh-generation one.[49] Mack could not have heard what he says he heard.

Mack went on with his charade. In 1978 an army of people arrived before dawn in Dealey Plaza to set up dozens of microphones and record a series of test shots that Mack, Larry Harris, and others also recorded. Mack was all over television talking about it. "Several of the shots on the Grassy Knoll sounded very much like the shots that I had on tape. There was virtually no difference. The gunshots were much louder than I expected."[50]

This question arises: Why, now, are there no shots audible on the tape? Rifle shots in such an enclosed urban space, echoing off buildings, would be very loud and certainly were heard by everyone in Dealey Plaza. Was there some technical reason why they might not record through an open mike located somewhere in Dealey Plaza?

The answer is that there was no microphone open anywhere near Dealey Plaza, and so the gunshots could not have been recorded. Jim Bowles was of the opinion that the open microphone was at the Trade Mart, and Todd Vaughan believes it was at Parkland Hospital. Their reasons will be given later. Bowles adds, "No motorcycle went to Parkland *before* the assassination. The defective unit *did* go to Parkland *after* the shooting. It left for Parkland when the open-mike episode ended."

But Mack got a lot of publicity at the time, appearing on radio and television talk shows, and various news reports.[51]

The Motorcycle

For the findings of the House Committee scientists to work, the motorcycle with the stuck microphone has to be near the corner of Elm and Houston. Gary Mack and Robert Groden tried to place him there, before the House Select Committee became involved. They argued that he was one of the three lead motorcycle police who separated from the motorcade[52] and parked in front of the Texas School Book Depository. This claim was made by Robert Groden during his many showings of the Zapruder film. Groden said one of the policemen (H. R. Freeman) disappears off the left side of the film. When photographs showed that Freeman could not be anywhere near the School Book Depository, they had to find another motorcycle officer, and McLain was it. Groden is the one who identified McLain,[53] scrambled the evidence, and blurred the line between one motorcycle officer and another.

With regard to this supposedly errant motorcycle, researcher Sim Heninger has the following to say: "While we've ruled out McLain's being the cycle in question, and have shown it to be unlikely that any motorcycle was in position to broadcast from the necessary position, we have not absolutely disproved it." Heninger writes, "This can be done beyond any doubt with the Elsie Dorman film, which Robert Groden told the HSCA showed McLain in the right place at the right time.[54] The Dorman film actually shows the direct opposite to be the case, and the logic is remarkably simple, using only the selected frames published in Volume V of the Committee's hearings. On page 711 of that volume a frame from the Dorman film, taken from a fourth-story window of the Texas School Book Depository, shows Mayor Cabell's car passing under a traffic light at the head of Elm Street. This frame obviously represents a moment in time after the famous Altgens photograph, which was taken while Cabell's car was further back on Elm Street. Since I don't have a complete copy of the Dorman film, I have to take Groden's word for the timing of what happens next: 'This sequence is shot nonstop from this point on and acts as a clock. From this point until the point when Officer McLain reaches the Elm Street corner, we have an accurate clock of six seconds.' Six seconds after the Altgens photo at Z 255 and the instant at which McLain reaches the Elm/Houston corner.'' ''The wording 'six seconds' may be too precise,'' Tony Marsh wrote me. ''There is no absolute proof that it was exactly six seconds. That was a guess that Groden made.''[55]

This means that McLain does not even begin to turn onto Elm until seconds after the head shot. Unless at least four bullets were fired at Kennedy *after* he was mortally wounded, McLain could not have broadcast the sounds of gunshots from Elm Street. Dorman sweeps with her camera pavement that cannot be seen by Altgens, so we can tell there is no motorcycle driven by anyone in the position required by the acousticians' calculations to have broadcast the shots.

''Finally, the Robert Hughes film, which was also presented to the HSCA as evidence of McLain's being the cycle in question,[56] actually proves that McLain was barely past the intersection of Houston and Main streets when the shooting began. . . .''[57] ''Which is what McLain has always said,'' Sheriff Bowles adds. Jim Bowles told me, ''Blakey says, 'Well, maybe McLain forgets turning his siren on. . . .' When you're running your motorcycle Code-3, you don't forget to do what you're paid to do, and that's to protect yourself, because if you have a wreck, it's your own. 'Well, maybe McLain lingered around in Dealey Plaza while . . .' Yeah, he probably stopped and struck up a conversation or fired up a cigarette because it's been a long ride . . .''[58]

''When McLain was taken to Washington by the Assassinations Committee,'' Bowles said, they showed him selected things and asked him, 'could it be—is it possible?' McLain didn't have a look at the whole picture. It's like if you took a movie and cut out a shot of an ocean, 'could this be taken from the *Seahawks*?' Yeah, it could have been. It also could have been *Submarine D-9* and a dozen other sea movies. He couldn't say it definitely wasn't, though, and answer the question under oath. The question is, 'Could it have been?', the honest and only answer is, 'Yes, it could have been.' It also could have been something else. Now, he had no idea that the government attorneys would play a mind game with him. He thought they were being level and honest and he was being as honest and level as he could be.''[59]

As for the Zapruder film and Groden's claim that the right-hand motorcycle left the motorcade, Zapruder failed to pan far enough to the left, and so the motorcycle (Freeman) is lost from his view. The same police officer is seen clearly in the Bell film going beneath the Triple Underpass, and in Mel McIntire's photograph No. 1. Mack claimed in his initial article on the subject in *The Continuing Inquiry* that this officer was H. R. Freeman and that he "testified before the Warren Commission that he was, indeed, positioned in front of the TSBD immediately after the shots were fired.''[60] But why? Why would a lead motorcycle leave the motorcade at that moment?

There is no such testimony in the Warren Report by any Freeman, but there is a mention of H. R. Freeman and he is described by officer Thomas Alexander Hutson, who came up to the TSBD moments after the shooting and who said that he found two motorcycle officers at the door: "I am not positive, but to the best of my knowledge it was J. B. Garrick and H. R. Freeman." Was there more than one Freeman on the roster of Dallas cops that day? All this happened some minutes after the assassination when police from all over returned to Dealey Plaza and began investigating the crime.

The House Committee could only·have a finding of conspiracy (i.e., more than one shooter: four shots on the recording) if they could find a motorcycle police officer in the precise spot at Elm and Houston for the patterns made from the Dallas Police recordings and from recordings of test shots and their echoes on an oscillograph made by the House Committee to match. The placement of microphones by the House Committee's scientists conducting the tests throughout Dealey Plaza, including up and down the streets from Elm around the corner and south on Houston to the corner of Main, showed that the open microphone, which was claimed to record the shots, had to be at the corner of Elm and Houston just at the moment that the shots were fired at Kennedy, farther down Elm Street.

Because of the gunshot echo patterns claimed by the scientists to be that of Dealey Plaza, any microphone farther than nine feet away from the microphone placed at Elm and Houston by the Committee for its tests could not record shots yielding the same echo patterns.

It was determined absolutely by all parties that the open microphone was on a motorcycle, and this fact is not in dispute by anyone.

"If those are real shots on the tape, there is no doubt that they are at the wrong time, because of the crosstalk," Todd Vaughan says. "So the recording of the shots would have had to have been superimposed on the Dictabelt accidentally or on purpose, at a much later time."[61]

There is a remote possibility that another microphone in the motorcade could have been open for a moment during the shooting. The car most likely to have made such a broadcast during the shooting was the Vice President's Secret Service follow-up car, because the car is the only car that is consistently near the positions where BBN says the shots were recorded from.[62] Bowles writes that "the Secret Service were *not* on our frequency." Todd Vaughan adds that the Secret Service may have had their own recording set up for their own broadcast from their car, such as at the airfield on *Air Force One* or at Secret Service headquarters in Dallas.

The Vice President's Secret Service car had two radios with two different Secret Service radio frequencies. It is unknown if the Secret Service recorded their transmissions that day.[63] The transmission, if made, would have had to end the moment the shooting was over, since there are no sirens audible for two more minutes, and most of the vehicles in the motorcade with sirens turned them on. Such a recording would have had to be overlaid at a later date on the Dallas Police recordings. To what purpose?

"Even if the Ramsey panel was right about synchronization between Channel 1 and Channel 2," Tony Marsh writes, "the time when the shots would have occurred would be during the time when the microphone was stuck open. So the shots would still be on the tape. How could BBN have not found the real shots when they supposedly found the others? Let's assume that the real shots were recorded on the tape, but that the segment was moved out of sequence. So BBN really did detect the shots. If that was the case, the BBN and W & A studies are inconsistent with the open mike being in a car rather than a cycle for many reasons. (1) The sound of the exhaust from the cycle is much too loud to have been recorded from any other location than on the cycle. (2) The BBN study found that the open mike was outside the cone of the shock wave for the first two shots, whereas the VP SS car would have been inside that cone. (3) The VP SS car was already on Elm when the first two shots were being recorded by a mike on Houston. (4) W & A identified the location of the open mike at the time of the Grassy Knoll shot as being near the traffic line dividing the left lane from the middle lane, and up at the top of Elm. The VP SS car was farther down Elm at that time and in the middle of the street."[64]

The in-house staff photographic consultant who gave the Committee what it wanted was Robert Groden. He stated that the motorcycle of

H. B. McLain could be found photographically at the corner of Elm and Houston.[65] Although McLain is seen in the Dorman film at the corner, it is long after the last shot. This is simply beyond dispute, and is found by showing the position of the Vice President's Secret Service car in the Zapruder film at the time Kennedy is receiving shots, and McLain as seen in the Hughes film is *one block away* from the corner he needs to be on to have recorded the shots. The Dorman film shows that six seconds before McLain reaches the corner of Elm and Houston, where he needs to be to record the shots, the mayor's car is visible on Elm Street beneath a traffic signal. However, James Altgen's sixth photograph, taken at Zapruder frame 255, again when Kennedy is receiving shots, shows that the mayor's car has not yet even turned onto Elm Street.[66]

McLain strongly protested. He insisted that he was at the corner of Houston and Main streets, a block away, and in fact we see him there in the Hughes film. The Robert Hughes film, taken at the corner of Houston and Main, shows McLain making the turn onto Houston from Main, and the limo has come to the corner of Elm, a block farther on. Both are in view in the film. McLain identified himself to the House Committee at that place.[67]

Richard E. Sprague wrote the Committee, the FBI, and the Ramsey Panel that there was no police officer photographically at the corner of Elm and Houston at the moment of the assassination. At first he was ignored.

Bowles commented to me on this issue: "Now, what the Committee said was that shots 1 and 2 from Oswald's window was as McLain approached, and they put him at two different places as he approached the corner. Then they had shot 3 as he reached the corner and went around the corner, and shot 4 had a little bit of variance in it, so they said, 'Oh, we forgot to consider, that third shot was a little bit out of whack, and he says that was because of the loss of resonance that would come because the sound wave had to pass through his windscreen,' and that they had him then taking the fourth shot as McLain was going down Elm Street, quite some distance from and west of Houston. McLain's recollection if they'd bothered to ask him, he says, 'No, when we stopped at the congestion on Houston, I was looking through the opening in the wall behind the fountain there . . . I looked through the screen, those holes in the top . . . and couldn't figure out what in the Sam Hill that special agent was doing running behind the President's car and jumping up on it, and what was Mrs. Kennedy doing climbing out the back?' And he says, 'He thought she was trying to fall out and that he run up there and caught her.' "[68]

G. Robert Blakey was confident, and appeared on *Good Morning America* in early 1981, and leaked that they had confirmation from the National Science Foundation that "there are two shooters in the Plaza."

"While Blakey did not specifically state the NSF conclusions, he did reveal some of the evidence it has received."[69] Blakey makes an attack on the FBI and their own disputation of his findings, and Mack preaches at us: "As for the FBI, the retraction of its ludicrous report was inevitable. The science of acoustics in this electronic age is proving to be a valuable law enforcement tool...."[70] Sheriff Bowles of Dallas wrote in this place on my manuscript, "... and it should not have been compromised!"

Tony Marsh says that he thinks "the HSCA identified McLain as the open microphone before Groden was asked to look for him in photographs. I think the wording in 2 HSCA 92, 5 HSCA 679 and 616–17 suggests that the HSCA was sure that it was McLain and only asked Groden if he knew of any photographic evidence which showed that McLain could have been in the right place to record the shots."[71]

Explanations and Comments

The House Committee said that the "Equipment that was used in the DPD radio dispatching system in 1963 would have distorted the sounds of gunfire. The effect would have been to compress the peak amplitude of the sounds of the muzzle blast and of its strongest echoes, making them only slightly louder than those of some of the weaker echoes. Furthermore, if the microphone was on a DPD motorcycle in the motorcade, most of the many very weak echoes of the muzzle blast would have been obscured by the noise of the motorcycle engine. Consequently, the sounds of a gunshot would have been recorded as a sequence of very brief impulse-sounds (the muzzle blast and its loudest echoes), only a few of which have been larger than the accompanying engine noise, and none of which would have sounded to the ear like gunshots after being distorted by the amplitude limiting circuitry of the DPD radio and recording equipment."[72] "Lame," says Todd Vaughan. "That excuse is false. Everything else comes through just fine on the recording, and the same microphone and equipment they are criticizing also record things that they could not do if they were of such poor technology.

"Had Bolt, Beranek, and Newman found the crosstalk before they found the gunshots, they would have used that to work backward on

Channel 1 to determine where on Channel 1 the shots should ⟨
had they been recorded."[73]

Weiss and Aschkenasy provided at least five possible explanat⟨
as to what the impulses could be if they were not gunshots recor⟨
during the assassination.[74]

Dr. Norman Ramsey of the National Science Foundation found sev⟨
eral flaws in calculation by the defense contractor scientists who explained the above to the House Committee.[75] Ramsey writes, "The
impulses selected for the BRSW study were not always the largest
impulses. Frequently, large impulses were omitted and some impulses
close to the noise level were retained. There are far more impulses that
do not fall into the BRSW classification of 'probably sounds of gunfire'
than do. Since the results of correlation coefficient calculations are
highly dependent on the impulse and echo selection process, it is especially critical that the scheme used to distinguish these sounds stand up
to close scrutiny, with the process used being spelled out in detail so
others can duplicate the analysis. From the published reports, *it is impossible to do so*. Furthermore, weak spikes on the Dictabelt often are
selected to correspond to strong patterns, in the test patterns and vice
versa."[76]

It was necessary to find photographic evidence that there was a motorcycle in the right spot to record the alleged gunshots. Ramsey writes:
"Although the conclusions of the BRSW analysis were supported by
some later interpretations of photographic evidence as being consistent
with a motorcycle in the procession at approximately the position indicated by their analysis, it is by no means certain that this was the
motorcycle with the open microphone, that its radio was improperly
tuned to Channel 1, that the open microphone was even in Dealey
Plaza, or that the relative times of the four sets of impulses studied by
BRSW and WA were consistent with the three known actual shots.
There is important evidence to the contrary on all four of these points
that should not be ignored."[77]

Todd Vaughan writes, "There are serious problems, flaws, and errors
in the methodology used by BBN (Bolt, Beranek, and Newman, the
firm first hired by the HSCA), WA (Prof. Mark Weiss and Dr. Ernest
Aschkenasy, two scientists hired by the HSCA to further work with the
findings of BBN) and the FBI, several of which were reported by the
CBA. These relate to, but are not limited to, the identification and
selection of the impulses, the accuracy of the statistical probability calculation, the acoustical reconstruction, and the graphing and plotting of
the estimated motorcycle path."[78]

*   *   *

s the possibility (I had written here that it was a *fact,* but Bowles
cted me and said that it was "not really a fact") that the recording
nine for Channel 1 was operating at a 5 percent slower rate than
clock affect the findings of shots theoretically occurring at the time
identical conversation (crosstalk) on both channels and their
ccorders?

How poor were the time checks given by the dispatcher, and does
this affect the findings? "Very much!" Bowles wrote on this page of
the manuscript.

The following is an example of how, with all the money spent by
so many to investigate this case, we were shortchanged on almost every
major point of evidence. In the case we are discussing, the original
scientific investigators had only three days to do this work.[79] One would
wonder, since the House Committee was told at the very beginning of
their effort in 1977 that there was such a recording that might have the
shots on it, why was everything done at the end of 1978, just as the
Committee was closing up? Dr. James Barger, who conducted the first
study for the House, wrote, "Owing to time and funding limitations,
our original study devoted only about three days to the process of
matching the acoustical reconstruction echo patterns with the sound
patterns we had found on the DPD recording."[80]

Todd Vaughan went to see Dr. Barger in the summer of 1981, not
long after Barger issued his report, which was published by the House
of Representatives as the basis of their findings of conspiracy. Vaughan
was just a kid but he had a manuscript with him that poked a few large
holes in Barger's work. "I was only seventeen years old at the time
and he didn't want to talk to a seventeen-year-old kid or look at my
manuscript."[81]

The later indictment and trial of leading executives of Bolt, Beranek,
and Newman for serious improprieties in their accounting lead us to
question the veracity of their dealings with the House Committee. Whatever the true story, it was pretty serious: "Two top officers of Bolt,
Beranek, and Newman, a leading acoustics firm, were stricken yesterday
in a federal courtroom during a hearing on charges stemming from an
alleged scheme to overcharge the government." The vice president and
chief financial officer dropped to the floor moments after the proceeding
began. . . . Then "another man charged in the alleged scheme, Salvatore
P. Luciano, head of corporate services for the firm, complained of not
feeling well. Judge Skinner took him to his chambers, and within 30
minutes Luciano was wheeled out on a stretcher.

"The firm, which studied the 18 ½-minute gap in one of the Watergate tapes, was accused of conspiracy and making false statements in the alleged plot to overcharge the Defense Department, one of its biggest customers."[82]

The plot thickens because this happened in October 1980, just before Dr. Norman Ramsey's panel was reviewing their work. It was also BBN that studied the tapes made during the Kent State University shootings and determined that the U.S. National Guard was the first to open fire on the students.[83]

One can never put it past the government to indict those who have findings that conflict with somebody's political interests. On the other hand, though we don't mean to imply Dr. Barger's guilt by association merely because he worked for the company, the company was eventually fined $500,000. Both Luciano and Kirsch were indicted.[84] One of the criminal acts was "On or about December 18, 1973, the defendants caused to be sent BBN invoice No. 9112 to Judge John J. Sirica, U.S. District Court, Washington, D.C."

So where does that leave us with the Dallas police acoustical recordings? The answer is that the scientific results must be subject to duplication, and stand whatever tests are put that will either corroborate or disprove them. Since the tests conducted by the National Science Foundation, a prominent scientific facility, refute the findings of the firm hired by the House Committee, the issue of the credibility of the source of the House Committee's findings is very much an issue.

It is important to bear in mind that the original studies for the House Committee were made under great time constraints and were hasty. Both those investigators and the National Science Foundation recommended that extensive and (expensive) additional tests be made before any findings could be considered final.

The Transcripts

Sheriff Jim Bowles was the police dispatcher who transcribed the DPD tapes in 1964. He wrote Todd Vaughan to explain his work with the police recordings as follows: "The transcript I did for the Warren Commission was very shallow, as the request was for a more general idea of radio traffic, with no view toward evidentiary value. That did not become a consideration until the House Select Committee decided to make it so. My reel-to-reel covers longer periods on both channels than my transcription. I made Dr. Ramsey studio-quality cassettes of the entire content of both channels. As for further transcriptions, I made no more than you noted in my manuscript. I started enough ahead of events to set the mood, then ended after the units were well into the Parkland Hospital period. My intentions were to clarify the period in question rather than to provide irrelevant reading.

"I know of no other DPD recordings from that weekend. The Oswald-Ruby shooting was well recorded by the media, but not at all by DPD. . . . I am wholly unaware of any Secret Service radio recordings or transcriptions."[85]

Summary

The suspicion arises as to the possibility in this case that certain of the criminal conspiracies surfacing since the assassination with regard to the cover-up extend to the acoustical tapes. Some of those involved have repeatedly put forward false stories and false evidence in the case.

The House Committee and those who told the House Committee about the recordings should have known there were no shots on the tape—unless, of course, there are two sets of evidence.

We have seen showings of the Zapruder film many times on national television with sound effects of the loud crack of rifles added to it. The public does not always know that these effects are added on.

The answer to the acoustics puzzle may be one of fraud. Those who helped bring the police recordings to the attention of the House Committee insisted that they could hear loud shots with little enhancement. Sound effects added to showings of the Zapruder film since then have helped to draw a veil over the actual fact that there are no audible gunshots on the tapes and that the alleged impulses charted on printouts cannot be related to any open mike known to exist. The matches of the impulses with echoes of shots test fired years later have been found to be mathematically in error.

What comes through loud and clear is the possibility of two completely different tapes and the manipulation of evidence for political reasons. That is why we can't be too certain about any of this. The misidentification of McLain is a case in point.

I admit that I was fooled by the evidence as I understood it. It won't be the first time. I trusted those who were supposed to be the "experts."

The rifle shots (and some Secret Service agents say pistol shots) heard by everyone in the plaza were quite loud as they progressed. It is not reasonable to imagine that the recording equipment could not record them had there been an open mike available. The issue is: Could there have been an open mike in the Plaza, and were there ever any shots on the tape? If not, what did Gary Mack hear when he started this, writing that he heard gunshots? Were the recordings taken away from the Dallas Police days after the assassination, and copies substituted?

The weight of the evidence tells us that the shots were not recorded, but we simply don't know if the tape had been tampered with. If the evidence and the authorities and researchers were on the up and up, we wouldn't have a fog and conflicts over each piece of evidence. Everything seems tampered with, even without reason, to confuse. The only thing *sure* is that *all* of the evidence may have been tampered with. That is the key to the case. There were many red herrings.

Because of the fact that the government controls and monitors new technology through the Patent Office, government agencies have access to new technology long in advance of commercial marketing. This would enable those privy to such advances to be able to alter films and recordings without anyone suspecting, and long before such technology became known or available to the public.

"I have tried to corroborate the work of the scientists," Tony Marsh, a student of the acoustical evidence, says, "but I'm hampered by the lack of access to the data from BBN and the unavailability of good copies of the tapes, which are withheld by the Department of Justice. This material should be made available through the National Archives for all to study for themselves."

"First off, the House Select Committee picked the wrong time for the shooting. They tried to do a 'forced fit.' They had what they thought was there, and then they had to prove the fit so the time was according to what they needed it to be, but they put it in the wrong time," Sheriff Bowles told me. "This is called self-fulfilling prophecy. When I want something to be, I find a plausible reason and declare that it is inevitable. If I have something that is inevitable, and it doesn't fit my pattern, I say well, uh, that's just one of those unexplainable things.' In other words, I will explain what I want it to be, and deny the existence of anything to the contrary."[86]

That seems to sum up the problem with the acoustic evidence, and whatever attempted fraud that went with it. It was a "forced fit."

They're all like a squirrel with a
prize nut.

—Farris Rookstool, FBI

Of course there was a conspiracy
in the case!

—Deputy Al Maddox

What if a man gain the whole
world, and lose his own soul?

CHAPTER 13

TREASON AND THE SMOKE SCREEN

There is another side to the research in the assassination of John
Kennedy, and that is the world of the researchers and critics themselves:
what they do, what kind of people they are, how they treat each other,
and what really motivates them.

This chapter is highly personal. I write it because by telling my own
personal experience, it may have meaning for the reader and the history
of what lies behind the masks.

I have come to the frightening realization that part of the research
community (AKA "critical community") is an operation of some kind
and has co-opted the case. This chapter may be the most difficult thing
I have ever undertaken to write. I feel that I have reached into Orwell's
world where things are never as they seem. I arrived here after a torturous journey. Investigating the case is torturous, because few are interested in the truth. Many have built their careers on wild theories. And
now, to protect themselves, they would rather kill the truth than have
their pet theory disproved.

There is a smoke screen erected to prevent us from getting close to
those who might know something about the actual plot's continuing
cover-up. Those witnesses are in Dallas, and there is a wall of silence
there to prevent us from learning what did happen and what is happening. There is an almost impenetrable smoke screen.

I penetrated this wall enough to know what was behind it. There
must be a *real* investigation, and it should start with those involved in

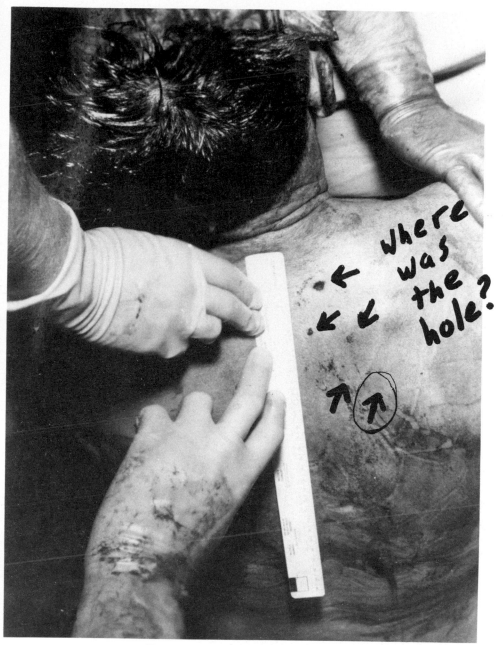

Notation made by Diana Bowron on a copy of an official photograph alleged to be that of the back of President Kennedy. "This is not the back I saw," she wrote. The circle around the lower arrow was made by Diana Bowron to denote the approximate place where she saw a bullet entry wound on President Kennedy's back.

Drawings made by Diana Bowron of where the large defect was on the head. The lower drawing shows the placement of missing brain and roughly the amount missing.

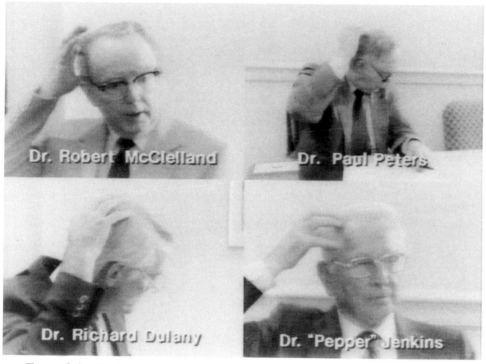

Four of the Parkland doctors demonstrating the position of the large defect on the back and right side of the President's head.

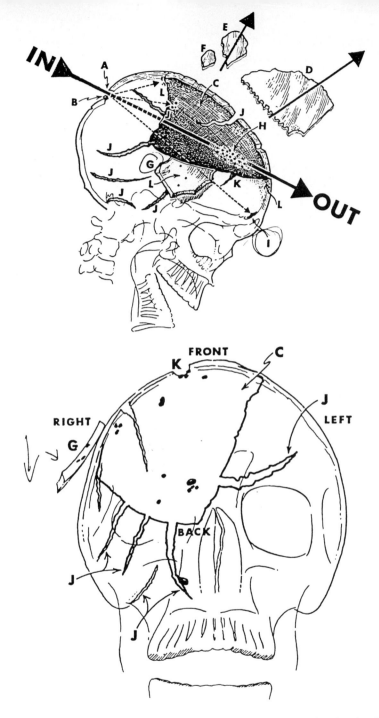

Dr. John Lattimer's 1972 drawings of the X-rays he saw in the Archives. Note that the placement of the large defect is not identical in the two drawings, but is well forward on the head in both. I made the point in *High Treason 2* that the AP X-ray does not have the defect in exactly the same place as the lateral view. There is no posterior bone missing. His drawings correspond exactly to the published X-rays.

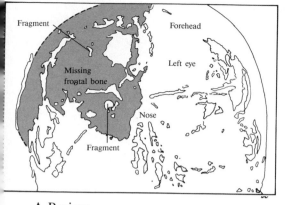

A.P. view

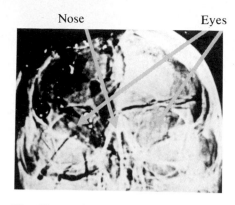

The Kennedy Anterior-
Posterior skull X-ray

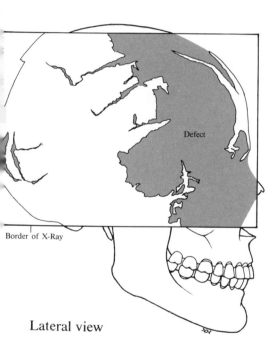

Lateral view

The Kennedy lateral
skull X-ray

Groden possesses a color copy of this photograph, which is identical in all respects. On the left side, note the lip of a specimen jar just visible alongside the neck. The right side of the head is by the hand, and the right side of the neck is at the bottom right of the picture, with the left side of the neck on the left margin. The hairline is just barely visible. Note the scalp reflected back to the left. This was "just like a window shade," as Jim Metzler and Audrey Bell described it, and could be peeled aside to reveal the large bony defects beneath, which we see here. No part of this photo appears faked, but the problem is in knowing which part of the head it is in or whose head it is. It proves there was a major hole in the back and right side of the head. The thickness of the bone, which appears almost to be sawn, shows that it cannot be from the front part of the head.

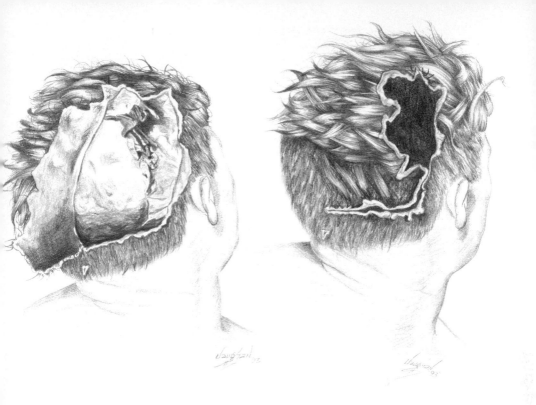

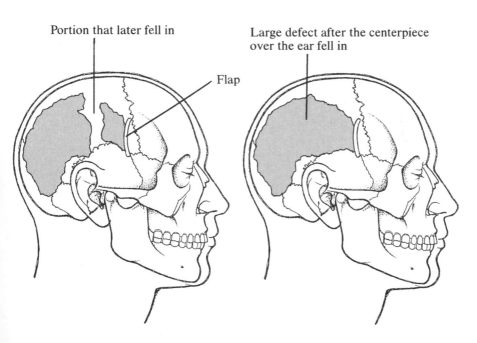

Portion that later fell in

Large defect after the centerpiece over the ear fell in

Flap

Side view of skull

From author's sketch

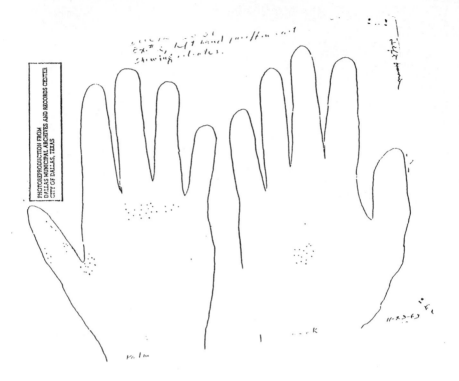

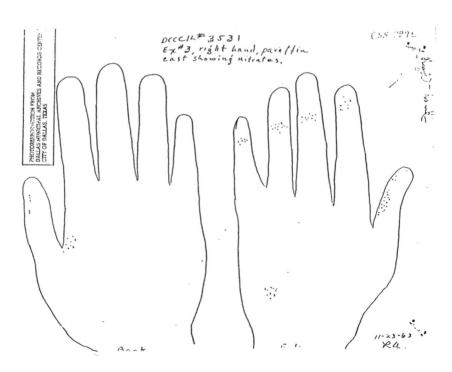

Oswald's paraffin tests.

The view from the fence.

The Main Street curb which the motorcade couldn't get over to enter Stemmons Freeway without changing its route to Elm Street. New layers of asphalt have built up the street since 1963.

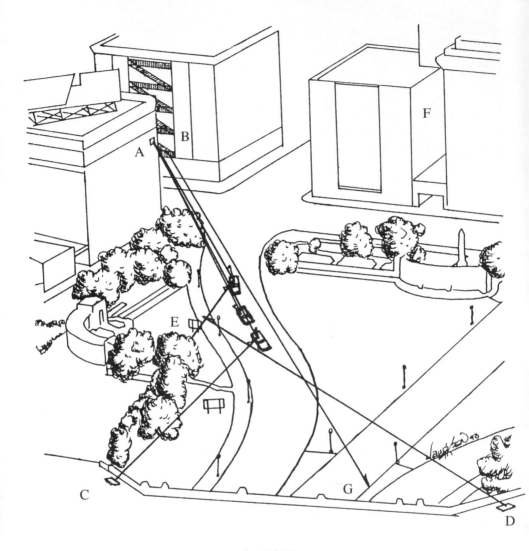

A. The Sixth Floor window at the TSBD
B. Sniper at the Dal Tex Building.
C. The storm drain facing the car.
D. The south storm drain. The bullet strike on the sidewalk pointed directly to it.
E. The possible Grassy Knoll gunman
F. The "cave" where a shot may have been fired.
G. The place where a bullet struck the cement, and debris hit James Tague

View of Elm Street from the Triple Underpass curving to the left in Dealey Plaza, with the TSBD seen just above the tree, the Dal Tex Building at the end of the street, the jail and the County Records Building along Houston Street facing the camera, and Main Street on the right. Had the car continued straight down Main Street to the underpass, a sniper on the Knoll could just as easily hit a target on either street.

The south side of the Triple Underpass. The pavement has covered over a storm drain identical to the one on the north side of the bridge facing Dealey Plaza. It was a parking lot in 1963 and a car could have been parked over the top of the drain. With the grate removed, it was a perfect firing position and the scar on the sidewalk pointed directly to it. The TSBD and the Dal Tex Building are in the background.

The storm drain on the north end of the Triple Underpass, facing east.

Jack Brazil stands in the storm drain and sights along the perfect line of fire for the fatal head shot. The wooden fence joins the bridge just to the right. The pickets were recently removed.

A view of the shooter with the pickets removed. Only a very small space at the bottom of the fence was needed through which to fire.

The Grassy Knoll. This shows how close everything was.

Another view of the storm drain and drainage pipes.

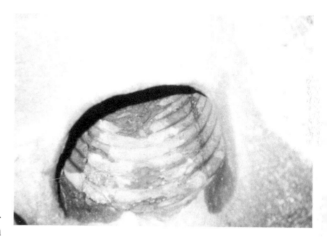

The large drainage pipes leading away from the storm drains provided a safe escape.

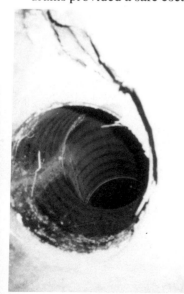

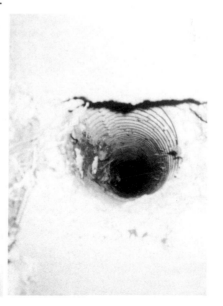

The retaining wall.

Jack Brazil standing behind the wall.

Zapruder's pedestal. The small ornamental tree is just a few feet in front of the pedestal. The presence of a shooter in this location would be impossible, unless the shooter knew Zapruder quite well.

Jack Brazil demonstrates how the storm drain alongside the car may have been used. The fatal head shot was received at approximately this location on Elm Street.

The railroad control tower behind the TSBD.

Another possible shooting location on Houston Street between Main and Elm streets. Some shots were heard in this area as though they came "out of a cave."

Jack Brazil.

Robert Johnson at the JFK Assassination Center. Robert has always been unfailing in his assistance to me.

Former Dallas Police Vice Squad Lt. Tony Ingargiola. He knew Ruby well.

August 1980. Richard Ducar, Robert Groden, and Steve Barber at Groden's home. Groden showed his color autopsy photographs from the National Archives, and his films. Photo courtesy Steve Barber.

the cover-up. People have known for some time that there was some-thing suspicious about certain researchers and the official investigations.

To determine such involvement, we look first at what some of the leaders of the research community have done, whether their behavior makes them consciously a part of the smokescreen.

I investigated these people because of the signs in their behavior and ''research'' that what they were doing was not on the up and up for many years. Often what they accused others of, including myself, in their smears was a reflection of their own dark souls and acts.

The facts are that there is fraud and misrepresentation in the critical community: hoaxes, opportunism, territorialism, copyright violations, bootlegging, vendettas, misinformation, serious misdirection by critics of other critics, disruption, suppression of vital evidence for commercial purposes, slandermongering, and interference with other researchers and witnesses. These people have been throwing rocks for a long time. It's time to throw back.

Some prominent researchers use the case to mask their activities. Their method is to offer some believable evidence or theory to establish credibility, and then sabotage any real and objective evidence of conspiracy.

Vincent Salandria, an attorney in Philadelphia, wrote, ''I have long believed that the killers actually preempted the assassination criticism by supplying the information they wanted revealed *and also by supplying the critics whom they wanted to disclose the data.* Does it not make sense that if they could perpetrate a coup and could control the press, they would have endeavored to dominate likewise the assassination criticism?''[1]

Anyone who looks to the critical community for support and validation is a fool because the critical community is a madhouse. Stay away. Find your own network and do your own thinking. Don't be fooled.

Some more of what Salandria had to say in 1971 is appropriate here. ''The federal government's intelligence agencies must have known that the material which the government issued would indicate a conspiracy existed. Then why did we get the evidence? The people would not have tolerated an overt coup against such a beloved man as President Kennedy. Because of the covertness of the coup, I propose the explanatory thesis that the new governmental rulers were eager to reveal their work at differing levels of certainty to diverse people at different times. In this way, they could avert a concerted counterthrust to their illegitimate seizure of power. Democratic forces could not unite against the new illegitimate governmental apparatus because of timing. The insights of what had occurred dawned in the minds of decent citizens at different imes and with different degrees of clarity. The transparent aspects of the conspiracy were permitted to flash signals to various elements of our population, much in the fashion of spot ads slanted at different times for selected audiences. The new rulers carefully and selectively orchestrated revelations of their bloody work, so as to gain therefrom the deference to which they felt they were entitled by their ascendancy to absolute power."[2]

"Where evidence of conspiracy with respect to the Kennedy assassination surfaced—and much did—thanks in the main to the government's disclosures, that same government from the very first and continuously to date has publicly refused to act on that evidence. Wherever any data appeared to be thoroughly ludicrous and incredible—and much of the lone-assassin evidence did violence to common sense—the federal government publicly and solemnly declared those data veracious. The unvarying governmental pattern of consistently and publicly supporting the lone-assassin myth, and equally uniformly rejecting the irrefutable conspiracy evidence, was too studied to be the function of mere bureaucratic stupidity or accident. I propose the thesis that this uniform governmental pattern did not speak to official innocence or ignorance but rather to the guilt of the government at the very highest echelons."[3] "In my judgment, the assassination critics came up by and large with the evidence of assassination conspiracy which our new rulers wanted us to discover."[4]

Vincent Salandria credits Professor Thomas Katen of Philadelphia for coauthoring the theories of a transparent conspiracy we are presenting here.

The CIA did not kill President Kennedy. The FBI did not kill President Kennedy. The Mafia *did not kill* President Kennedy. Neither did Castro or Khrushchev, Somoza, or Corsican mobsters. The body wasn't stolen, and it did not arrive at Bethesda in a military shipping casket or a body bag. The body and its tragic wounds were not altered, and Lee Harvey Oswald did not shoot John Kennedy. How do I know any of this? This is the point of all my research and the books I've published.

Let's take a closer look at ourselves. Some may say, "Don't do this now." Remember Robert Groden attacking Steve Barber for performing his intellectual duty when he pointed out that there was crosstalk at a seemingly wrong place on the police recording—made during the assassination? No one suggested that someone might have doctored the tapes before Dallas/Fort Worth researchers handed them to the House Committee, containing the seeds for discrediting the pap Robert Blakey flung at us in 1979 with a finding of "probable" conspiracy. Just "probable." That was the "limited hangout." The limitation was that the recordings were a time bomb.

No one then suggested or even thought that, as Steve Barber and others now believe, there may have existed a secret deal between researchers and the House Committee to find shots on the audiotape where there are none. It would later blow up in our face when the National Science Foundation ridiculed their findings.

Now that I've thrown down the gauntlet, let's look at some facts. Why do we have to examine ourselves? Why cast the first stone? I'm not perfect or without fault or blemish. We're already in a war hidden from the public, so let's get it all out in the open. There are people involved in this research with the worst character I've ever known. They'll take perfectly good, honest people and all but kill them, ruining their reputations with lies, walking over the quivering bodies to achieve their goal, and making others crazy with theft, dishonesty, and false accusation. Somebody is waging political warfare among the researchers and against this nation.

That's why we have to examine what we are doing and our methods of doing business because the ends here *do not justify* the means. We have to police ourselves and think about what we do. There are many unsung researchers who have some small but important point they devote themselves to who normally would never be heard from because the big-name writers have shouldered them and everyone else out of the way. There are many early researchers who were once well known but who have been driven out.

Sometime in life, it's good if we can face the darker side of our character. Perhaps many or most never do, and never "know thyself," as Socrates told us to do. Sadly, some of the opportunists, publicists, authors, and operatives in the JFK case will never look at themselves for what they are.

One researcher was intimately involved with various arms dealers, gun runners, and other notorious figures in the case, not to speak of some of the principal con men and frauds of our time. One of the most famous has a self-inflated view of himself that "justifies" his thefts—which extend into all other areas of his life, not just his alleged research—for the ends he thinks he is trying to achieve.

The case is important, but it can be dealt with honestly.

There is something we all have to face, and that is that once again in our national life, we have a choice of ends over means. The fact that unscrupulous critics and researchers are robbing each other's work—

and who have planted a vast amount of false information in this case—and doing so much that is dishonest is a clue to the real game being played with us.

When I began to look beneath the surface in Dallas, I dug fast and deep. I got the story from both ends: the first being to backtrack on the trail of some of the researchers, and second, to investigate high-level people in Dallas who had been involved with the oil men and leading politicians.

It is clear that reporters and commentators are put off by the vast amount of disinformation flying around in this case. "How do we know that what you are saying is right? How is it any different?" They are simply too exhausted by thirty years of bullshit. I don't blame them.

For years I was the victim, off and on, of character assassination. Over the years vast damage was done to my personal life. Deliberate smears are not without a hidden motive. We have a right to criticize each other's research, but with such an undisciplined bunch of amateurs as we have in this case, nobody is safe to exercise that right without harassment.

Tell me, reader, what would you think if you found out that someone was spreading the story that your spouse was unfaithful when you knew it was not true, and it was emotionally killing your spouse? What would you think if someone was spreading the story that you were an ex-con and had killed or raped or molested someone? What would you want to do to the person who spread such lies? Suppose your career was being ruined by secret, slanderous stories?

As everybody knows, anyone who is reaching out beyond the ordinary will have someone trying to take a shot at that person behind his or her back. This is how other researchers try to discredit my research: by discrediting *me*.

I had a number of quite terrible things happen to me in connection with this case, and all of it was traceable to six leading researchers who didn't want me working on the case. These problems began with one of my trips to Dallas, in 1975. The Kennedy case is like an exclusive poker game, and if you can't get in that game, you have to start your own or not play at all. Any other games threaten the big one, and they will mess with you once you are in their territory. This tells you that you might be on the right track. The trouble is in distinguishing between legitimate dissent and provocation and who is the ultimate cause of the trouble. The leading researchers in this case were here to *disrupt* the rest of us.

Does it make any difference if researchers use criminal methods to uncover evidence or to concoct theories they think will sell? What does their personal life have to do with what they are saying and the value of their work? Ordinarily, it should not be a factor, except as they use this case as a mask for ill-gotten gains. I'm talking about everything from copyright piracy to accessories after the fact in *treason*.

The case is filled with fakers. We have in our midst wolves in sheep's clothing who were pointed at us by those who helped kill John Kennedy. There are those who have obtained a position of leadership in the research community who bitterly hated John Kennedy and who were put among us to watch what we do and say, and to mess with us if we get too close.

I know that what I write here seems extreme, but it is the truth.

"He's an agent," or "She's an agent," Penn Jones said about this or that famous researcher.[5] He ought to know, but those who revered him will quickly excuse Jones as simply being senile.

Even the chief counsel of the Assassinations Committee comes among us as a "critic of the Warren Report." He participated in a staged investigation where experts were used by the House Committee to give them only the results they needed. And they did it.

To illustrate, a statement was made before the American Bar Association[6] when Dr. Robert Piziali, a scientist, was asked, "Excuse me, you've located the car at 224. Now, isn't it so, sir, that the House Select Committee in 1978 brought NASA in—the space agency—and they did an analysis to place the car in the plaza, and they said the car should be located according to frame 190 on the Zapruder film—34 frames earlier, isn't that so?" "No. What happened is NASA was told by the Select Committee to please locate the car at frame 190." That is where they wanted the shot to happen.

The House Committee told one of its staff photographic consultants where to locate the motorcycle they needed in Dealey Plaza to record the assassination, something that did not and could not exist on the recordings made by the police because there was no open microphone there. They told the medical and firearms panel and the photographic and X-ray authentication panels and experts to give them the results they wanted.[7] The result was a mishmash that nobody believes, with no hard evidence, and a deliberate ignoring of powerful witnesses from Dallas whose files they seized and buried.

The truth is that some of the leading researchers discredit the very evidence they need, and shoot down the researchers bearing the messages in the process. Why? One would have to ask why a well-known critic would get up at four in the morning and drive to New York to disrupt another researcher's press conference that presented powerful autopsy witnesses for the first time at a press conference and that would help expose the cover-up in the case.

There are those who take money from other researchers and then stab them in the back. There are those who extort money from witnesses. There are those who hold priceless original evidence on the pretense of "enhancing" or "studying" it, then sell it or show it for a high price.

Harold Weisberg

One of the most powerful leaders of the "critics," who aspires to be dean of them, "former Senate investigator" Harold Weisberg, has a strange history. At the time of the assassination he and his wife, Lillian Stone Weisberg, owned a fourteen-acre place they called the Coq d'Or Farm, and raised chickens, ducks, geese, pheasant-chickens, and Rock Cornish game hens. Weisberg, before World War II, worked for the La Follette Civil Liberties Committee "and was discharged for permitting certain information to leak to the press. Senator La Follette stated that Weisberg had been dismissed for a breach of trust involving the release of confidential information to a newspaper and the Senator was quite certain the newspaper involved was *The Daily Worker,* former East Coast Communist newspaper."[8] Sound familiar? Weisberg is the man who leaked Oliver Stone's filmscript to *The Washington Post* in 1991, and all but wrecked the film before it began.

Harold Weisberg has followed a pattern of running power trips on people and asserting himself in their affairs for years.

He is the man who moved into Jim Garrison's investigation around 1967, and in his own words (which follow in this chapter) all but wrecked it.

"Weisberg was one of ten employees fired summarily by the State Department in June 1947 because of suspicion of being a Communist or having Communist sympathies. He was later allowed to resign without prejudice."[9] The fact that he was a member of organizations that were cited by the Department of Justice as subversive does not necessarily mean too much. But is it not passing strange that the same Department of Justice dumped tens of thousands of files in the JFK and other cases on Weisberg and nobody else in the United States?

Weisberg resisted forgery of the autopsy materials as a viable explanation when it appears that *everything* in the case is probably forged. He always put forward this argument: Why would the conspirators forge something if it could be found out? He used this conundrum to damage important discoveries. His philosophical question simply evades the real questions that arise from statements of witnesses denouncing the autopsy photographs and X-rays.

Weisberg wrote a letter to officer Richard Waybright of the Baltimore City Police: ". . . had jumped to the conclusion that I [Weisberg] was helping H. L. Hunt. I did not go to Hunt to help him. I sought help, in an effort to kill the potential of the book *Farewell America,* and the film made of it. It after [sic] happened that I was able to do what I wanted to do without any outside help and the movie just dropped dead because of it and with it the objective of the French CIA in making it.

"[Hunt's man] used me to check out some of the right-wing nuts he knew were approaching the old man for money, so if they did something bad, the old man would not be involved.

"In return, he [Hunt's man] gave the Dallas FBI some of what I had given him, telling them it was mine when in fact he knew it was not and I gave it to him as a joke. So, the FBI files have a monstrosity I regarded as ridiculous and laughable as my theory of the assassination— and you know I have none and never did."[10] He goes on with his threats: "There will yet be something big that Harry is onto and I hope neither he nor you is hurt by it. A big blowup."

In fact, the whole issue of the government dumping tens of thousands of pages of crucial evidence in the murder of President Kennedy on an old and frail man without any staff at all in a private house ought to be an issue.

Weisberg poses another question: "Why would anyone fake photographic evidence to disprove what the alleged faking is supposed to validate? Until you can answer this question, I see no purpose served in doctoring any of the film. As you will see in *Post Mortem,* it entirely destroys the official 'Solution.' "[11] I repeat this as an example of the sort of extraordinarily muddled thinking that has kept this nation in turmoil over the years.

This is the man who has been the so-called premier authority on the medical evidence for thirty years.

I had written Weisberg the following: "Why did you accept so easily the Clark Panel's report? That is, you just assumed that the new descriptions of the autopsy photos and X-rays represented authentic X-rays and photos. You automatically assumed that the original (supposed) stuff was fake [Author's note: Here I quoted from one of Weisberg's letters to Hunt Oil without telling him *the quote was his own*]: 'Clark did blow his cool. In the course of doing it, he made available for the first time two things: a reading of what the X-rays show and the fact that both X-rays and pictures have been eliminated. (Harold: What does this mean?) There has, without any possibility of doubt, been the most serious tampering with the film . . . I had some of the evidence on the pictures for more than a year.' " And he has never done anything about it but try to block it. The letter was addressed (along with many) to the chief of security of the Hunt Oil Company.[12]

Weisberg wrote a violent letter back to me on purple, green, orange, and yellow paper, not realizing that the above quote was from his own letter written in prior years. At no time did Harold answer my question, which was "How can you say the Clark Panel Report disproves the Warren Report?"[13] He has never answered it. His problem is that he systematically takes opposing positions for the sole purpose of defeating you personally, of being cantankerous and contrary. (In private conversations, Harold puts out the backup position that the Warren Commission covered up to prevent a war, which is preposterous in view of the real nature of the evidence the Warren Commission knew about and covered up that show a domestic conspiracy. Harold knew what that evidence was, too.) Harold's written tirade said, "You are ignorant in saying that 'Clark did lose his cool' on it. The panel (Clark) was not even his idea. It was from the White House, where it was John P. Riche's idea. The rest of what you say in this paragraph, penult on page 2, I cannot understand. But the only reason that report was disclosed is that it was essential in preventing Garrison from having the right to use that evidence and the paranoid Garrison dropped it as a CIA plot against him—it was his own idea!!!—the minute he won in court. I was there and I made his winning possible, so I know what I am talking about. . . . I'm not going to waste any more time trying to explain or to argue with you about the autopsy film. Not at least until you answer the question I've asked you first. If you do not understand the report of the Department of Justice (Clark) Panel, that is your problem and it exists only because you begin with a preconception that was not based on fact and are unwilling to face the fact that you did and cling to it still. In a simple response, that report utterly destroys the Warren Report and if you cannot understand that without any explanation, you are far out of your depth on the entire thing."[14]

My question, which was "How can you say the Clark Panel Report disproves the Warren Report?" had the following comment to Weisberg: "Superficially that seems like the *wildest* statement ever made. I won't tell anyone. The Clark Panel found the entry in the head four inches from where it was in the autopsy report. How does that disprove the Warren Report? What it does is throw into question the autopsy pictures. There was no bone or scalp in that area. I know that beyond a shadow of a doubt, and when you sent me down to the National Archives, I found proof of it. Hopefully, I will be able to get copies of that and prove it to the world. Harold, I was quoting one of *your* letters about 'Clark losing his cool.' So you are saying that you are really ignorant. That is the problem. You constantly reverse yourself just to criticize people."[15]

Discussing the research community, Weisberg wrote: "I hope this gives you an idea of what you are silly enough to immerse yourself in. Cut it out completely before you have real trouble from it. And from them. Those people lie without realizing they lie because what they say is what they want to be and they then believe it."[16] He's got that right, as we sort our way through this psychiatric labyrinth, making our way to the funny farm. There was an implicit threat from Weisberg about the power of these people, which I resolved to test.

He wrote that "Mary Ferrell is as right wing as she seems to be. She has never been secret about this or pretended to anything else. She has never, to my knowledge, defended the Warren Report. She is not part of any plot of any kind. You will harm yourself greatly if you push that kind of notion because while there are many who do not agree with her beliefs, they will all resent this kind of baseless charge. Where she worked and for whom is irrelevant."

Weisberg's November 20, 1992, letter goes on to say, "You ask why Jim Garrison wound up flogging the CIA. He actually began that way. You do not understand Garrison: What he did not crib and enlarge upon he just made up. No substance to anything at all from him."

Harold repeatedly in his letters gloats on his turning on Garrison and destroying him when he thought it was justified. And, interestingly, who does he report all of his activity to, currying favor? H. L. Hunt and the Dallas Police, who received copies and reports of all of his communications to Dallas.

It was Harold who launched an all-out assault on the book *Farewell America,* in the United States in the 1960s. "There is intense interest in *Farewell America* because the ignoramuses pretending to be researchers like the crap that SDECE made up to disinform the critics, especially that Pink Panther, Garrison. My taking the manuscript to Garrison and my later preventing Garrison from going ape, as he'd planned and the CIA's French pal SDECE intended, over that stuff that Lamarre just made up. Garrison suggested the [English] title *Farewell America.* That zany actually believed it was the KGB leaking it to him! I broke up the last effort Lamarre made and he has been silent since. He was known as an oil specialist for French Intelligence in this country, under the name Lamarre. I do not know if it is his real name."[17]

It is easy to see why Garrison was destroyed with advisers such as this: men who came to him first with one story and slant on things, who promptly change their position on the facts, and who lead all who come near them to their doom.

The book, *Farewell America*, had its origins with French Intelligence, just as Weisberg said, but the real sources were the Kennedys and Senator Daniel Patrick Moynihan who was asked to set up a team to investigate the assassination the day after it happened, by Robert Kennedy.[18] There were direct lines of communications between the Kennedy family and President De Gaulle of France.

Former FBI agent William Turner and Steve Jaffe authenticated *Farewell America*, tracking it to President De Gaulle and the presidential palace. The book said that ''President Kennedy's assassination was the work of magicians. It was a stage trick, complete with accessories and fake mirrors, and when the curtain fell, the actors, and even the scenery disappeared . . . the plotters were correct when they guessed that their crime would be concealed by shadows and silences, that it would be blamed on a 'madman' and negligence.'' This is great writing and absolutely the truth as I now understand it in the assassination. The above paragraph describes what happened better than anyone else could have said it.

After criticizing the Secret Service agents for drinking the night before and for other serious mistakes, the book went on to credit them with professionalism: ''They were the first in the President's entourage to realize that the assassination was a well-organized plot. They discussed it among themselves at Parkland Hospital and later during the plane ride back to Washington. They mentioned it in their personal reports to Secret Service Chief James Rowley that night. Ten hours after the assassination, Rowley knew that there had been three gunmen, and perhaps four, at Dallas that day, and later on the telephone Jerry Behn (head of the White House detail) remarked to Forrest Sorrels (head of the Dallas Secret Service), 'it's a plot.' 'Of course,' was Sorrels' reply. Robert Kennedy . . . learned that evening from Rowley that the Secret Service believed the President had been the victim of a powerful organization.''

Who were the sources of this for French Intelligence? *Robert Kennedy. Jacqueline Kennedy. Senator Daniel Patrick Moynihan.*

A book like this, ''explosive as a bomb,'' as *Bild* called it in Germany, was almost completely suppressed in the United States.

It is my opinion that in the face of the evidence and the contents of the book that any one of the researchers who speaks against *Farewell America* is suspect. Just as Weisberg was catastrophically wrong when he unquestionably accepted the Clark Panel's movement of the wounds in 1968, after seeing the same photographs and X-rays. None of them questioned the authenticity of the evidence relied on: the phony photographs and X-rays.

In the early days after Kennedy died, Weisberg thought that H. L. Hunt might have been involved in Kennedy's murder. Hunt was one of the conspirators, put money in Weisberg's hands as though from other sources, and one of Hunt's men paid for his several trips to Dallas. On one occasion, Weisberg spent six weeks in Dallas at the home of Mary Ferrell. Weisberg spent a great deal of time with SMU law professor Charles Story (who was one of the judges at Nuremberg) and with Paul Rothermel and Henry Wade. Wade undoubtedly has a good grasp of what really happened in the murder of John Kennedy, but plans to take most of it to the grave. He told Weisberg nothing of importance.

Weisberg never again accused Hunt of being involved in the crime.

It is interesting that this critic, one of the revered idols of younger people in the research community, was trained in political warfare and intelligence operations.[19] He worked for one of the granddaddies of secret intelligence agencies, the Office of Strategic Services (OSS). So did Warren Commission members John J. McCloy, and Allen Dulles. Senator Richard Russell, for whom Harold Weisberg worked, helped supervise these intelligence agencies.

Sue Fitch

Sue Fitch distributed a tape, claimed to be of John Kennedy making love to Pam Turnure, which she evidently got from the FBI or the John Birch Society, of which she was a prominent member, to the Dallas community of right-wing political activists. Fitch was a radical rightist, and she greatly disliked Kennedy.

Mary Ferrell was close to Sue Fitch. Fitch was a close friend of General Edwin Walker, who was fired by President Kennedy for disseminating neo-Nazi propaganda among his troops. Fitch hated Harold Weisberg. H. L. Hunt received a report in 1969 saying that "Sue Fitch advises that she has a low regard for Harold Weisberg in that he was fired from a government position for associating with Russian Nationals believed to be espionage agents. I told her that my dealings with Weisberg had been at arm's length; that I had done some favors for him and that he had provided some information for me. He has done more for me than I have for him, including furnishing to me copies of interoffice correspondence between members of the Warren Commission and the staff, which was highly enlightening. She said that she had heard that even though Boxley [William Boxley was an investigator for Jim Garrison] was fired by Garrison and was trying to implicate Mr. Hunt and myself in the Kennedy Assassination, he [Boxley] was still thinking about coming to see me to ask for a job. I thanked Sue Fitch for the information and told her that I had read Weisberg's books; I did know that he was anti-H. L. Hunt in the beginning but that I had an idea that I had converted him based upon some material Mr. Hunt had written which tended to show that Mr. Hunt was not anti-Semitic."[20]

The author of the above memorandum, a close associate and source of mine, stated that it was unlikely that Hunt knew Abraham Zapruder because Hunt "was anti-Semitic. The only Jew that Hunt knew or talked to was Ben Freedman in New York who printed anti-Semitic material."[21]

Fitch, whose maiden name was Boren—an old Texas family—was an attorney at Locke, Purnell, Boren, Laney, and Neely, where Ferrell worked for about twenty-five years. Fitch's brother, Ben Boren, was a senior partner in the firm, and the Boren family was descended from Senator Boren and others prominent in Texas history. This law firm helped plan Kennedy's fatal visit to Dallas and his motorcade. Fitch died October 2, 1991.

Some General Considerations

What we are looking at here is a criminal conspiracy by certain people in the city of Dallas in alliance with some of the alleged researchers, some of whom are highly trained in intelligence operations. What we get is a wall of silence and many closed doors. There are those witnesses who know something today, but who hide behind the Warren Report, mouthing the findings of the Commission in a very unbelievable way. There are also those researchers and authors who came to Dallas seeking to be paid off. Yes, there is big money in this game. The police officers with me during one trip heard of offers as high as $35,000 to buy the "research time" of some of those relatively unknown but crucial researchers working on the case *in Dallas.*[22] I emphasized "in Dallas" because that is where their greatest fear of exposure is.

The most serious researchers who go to the core of the evidence can expect constant interference and harassment. One technique is to tie up witnesses by dangling dollar signs in front of them for movie and book rights. Time after time I found I could not get an interview because someone was forbidden to talk in order to protect their film or book contract or chances. In most cases, these films or books never materialized. Some of the most important witnesses have been gotten to in that way.

The FBI in Dallas is there to watch everyone and to debunk any new evidence in the case. The most recent Special Agent in Charge of the FBI office in Dallas, Oliver Buck Revell, made it quite clear in the media that he was there to debunk whatever researchers come up with. That is one of the results of so much hokum in the case: Serious work has no chance to get a fair hearing from law enforcement or the authorities after running the gauntlet.

My use of a radio frequency detector shows that the JFK Information Center, run by Larry Howard, is bugged with ''drop-ins'' all over, even in the walls, as Howard says. The FBI makes frequent visits to his Center, and asked Howard's neighbors to keep an eye on him. He claims he had to remain neutral, a task that makes him a target of suspicion by all sides. Neutrality to Howard means denouncing one side to the other, hurting both. Often, anyone who tries to be neutral in the middle of a war in this life ends up hated by all.

The FBI, in the JFK case in general, cannot be trusted. They are not interested in pursuing any real evidence of conspiracy, and in fact are a lot more interested in learning about the researchers, which is clearly not without reason. But their priorities are not right. Had the FBI done its job and properly investigated the assassination of President Kennedy, the hunt for the killers never would have become an industry of amateur investigation and wide-open banditry.

The FBI could not do its job because its leader at the time of the assassination, J. Edgar Hoover, participated in the conspiracy. In fact, an FBI sniper may have been one of those who shot Kennedy in Dealey Plaza.[23] Certainly one of Hoover's closest pet gunmen may have killed Martin Luther King, Jr., while James Earl Ray was framed for the crime.

It is unfortunate that the Dallas FBI in charge of the JFK case at the time of this writing is considered very treacherous by all. I can understand their attitude when dealing with so many crooks in our midst. To law enforcement looking at this case and the people in it, soon *everyone* becomes a suspect, or is thought of in that way, and soon they begin mentally roughing people up, scaring us, trying to trick and trap us in statements that aren't true. But here we can see the effect of many years of dishonesty by the Dallas-based research community on law enforcement. Not that the FBI there did not have its own agenda for cover-up. I personally felt that Farris Rookstool had a certain amount of good will and a somewhat open mind for evidence in the case, but it was impossible to deal with him due to the immense damage already done by both sides. Even worse was the fact that Mary Ferrell seemed to attempt to manipulate the FBI for her own purposes, chief among them to get other researchers into trouble, never mind the fact that she was pushing a great deal of false evidence on this nation, such as the acoustical tapes with alleged shots on them, though even she might have been unwitting in this fraud.

The FBI comes in for some unfair criticism. I'm sure they made mistakes twenty-nine years ago, but their files show they performed a massive job of trying to track down many leads. What some people at the top of the FBI or in that one Dallas office did for political reasons does not convict the whole agency of JFK's death. The questionableness of some of the FBI's other activities is another story.

We are dealing with a stacked deck. Many well-meaning people have had the wool pulled over their eyes and are being denied the truth. Certainly the American people are unaware of the major scams and brutal internecine warfare that occurs among us. It would be too easy to explain the affairs and people I describe in terms of personality disorder, territorialism, and ego. Our problem is to grasp just how deep the conspiracy in the murder of John Kennedy went. We cannot understand it if we seek only to interpret various minutiae of evidence.

At all times we have to proceed from a fundamental understanding of the true political nature of our country. And we have to keep in mind the nature of Texas politics then and now. With regard to the latter, when I scratched the surface of Dallas, the City of Fear and Hate, it was like picking up an old fallen log in the forest. Beneath it seethed a seamy, primeval underworld struggling in the darkness. It made me sick, and for the first time, afraid.

As time went by and I knew for certain from my interviews with witnesses that the conspiracy that murdered John Kennedy came from Texas, and all that we have heard from New Orleans and other places was a dodge to get us off the track, I realized that there was a pattern to the many false stories that have come out of Dallas. It will take some effort to point out the degree of misrepresentation and fraud in many of the stories that have originated in Dallas, and the degree of control that the Dallas research community has exercised at one time or another over other critics living elsewhere in the nation.

Therefore, we first have to accept that the **pattern** of misrepresentation in the stories from Dallas is not accidental. We are having false information planted on us deliberately. False information was planted on the House Assassinations Committee. Agents planted such information to tie up the resources of the Committee. The effort needed for us to investigate each allegation is enormous and exhausting—and part of the plan. The effort wears us out until we quit. The public has no hope of sorting through it to the truth.

There are often two sets of each piece of evidence, such as two apparently different acoustical tapes, one with gunshots and one without, two Bronson films, two versions of the Nix film, two Zapruder films, two sets of autopsy pictures, two different sets of wounds for President Kennedy, two different sets of bullet fragments, and so on. (See the outline in *High Treason 2,* "Some Conflicts in the Evidence," p. 145.)

Most researchers (as is the public) are operating at a serious disadvantage because they are either unaware of the true nature of our political and social organization, or they ignore it. You have to start from the top to understand the way things work. As long as we had Soviets and Communists to point to and could talk about brainwashing their peoples, we ignored the brainwashing going on here.

The view from the top tells us that there are very rich people in our country with far more money and power than is comprehensible to the average struggling, middle-class person. It is almost impossible to have that kind of money and power without operating with different ethics and precepts than is expected of the rest of us. Certainly the concept of democracy is an illusion because, no matter whom we elect, the chances are that the elected representative, whether in the House, Senate, or White House—if not already compromised—will be overwhelmed by powerful and wealthy people. The problem they had with Jack Kennedy was that he was a true democrat, and his refusal to take orders cost him his life.

Each new president is deliberately destabilized when he comes into office. He is publicly embarrassed by well-planned events over which he has little control, and let known that *the power* lies elsewhere. They've done it to every president at the start of his term for decades, and they've done it to Clinton, as should be obvious to all. It's all part of the program. Clinton's additional problem is that he is not his own man, as Kennedy was.

The nature of Texas and its politics is particularly corrupt and violent. There is the undercurrent of a fascist police state controlled by very wealthy people from oil and gas and, later, the defense business. I found ordinary people in Dallas who knew more about the case and what really happened to John Kennedy than most researchers. That is because they well understood their state, their city, and their politics. That is because they understood that people in their city did in fact kill John Kennedy.

So what we have is a massive disinformation campaign coming from Dallas/Fort Worth. There was vast wealth and power based in that area, and it was so great that they were able to back and install President Dwight David Eisenhower. True, Eisenhower also had backing in the blue-blood eastern Establishment, but his primary financing came from Dallas/Fort Worth, and to some extent, Houston. It is worth asking why George Bush left his native New England for the richer prospects of Texas, where he made his financial fortune with a nondescript oil company that was perhaps little more than a government front.

The filth of Texas politics was perhaps best described in Evetts Haley's book *A Texan Looks at Lyndon.* It is worth it to read at length some of his descriptions of how elections are run there.

That Establishment is vicious and unscrupulous and sometimes will do anything to preserve its power, up to and including killing one of their own when the power, control, and destiny of a great nation is at stake. Kennedy was considered by some a traitor to his class, as was Franklin Delano Roosevelt.

Kennedy was a victim of a massive conspiracy that involved the new-rich Establishment in Texas and some elements of the blue-blood Establishment in Washington, D.C., and New York. *The Establishment is a conspiracy!*

There is so much money in Dallas and there are so many reputations at stake with some of the big families there that they cannot allow the truth to come out even today. Not only can we decode the conspiracy that murdered John Kennedy in these terms, but we can also find a trail leading back to the plotters through some of the researchers themselves. In other words, money translates into power in Dallas, and it means that they own the police and intelligence operatives in the area. Those people are able to motivate some of the stories that creep into our awareness, and other members of the assassination community based in Dallas spring from that police power and wealth. It's not so hard to compromise someone or get that person in trouble, or take someone already in trouble and make an informer or operative out of him or her.

Trying to find honorable people among the big names in this research is like Diogenes' quest for an honest man with his lantern in a Stygian darkness. But there is a reason for it. Any conspiracy would have to have left operatives in place to serve as watchers. There would have to be active provocateurs created to screw up people like us. You and I have seen the patterns of those who moved in to co-opt this case. Such people usually are of very bad character.

What has happened has been the gradual abandonment through death and attrition over thirty years of the operatives who were programmed, wound up, pointed at us, and set loose. Some of the operatives can be unwitting. Those who find themselves cut loose without their case officers and money would become desperate.

When you remove the program, the case officer, or the memory chip from the actor or provocateur, that person reveals his basic lack of intelligence—as we see in the patterns of some of their recent actions. He or she has been abandoned. Whenever an asset becomes a liability or when the asset fails in his or her mission (control of another, for instance), the asset is abandoned and starts to die, like a withering plant. They are programmed to self-destruct.

The plotters put out a smoke screen all of these years. I realize that this chapter will cause a severe identity crisis in the already fractured minds of those in the ''community'' who have nowhere else to go in society.

Entertainment and Tourism

For a long time, the Dallas research group of critics played fast and loose. Eventually I realized that their primary intention was to set up first their own assassination research tourist business in Dallas, and second, to control the national effort in this research through what became the ASK conferences—which are run by a commercial rock concert promoter (South by Southwest Corporation) in Houston.

Gary Shaw has admitted that some of the press conferences he held at the JFK Assassination Information Center (AIC) were done in part for publicity.[24] The Center needed money. All the noise brought in the biggest shill (sucker?) of them all for this carnival, Oliver Stone. Bud Fensterwald spent a hundred thousand dollars on the AIC prior to Oliver Stone. The flimflam artists worked Fensterwald for all he was worth and offered him a vast amount of phony material.

The souvenir shop better known as the Dallas Center serves a variety of purposes, chief among them the receipt and dissemination of information. What it does with the information it receives is another story, which is to sell it.

This assassination research business is no place for decent people. Among the leaders, I have never known or imagined such unscrupulous and dishonest characters. Too many seem to have a secret agenda, or some other motive for which they use this tragic case.

Beware, all you researchers from other parts going down to Texas: Get your shots, passport, a tour guide, and say good-bye to your mother, because you are about to fall prey to vicious predators and rattlesnakes in another country. God help you. They don't want you snooping there.

Mary Ferrell

There was a woman, known as the Mother Goose or the Dragon Lady, in Dallas and of whom many people were greatly afraid. She is supposed to be the grandmother of assassination research, but nobody knew what she really was or believed. Everyone was fooled while she lived a double life, like a spy in a foreign country during a war. Ferrell and Mark Lane were both from Memphis, where Martin Luther King, Jr., was assassinated.

She was a secretary to the executive assistant to the governor of Texas, Dolph Briscoe, in 1973–74.[25] She was on loan from the Dallas law firm of Locke Purnell, the largest and most powerful firm in the city then. Eugene Locke, her longtime boss, was John Connally's closest friend and went to college with him, and was ambassador to Pakistan in 1966–67 and deputy ambassador to South Vietnam in 1967. That later post, under Henry Cabot Lodge, represented a key moment in the escalation of our war there, and the fortunes of the Texas Defense industry so well represented by the Dallas law firms. When Locke returned to the States, Ferrell went to work for him. From that moment forward, from the time of her return from Austin, she was "the keeper of the Keys" (as many call her) in the JFK case. I think she isn't just that, but a key itself. There is a conflict in the record, as she says that she began working for Locke Purnell in 1967,[26] and in a later interview said that it was not until January 1970. Eugene Locke, whom she says she never spoke to, died in 1972.

The whole time I thought I had made some friends in Dallas, they hated me. The Dragon Lady finally came after me, breathing fire. Ferrell was quoted on network television as supporting the Warren Commission at the time Jim Garrison died, during the second ASK conference, in October 1992. It took *thirty years* to find her out. Officially, she never did not believe the findings of the Warren Report, as anybody who truly knows her understands. But researchers had the impression that she believed there was a conspiracy. Yes, but what kind? She is a critic of the Warren Commission because she believes a Communist conspiracy killed Kennedy, if there was a conspiracy.

Some people can accept the Warren Commission's findings of a lone-nut assassin acting without other guns to kill JFK, but can claim that the Communists put Oswald up to it, as Edward J. Epstein implies, and as Mary Ferrell will sometimes profess to suppose. "I never said Lee Harvey Oswald had nothing to do with it. He could have been used unwittingly."[27]

Mary Ferrell attempted to give the impression that she was merely one of numerous secretaries in a secretarial pool at Locke Purnell. But this is a misleading impression, and she appears to have been more than that.

Locke went to Vietnam at a time when our war effort there was rapidly escalating. Locke was a member of the Petroleum Club of Dallas, the Petroleum Club of Houston and Austin, and, of course, the Dallas Club, the City Club, Idlewild, and various other organizations. Locke was John Connally's campaign manager in 1962 for governor and was a power in Democratic Party politics before Connally switched to the Republican party. Connally's brother managed Locke's campaign for governor in 1968.

The law firm of Locke, Purnell, Rain, and Harrell was run by Eugene Locke. Charles G. Purnell went to school with John Connally at the University of Texas, graduated from Yale Law School, and was in the Office of Naval Intelligence. Connally had been secretary of the Navy. The firm helped organize the motorcade, and Buck Ferrell, a car dealer, provided cars, including Mary Ferrell's personal car, for the motorcade. The law firm was deeply involved with various oil companies, including Hunt Oil in Dallas, and was instrumental in the case when Earl Golz was let go from his newspaper, *The Dallas Morning News.*

Eugene Locke was Mrs. J. D. Tippit's attorney before the assassination.[28] Brigadier Jones writes that the decision to route the car and the parade route past the Texas School Book Depository was made by the group meeting in Locke's office.[29] Judy Amps, Sam Bloom, and Elizabeth Forsling Harris met there with him.

Locke was chairman of the Texas Democratic Party at the time of the murder, and he was going to introduce President John F. Kennedy in Austin that fatal Friday night. Locke was a director of Trinity Steel Co., Trammell Crow Realty Trust, and a director of the Sam Rayburn Foundation. He was a director of the Mid-Continent Oil & Gas Association.

* * *

One writer reported the following: "Mary Ferrell said she had disliked Kennedy, did not vote for him, and would not vote for him if he were alive today. In the early 1960s, she explained, she had belonged to a right-wing group that was violently opposed to Kennedy's integration policies and to the Kennedy family in general. The group thought Kennedy was soft on communism.

"When pressed for specifics about the dislike for Kennedy, all Mary would say is that she had heard a tape recording of Kennedy making love to Pamela Turnure, Jacqueline Kennedy's secretary. She explained that Turnure's landlady had placed a microphone under Turnure's bed and had made a recording of her affair with Kennedy available to various right-wing groups in Dallas. This tape was played often in Dallas, fueling a hatred for Kennedy. Mary said all the Kennedys were arrogant and that they wanted to establish a dynasty in American politics.

"Mary's explanation of why she has spent so much time and money researching the death of a man she despised was evasive. She offered a view of her childhood, in which she painted herself as a poor southern girl who was often abused by her first husband, an alcoholic and a thoroughly miserable sort. She had escaped a life of 'being barefoot and pregnant' and had gone on to accomplish things she never dreamed possible. She mentioned traveling widely, meeting important people, and holding an important job as some of her accomplishments.

"We went on to talk about the researchers, and she had some harsh comments about some of them. . . . She praised the work of Gary Mack and Gary Shaw, naturally. She went on to say that researchers should pay close attention to the information contained in the book *The Man Who Knew Too Much*. Ferrell pushed hard for a theory of Communist involvement in the assassination. She also defended the accuracy of the Dallas police audiotapes that allegedly have the assassination shots on them, which she allegedly uncovered and transcribed." Ferrell refused to discuss the possibility that Locke, Purnell, the military, her husband, defense contractors, or organized crime played a part in the assassination.

"She did admit that she had met Carlos Marcello. She said she met him once in a New Orleans restaurant, and found him to be a 'a charming gentleman.' I enjoyed his company," she said. Larry Howard, who dislikes Ferrell, says that the relationship was more than that, and that Ferrell has been in Marcello's home.[30]

As for the alleged tape of John Kennedy making love to Pam Turnure, Ferrell told me that Sue Boren Fitch, the radical right John Birch lawyer at Locke Purnell and her closest friend, had received it from one of the oilmen's executives, a former FBI man in a position to receive such things. Ferrell said she heard it many times and was unable to verify that it was in fact Kennedy on the tape, since there was little or no talking but only the sounds of making love. Everybody in Dallas who heard the tape, she told me, believed it was Kennedy and Turnure because that is what they were told by people they respected, and it had a claimed chain of evidence going back to the beautiful Turnure's landlady.[31] The tape served the function of bolstering great hatred for Kennedy in the Dallas Establishment. They also avidly passed about an alleged wedding certificate of John Kennedy to Drurie Malcalm, which said that they were married in Newport, Rhode Island, a marriage that was later annulled.[32]

Ferrell denied that she had ever received training in intelligence-gathering, though there was no trouble in admitting her to the retired intelligence officers' association Forth Worth's David Atlee Phillips set up (she says that she joined only to receive their publications).[33] She said that she began indexing news articles dealing with the assassination the day Kennedy was shot, and never quit for the next thirty years.

Ferrell claimed in another interview with me to have voted for John Kennedy for President, but would not have voted for his reelection. She says that she voted for him because he was Catholic, which she says that she is, and she voted for Barry Goldwater because he was Jewish and for no other reason. She believed that the traditional religious barriers to public office should be broken down.[34] Many other sources say that the real reason she would have voted this way was because she was opposed to the Civil Rights program, a charge she vigorously denied to me.[35] Goldwater and his family were Episcopalians.

Ferrell has built her reputation on a seeming command of myriad facts in the case, and at one time or another nearly every researcher in the country comes to her for information, not thinking that the facts could be wrong. For instance, Ferrell long put out the story that Abraham Zapruder, Morty Freedman, and Sam Bloom owned the Dal Tex Building. A title search by my attorney in Dallas, Judge Paul Rothermel, proved that nothing could be further from the truth.

Mary told my research associate that her husband, along with Gordon McLendon, had founded Downtown Lincoln Mercury in Dallas. The company had agreed to supply cars for the Presidential motorcade on November 22, 1963. "They quickly ran out of cars," Mary said, "so my husband called me and asked to use my car. That's how my car came to be photographed in pictures of the assassination." Later, Mary retracted this and said that the cars—except for the Chevrolets—for the motorcade were provided by Eagle Mercury, where she says her hus-

band worked. The whole issue of Downtown Lincoln Mercury is suspect. We found many conflicting stories as to who owned it and when.
In 1963, W. O. Bankston apparently sold it back to Ford, and it was
incorporated in Delaware. Bankston retains another dealership to this
day. Buck Ferrell, Mary's husband, became president of Buckner
Chrysler.[36] Ferrell then denied that they were ever involved with Gordon
McLendon.[37]

My informant wrote, "I asked Mary why her husband, who also
disliked Kennedy intensely would have cooperated with a request to
provide cars for the motorcade. She avoided the question. It was on
this note that she ended the interview."

It is worth noting here that Gary Shaw wrote that a car belonging to
Downtown Lincoln Mercury was found parked on the Grassy Knoll
after one of their employees, Jack Lawrence, who, according to Shaw,
was thought by some to be one of the shooters, was found to be acting
strangely.[38]

My informant, a former editor at *The New York Times,* went on to
say, "I uncovered no absolute proof that Mary Ferrell had anything to
do with the assassination, but it is indeed odd that she has become the
grand old lady of the assassination research effort. She truly disliked
President Kennedy. She says her involvement stems from patriotic feelings and her love of our democratic system. I find this weak and thin.
Her concept of democracy is diametrically opposed to everything that
John Kennedy stood for. She openly admits to connections with groups
and people who hated Kennedy, yet she has involved herself year after
year with an effort to find his killers. She counts herself among the
right-wing Dallasites who listened to a tape of Kennedy making love
and scorned his immorality, yet when he came to town she provided a
car for his motorcade. She is a tough, pragmatic woman who does not
openly display the concern for democracy she claims to feel.

"Perhaps there are good reasons for her behavior. But for now, her
involvement with the research community raises more questions than it
answers."[39]

At the time of the Garrison circus and dating from the assassination
itself, there was a propaganda effort in Dallas to pin the murder on
leftists, if not the Soviets or Cubans. The primary effort of Ferrell,
who to this day holds authority over very many critics nationally, was
"information showing that [Warren] Commission Counsel Norman
Redlich, Leon D. Hubert, Jr., and Albert E. Jenner, Jr., were involved
in the defense of certain Communist individuals or matters related to
Communist organizations. I did not take notes while Mrs. Fitch related

this information to me because this was the information Mary had told Tom Bethel, Bill Boxley, and myself that was so supremely important. This is the secret data which is documented with papers which belong to Mrs. Fitch and which are in a safe deposit box belonging to Mary. This is the information which Mary feels will be so damaging to the Federal Government's cover-up because a close association can be shown between some or all of these individuals and President Johnson. Now, obviously there is an association between individuals on the Warren Commission staff and the President. We also know that it would be a matter of public record as to what work these attorneys had done in court before the Commission convened. I do not see the overwhelming importance of this entire point except to someone who is trying to establish a Communist-based conspiracy. . . . This discovery made me wonder why Mary [Ferrell] had considered it so important. . . . Why would Mary consider this of such supreme importance unless she herself felt there was a left-wing conspiracy? To me, the answer seems to be that Mary still believes her earliest suspicions that it was a Communist conspiracy and she clung to this as a most important lead in that direction. . . . she had hoped we would consider this an important possibility and investigate it as such.[40]

". . . They felt that the Mafia was an extension of the Communist Party in America and that therefore made the Communist 'ties' of those Commission staff members all the more important."

Of course, we have a problem with one of the leading Warren Commission members being well connected in Dallas and his having been there at the time of the assassination. Claiming that there were Communists on the Commission is an effective way of protecting the radical conservatives on that same Commission who covered up the crime and perhaps participated in the plot itself.

At one time or another in the late 1960s and throughout the 1970s and the 1980s, everybody who was anybody trooped through Ferrell's home to sit at her feet.

She collects *everything* in the case. Why?

The first time people go to see her, she suddenly enters the room with a camera and takes pictures of them from the front and side, creating mug shots for her dossiers which she then pins to the bathroom door.[41]

Ferrell first worked for Mobil Oil Company, and at the time of John Kennedy's murder, worked for Philip Burleson of the firm of Abney, Howell, Abramson, and Burleson. Burleson was one of Jack Ruby's attorneys and key defense information passed to District Attorney Henry

Wade. Mobil Oil was based in Dallas and had its origins in Humble Oil in Texas; both firms were bought by Socony. Mobil's headquarters was across the street from the Adolphus Hotel in Dallas, on Commerce Street, and still maintains its beautiful neon sign on its roof of a red flying horse.

"Why does she do this for nothing?" those close to her ask. "Look at the work she has put into this case for many years." Ferrell told me that nobody put her on the case—nobody suggested that she do this research.[42] Ferrell certainly has the most extensive collection of JFK assassination materials in existence, and for no admitted training in intelligence-gathering, certainly has done a bang-up job. The question is, who is she reporting to? Perhaps she herself is simply monitored by governmental agencies in Dallas, who listen to her phone and otherwise watch everything. Between her and the JFK Assassination Information Center in Dallas—which is completely bugged—they learn everything they need to know. Just like a sting operation.

George De Mohrenschildt was Oswald's case officer, reporting to Jim Moore (J. Walter Moore) of the CIA in Dallas. De Mohrenschildt, whose wife, Jeanne, worked for Abraham Zapruder, was used to debrief Oswald and keep tabs on him. Something caused De Mohrenschildt seemingly to panic and move away from Dallas in April 1963, perhaps sensing the plot involving Oswald and De Mohrenschildt's unwitting role in setting up Oswald and keeping tabs on him. The Paines, who took in Marina and befriended Oswald, were undoubtedly used for this purpose later on. As long as Marina was staying with Ruth Paine, the plotters could keep tabs on him and get him to his appointed place the day of the murder.

Melissa (not her real name) was a young researcher I employed in Dallas at Larry Howard's behest. This girl, "Melissa," wrote a short report for me once that had one mention of Ferrell's and Gordon Novel's names. One of Ferrell's people, Duke Lane, promptly reported to her that "Melissa" was working for me and investigating Ferrell (not true), told Ferrell the girl's real name. Ferrell went haywire when she heard this.

Shortly before, I had enclosed a report from another individual that dealt with Ferrell in a few more sentences and that said she needed serious investigation. I took the officer's name off the report and sent it to Ferrell. Ferrell promptly claimed that she got another copy of it from another source with "Melissa's" real name on it, which she had found out from Duke Lane. I heard about it when "Melissa" called me crying her eyes out, in great fear of Ferrell, who called her just prior to our March 1993 trip to Dallas. The operative description here is *"great fear."*

Nothing like this ever happened—that is, I would not have sent the girl's report or anything by her to Ferrell. I sent Ferrell something a police officer had written to see if she would falsify it, and she did. How *paranoia* got the better of these people on Melissa's account, I'll never know, other than that they were trying to terrify and make a target of the poor girl, a college student. Howard himself had warned us against the Dragon Lady: "She's very dangerous!" he told us.[43] I'd be safe in saying that half the city of Dallas told us that for the same reasons. Why was she so dangerous? We would find out fast.

Unexpectedly, Melissa had inadvertently found one piece of information that linked the Dragon Lady with Gordon Novel. Melissa came to me with this as though it were the greatest treasure of information in the world, but we already knew it. That was the end of it, but Mary learned from her spies at the JFK Assassination Information Center in Dallas that Melissa was doing a bit of work for me.

Stunned, I began making calls. Almost every day there was interference with my regular research and interviewing due to some brush fire that sprang up and the necessity to deal with it.

I made Larry Howard go to Ferrell's house in Dallas, a little yellow cluttered cottage on Holland Street, and asked to see the paper with "Melissa's" name on it. He reported back that Ferrell refused to produce the paper. Months later, Ferrell was still claiming to have this document but refusing to produce it.[44] I wrote Ferrell an angry letter about trying to draw the girl into our dispute.

The upshot was that I escaped their attempted frame-up again, and Melissa and her family were satisfied that I had not sent Ferrell her reports to me. The question remained: How did Mary find out the girl's real name? Once again, the suspicion was that she was having help from the FBI. But Howard determined that Duke Lane had told Ferrell that Melissa was helping me, so Ferrell framed the girl with a report she did not write—which was in fact written by an off-duty police officer working as a detective. It was nothing compared to the attempt in an early version of Operation Firehel to set up police officers for arrest or the loss of their jobs. Typical, I'd say.

She didn't have help from the FBI. "She *is* the FBI," Gordon Novel told me.[45] The entire leadership of the assassination research community appears to be an FBI COINTELPRO operation from out of our dim past, but if she knows how to run such an operation, she may merely be using the FBI and their past methods (unbeknownst to the FBI!) for protective cover.

Within days, she was on the phone calling Farris Rookstool of the Dallas FBI and telling him that *"it's all coming down this week!"* and boy did they have a hot reception for us on our next trip. Of course, it didn't work, because sometimes you can't beat righteousness.

Mark Crouch called Ferrell shortly afterward to tell her that somehow I knew everything that was going on in her house! Fancy that?! Well, it was true because, as all this was going on, a retired Baltimore City police officer was sitting in her living room and noting it all down.

But now we knew how they operated and what their depth was, and here it is for you to read, for history to know. The constant interference with legitimate investigation was unbelievable.

"Mary is the keeper of the key to this case. She got involved to see who knew what."

"She's the gatekeeper," Greg Lowrey says.

The delicately prepared friendships of some researchers with vital witnesses, such as Ruth Paine, Marina Oswald, and Jeanne De Mohrenschildt, were ruined by some of these activists, provocateurs, and saboteurs. Greg Lowrey, in the midst of trying to deal with an ongoing family tragedy, was so afraid of Ferrell's power that he came to be in a state of terror, suspecting enemies at every knock or call.

Meanwhile, Ferrell went out to dinner the night of March 3, 1993, with the local FBI agent (Farris Rookstool), Marina Oswald, Norman Mailer, and Larry Schiller, Mailer's associate for *The Executioner's Song,* about the mass murderer Gary Gilmore.[46] Mailer will be giving us the word on Lee Harvey Oswald in a new book Schiller is researching, smelling big money in America's hottest cottage industry. Mailer personally hates David Lifton who is writing a book on Oswald.[47] They are both from Brooklyn Heights in New York. Of course, there is another element in the equation: David Lifton's mother's personal calls to Mary Ferrell about her son. "He's a little strange, don't you think?" Ferrell reports about Mrs. Lifton's opinion of her son, whose phone bills caused his dismissal at their home.[48]

Schiller researched *The Scavengers and Critics of the Warren Report,* written by Richard Warren Lewis, which should tell us something about where Mailer's new book on Lee Harvey Oswald is coming from. Schiller and Lewis's book was "the first book to comment on the critics with the truth about the facts, and gives us the poop on Mark Lane, Edward J. Epstein, Harold Weisberg, Penn Jones, Jr., the Housewives Underground, and Superbuffs David Lifton, Vincent Salandria, Harold Feldman, Raymond Marcus, and Jones Harris."[49]

Ferrell's son, Larry (Lawrence Afton Ferrell), a well-known drug dealer, was murdered in a bizarre incident in about October 1986, according to Ferrell. "We think he was murdered," she told me. "We know he was involved in drugs."[50] There were some thirteen criminal charges against him between 1973 and 1986 in Dallas, with five of them felonies. One of those is "felony aggravated assault." In one case he slugged Gordon Novel's girlfriend, "Hi," and popped her eye clean out of her head.[51] Ferrell was truly the Ma Barker of the assassination research community.

I had quite a talk with Ferrell one day.[52] I told her that I was writing about the medical evidence in the JFK case, and she says, "You talkin' about medical evidence! Harry, do you know that there are people digging up your medical records even in Canada? It's somebody a lot higher up than Bob Artwohl that has dug up a lot of stuff about you. I mean they're getting ready to really lower the boom! They're trying to make it sound like you have been insane." I never denied being nuts.

"Who is 'they'?"

"Well, I can't tell you. I've never thought you were crazy in the last seventeen years that I've known you. I told this to someone who came up to me with some records saying that you had been in a mental institution." I tell her this is untrue, and asked who showed it to her. "Well, they've got some records saying that you had a breakdown. . . ." She swears on her mother's grave that it is not Bob Artwohl. ". . . on your hospitalization. . . . Well, they've got those records. I think every time since the day you were born . . . why, they've got everything in the world on you!" She had my place of birth right.

I ask her about the medical background on me. "Oh, well, they have got a stack of stuff on you that you wouldn't believe it!"

"Who is 'they'?" I want to know. I tell her that my medical file disappeared from where Dr. Robert Artwohl works at Union Memorial Hospital in Baltimore. "I haven't heard from Bob Artwohl in a long time. The only thing I know is that he called and wanted to know if I knew you. I said yes, and he said, 'What's a matter with him? He wrote a letter on City of Baltimore Police stationery. . . .'" I tell her that it is false and I demand to see the papers. She refused, and changed the subject quickly.

Do I have to explain more why I dislike these people? How come this case has collected such riffraff? This fact was noted by commentators twenty-five years ago or more, and not just because those commentators might have been opposed to conspiracy theories. It may be because such creatures are made to order for sowing discord and disruption, misinformation and disinformation. They are easy to use, and easy to point at others.

We're talking about the organizer and keynote speaker at the 1992 ASK conference in Dallas and key organizer of the 1993 ASK conference,[53] which has become the centerpiece of the "critical community." The sort of troublemaking and endless and exhausting personal inquiry, having nothing to do with the case, like a bunch of old gossips, are what consume the energy of the critical community. Everyone has been set against each other, and if the government did it and planned it that way, they couldn't have done a better job.

I'm trying to demonstrate what form a police state takes in the United States. The dead President's brother Senator Edward Kennedy, in talking about crisis creation in the United States, said, "Now I fear that we are entering another era of crisis, an era of inaction and retrogression and repression. . . . Growing use of domestic spies—in schools, in political groups, at public meetings, of informants who sometimes help to foment the very acts they are supposed to be investigating."[54] That is what has happened in the assassination research community.

I believe that what we are looking at is a sophisticated private intelligence operation. It flows from a *de facto* secret society in Texas, run by powerful people there, to protect the name and reputation of Texas and to protect those who were involved in the murder of John Kennedy.

J. Gary Shaw

What Gary Shaw and his coterie of "critics" had done was to cut out of the herd certain witnesses, sign them up as their agents, and make them professional. We now have professional witnesses in this case, such as "The Lady in Red" (Jean Hill), Dr. Crenshaw (though he had the sense and money to quit), Paul O'Connor, Marina Oswald, Beverly Oliver (the "Babushka Lady"), and numerous others.

It isn't long before witnesses embellish their stories, ornamenting them with little touches here and there, go on the circuit, and make fools of themselves.

The ASK conference was free of the watchful eye of the press while the research community could be repropagandized and separated from the cutting edge of the research. Things had become compartmentalized.

The program is for the controllers, the big-name leaders to suck out of the little people what information they have and to take the pulse of things, whether they do it at a community college or at big conferences. David Lifton spoke for two hours on the Zapruder film at a panel he headed in 1992, and he managed not to say a single word that was new. Not once did he reveal what it was that he thought was fake about the Zapruder film, which was his announced purpose.

Gary Shaw and his gang in Dallas and Fort Worth are the ones who gave us the Roscoe White hoax. They came up with a phony buried canister with phony CIA cables inside ordering Roscoe White, a Dallas police cadet and former Marine, to murder Kennedy, as a "national security problem."

Several of us interviewed Roscoe White's family, and we know that the dog tags found in the canister were given to Gary Shaw by Roscoe's sister and mother, so the whole thing was a fake.[55] (A statement from the family is printed in this book's appendix.) Detective Joe West had the cables studied by a firm in Arizona that determined that the cables were fake.

"But experts disagree about the authenticity of three vaguely worded cables—the only physical evidence in the case—that Ricky White said ordered his father to kill the president. . . . In any case, the story presented that day differs from one presented a few months earlier by Mr. West, a Houston private investigator, and J. Gary Shaw, vice president of the JFK Assassination Information Center. The two held a news conference in May at which they blamed the Mafia for the assassination. Mr. West said then that Mr. Kennedy was killed by Charles Nicoletti, a hit man for the Sam Giancana crime family of Chicago, and was backed up by another Mafia hit man, John Roselli."[56]

Gary Shaw is the one who gave us Jean Rene Soutre (Michael Mertz) as QJ/WIN on the Grassy Knoll some years before this,[57] the military as the murderers of John Kennedy,[58] and so on and on.

Shaw, who lives near Forth Worth, is a primary backer of the Robert Easterling story, which holds that Easterling was involved in the assassination, and pushed that on author Henry Hurt. One of the notable things about Shaw is the manner in which he creates suspects so easily, such as Easterling, White, Roselli, Nicoletti, Jack Lawrence, Gordon Novel, and Jean Soutre.

Shaw also put forward one Tom Wilson, a prodigy of Cyril Wecht. Wilson came out of the blue to make fantastic claims that his computer system had confirmed all my findings of forgery of the autopsy pictures. The trouble is, he has not been able to prove what he says. Instead, he is in the business of suing people who suggest that he is a fraud.

Gary Shaw, pointing the finger at the other guy with the best of them, told me that Gary Mack was the one planting disinformation in the JFK case. Shaw has cried "Wolf!" so many times, it's going to come as a big shock to him that nobody listens anymore.

The second ASK (assassination symposium) conference in Dallas, in

1992, had little that was notable to report. *The Dallas Morning News* told me, via reporter David Real, that the paper had decided not to cover the 1992 conference. "They had their chance last year, and they blew it!" he said. "There was nothing new, and there was Tom Wilson." (This is in reference to the unsupported claims of Wilson regarding forgery of the autopsy pictures. Some months before the conference, I tried to arrange with the sponsors—the AARC in Washington, and the AIC in Dallas—to set up a panel of doctors to get to the bottom of the medical evidence, and to speak to the entire gathering on ethics in this research community.)

Oliver Stone

The most unfortunate result of Oliver Stone's film *JFK* was to drag out of the woodwork many false ideas, kooks, and writers that serious researchers are now forced to compete with and who are all but buried under the deluge of misinformation. The fact is that Hollywood and show business have caused vast damage to this case. There are those who feel that any publicity is good, but *JFK* trivialized the assassination of JFK. The result is that the public drowns in a mountain of dross, making it impossible to sort through and find the truth.

Stone and many others are simply too dense to grasp that all of those newspaper commentators who denounced Stone are the very people we have to convince. Half-baked minds were easy enough for Stone to convince, but not a hard-nosed journalist. If you can't make your case to them, then you'll never convince the Establishment—who are our only hope to get the truth out in the open. And I don't mean the files he seeks to open, because there can be little if anything of real value in them. Stone's film co-opted and ruined the real investigation that was going on.

I should be happy if anything that draws attention to the evidence I'm trying to develop, which is the fake autopsy pictures, helps me make my case. No, I'm not happy, because there is a dignified way to draw attention to what I'm trying to say, and the comic-book way. Stone's movie is a cartoon, and it's not at all funny.

"... You've got to prove what didn't happen as well as what did happen if you want to make it count ... what Oliver Stone did with his movie *JFK*. He made millions of dollars making a plausible, potential, and in a lot of people's minds, an exposé of what happened, which is nothing more than a cheap drifter's way of making a buck!" Sheriff Jim Bowles of Dallas told me.[59]

More Considerations

If there was not such a circus here, not such an abuse of our responsibilities, the case would have been solved long ago. But we have been screened from those who knew the truth.

We have to police ourselves just as medical and bar associations must do. The alternative is that we're *being policed.* I had police at my door every day for eighteen months after I published my first book, *High Treason.* They moved in close to take a good look, and it was very hard on me.

But I'm glad the police came because I began to look at myself, and all of us, through their eyes. That was quite a revelation. I woke up. I realized that a lot of this is *crooked.* It is a *scam.* Some of the biggest hoaxes of the century are being perpetrated by so-called assassination critics. It's an open field. And a lot is because we're amateur, halfbaked, and untrained investigators.

After one of my crucial trips to Dallas to talk to the doctors, I was set up and framed by other researchers who needed to cover for their own thefts of evidence by laying a false trail to me. I was supposed to be selling autopsy pictures that I, in fact, did not possess. Nothing could have been further from the truth. The story was retracted the next day, but the damage was done.

The story I am trying to tell here is one of political warfare, although a lot of it has to do with protecting one's own turf.

David Lifton

"Paranoid grandiosity tends to be well organized, relatively stable and persistent. The complexity of delusional conviction varies from rather simple beliefs in one's alleged talent, attractiveness, or inspiration to highly complex, systematized beliefs that one is a great prophet, author, poet, inventor, or scientist. The latter extreme belongs to classical paranoia."[60]

Attorney Roger Feinman recently wrote a marvelous analysis of the once proud leader of the assassination community. Or at least one of those who thought he was the leader. In the preface to his manuscript, *Between the Signal and the Noise,* Feinman outlines his thesis "that *Best Evidence* is a literary deceit in multiple dimensions."

> As Mr. Lifton explains in the preface to his work, he was unable to obtain a publisher until his agent persuaded him to rewrite his

first attempt at a manuscript as an account of his personal history
in researching the assassination of President Kennedy. The motif
of *Best Evidence* thereby became Mr. Lifton's reconstructed rumi-
nations over the medical evidence during a period of fifteen years,
ranging from his earliest exposure to the subject, to an inspiration
in late October 1966, through seemingly laborious and detailed
investigations, and finally to a new synthesis purporting to explain
how the assassination was accomplished. . . . [H]owever, where
Mr. Lifton tells his readers what he was thinking at certain points
in his odyssey . . . his formal and informal contemporary writings,
prove beyond doubt that the views he professed then were precisely the opposite. Furthermore, he garnered the chief evidence
that allegedly supports his assassination theory only while he was
in the final stages of writing the manuscript that Macmillan Publishing Company eventually published.

If autobiographical revisionism was merely ornamentation on
the structure of *Best Evidence,* no matter how lamentable, it might
be forgiven as taking literary license to the extreme in a work
promoted as nonfiction. Unfortunately, the pattern of the author's
dissimulation attenuates to obscure his long-standing predilection
for bizarre hypotheses to explain the assassination, as well as the
crude political philosophy that drove him, at least during his for-
mative years as an assassination researcher, to erect the type of
convoluted rationalizations of the evidence that are the bedrock of
his book. The second dimension of literary deceit, then, is the
deliberate concealment of a past that is prologue to the present
and future.

Ostensibly, *Best Evidence* is the story of one of the true originals among all the Kennedy assassination conspiracy theorists. Underlying the edifice of his book, *nevertheless,* one discovers an
unsettling theme of derision and disparagement regarding the early
critics of the Warren Commission. . . . There is, however, an
equally distressing parallel to this theme running throughout Mr.
Lifton's body of work. Specifically, it is his affirmative exonera-
tion of the Warren Commission, its staff attorneys, and several
key participants in the events surrounding the assassination from
any intent to deceive or conceal, notwithstanding abundant evidence to the contrary, as Mr. Lifton himself asserted before the
promises of literary fame and fortune were held out to him. Here
is the third dimension to the artifice of *Best Evidence*: a subtle,
though repeated assault against those with whom its author is supposedly in sympathy, coupled with absolution for their adversaries.

Finally, there is Mr. Lifton's central theory of body-snatching
and the artificial creation or alteration of President Kennedy's
wounds. Through the selective use and misuse of the evidence,

and with his autobiographical interludes serving to distract his readers from the development of his argument, Mr. Lifton almost succeeds in making the impossible seem credible. At bottom, however, his theory is not only absurd, but also redolent of the worst caricatures of Warren Report critics drawn by apologists for the official fiction.[61]

Lifton perpetrated one of the biggest and most preposterous hoaxes of all time, and yet persists in attempting to establish personal and intellectual credibility, hoping to take over as the elder statesman of assassination research when the present gang dies out. His theory of body alteration in order to fool the camera's eye was blown to smithereens by his own witnesses who described wounds quite different from what are shown in the photographs and X-rays on KRON in 1988.[62]

An example is a letter to Gary Rowell wherein Lifton attempts to write Rowell's article for him. Rowell had told Lifton over the phone that a new book would destroy his theories "once and for all," and Lifton "objected to the use of inflammatory language. . . . I don't see any justification for your putting such inflammatory language into the minds of 300 odd readers."[63]

Lifton tells Rowell to "report in your column that you think there's a book that will attack the 'head reconstruction' theory set forth in *Best Evidence*." How about the bullet hole in the President's back that he thinks was manufactured?

David Lifton tried to make himself look simon pure, as though he would never try to sell the autopsy pictures himself, something he accused others, including me, of trying to do. Then Lifton tried to sell the pictures to the *Star* almost as quickly as he had them in his hands.[64] Of course, Lifton never told James K Fox that he was trying to sell his pictures, while Fox was trying to have Mark Crouch sell them for him.[65]

In 1979 a story appeared in *The New York Times* saying that I was trying to sell the autopsy photographs. It was completely false, and Mark Crouch knew what only I thought I knew, that two researchers conspired to plant the story and frame me for this, trying to take me out of the case then, and they succeeded for a period of years. I had just returned from my startling investigation in Dallas in 1979, where I had shown the House Assassinations Committee tracings of some of the autopsy photographs to the Parkland doctors.

A dispute arose between Mark Crouch and David Lifton about the concept of body alteration in Lifton's 1981 book on the Kennedy assassination. Crouch told Lifton that he failed to attribute several articles that preceded his book with the same theory. Lifton wrote, "This article, by Fred T. Newcomb, was the result of a serious breach of confidence in my relationship with Newcomb, who lived nearby, and with whom I developed a close relationship in the period 1969–70. He found out what I was working on, and quite simply, decided to *steal* it."[66] Newcomb and Adams's book *Murder From Within* was completed in 1974 but not published. It contained the complete body theft and alteration theory many years before Lifton published it, and was massively researched and documented. In addition, the book contains a very extensive study of forgery and tampering with the Zapruder film, something Lifton claims to just be developing and preparing to publish. Mary Ferrell passed *Murder From Within* to Dave Hawkins in Canada, who sold the copies from his base in Québec.

Lifton claimed that in 1988 he had discovered the conflict between the X-rays and the photographs, one showing that the face was blown out, and the other showing the contrary, and so wrote in the Afterword of his reprinted book.[67] I produced affidavits from several doctors that showed that I had discovered and written about this in 1978. Lifton learned about it in 1988 from Robert Groden, who spread the word about my discovery when he obtained my manuscript prior to publication, and sold or gave it to Jim Marrs prior to publication of his compendium of other people's work. Marrs promptly used my book, not thinking it would be published.

Lifton then claimed in a famous Fax to the president of Emerson College that he had written about the "fakery" of the autopsy pictures in that same Afterword. "I conducted a series of interviews with the Dallas medical staff who treated Kennedy that day. Subsequently, after both Fox and his wife passed away, I published the pictures in the 1988 edition of *Best Evidence,* along with my analysis indicating fakery, and also gave them to the TV program *Nova.*"[68]

Lifton conducted three interviews with Parkland doctors some four years after I had gone to Dallas, quizzed many doctors, and published my findings. In no part of his Afterword does he indicate forgery of the autopsy photographs. Lifton privately admits that the pictures have been tampered with, but he knows that forgery invalidates any reason to alter the body for the purpose of fooling the camera's eye. In fact, in his book he strongly denounces the whole idea of forgery of the photographs.[69]

Lifton is trying to stride both sides of the fence in the forgery issue, something he denounced in his book *Best Evidence.* He wrote (privately), "The irony: I am very sympathetic to the idea that the autopsy photographs in some important areas, may have been photographically altered—my big turning point on this coming in October 1988, and having little to do with Groden, who apparently can't distinguish between hypothesis and fact."[70] October 1988 was the KRON show.

There it is again: That wonderful one-hundred-dollar word that shines so brightly in David Lifton's eyes, that rings with authority and the intellectual, with art and artifice, with crime and the big con—*hypothesis!*

But more appalling is the spectacle of a man who had to be helped out of KRON's studio in October 1988 when his own witnesses told reporters that the autopsy pictures did not show the wounds they saw. At a trice, Lifton's entire hypothesis of body alteration was demolished by his own witnesses. He should have known after seven years what they thought. Here we have Lifton in a paragraph above admitting that he was shown to be wrong in 1988. What did he do next? Try to appropriate someone else's discovery of the incompatibility of the X-rays with the photographs, and from that moment on try to destroy his new competitor who was developing the thesis of forgery of the pictures. Look when Lifton tells the president of Emerson College in 1992 that it was *he* who was revealing evidence of fakery in the autopsy pictures.

I try to bring people together. If it's necessary to confront things or disrupt them, I bring it to a boil and get everything out in the open. I put all the witnesses together.

In other words, *Lifton's book actually discredits what he appears to be trying to prove.* Think about what this means . . . about who he really is and what he is actually doing.

An even worse error by Lifton in dealing with the evidence is what he suppressed. His witnesses told him vastly more than he cared to report, as you see in my book *High Treason 2.* Lifton had access to Groden's stolen autopsy photos in 1978 and knew that his witnesses would tell him they were forged. The witnesses described the same wounds that were seen in Dallas, but he concocted a major distortion of the facts. Lifton had to keep his witnesses apart, too, preventing old friends from finding each other, instead of having them work in teams, as I've helped them do many years later.

Paul O'Connor originally told the HSCA that the body was wrapped in a body bag, but by the time Lifton got through with Paul, the body was *in* the body bag. Paul didn't see every little thing because he wasn't there every minute. Paul described a basic viewing casket, and that's exactly what was used to ship the body. In Dallas, the bronze colored casket was described as a "cheap plastic casket." Lifton fell for the crooked undertaker's scam and decided it was a casket fit for a king. No, the body wasn't stolen. It couldn't have been, because Jackie would know it. After all, Texas was the land of shell games and flimflams, and the old bait-and-switch scam with caskets was as old as the frontier.

In the 1960s, Lifton promoted the idea that Brown & Root built a concrete bunker on the Grassy Knoll from which the assassins, hidden behind papier mâché trees, shot Kennedy. Another sniper was in a cherry picker overlooking the plaza from behind the stockade fence. ''He suggests that camouflage may have been used in Dealey Plaza and left there, at least for a few days.... At this time, and perhaps at all times, he cannot be taken seriously,'' Robert Richter wrote.[71]

Lifton believed that the only shots came from the front and that wound alteration was preplanned. As Roger Feinman points out:

> Simple logic, as well as the indisputable history of the government's handling of the medical evidence, both militate against Lifton's before-the-fact, pre-planned scenario and in favor of an after-the-fact, ad hoc response to the developing situation.... Unfortunately for Mr. Lifton, a number of his autopsy witnesses describe the large wound in the head as being in the same posterior location where some of the Parkland doctors placed it. This, after the head was supposedly altered to remove evidence of a front-to-back hit.[72]

I am making a target out of myself in this book in hopes of instructing the public. I may come off as petty or self-aggrandizing, or wearing my heart on my sleeve—overly sensitive, but I have to weigh what I experienced with this crowd and what normal human experience might be. The conclusion of myself, those I talked it over with, and my publisher was that this whole sordid story has to be told. It is instructive to the dark side of human nature, the dark side of the JFK assassination research community, and the actual facts and history of so much that has consumed the generation of those who were caught up in the mystery of what happened to John Kennedy.

''On the question of Harry's credibility,'' Lifton wrote Robert Groden, ''Harry implies on the back jacket of *High Treason* that he went to Harvard University. Indeed, he implies he attended the law school at Harvard. The description starts: 'Harrison Edward Livingstone, a graduate of Harvard, studied law.'

''Harry Livingstone neither attended nor graduated from Harvard University. Nor did he graduate from its law school. Moreover, if he tells you he did, he is simply lying. Harry Livingstone attended Harvard Extension School. This is the 'night school' of Harvard, and is quite a different animal than Harvard University. Anyone can attend Harvard

Extension—you simply sign up, and pay for the courses. For your information, Harvard University will not—I repeat, will not—accept credits from Harvard Extension School. [False. All the degrees of its schools are from Harvard colleges.] Harrison Livingstone first enrolled at Harvard in 1966–67; he received a B.A. on June 11, 1970. He never attended or graduated from Harvard College [false]: he never attended or graduated from Harvard Law School [I never implied that I did]."

I had the unique experience, along with Henry Kissinger and Eric Erikson and probably nobody else in three hundred years, of being undergraduate members of the faculty at Harvard, but this is an achievement that Lifton, in his zeal to destroy or discredit imagined enemies, would overlook.

Magnanimously, Lifton wrote me, "For what it's worth, I want you to know that I have never judged a person by what school he went to, or his degree, etc. I am sure that Harvard Extension is a fine place to study; and it wouldn't surprise me in the least if someone who went there had just as good an education as someone who graduated Harvard College. None of that is at issue.... The issue is one of falsifying one's own credentials and not telling the truth about ourselves—on the back jacket of a book whose major thesis is that the government didn't tell us the truth about a President's murder.

"As to how this whole matter came up: I called the Registrar at Harvard University and Harvard Extension not because I am (or was) out to hurt you, but because I had heard from some third party that you in fact had not graduated from Harvard College [there it is again! *Slander!*], despite what your book jacket implies.... Being the kind of person who doesn't accept someone else's word, I made the phone calls I did—only to discover that the allegation was correct; that you in fact didn't graduate from Harvard College; your degree is from Harvard Extension.... since you went to Harvard Extension, what's so difficult about stating exactly that on the book jacket? That's the proper and honorable thing to do."[73] He says he would not impugn my credentials publicly, but he certainly went on right up to the present day passing this slander around, in spite of the fact that a dean at Harvard wrote him to tell him that he was wrong. This is a typical Lifton distortion.

Harvard wrote Lifton back as follows: "Dear Mr. Lifton: Mr. Harrison Livingstone, author of the new book *High Treason,* asked me to confirm to you that the dust jacket statement on that book ("Harrison Edward Livingstone, a graduate of Harvard ...") is indeed correct. I am happy to do so. Mr. Livingstone is an alumnus of Harvard University, and is so listed in the official Harvard University Alumni Directory. While a student at the Harvard Extension School, he took courses, as a Special Student, at Harvard College, and officially received his A.B. in Extension Studies degree from Harvard University in 1970. It would not be correct for Mr. Livingstone to claim that he was an alumnus of Harvard College, but it certainly is correct to claim, as he does truthfully, that he is an alumnus of Harvard (i.e., Harvard University, 'Harvard' being the customary shorthand expression for 'Harvard University.').''[74]

There never was any doubt that Governor Connally was struck from the rear, and we now know from Diana Bowron and Dr. Marion Jenkins that rear entry wounds were identified at Parkland. Feinman asks, "Would Lifton have us presume that Governor Connally volunteered to take a near fatal shot from behind to assist the conspirators in persuading the world that someone was indeed firing from the rear?"[75] After concluding that "only the Marx Brothers had the skill and impeccable timing to execute" Lifton's kidnap-and-alteration theory[76] Feinman notes:

> The tragic irony of David Lifton's work is that, like the Warren Commission itself, he was constrained by the lack of solid fact to resort to speculative improbability in constructing a 'logical' explanation for the assassination. It is noteworthy that this technique achieved currency in several more recently published works. Sadly, Lifton's book inaugurated a trend in the publishing industry, whereby it has seemingly become impossible for a serious, responsible student of the assassination to see his work commercially published unless he posits a neat and fanciful solution to the crime. . . .[77]

Roger, whose manuscript is not yet commercially available, also sees "a striking parallelism" between the way in which both David Lifton and the House Select Committee on Assassinations treated the Warren Commission critics: "Both the HSCA and Lifton exonerated everyone in sight of complicity in the murder, and of the cover-up of the crime, leaving only sinister ghosts to blame for the assassination."[78] In his view, "Mr. Lifton seems not primarily concerned with Oswald's guilt or innocence or (in the latter case) the undoing of a vicious injustice; he seems not concerned with tracing the assassination conspiracy to its source; whatever may be his aspirations, the least one can say is that his work is fundamentally irrelevant to the objectives of the critics and mainly supplies diversion."[79]

Recalling that the late Sylvia Meagher, a highly respected author and critic, begged Lifton to abandon his "papier-mâché tree theory," Feinman laments that "somewhere along the line David Lifton lost sight of the distinction between hypothesis, theory, evidence, and proven fact."[80] He sums up his argument as follows:

> At bottom, the immutable facts are these: Mr. Lifton professes to believe that the critics of the Warren Commission were ill-motivated and fundamentally in error. He reserves his venom for them, not for the perpetrators of a monstrous frame-up. He further professes to believe that none of the known key participants in the creation and handling of the medical evidence acted less than honestly. He shouts "conspiracy!", but his message boils down to: "Well, something must have happened, and maybe someday they'll tell us."
>
> It is these broad and basic truths that far transcend the interpersonal rivalries, the quibbles, the different shadings of emphasis and interpretation of the assassination evidence and motive among critics, to set David Lifton and the continuum of his activities in the case distinctly apart from the rest. . . .
>
> Whoever David Lifton is, to label him as a "critic" is nothing less than fraudulent. Rather, he plays into the hands of the very forces we are all opposing. It is therefore a source of deep regret that no voices among the critics have been raised against him. . . .[81]
> David Lifton's attempt to persuade the American public to buy this hideous, ghoulish, sick, perverted, twisted, and insane fantasy of body-snatching, postmortem wound infliction, and alteration mocks the assassination researchers and critics of the government's case. . . . Wherever or whoever David Lifton may be, he is the perfect public spokesman for the assassination research community only if we look at things from the perspective of both the government and the established news media.[82]

Roger Feinman, in his anger, is a better writer than I.

Lifton gave us "the body, disguised as luggage" leaving *Air Force One;* that false wounds on the head and back were made; that there were no gunmen at all from behind; that the gunman was on top of a cherry picker behind papier-mâché trees in Dealey Plaza; that there were two caskets and the body was reintroduced to its casket at Bethesda; that the wounds changed drastically between hospitals (how could they, if there was no gunman from behind?); that the brain, disguised as a baby, was taken into Bethesda on a gurney and inserted back into the head during the clandestine intermission. Lifton states as a fact that Andrew Purdy or the HSCA simply wrote an affidavit and had Sibert sign it, saying that the statement "surgery to the head area" was a mistake. Lifton stated that the body was altered to make a "perfect medical forgery" to fool the camera, instead of simply forging the pictures. He ignored many statements of his own witnesses that disproved or conflicted with his theories.

Jim Marrs

Of the Texas wild bunch, one of the leaders is journalist and freelance author Jim Marrs. He sold his book *Crossfire* to Oliver Stone for $300,000 for Stone's movie *JFK*. No more than a month after *High Treason* was published, to my horror I saw *Crossfire* come off the press, and some of it seemed to be my own book. The very first thing I opened the book to was a verbatim paragraph from my book. This was a terrible and stunning shock.

There are verbatim "borrowings." In quite a number of places in *Crossfire* there is essentially similar or identical language, not just the alleged Groden quotes, which I wrote ten years prior to teaming up with him.

For example, compare the language in the middle of page 378 of his book beginning with "The Key to understanding" with that at the bottom of page 7 of my book. Marrs says at the beginning of that "As Groden later told his [sic; this] author . . ." Same slip of the pen.

And on his page 377, he has "Groden wrote" and then the exact language from the top of page 8 of my book, which I let Groden participate in, at his insistence. But my book was *printed* before Marrs's book. I knew nothing of the Stone contract or that he was going to make a film on the case, but Stone planned to hire Groden and he needed to buy a book to cover himself, so people frantically scurried through the industry looking for a suitable compendium. I had a manuscript and Groden had a copy of it. For two years I tried to get him to correct it but never could get any movement. Since the dot matrix print was so dim it could not be copied well, it is logical that he did not have it, and the next thing I knew, many sections of Marrs's book had identical sourcing. In other words, page after page has sequences of fact, sometimes not changed around at all, without any attribution to me. Since much of what was unique in my first book was the synthesis of the evidence I was responsible for, nobody else had that, or, for instance, the history of the House Assassinations Committee in the unique manner in which I wrote it.

Marrs would have come out with this before my book ever saw the light of day, if at all, but I suddenly got credit from a printer and was able to print my book in the winter of 1988–89. *High Treason* came out first, and the above quotes and sourcing show that Marrs had access to my manuscript from Groden, with whom he was about to work on Stone's project. Marrs told me, "he let me have it," then later denied it. This is kind of like Groden saying that Michael Goldsmith let Groden copy the autopsy pictures.

Plagiarism, endemic in the "critical community" or "research community," is a criminal act wherein the *structure* or outline of even part of someone else's work is used for the framework of your own.

Marrs told me on May 14, 1991, that Groden gave him my *manuscript* in 1988 and told him it was "all right to use it." Groden has stated that he had done so and that none of this could have happened after *High Treason* was published as he now claims.

Shortly after I printed *High Treason*, Groden published an article saying that he wrote the book and why he wrote it.[83] Nowhere in that article did it mention that I in fact researched, wrote, and even published the book. My name was nowhere in that article. Later I learned that he was whiting my name off the book on some television appearances. Meanwhile, my business was being sabotaged, and I ended up in a few months with 5,000 books gone and the printer not paid. I owed $30,000. I was caught up in a nightmare. I still did not know about the Stone film, and it never occurred to me that this bunch had to wipe me off the face of the earth for the sake of that project, which they all sought to control.

In a news article about Groden not long before I managed to print the book, he is quoted as saying that he was trying to place "his" book, and that if he failed, he would try to publish it himself.[84] Again, my name was not mentioned. But too often I had no idea of the things going on behind my back.

Lifton, Groden, and others extensively interfered with my later publishers on a number of occasions. This to me is the worst crime that can be committed against an author. I was fortunate to find owners who had the exact opposite reaction to being pushed. Pushing bureaucrats at a big publishing house is one thing, and they are more easily threatened, than pushing people who have a great deal of life experience and can look right through the types we have in this case. It's like those in Dallas and elsewhere who try to scare me now and who try to tell me what I can write and not write. Like all those who tried to stop this book and who don't want me to bring this story to you.

A reader wrote me that "In the Oliver Stone movie *JFK,* my first thought was that it seemed he used a great deal of your research to make his case. I know Director Stone has taken many hits in the press over this film. . . ."

Let's look at some of the other big-name hustlers on the lecture and chicken dinner circuit in this business. Think long and hard about the character these facts represent. It isn't enough just to latch on to a good issue in this life and ride it for all it's worth. We have to be worthy of it. There is a question of character here, and I'm sure they'll find lots of bad things to repeat about me for saying that. At least I don't falsify evidence.

Cyril Wecht and Tom Wilson

Wecht originally told me that the Dallas doctors were wrong about there being a throat entry wound and were wrong about a large hole being in the back of the President's head. "It's all semantics," he told me. "The pictures don't show any hole in the head."[85] Like Harold Weisberg, Wecht didn't question the pictures. Wecht *noticed* that the top right front of Kennedy's face was missing in the X-rays. But after noting it in 1972 in an article, he ignored it.[86] I am the only writer who noticed that and made an issue out of it in ten years before others tried to claim they just discovered it. Their information came from me. But those alleged critics always made a living sponging up other people's information and claiming it as their own. That's when they try to shoot your head off if you poke it aboveground.

Wecht bitterly resisted the proposition that the autopsy photos were forged. For ten years he told me that I was wrong. Then I published my book *High Treason,* and Wecht came to my press conference and praised it to the skies. I thank him for that, but *why then*?

Cyril Wecht together with Gary Shaw launched Tom Wilson, who claims his method of computer image processing proves the autopsy photos are forged and much more. Wilson (and Wecht) told us he won't publish his work because their plan was either to get someone to sue him, or to sue anyone who says he is wrong, and then they'll get to prove everything in court! Great plan. Kind of like Joe West suing to exhume John Kennedy's body without employing a lawyer. He had only a fool for a client, and nothing to gain but publicity.

Frankly, the Wecht and Wilson plan is not just imbecilic but also damages the ongoing inquiry. This research is an academic discipline, an academic effort, and we *have to* be able to duplicate Wilson's work. But he refuses to spell it all out, and so famous professors say Wilson is a fraud. Wilson refuses to be filmed or taped. Everyone naturally concludes that he's hiding something.

Wilson claims that he sees an exit hole in the back of the neck. "It's in the folds of the neck," he says.[87] The trouble is, the nurses who washed off all of the President's body saw no such wound.

I believe that Wilson was launched in order to co-opt this field of study: *the forgery of the autopsy pictures.* He completely deemphasized the absolute proof I developed through the statements of the men who took the photographs and all those medical witnesses who saw them. Now we are saddled with a trial of Wilson's evidence that can only blow up in our face like the police recordings with the alleged shots on them.

Wilson is a Republican and certainly no Democrat.

Wilson represents what we've been getting all along— pseudoscientific gobbledygook designed to overwhelm the untutored mind. It's all a charade, a smoke and mirror show. The trend is to rely on anything that sounds scientific and discount the eyewitnesses.

What we have are people using this case to promote their own businesses by keeping their names constantly before the public. Some are professional witnesses and are paid high fees for testifying.

There is another kind of responsibility, and that is the responsibility we have to our witnesses. Some witnesses, as previously stated, have turned into professionals, and gradually the force of what they have to offer is diluted as their words and memories become twisted and they become "critics." They have become "properties," and with a price tag.

Fletcher Prouty

Extensively false information was planted on Oliver Stone. I've known and liked Fletcher Prouty for years, but I've taken to checking out, or trying to, whatever he tells me. Fletcher offered me, after *High Treason* was published, a number of items that later cropped up in that exercise in public entertainment *JFK*. One of them was a Christchurch, New Zealand, newspaper story carried on the day John Kennedy died. Fletcher's claim is false, which is that he saw that story announcing JFK's death *before* the assassination, too soon after for them to have the information. Forced to retreat from this, he claimed that the biographical data on Lee Harvey Oswald in the story had to have come from secret Pentagon files. He was shopping a bunch of other questionable stuff, too, such as the hearse driving off at Andrews without Jackie in it. It takes a lot of time to find the films and see that she is in the hearse. This could have been the same mix-up as some made at Parkland when newscasters announced from live video that day that Jackie had arrived at Parkland and was going inside. They saw Jackie's look-alike Pam Turnure, and that's whom they saw at Bethesda.

Prouty's *Christchurch Star* story (dated November 23, 1963, because of the international date line, but actually the same day that Kennedy died—November 22) is preposterous because it was an Associated Press story partly compiled from what was already known—*before the assassination*—about Oswald. Any news office had it all in their files on Oswald from the time he defected to the USSR. These were public stories about Oswald in the newspapers in New Orleans and elsewhere. There is *not a single fact* on that bio in the first extras that was secret or not publicly known beforehand.

The *Star* carried the AP article about Oswald, from the United States, and this is what the *Star* printed about Oswald: "Police said Oswald was an employee in the building where the rifle was found following the President's assassination.

"Oswald had defected to the Soviet Union in 1959, it was learned later.

"He returned to the United States last year.

"He has a Russian wife and a child.

"While in the Soviet Union he worked in a Minsk factory.

"He went to the Soviet Union following his discharge from the Marines.

"While in Russia he apparently became disillusioned with life there.

"Soviet authorities gave him and his family exit permits to return to America.

"Oswald was later identified as chairman of a 'Fair Play for Cuba Committee.'

"He became the prime suspect in the assassination of the President."

There is *nothing* in the above that had not already been published by the AP and carried in newspapers with regard to Oswald's defection and so on.

There is, however, a significant difference in something else in the story and what we have been told. "Oswald had been chased into the cinema by two policemen. The officers, J. Tippit and M. MacDonald, had received a tip that the President's assassin might have gone into the cinema. Tippit was shot dead as he ran into the cinema, British United Press said.

"MacDonald grappled with the man and they sprawled over theatre seats. He received a four-inch gash before he overpowered the man."

This is such a major difference in what Americans were told, that Tippit died in his patrol car some distance away, that we ought to think about why the rest of the world is so certain that there was a major domestic conspiracy in the case. The rest of the world has been exposed to different information than we have, and the question is, which is more accurate? What about the pool of blood on the sidewalk in Dealey Plaza and the AP report that day of a dead Secret Service agent there?

I checked it by calling the editors of the *Christchurch Star,* and they got back to me with the exact schedule of when they received the AP wire, when they went to press, and when the paper went on the streets. There was plenty of time. Prouty's story is false. Stone had to know that. We can put this in a class with Paul Groody's severed Oswald head, LBJ's order to Crenshaw to *kill* Oswald when they had him at Parkland after Ruby shot him, and the phony canister contents and fake CIA cables in the Roscoe White story. Roscoe was the newly hired Dallas police cadet whom Gary Shaw claims was on the Grassy Knoll behind the fence in uniform along with Johnny Roselli and Charles Nicoletti shooting at the President.

Along with body theft and alteration, there are many fake stories in this case. The latest we heard is that someone shot the body on the plane to alter the wounds, and the hearse was taken away from Dallas on one of the planes for sixteen years. Our informant tells us that the best reconstruction artist in the country was taken aboard *Air Force One,* and while Lyndon Johnson was being sworn in as the new president, the reconstruction artist rebuilt Kennedy's head and body. This is a country undertaker's idea of a new twist, a hot new angle that is going to make a great movie. "And I can *prove* it, too!" this Texas charlatan tells us.

It is unfortunate that Fletcher's zeal for pointing the finger at the CIA for every misdeed distracts attention from the Pentagon's own complicity. Remember, Prouty worked for the Pentagon, and they hated the CIA, the way city cops hated the FBI in those days.

The problem we have is one of misinformation. Each of these folks gives us some truth to establish credibility, but then there appears a great deal of false and misleading information.

Jones Harris

Then there's Jones Harris. Who knows who he is? Harris is in the literature as hanging around Jim Garrison's circus. I see him appearing at press conferences, a battered old suitcase in hand. He thinks or says the Japanese killed John Kennedy.[88]

"Harris had studied and meticulously enlarged an 8-millimeter motion picture showing Kennedy's mortal wound, taken by a spectator, Orville Nix. In one of the Nix frames, he sighted an object behind the wall on the grassy knoll. He had enlargements made of the critical area. It then became even more apparent to Harris that he could see a station wagon on the grassy knoll. And on the roof of the vehicle he discerned a figure aiming what seemed to be a rifle," writes Lewis and Schiller.[89] Of course, the fence is more than five feet high and it would be impossible to see a car behind it except from a very high angle, not below it, as Nix was.

"Harris journeyed to Dallas to investigate first hand. He talked to Nix and to Abraham Zapruder. He even interviewed Zapruder's secretaries. His big find was a big fizzle. This was proven by other candid color pictures taken by another spectator. From this position, at a different angle and at a slightly higher elevation, the Harris murder car turned out to be nothing more than a space between a clump of trees.

"It was Harris who was the catalyst in helping arrange the publication of various books concerning the assassination. Showing no favorites, he first introduced Josiah Thompson, Edward J. Epstein, Sylvia Meagher, and Wesley J. Liebeler to interested editors. As a result of these selfless endeavors, Harris has gained recognition as the unofficial arbiter among the in-group of superbuffs."[90]

Mark Lane

Mark Lane represented the Reverend Jim Jones at the time Jones and his American followers in Guyana had been accepted en masse to defect to the Soviet Union. Almost a thousand were murdered, and Lane was on the spot. Jones, Congressman Ryan, and *a thousand* of Jones's followers died while Lane was protected by armed guards.

One client Lane didn't lose was the Liberty Lobby and Victor Marchetti. The Liberty Lobby is a far-right-wing operation on a par with the John Birchers. Victor Marchetti, the author of *The CIA and the Cult of Intelligence,* wrote an article for the Liberty Lobby's magazine indicating that E. Howard Hunt, who had been arrested in the Watergate caper that forced the resignation of President Richard Nixon, was implicated in the assassination of John Kennedy and may have been in Dealey Plaza at the time of the murder. Either Lane has no scruples or he has another political agenda we don't know about. Lane's excuse is that he was defending the idea that Howard Hunt was in Dallas on November 22, 1963.

Lane made big claims about this case, and one of them was that the jury was convinced that the CIA killed John Kennedy. This is patent hogwash. Lane quoted only one juror, Leslie Armstrong, and ignored the others for obvious reasons, since the question of whether the CIA killed Kennedy was not the issue in the case. To the contrary, another juror—Suzanne Reach—denied that she was convinced that the CIA was involved in the case.[91] In addition, UPI wrote that juror No. 11 (Cobb) "Said the jury did not address the allegations brought out by Lane throughout the trial that Hunt was involved in a CIA conspiracy to kill Kennedy. She said they were more concerned with whether the article was damaging to Hunt." These are two jurors Lane does not mention in his book.

Lane defended the Liberty Lobby in cases involving Jack Anderson and William F. Buckley, Jr., as well. He called them "political cases." He says that Anderson settled that case with a "financial contribution." The Liberty Lobby was found to have libeled Buckley. Lane calls Willis Carto, the founder of the Liberty Lobby, "a true believer in the Constitution." The Anti-Defamation League calls Carto possibly the most influential anti-Semite in the United States. Some of those Texas farmers with a lot of oil wells and more radical political ideas help back the Liberty Lobby and its campaign of hate.

Martin Shackelford, the indefatigable and unconquerable longtime assassination researcher from Saginaw, says, "I am about as excited about Mark Lane's association with Liberty Lobby since the Hunt case, as I was about his association with Jim Jones and the People's Temple prior to the massacre/mass suicide in Guyana. Lane has made some contributions to the assassination field, but he has also been caught in errors and misleading attributions. Even more than some other books on the case, his [books] need to be read cautiously, not repeating anything as fact until you have verified it in a solid way."[92] "Mark Lane has often been justifiably accused of playing loosely with the facts."[93]

Norman Mailer said on the dust jacket of Mark Lane's book, evidently being quoted from a letter he wrote stating ironical ridicule of Lane's piece of shit *Plausible Denial,* "*Rush to Judgment* will live as a classic for every serious amateur detective in America." Kathlee Fitzgerald asks if this is a rip on Lane. *Amateur detective?*

I don't know how Lane or anyone else can convert an alleged statement by David Atlee Phillips into an admission that the CIA invented Oswald's visit to Mexico City. That isn't what the statement by Phillips says.[94] It's what people choose to *hope* it says, like Ruby's last note to his jailer before he died. That note may say the exact opposite of what it sounds like. It's too easy to take a phrase out of the context of its sentence, as in the case when Ruby appears to say he killed Oswald to silence him. He actually seems to say, "I'm being framed in the conspiracy, and killed Oswald to silence him." (I added the comma.) He is saying he was framed for the *idea* that he was silencing Oswald. In other words, he had other motives in killing Oswald.

"Lane has never seen a lily without wanting to gild it," complained rival conspiracy researcher Harold Weisberg to *Mother Jones*. "*I* only wish he were content to steal from others, but he has this urge to invent his own stuff."[95]

Bob Katz said in his article "Mark Lane, the Left's Leading Hearse-Chaser" in *Mother Jones* that "Lane had developed a methodology over the years that was as distinctively his in style and content as a thumbprint on a police blotter: leap like a tiger at a hunch or a tip, call a press conference, make dramatic changes to illustrate that the issue— be it nuclear proliferation, assassination cover-up or dishonesty in the media—boils down to nothing less than the age old tussle betwixt good and evil. Then crank up an investigation, borrow and magnify other people's evidence and, finally, never let up so long as there is a virgin ear unassailed by the accusations."[96]

It was Lane who recruited Arlen Specter's partner in the Philadelphia district attorney's office, Richard A. Sprague, in the fall of 1976 to become the first chief counsel of the Assassinations Committee.[97] It was Sprague who all but destroyed the Committee before it could get off the ground with his and Robert Groden's proposals for secret bugging devices and PSI tests. Groden is proud of the fact that he got the voice stress analyzers included in the budget. See *High Treason* for how this affected other congressmen and caused the near death of the Committee.[98]

Marvin Watson, special assistant to President Lyndon Johnson, had the FBI prepare some reports on the leading critics of the Warren Report. The targets included Mark Lane, Joachim Joesten, Penn Jones, Jr., Edward Jay Epstein, Professor Richard H. Popkin, Leo Sauvage, and Harold Weisberg. The reports were sent over to the White House on November 8, 1966. The main information the FBI was concerned with was Lane's extreme leftist background. "Lane has a long history of affiliation with Communist Party front groups and organizations which have been cited as subversive."

Granted, the House Committee on Un-American Activities named some organizations that may have been perfectly innocent, but nevertheless there is a long litany of Lane's speaking before countless groups from the extreme left. Either he was a double agent, or he believed all that crap. One of the things that condemned Lane in those days was his close association with Isidore Gibby Needleman, "an attorney who was formerly employed by Amtorg Trading Corporation, the registered Russian trade agency in the United States. Needleman was reportedly interested in assisting Lane during his political campaign in 1960 when he was elected to the New York State Assembly. Needleman has represented current and former Communist Party members in court and before various congressional committees. He has had custody of Communist Party funds and has described himself as a strict adherent of Marxist-Leninist doctrines. It has also been reported that Needleman has acted as a Soviet espionage agent in the past."

It did not help the cause of those who believed that Oswald didn't kill John Kennedy, and was not really a Communist, to have Mark Lane take over and represent Marguerite Oswald, Lee Harvey's mother. Maybe that was the plan, because, like Lane's dead witnesses, Oswald rapidly was convicted of being a Communist posthumously through guilt by association with Lane via Oswald's poor old battle-ax of a mother.

That's how it works.

Carl Oglesby

Speaking of leftist influence seeking to control the JFK case, there's Carl Oglesby, a former head of Students for a Democratic Society (SDS), who claims to be an assassination researcher and, in fact, harbors a deep resentment for John Kennedy.

Oglesby brings with him the rusty and antique baggage of radical Marxist dialectic. His "research" comes within the confines of talking to other researchers; footnoting footnotes; and helping set up the Assassination Information Bureau, which was an umbrella organization for some of the popularizers and opportunists in the JFK case.

Oglesby's venom for John Kennedy comes through loud and clear in his television appearances, where he grits and hisses between lines like a snake, hating the capitalist Kennedy.[99] It's visible every time he mentions Kennedy's name.

I object to any Marxist interfering in this investigation, because the historical bias they bring with them colors their and our perception of the facts. I don't need anyone like Oglesby to tell me or the public what the facts are, all the while he is hating the man he's talking about. We care and we care deeply for John Kennedy and what happened to him. It is wrong for those who don't truly care to, in any way, mix in this criminal investigation. And that especially goes for Republican leaders and leftist Democrats. Stay out of this. They screwed up the Warren Commission and now they've basically ruined this nation's finances, hopes, and dreams.

Conclusion

The bottom line is that there are certain powerful figures in this research, often all over national television, who are going to die. There is a fierce power struggle for the succession. Worse, a common Modus Operandi is being utilized by the leadership of the "critical community." Those *modus operandi* start with the gaining of trust from the neophyte researcher, leading to the taking over of that person. The evidence being dealt with by the researcher is then deobjectified. This is done by modifying each piece of evidence as little as a millimeter, but it works to discredit both that hard piece of evidence, if such it is, and ultimately to discredit the researcher or the witness. The ultimate object is to protect the plotters, those who took over the direction and control of the United States.

What we are talking about is *psy ops,* or psychological operations, intended to control the flow of information in the assassination of President John Kennedy and to protect the murderers. We have a research community, or a "critical community," some of whom are the real accessories after the fact, protecting the political party that gained by the murder, and those powerful forces that remained in place as a result of the assassination. And it is very, very deliberate.

Every time a researcher embellishes a story—adds something to it, as the Dallas bunch has been doing to the witnesses they have been representing and agenting to publishers, TV shows, and film companies—this case is that much more irretrievably damaged in the commercialization of JFK's death. Those members of the cult don't want the case to be over. Their identity is terribly threatened by the game ending, so they keep going down wrong trails, knowing what lies at the end of the right trail: down the center. They have to avoid that at all costs.

We should never underestimate how vulnerable people are to persuasion, and the fact that there are a lot of smooth talkers in the assassination information business. They are very persuasive and appeal to our emotions and play upon our idealism. It all sounds very reasonable, but it is largely just another scam. We have got to put an end to it, because we have spawned an industry and a tradition with this tragic mystery that will go on for centuries, like a monastery full of monks devoted to protecting the sacred bead.

The only thing most will get out of this is betrayal. These people have fundamentally betrayed this nation, not just those of us who do this work. The top dogs in this business know not the meaning of loyalty or honesty and are not decent people. The former leaders of the assassination research cult for the first three decades following John Kennedy's death are the Stalinists of our time, who will crush anyone who gets in their way, or try to. They have a lot of bad things to say about me, most of it false, and I expect many bad things to happen to me for having written the truth. But so be it. That is my job as a writer, and I will perform it come hell or high water.

After reading the above long mudslinging smear, the subjects will sigh deeply and once again tell themselves and anybody who will listen that I'm crazy and shouldn't be taken seriously. Well, I'm the Art Donovan of this case, and I can live with myself! He's authentic, and so are those who are with me. The rest are not!!

For every enemy I make by being outspoken and honest, for telling it like it is, I make a hundred or a thousand new friends. So let all the fakers beware. I've told only a small part of what I know about these people.

Bearing false witness is a terrible thing. That's something I never want to do. I myself have often suffered from false accusations like those described above. It happens often to people with what is known as a "strong presence," which makes one a target. We make some people afraid, though it is completely unintentional. And, often, people try to hurt us. I try to remain humble before God and cultivate my flowers.

To quote a friend: "They're a bunch of lunatics!" I think they are a lot worse than that, in view of the often criminal and unethical activities on the part of the leaders, not to speak of their betrayal of this nation. They have made themselves a party to treason.

There is nothing knowingly false in this chapter. It is not malicious. It is the truth about these folks as I know it. These are truly the scavengers and critics of the Warren Report. Unfortunately there is much more for which there is no space here.

They abused their power.

CHAPTER 14

ROBERT GRODEN

"Robert Groden stole everything we had!" Michael Goldsmith and Jane Downey, both former staff members of the House Assassinations Committee, told me.[1] Groden was later to claim that Goldsmith, head of the Committee's photographic panel, gave him permission to copy the autopsy pictures of President Kennedy,[2] which Groden later sold to the *Globe,* a supermarket tabloid, for $50,000.[3] Groden's company was "Artificial Intelligence," one of many names he uses for his operations, and the money was to be paid half to him and half to the company.

Groden has been the most public of the Kennedy assassination researchers for years. His notoriety is based not so much on his knowledge of the case as in the use of visual material upon which he makes various claims. Possession of an early copy of the Zapruder film gave him high visibility. Martin Shackelford writes, "It is unfortunate that someone with such unique access to the photographic evidence, someone in a position to influence millions of people, betrayed their trust and the trust of colleagues who welcomed him into the community of researchers, by abusing the power that access gave him."[4]

The *Globe*'s publication of some of Groden's color photographs and (unknown to them before publication) some of Mark Crouch's Fox photographs in 1991 also were advertisements for Groden's dubious business. "The *Globe* agrees to credit in each article the photographs and interview as 'new evidence to be contained in the new book, TV documentary and videocassette, *JFK: Proof of the Conspiracy,* by Robert Groden, forthcoming from SCS Management Co., a Beverly Hills, California, production company 212-273-0220).' " SCS Management refers to Groden's agent, Steven Sanford. Interesting that Groden holds back materials for many years until he can get a deal like this, with advertising included in a supposed news story about "new" evidence.

Groden's December 30, 1977, contract with Larry Flint's L.P.F., Inc., the publisher of *Hustler* magazine, conveyed to Larry Flint his enhanced Zapruder slides and other material, certain photographs, documents, and information. He gave up control or ownership in the material to Flint's *L.A. Free Press.* The contract read that "Licensor hereby conveys to Licensee all right, title and interest to the property more particularly described in Exhibit '1' for its exclusive use without restriction [and] ... further licenses the use of said material for the period of July 1, 1978 through June 30, 1998 to each signatory to this Agreement as co-licensees with all incumbent rights."

Groden's primary conspiracy scenario is one most conspiracy theorists have never accepted, that Joseph Adams Milteer's group of right wingers shot Kennedy. He implicates the John Birchers. Radical rightists though they may be as an organization, they did not undertake to kill the President.

I cannot believe, for reasons outlined elsewhere, that there was a gunman on the Grassy Knoll, as he says. Instead there were gunmen facing the oncoming car on each side of the bridge in manholes there. One of those storm drains adjoins the Grassy Knoll but was some one hundred feet from where Groden sees a shooter in the Moorman photograph.

Groden has espoused every wild theory from gunmen in the Moorman photograph of the picket fence to a gunman behind the cement retaining wall in front of the fence and in front of Zapruder. He believes that the body was stolen and altered. In the early 1970s, Groden said in his lectures that the Dallas doctors were wrong about there being a hole in the back of the head. For apparent reasons of convenience, he later reversed this.

Obtaining the Autopsy Photos

Groden's original story was that he copied the autopsy pictures when no one was looking. Later he said Blakey let him copy the pictures. Jane Downey denies that Groden ever copied them in her presence, and states that she was with Groden at all times when he viewed the pictures. And who set up Regis Blahut, who lost his CIA job because his fingerprints were found on the sleeves of the pictures?[5]

Groden holds a great deal of his materials back until he gets the right price. We were being denied vital evidence in this case—by some of the critics.

Groden has either the original or a copy of the Bronson film, and we are unable to verify what it shows. He may have obtained the original from Bronson for study, but until now the film has not been available to researchers.

Chris Sharrett, Steve Barber, and numerous other researchers who knew Groden told me that Groden said he copied all of the visuals that came into the hands of the House Assassinations Committee. This was confirmed often enough by what they actually saw in his possession. Sharrett said Groden told him he had *kept the originals* and returned the copies to the Committee and the National Archives.[6] Shackelford adds, "I still find the charge that he kept the originals very hard to believe, as it is not that difficult to tell an original from a copy. Original films have the sprocket hold information."[7] *Every* staff member of the House Committee quizzed by me told me that Groden "stole everything we had."[8]

Think about that. The color autopsy photos that Steve Parks and I saw at Groden's house had stamped on them "Property of the National Archives." He had black-and-whites then, too. Groden told us that Blakey leaked them to him because they wanted to get them out.[9]

Naturally, I became one hell of a target perhaps because I'm one of the few researchers developing criminal evidence and witnesses in this case. I know too much about some of the operatives among us. Some say they know how close I'm coming to the truth in my investigation by how much of an operation is pointed at me by other researchers.

On Writing *High Treason*

Robert Groden did not write *High Treason.* He proclaimed that fact to David Lifton and others when he attempted to get out of responsibility for the book. A total of five pages in the book are his. I made a few changes and additions at his request.

Lifton wrote in a letter to Groden, "I wrote Harry directly because you have consistently maintained that he did the actual writing—and, from what you say, he seems to have editorial control and final say regarding what goes into the book. Moreover, from what you have said, Harry is not only the actual writer, he is in fact the publisher. . . ."[10]

One major issue with Groden is his relationship with Jamie Silverberg, lawyer for Henry Zapruder. Groden admitted during depositions in our court case in 1993 that he was receiving money back from Silverberg after Silverberg collected from New York publishers for use of the frames from the Zapruder film in publications. Groden said that the checks were for his "enhancements" of the material. What would Silverberg want with them? Groden claimed that Silverberg was now one of his lawyers. According to Groden's testimony on "Grodenscoping," his "enhancements" appear to be nothing more than recentered new photographs, with Groden deciding what is extraneous in each frame or photo and eliminating it. What is meant by "optical enhancement" is not clear.

David Lifton has made many public accusations against his longtime partner Groden. At the ASK conference in 1992, Lifton made some twenty-five charges against Groden in public, in Groden's presence, to which he said nothing. Groden never sued Lifton for such criticism.

David Dudley wrote a long and perceptive article on the 1992 ASK conference and went on to say, "Harry Livingstone flies back to Baltimore later that Saturday, having made good his promise to shake things up. But what's the point? This was like an academic conference of angry cokehead professors. The infighting. The backstabbing. The vindictiveness, the outright paranoid weirdness. The petty squabbles between big, dangerous egos. Everyone seemed to have something terrible to say (off the record, usually) about one of their colleagues. David Lifton was a 'pompous jerk' who refused to share information. Bob Groden, according to one of the organizing parties, 'is the smarmiest lying son of a bitch in the world,' the kind of guy who whined that his kids would go hungry unless ASK paid for his airfare and hotel room for the symposium. And then he showed up with an entourage and demanded an extra room for them, too."[11]

There were hundreds of mug shots of me brought to the 1992 ASK conference and passed out by Robert Groden and his son. Groden even paid a boy in Dealey Plaza to hand out mug shots of me as though I were "Wanted for Treason." Conducted by others, this ferocious campaign of slander had been going on since 1976. Few people might have ever experienced such a nightmare. The story Groden passed out along with this, in an attempt to destroy his old associate, was that I had done time in prison for child molestation. I was shunned by the leadership of the research community and abused everywhere. There was no truth in the story Groden perpetuated at ASK. It is clear to anyone studying my research and what I have to say about these people, who brought our investigation on themselves and that you are reading about herein, that they had to try to knock me out as a means to hide the fact that the most prominent people in this case have ruined it, as Sheriff Bowles has said.

Paranoia, accusation, suspicion. That is the rock bottom of the research community. The key was not to be involved, but we all got sucked into this maelstrom. It was the human thing to do to seek colleagues, and I never dreamed that part of the whole thing was an operation. The first meetings of assassination researchers in Dallas were said to have more FBI agents than researchers present. I can see why. Far too many have come to the assassination research conferences with the intent of disrupting important research because they have a commitment to the findings of the Warren Report or some other theory.

Not long after the ASK conference, David Lifton wrote the president of Emerson College, Jacqueline Liebergott, complaining because he had not been asked to speak there: "I have known Robert Groden for some twenty years. Unfortunately, he is someone I have had to deal with—as almost everyone has who has to do a film on the subject. Back in the early 1970s, Groden—through a coincidence as to where he happened to be employed—acquired a copy of the only copy of the Zapruder film (then owned by Time-Life) that was available. Indeed, some would use a less polite word than 'acquired.' That acquisition of the film had a morally ambiguous quality to it. I for one was happy to see the film publicized. Often the way information gets out in our democracy is as the result of acts such as the journalistic 'leak' acts that have a morally ambiguous quality. Such transactions occur daily between journalists and their sources. It's food for thought, and for philosophy classes. But Groden isn't a journalist; and he didn't just obtain information and make it available—he then went into business, selling the film for substantial sums of money to anyone who wanted to make a documentary. It would be as if Eilsberg, having stolen the Pentagon Papers, and claiming a higher moral purpose in doing so, then attempted to copyright them and make a living by selling them to various publishers."

Groden claims that the Zapruder film was first copyrighted by Time Inc in 1967, which would seem preposterous. He argues that his copy was made in 1966, and therefore, "since it was made before the film was copyrighted, that it could have been used before it had been—since it had not been published, Time, Inc, had never used the film and did not copyright it, they did not have a statutory copyright because they had not used the film intact, just the individual frames copyrighted and, again, by publishing them, gave them a statutory copyright just as it is our feeling that the publishing of this photograph in *High Treason,* the one that we're talking about now . . . by publishing it in *High Treason* gave us statutory copyright since it's the first time it's ever appeared anywhere in print." Who is we? Groden and his wife? Or Groden and me? He seems to be saying that publication gave him copyright, ignoring the owner of the underlying materials, which is an assertion of squatter's rights without the statutory time period. If he means by "we" that we both owned it upon publication, since I owned half of the book, then he gave up his interest when he assigned his half of the copyright later. Zapruder's own lawyer told Jane Schwartz that Zapruder sold copyright in November, 1963, to Time Inc. then. Several years later it was transferred back. I never wanted the pictures.

For a while in 1991 and 1992, Groden was claiming to be writing a book called *Inside the Conspiracy,* a title already used by someone else. How could Groden get inside the conspiracy, anyway? Peter Model told me that Model wrote 100 percent of the first book that had Groden's name on it as coauthor.[12]

Groden claims that in frame 413 of the Zapruder film there is a rifle poking out from the bushes at the limousine. (See further information in the film chapter in this book.) I took this on faith and was foolish enough to print it in my first book. After all, *Rolling Stone* printed the picture. I took far too much on faith from this person. We all have. It takes a long time to awaken to his misinformation, like his story of Oswald in the doorway of the TSBD, who turned out to be Billy Lovelady. A better example of his misinformation is the story of the motorcycle leaving the motorcade at Elm and Houston.

Go to Dallas and look at that short, three-foot-high cement wall from the steps leading up from the sidewalk to the pedestal where Zapruder stood with his camera, and try to imagine a gunman there in front of Zapruder. (See the photo section.) If there was a gunman there, what does that tell us about Abraham Zapruder?

Once I asked Groden, "What did you discover in this case?" He came up with only one answer: "Black Dog Man."

"You are right if you think you've been had by Robert Groden," respected researcher Simmie Heninger wrote. "We all have! He is one of the main reasons that the HSCA investigation failed to resolve the controversy but only muddied the waters. His consultations with them were incompetent in every aspect of the assassination photos.

"I can't really say exactly where he is mistaken in his film analysis. The problem is that he makes a lot of speculations that either cannot be proved or can be disproved. This confuses matters and makes the things we can be sure of in the films less obvious. Groden's claims that assassins can be seen in the bushes, and that Kennedy and Connally can be seen reacting to various shots just because their bodies move suddenly are good examples of this.

"Frankly, whenever I'm confronted with a Groden statement, I check it out myself to see if the films, which do not lie, bear him out. They usually don't. I am unable to check out the Bronson film, because Groden by agreement has to keep it under wraps—he doesn't seem to cooperate with other researchers. I have been studying the films for more than fifteen years and I do consider myself more expert on them than Groden."[13]

So do a lot of other film experts.

Groden sued over the use of a few still frames from the Zapruder film which he claims were enhanced by him and have a unique value as such, for which he wanted thousands of dollars. Yet he says "I said the way of noticing a specific degree of enhancements is far more readily apparent when you have it in motion. A specific individual frame becomes very, very difficult to determine what the overall enhancement is." He was asked to look at one of the frames in my book which he claims he enhanced: "Can you recognize your enhancements in the picture?" "This particular frame does not have a specific enhancement unique to that frame, except for the contrast control. . . . The cropping and positioning and degree of enlargement, things of that nature."

He admitted that my statement in the book was correct that the picture had been altered. "Do you claim that you can recognize your original work in the (autopsy) photograph opposite page 321?" "The photograph opposite page 321 is an unauthorized photocopy from the *Globe,* which is the only place I ever published this particular photograph, and unfortunately, the *Globe* took the liberty of altering the color from my original copy." Altered not once but *twice,* and he sued for defamation for saying this as well: "The original copy that I made of this photograph enhanced the color that was there to its natural color state. The cropping of the picture made it more coherent as well, it eliminated extraneous materials. The *Globe* cropped my work to fit their format and changed the coloration of the blood and the hair."

"Do you recognize or can see your original work in here, 'here' being the picture opposite page 321." "The only thing that I can see that is still remaining in this from the copy that I originally made as opposed to the original source material is that the skin tone, even with the coloration of the hair or the color change of the hair by the *Globe,* is still more natural the way I made it than it was in the original."

"And so the skin tone that you see at the very top of this picture and at the right side you are showing there is, you say, more natural and reflects your enhancement?"

"Yes, over the original source material."

"Why is it that you are not claiming a violation of your copyright in that enhancement work with respect to this particular photograph?" Groden answers that "I'm not clear that there is."

With respect to the back of the head autopsy picture printed opposite page 320 of *High Treason 2,* he admits to having changed the original with that one, also: "Outside of eliminating a D Max blue tint and D-Min magenta—yellow tint to the original, this is so heavily cropped, this photograph opposite page 320 was one which Mr. Livingstone made as a video print.''

Groden did not want to admit that he had an agreement with Gamma Liaison for the raw sales of the pictures, and that one of them ended up in a comic strip in *Details* magazine.

He is asked if he knows Mark Crouch, with whom he has a secret agreement to market the pictures. "Has Crouch ever made any statements, to your knowledge, that question your integrity or are harmful to your reputation?" "There was a—his lawyer released a statement to newspapers about a year and a half or two years ago—which—there was some use of his pictures by a third party. I can't remember what the particulars were, but it was resolved, and I can't remember what the issue was. I can find it for you.'' This is another example of Groden's memory loss. Groden sold some of Crouch's pictures to the *Globe,* saying that they belonged to him, and Crouch went public with a demand to set the record straight and to be paid. The *Globe* corrected the oversight in its edition of January 14, 1992 and wrote that Crouch owned some of the pictures.

The ever-ready opportunist, Groden jumped on the Roscoe White story put out by the Dallas JFK Information Center, smelling opportunity. " 'Mr. White now is trying to reconstruct the diary passages from memory,' said Robert Groden. 'Seven other people have come forward since the news conference saying they saw and read parts of the diary without the knowledge of Ricky White or his mother,' said Mr. Groden. But experts disagree about the authenticity of three vaguely worded cables—the only physical evidence in the case—that Rickie White said ordered his father to kill the president.''[14] (See the appendix for a statement by Roscoe White's family with regard to the hoax in this whole matter, and their feelings about it.)

Groden got the community of assassination researchers to refer to his stolen autopsy pictures with the code name of the "The Family Jewels.'' Nobody wanted to say what they were. Nobody ever thought to ask if he might have "enhanced them" himself.

What was the education of "Dr. Groden,'' as the congressmen used to call him in public hearings of the House Committee when he was employed by the government, thus misrepresenting him to the public. How did they get that idea? He enlisted in the Army in June 1964. "And how many years had you attended Forest Hills High School?" "Three.'' "Had you just completed your junior year when you enlisted?" "Yes. Well, wait a minute, strike that. I have to think about that. I'm not really sure. I don't remember.''

"Do you remember what your graduating class would have been at the time you entered Forest Hills High School, if you had gone straight through for the four years?" "I believe 1965." "Was Forest Hills High School a three-year or a four-year school?"

"At the time. At the time it was a three-year school."

"And you were there for three years?"

"I was in my third year."

"How long were you in the Army?" Groden got out of the Army after one year in 1965 and began working in record stores and very shortly began acquiring the knowledge needed to manipulate and enhance photographic images and, as he said, create them on film. He never attended a college after leaving the Army.

The following was written by Mark Crouch, which he wished to publish in this book. It's called "What's the Real Story . . . Robert?"

There's an old joke among the veterans of the assassination research community that goes, "So this critic died and when he went to heaven God offered to answer one question. The critic asked, 'Who shot JFK?' and God replied, 'I have a theory about that.' "

I have recently come to the realization that should I be that critic I might instead ask, "What's the story with Robert Groden?"

On March 30, 1981, James K. Fox, a retired Secret Service employee, showed me nine black-and-white autopsy photographs of John F. Kennedy. Later that year Fox allowed me to make copies of his pictures. In 1982 I shared a set with David Lifton. Fox retired to Florida in 1982 and died in 1987.

Jim Fox and I had a gentlemens [sic] agreement. If, upon his death, the photographs had not entered the public realm, then I was free to proceed with releasing them as I saw fit.

In 1988 Lifton informed me of the pending rerelease of *Best Evidence* and the publisher's willingness to print the autopsy photographs. Since I had shared a set of photos with Lifton there was really nothing I could do to stop their publication. I did, however, according to Lifton, have to be willing to vouch for the "pedigree" of this evidence. At first I was reluctant to allow my identity as the bridge between Fox and Lifton to be revealed. During several lengthy and exhausting phone conversations with Lifton I finally consented.

The logic in Lifton's argument was simple. If the Fox autopsy photographs were to be used to challenge the "official version" of what happened in Dallas on November 22, 1962 [sic], then there must be a clear chain of possession. Jim Fox had access to the pictures (HSCA Volume 7, page 23) and Jim Fox shared them with Mark Crouch. (See "Witness List.")

Since 1988, the black-and-white autopsy photographs have found their way into numerous publications and productions. Despite the seemingly great variations in quality among these reproductions, *all of the black-and-white photographs published to date originated with the Fox set.*

I make this statement not for the purpose of cementing for me a small footnote in the annals of this case, but rather to confront a growing counterattack being launched by those wishing to discredit the expanding list of witnesses whose recollections are severally at odds with these official photographs.

The basis of the argument that the Fox photographs have a suspect origin within the critics' community has grown out of a continuing confusion drawn from statements made by a man who should be equally concerned with "photographic pedigrees." I refer to Robert Groden.

In early 1989 an employee of my radio station, WCHE-AM West Chester, Pa., rushed into my office with word that "there's some guy on WWDB (a Philadelphia talk station) who's just put out a book with autopsy photographs." The man was Robert Groden.

I hastily obtained a hardcover of *High Treason* and observed that all but one of the photographs were clearly identical to the Fox set. I phoned Lifton, who confessed that he had given Groden permission to "copy" the Fox pictures directly from *Best Evidence.*

During the ensuing weeks I learned that Groden was the keeper of the infamous color autopsy photographs. It was these color photographs which had created a great controversy in 1979 when it became known that they had been "leaked," presumably in the course of the House Select Committee investigation.

After reading *High Treason* I realized that there was no attribution for the Fox photographs nor for the curious right superior profile picture which was not in the Fox set. I soon learned that this was a black-and-white reproduction of a Groden color picture. My preliminary observations of this photograph indicated that there were several striking contradictions with the closest comparable Fox photograph.

The need for maintaining the "pedigree" of the Fox pictures suddenly became apparent. If the Fox photographs, which by all indications were leaked within a few weeks of the assassination, differed noticeably from the Groden color pictures which were obviously leaked years later, then a clear *prima facie* case of photo alteration existed. I was anxious to meet with Groden and compare photographs but instead I found myself caught up in a heated argument between Lifton, Groden and Harrison Livingstone.

Lifton and Livingstone exchanged stinging letters and phone calls over certain points in *High Treason,* chiefly the photo credit for the Fox pictures. During this almost year-long battle I attempted to maintain a cordial relationship with Groden.

Groden had told me that he had no argument with the photo credit and that the issue was really a major personality conflict between Lifton and Livingstone.

The issue remained unresolved until the November 1990 Berkley paperback release of *High Treason.* The argument over photocredit [sic] had escalated to the point that Groden was forced to come to my office in September of 1990 and ask for a signed release on the pictures in order to allow the paperback project to proceed. All autopsy photographs are attributed to me, from Fox, via Lifton on page 484 of the Berkley edition.

Prior to January of 1991, I had only brief communications with Livingstone. His comments, as relayed to me by Lifton and Groden, characterized him as nothing short of a raving lunatic. Still, I was mystified why a man, who had authored and published several books, among them the very notable *High Treason,* would be so obstinate over such a minor point as a photo credit. The reason for Livingstone's behavior didn't become apparent until later in 1991 when we began comparing notes on the autopsy photographs.

Groden had allowed me to examine his photographs at his home in Boothwyn, Pa., in July of 1990. The three-hour study is preserved on audiotape. During the session I describe in great detail each of the five color autopsy photographs. There was the right superior profile published in *High Treason,* along with two slightly differing close-up views of the back of the head. There was also a left lateral profile and a top-of-the-head view taken from the head of the autopsy table.

In January of 1991 I found myself in direct debate with Livingstone over the origin of the photographs. Over the course of the next several months I realized the reason for Livingstone's hard line on the photo credit was due to his belief that "most" of the autopsy photographs in *High Treason* had come from Groden.

Livingstone repeated in detail the events on the night he met Groden near Baltimore and proceeded to the printer's factory in Pennsylvania. He was and still is unrelenting in his assertion that Groden brought with him "color" autopsy photographs to be printed, but apparently substituted Fox pictures at some later point.

I was finally able to convince Livingstone that all of the photographs in *High Treason* except for the right superior profile, had come from the Fox set but not before an interesting contradiction arose.

During my debates with Livingstone he asserted that the Fox right inferior profile, the so-called Stare-of-Death picture, was definitely in Groden's collection. He wasn't certain if the color version had been used in the book, but he was adamant that Groden possessed one. I countered with a detailed inventory of the 5 photographs, which Groden claimed was his entire collection.

What followed was an avalanche of supporting documentation from Livingstone. It included:

1. Statements by Groden concerning a 1979 meeting with Dr. Malcolm Perry and Perry's shock at the size of the tracheostomy. (The wound is only partially visible in two of Groden's five pictures.)

2. Drafts of a 1981 manuscript of *High Treason* where Livingstone vividly describes the "eyes open and askew." No such observation could be made from the photo's [sic] Groden showed me.

3. Copies of 1979 newspaper articles authored by Livingstone which contain observations consistent with viewing a right inferior pose.

In an attempt to resolve the issue I went to the only person I knew who'd viewed the Groden collection in 1979, David Lifton.

In *Best Evidence,* Lifton had briefly described seeing "poor quality black-and-white" autopsy photographs. I phoned Lifton, who'd previously confessed to me that the 1979 pictures he'd seen were Groden's. I asked him if he could recall for certain if he'd seen a Stare-of-Death shot in Groden's collection. Lifton waffled and would only say that he stood by whatever was in *Best Evidence* because it would have come directly from his notes.

I confronted him with the fact that he was making observations which could not have been made from the 1990 Groden collection. He'd written that he could clearly see the head resting on a towel and imprinted on the towel was, "Bethesda Naval Hospital Bethesda Maryland." The imprint on the Fox photographs reads, "U.S. Naval Hospital Bethesda, Maryland." The point was not the wording but the simple fact that in Groden's uncropped "best copy" of the right superior profile the lettering is totally illegible.

I soon discovered the reason for Lifton's reluctance. He confessed that in 1983 he'd visited Groden and shown him the Fox set I'd provided. Lifton recalled that Groden was "very excited" when he saw the Stare-of-Death. So excited according to Lifton that he (Lifton) was "afraid to go to the bathroom for fear that Groden would make off with the picture." This seemed highly inconsistent behavior for a man who possessed a color version of the same picture. Regardless, I was left with only two explanations. Either Lifton and Livingstone were lieing [sic] or Groden was.

In July of 1991 a local reporter at the West Chester *Daily Local News* did a profile piece on my research and my limited involvement in Oliver Stone's *J.F.K.* The story was picked up by the Associated Press and ran in many other papers around the country. Shortly after the story ran I received a phone call from a researcher, Warren Graham of Charlotte, North Carolina.

I sent Graham a set of the Fox pictures along with my inventory which outlined the Fox and Groden pictures. Graham phoned me later to inform me that around 1988 he had personally seen a color Stare-of-Death photograph. He stated that the picture had been in the possession of a man who'd reportedly obtained it from a Charlotte doctor who's [sic] gotten it from Dr. Cyril Wecht who'd in turn received it from Robert Groden.

Groden laughingly dismissed the story and the young man who reportedly had these pictures was of dubious character and has since disappeared. While it's impossible to say where exactly the pictures Graham observed came from, I believe he did indeed see such a picture. His story was corroborated by another North Carolina researcher, Richard Sullins. If, as I believe, these men are telling the truth then there is either an undiscovered third group of autopsy photographs outside the Archives or once again Groden is not telling the truth.

Another researcher, Steve Barber, has also reported seeing a photograph in the Groden collection, in Groden's possession, which was not there during my 1990 inventory.

In late December of 1991, Groden phoned me to warn that "something big" was about to happen. I soon discovered this major event was his sale of the color autopsy photographs to the tabloid *Globe*. I was glad his pictures were finally being published, but when I saw the article my mood turned to rage. Groden had given the *Globe* three of his color pictures along with two of my black-and-whites along with a story that all had been given to him by a dieing [sic] Secret Service agent.

I threatened Groden and the *Globe* with legal action and a minor correction was printed in a subsequent issue. Then to my amazement a subsequent story appeared in a local paper (*News of Delaware County*—Jan. 8, 1992) where Groden claimed that all the autopsy photographs were "given to him by his friend Mark Crouch who got them from James Fox, a dying Secret Service agent."

Groden claimed the *Globe* story was a mistake by the reporter, while the second story was his attempt to "set the record straight." The most revealing statement made to me during this time was concerning the pictures in his inventory. When I asked him why he'd not published the right superior profile picture in color in the *Globe* he responded, "I'm saving that for my book." I responded casually, "and the other back-of-the-head shot, too?"

His response, "what other picture? . . . I only have four."

I have replayed the tapes of our July 1990 session and I find it hard to believe what was clearly five pictures then is only four pictures now.

In *High Treason 2*, Livingstone published a letter I wrote him during our debates in which I stated that this second color back-of-the-head shot was most visibly altered of any of the photographs and would have been far better at proving Groden's thesis of matte insertion. When Livingstone, still defending his former co-author asked what possible motive could explain Groden's behavior I responded by saying, "I don't know why he's playing a shell game with the pictures."

From our first meeting in 1989 until the present I have consistently urged Groden to not only properly attribute the Fox photographs but also his own. As of this date, in every case I know of, he has either offered no attribution, attributed all the photo's [sic] to himself or all the photo's [sic] to me. The result has been the creation of a fertile field for those who wish to challenge the chain of possession of this vital evidence.

I have spent the last three years trying to get Robert Groden to acknowledge his pictures. In 1990 I requested an FBI acquaintance to assess any criminal liability and was told there was none. This I passed on to Groden but it did not alter his position. I have pleaded and demanded on numerous occasions that even if he does not wish to explain how he obtained his pictures he owes it to me and more importantly to future historians to at least set the record straight. I wish only for him to say publicly, "I am responsible for the color autopsy photographs being brought forth . . . and I choose not to say from where I obtained them." Is this asking too much?

It is said that to determine the motivation behind consistently repeated illogical behavior one need only look as far as the consistent result of such behavior. It would certainly appear that Groden does not wish there to be a clear distinction between the origin of the Fox photographs and his own. In so doing he places in the public record consistently inconsistent explanations and thusly taints the pedigree of all autopsy pictures. The only possible result of this behavior is the weakening of the arguments which are drawn from the autopsy photographs. The powerful contrasts offered by people like Paul O'Connor, Gerald [sic] Custer, Floyd Reibe, Dr. Charles Crenshaw, Dr. Robert McClelland and others are weakened when the credibility of the autopsy photographs is brought into question.

Groden's actions are the fodder for counter-critics like Dr. John Lattimer who recently wrote researcher Steve Barber, "All the alleged autopsy photos I have seen are fakes or later models. Don't trust the authors out of your sight."

The end result is that arguments such as the photo/X-ray conflict which are black-and-white, are suddenly cast into a shade of grey. Defenders of the status quo (Warren Report) can counter-attack the autopsy personnel and the Dallas doctors by attacking the pedigree of the pictures instead of personal attacks on the witnesse's [sic] credibility.

Could Groden actually be too naive to realize the consequences of his actions? Could there possibly be some motive, greater than preserving the integrity of this evidence? Could Groden be deliberately trying to dilute the strongest arguments in the case ... the ones which really underscore "official corruption of the evidence"? There's only one question that remains. What's the real story ... Robert?

1/25/93

MEMORANDUM: Visit to Robert Groden's Home:
385 Florida Grove Rd.
Hopelawn, NJ 08861

In early August 1980, I visited the home of researcher Robert J. Groden in Hopelawn, New Jersey. I traveled there on behalf of two other researchers who had invited me along, hopefully to get a glimpse of the mountain of photographic evidence Groden had pertaining to the assassination of JFK, since he was the photographic consultant to the HSCA.

During my visit, *nothing*—out of the many films that Groden had—made an impression more than the extremely clear and unbelievably sharp print of the Zapruder film he owned. It was, in fact, so near to—if not THE—original copy. He remarked that the film has "mold stains" on it—from sitting around all those years.

After viewing it several times, I couldn't help but think just how clear a case could be made against the lone gunman theory even more vividly with this print of the film. I wondered why this man didn't use this print during his lectures and TV appearances. His 16mm, rotoscoped, enhanced, slow-motion copy (sold through Penn Jones in the late 70s) didn't compare to the high quality of the print I was now seeing. Even the 35mm slides he (Groden) was selling didn't have this sharpness & clarity.

So, I ask this question: What is the reason behind his presenting visual evidence using multigeneration prints of the Zapruder film—when he could just as easily for all of our benefit use an extremely close to the original print of the film to present the case for conspiracy? Unfortunately, I don't have the answer. I didn't ask him.

To make a long story short ... Later in the day—to top it off—Mr. Groden asked all of us what we thought about the autopsy photographs, meaning, did we think they were authentic. As I recall, I really hadn't formed an opinion to this question—even when the HSCA said they were examining them, there were rumors that the original photos weren't authentic. My answer, however, would turn out to be something to my advantage. He walked over to a shelf full of reels of film in metal canisters and pulled out a manila envelope—large size. He opened it and pulled out the contents. It was photographs—5×10 glossy black-and-white photographs of JFK in the autopsy room. I was astonished to say the very least!

There were at least five of these photos. One in particular stood out in my mind. It was a right profile of the upper torso and head of the President. This photo showed a very large wound above the ear that extended into the middle of the head. A large flap of skull was hanging down by the ear, with brain tissue protruding. His eyes were open, his upper teeth were showing and touching his lower lip.

I have never been able to forget that photograph nor the other four in the envelope. For one thing, it was the first time I had ever seen a dead person. Here I was seeing the 35th President of the United States just prior to his autopsy. I couldn't believe my eyes.

Later that day, we discussed numerous aspects about the assassination, all based around the films & photographs taken that day. Much to our surprise, Mr. Groden did say something that, to this day, has disturbed me. He said that when he was given access to all the original films & photos taken, that he made copies of them. But, instead of keeping the copies of the films, he kept the originals. This means that the films in the HSCA files are not the original prints but rather copies—all because he kept the originals.

First of all, I couldn't understand why Mr. Groden was telling us this. We were strangers in his home. He didn't know us from Adam. Apparently, he's proud of this performance. Years later, I would learn that he told the same story to a researcher from the East Coast. Whatever his reason was—we are not going to see the original films taken November 22, 1963, if and when the HSCA files are opened.

And for whatever reason, why he hasn't made available copies of that clear print of the Z film—or used it to present the case for conspiracy—is equally baffling. The print was so clear & crisp that you could see President Kennedy's squinting eyes just after his hands and arms fly up in front of his mouth—without straining to see—in frames 235–236–237. It was unbelievable. You could actually see how powerful that shot to the back must have been. He certainly did not use this copy of the Z film to make his 16mm print available through Penn Jones—nor does he use it or anything close to it—in his videocassette, available again through *The Continuing Inquiry* in 1980's WNEC New England College Production "The Assassination of President John F. Kennedy" and "The Case for Conspiracy."

He also had an extremely clear print of one of the four photos taken by eyewitness Jim Towner. One photo in particular showed people rushing up the Grassy Knoll—and in the foreground of the photo was the pergola and retaining wall. Groden handed me a magnifying glass and told me to look on the retaining wall, and that I'd see a partially drank bottle of soda pop sitting there. In fact, there it was plain as day. It was in the spot where black-dog man would be standing.

This day in August 1980 turned out to be more than I bargained for. A lot more.

(Signed) Stephen N. Barber, January 25, 1993.
1-25-93

Groden's Color Autopsy Pictures

Here follows the story of how Groden obtained his color autopsy photographs as Groden told it in sworn testimony to Kevin Brennan.

Q. What response did you receive to your request?
A. I was allowed to see them.
Q. Where was it that you saw them for the first time?
A. The very first time was in the offices of the House Select Committee on Assassinations.
Q. Was anyone else present?
A. Yes.

Q. Who?

A. Let's see.

There were several people. I can't remember exactly who.

I remember one was Ed Lopez.

Q. Who was Mr. Lopez?

A. He was a researcher and investigator for the House Committee.

Q. Do you remember anyone else who was present?

A. Not by name.

Q. In what form were the pictures when you saw them for the first time?

A. Black and white and color photographs in an album.

Q. How long did this viewing take place?

A. I could only guess.

Probably an hour.

Q. During that hour, were the pictures removed from the album, any pictures?

A. No, never.

Q. How were the pictures secured in the album?

A. They were placed within plastic protective sheets.

Q. Were the pictures catalogued or numbered in any way?

A. I don't know.

Q. Was it one album or more?

A. As I recall, it was one album.

Q. Did the album cover bear a title?

A. I don't recall.

Q. Were the pictures of uniform size?

A. As I recall, they were all approximately 8×10 or 8½×11, somewhere in that area.

Q. Do you know exactly how many pictures there were?

A. No.

Q. Do you know approximately how many pictures there were?

A. No. Several dozen, I would say.

Q. Was it communicated to you at or before the time you first saw them whether this album contained all of the pictures of the autopsy?

A. It was not.

It was implied that this is what they had, and it was also implied that this is what there was.

But nobody specifically said this is all that exists.

Q. Presently, do you have any reason to believe that there were other autopsy pictures that you did not see at that time, this first viewing?

A. Yes.

Q. What is the basis for that belief?

A. I found more of them in the National Archives.

Q. *When was that?*

A. That was when I had requested to view the original materials.

Q. *What do you mean?*

Can you explain your request to "view original materials"?

A. Yes. The photographs I was shown in the album were duplicates, some of them not very good quality.

From what I saw, and my knowledge of the statements of the Dallas doctors who had seen the body, there was a conflict, a severe conflict between what the photographs showed and what the doctors had said.

I requested to view the originals to see if there was anything that would indicate a degree of forgery.

Q. *When was that in relation to this first viewing in the beginning of 1988; when was it that you viewed pictures at the National Archives?*

A. I don't remember the specific date.

Q. *Was it within a month?*

Was it within a year?

A. Oh, it's well within a year.

Q. *How about within six months?*

A. I would say well within six months.

Q. *So, it was during the calendar year 1977?*

A. I would believe so.

Q. *From the time you first saw the album with Ed Lopez and, perhaps, others, until the time you saw the pictures at the National Archives for the first time, anyway, did you see autopsy pictures at all in between?*

A. I don't recall whether I did.

I may have. I would like to correct a statement which you just said, which was not correct. You said when I viewed the pictures with Ed Lopez. Ed Lopez was not viewing the pictures with me.

He was in the room.

Q. *That's what I mean, with Ed Lopez being present.*

When you viewed the pictures from the National Archives, where did you actually do that, look at them?

A. In the National Archives.

Q. *In a particular office or room?*

A. In an inner room, a sealed room.

Q. *Do you know if that room has a name, or was it assigned to a particular person, do you know?*

A. I don't know.

Q. *Who else was present with you then?*

A. As I recall, there were two members of the—with the originals, there were two, as I recall, two employees of the National Archives.

Q. Do you know their names?

A. No.

Q. Did you have to register the fact of your viewing, or record the fact of your viewing in a log or some other type of book or record?

A. As I recall, I had to sign in, but I don't know if there was any specific record.

Q. In what form or containers were the pictures that you viewed in the Archives?

A. The color originals are 4×5 transparencies.

And, as I recall, each of them was in a plastic sleeve, individually. The black and white originals are 4×5 negatives, and I believe they were also in transparent sleeves.

Q. Did you use any type of a device to view the pictures with at the Archives?

A. As I recall, an optical loop.

Q. What is that?

A. It's a magnifier.

Q. Going back to your first viewing at the House Committee offices when Ed Lopez was in the room, did you make any notes about your viewing?

A. I made notes.

Q. Can you describe the notes you made?

A. Let me correct that.

I believe I made notes at that first viewing. I may not have.

Q. What causes you to change your answer and doubt whether you made notes?

A. I made notes in the National Archives. I am aware of that.

But, I'm not sure that I actually made notes the first time.

Q. Why are you confident that you made notes in the National Archives?

A. Because I remember specifically they would not allow me to make diagrams or drawings or tracings of the pictures. I could only make notations.

Q. Do you still have the notes?

A. I probably do, yes.

Q. On what did you make the notes? On loose paper, in a book?

A. As I recall, loose sheets of white paper.

Q. Were you able to compare at this viewing at the National Archives your impressions of what was available with what you had seen before?

A. I don't understand what you mean by "compare."

Q. Had you been to the National Archives this one time only to view autopsy pictures, or had you been there more than once?

A. More than once.

Q. How many times had you been there all together?

A. From memory, I would say twice.

Q. When you say "from memory," is there some other way you could determine from your records or materials that you have access to, how many times you have been there?

A. No.

Q. The second time that you went, when was that in relation to the first time?

A. That was, as I recall, after the House Assassinations Committee had broken up. That was part of a photographic panel with the Baltimore—I mean the Boston Globe.

Q. What year was that?

A. I don't recall exactly. Probably around 1979 or 1980.

Q. How did the panel from the Globe get access to the National Archives?

A. They were granted access by Burke Marshall, the lawyer for the Kennedy family.

Q. In your first visit to the National Archives, did you note, did you record how many different views there were?

What do you call each different negative or transparency?

Is there a term of art to describe it? Is it a shot? Is it a picture? What would you call it?

A. It was a specific shot. It would be an individual shot.

Q. How many shots did you see during your first viewing at the National Archives?

A. I don't recall.

Q. Is there anything that you have here, or anywhere else, or have access to, that would help you recall?

A. No. I did not take notes as to the number of pictures.

Q. When for the first time did you become aware that there were more shots in the National Archives than there had been in the files of the House Committee in that album?

A. When I was reviewing the materials, I came across a roll of 120 Ektachrome film, and this roll had very dark images on it, but there were images of the President.

As I recall, between three and five. Some of them were so dark, you couldn't really tell whether or not there was an image there.

Q. You said there were three to five shots of the President. Three to five shots of the President or total from this roll?

A. The same thing. Three or five shots, all of the President.

Q. Other than those three to five shots of the President that you described, were there any other shots that you noticed during this visit to the Archives that you had not noticed in the album?

A. No.

Q. Up until the present time, are you aware of any other shots that exist of the autopsy of President Kennedy, taken during the autopsy, other than those that you have already—that you had seen either in viewing the album in the beginning of 1977 at the House Committee offices, or during your first National Archives visit?

A. First-hand knowledge?

Q. No, any knowledge at all, first-hand or second-hand.

A. First-hand knowledge, no, I have not seen any others.

I have received two phone calls through the years of people telling me there were additional materials that I have not seen, but I have no way to verify that.

Q. Your complaint mentions autopsy photos; am I right?

A. That's correct.

Q. The first point in your complaint that discusses an autopsy photo is the second cause of action, specifically Paragraph 17; is that right?

A. It appears to be, yes.

Q. The second cause of action concerns the use in High Treason 2 of one particular autopsy photo which you, in the complaint, describe as the "Groden superior right profile"; is that correct?

A. That is not the way I describe it. That is the way it's described in the book by Mr. Livingstone.

Q. When for the first time did you see the shot which is described in the second cause of action of your complaint?

A. When did I first see it?

Q. Yes.

A. On that first viewing in the House Assassinations Committee.

Q. Do you know who took that shot?

A. No.

Q. Do you know the status of the person who took that shot?

A. Since I don't know who took the picture, I don't know what his status is.

Q. Do you know who took any of the autopsy shots?

A. The ones that I saw?

Q. Yes.

A. Specifically, no.

I was going to say there were three separate people credited with taking the pictures, and I have no idea who took which ones, which one—

Q. Do you know the identities of those three people?

A. Yes.

Q. Who are they or were they, if they are not alive?

A. One is Floyd Reibe, one was a fellow by the name of Stringer, and the third man's name escapes me for the moment, but I do know his name. I just can't think of it right now.

Q. Do you know whether they were government employees or the employees of some other organization at the time they took the pictures?

A. I believe they were Naval Corpsmen, or at least I believe they were Naval personnel.

Q. Can you describe for me your copyright interest in the photograph described in the second cause of action of your complaint?

A. That particular photograph?

Q. Yes.

A. I created the photograph. I took the photograph.

Let me clarify that. When I say "took" it, I did not physically take a photograph.

I made the photograph. Using photographic materials, I made that photograph.

Q. Do you mean that you copied that shot?

A. Yes, I duplicated that shot.

Q. Other than duplicating it or copying it, have you changed it in any way from the way it was, from the object that you copied?

A. The original photograph was a color photograph. I made this in black and white, adjusted the contrast, cropped it, and I would say that's probably it.

Q. When did you copy it in black and white, crop it and adjust the contrast? When did you do those things?

A. I have no recollection of the exact time or even close to when.

Q. Can you tell me the decade you did it in, 60's, 70's? It couldn't be 60's, right. So, was it 70's, 80's or 90's?

A. 70's or 80's, I would say.

Q. Where did you do those things?

A. The black and white?

Q. Where did you copy it in black and white, crop it and adjust the contrast?

A. I don't have the recollection of the time or even the location where I did the black and white version that is in that book.

It should be mentioned, I think, that the black and white copy was from my own color copy.

Q. In other words, you made a black and white copy from a color copy that you had?

A. That is correct.

Q. Was the shot originally taken with color film?

A. Yes, it was.

Q. When did you obtain your color copy?

A. Sometime around 1978.

MR. MENDOLA: Is "obtain" the word you want to use?

MR. LIVINGSTONE: Excuse me?

MR. BRENNAN: Don't worry. He can talk to his client all he wants.

MR. MENDOLA: Is "obtain" the word you want to use here?

A. Would you define "obtain"?

Q. Are you familiar with the word "obtain"?

A. Obtain is to receive.

Q. When did you receive your color copy?

A. I did not receive the color copy. If you are suggesting someone gave it to me or that I obtained a print from some other source, I did not.

Q. Was there a point in time when you held in your hand a color copy of the photograph, of the shot described in your second cause of action?

A. Yes.

Q. The first time you held that color copy in your hand, where were you?

A. The first time?

I have no recollection.

Q. When was it?

A. I don't know. The first time, I don't know.

Q. How did you obtain it?

A. I was allowed to hold it and photograph it by the House Assassinations Committee.

Q. Who allowed you to do that?

A. I don't know exactly who had the final say to allow me to do it.

Q. Who communicated to you that you were allowed to do that?

A. I would only have to guess. Possibly, Mickey Goldsmith.

Q. Why do you have to guess?

A. Because I don't remember specifically who it was who gave me permission to duplicate those.

Q. Did you, yourself, make a duplication from a photograph in the custody of the House Committee?

A. That is correct.

Q. When you are referring to obtaining permission from Mickey

Goldsmith or someone else to do that, that's permission to make the copy?

A. That is correct.

Q. Did you obtain permission to make a copy of more than one shot?

A. Yes.

Q. Did you obtain permission to make copies of all the shots in the possession of the House Committee?

A. No.

Q. Which other shots did you obtain permission to make copies of?

A. Two photographs of the rear of the head, one photograph of the top of the head, one photograph of the left side of the head, and one photograph of the right side of the head.

Q. Is the one of the right side of the head the one that is mentioned in the second cause of action of your complaint?

A. That's correct.

Q. So, that's a total of five?

A. As I recall, that was the only five.

Q. Is Mickey Goldsmith a man or a woman?

A. A man.

Q. Did you seek permission from Mr. Goldsmith or someone else to make those copies?

A. Yes.

Q. For what purpose did you seek that permission?

A. To prove the hypothesis that the autopsy photographs were forgeries.

Q. Did you seek that permission in writing?

A. I don't recall.

Q. Do you have any documents, and I use that, whenever I use it, in the broadest sense, about your seeking or obtaining permission to copy shots of the autopsy?

A. I don't believe so.

MR. BRENNAN: Please read back the question as to why he sought permission, and the answer.

(Last question and answer were read by the reporter.)

A. I could modify that answer to state—okay.

Q. Just for the record, your attorney held his hand up and you stopped answering the question.

MR. MENDOLA: Only because there was no question pending at the time.

Q. If you want to modify an answer at any time, as I think I said before, feel free.

I want an accurate and complete answer. So, go ahead and do that.

A. The point I was going to make was the hypothesis was that specific autopsy photographs were faked. Not all of them.

Q. Was your effort to prove your hypothesis that specific autopsy photographs were faked, intended to be carried out as part of the business of the Committee?

A. This is correct.

Q. Was your copying of the photographs, the five copies that you made, for the purpose of carrying out the business of the Committee?

A. That is correct.

Q. Were you paid government funds for your work in doing so?

A. I don't believe I was.

That was voluntary.

Q. Did you make the copies in the course of your employment for the House Committee?

A. Would you define "during the course of."

Do you mean during the time frame, or do you mean was I—

Q. Let's go back, then.

Can you describe for me your relationship with the House Committee?

A. I was staff photographic consultant to the Committee.

Q. Did a particular person retain you as staff photographic consultant?

A. I don't know it's possible for me to even answer that question.

Q. How did you learn that you were retained as a staff photographic consultant to the Committee?

A. I was requested to do so.

Q. By whom?

A. Initially, as I recall, Congressman Thomas Downing and Richard Sprague, and then G. Robert Blakey.

Q. Which Richard Sprague?

A. The Richard Sprague who worked for the House Assassinations Committee as chief counsel.

Q. Did you ever receive any written notice that you were retained as a staff photographic consultant to the Committee?

A. Specific written notice?

Q. Right.

A. I don't recall. I honestly don't recall.

Q. Did you talk with anyone from the Committee about how you were to be paid for your services as a staff photographic consultant?

A. Somewhere early on, it was established that I would be paid per diem for the days I did work, when these days were requested by the House Committee.

Q. Were you paid per diem for work that you performed for the Committee?

A. Sometimes. Not always.

Q. Under what circumstances were you paid, and under what circumstances were you not paid for your work?

A. If the House Committee specifically requested me to do something for them, such as testifying before the Committee, or as a witness, or performing photographic services, certain photographic services, then I was paid.

If there were specific areas of investigation that I initiated, then I usually was not paid.

Also, when the Committee ran out of money, I volunteered very many days of my own to work with them and for them.

Also, before they formally existed and had a budget, I also volunteered my time.

MR. BRENNAN: If we can, let's just take three or five minutes.

(At this time, a brief recess was taken.)

BY MR. BRENNAN:

Q. Can you help me pinpoint during what time period you worked for the Committee, including any voluntary work?

As best you know, when did you start working and when did you finish your work?

A. Again, that is very hard to define, because I worked for the Committee before there formally was actually a committee.

Q. I am asking you to include that time with the Committee, when did you first start working for them?

A. I was working with Congressman Henry Gonzales as early as May of 1975. I worked all the way to 1977—1976, 1977, 1978, and I believe my last contact with the Committee was May, June or July of 1979.

Q. Did the Committee ever issue a report?

A. Yes.

Q. When did the Committee issue its report?

A. Sometime mid or late 1979.

Q. What was Mickey Goldsmith's position with the Committee?

A. He was the head of the photographic panel.

Q. Was he a full-time employee of the Committee, to your knowledge?

A. I believe he was.

Q. What was his background?

A. As I recall, he is a lawyer.

Q. Do you know where he is now?

A. No.

Q. Do you know where he came from before he worked on the Committee?

A. No.

Q. How was the Committee organized? Specifically, in addition to the photographic panel, were there other similar categories or sections of the Committee?

A. Yes. There was a photographic panel. There was an acoustics panel. There was a ballistics panel. There was a medical panel. There was an organized crime panel, and probably others, too.

Q. When you describe yourself as a staff photographic consultant, was your work entirely with the photographic panel?

A. No. I worked with a photographic panel for the most part, but I also worked with the acoustics panel, and with the medical panel.

Q. Was it the photographic panel that controlled access to the autopsy photos?

A. As far as I know.

I do know that the medical panel did have access, as well.

Q. When you obtained permission to make copies of the five autopsy photos, did you do that through the photographic panel or the medical panel, or some other way?

A. Through the photographic panel.

Q. In addition to Mickey Goldsmith, who you describe as the head of the photographic panel, who else held positions of authority with the photographic panel?

A. This is very difficult to say. Starting with the chief counsel, Professor Blakey, and then there was Mr. Goldsmith's assistant, Jane Downey.

Q. Anyone else?

A. I'm sure there were.

Then the photo panel itself was made up of photographic experts. They might have had a chairman. I'm not really sure.

Q. Did the photographic panel itself issue a report?

A. The main report itself had specific issues as to the photographic panel, their results, their conclusions. Whether or not you could categorize that as a separate report, I wouldn't think so, but it's possible.

Q. Did the report discuss the hypothesis that you referred to earlier that certain autopsy photographs were faked?

A. As far as I know, they never seriously considered the charge.

Q. Who originally formulated that hypothesis?

A. I did.

Q. What did you do to test that hypothesis or develop that hypothesis between May of 1975 and June of '79?

A. During that period of time, there were several things I tried to do.

The testing I did for the House Committee on the autopsy photographs to show contrast build-up in the photographs of the rear of the head.

The stereoscopic views that I created showing the incongruity of the rear of the President's head in the photographs.

The constant requests to Professor Blakey and other members of the Committee to get the autopsy—not the autopsy—the Dallas doctors, the Parkland Hospital doctors and the photographs together in one place to verify or challenge the authenticity of the photographs.

Those requests were never heeded, and I suggested them, I requested them countless times through my involvement with the Committee, and they just refused to do it, which, of course, piqued my curiosity.

Q. Did you do anything else to test the hypothesis?

A. There was a time when we brought copies of the autopsy photographs and diagrams to Dr. Malcolm Perry in New York City, myself and two reporters or two employees, one reporter, and I think a photographer and editor for the Baltimore Sun, and we showed the items to him.

A. My initial report to the House Assassinations Committee upon my first viewing of the autopsy photographs was to point out the inconsistencies between the photographs and the reports the Dallas doctor made on the day of the assassination, and very soon thereafter.

I noticed a contrast build-up, what appeared to be a contrast build-up around an area in the rear of the President's head, and I wrote a report for the Committee about that, and requested at that time to view the original autopsy materials to see if that build-up was as apparent in the original as it was in the duplicates.

That was my reason for the request, to see the originals in the first place.

Q. So that report came before you saw the originals at the National Archives in the first place?

A. That's correct.

Q. Okay.

A. Upon examining the original photographs, I found that the originals did not display the degree of contrast build-up that the duplicates did, and my hypothesis was, having been in the photographic field for some time, that as with any mat insert situation, contrast picks up upon multiple generations.

The idea was to run additional generations off of the duplicates to see if they did, indeed, pick up additional contrast, which they did do.

Q. Is that the extent of testing that you did to show the contrast build-up?

A. Along that line, yes.

We did use high-contrast film. We did different generations.

Q. What testing did you do with stereoscopic views to show the incongruity in the rear of the head?

A. We made reduced-size images, color images of two separate photographs of the rear of the President's head. Much in the way you would end up with a View-Master type of situation, where you end up with—since the cameras were in slightly different views, it created a quasi-kaleidoscopic effect.

Q. You did that on two shots only?

A. Yes.

Q. The testing to show the contrast build-up, how many shots did you do that of?

A. That, I don't remember. We did multiple generations.

Q. Where did you do that testing that you described, physically where?

A. Two different places. We did some in the offices of the House Committee, and we did some at a photographic laboratory in Maryland.

Q. What was the name of the photographic laboratory in Maryland?

A. I don't remember.

Q. Did the laboratory in Maryland have a formal relationship or a contractual relationship with the House Committee?

A. They did work for them. I assumed there must have been some kind of a contract.

Q. Did you do work yourself at the lab in Maryland?

A. I supervised the work in Maryland.

Q. Did you go there?

A. I went there with them, yes, along with an agent of the FBI.

Q. Were you the person in charge of this testing, the part of it that was performed at the laboratory in Maryland?

A. Yes. I was the one who was supervising it and giving the instructions and the specifics, but the manual labor was done by the people who were employees of the laboratory.

Q. How about the testing that was done in the House Committee offices, were you supervising that, as well?

A. That is correct.

Q. Other than the visit to Dr. Malcolm Perry, and the requests to bring the doctors from Parkland in, are these all the things you did to test your hypothesis?

A. You made a statement that I'm not sure would be representative correctly in the record.

Q. All right.

A. The majority of the work that I did was for the House Committee. The interview with Dr. Perry, which was set up by the two members of the Baltimore Sun, was not for the House Committee.

It was a totally separate issue, and they had set it up and contacted me, and I met them in New York City on 86th Street and Second Avenue, and we drove down by taxicab to New York Hospital, where we met Dr. Perry in his office.

Q. Who was Dr. Malcolm Perry?

A. Dr. Perry was the doctor who performed the tracheotomy on President Kennedy's throat.

Q. That is at Parkland?

A. That's correct.

Q. When they were trying to save his life?

A. That is correct.

Q. Did you speak to Dr. Perry that day?

A. Yes, I did.

Q. Who else was present when you spoke with Dr. Perry?

A. I don't remember the names of the two people

I know that one of the people involved in setting this up was Jeff Price, but I don't know whether he was physically there or not.

There were only two others. They both worked for the Baltimore Sun. At the time that we met Dr. Perry, Dr. Perry gave me his business card, which I still have, and immediately after the interview we went down to a coffee shop directly across from New York Hospital, sat in the corner booth and discussed.

They were very excited, because Dr. Perry had told us that the autopsy photographs did not represent the President's wounds as he left them.

Q. When was this visit to Dr. Perry?

A. I don't have a record of the specific date.

Q. How about a month and a year, a season of the year?

A. I would say in all probability, it was winter, because it was freezing cold.

It had to be very late in 1978 or very early 1979.

Q. Did you bring any photographs or photographic material with you to this visit with Dr. Perry?

A. Yes.

Q. What did you bring?

A. I do not remember the exact specific items that I brought, but as I recall, I brought the photograph that is in question as to the—that we have been speaking about, however it's referred to, the right superior.

Q. Superior right photograph?

A. Superior right profile photograph of the back of the head, diagram; as I recall, I brought the diagram or drawing done by Dr. Robert McClelland, showing the exit wound of the President's head and, I believe I brought a Xerox of a medical illustration done by one of the House Assassinations Committee. She was their artist.

Q. So, you know of two autopsy photographs you brought with you, or more than two?

A. As I recall, those were the two I brought.

Q. Where did you get those photographs from?

A. Those specific ones?

Q. Yes.

A. I don't recall. I don't know if they were originals or duplicates. They weren't camera originals. Whether there were my originals or duplicates, I don't recall.

Q. Had you made the five copies with the permission of Mr. Goldsmith or someone else before this visit to Dr. Perry?

A. I believe so.

Q. Were the two photographs that you took with you two of the copies that had been made of the five photographs?

A. I'm not sure I understand the question.

Q. You made copies of five color autopsy shots with the permission of Mickey Goldsmith or someone else?

A. I didn't say with the permission of Mickey Goldsmith. I said I think it might have been Mickey Goldsmith.

Q. Right, I didn't finish my question.

A. I'm sorry.

Q. With the permission of Mickey Goldsmith or someone else, you made those copies of five photographs, sometime in 1978, you believe?

A. I would say that's correct.

Q. My question is: Were the two photographs that you brought with you two of the copies of those five copies that you made?

A. They were either my originals or copies of the copies.

Q. Did you tell anyone from the Committee staff before you went to see Dr. Perry that you intended to go see him?

A. No.

Q. Why not?

A. Because at that time, I no longer trusted the House Committee.

Q. Was Congressman Downing still on the Committee—

A. No, he was not.

Q. Was Congressman Gonzales still on the Committee?

A. No, he was not.

Q. Was Mickey Goldsmith still with the Committee?

A. No, he was not.

Q. Who were the Congressmen on the committee at that time?

A. It would help me if I had a list of them. There were several.

But to generalize, and answer your question, no, I did not inform anyone.

As a matter of fact, I was forbidden to personally speak to any Congressman on the Committee.

Q. Who forbade you to speak?

A. There was a gag order enforced against all or with all employees, contract employees or straight employees of the House Committee.

Q. So that no staff was to speak with any Congressmen?

A. Or other staff. We were not allowed to initiate any conversation or any dialogue with anyone else. It was basically a need-to-know basis type of situation.

Q. Who then initiated any conversation between staff of the Committee?

A. It always came from up above, heading downward. Chain-of-command type of situation.

Q. Are you saying that the gag order said you could only answer the questions from a superior or up above, and you were not allowed to initiate any questions or other communication to someone up above?

A. Out of the chain of command, yes, that's correct.

Q. In the winter of 1978 or 1979, when you went to see Dr. Perry, were you in a chain of command?

A. No. As I said, I did that on my own.

Q. I'm not asking you if you did that on your own.

I am saying, at that time, you were still involved with the House Committee; correct?

A. If it was until December of 1978, yes.

If it was after December of 1978, then no, because the Committee no longer formally existed.

Q. But didn't you tell me you continued to work for the Committee until June of 1979—

A. Yes.

Q. —after it formally existed?

A. As I said, after it formally existed, yes.

Q. When did the Committee formally disband?

A. As I recall, their formal life ended December 31, 1978.

Q. During the winter months before December 31, 1978, and including that day, were you in a chain of command?

A. Would you repeat that?

Q. During the winter of 1978, up to and including December 31, 1978, were you in a chain of command in the framework of the House Committee?

A. That's correct.

Q. Describe your chain of command.

MR. MENDOLA: Do you understand what he means by "were you in a chain of command, and describe that chain of command"?

MR. BRENNAN: It's not your turn to ask the questions yet, and I consider that an unwarranted interference.

This is a bright guy, and if he doesn't understand a question, he could say so. I am entitled to an uncoached answer to a question.

MR. MENDOLA: I merely asked if he understood the question.

MR. BRENNAN: You are not supposed to ask that?

A. I don't fully understand.

I understand what a chain of command is.

Was I in a chain of command?

Q. Yes, were you a part of a chain of command?

A. I was at the bottom end of the chain of command.

Q. Starting at the bottom of the chain you were in, in November and December of 1978, please describe the chain as it ascended upward.

A. I would say, and again from memory, pretty much, it would be from myself to Jane Downey, to Mickey Goldsmith, to, I can't remember his name—the assistant chief counsel, Gary Cornwell, and then G. Robert Blakey.

Q. In December of 1978, who was the chairman of the Committee?

A. December of 1978?

Q. Yes.

A. The chairman was Louis Stokes.

Q. Approximately how many Congressmen were on the Committee in 1978?

A. Well, this might sound sexist, Congressman Pell, Yvonne Burke was not a Congressman.

I don't really remember the exact number.

I would say it was approximately around a dozen.

Q. Can you tell me as specifically as you are able, precisely or approximately when it was you made the copies of the five shots you described?

A. I believe I have already told you I have no memory of the specific date or even exactly when, or even within a specific season.

It would have been sometime, most probably, in 1978.

Q. *How is it you are able to recall that? How is it you are able to place it in 1978?*

A. Because it was toward the end of the Committee's life.

Q. *How do you know that?*

A. I just remembered that it was basically toward the end of Committee's life. It was during that last year.

The Committee only formally existed for two years.

Q. *Did you use equipment or devices of some type to make the copies?*

A. Yes.

Q. *Can you describe the equipment or the devices that you used?*

A. A 35 millimeter camera, a copy stand.

Q. *What is "a copy stand"?*

A. A copy stand is a horizontal platform with a vertical appendage to which a small piece of metal is attached, that the camera attached to.

It has lights on either side where you can duplicate original flat art.

Q. *Did you use any other devices?*

A. Not to my knowledge.

Q. *Did you make the copies at one sitting or one event?*

A. Would you qualify that?

Q. *Yes.*

When you made the copies from the five shots with the 35 millimeter camera and the copy stand, did you do that at one time, or did you do that in a series of events?

A. It was all in one afternoon.

Q. *Where did you do that?*

A. In the office of the House Committee.

Q. *Specifically, where in the office of the House Committee?*

A. I don't remember.

Q. *Are you able to narrow it down for us at all?*

A. They had an entire floor. I don't know the exact position or spot.

Q. *Was part of the House Committee's space a photographic laboratory or work space or spaces or laboratories?*

A. Not formally, no.

Q. *What do you mean by "not formally"? Do you mean informally this was a laboratory or work space for photographic work?*

A. Not usually.

This was a specific one-time situation.

In other words, they weren't set up to do this as a standard.

Q. When you did some of the testing that you described to test your hypothesis, to test the contrast build-up and the stereoscopic views, some of that was done in the offices of the House Committee; is that correct?

A. Correct.

Q. Where was that done?

A. Well, wait a minute. Let me go back. Ask me that last question again. I'm sorry.

Q. Let me back it up some more. The testing you described before to test your hypothesis that some of the autopsy photographs were not genuine, involving the testing to show contrast build-up and the testing involving stereoscopic views, some of that testing was performed at a lab in Maryland, and some of that testing was performed on the premises used by the House Committee; correct?

A. That's correct.

Q. The part of it that was performed on the House Committee premises, specifically where was that performed?

A. That's what I said, I don't know. I don't remember specifically where that was done.

Q. Presumably, that was not done, for example, at Congressman Stokes' desk in his office, it was done in some other location that was more suitable for photographic testing?

A. Considering Congressman Stokes did not have an office in that building, yes, I would say that was accurate.

Q. All right. Touché.

Were there spaces in the offices of the House Committee where photographic work was never done?

A. I can't answer that. There were areas that were not done by me.

Q. Let's limit this to your knowledge.

To cut to the quick, what I am trying to establish, were there spaces where, you may not call them a laboratory, but these were spaces where if you had to do duplication of photographs, or blow-ups, or other types of photographic work you have described yesterday, and that some of it you described today, that they would customarily be done, this is the place where we do this or this is one the places where we would do that kind of work?

A. I would say no. I would say no.

Q. Where were the House Committee offices? What building?

A. I believe it was originally called the FBI Annex Building. It was right near an entrance to a highway in the southern part of Washington, D.C.

Q. *Did the offices ever move, or were they always there?*

A. As I recall, initially, they may have been somewhere else.

Q. *But in 1978?*

A. In '78, that's where they were.

Q. *Did you have a desk or other space that was yours?*

A. No.

Q. *The House Committee, you said, had an entire floor?*

A. As I recall, they had an entire floor, or at least one-half of the entire floor.

Q. *Were the offices during the time, say, during 1978, monitored by security personnel at all?*

A. Yes.

Q. *Was access limited to authorized personnel?*

A. Yes, it was.

Q. *Were the offices open 24 hours a day?*

A. I don't know.

Q. *Did you ever go to the offices at other than, say, 9 to 5, Monday through Friday?*

A. Oh, yes. I was there weekends. I was there in the evenings.

Q. *Whenever you were there, say, on weekends or evenings, was a security staff there controlling access?*

A. At all times.

Q. *Did you have any keys to any of the doors at that space?*

A. No.

Q. *Are you able to narrow down in any way where it was that on this one afternoon you made the copies?*

A. No.

Q. *And you are not able to tell us what season of the year it was?*

A. No.

Q. *And certainly you are not able to tell us what month it was?*

A. No.

Q. *Was anyone present with you?*

A. Yes.

Q. *Who?*

A. An agent of the FBI.

Q. *What was his or her name?*

A. I have no—it was a him, but I don't remember his name, if I ever even knew it. I probably did, but I don't remember it.

Q. *Was he regularly, do you know, assigned to the Committee staff?*

A. I can't recall that I had ever seen him before or since.

Q. How did he come to be present?

A. He just was making sure that no one walked out with the original copies.

Q. Did you take rolls of film?

A. I believe it was all on one roll.

Q. What kind of a 35 millimeter camera was it?

A. It was either a Nikon or a Minolta.

Q. Was it your personal camera?

A. Yes.

Q. Was it your personal copy stand?

A. Yes.

Q. Why do you say it was a Nikon or a Minolta?

A. Because I don't remember which one it was.

Q. But you are certain it was one of those two?

A. Those are the only two kinds I have, at least professional type cameras.

Q. After you finished shooting, what did you do with the film?

A. Specifically, I don't recall what I did with it initially.

Q. Did you leave it in the building when you left that day, or did you take it with you?

A. I believe I took it with me.

Q. Why do you believe that?

A. Because I paid for the processing.

Q. Where did you have it processed?

A. As I recall, and I could be wrong about this, but as I recall, I had it processed at a laboratory in New Jersey, in Linden, New Jersey, but it wasn't Linden Color Labs, it was an exception.

Q. How do you recall that?

A. Because I had already left at that time Linden's employ, and had no desire to have any dealings with them.

So, I had done with work with this other lab which was more professional, had done more work like that.

Q. Did someone else do the processing, or did you do it yourself?

A. Someone else did the processing. It was machine processing.

Q. Do you know the name of the person who did it?

A. No.

Q. Were you employed at the place where the processing was done?

A. No.

Q. Did you discuss with the outfit that did the processing, before they did it, what it was that they were processing?

A. I don't recall. I remember saying it was very sensitive, and I was going to stay with the film until it was processed.

Q. Did you do that?

A. Yes, I did.

Q. After the film was processed, how many copies were made at the time you had it processed?

A. I don't recall.

If I remember correctly, one of each.

Q. One of each shot?

A. Yes.

Q. What came out of the processing? Prints?

A. The processing was negatives, and then prints were made from the negatives.

Q. Were the prints made at the same time the negatives were made?

A. Yes.

Q. How many prints were made of each shot?

A. As I said, one of each.

Q. What kind of prints were they, what size?

A. 8×10.

Q. Color?

A. Color.

Q. What did you do with the negatives and the 8×10 prints?

A. I retained them.

Q. Where did you retain them initially?

A. In my home.

Q. And you were living where at the time?

A. In New Jersey, 385 Florida Grove Road.

Q. What was it that you had copied with your 35 millimeter camera?
Had you copied from a negative?
Had you copied from a print? What did you copy from?

A. From prints, from duplicate prints.

Q. And the duplicate prints that you actually copied, where did they come from, the album?

A. From one of the albums.

They had several albums.

Q. You did the copying in a particular afternoon.
When in relation to the time that you did the copying that afternoon did you obtain the duplicate prints?

A. The FBI agent brought it with him.

Q. He brought it to where?

A. To wherever the room was that we did the duplication.

Q. How did it come about that you knew to go to that room?

A. I was told where to go.

Q. By whom?

A. That, I don't remember.

Q. *In writing or orally?*

A. Orally.

Q. *Did you communicate to the FBI agent to bring it, or did someone else?*

A. Someone else did.

Q. *Did you have your 35 millimeter camera and copy stand there on the premises already from a prior occasion, or did you bring it there that day?*

A. I brought it there that day.

Q. *Did you leave it when you left that day?*

A. I brought it with me when I left. I took it with me when I left.

MR. BRENNAN: I would just like to take a short break, please.

(At this time, a brief recess was taken.)

BY MR. BRENNAN:

Q. *After you took the negatives and the prints to your home, when was the first time you did anything with them?*

A. That may be impossible to answer. I don't know. As far as reviewing them, instantly. I did not publish them. I had no intention to publish them.

Q. *Did you do any work with respect to those negatives and prints that you took home at some point?*

At some point, you told us you did.

A. Yes.

Q. *At some point, you copied them in black and white, you cropped them, and you adjusted the contrast on them; is that right?*

A. That's correct.

Q. *When did you start doing that?*

A. I don't have a specific date. I don't know.

Q. *Did you start doing that within days after you brought them home?*

A. Probably not.

Q. *Within a month?*

A. I have no memory. I don't know exactly when I started doing it.

Q. *I am not asking exactly. I am asking approximately.*

Let me ask you this:

Did you start the work on them during calendar year 1978?

A. I don't know. Probably not. I probably did not actually physically start working on them until after that, but I may have

I don't have records of specific things I did with them.

Q. *Why do you believe, at least, that you probably did not start doing anything by way of work with those negatives and prints you brought home until calendar year 1979 or later?*

A. As to the best of my recollection, I don't think I did anything physically with them, because all I had in my files for quite some time after that were the original set of prints and the negatives.

Q. *Do you have a recollection at some point of beginning work on the negatives and one set of prints?*

A. No specific recollection.

Q. *Do you have a general recollection or any recollection at all of starting to do work on those?*

A. I would say no.

I did nothing with those pictures until—as a matter of fact, as Mr. Livingstone is well aware, I had no intention of doing anything with them at all, and it was at his urging and his insistence that we publish them in High Treason 1.

MR. BRENNAN: Off the record.

(Discussion held off the record.)

Q. *You had already met Mr. Livingstone at the time that you copied these; right?*

A. I don't know.

Q. *My notes show that yesterday you believed you first met Mr. Livingstone, and I am not trying to—you first met Mr. Livingstone in 1976 or 1977.*

Does that sound right?

A. Possibly right. As I said, it was some nebulous time.

Q. *Do you have any recollection of discussing this with Mr. Livingstone before you made the copies?*

A. As I recall, I believe, and again, I can't swear to this, but I believe I already had the prints when I met Mr. Livingstone, because while he was in my office, he started going through my files, and he said what are these, what are these, and he pulled the file out with the pictures in it.

I had not initiated showing them to him.

Q. *The file that you had at this time, when Mr. Livingstone was in your office, did that file still contain simply the negatives and the prints and nothing else that you had, in effect, in the same condition you had brought them home from the processing lab?*

A. As I recall, and again, it's just a matter of memory, I believe that that file folder only had the photographs. I had the negatives in a separate place.

Q. *In relation to your last involvement with the Committee or the vestiges of the Committee in June of 1979, do you know if you began to do any work on the negatives or the prints that you brought home with you from the processing lab before the conclusion of your involvement with the Committee vestiges in June of 1979?*

MR. MENDOLA: Do you understand that question?

MR. BRENNAN: Again, I object.

THE WITNESS: I think he saw the question mark in my eyes.

MR. BRENNAN: I will rephrase the question.

MR. MENDOLA: Thank you.

BY MR. BRENNAN:

Q. *Did you do any work on the negatives or the prints you brought home from the processing lab before you ended your involvement with the Committee or its personnel in June of 1979?*

A. I don't believe so.

Q. *Why is it that you think you did not do it until after that?*

A. It was very soon after that, that basically two events happened.

Number one, the House Committee was winding down and running out of money. That was number one.

Number two, a new film of the assassination had been found, and I started focusing my energy very heavily on that.

Q. *Were you authorized by anyone from the House Committee to take the film that you made on that one afternoon with your 35 millimeter camera and process it at a laboratory of your choosing?*

A. I wasn't forbidden to. Nobody had a specific suggestion as to where it should be processed.

Q. *During the work of the Committee that you knew of, was any other film processed for the purpose of copying it or enhancing it in any way?*

A. Yes.

Q. *Was there quite a lot of film that was processed during the work of the Committee?*

A. Yes; I did a lot of that work for the Committee.

Q. *Was any of that other film processed at the laboratory in or near Linden, New Jersey, that you took this film to?*

A. Yes.

MR. MENDOLA: Before you ask a question, are you asking him about film that he took, or film in general?

MR. BRENNAN: I just—

A. I assumed that you were asking film I had done, other duplication work that I had done.

If that was your question, the answer is yes.

Q. *Did anyone from the Committee authorize you to retain the negatives and the prints that you put in your files?*

A. When you say "authorize," you mean specifically tell me to?

Q. Tell you that you could.

A. No.

Q. Did you advise anyone from the Committee, before you did it, that you intended to make the copies with the FBI agent present at that time for the purpose of bringing it home to your house?

A. I don't recall that it was specifically stated, but again, it wasn't said yes or no. They knew that I was doing it, and they authorized it.

Q. Did they authorize it for the purpose of proving a hypothesis that specific autopsy photos were faked?

A. That is correct.

Q. Why was it that you didn't do anything with the material that you created, that you copied, to prove your hypothesis?

MR. MENDOLA: That's not his testimony.

A. That's not what I said at all. I didn't say I did anything. You asked if I performed any other work on them. I said no, based on the report that I had there. That was my guide for writing this report to the House Committee, stating that the House photographs were fake.

In that report, I cited the multiple statements of the doctors, specifically the avulsed exit wound in the rear of the President's head.

Q. Do you have a copy of that report?

A. Not with me.

Q. What is that report called?

A. I don't know that it was specifically called anything.

Q. How do you identify it?

A. I would say, Report to the House Committee or the House Select Committee on Assassinations as to the condition and/or as to questions—it's silly, I never titled it, but I have to title it now.

Q. How did you identify it? If you were going to refer to it, how would you refer to it?

A. I would say, My Report of Robert Groden to the House Select Committee on Assassinations in reference to the question of authenticity of the autopsy photographs of President Kennedy.

Q. Was that report in the form of a letter, or some other form?

A. It would have been in a letter form.

Q. To whom was the letter addressed?

A. It would have been addressed to either Professor Blakey directly, or to Mickey Goldsmith, or to Jane Downey.

Q. Did the report make specific reference to each of the five shots that you copied?

A. I believe that the report related only to the photographs of the rear of the head and, again, I would have to think about this, but probably how they related to the other photographs showing that area.

I remember noting there was a marked difference between the area of the top of the head, in relation to the area in the rear of the head; there was an overlapping area that was inconsistent.

Q. Did your report discuss the two profiles, the left and right profiles?

A. I don't recall.

(At this time, a brief recess was taken.)

Q. Were the left and right profile shots relevant to your report?

A. There were other issues that I was interested in trying to see. For instance, there had been three reports or three statements made of an entrance wound to the left temple of President Kennedy, all of which proved to be not true, and I was interested in that hypothesis, as to whether or not there was a contrast build-up in those areas, as well.

So, I wanted to deal with that.

That was a separate issue.

Q. Did you obtain copies of any other autopsy photographs in addition to these five?

A. From the Committee or from other sources?

Q. Let's start first from anywhere.

A. Yes.

Q. From where did you obtain copies of any other autopsy photographs?

A. When we were ready to start publishing High Treason, and Mr. Livingstone insisted that we have photographs in the book, I felt we should have more than just the few that I had, and I asked David Lifton, who had already published photographs, if I could have copies of his.

He said, just take them out of the book, copy them out of the book, which we did do.

I then later obtained copies from Mr. Lifton after the book was already published, but we never updated the book. We left the photographs as they were, as per my agreement with him.

Q. Other than Mr. Lifton and the House Committee, have you received autopsy photos from anywhere else?

A. Yes.

Q. Where?

A. Mark Crouch.

Q. Anywhere else?

A. Paul O'Connor.

Q. Anyone else?

A. From a source in England, whose name I cannot quite recall. If I think of it, I will tell you.

Q. That's okay.

Why don't you tell me all of your sources?

A. As far as I know, that's it. As far as I can recall.

Q. *Have you ever obtained from the House Committee any other photographs other than the five that you described that you have copied for us?*

A. Sections of photographs, yes, of other photographs.

Q. *Under what circumstances did you obtain the sections of the other photographs from the House Committee?*

A. When the House Assassinations Committee was breaking up, at the very, very end, they had, I believe, 16×20″ or maybe larger exhibits of small sections of the wounds, the back wound, the throat wound, and they were given to me at the end of the Committee's life.

Q. *Who gave them to you?*

A. Professor Blakey.

As I recall, it was Professor Blakey. I think I went through Mickey Goldsmith first and asked him.

Q. *They were given to you after you asked to receive them?*

A. That's correct.

There were also many other exhibits, too. They were just throwing them away anyhow.

Q. *Anything else that you received from the House Committee other than the five you copied, and the 16×20 exhibits of small sections?*

A. In relation to just the autopsy pictures?

Q. *Yes.*

A. Except for the ones that were actually published in the House Committee volumes, no.

We're not so much American as
we are Texan. . . . Don't mess
with Texas.

CHAPTER 15

THE TEXAS CONNECTION

I have written that elements of several groups constituting what might be called "the secret team" came together to organize and operate the conspiracy that resulted in the death of John Kennedy. The planners and case officers at the operational level were financed by prominent Texas oil and business figures who had, for some time, sought to control the direction and policy of the United States. These same oilmen had placed Dwight David Eisenhower in the White House.

These men were diversifying their investments, and plowed their earnings into the defense industry in Texas, ultimately culminating in the vast growth of General Dynamics, Brown & Root, Bell Helicopters, and the establishment of the Space Science Center in Houston. They sought to develop a desert and farm country to an industrial base that would survive their oil reserves. This plan depended on defense spending by the United States. For that, they needed the Cold War and some smaller hot wars that might drag on for a long time.

These wealthy Texas oilmen had few scruples, and the politicians who worked for them, worked for *them,* and not for the public. People owned other people. Wealthy men backed people of either political party. Party labels meant little, since principles changed according to circumstance. At the top, things are pragmatic.

Craig I. Zirbel, an attorney, self-published an important book on the assassination in 1992, *The Texas Connection.*[1] Zirbel presents the case for Lyndon Johnson's involvement, along with powerful businessmen in Texas, in the assassination. Although Zirbel seemingly has no actual evidence to back his case, his argument for Johnson's involvement is strong.

As I have previously stated, I found it difficult to believe that Johnson would have had knowledge of the plot, even if his friends were behind

465

it. But considering Johnson's unscrupulous background (and there is evidence that Johnson was, in fact, behind certain murders in Texas), it is plausible that the plotters would want him to have plausible deniability. In other words, the man who would benefit—a man who could be controlled and who would be a proper puppet—should not know about the plot. Unfortunately, there is evidence that Johnson was part of the plot.

I know Madeleine Brown, a former mistress of Johnson, rather well and find her mostly credible. It is hard for me to believe that she is making up all she says. Brown has, in the past, maintained that LBJ told her that John Kennedy was going to be assassinated in advance of it happening.[2]

In my talks with her, she confirms the portrait given in *The Texas Connection,* and then some. She says that Johnson was a totally amoral man who slept with any woman who came along, betrayed all his women, and who was often drunk and abusive.[3] She said that she believed he worked together with H. L. Hunt and others on the murder.[4]

I. F. Stone wrote, "Johnson has ruined morally all who deal with him at home and he will ruin all who deal with him abroad."[5]

Johnson was a power broker and a political bagman. This was the source of his power in the U.S. Senate. Johnson paid off everybody, and throughout his career, scandal swirled around his head. But his power was larger than those who sought to investigate him. More than one death, such as that of an Agriculture Department agent, Henry Marshall,[6] was imputed to LBJ.

Marshall's was one of those strange deaths of which we hear so much. He was found dead with a single-shot bolt-action rifle alongside him and ruled a suicide. The trouble was, he had been shot five times in the head.

The lesson from that story is that Texas justice operates differently. There is less compunction about killing someone in Texas. Bank robbery, horse stealing, and cattle rustling are so much a part of the tradition and social mores of the state that violence, lynching, and public execution became so ingrained that they were the answers to any sort of problems, including political problems. In the rest of the country, frame-ups by police and the criminal justice system, and cover-ups by coroners, are more discreet. In other words, we all have different concepts of right and wrong, and in the rugged old Wild West, justice was sure and swift, even though it may have had nothing to do with the law. "We'll try him today and hang him in the morning," the refrain went. Sort of a lynch law, and when a *Texan* was offended by President

Kennedy, the best thing to do was to shoot the damned Yankee in public.

Johnson, after all, had eulogized Joe McCarthy in 1957 as follows: "Joe McCarthy had strength, he had great courage, he had daring. . . . There was a quality about the man which compelled respect, and even liking, from his strongest adversaries." Joe McCarthy was a red-baiter with his terroristic campaign of Communist-hunting in American government and the media. A generation later, when we faced the true natures of J. Edgar Hoover and of Joe McCarthy and his chief assistant Roy Cohn, we can only shudder. These monsters led double lives, sitting in judgment on our morals and political affiliations, while all the while they wallowed in filth. Now, we are faced with their friend LBJ.

There is a quite accurate portrait of Johnson in *A Texan Looks at Lyndon: A Study in Illegitimate Power,* by J. Evetts Haley.[7]

Zirbel makes some telling points: Johnson was one of the main figures involved in urging the President to make the trip; Johnson was the one directly involved in planning the President's death trip; on the day before the assassination, Johnson and the President got into a fight over switching seating positions in the vehicles for the upcoming motorcade (Johnson wanted Connally out of JFK's car and his enemy Senator Yarborough to sit in Connally's seat); Johnson's strongest supporters for his presidency lived in Dallas; some of Johnson's strongest supporters in Dallas made threatening remarks against the life of President Kennedy; Johnson's appointees as secretary of the Navy each had preassassination contact with the Oswald family, and one appointee even had contact with Oswald less than two months before the assassination; one of Johnson's strongest supporters in Dallas was visited by Oswald's murderer (Jack Ruby) the day before the assassination; Ruby was found to possess evidence directly linking him with one of Johnson's strongest supporters in Dallas; Johnson's friends had contact with Ruby's trial court judge (who committed reversible error) and gave him a California resort trip and a book contract; and Johnson created the Warren Commission, which seized the evidence, investigated the murder, and reported only to him.[8]

Johnson personally intervened at the Dallas Police Department, and later at Parkland Hospital when Lee Harvey Oswald lay dying.

Cindy McNeill, a Houston attorney and assassination researcher, has read Zirbel's book closely. She has this to say: "From a lawyer's standpoint, I found it to be weak. While Zirbel spends a lot of pages on Johnson's alleged motives to kill JFK and Johnson's lack of moral fiber, he doesn't really tell us how Johnson put together an assassination team and implemented the plan to murder JFK. For a number of reasons, I personally believe that Johnson was not involved in the plot. But every stone must be overturned and I remain open to new evidence."

McNeill goes on to argue, "There is a great deal more solid evidence pointing to Richard Nixon's complicity. This is my present area of research and I would appreciate any new or previously unpublished evidence or information connecting Nixon with Kennedy's death."[9] You see, they were all in it together, as was Caesar killed.

Zirbel makes some errors. Like many, he ascribes a great deal of weight to the fact that the motorcade did not proceed straight down Main Street and instead turned on Houston and again on Elm to get onto Stemmons Freeway.[10] There are other issues involved—for instance, whether the luncheon should have been at the Women's Club and not at the Trade Mart, which would have changed the motorcade route without routing it down Elm Street. Others wonder why the motorcade did not come down Elm Street in the first place, which would not have forced it to slow down in its final turns.

Jerry Bruno, the President's advance man, had argued vigorously not to have the lunch at the Trade Mart, and for the car to proceed straight down Main Street without making the turns.[11] Many felt that this would have put it out of range of the sniper in the sixth-floor window, which I consider ridiculous. There was no extra-long block involved, only a very short one where the real snipers still faced the car from their hiding places on either side of the overpass. The shot would still have been simple.

Critics had pointed out that the motorcade should not have been rerouted off of Main Street onto Houston and then down Elm before entering the freeway, and should have gone straight down Main Street and either gone over the top of the curb to get over to Elm and the entrance ramp, or continued straight and traveled to the Trade Mart on Industrial Boulevard. Zirbel makes the argument that there were only minor speed bumps separating Main Street from Elm and which were located where the two streets come close together shortly after passing under the bridge. This is false because there is a normal curb between the two and a concrete island between the curbs. It would have been all but impossible for the cars to get over the curb, and even then not sure of hanging up their undersides and getting stuck. I don't doubt that no motorcade planner in the world would have chosen such a route, since every car in the motorcade would have had to crawl up over the top of the curb. In spite of such a mistake (we all make them), it should not be used to discredit Zirbel. (See photo section.)

The southern wing of the Democratic Party was always conservative. After Kennedy's death many joined the Republican Party. Johnson was a leader of this conservatism: "Under the banner of Senate Majority Leader Johnson, the congressional Democrats have become practically indistinguishable from the party they allegedly oppose," said Joseph L. Rauh, the national chairman of Americans for Democratic Action, on March 23, 1956.

The old alliance of the northern liberals, unions, intellectuals, and southern conservative Democrats could not continue. Bullets would change the alignment, and the Republican Party benefited. There can be no doubt that Kennedy was lured to Texas, where they could kill him and cover it up. Johnson handpicked the Warren Commission, and he locked up the evidence until the next century. The lure was the mess in Texas politics. Kennedy always rose to those challenges, and Texas was needed in the year to come if the Democrats were to win the presidential election again. But the problem remained long after Kennedy was so brutally murdered:

"The pro-Johnson and anti-Johnson factions are so violently opposed as to make Texas politics almost unbelievable. If you haven't seen it, you wouldn't believe it," said Senator Wayne Morse in 1966.

With regard to the Dallas police, Zirbel makes far more telling arguments. He writes, "The actions of the Dallas Police Department described in this chapter when looked at in total defy all logic and common sense. Why did they: never follow up on the miracle bullet; fail to explain Officer Tippit's patrol assignment in Oswald's neighborhood; refuse to say why a Dallas police car stopped in front of Oswald's rooming house; not explain why Officer Tippit was seen casually talking to Oswald before Tippet's death; not investigate how and why Oswald killed Tippit; fail to answer how Oswald could have single-handedly stacked over a ton of books to create a sniper's nest; not question why they only could find a few of Oswald's prints in the sniper's area; not ask why the sniper did not fire at a closer unimpeded range; not supply an explanation as to how an Oswald fingerprint could surface on the alleged assassination weapon, days later; not allow Oswald to have a lawyer; take no contemporaneous notes of Oswald's interrogations; permit Oswald to be an execution target for Ruby on the late Friday evening; never allow Oswald to publicly talk; not transfer Oswald out of the Dallas jail within twelve hours as required by law; choose to make the transfer of Oswald instead of the sheriff as was customary; permit the Chief to ignore reliable warnings of a possible execution attempt of Oswald; perform a public transfer of Oswald; not use a human police shield to protect Oswald; let Ruby get into a secured area twice with a gun; and, have an ambulance ready in advance of the shooting?"[12]

Zirbel suggests that "Police Chief Curry's personal relationship with Lyndon Johnson may offer some insight" into why all of the above happened.[13] He describes Curry remaining at Parkland Hospital when he might have been leading his investigation in the field, and why did Johnson remain there? "Any reasonable man under the same circumstances who was repeatedly advised to get away from a crisis area for his own safety and the good of the nation would have immediately left. . . . Unanswered questions remain. Why did Chief Curry not lead his police investigation, but rather stayed with Johnson? And why was Johnson so unconcerned about fleeing Dallas? One possible answer is that one or both of these men knew that Johnson had nothing to fear concerning his own possible assassination."[14]

Look at some of the things Johnson did within hours or days of Kennedy's death. He had his own baggage removed from his plane and put on *Air Force One,* and insisted that the coffin ride with him. He forced the widow and Kennedy's men—all of whom were in deep shock and disliked Johnson—to stand with him while he was sworn in as president. He took over Kennedy's cabin. He would not allow the plane to leave until a federal judge was found who swore him in as president. As soon as he was in Washington Johnson gave Mrs. Kennedy three days to get out of the White House, and had all of Kennedy's possessions removed at once.

"These types of callous activities demonstrate the cold ruthlessness of a man who was neither stricken with fear over a possible conspiracy, nor in any way mourning the loss of a leader," Zirbel writes.[15] Johnson took over with great force and speed.

The night before Oswald was killed, someone called the FBI to tell them that the transfer route ought to be changed and that Oswald was going to be killed.[16] This had to be Ruby. In addition, police communications officer Billy Grammer received a call the night before Oswald was killed asking that the transfer route be changed. He recognized the voice as that of Ruby, whom he knew.[17] "As we talked, he began telling me that we needed to change the plans on moving Oswald from the basement. That he knew of the plans to make the move and if we did not make a change he—the statement he made precisely was, 'We are going to kill him.' "

Grammer discovered the shooting of Oswald by Ruby when he turned on his TV, and "I suddenly realized, knowing Jack Ruby the way I did, this was the man I was talking to on the phone last night. At that time I put the voice with the face and I know within myself that Jack Ruby was the one who made that call to me the night before, and I think it was obvious because he knew me and I knew him and he called me by name over the telephone and seeing this and knowing what I knew and what he had said, to me it had to be Jack Ruby.''

Grammer also said, "He made the statement, 'We are going to kill him.' Which leads me to believe that this was not a spontaneous thing that happened on the spur of the moment. That he was watching Oswald coming out of the door and all of a sudden he decided to shoot him. I do not believe that. I think this was a planned event with him being the man to do the shooting.''[18]

Describing the moments after Ruby was arrested and thrown into a jail cell, his jailer, Don Archer, told a British film team: "His behavior to begin with was very hyper. He was sweating profusely. We had stripped him down for security purposes. He asked me for one of my cigarettes. I gave him a cigarette. Finally, after about two hours had elapsed, which would put it around 1:00 P.M., the head of the Secret Service came up and conferred with him and he told me that Oswald had in effect died and it should shock him, 'cos it would mean the death penalty.' So, I returned. I said—'Jack, it looks like it's going to be the electric chair for you.' Instead of being shocked, he became calm. He quit sweating. His heart slowed down. I asked him if he wanted a cigarette, and he advised me that he didn't smoke. I was astonished that this was a complete difference in behavior from what I expected. I would say that his life had depended on him getting Oswald.''[19]

In my many trips to Dallas, I found numerous people who felt that the power structure and Lyndon Johnson had something to do with John Kennedy's murder. Certainly the circumstantial evidence presented by Zirbel shows that the police chief and the Dallas police acted in strange ways. When Penn Jones and I drove to Dallas from his town, as we could see the tall buildings rise up ahead of us from the land, he would say without fail: "I hate every brick and stone in that goddamned town!'' Penn Jones is one of the original researchers into the assassination and authored several books on the case. Jones was one of those rare birds: a Texas liberal, or populist. They bombed his newspaper for some of what he wrote.[20] Penn believed that Johnson and the military who backed him killed President Kennedy.

Through reason and common sense, Zirbel arrives at his conclusion that Johnson had Kennedy killed, and he constructs a massive case of circumstantial evidence. I don't think he has the story quite right (this is not explained well in the book) because Johnson would have been only one part of the plan. Zirbel gives the impression that Johnson ordered the murder.

The problem that most Americans have is that they are now too far away from political realities to understand how our politics operate: trades, payoffs, pork barreling. There is no loyalty. Men who are allies one day will be enemies the next, and enemies will get into bed with one another for the sake of expediency. Idealism has little or no place in the system.

So much scandal swirled about Johnson that it all but destroyed Kennedy's presidency. Johnson was known to have stolen elections,[21] and history has it that the Kennedy/Johnson ticket had the election stolen for them in Chicago, West Virginia, and Texas. The Billie Sol Estes scandal involving Johnson was followed by the Bobby Baker scandal. As Zirbel points out, had not Kennedy died and Johnson become president, Johnson would probably have been forced from office and indicted in the Bobby Baker case. Baker was a former Senate page boy who rose to be Lyndon Johnson's right hand when he was the majority leader, perhaps the second most powerful position in America.

Baker was an influence peddler who collected a cent for every pound of beef that came into the country from Argentina and the Caribbean, and he was on the take from many other sources. He became rich, and built the Carousel Hotel in Ocean City, Maryland, noted for its upscale Washington prostitutes.

Zirbel writes, "When Johnson seized power the Senate investigation into Baker was temporarily stopped. It was then 'deferred' until after the 1964 presidential election because of the assassination. Even the criminal pretrial hearings against Bobby Baker were deferred for no other reason than that was what Johnson wanted. And in a direct threat to the Republicans, Johnson told them to leave the Baker scandal alone during the 1964 campaign because he had the goods on them. How Johnson stopped the press from continuing their investigation is unknown, except the facts demonstrate that this did occur. What is known in retrospect is that Johnson's order was obeyed by all.

"If Jack Kennedy had not been murdered, the Baker investigation would not have ended. If Jack Kennedy had not been murdered, the Baker scandal would have either destroyed or tarnished Johnson's image so completely that he would not have been on the 1964 ticket. If the president had not been slain, the truth about LBJ may have put him in prison, as his grandma predicted, rather than into the White House."[22]

* * *

Too many people stood to lose too much if Kennedy lived. Johnson would have been forced out by Kennedy and/or the media over the Baker scandal, and Johnson's power would have been forever destroyed. All those Texas interests that stood to gain from the Vietnam War would have lost because Kennedy was determined not to get involved in combat anywhere in Southeast Asia.

Kennedy's speech at American University in June 1963 perhaps wrote his death warrant because he announced a unilateral halt by the United States on above-ground nuclear tests, and this threatened far too many financial interests with a stake in nuclear armaments. Kennedy pushed for an end to the Cold War and for a nuclear test ban treaty.

His appearance before a million to two million people in West Berlin that same month, followed by the conclusion of a nuclear test ban treaty with the Soviet Union in July, *signed* his death warrant. In August 1963, Kennedy met with civil rights leaders who led a vast march in Washington. In September he spoke at the United Nations and proposed that the Soviet Union and the United States go to the moon together. In October he negotiated to sell wheat to the Soviets.

The argument that I have repeatedly made is that a consortium came together from the conservative right to kill Kennedy, and it included either Nixon (whose chief backers were these same Dallas oilmen) or those interests whom Nixon represented, and his personal gang of agents. This later led to Watergate. Texas was chosen because the situation could be controlled in Dallas. The levers were there to plant evidence on the police. Each big city police force has men allied with military intelligence who will do their bidding. Men trained in the military get civilian jobs and go on doing this sort of work, and coroners are in place to cover it up.

There were backup patsies in case something happened to Oswald. The conspirators had a lot of money, and none of this was any problem, since the number of informants and other operatives available for clandestine operations at the time in the United States was large. It has been admitted that there were at least fifty thousand Pentagon spies, operatives, and informers on college campuses during the Vietnam War that followed.

Whether or not Lyndon Johnson knew what was going to happen to JFK, I am sure that he actively helped to cover up the murder.

A major propaganda effort was needed to counteract evidence of conspiracy, and that could best be done in Washington with a blue-ribbon and high-blown presidential commission. Once the press was trapped into accepting the findings of the commission, and failing to investigate the crime themselves, the media forever after had to ridicule and humiliate those who continued to look into the murder and not accept the official story.

CHAPTER 16

DALLAS

I began my own investigation in Texas. For a long time, I had been told by liberal Texas Democrats that Lyndon Johnson was fundamentally evil and capable not only of murder but also of having killed John Kennedy. Johnson has had imputed to him other apparent murders prior to his assuming the presidency. But, in addition, there were always rumors that oilmen—in particular H. L. Hunt—might have had something to do with the murder of Kennedy.

One of the discoveries that stands out the most in my mind about Dallas is that there is a great deal of fear under the surface. The wealthy people and their detectives, smear campaign artists, and hit men have so terrorized the city that when people get too close to the truth of some piece of criminality, corruption, killing, or assassination, fear takes over.

So we will call Dallas the City of Fear. Football and television may mask some of what goes on there, but the real truth of Dallas needs to be told.

Years ago, somebody went to a lot of trouble to publish a book, *Farewell America,* that pinned the crime on the Texas oilmen, Lyndon Johnson, and elements of the intelligence and local police agencies. The book was published in Europe and offered to *Ramparts* magazine, a bastion of the New Left in the sixties, and which attempted to investigate its origins. The fact was that the author knew an awful lot about the inner workings of the CIA, and this seemed to establish the book's authenticity.

Farewell America was always looked down on by the community of assassination researchers, but it is not clear why, other than the suspicion that it came from the KGB, which does not necessarily impugn the truths in it. Warren Hinckle tells the story in his book *If You Have a Lemon, Make Lemonade.*[1] The consensus was that the book originated with French Intelligence. It was possible that the Kennedy family had something to do with it. Daniel Patrick Moynihan had conducted an intense private investigation for Robert Kennedy and the Justice Department concluding that Jimmy Hoffa and other mobsters were not involved in the assassination, but crucial evidence was developed during the course of this indicating a domestic plot.

I had developed several witnesses whom I judged to be in a position to know what had really happened to John Kennedy. The problem we have in proving anything—getting corroborated or credible testimony— is enormous. There is a certain amount of luck and guesswork in investigating. We often have to follow our hunches. I follow many trails to see where they lead. That can be a great drain of energy.

I came across certain people who were in touch with the Dallas researchers. These people were often kept hidden from view by those same researchers. As explained elsewhere, it eventually appeared that this same Dallas research group was responsible either deliberately or unwittingly for a great deal of misinformation. They were cutting out a bunch of witnesses and turning them into professionals, and staging various press conferences and meetings that promoted a massive amount of false information.

The result of the activities of this Dallas group of researchers was to alienate many others in Dallas and the national press familiar with the case. Bear in mind that what the public may believe and what hard-nosed journalists and editors as a group may believe are often opposed, because journalists take a tougher look at the sort of information being fielded by researchers and other publicity-seekers.

I gradually uncovered this disaffected underground of witnesses as well as a group of largely unknown researchers and sympathetic observers. Some of them led me to high-ranking citizens who, at one time or another, were in a position to know.

The Dallas Charter Committee ''was the political leadership'' of the city in 1963. There were about fifty or sixty people on this committee. Its right hand were the thirteen men of the Crime Commission, an arm of District Attorney Henry Wade that was dedicated to keeping outside crime out, or so we are given to believe. The Charter Committee rubber-stamped the decisions of the Crime Commission. ''Dallas was wide open, kind of like Galveston. Whorehouses, gambling joints, Dixie Mafia. When Henry Wade got in power, he said. 'The Mob is not going to control this city!' They cleaned Dallas up, and to this day there is very little Mob control in the city.''[2]

"Concentrate on the Crime Commission," one native told me, "if you want to get some leads on who killed John Kennedy. Look at who was in the City and County offices." One of those who might provide leads who worked for the Crime Commission was Bob Denson. Denson was Melvin Belli's investigator when Belli represented Jack Ruby. John Stemmons and Fred Florence were on the Commission, along with Alan Merrieman, the editor of the *Dallas Times Herald,* and A. H. Below, the editor of The *Dallas Morning News.*

Someone who knew everyone on the Crime Commission was "The Little Pallbearer," Bobby Freedman. "All the people in power were his friends. They all grew up on Forest Street." Speaking of the Texas Mafia, or "The Power," as some call it, "The strength of it is they can break who they want to break. The concept of *how* this works tracks back to the Kennedy assassination. If their hands weren't dirty with the blood, their skirts were."

One of my informants—from Tennessee, but long settled in Dallas—said, "The circle of Sheriff Bill Decker, Morris Jaffe, Judge Lew Sterrett were either involved or definitely involved with the people who were. It's all one thing. It goes into Nixon and Reagan," she told me.

"All these people are intermarried way back, all from South Dallas and those big houses. They grew up together and were born just after the turn of the century."

"Anybody they couldn't control, they did something to! That's what happened to Connally," one important source told me. Several years before Connally died, he was broken financially, it was said, because he was talking too much about 1963. Connally believed that they were also trying to kill him.

There was a rash of deaths, disappearances, and apparent arrests in law enforcement after the assassination, some of which were very suspicious. Dallas police officer Nick Christopher apparently died of a heart attack, it is said. Also meeting with untimely demises were Dallas policemen Maurice "Monk" Baker, Lieutenant George Butler, John Liggett, Lieutenant H. M. Hart, and Bill Biggio. Henry Wade's investigator, Clarence Oliver, died in 1966. U.S. Marshal Clint Peoples was recently murdered.

Baker blew his brains out on December 3, 1963. He was a friend of Jack Ruby and lived in Oak Cliff on North Beckley, the street where Oswald lived.

The Murchisons

The Murchison brothers were the sons of Clint Murchison, Sr., from Athens, Texas, southeast of Dallas. South of there, where Big Clint roamed, are many spring-fed lakes, grazing meadows, and pine and hardwood forests where cotton once ruled. "Clint, Sr., was one of the first to create the grand metamorphosis from patchy croplands and eroded fields, back to thickety forests interspersed by lush pastures producing enough hay and other chlorophyll to carry cattle safely through the winters, without supplementary feeds. The surrounding ranchers and farmers followed Clint's scheme of restoring the health of the land for the benefit of both mankind and wild creatures."[3]

Clint, Sr., had grown rich buying and selling oil leases in the newly discovered oil fields near Wichita Falls, Texas. The roots of his family were in Athens, where three generations of Murchisons had worked at the First National Bank of Athens—so writes Bill Deener of the *Dallas Morning News* when Clint Sr. died. Gambling was more to Big Clint's liking, whether in oil leases or dice, and he "briefly attended Trinity College, but he was caught shooting craps within two months of enrolling. He refused to sign a pledge to quit gambling and was kicked out. He and Sid Richardson, founder of another of the state's oil fortunes, were early partners. By 1927, when he was thirty-two, Clint Sr., sold his oil properties for $5 million and announced his retirement. He later reconsidered, however, and headed to West Texas, where he bought rights for natural gas—then considered a waste product. The company he formed, Southern Union Gas Co., essentially created the natural gas industry. Along with his East Texas oil holdings, it became the foundation of what was at one time the third largest of the great Texas oil fortunes, behind only those of H. L. Hunt and the Richardson and Bass families."[4] The Bass family of Fort Worth worked as partners with Richardson, who took care of the Bass children and set them up as his successors with his wealth and power, with John Connally as administrator of the trusts.

The senior Murchison's three sons—Clint, Jr., John Dabney, and Burk—were raised in a palatial mansion on Preston Road north of Dallas. Their mother, Anne, died after surgery, and Burk died at ten. "A close friend of the Murchison family said Clint, Jr., was profoundly affected by not knowing his mother. He was raised by his father and aunt." Clint became a Marine in World War II and attended Duke, receiving engineering degrees from there and MIT.

For his two surviving sons their father set up a firm: Murchison Brothers. John went into banking, and Clint created construction projects, such as widening the Panama Canal, the St. Lawrence Seaway, New Orleans II, and Texas Stadium. He also put a lot of money into the banking business in Nevada, Minnesota, and Texas.

Clint, Jr., bought a National Football League expansion franchise in 1959. He created the Dallas Cowboys. The team became part of the propaganda assault launched by his cohorts to restore the good name of Dallas after the assassination of John Kennedy there. He had to drive the American Football League team owned by Lamar Hunt out of town. Baltimore got the previous Dallas football team, which became the legendary Colts. When Clint, Jr., had to give up ownership of the team, it all but broke his heart. "Selling the Cowboys would be like selling one of my kids," he said, but needing money, he eventually had to do it. He sold it to H. R. "Bum" Bright, the owner of a trucking company and a large bank, which failed in 1989. Clint, Jr., had bought the Cowboys for $600,000, and he sold it for $60 million.

Clint Murchison, Jr., put together a fortune "estimated to be $350 million from banking, real estate, oil, and innumerable other projects. But a series of highly speculative real-estate ventures in the early 1960s turned sour and forced him into bankruptcy in 1985."[5]

"His political leanings were as conservative as his crew cut hair."[6]

Clint, Jr., adhered to his father's advice to have diverse investments and "owe more than you own." Murchison invested in barbecue (Tony Roma's), banks, condominiums, railroad lines (the New York Central among them), and hundreds of other projects.

Clint, Jr.'s, brother John Murchison was also fabulously rich and lived in a virtual palace. "There was no social invitation in Texas that was more sought after than one from John and Lupe Murchison."[7] Many of the most famous people in the world, including kings and queens, came to their house. President Gerald Ford, formerly a member of the Warren Commission, often stopped by their home in Vail.

"Lupe's parties were unarguably lavish and important in the annals of high society. But what made her one of the best hostesses in Texas was that her parties were always fun. Lupe was as loquacious as John was laconic. She shot around her parties, flailing her arms, hugging her guests, laughing and shouting gleefully. She was never still a moment, with the result that first-time guests relaxed immediately. Lupe had an extraordinary knack for putting her guests at ease and making them feel wanted. During dinner she was the first one to jump up from her chair and make a toast to everyone at the table. Lupe's guests felt appreciated, as though they individually played an important role in the success of the party."[8]

The property the brothers owned in New Orleans comprised thirty-six thousand acres, which was slightly less than one third of the land within the city limits of that town.[9] This gave Clint an escape route to the East, and "between Super Bowls and business, Clint was spending so much time in New Orleans that he decided to buy a house in the French Quarter. He bought an elegant, old three-bedroom house with a beautiful garden and courtyard and three separate guest houses all hidden behind a high brick wall. Like his other homes around the country, the New Orleans estate became a wild party place, and, to no one's surprise, there soon developed a New Orleans contingent of Clint's hangers-on."[10]

Clint, Jr., had his own problems after he married Anne Ferrell in 1975; she had been married to Gil Brandt of the Cowboys. Anne never was accepted in Dallas society, so to speak. "Liquor, drugs, even many of Clint's longtime buddies were off limits under Anne's stringent new house rules. Anne had found a new purpose in life, and she was determined that Clint share in it. . . . Her deep insecurity manifested itself in a violent temper, as she went into tirades that lasted for as long as three days. 'I wouldn't even let Clint sleep,' she said. 'I would kick, scream, bite.' "[11]

As for business, Clint "left most of the managing of his projects to others. This style worked with the Dallas Cowboys for two decades, and the team became the pride of the National Football League. But those close to him said the days of doing business with a nod and handshake were over long before Murchison chose to believe it."[12] He made the mistake of trusting too many of those who worked for him. The people he delegated management to lost most of what was in their trust, finally breaking him financially.

"With failing health and creditors at the door, the last three or four years of his life were seen by his family and associates as a tragic epilogue to a once proud life." Falling oil prices speeded his descent.

The first action against Clint, Jr., and his partner Louis A. Farris, Jr., was filed by a Cleveland bank in 1983 for a $2 million judgment, and it "should have represented nothing worse than an ant bite to an entrepreneur like Murchison. Instead, creditor demands began cascading into state and federal courts, eventually totaling more than $500 million."[13] He had to file for bankruptcy.

Clint, Jr., who died in 1987, had to sell his big mansion on Forest Lane in Dallas, and he moved across the street with his wife, Anne Ferrell Murchison, into a smallish cottage, where they lived quietly for the next three years. Anne Murchison was saved, as they say, and became hyperreligious in the fundamentalist, charismatic sense. She "constantly proselytized as a born-again Christian. 'I still sin but I confess and ask for forgiveness,' she said, "adding that she relied on Jesus to help her find a parking place at the supermarket."[14] This was someone who had previously lived in the fast lane.

Jane Wolfe writes that "The enigma of Clint, Jr., was that outsiders saw only the dark side of him. They recognized the arrogant egotist but ignored the brilliant and inventive businessman. They condemned the flagrant adulterer, unaware that he was also a loving and sensitive father. They saw only his distant side and never the immense wit and charm he reserved for making a deal or a woman."[15]

"There were very few people that Clint associated with who were of good character," said his ex-wife Jane Murchison Haber. "After the downfall the mention of Clint Jr.'s, name often brought the reply, 'He was a rich, arrogant son of a bitch. He probably deserved what he got.'

"Equally unmoved by Clint, Jr.'s, financial crisis were those who disapproved of his constant philandering. The mystique of Clint, Jr.'s mythic wealth did not mask from his friends and associates a severe psychological problem. He was sexually obsessed, priapic. The brilliant mind that had impressed his teachers at MIT was, for most of his adult life, focused largely on the tactics and strategies of serial seduction. Every young, pretty woman he met was a potential bedmate. His was a sexual hunger that could not be satisfied, a thirst that could not be slaked. The more he got, the greater his need."[16]

Jane Wolfe tells the story of the new headquarters he built for the Cowboys and himself, but Clint rarely used it, except for the fact that he'd leased space to a health club and had "built a one-way mirror into the women's dressing room and invited his buddies to come by and watch the women undress."

"By the midseventies about eight out of ten of Clint's projects were failures," Lou Farris told Jane Wolfe. "Clint was busy experimenting with new hedonistic pleasures. Clint's life-style took a dramatic turn in the mid-1970s when he started using drugs other than just marijuana. 'Some of the guys he was hanging around with on the West Coast lured him into a lot of bad things.' One of his girlfriends described his use of cocaine. 'He started calling me in the middle of the afternoon and I could tell he was on some drug or other. It got to the point where he needed drugs in order to perform in bed. Without cocaine, sex was impossible for him.' "[17]

Clinton Murchison, Jr., was also tied in with the Mob and Carlos Marcello in New Orleans. Clint's extensive holdings of vacant land in that city where he eventually literally built a new city (New Orleans East) was another key to the murder of John Kennedy.

Gordon Novel tells me he was partners with Clint Murchison on New

Orleans East when Novel was arrested in the Watergate affair—perhaps to get him out of the deal.[18]

Marcello had an interest in car dealerships in Dallas, and his son, Carlos, Jr., settled in Highland Park, the ritzy suburb of Dallas where he lives today. Aubrey Rike, the ambulance attendant who helped put John Kennedy into his coffin, is the police chief of Highland Park today. Marcello was closely tied to Sheriff Bill Decker through W. O. Bankston and Joe Civello, the local Mob chieftain. The fact is that at the top of Dallas's power there sat the don of New Orleans through his contacts with Murchison, the sheriff, Civello, and Bankston in Dallas. They insulated Marcello from Hoover, but they all (including Hoover) had gambling, the track, and Las Vegas in common. Of course, Clint, Jr., was very tight with Hoover, and they shared a common love of the racetrack.

Several sources say that Marcello was financially involved with Buckner Chrysler,[19] whose president was Buck (Hughbert) Ferrell. He is the husband of prominent assassination researcher Mary Ferrell, who worked for a number of very powerful people in Texas, including Phil Burleson, Jack Ruby's lawyer; former deputy ambassador to Saigon Eugene Locke, who was John Connally's closest friend (whom she knew quite well); and former governor of Texas Dolph Briscoe. Marcello primarily dealt through Jo-Jo and his brother Sam Campisi in Dallas, along with Joe Civello, the local Mob head.

On Bill Decker, a judge told me, "The man really didn't know his own power. He could do any damn thing he wanted to do! Nobody challenged him, not even Henry Wade, but they were on the same wavelength." Al Maddox told us that Decker "was mean as hell. The only eye that had any life in it was his glass eye" (Decker had lost an eye).

When Decker wanted to talk to someone he was about to arrest, he didn't bother with warrants. A call was made to the person, and that person knew that he had to come downtown of his own volition. This was called a "Decker Warrant." There were countless cases of people who were incarcerated on a "Decker Hold"—that is, without benefit of being booked or making mug shots or fingerprints. Therefore no records were kept. Important prisoners and those considered "in the family" were kept on the fifth floor of the Adolphus Hotel, one of the ritziest places in the United States.

No wonder so many had a great terror of these people! They had no hesitation about using their power. Fear of the great power of the grown children is there to this day.

In 1983 Clint, Jr., was diagnosed as having olivopontine cerebellar atrophy, an extremely rare degenerative nerve disease similar to Lou Gehrig's disease. The disease would not affect his mind but it would incapacitate him.

Clint and his wife had found God after a wild life. "The church he entered was nondenominational and relentlessly fundamentalist. Its working-class members were mostly 'charismatic Christians' who sang and danced and clapped their hands, spoke in tongues, and were thoroughly washed in the blood of the lamb. It was not a church for the undecided or questioning, but only for 'people who have been saved, who have given their lives to Christ.' Others of Clint's friends were cut off from him by Anne. One of Clint's closest friends had made it a practice to drop by each week with videotapes of classic movies. 'Each time I went to the house, Anne met me at the door and looked over each tape closely to make sure it wasn't pornographic. She said she didn't want anything in the house that wasn't allowed in God's eyes.' "[20] Some sixteen hundred people came to his funeral "to witness the last memorial to a man who had risen higher and fallen farther than most men. Obituaries throughout the world explained that Clint Murchison, Jr., had suffered one of the largest personal bankruptcies in history, but the enigma of the man himself was perhaps the most fascinating aspect of his life."[21]

One more of the killers of John Kennedy did not have a pleasant end. He became increasingly ill. "The great house on Forest Lane, on which Clint had lavished a decade of thought and planning before even moving in, stood vacant from the time he and Anne left it in early 1987. During the next two years it was badly vandalized, and hundreds of trees and shrubs were left to die. But the news about the once-fabulous Forest Lane estate became even worse. When it was finally sold in March 1989 for a much-deflated $6 million to a residential real-estate developer, friends and family were crushed to learn that the twenty-five acres on which Clint had spent years of effort and millions of dollars will be subdivided into one-third-acre residential lots and that the home will be demolished."[22] The ultimate humiliation for the once rich and mighty: a subdivision.

Murchison's Party

On the night of November 21, 1963, there was a big party at the home of Clint Murchison, then one of the wealthiest oilmen in Dallas. Some have called this a "victory" party or a "command conference," celebrating the planned murder of President Kennedy the next day.

Many of these people had supported Kennedy's election, but his stance on civil rights had alienated them. These people had vast power reaching out through the nation. They had financed the removal of major defense industries from the Northeast and relocated them in the Dallas/Fort Worth area.

Word of this party was first mentioned by Penn Jones, Jr., in one of his books, and he states that it was one of the rare ones that was not reported by society columnist Val Imm, who later married Dr. Fouad Bashour, one of the Parkland emergency room team that tried to save President Kennedy's life.[23] I interviewed Imm, and she has no memory of being there.[24] Madeleine Brown attended the party. She gave me an extensive description and list of those present.[25] She verified Jones's published report that Richard Nixon, who was in Dallas that day, was at the party, driven there by Peter O'Donnell.

I have verified that at least the following were at the party: J. Edgar Hoover, Lyndon Johnson, H. L. Hunt, John Curington, George Brown of Brown & Root, former Texas Republican congressman Bruce Alger, and John J. McCloy of Chase Manhattan Bank and the Rockefeller interests. McCloy was placed on the Warren Commission within the week. The Rockefeller fortune was made in oil, much of it in East Texas, but their two major banks in New York overextended themselves in real-estate loans and threatened to go bankrupt. Everybody needed a new and major source of income. If a national debt could be generated, the interest the U.S. Treasury would pay the banks would replenish everybody's coffers at the expense of the taxpayers—and mortgage the future of our youth and nation in the process.

Some typify the party as a coming together of the financial interests of the eastern Establishment and those of the Texas oilmen. Kennedy's threat to remove the oil depletion allowance that made them all rich was the straw that broke the camel's back, though there was much else he was doing that they didn't like. There was no "Yankee-Cowboy War" when seen from this aspect. They were all in it together, and they were all in the same house the night before the murder.

George Healey told me, "They believed Kennedy was going to flood the country with cheap money, and they were not going to get any more money for their oil, except for what might go up as a result of inflation. Inflation always catches up with oil and gas products later. They considered the flushing of money through the Federal Reserve an act of treason. Secondly—"

"You mean, to remove it from the Federal Reserve?"

"Yes! Yeah, it had no constraints on how much money was printed. The Federal Reserve was independent."

"They were going to flood the country with cheap money—you mean the Kennedys?"

"Yes. That's what they thought they were going to do. That was the great fear. And the second thing is the depletion allowance was the only way the oil people could corner and preserve wealth. Because 27½ percent they could stick in their pocket, and the rest of it they drilled up. None of these big oil people ever paid any taxes. They just went out and drilled for more oil, stuck another 27½ percent in their pocket. They drilled it all up in intangible drilling costs, so they didn't want anything to happen to the 27½ percent depletion allowance (as JFK threatened). The talk around was, 'How could Kennedy do this? He is hurting himself.' " It's true, he had some oil interests. "If oil in the ground had had some kind of value at that time, no one would have been concerned about it. If oil in the ground had had a value like it has today, nobody cares. But at that time, it was taking away their livelihood—it was in effect a tax on them.

"You couldn't build up any wealth because of the income and inheritance tax structures. You couldn't pass wealth on unless you had some method of getting tax-free money. Twenty-seven and a half percent is damn near a third. You could put all your friends and whoever you want in oil deals and when you get your money back out of the deal, you get to stick 27½ percent in your pocket because you get to knock that off your income. That was the first time anybody had ever mentioned taking away that depletion allowance, seriously, and that was Kennedy, and that was a real biggie. On the other hand, Lyndon Johnson was deeply beholden to the oil and gas industry. And that was one of the reasons Lyndon Johnson was tugged in several different directions. No one wanted him to be vice president for fear they wouldn't have their man in the Senate to keep the depletion allowance."

"Did you yourself hear these fears and angers?"

"Well, yeah, sure! All these things were freely bandied about."

"Must have been the talk of Dallas?"

"Well, of course. Letters. Little comments in the paper. One oilman would write another and they'd form a committee to preserve the depletion allowance. It was the same old argument: We'd be dependent upon foreign oil if we take away the incentive to drill."[26]

Richard Nixon's presence at the party at Murchison's also represented the Rockefeller interests, as the law firm of which he was a partner served the Rockefellers. Some enterprising newspaper reporter ought to ask Nixon what he was doing there behind closed doors.

"There was a real atmosphere of uneasiness at that party," Madeleine Brown told me.[27] If they were afraid their plan to kill the President would fail, that might make them acutely uneasy. It must have been quite a scene with the women trying to affect gaiety and not getting a rise out of the men.

This was a social gathering, with a private meeting of the men behind the big double doors of the drawing room. Women were excluded. I have had this description from more than one source. Therefore I feel that Jones's description of a "command conference" is possible. Certainly the party seems to have been a cover.

It was at this party that Lyndon Johnson made his now famous statement to Madeleine and those standing with her. He had come late to the party and, as Madeleine Brown was preparing to leave, he came out of the private meeting red-faced and told her, "After tomorrow, that's the last time those goddamned Kennedys will embarrass me again!"[28]

Some members of the Texas "8F" group were at the party. Of course, the host, Clint Murchison, was present. 8F is a term taken from the suite where they used to meet at the Lamar Hotel in Houston, where the Browns of the Brown & Root construction company had their offices. Herman Brown was a principal backer of Lyndon Johnson, and Brown & Root ultimately found vast benefits in the Vietnam War, which included building the artificial port at Cam Ranh Bay.

Among the original members of the 8F group was Jesse Jones, who built the Democratic Party in Texas. In 1936, during the Depression, he gave the party more than $200,000. Some of the members were Sam Rayburn, who died in 1961; Lyndon Johnson; John Connally; Alvin Wertz; Abe Fortas; and Herman and George Brown. Also closely connected to this circle was Clark Clifford, later indicted in the BCCI bank scandals in 1991, and J. Edgar Hoover.

Penn Jones wrote, "The killing of President Kennedy was the most important takeover of a country in our world history. All the major forces in this country were involved, and had to be accounted for at the final conference before the strike."[29] Jones says that a conference was necessary. The party was the cover for the conference that occurred. Jones feels that J. Edgar Hoover was the commander and "present to confer with his troops, to issue last-minute instructions, to review the final plans and to give the word to 'go' or to cancel as necessary."[30]

If the occasion of John Kennedy's death prompted schoolchildren in Dallas to jump for joy and cheer in their classrooms, and for the wealthy and powerful in Dallas to have the above-described soiree, the virulent antiliberal lawyer Roy Cohn had a similar victory celebration in New York City the evening that John Kennedy died, attended by Shirley McKinley, among others.[31]

Cohn was the man whom Senator Joe McCarthy relied on, and the two of them sat in judgment on the nation, both of them drinking heavily and engaging in homosexual saturnalias. Cohn ultimately died of AIDS, but not before destroying the lives of innocent victims with charges of being Communists or "com-symps." Many took their lives because of these two. Cohn hated Robert Kennedy, who was the minority counsel when McCarthy harassed the U.S. Army for their refusal to grant special treatment to Cohn's lover David Schine.

Drew Pearson's published diary tells the story that in 1952 he got a call from Texas "to tell me about a conspiracy which began about two years ago by H. L. Hunt, the big oilman, and a publicity firm called Watson Associations, to put Nixon into the vice presidency. He claims an untold amount of oil money had been behind Nixon for some time, and that all this was put over on Eisenhower without his knowing it."[32] Bernard Fensterwald notes that Hunt backed Representative Gerald R. Ford and "personally buttonholed various party officials at the Republican Convention in Miami to recommend a favorite conservative congressman as Richard Nixon's running mate."[33]

An interesting letter was written by H. M. Hart, a detective with the Criminal Intelligence Section of the Dallas Police Department, to Captain Gannaway, with regard to Lee Harvey Oswald's diary. "Sir: The following information was received from confidential informant T-1 regarding SUBJECT, reportedly sold to the DALLAS MORNING NEWS without permission of MARINA OSWALD.

"Source states that REPRESENTATIVE FORD (fnu), a member of the WARREN COMMISSION, sold SUBJECT to the DALLAS MORNING NEWS. MR. FORD had a copy of the diary and took it to executives of LIFE MAGAZINE and also NEWSWEEK magazine. Source states that these executives paid MARINA OSWALD, widow of LEE HARVEY OSWALD, $16,000 for the world copyright of the diary.

"Source further states that proof of this is in the hands of the DALLAS COUNTY DISTRICT ATTORNEY'S OFFICE."[34]

H. L. Hunt

Three days before President Kennedy was assassinated, H. L. Hunt parked his car in the same lot where Madeleine Brown left her car. They knew each other quite well, and Hunt called her over: "Come here, honey pie, I want to give you something!" and he handed her one of the flyers that was flooding the city of Dallas prior to Kennedy's visit on November 22, 1963. The flyer was a police-style mug shot of John F. Kennedy, front and side views, with the legend "Wanted For Treason" on them. They were later handed out all along Kennedy's parade route. H. L. Hunt had paid for the flyers, just as Hunt Oil money paid for the full-page add denouncing Kennedy that was carried in *The Dallas Morning News* the day of the murder.

Madeleine said, "Why, H.L., you can't do the President that way!"

Hunt snapped back with a sugary smile, "I can do anything I want. I'm the richest person in the world!"

Who was Haroldson Lafayette Hunt? The richest man in the world at the time, just about. The problem most people have in understanding all the mysteries we are faced with in this case flows from human nature. Too many are unaware of just how much power there is in being a billionaire, as Hunt was.

Hunt's children, after serious fighting among themselves over the inheritance when Hunt died, are interested in protecting their family name. They may be retaliating when some of us get too close. There is a lot of money out there paying some of the leading people in the research community. Often the way it works is that some wealthy person in Dallas or Houston backs a documentary show in England, let's say, that is later shown in the United States, and they pay an alleged witness $25,000 for an appearance, which, for example, Beverly Oliver, the alleged "Babushka Lady," allegedy received for her appearance in *The Men Who Killed Kennedy*, a movie that put forward one of several wild French assassin theories.

Hunt, a fifth-grade dropout, remained a recluse for many of his early adult years until *Life* published a photograph of him in 1948 and announced that he was the richest man in the nation. Until then, he had never been interviewed.

His obituary in *The Washington Post* said he may have been worth $5 billion when he died, "but nevertheless carried his lunch to work in a brown paper bag."[35] Hunt was the great anti-Communist fighter: "A self-made man who feared the Communist menace and said in 1967 that 'we have perhaps three, four, five years to save the republic,' he devoted much of his time and money that he did spend to efforts to spread his conservative views. He called them 'freedom education.' "[36] A main vehicle for that was the radio show *Life Line*.

Hunt was such a skinflint, according to those I talked to who knew him well, that "I don't think they had any friends in Dallas. He never gave to any charities much."

"Mr. Hunt gave me an eleven-cent tip and he thought he was giving me a life income," a waitress who remembers Hunt well told me at the Stonleigh Hotel. "But he was a sweet old man." Another working girl told me, "They judged people by their cars. They judged people by their looks, the way they dress. I didn't find Los Angeles as fake as this town!" She also told me that Dallasites are "judgmental, superficial, and bigoted. I just thought that was how all human beings are, growing up here. There is no integrity, no honor. Integrity and self-esteem go together." "In Texas, the outlaws are the good guys!" a waitress named Annie told me. "To live outside the law, you must be honest. In Dallas, money doesn't talk. It swears."

Hunt wrote a novel called *Alpaca,* which proposed a new constitution having elections based on educational qualifications and the ownership of property. The more taxes you pay, the more votes you get. Born in Vandalia, Illinois, Hunt roamed Arkansas, Louisiana, and Texas seeking to make his fortune, first buying cotton land and then buying oil leases in El Dorado, Arkansas. By 1923 he was starting to get rich in the oil fields, and six years later he made a fortune from the richest pool of oil in the world, which he got from Dad Joiner.

Hunt built a home in Dallas with his winnings. It was a replica of George Washington's Mount Vernon, only several times larger. "You have to be lucky," he once said about making money. "You have to be of an acquisitive nature, aggressive, and thrifty. You have to be honest and fair or at least have people think you are. You can't do a great volume of business unless your word is accepted."[37]

"Calvin Coolidge turned in the last successful administration. There was no subversive buildup whatever in Washington during Coolidge's term," Hunt said.[38] Hunt financed the printing of an anti-Kennedy, anti-Catholic sermon by the minister of his Baptist church, the Reverend W. H. Criswell, who officiated at Hunt's funeral. A Senate subcommittee and the Department of Justice investigated the pamphlet, and looked into both Hunt and his chief of staff, John A. Curington. "They are believed to be the source of some of the anti-Catholic literature being mailed in the campaign against Senator John F. Kennedy."[39]

Hunt was a bigamist, but he could get away with it because he had the money. His estate was sued by one of his wives, and a large settlement made on Frania Tye Lee, who married Hunt in 1925. She did not discover until 1934 that Hunt had another wife and six children living in Tyler, Texas. That was Lyda Bunker Hunt, whom Hunt had married in 1914. Lyda died in 1955, and Hunt married Ruth Ray Hunt in 1957.

Something had happened since Johnson became president in 1963. What? Hunt was asked if he liked all that the Johnson administration had done. "Not all of it," he replied. "When I backed Mr. Johnson for the vice presidency, he was more of a conservative.''[40] Johnson had put forward his civil rights program, and Hunt did not like him for that.

A mere four years before this, Hunt had said, ''that he thought that the United States faces imminent danger of bankruptcy and 'is moving toward communism.' He thinks the United States should pull out of the United Nations unless it gets a greater voice in that body, which, he says, 'already is dominated by the Communists. . . . and if we go along as we are, as we get sold on con-existence, we ourselves will become a Communist country.' Hunt thinks the times call for a 'strong man' in the White House and feels Senator Lyndon Johnson may be the answer. Curiously, Johnson is not among Hunt's favorite senators because of his 'New Deal voting record.' He much prefers the work of Senators Eastland, Talmadge, Bridges, Goldwater, Byrd, and other conservatives. . . . 'If we are to be saved from Communism, a strong man will have to do it. Johnson has shown he can be a strong man the way he leads those Democrats and Republicans around in the Senate as though they had rings in their noses.' ''[41]

It is well documented that various people connected to the crime trooped down to the Hunt offices shortly before the assassination. The Warren Commission had Jack Ruby there with a ''young lady who was job-hunting in Dallas.''[42] She was Connie Trammel, and Ruby took her to Lamar Hunt's office. He took her there the day before the assassination, and ''at roughly the same time that Mafia figure Jim Braden was visiting there. Strong possibilities exist of Braden connections to both Jack Ruby and David Ferrie in the days and weeks immediately preceding the assassination.''[43]

The Warren Commission tried to get Richard Helms of the CIA to tell them about any possible ties to H. L. Hunt and his son Lamar Hunt.[44] Why did they go to the CIA, an intelligence-gathering and covert-activities agency that was supposed to be dealing only in foreign countries? Helms did not respond to the Commission's request until the Warren Report was being printed. The Commission asked the following: ''H. L. Hunt and Lamar Hunt. . . . Name Lamar Hunt found in notebook of Ruby. Ruby visited his office on November 21. Hunt denies knowing Ruby. Ruby gives innocent explanation. Ruby found with literature of H. L. Hunt in his apartment after shooting Oswald.''[45]

There was a suspect in the case, Sergio Arcacha Smith, who had worked for H. L. Hunt. He was subpoenaed by Jim Garrison and refused to leave Texas. Governor John Connally refused to extradite him, and there Smith remained. Smith had been the New Orleans director of the Cuban Revolutionary Front (FRD), which was a linchpin of the Bay of

Pigs operation. Another group he belonged to was the Cuban Revolutionary Council, a CIA organization that was based at 544 Camp Street, in the same building where Guy Banister had an office. Smith worked closely with David Ferrie from the time of the Bay of Pigs.[46] Smith provides one link between Howard Hunt and H. L. Hunt because he knew and worked for Howard Hunt. Smith had been a diplomat under the brutal right-wing Cuban dictator whom Castro overthrew, Fulgencio Batista.

Hunt was so concerned about Jim Garrison's snooping around that he "Asked his security director, a former FBI agent, to keep up with developments in the case."[47] The memo was written by J. Walter Moore, the Dallas CIA chief who knew several players in this drama. He said that Hunt had been in touch with them.

As for the story in *Farewell America*[48] that H. L. Hunt had fled Dallas shortly after the assassination, this was verified to me, but he did not go to Mexico. He was in Washington, D.C., at the Mayflower Hotel the whole time, under the protection of the new president, Lyndon Johnson, and J. Edgar Hoover.[49] Hunt probably helped dictate the shape of the new administration.

Harold Weisberg and other "researchers" mounted a major operation to determine who wrote *Farewell America* and who was behind the book.[50] It is unclear why they went to such trouble, except that Weisberg's trips to Dallas were being paid with Hunt oil money, and the main point of *Farewell America* is that the oilmen were behind the murder of JFK.[51] For example, the book says, "Only the solidarity of the oil industry and, in some cases, fear kept certain habitués of the Fort Worth Petroleum Club, the Bayou and International clubs in Houston, The Club Imperial, the Cipango Club and the Public Affairs Luncheon Club of Dallas from talking in the months and weeks preceding November 22. Instead, they let matters take their course."[52]

An idea of the way Hunt thought in 1968—in sweeping generalities that left the specifics only for himself to know—was contained in one of his many letters to Dallas newspapers. In "Taking a Stand," he wrote the following: "The danger of loss of our Republic will be greatest during the next five years. Patriots should lay aside every other motive and do whatever they can in behalf of liberty versus slavery. It should be known on which side of any controversy each writer, speaker, or worker stands. Wolves in sheep's clothing can do more harm now than ever before. Fancy and unusual words affording a cover for evil design must be analyzed and the cover penetrated. Truth, moderated, may be made a lie.

"A title acquired a few years ago must not permit anyone to sabotage liberty and defame actual patriots. If we cannot possibly understand why someone has turned against freedom, their guilt is not less and they can do far more harm."[53]

Here is a man with the power personally to install a president, revealing the poverty of his mind, espousing a virtual police state over writers and thinkers, and exposing a kind of philistinism that feared words he wasn't familiar with. I ask every reader to take a long, hard look at the unique tale of a police state presented by Herbert Mitgang in *Dangerous Dossiers* and "Policing America's Writers."*

That police state was perpetrated by J. Edgar Hoover, one of the killers of John Kennedy, Robert Kennedy, and Martin Luther King, Jr., not to speak of many other political murders. Yes, the Mob was involved, but they didn't have to be involved *directly,* when they *owned* a piece of Hoover, just as Murchison and Hunt did. "In the case of the head of the FBI, a man who's responsible for national security, it takes on a special relevance of the possibility that he would be compromised by his sexuality,"[54] Anthony Summers writes. Summers says that Hoover was compromised by mobster Meyer Lansky, who, the author claims, used evidence of Hoover's alleged affair with associate Clyde Tolson to protect the Mafia. Many have written that Hoover blackmailed presidents, and that culminated, according to Summers, when Hoover used evidence of John Kennedy's sexual indiscretions to force JFK to pick Lyndon Johnson as his running mate.

Summers was quoted by reporter Bob Hoover as saying that Evelyn Lincoln, Kennedy's secretary, was the source of this story. "She said the reason was that [J. Edgar] Hoover had been supplying Johnson with sexual smear material and that if the Kennedys didn't pick him, John Kennedy would be exposed."[55]

Was H. L. Hunt Involved?

We should also ask if any other members of his family were involved.

Let's digress a moment. Apologists for H. L. Hunt argue that there wasn't anything in this for Hunt. Why would he be involved?[56] Ray Carroll published an article in *The Third Decade* dealing with the question of Hunt's involvement, which Carroll discounts. Carroll has raised some important issues so let's deal with them one at a time.

Craig Zirbel cites the following material:

*Herbert Mitgang, *Dangerous Dossiers* (New York: Donald I. Fine, Inc., 1988), and "Policing America's Writers," *The New Yorker* (October 5, 1987).

1. Hunt's son Bunker admitted contributing toward the cost of the "Welcome Mr. Kennedy" advertisement that appeared in the *Dallas Morning News* on November 22, 1963. Ray Carroll comments: "Not very clever on Bunker's part, to insult the President publicly if he was also planning an assassination."[57] Insult wasn't the word.

Well, consider that Bunker was one of the radical right John Birch Society's largest contributors.[58] He was one of the three owners of the Birch Society's *American Opinion* in 1964,[59] but it took him more than a decade to join the national council of the Society, in 1976, trying to keep a low profile after being prosecuted for wiretapping, obstruction of justice, and other crimes prior to his great scheme to corner the world's silver market. Bunker gave more than $250,000 a year to the Birch Society.[60] In one instance he gave more than $10 million for "Here's Life," part of Bum Right's Campus Crusade for Christ. His brother Herbert, also a radical right winger, put up only $1 million.[61] Actually, compared to other wealthy Texans, these and other gifts were a drop in the bucket, but it should give you an idea how much money the rich Texas political activists have to buy doctors, witnesses, medical associations, politicians, investigatory commissions, police, jet fighter, pilots and generals for hustling back and forth bone fragments, film, and testimony. This is not to say that Hunt's children did such a thing.

"Bunker's political activities also extended into more mainstream associations. Though larger than most of his father's contributions of record, many of Bunker's political gifts were of moderate size. . . . Bunker reserved his biggest political money for the 1968 presidential campaign of George C. Wallace. At one point, a disgruntled Wallace supporter charged that the John Birch Society was trying to 'take over' the Wallace campaign in Texas."[62] Wallace was the archsegregationist governor of Alabama who had bitterly resisted the Kennedy brothers' push for school integration in the South. His running mate was General Curtis LeMay, who had headed the Strategic Air Command and was a close friend of Air Force general Charles Cabell, whom Kennedy had fired. LeMay was a great hero of the far-right-wing militaristic element in the United States. Bunker had given $1 million to cushion LeMay and carry him through the campaign for the White House, which he and Wallace lost, though making a respectable showing.

With regard to 1., Ray Carroll cannot imagine the mentality of the Texas rich. Certainly the Hunts needed plenty of backing in their own backyard for what was about to happen, and the list of charges distributed against Kennedy the morning he died, along with a mug shot, made Kennedy an object of hatred and justified his murder in some minds. There are those who think Bunker and Lamar Hunt (who claims an alibi that day) were not told about what their father planned to do and therefore could have been led to distribute the mug shots to fool just this sort of research. Of course, those in Texas who have something to say about it, who believe that Lamar and Bunker did not have foreknowledge, are in a minority. Billie Sol Estes, it must be said, thinks the two brothers had no idea what was going to happen. And he ought to know. Carroll has proved nothing either way with this charge.

2. "H. L. Hunt had gambling contacts with Ruby in the 1950s." Comment: true. Ruby helped set up a scam designed to fleece Hunt and others of large sums of money.[63]

I uncovered evidence that Hunt and Ruby continued their association right up to the time of the assassination, and that Ruby supplied him with women, including one or two who became Hunt's close girlfriends. Hunt was glad to pay for what he got.

3. "Ruby stopped outside the offices of Lamar Hunt on November 21." Comment: true. Ruby was even thoughtful enough to arrange for an independent witness.[64]

The plotters really had nothing to fear. The attitude of gangsters when they own a local government is that it doesn't matter what they do, or who is seen with whom.

4. "Ruby had some of Hunt's conservative *Life Line* literature in his apartment." Comment: true. Ruby had picked up the literature three weeks previously and promised to send it to the White House. "Nobody has any right to talk like this about our government," he reportedly said.[65]

The fact that Ruby had some of Hunt's literature in his apartment does not mitigate against Hunt's having been involved. A guy like Ruby could say to one person, either as a joke or as a deception, *anything,* such as "Nobody has any right to talk like this about our Government," and it is one more enormously worthless statement from one more enormously worthless individual, unless you enjoy clubs like that, and it takes guys like him to run it. It was a popular place, obviously.

5. "In 1975 a curious letter surfaced, apparently in Mexico. It was directed to a Mr. Hunt, address unknown, and was purportedly written by Lee Harvey Oswald on November 8, 1963. Zirbel presents this letter, apparently expecting us to believe that it proves that one or another member of the family of H. L. Hunt was involved in an assassination plot with Oswald. Curiously enough, the FBI investigated the letter on the assumption that it was intended for Bunker Hunt. The results of the FBI probe have not been released,[66] but Zirbel appears to have the distinction of being the first Warren Commission critic to be on the FBI's wavelength." (It's not clear what Carroll means here.)

I agree with Ray Carroll on this one, that the letter addressed to "Mr. Hunt" proves nothing at all, since we have no idea which Hunt it was intended for.

6. "Zirbel cites a disgruntled former Hunt employee as claiming that he saw Marina Oswald in Hunt's office shortly after the assassination."[67] Comment: Zirbel neglects to mention that the Hunt family and Marina have repeatedly denied this allegation. Anyway, Marina and old man Hunt could not have had a very exciting conversation because Zirbel's witness apparently forgot to notice whether there was a Russian translator present. One question for Zirbel: If Hunt really was as fanatical an LBJ supporter as Zirbel would have us believe, why did he throw his support behind Barry Goldwater in 1964?[68]

Carroll argues that Marina Oswald and the Hunt family deny that Marina was ever in the Hunts' offices as described by John Currington. Marina said a lot of things she was coached to do, and often contradicted herself. She did not speak English well, and perhaps did not always understand the question, or was a victim of inaccurate translations. In addition, neither Carroll nor anyone else who was not present has any idea if a translator was present. But whether Marina was or was not at the Hunt offices a month after the assassination is of little importance with regard to Hunt's involvement in the conspiracy. Hunt helped a lot of people, and perhaps he passed some money to Marina, which she would understandably be forbidden ever to mention. We know that the poor woman got a lot of help and financial support. Quite clearly, Marina was well protected and provided for.

Ray Carroll's article ends with an interesting quote from H. L. Hunt: "For the continued progress of the country he so courageously served, the assassination of President Kennedy should not be soon forgotten and should be openly and often reviewed, discussed, and analyzed. The tragic event and its catastrophic results will be with us for years. The better it is understood, the less paralyzing the tragedy will be; and John F. Kennedy would be last to desire that blame be ascribed to anyone who is blameless."[69]

As far as this quote is concerned, it was the safe thing to say when one is so politically active. What most political people say and what they do are entirely different things. Knowing what I know about 1963, I cannot believe that Hunt was moved by Kennedy's death. In fact, he not only was glad to see Kennedy go, but also toasted his death, and went immediately to Washington to assume control with Lyndon Johnson and J. Edgar Hoover.

Finally, Carroll asks why Hunt then backed Goldwater in the following election in 1964. Easy. Hunt hated black people and certainly did not like the idea of their voting. He wrote *Alpaca,* his crazy novel, about not allowing popular elections. When Lyndon Baines Johnson tried to act like a statesman and salve his guilty conscience by passing his monumental Civil Rights Act, Hunt could not abide that. Besides, Hunt basically was a Republican in philosophy, and why should he go on supporting Johnson, when Johnson turned out to be such a liberal in other respects? Hunt was a fiscal conservative, and Johnson promptly began to betray those who had backed him. The Romans and the Praetorian Guard repeatedly overthrew emperors and then turned on their replacements. There is nothing new in this.

Another view comes from someone close to the principals in the case, someone who grew up with Billie Sol Estes and who has been privy since adolescence to the discussions of people knowledgeable of the plot itself.

Kyle Brown should know. He worked for Brown & Root for years, and he was a private investigator. Brown & Root was a huge construction firm that financed Johnson and was a principal benefactor of the Vietnam War. We had a discussion about the plot in early 1993, and I asked him if they brought the eastern Establishment from New York into it.[70] "Well, *they had to*! But it wasn't just New York. This thing had to be agreed upon across the board, because you can't . . . they all had a stake in it, in what they could or couldn't do."

The point is this: Any group that tried to overthrow the government or kill a president in this country without obtaining the consent of the most powerful people in the American Establishment—who in fact have more power than the government, which is nothing more than their hired administration—would be crazy.

Carroll wrote me that he thought Hunt had no motive, unless he was upset about the oil depletion allowance: "That would give him . . . a motive. Johnson and Hoover had a motive, but Hunt did not. If he was minded to engage in criminal activity, to bribe a few senators, it would not, in my judgment, provide an adequate motive for murder. We can infer a motive for Johnson or Hoover based on the possibility or probability that JFK was planning to send either or both into retirement, or that even if JFK had no such plans to the extent it could be shown that either Johnson or Hoover or both *believed* he had such plans."[71]

Hunt had a long history of financing radicals, some of whom were involved in violent activities. His MO was political action, so he would need only his own ideological agenda to back any sort of plot. He was not beyond killing people. Numerous people have commented that Hunt maintained a stable of assassins in Mexico. How can someone build such an enormous empire so quickly? One way is as follows: "If they didn't play his game, they went in and took it. They pulled no punches. They had no morals. They had no rules. It was strictly power. They were absolutely ruthless.''[72]

"H.L. had every lawyer in Dallas doing something for him. That way he owned them all. He'd give them a little piece of the pie, and nobody could find a lawyer big enough to stand up to him.''

I have established through personal interviews that Hunt was greatly incensed at Kennedy's plan to remove the oil depletion allowance. How *could* he have accepted it?

Dan Smoot, who had been an FBI agent and worked for J. Edgar Hoover, was transferred to Dallas, where he resigned and went to work for H. L. Hunt and his *Facts Forum* national radio show. He was a radical right winger and involved in the printing of some of the anti-Kennedy material. An example of Smoot's thinking is the following: "... People were blindly following the philosophy of the New Deal, which stands for a total transfer of power from the individual to the federal government under the claim of using the power beneficently. This is the same philosophy of the Fair Deal, the New Frontier, and modern Republicans. ... It is also the basic philosophy of communism, fascism, and Nazism."[73]

Note that this is one more link with Hoover, Dallas, and violent anti-Kennedy sentiment.

Hunt, according to Kirkpatrick Sales, gave "most of his propaganda money to his own Life Line Foundation (which puts out a magazine, pamphlets and radio broadcasts to some 100 stations with over a million listeners), but had something left over for his friend Dan Smoot, for Texas rightist groups like Youth Freedom Speakers and a Public Service Educational Institute, and for every conservative politician coming down the pike (George Wallace, Douglas MacArthur, Joseph McCarthy, General Edwin Walker, and various local mossbacks); Hunt was even magnanimous enough to have given money to such dangerous people as Barry Goldwater, Lyndon Johnson, and Richard Nixon, despite his stated belief that the United States is run by a Communist government."[74] Hunt gave at least $250,000 to support Alabama segregationist Governor George C. Wallace in his bid for the presidency,[75] because "he's like us on the nigger situation," as Henry L. Seale, a Dallas millionaire, said.[76]

There are many people from Texas who feel that when John Connally blurted out after receiving his wound, "My God, they're going to kill us all!" that he had foreknowledge of the murder. It also would appear that the shot that hit him wasn't a miss or "magical," but an intent to kill him. This shot almost made for too many bullets from one rifle in a limited amount of time. But that was no real problem in a state where people with five gunshot wounds are routinely ruled "suicide." It's no problem when coroners routinely cover up police murders.

Then there are those who are run off the road and killed. "That is the way they do it in Texas when people get decrepit and have outlived their usefulness, or who have come too close to the truth. They get themselves run off the road."

Clint Peoples

In Texas, it happened to U.S. Marshal Clint Peoples of Waco on June 23, 1992, and it happened to Malcolm "Mac" Wallace, a suspect in the case and named as one of the trigger men by those who should know. Wallace was an employee of the U.S. Department of Agriculture and was part of the matrix in the department that got into so much trouble with Billie Sol Estes. Estes survived. Others closely involved with Johnson and Estes did not.

"There were about eight or nine murders around Estes," Madeleine Brown told me. Estes says it was to protect Johnson.[77] After all, he was the President. But the murders started before LBJ was president.

Clint Peoples was well known. He had been a famous Texas Ranger. You would think that killing a U.S. marshal would be forbidden, for the same reasons that the Mafia normally does not kill citizens. Just their own. But in Texas, a U.S. Marshal is of little account.

Peoples told Madeleine that he had documents saying that Mac Wallace was on the grassy knoll and was one of the gunmen.[78] Peoples helped Henry Marshall who was one of those killed over Johnson's dirty deals. Marshall lived two hours after the accident.

Madeleine Brown spoke to Peoples on Friday, June 19, 1992. Peoples died on the twenty-third, a Tuesday. Of importance is the fact that Madeleine Brown and an investigator for Oliver Stone, Jeff Flach, were going to meet Peoples that Tuesday. "Clint was apprehensive," she said.

I have seen the concern in the faces of those who knew about Peoples' fate. There is pain and fear in their eyes. They know what that death meant: Peoples had told those who found him that he had been run off the road.

Peoples told Brown that there was a Wallace plumbing truck in Dealey Plaza. Mac Wallace was from Dallas, and his family owned a plumbing business.

The Order to Kill

Madeleine Brown says that she thinks it worked like this: Vice President Lyndon Johnson got the order from H. L. Hunt to kill Kennedy, and Johnson called Mac Wallace.

Wallace called Jack Puterbaugh to change the route of the motorcade, Brown says, and just before they all got into the car, there was a violent fight between Connally and Johnson.

"Wallace was the mastermind and he hired the other two shooters. There were three shooters." How does she know this? Did she hear it, and if so, from whom? Or is it her opinion? Brown is friendly with a former FBI man and chief of security for one of the oilmen. He ought to know. Did she hear it from him? "No. I heard it in bits and pieces from Johnson and the others around him. From Billie Sol."

She went on. "Meanwhile, people were dropping dead in Texas all over the place from the agriculture scandal. And Billie Sol was in deep shit," she said, with true Texas flair. "Lyndon was in trouble over Estes, Bobby Baker, and Walter Jenkins, who was caught in a gay bar. Hoover framed him, I think. Hoover was real good at making trouble like that for people."

I liked Madeleine. My assessment of her was that she was about 65 percent accurate.

One could interpret the actions of Ricky White accusing his father of being one of the shooters as a need for money and fame, but maybe not. It is hard to imagine people exposing crimes of their family or former loved ones. Madeleine had taken many years to come full circle from the time she had loved LBJ toward trying to get out the truth about Lyndon. When we are in love or impressed by big money and power, we don't easily look at what is wrong with the person with whom we are involved.

"Charles Cabell handled the rest."

"What do you mean?!"

"He took care of the Washington end of it, and kept his brother [Earle Cabell, the mayor of Dallas] in line. They needed the Mayor's help to cover it up." Earle Cabell went to Washington the following year as a congressman.

My information is that Lady Bird Johnson, still alive, is one of only two living people who can bear witness to most or all of the story of what happened to John Kennedy. Billie Sol Estes is the other person, but there are others in this chapter who knew a great deal.

John Curington

We started at the top, so to speak, when Larry Howard and I went to see John Curington, former No. 1 aide to H. L. Hunt in those years.[79] "I sure wish you fellows had come through here a long time ago!" he said over the phone after our first meeting.[80] At first we thought we were going to get the gate when we went out to see him at his ranch, but both he and his wife, Mary Anne, were most gracious.

"I ran the entire operation," Curington said of his job with Hunt.

Unfortunately, Curington was taken away to jail not long after we talked to him, and the feds wouldn't tell me where they took him. I spoke to his son and learned that they had been forbidden to reveal where he was. The indications were that he had been set up and his conviction was some sort of retaliation for opening his mouth to the wrong people. Of course, others who had known him well said that he would do anything for money. When I interviewed Curington, I had no idea he was going to go to prison. Sometimes I am too late and they are already dead or taken away, so I was lucky to have had the opportunity to talk to him. Eventually I learned he was in a facility in Tennessee.

His lovely and gracious wife was caught in the middle—like most wives—because she had no idea what her husband was doing. He pled guilty to a charge of uttering a false statement to a financial institution, probably something of which many people are guilty. This is not to say that I condone lawbreaking, because I don't.

Since I was able to corroborate what Curington told us, I feel that much of what he had to say was good information. I hope to learn more from him.

H. L. Hunt had told Curington that there was a conspiracy in the assassination. "Whenever we had a message to give to Lyndon, it went through one person, Boothe Mooney, and was directly communicated by him to Johnson. He'd have a world of correspondence."

Curington, an attorney, was a wiry good ol' boy, affecting the costume of old-time Texas hard-ass, just like in the movies: cowboy boots, handlebar mustache, and a black Stetson wide-brim cowboy hat. Having worked the oil fields of West Texas and Hobbs, New Mexico, as a roustabout was an advantage because I could talk the native language.

"I have no doubt that Lyndon Johnson may have ordered John Kennedy's murder. He or his wife. She was more vicious than he. Even more brutal." Curington explained that Johnson was about to be destroyed forever politically. "It was either him or Kennedy. He might have brought down the whole Kennedy presidency with the scandals he was involved in. And Johnson was valuable to us and a lot of people in office.''

He recalled seeing Marina Oswald visiting Hunt's private offices. Marina has denied this story, but perhaps she had compelling reasons to do so. I cannot believe that Curington made this up. He had been asked to clear the executive offices one night a few weeks after the assassination. ''Hunt asked me to lock everything up and prevent anyone from coming upstairs on the elevator. As I waited, an elevator came down and Marina Oswald came out of it, left the building, and got into a waiting car. I'm absolutely sure it was her.''

It was Curington who came into possession of the alleged Oswald letter to a ''Mr. Hunt'' and gave it to the FBI. Penn Jones received it with a Mexican postmark. Handwriting tests demonstrated that the letter was, in fact, written by Oswald. We might assume, therefore, that it was not addressed to E. Howard Hunt of Watergate fame and suspected by some of involvement in the assassination. Curington believes that H. L. Hunt wanted to question Marina about what Oswald had told her and what she might know of Oswald's letter to him.

Curington said that H. L. Hunt had daily reports from Washington on the investigation conducted by the Warren Commission. He was intensely interested in what went on there. Hunt's statements to his top aides about there being a conspiracy was confirmed to reporters by Walter Tabaka, his longtime lobbyist in Washington.

Curington said that Hunt had often said that the United States would do better without Kennedy, but that right wingers who heard this took it to mean that they ought to kill Kennedy. He thinks that some of those who were close to Hunt did, in fact, participate in the murder. Some of the groups involved with H. L. Hunt were the KKK; the Minute Men; the John Birchers; and Liberty Lobby, whom Mark Lane later defended in a lawsuit brought by Howard Hunt.

Curington also maintained that some of those intelligence operatives and free-lancers who were close to Nixon were also close to Johnson. The *same men,* in other words, were working for both men, and they may have organized the plot. ''Oh, I think so!'' Mr. Curington said in answering my question if some of the Watergate operatives and other longtime Nixon intelligence agents were close to Johnson.

''Lyndon wasn't dumb. He knew he was going to be dumped. Those people with that kind of ambition will do just about anything,'' Curington said.

Did Hunt have actual personal knowledge that there was a conspiracy, or were his statements to his aides in 1967 just speculation? "He knew," Curington told me.

Curington had previously told reporters William Dick and Ken Potter, "These Hunt followers overreacted. Believing they were acting on Hunt's veiled instructions, they set out to eliminate Kennedy—literally."[81]

For Curington, Hunt was a patriot whose views were distorted by the radical right. "They plunged America into tragedy."

My impression of Curington is that he was just performing a job when he worked for Hunt and did not necessarily share Hunt's political views. Curington seemed to me a liberal, tolerant, and gentle man who could not have been a fanatic of any kind. He may have also been ruthless and a crook who would do anything for money, as others say.

Interestingly, Hunt asked Curington to go down to Central Police Headquarters after Oswald was arrested and check on how the security was. "I reported to him that there was no security there. Hunt was very happy about that. I wondered why he wanted this information, but I never questioned him. I just did what he asked me to do. That's what I was paid to do. Fortunately, there wasn't anything I was asked to do that was unconscionable."

Curington also told us that Hunt had asked him to check on the elevators in the building that transported the prisoners. "I thought this was rather strange, but I did so, and even ended up in the same elevator with Oswald and his police escort, quite by accident. I could have easily killed Oswald right then. Hunt was right glad to hear that the elevators had no security. I walked in and out of the building three times and nobody ever checked me or my briefcase," he said. Of course, Roy Vaughn, the patrolman who was assigned to guard the ramp, passed lie detector tests at the time showing that he was telling the truth when he said Ruby never came down that way nor could Ruby have slipped by when Vaughn wasn't looking. Ruby came down the elevator with the assistant chief of police, but nobody dared admit that.[82]

"Don't forget that Johnson had one goal from birth: to be president. That's all he thought about, and he would do anything to achieve that goal. He lived, ate, and slept being president, and when he knew that he was going to be dumped in 1964, he knew that it was either him or Kennedy. In fact, his career was probably over right then because of the Bobby Baker scandal. So it was him or Kennedy."

Our problem is that we are walking through a minefield.

I also want to add that Curington confirmed every point in the article in the *National Enquirer* tabloid in 1977.[83] He thought a few adjectives were not true to his speaking style but that it was good journalism. Meanwhile, the *Enquirer* checked up on him with voice stress analysis, and wrote that Curington had a clean bill of health: Everything he said was what he believed to be the truth.

Curington had told me what I've just written before I knew about or read the article about him that appeared years before in the tabloid. In fact, he gave us the article as we were leaving. All this was before I corroborated what he said with considerable detail from other witnesses.

Curington knew far from the whole story, but he had part of it, and was wrong on an essential point: H. L. Hunt probably ordered Johnson to have Kennedy killed.

Madeleine Brown

Brown is widely known to have been one of Lyndon Johnson's many women, though she was closer to him than most, and had a son by him. The son died in 1992. She came under fire for going public with the story but, in my talks with her, I thought she had genuinely become repulsed by the memory of Johnson and what she believed to be the conspiracy that murdered John Kennedy.

Brown began to see the good in Kennedy, and looked back on him more fondly. She says, "It is a terrible tragedy that he is gone, and that we have lost that forever. Kennedy was a good man, and I don't think anyone here in Dallas understood him." She said she realized they were all wrong about Kennedy and deeply regretted her past hostility toward him, which was learned from the big money in town.

Madeleine Brown took a chance talking with me. Never before had she said very much of what she knew about the murder, other than that Johnson had indicated to her that he had knowledge of it the night before Kennedy was killed.

Madeleine did not choose to reveal any of this even in her own unpublished book *Texas in the Morning: My Secret Life with LBJ,* which she said was more of a love story. "It's a romance," she told me. On another occasion, I asked her what Lyndon's attraction was. "Well, it certainly wasn't the way he talked, because he had the foulest mouth imaginable. I can swear like a trooper myself, but he was pretty filthy. He used to do a lot of filthy things, too, like pee in public, though I guess that isn't so bad.

"I suppose it was sex appeal. He was a big stud in bed and took care of a woman. He was a good lover. But I was attracted to the money and power that surrounded him, and that enchances sex appeal."

*   *   *

"John Connally knows something about the assassination but won't talk about it. They tried to kill him because he knew what happened,"[84] Madeleine Brown told me.

"There was some sort of serious break between John Connally and Lyndon," she told me. She said that C. Horace Busby, who was on *Air Force One* that tragic day, knew something about it. Connally had control of the Syd Richardson estate, and received a large sum of money each year for administering it. The control of that estate gave him considerable power in addition to what he already had.

"Lyndon Johnson did not die naturally." She thought that his Secret Service people killed him. "They hated him," she said.

"I just knew H. L. Hunt on a one-to-one basis. He pulled no punches. He said, 'Why, me and R. L. Thornton own Dallas and we run it like we want to!' " R. L. Thornton, a banker, built the Mercantile Bank Building, where Hunt occupied two floors.

The most likely place for some of the shots from behind was the Dal Tex building, across the street from the TSBD. The owners of the Dal Tex Building were Morris J. Russ and D. R. Weisblat in 1963 at the time of the assassination. Dallas Uranium and Oil was on the sixth floor of the Dal Tex Building. The second or third floor was a good place to shoot out of a window down Elm street at a car going away. It was a better place to shoot from than practically straight down through the floorboards of the car from the Texas School Book Depository Building. In fact, it was there that Jim Braden was picked up.

"Talk to John Norris," Madeleine said. "First he'll tell you that Khrushchev killed Kennedy. But keep working on him. Then you'll find out that there were three plots to kill Kennedy, and the other two were backup plots. One of them was LBJ's plot, which took JFK out with the KGB's help." John Norris was a Secret Service man who worked for Hoover and for LBJ.

We were having dinner at her club, The Top of the Cliff, in Oak Cliff, where Ruby and Oswald lived.

"Brown & Root were in bankruptcy in the thirties, and in trouble with the IRS. Roosevelt and Lyndon got them off the hook," Madeleine told me.[86] Both Herman and George Brown became among Lyndon's biggest backers, along with H. L. Hunt and the other oilmen. Clark Clifford was an important man in Democratic administrations, including those of John F. Kennedy and Lyndon Johnson. Not until the BCCI scandal did the other side of the Clifford coin reveal itself. That bank was, of course, up to its ears as a government front for many covert activities throughout the world.

Madeleine Brown says that when Averell Harriman died, Clark Clifford sealed all of his files and records. Why? His widow is Pam Harriman, who was Winston Churchill's daughter-in-law.

Another source, highly placed, told me, "I think that Herman Brown may have been as close to Lyndon Johnson as any of the business establishment ever was. You understand that Herman Brown was in the construction business primarily. Lyndon Johnson bailed him out during the time he was congressman. He got Herman a contract to build a highway. It rained like hell and Herman couldn't make the deadline, and Lyndon intervened for Brown—and I don't think it was Brown & Root at that time, it was just Herman Brown & Co. And he was something like a hundred days over and there was a penalty on that, and as a result I believe he intervened and got them to waive the penalty because of an act of God. And that saved Herman from going busted."

I wanted to know if Hunt knew Ruby. "I'm here to tell you he knew him!" she exclaimed. She knew both men, of course. Brown stated that it was probably Hunt who called Ruby and ordered him to kill Lee Harvey Oswald.

Madeleine Brown knew Roscoe White, who used to work for Clay Page's pharmacy on Jefferson in Oak Cliff, now a Rexall drugstore. White worked there before he was hired by the Dallas Police Department in 1963. Madeleine followed the 1990–92 stories emanating out of the Assassination Information Center in Dallas with great interest, since she knew Roscoe. Gary Shaw and the local research contingent claimed that Roscoe was the gunman on the Grassy Knoll, whom they all claimed they could see in the fuzzy Mooreman photograph. They claim that the gunman is standing on the bumper of an automobile to explain why his badge and chest are visible over the high fence. This is a highly unlikely scenario, since a shooter would want to use the fence to hide behind, for cover.

"Why, I knew Roscoe pretty well," said the lady who seemed to know everybody, "and he couldn't have done anything like that. He was kind and gentle. He could not possibly have participated in such a crime!" Dallas was a big small town, and everybody knew everybody else.

Madeleine believed that the Rickie White story that his father, Roscoe, was one of the shooters was hokum because she had knowledge of one of the leading researchers in Fort Worth fabricating one of the photographs backing the story. She knew an awful lot about what went on with the publication project for Rickie's book about his father's role in the assassination. When there was a falling out with Gary Shaw and the others, White told an editor at Viking that the whole story was a lie. The book deal fell through. Viking also had Gary Shaw and Jens Hansen tone down their book with Dr. Charles Crenshaw, which had Johnson ordering the Parkland emergency room team to kill Oswald.[87]

Brown was one of the many people in Dallas and perhaps elsewhere in Texas who kept track of who was dying and how.

She told me that Cliff Carter, a former aide to Johnson, died a day or two after he told U.S. marshal Clint Peoples that he was "in fear of his life over Watergate" in 1972.

Billie Sol Estes says that he was present for some of these planning meetings and saw Cliff Carter there.

"Peoples hated Barefoot Sanders!" she told me. Sanders was appointed a U.S. attorney by Lyndon Johnson.

"Don't you know that they were all connected?" she asked me.

"What do you mean?"

"Nixon and Johnson's men! They were all working together," she said. Of course, this was an argument I was establishing in my writing and she had read.

I pursued this matter further with her. *"Why,* Harry, *why* do you think that John J. McCloy and Richard Nixon were there when Kennedy died? Don't you know it was a joining of the forces, that they put aside their warfare and came together to kill Kennedy? Don't you know it was the same men working for both? The same agents? Whatever party it was didn't matter."

This was in line with my own feelings. She went on, "The oilmen were Texas Democrats. They were as conservative as the day is long. They wanted Eisenhower to run as a Democrat, but he wouldn't, so they backed him anyway as a Republican, and they still owned him. Party doesn't mean anything. It didn't mean anything then and it doesn't mean anything now."

This was a woman who was making love to a President on a regular basis and had a son by him. We need to pay attention to what she says. She wasn't always right, and it was necessary to sort out what she actually saw or heard from what was secondhand, but much of what she said, I found, was verifiable.

"There's only two living people," she said, "who know most of what happened to John Kennedy." Lady Bird (Johnson's wife) seemed to be one of them. The other was Billie Sol Estes. "Billie Sol took the fall for Lyndon," she said. She ought to know. Both she and Larry Howard talk to him every week.

"Bobby Kennedy went to see Billie Sol Estes when he was in jail in 1965 or so to find out what he knew about his brother's death. He wanted him to tell everything he knew.

"Billie Sol told him, no, that he wasn't ready to die yet." Madeleine said that the source for this story is Billie Sol, and Kyle Brown, who had been employed with Brown & Root.

Brown says that Billie Sol knows all three shooters.[88]

Malcolm Wallace is one of the suspects. He was named to me by several people as having been one of the triggermen. He was a hatchet man for Johnson. He died in Pittsburg, Texas, in about 1971.

Did Lyndon Johnson have anything to do with the assassination of Kennedy, or did he have foreknowledge of it? There are some other arrows also pointing in his direction. Jack Ruby wrote a letter in jail that denounced Johnson: "In all the history of the U.S. never has a president been elected that has the background of Johnson. Believe me compared to him, I am a saint."[89] Would anyone writing such a statement have been a part of a plot to put Johnson in power? Ruby went on to say, "I walked into a trap the moment I walked down that ramp Sunday morning. They alone planned the killing, by they I mean Johnson and others."[90]

We know from Dr. Phillip Earle Williams and Dr. Charles Crenshaw that Johnson called the emergency room at Parkland when Oswald was nearly dead.[91] He also called Captain Will Fritz during the homicide investigation.[92]

Fritz said that in the twenty-four hours after Oswald's arrest, people called him to tell him to stop his investigation. "You have your man," they said. Finally a phone call came from Lyndon Johnson. "When the President of the United States called me and *ordered* the investigation stopped, what could I do?"[93]

Madeleine says that Bill Alexander, the Assistant District Attorney, told her that "nobody fired through that window" (the sixth floor of the Texas School Book Depository). She says that Roy Truly gave Lee Harvey Oswald's description to Bill Alexander and Captain W. R. Westbrook, and Westbrook said, "I think this is who I am going to arrest!"

She told me that Jean Hill's book was not on the up and up. "That book is fabricated. Jean Hill is another straw witness," she said. Jean Hill was a sort of Dallas Police groupie in 1963. Madeleine told me a story about going to see Jean Hill with Ken Bradbury and Billie Sol Estes in 1990. "Ken knew the way to Jean's house without ever looking at a map or anything else. Maybe he knew that street for some other reason, but I was just stunned at how he went right there without asking directions. It's not an easy place to find."

Madeleine thought they were going there to see if Jean recognized

Ken Bradbury, whom she thinks was in Dealey Plaza when Kennedy got shot. Was Bradbury one of the men standing across the street from Jean by the Umbrella Man?

With regard to Jean Hill's book, one might bear in mind that there were certain embellishments added to many of these books. Madeleine put me in touch with Gayle Nix Jackson, and there I learned quite a story about the theft and suppression of her father's film.

Jackson had insisted that the film had been stolen, but months later she indicated that she had received payment and the matter was settled.[94]

Along with numerous others, she said that Beverly Oliver, identified by Gary Shaw as the Babushka Lady—the woman seen on the Zapruder film near Jean Hill with a scarf over her head—isn't the Babushka Lady in the photos. One of the problems with Oliver, who was married to gangster George McGann, is that she claimed to shoot a moving picture during the assassination with a super eight camera that was not publicly available at the time of the assassination.[95] She says Yashika wrote her recently, saying the camera did, in fact, exist. Her cousin, former deputy sheriff Al Maddox, says that Oliver really is the Babushka Lady. Oliver wrote a strong defense of her story in *The Third Decade* in July 1993 but said that she is not the dark-haired woman in the photographs published in Shaw and Harris's book *Cover Up*. Oliver answered charges that she is not who she says she is, and took issue with Shaw on a number of points he should have known better about, since he discovered her. Her complaint is that once someone writes a false statement about a person in this case, as Shaw did about Jack Lawrence, many other authors repeat it, without investigating, to the damage and emotional trauma of the victim. We are all guilty of this.

"Do you want to know why Nixon and Hoover were at the Murchison party? Because they supported the oilmen's interests. They put Ike in power because they felt the times required a military man." And the Cold War, I might add. "Nixon, Nolan, J. Edgar Hoover promoted the oil interests, and General Douglas MacArthur's top aide was one of Hunt's top guys," Brown said. We couldn't find the aide's name, though.

"Hunt hated with a passion John Kennedy. This was right down LBJ's alley," she said. "Allan Dulles, LBJ, and Charles Cabell were all in bed together." Connally worked for Sid Richardson until he died. Sid and Clint Murchison, Sr., came from Athens, Texas. "They were lifetime buddies."

LBJ

Lyndon Johnson, with a lot of fingers pointing at him for involvement in the assassination of JFK, was well aware that in spite of the official findings of his handpicked Warren Commission, everyone who knew the case spoke of the "conspiracy" long after the Warren Report was released. So Johnson established false trails leading everywhere but to him and his friends.

Johnson confided to his aide that the CIA was involved. Johnson staffer Marvin Watson told FBI executive Cartha DeLoach that Johnson had told him he believed that the CIA had something to do with the assassination of President Kennedy and that there was a plot.[96] From this we are supposed to infer that Johnson would not have known about J. Edgar Hoover's involvement and was making a clumsy attempt to direct the FBI at the CIA, whom he was afraid of, evidently. At the same time, we are to get the idea that Johnson was trying to direct attention away from himself and his friends.

The FBI and Dallas

The order came down from LBJ after the assassination for the FBI to take over the case from the Dallas Police. Retired FBI agent Robert Gemberling told the story to Mark Oakes.[97] "We put the Dallas Police in a bad spot," he said. "We had absolutely no legal jurisdiction in the case, and we went in there like gangbusters and took away all of their evidence and investigation." In the same interview with Oakes, Gemberling confirmed that it was FBI agent Robert Barrett who picked up an apparent .45 slug from the grass across the street near the triple underpass. Photographs have been widely published. Patrolman Joe Foster stands in the background of the picture, along with Deputy Sheriff Buddy Walthers. Barrett himself indicated in a letter to Oakes that it was he. A week later Barrett retracted the identification.[98] The bullet disappeared from the evidence. There are indications that a pistol was fired that day and that Kennedy was hit with a .45 slug. Some of the Secret Service men said that what they heard were pistol shots.

Some of the other members of the FBI office in Dallas who worked closely with Barret were Robert Gemberling, James Hosty, Vincent Drain, Arnold J. Brown, Charles Brown, Robert Lish, W. Harlan Brown, Walter Bent, Burnett Tom Carter, Manning Clemments, John W. Fain, Bardwell Odum, Will Hayden Griffin, Arthur E. Carter, Walter Heitman, Emory E. Horton, Milton L. Newsom, Regis Kennedy, Edwin D. Kuykendall, Al Manning, and Ivan Lee. The head of the office was Gordon Shanklin. My source says that both Barrett and Bardwell Odum were Hunt's men. Warren de Brueys followed Oswald back and forth from new Orleans to Dallas.

Shortly after completing their search of the Texas School Book Depository and entering the basement of City Hall en route to the Special Service Bureau office, Detective V. J. Brian and Lieutenant Jack Revill met FBI agent James Hosty "walking very fast toward the entrance of the City Hall from the parking area. At this time Agent Hosty made the statement that Lee Oswald had killed the President and that Oswald was a Communist. Hosty also said that he knew that Oswald was a Communist and that he knew Oswald was working at the School Book Depository."[99]

The statement in the above letter had been written by Detective V. J. Brian several months after the assassination, but another letter, ostensibly written the day of the assassination by Jack Revill to Captain Gannaway, described the same meeting with Hosty. "At that time Agent Hosty related to this officer that the Subject was a member of the Communist Party, and that he was residing in Dallas. The Subject was arrested for the murder of Officer J. D. Tippit and is a prime suspect in the assassination of President Kennedy. The information regarding the Subject's affiliation with the Communist Party is the first information this officer has received from the Federal Bureau of Investigation regarding same. Agent Hosty further stated that the Federal Bureau of Investigation was aware of the Subject and that they had information that this Subject was capable of committing the assassination of President Kennedy."[100] So why didn't the FBI do something about it? Why didn't they alert the Secret Service prior to November 22, 1963?

FBI agent Robert Gemberling told Mark Oakes that Hosty's destruction of Oswald's note to Hosty "did more to damage the credibility of the Bureau than any other act."[101] Gemberling went on to say that there were two versions of the note but that it had no bearing whatsoever on the assassination. The note said that Oswald would retaliate if Hosty didn't leave his wife alone.

Lieutenant Jack Revill wrote Captain Gannaway the following memorandum: "On November 22, 1963 J. E. Curry, Chief of Police, Dallas, Texas appeared on a television broadcast and made a statement to the effect that agents of the Federal Bureau of Investigation had prior information and knowledge regarding the SUBJECT, and that the SUBJECT was a communist. The source reported that shortly after this appearance, GORDON SHANKLIN, the Senior Agent in Charge of the Dallas office of the FBI, received instructions from his superior in Washington, D.C. to obtain a retraction of the above statement from Chief J. E. CURRY.

GORDON SHANKLIN was told that if he did not obtain this retraction, he would be terminated from the Bureau. Mr. SHANKLIN visited Chief J. E. CURRY and the following news release was made: Chief CURRY stated that to 'his own personal knowledge, the FBI did not have any previous information regarding Lee Harvey Oswald nor about Oswald being a communist.''[102] The FBI covered its ass.

Files are missing from the local library and the newspapers for the history of Mayor Cabell, and so on. Light-fingered researchers—a common problem in the critical community—might explain part of it, and cover-up might explain the rest.

The Dallas Police had kept their files secret until 1992, when they voluntarily released them, with the prodding of Domingo Garcia, a city councilman who pushed for their release.

Vickie Mayne

Vickie Mayne was sixteen on the day that John Kennedy died. She helped do the work in her parents' film lab when the Secret Service brought in all of the photos, films, and the Zapruder film they had rounded up in Dealey Plaza. She told me that she had seen photographs of Kennedy's body taken at Parkland Hospital, a fact that no outsider was aware of. She remembered this with great clarity because she threw up upon seeing them.[103] What else could make her throw up but pictures of a dead body and its terrible wounds?

Two couples owned the lab, the National Photo Company, and the Secret Service supposedly allowed them to retain copies of all the pictures they developed that day.[104] If this is true, it would seem an unlikely scenario that the Secret Service conspired to kill President Kennedy.

Another interpretation is that the passing of copies to outside witnesses was for their (the Secret Service's) own protection. Some of the Secret Service agents had testified to other guns and the sounds of pistols. They must have known it was a conspiracy, and their later descriptions of the wounds was not in line with the Warren Commission story.

In any event, the home of Vickie Mayne's parents burned down some time later, and the treasure trove in it—if that is where it was—burned with it.[105] "There were hundreds and hundreds of rolls of film," she told me. Mayne said the fire was determined to be arson. Healey told me that he knew of the trove and that Mayne's parents had had this material. Vickie told me that her family still had the materials when her mother died in June 1987.

Her parents were Robert and Pat (Edna) Hester. The other couple was Fritz and Helen Holland, both deceased and leaving no children.

Billie Sol Estes

Billie Sol Estes was one of the hosts at a $1,000 table at President Kennedy's birthday bash in Washington, D.C., in 1961 as well as at another anniversary party for Kennedy, on January 29, 1962, where Estes sat next to Vice President Lyndon Johnson.[106] Not too long after that, Estes was in jail.

Estes was a close business associate of Lyndon Johnson. Scandal swirled around Estes during the Kennedy presidency, and it seemed that Johnson would have to resign. That and the Bobby Baker scandal threatened to destroy Johnson. Johnson's backers could not have it. Estes says that the numerous deaths that lurk in the background of all these affairs were to protect Johnson.

Estes told Larry Howard and others that he sat in on one of the planning sessions for the assassination of President Kennedy, a meeting at which Lyndon Johnson was present.[107] Estes maintains that Hunt and Murchison paid for the murder, and Hoover orchestrated it with special agents trained by the CIA. General Charles Cabell took care of the problems at the autopsy, and Hoover and Johnson were able to cover it up by creating and controlling the Warren Commission.

All the leads I explored in Dallas point to Estes as having knowledge of what really happened in the assassination. Certain people remain his confidants to the day I am writing this, and that includes Madeleine Brown and Larry Howard of the Assassination Information Center.

Billie Sol financed loans on soybean and grain and cottonseed oil stored in tanks that didn't exist. The stories that brought about his downfall began with a newspaper article on February 12, 1962.

Craig Zirbel writes that the FBI's investigation "reached an impasse when LBJ's personal legal counsel showed up as Estes' principal attorney; Billie Sol refused to talk; and Billie Sol Estes' accountant (who was the only other man besides the dead Henry Marshall who could unravel the fraud) was found dead in his car."[108] Zirbel also tells the story that "By March of 1962 Estes was arrested and charged with a host of crimes, and by May of 1962, the Estes affair had reached such a boiling point that Vice President Johnson flew to Dallas aboard a military jet to privately meet with Estes and his lawyers on a plane parked away from the terminal. What was discussed has been kept secret but it has long been suspected that during this meeting LBJ told Estes to keep his mouth shut and leave Johnson out of the scandal.''[109]

An unnamed informant wrote a report in the fall of 1963 about gathering information concerning the activities of Billie Sol Estes. He talked to Dr. Dunn, who was investigating and writing about Estes. He discovered a huge land deal where Mrs. Lyndon Johnson's brother and a U.S. senator sold land to the federal government "at a figure of 2,600 times the purchase price. This land was to be used for a satellite hard landing program which never did come off." But the federal government drilled wells, ran in large power lines, erected fences all the way around (2,000 acres), and built buildings. "The federal government did all this."

The person who wrote up this investigation described how the Johnson family obtained control over a radio station and took the ranch that Lyndon Johnson came to live on. They simply drove away the lady who owned it. "One of JOHNSON'S people came to the ranch and told her that there was going to be an epidemic of cattle poisoning in that area and that she should sell the ranch immediately so that all her cattle would not accidentally die."

"I talked to DR. DUNN in Grapevine, he said that on a particular day an investigator whom he was working with called on him and indicated that he had gathered information and that he was going to go and confirm one more piece of information which directly connected Mr. JOHNSON and MR. ESTES in a partnership deal. Three days later this man committed suicide by shooting himself eight times in the head with a .22 rifle."

Zirbel writes: "A source with which I am connected in Washington told me that the Congressional Committee investigating BILLIE SOL ESTES on the fertilizer fraud, of which he was a member, were drawing up the papers for the impeachment of JOHNSON, the Vice President, and that they were within a week of presenting these papers to the Department of Justice at the time of the assassination. Shortly after the assassination, the FBI picked up the papers that the Committee had in order to make copies and they never returned the papers; when my source directly called the FBI to ask about them, the FBI replied, 'what papers?' ''[110]

Estes's daughter wrote in her book, "I firmly believe that if Daddy had been operating out of a big city like Houston or Dallas, the tank financing scheme would have perked right along until the debt was retired and it would be obscure financial history. Daddy, and the farmers, and the finance companies would all have made money and everybody would have been happy and moved on to something else. However, since Daddy operated out of Pecos, everybody knew everything about everybody else. In a small town whenever somebody records a deed or mortgage at the courthouse, some busybody will always know about it, and soon everybody in town will know. In this case, the newspaper that was rival to Daddy's newspaper, the *Pecos Daily News,* began its crusade against Daddy and sparked the investigation."[111]

Three newspaper articles in a biweekly West Texas newspaper brought the vast financial empire of Estes down, and the writer, John Dunn (a physician), got a Pulitzer Prize. He was then promptly destroyed. "He was threatened, hounded, and condemned. His business holdings were sacrificed . . . by corrupt and ruthless power in his hometown, he was destroyed, professionally and financially and in virtual penury was forced to move away to seek another start in anonymity.

"John Dunn became the culprit because he had stripped the garments of simulated decency from the popular idol—the reflected image and ambition of the gross and corrupt who admired him, as well as the immoral nature of the government policies which had made him.

"Dr. John Dunn was guilty of but one thing and that was mistaken judgment. He had dared to believe that truth and virtue would prevail where public apathy condones illicit power, and he had paid the price exacted by faith while denied in reason. This is the second profound historic principle—and tragic truth, that his marvelous investigation proved."[112]

Estes made a statement to a grand jury about Johnson's orders to kill people, in 1984. He said that LBJ told Estes to "get rid of him," referring to Henry B. Marshall.[113] Marshall, an Agriculture Department official, "could have linked Johnson to Estes' illegal activities." Estes said that "illegal cotton allotments and other business deals he arranged with Johnson's help generated $21 million a year, with part of the money going to a slush fund controlled by LBJ."[114]

As a result of Estes' testimony to the grand jury, the ruling of suicide in the death of Marshall more than twenty years before was changed to one of homicide. Estes said that Malcolm Wallace killed him. Wallace worked for the Department of Agriculture but took orders directly from Lyndon Johnson.

Those who worked for Johnson in the White House were quoted in these newspaper articles as saying Estes' comments were "scurrilous." Some of the aides who commented on it were Liz Carpenter, a helper to Mrs. Johnson, probably one of the few who know what happened to President Kennedy; Walter Jenkins; and Robert Hardesty. The Dallas papers headlined this news as follows: "LBJ ordered murder of witness, says con man Estes."

Attorney Craig Zirbel wrote in his book, "The only difference between Vice President Agnew's resignation in disgrace when compared to Vice President Johnson's tenure 10 years earlier, was that Johnson, in the midst of several scandals, rather than resigning in disgrace, stepped up to the Presidency. Johnson's tenure as Vice President was so clouded by turmoil that he was branded as the Vice President of Scandals. . . . They were matters of national significance that were publicized across the country. Three major scandals rocked Johnson while Vice President and all three surfaced less than 18 months before Kennedy's death." They were the TFX Missile Scandal (a.k.a. "the LBJ"), the Bobby Baker scandal, and the Billie Sol Estes affair.[115]

Morris D. Jaffe

Bankruptcy proceedings were filed against Estes, and he was declared a bankrupt on July 13, 1962. Morris D. Jaffe, of San Antonio, and "Vice President Johnson's warm friend"[116] took "one of the first steps to move in on the Estes Empire." In June 1963, Estes' "splendid installation at Plainview was taken over by Jaffe's American Grain Corporation at 'what was against it'—a drastically reduced note of just over $418,000 at the Midland National."[117]

Evetts Haley wrote, "Meanwhile Morris Jaffe took over—the newspapers seriously said 'bought'—the still vast and valuable Billie Sol Estes assets. 'The news' that Jaffe, a 'San Antonio businessman,' had offered $7 million for them broke in the summer of 1962 and it soon developed that the fine hand of Walter Heller, through his lawyers, Henry Strasburger of Dallas and Greenberg and Schimberg of Chicago, was playing an important if not dominant role—as well it might with seven million at stake, with Commercial Solvents in the favorable position of holding a lien on the principal assets. . . . Jaffe took possession of Billie Sol's assets; some thousands of acres of the best Pecos irrigated land, ranch holdings and the multi-million-dollar grain complex."

Haley wrote, "The conclusion is inescapable that the Johnson controlled political machine in Texas designedly set the stage for Jaffe's take-over, as the cleanup was without financial risk and potentially very good. . . . What the government was actually doing was destroying the value of his [Estes'] major assets, to which his hundreds of hapless creditors looked for some small percentage of recovery."[118]

Of course, the federal judge in the Estes bankruptcy case was a close friend and supporter of Lyndon Baines Johnson.[119]

There is more on Jaffe in this. It is important to note that there are two Morris Jaffes in this case. There is the San Antonio Jaffe, warm friend of LBJ, and there is the Morris D. Jaffe of Dallas. This Jaffe was known to be present at many gatherings of Joe Civello and Carlos Marcello when Carlos came to town.

Jaffe was often at the Dal-Tex Building to see Morty Freedman. The building had a sixth-floor window that looked at the same window Oswald was allegedly in and from which one gunman could communicate by hand signal with the other across the street, with a perfect straight-on view.

As for Lyndon Johnson's warm friend Morris Jaffe, the question Evetts Haley writes that everybody was asking at the time Estes lost his property was, "Who in the hell is Morris Jaffe?"[120] Haley writes that Jaffe and David Martin organized Jaffe and Martin Builders and went into construction work. This, naturally, leads us to a tale of chicanery in the construction of barracks at Lackland Air Force Base in San Antonio. Lackland is where Jaffe had made a friend out of an Air Force colonel, Roger Zeller. Jaffe was tight with LBJ, who got Zeller promoted over other officers with greater seniority, and had him sent to the Pentagon as a brigadier general.[121]

Jaffe acquired options on a vast holding of South Texas uranium deposits and "unloaded his leases and options at a fancy profit before the magnificent and expensive dream fizzled out like a cheap Chinese firecracker."[122] Jaffe then all but destroyed a military officer over an ice skating rink boondoggle the Air Force was compelled to buy. Jaffe was no "ordinary operator," as Haley tells us.

"By the late fifties, Jaffe had more to his record than some faulty barracks, a skating rink, some sour oil leases, and a magnificently abortive but personally profitable boom in uranium. As the president of the Texas end of the Fed-mart operations, he had become a merchandising tycoon. Politics is another and most important side of Jaffe's business, 'since my boy became President.' "[123]

"It may be asked what became of the interests of the hundreds of other Estes creditors. A committee of Creditors was set up with the approval of the Trustee in Bankruptcy, and through agreement Jaffe took over the entire shooting match with a lien of $6,500,000. . . . Jaffee took over for a song, and short one at that. . . . Walter Heller, Commercial Solvents and Jaffe are running the bankruptcy, lock, stock and barrel."[124] This is a brief background of Morris D. Jaffe, an old friend of President Lyndon B. Johnson who was unheard of in the Pecos area before he turned up to take over what was valuable and tangible after the crash of the Billie Sol Estes empire. The high point politically of Jaffe's career was his backing of Johnson for the presidential nomination in 1960 in Los Angeles. Jaffe, too, was there to lay his money on the line. An old-time San Antonio newspaperman came home admitting that Jaffe not only seemed to be the "money man" but also the "brains and the trouble-shooter and smart beyond imagination," the most effective man behind Lyndon B. Johnson. For whatever it was worth, it was one veteran's opinion, which provoked another to add: "When anybody's high in Johnson's organization, you can be sure he's the best. Lyndon hasn't got a bum working for him. This emphasizes a highly significant facet of Johnson's genius which makes him tremendously effective and infinitely more dangerous."[125]

Conclusion

What I learned in Dallas did not jibe with the stories that the CIA or the Mafia or others killed Kennedy, other than those elements of the agencies that were used by the Texas plotters. I found a lot of support from researchers that Jim Garrison had at least part of the story right and that some of those in New Orleans (Bannister, Clay Shaw, and David Ferrie) played some role in the assassination, if only to set Oswald up, but little if any evidence was offered to back that up.

What I found in Dallas was a plot that was plausible. It utilized elements of the military, and possibly the Mob, though in a very small way and at a low level.

It was simple, really. Many of the most powerful people in this country know how to subvert or control the appearance of democracy. John Kennedy got in the way, and his plans had to be stopped. His death was part of the Cold War as they perceived their goals. They had enough on Johnson and he had been one of the good ol' boys long enough for them to know that they could control him.

There was a trade: The eastern Establishment got the national debt for their banks to own and collect interest on, and Texas got the Vietnam War business. There was always money in war industry.

Johnson exacted a price for his cooperation, and that was the presidency and civil rights. That issue was the last shred of integrity and independence left to him. In the end, Johnson paid for his high office and was destroyed like so many others in this modern Rome.

As I finished this book, I heard repeated warnings that President Bill Clinton was in grave danger by planning to go to Dallas on November 22, 1993, to commemorate John Kennedy's death. "I fear for him," were the words of numerous people native to Dallas. "They hate Clinton and all that he stands for!"

"It's still the City of Hate, and it will always be the City of Hate," I was told time and again by people who knew it too well.

Texas killed President Kennedy.

There were sharpshooters in the
FBI and the CIA that could hit a
thousand bulls-eyes in a row.

—a former CIA agent

CHAPTER 17

THE SOURCE

I stepped out of the maelstrom into a large, quiet room. The room
had many doors. I had gone from the fiery confusion and conflict of
one intelligence operation into the measured reason of another. Masked
by a seemingly simple souvenir shop near the place where John Kennedy lost his life were a spy and counterspy games that sometimes
made intelligence operations between nations look like child's play.

But this was no game. Behind the scene, those covering themselves
with the mantle of "researchers" and "critics" worked for the highest
bidder or labored to draw a fog over the evidence in the case.

Only when I sprang free of the major researchers did I begin to
understand what had happened. Only when I made a public split with
them did the *real* researchers come out of the woodwork where they
had been hiding.

And the real witnesses.

And the real investigation.

There were actors posing as witnesses, actors playing researchers,
and actors playing investigators. The whole thing had been a show.

There had been a shadow investigation in the years following the
murder. Three former FBI agents conducted it, employing a network of
other agents and security operatives. Some were employed by the big
companies that had an interest in seeing John Kennedy dead: General
Dynamics, Bell Helicopters, Hunt Oil, Clint Murchison's empire, and
Brown & Root at the top of it.

I tapped into this network of aging, gracious, kindly southern gentlemen. Soon I was staying at the most exclusive hotels in Dallas and
lunching at the Petroleum Club, the Adolphus, the Top of the Hill, and

the Grill at the Anatole. The King's Club where the conspirators once hung out was no more. It had been across the street from Jack Ruby's place. Ruby had supplied them with women. Hunt particularly fancied a pretty girl named Lacie, and another named Chris Cole. With a police officer at my side, I met with a gentleman at his home in an exclusive, gated section of the city.

His house had been designed by Frank Lloyd Wright and relied on glass and soaring constructs, light and foliage, with an inner courtyard in a Spanish motif. The house contained illuminated aquariums filled with every sort of exotic fish. This was a man who was cultured and artistic, who abhorred so much of what Texas stood for—a rough-and-ready bravado, violence, and corruption. In this house I began to learn what really had happened.

I have to give him a name, so we'll call my source George Healey. For those readers who are puzzled, I have never made up evidence in my life, and this story is not made up. Healey is real, but he knows he is in danger for telling this story. The wealthiest and most powerful people in the city are perfectly capable of hiring "contractors" to mess with someone who reveals their more nefarious activities.

Not to speak of the assassination of President John F. Kennedy. "Dallas was the absolute perfect place for the assassination," he told me.[1]

Healey had the core of the story, and only two people were left alive who knew the story. No one had it all. "It was not designed that way," he said, repeating what several others familiar with the plot had to say.

This may not be the definitive story, but I believe it to be very close. I believe that I am as close as one might come thirty years after the murder, when so many are already dead, having taken their stories with them. On the other hand, after so long, with many of the principal players and killers dead, some have found the courage to tell what they know. Hopefully, as a result of what I am writing, more will come forward to tell their stories. Many in Dallas hope it comes out now.

Healey told me that only three presidents "knew what they were doing and where the power lay. That is Franklin Delano Roosevelt, Richard Nixon, and George Bush." The implication was that all the other presidents were puppets without knowing it. Roosevelt, Nixon, and Bush knew where the power was and how to use it. Conspicuously absent from his list was Lyndon Johnson, whom he met in 1936.

"The oilmen—except Al Meadows, who owned an oil company—washed their hands of LBJ over his civil rights legislation."[2]

"You are only one of two writers that are on the right track," Healey told me. "Some of the key people aren't around anymore. Theirs weren't natural deaths. Captain Gannaway and Will Fritz used to reel off the names of the dead to me. Money corrupts," Healey said. This was a different list from our "Strange Deaths" compendium.

George Healey and I discussed both the broad outlines of the plot, and the specifics. He helped me on another level as well, and that was to lead me to the doors I had to open to find what was in the rooms behind them. Some would be empty. There were double blinds, providing insulation for the individuals behind them. My inquiry would be compartmentalized as much as possible, just as the conspiracy was.

He gave me the addresses of those he wanted me to contact. He had kept secret a Rolodex with all of the addresses of those active in his political work at the time of that terrible minute in 1963.

He told me things he was afraid to say.

Healey told me that in 1977 the House of Representatives had sent men from the Select Committee on Assassinations to Dallas to collect evidence and materials—just as Jim Garrison had done ten years before, and just as the Warren Commission had done before that in 1964. The men had come to Dallas and delivered subpoenas to testify. This put deadly fear in the former FBI men who had conducted the shadow investigation. They knew that if they talked, their careers and maybe their lives were over. They were in fear of the powerful people of Dallas.

They could kill a person with slander or with a bullet. It made no difference.

There was the additional fear of prosecution for whatever they might say to a federal officer. Anything that might be misunderstood or distorted could result in a jail term. The FBI opened discussion with a quotation from the U.S. Code about making false statements to federal officers, and then wondered why nobody would talk to them. The answer is simply fear that their statements would be distorted, even if true. "Talk to him alone. Make sure no one is with him, because they could say you said something when you didn't, and you'd be convicted of perjury. Because of the Freedom of Information Act, nothing is secret anymore."

They got out of the subpoenas, begging off with sick wives and other excuses, but the House seized the records of their shadow investigation. These records were of vast value, for they explained in large part what the true nature of the assassination of John Kennedy was all about, where it came from, and who did it.

The source said that Paul Rothermel, H. L. Hunt's former chief of security, honored the subpoenas but he can't believe Rothermel gave everything he had, because it would cause him problems.

The question then becomes: What happened to the records? With certain alleged researchers secreting out of the House's vaults massive amounts of material including films, photographs, slides, and documents that were then sold on the open market, we can only imagine what became of this material. They could not have done this without the complicity of those high up in the staff of the Committee. The names of the former FBI men are nowhere in the index of the House investigation.

This shadow investigation had much of the real assassination story, but nowhere do we find it in the House investigation. Who was in charge of this material? Why was it ignored? The answer was that certain researchers who act as monitors or watchers in the case said there was nothing to the people who had conducted the investigation.

Years before, Jim Garrison had sent emissaries to Dallas. Prominent researchers had gone there and contacted these former FBI men. The researchers were blown off the scent because that was the job of some of the security men who worked for Clint Murchison, Howard Hughes, J. Paul Getty, Brown & Root, and H. L. Hunt. There had been accusations that Hunt had ordered John Kennedy killed. In fact, Jim Garrison had frequently and in public said that the oilmen were involved in the plot. Everybody knew that he meant H. L. Hunt.[3] This was before Garrison switched horses in midstream and pinned it on the CIA.

Healey went to see Paul Rothermel during Lyndon Johnson's tenure as president after Hunt had soured on LBJ. Under the guise of discussing another matter, the source produced the "Boxley" chart, which indicated that Rothermel and Hunt had something to do with the assassination. This was a drawing down by Bill Woods, who used the alias "Boxley" when he worked for Jim Garrison. Rothermel's cordiality toward Healey disappeared in a cloud of suspicion. Within days Rothermel had conducted a thorough investigation of Healey. The source feels that Rothermel would never have wasted the amount of effort that went into this investigation unless he was protecting himself and others.

"Hunt was not invited into the inner circle that did the dirty deed because they couldn't trust him to keep his mouth shut." Hunt's money, as is widely believed in Dallas, nevertheless found its way into the plotters' hands for their purpose, and Hunt knew what it was for. He asked no questions.

Another source very close to both people, close to Hunt, said on hearing the above quote, "But two or three men, very, very close to Hunt, may very well have been actively involved."

Rothermel told me that "Hunt was such a hick, so naive, so indiscreet that you couldn't plot anything with him. No one would have been stupid enough to draw him in. He got worse as time went on. He was a danger to himself, and everyone around him. His money could have been used in the plot, sure."[4]

There was an organized and funded activity in Dallas to turn away any threat to the security of the conspirators, so they blew off and even blew away snoops. Most of the time it wasn't necessary to kill someone when they could simply make the person out as crazy. "He has emotional problems!" became their refrain. Great way of trying to sweep someone out of the way and not dealing with what they are saying.

The goal was to shield Hunt and the other powerful people who had met the night before the murder at Clint Murchison's house with the operational head of the conspiracy, who outlined what was going to happen and how the aftermath would be contained.

"I guess a lot of people gave Garrison a bum steer," Healey said, laughing heartily. A lot of people buffaloed Garrison. He was easy.

Paul Rothermel had known there was going to be an incident at the Trade Mart the day of the assassination. He knew this because he was working in law enforcement and they had the word. They thought it was going to be an incident similar to the spitting on Adlai Stevenson. Rothermel never explained or was asked by any investigative agency what he referenced. Later it was reported that Rothermel told the FBI he did not know.

Rothermel refused to be interviewed about any former associates, and in answer to the memos quoted by prior writers attributed to him, told me, "That was my job: to deflect attention from them." From his employers. Then the questions were: Were they guilty? Did they conspire in the assassination of the President? Did he have foreknowledge? Hunt's program was to show a Communist conspiracy.

Rothermel told Earl Golz in 1970, at a time when Golz had access to some of his documents, that the assassination was too cleverly done, with too many safeguards for anybody ever to solve it.

The Plot

"There was no preexisting organization. The conspiracy was *ad hoc*," Healey told me. "There may never have been a plot until the decision was made to go to Texas." Did he have knowledge of this? Is this a result of his investigation, or a surmise?

Think about that. Well, we know that Kennedy was lured down to Texas. *He was lured.* Once they knew Kennedy had taken the bait, they laid down the net, and he was dead. These people had killed before.

There had to be a mastermind, and Healey told me that "he was a very brilliant one."

There had to be men who carried the messages, and those who were paymasters. Those involved all knew each other right down to the pilots and the shooters. They were so closely and tightly knit that no word had a hope of seeping out. "There's so many crossties that keep the cement together. Marriages, business, joint ventures keep the cement together," Healey told me.

There had been plenty of warnings of plots, but those occur from the moment someone accedes to the presidency. Some word of this plot leaked out—and Ruby appeared to be the leak—to Rose Cheramie and others. (Cheramie was one of Ruby's girls who told doctors about the impending assassination after she was thrown out of a car. She was later killed.) He knew that Lyndon Johnson's power was awesome, and he feared it. Ruby told reporters that Johnson was behind the events of November 1963.[5] Knowing this, Ruby had to die Because it was apparent that he might blow the whole thing out of the water after he won a new trial. Ruby had been drafted into the plot and had serious reservations about it. He had no choice.

In fact, this is how the CIA/FBI/Mob connection came in. They were all used to participate in the cover-up. Their clean-up squads went to work.

"My seat-of-the-pants feelings is that LBJ was up to his ears in it . . . he threw his weight around, and he usually got his way," one of the former FBI men told me. "This was Lyndon's last opportunity to become president . . . his swan song." And like a lot of others, he said that Lady Bird was even more dangerous than Lyndon. Some say it is possible that she played some direct role in the plot. "Not really," one source said. "If she had known about it, she would have ducked along with Lyndon when the gunfire started. He didn't tell her, hoping a stray bullet would kill the nagging old bitch." Johnson had ducked when the shooting started. Some say he ducked *before* it started.

"Walter Jenkins was the connection between LBJ and Clay Shaw," another source said. This was the homosexual pipeline in the case, and how Oswald was set up in New Orleans. Jenkins was connected to

Albert Thomas, the congressman from Houston connected to Brown & Root. Jenkins was arrested in a D.C. gay bar, and this seriously embarrassed President Lyndon Johnson. Jenkins, Tommy Cox (Clay Shaw's lover), and David Ferrie were the gay aides to Clay Shaw, Hoover, and Lyndon Johnson in all of this.

"You have to understand the tremendous closeness of J. Edgar Hoover and Lyndon Johnson," he told me. "Johnson carried Hoover's ball on the Hill, and got him his appropriations through his connections in the House, when he was majority leader of the Senate. They were joined at the hip, those two men. So when the finger of suspicion pointed at Johnson over the assassination, Hoover was able to cover it up and direct attention at the patsy."[6]

There was a committee, let's call it, that coalesced around the idea that John Kennedy had to go. These people lived far from the seat of power, and they had collected vast financial leverage in their state and city and were in a bid to make their city the focal point of the nation in terms of money and power. Culture they had not, preferring the vulgar. Like a lot of new rich, they could buy art and culture, but that didn't make them any better for it. They set out to destroy someone who was the embodiment of civilization and culture. One way of looking at it was that the assassination was the sort of deadly reaction barbarians have to that which they cannot understand.

Both Lyndon and J. Edgar Hoover stood to lose their jobs. Hoover and Bobby Kennedy hated each other.

Hoover commanded absolute loyalty from many of his troops, and those who followed his lead would have done just about anything he asked. Often enough, it was a criminal act: wiretapping, breaking and entering, and so on. Perhaps even killing.

"There were sharpshooters in the FBI and the CIA that could hit a thousand bulls-eyes in a row. They were as good as Tuperwine in San Antonio," a former CIA agent told me. Tuperwine, a legendary shootist, died around the turn of the century.

Regarding LBJ, not only the Bobby Baker scandal and the Billie Sol Estes affair threatened to overthrow Johnson that year, but also the fact that murders that had been committed might be laid at his feet. They had to act at once.

There were three topflight downtown hotels in Dallas at the time: the Adolphus; the Baker, across the street from the Adolphus; and the new Statler-Hilton, Stormy Meadows was the social director of the Adolphus, before she retired to Denton. She was in a good position to hear a lot of stories.

In his heyday from 1960 on, Murchison hung out at the Statler-Hilton from three-thirty to four o'clock on. "I'il tell you who was up there," Healey told me. The key people from "Eppler, Guerin & Turner, the big mortgage bankers. Eppler was there. Murchison was there." But nothing was ever discussed when someone who had no need to know was there.

It was a red room at the Statler-Hilton where they all drank. The decor was all in red, and the gals came around in red panties, and red garter belt and waited on you. It was some little watering hole.

"Did H.L. go down to the Statler-Hilton?"

"No. No. Definitely not. The thing about it is, I just don't believe Murchison and he would have been in the same room together. That's why I did question whether or not he was at this meeting with them. When I met with the Murchison's group, I never saw anyone from H. L. Hunt's 'clique' there."

"There was a lot of bad blood?"

"Well, it wasn't necessarily that there was bad blood. It's very odd that they never did any business together, so you have to presume that there was something there. Every wildcatter made deals with every other wildcatter. You know, they all need partners from time to time, and there never was one single thing between them and the Murchisons. The Richardsons and the Basses, who were kin, did all their business together, and they had a lot of backers over at Eppler, Guerin, & Turner."

Madeleine Brown recalled Hunt often coming into the King's Club at the Adolphus arm in arm with Jack Ruby, and Assistant Chief of Police Charles Batchelor. Batchelor, of course, lost both Kennedy and Oswald while he was in charge of security precautions in Dallas. Batchelor took Ruby down an elevator in the headquarters to kill Oswald.[7] He was rewarded by becoming chief of police.

Oswald

We know that DeMohrenschildt's job was to baby-sit Oswald for J. Walton Moore, the local CIA resident agent. Oswald was passed back and forth among intelligence operatives. In New Orleans he worked for Guy Banister, a former FBI man who had graduated from the Office of Naval Intelligence (ONI), an outfit that seems to retain an interest in the case to this day, littering the landscape and Dealey Plaza with their agents, former and present. Oswald *had to* be working for ONI when he was in the service and going to the Soviet Union. My sources knew Banister, and they knew that Oswald was an intelligence agent.

The lines get blurred as people change jobs and agencies, so it is difficult to say who or what they are at times. They are just agents, period. Of somebody.

"His mother, Marguerite, was hell-bent on telling her story," but LBJ made sure that she and the family were gotten under control. Johnson called the Secret Service shortly after Oswald was arrested and said: "I don't want anything to happen to that boy's family. You go down there and put them under protective custody!" They were taken to the Inn of the Americas at Six Flags, which was owned by Clint Murchison and Bedford Wynne. They were put in an as yet unoccupied but newly constructed wing of the motel. "That's where Marina was debriefed."[8]

"Do you think there is anyone who can confirm that Oswald was a PCI (Paid Criminal Informant)?"

"Anybody who was in the FBI at the time should have known it. I knew it, and I wasn't in the FBI. We laughed about it. It's kind of funny that the FBI would have as a security informant the very guy that killed the president. That is pretty embarrassing. The files were stripped in a hurry, you can bet your ass on that. And the paper had a lot about it, and Jack Revill ('Rebel'), the head of intelligence (DPD), and Hosty were very good friends, but they got crosswise in a hurry about who was lying about what. And I think Hosty was embarrassed, the Bureau was embarrassed, and Revill was *persona non grata* with the Bureau as a result of the statements that he made."[9]

Marina

Healey thought that the fact that Oswald had left an elaborate note for Marina before he was supposed to have gone off to shoot General Walker, detailing trivial household things to do, was significant. Oswald had left no such note the day of Kennedy's murder, but he had left his wallet behind. Had he intended to shoot Kennedy, Healey feels, he would have left directions to Marina. I might add, Oswald would have taken his wallet and not left it there. Since the police claim that they found a wallet on him and there is no indication that he used two wallets, there is something peculiar here, like so many of the conflicts in the record regarding Oswald.

One of the things Oswald directed Marina to do the day he was supposed to have gone off to shoot at Walker was to get ahold of Ruth Paine.

"I would doubt that anyone who was involved would ever try to help Marina," my source told me. "I think that would be the most foolish thing in the world. They didn't care what happened to her. They certainly didn't want to draw any attention to themselves."[10] But it was clear she was taken over and assisted by very powerful forces after the assassination of Kennedy and the murder of her husband.

"As far as the FBI agent that got transferred out, that was probably Hoover's style. I don't know whether in talking with Oswald that he ever got close enough to Marina—I'm sure he was out there at times when Oswald was not there. Because that is what the records reflected. So, you know, its problematical as to how many times he might have seen her, because he was the recordkeeper as far as contact with informants goes. I'm sure he was trying to make both of them informants."[11]

Michael and Ruth Paine

"I think that Ruth, of the two, would be the more interesting. I know that she knows a lot of information about the everyday comings and goings of the Oswalds."

Patricia Dumais writes, "I think it would be helpful to find out who 'leaked' the intercepted conversation between Ruth and Michael Paine [in which Michael made a cryptic reference to who 'really' committed the assassination]. Investigations are not supposed to divulge such information."[12]

Healey said he was not in touch with Banister that year. "If I was in touch with him that year, it would not have been over this." He says Banister had business everywhere. Everything was highly covert, on a need-to-know basis. Healey said he had to use Harry Roberts as the intermediary when he needed Banister. Roberts ran an investigating firm in Shreveport. "I never trusted Banister. I never wanted him to know my business. On occasion I would drop by and visit him for Houston business interests, mostly on high-level Louisiana politics. If I had contact with him, it was prior to the assassination."[13]

Healey told me that LBJ handpicked his own Secret Service men, and that he chose the former chief of police of Saginaw, Texas, near Grapevine. "He drove LBJ."

The FBI sighted in on a radical group in Denton, a town near Dallas, as the ones behind Lee Harvey Oswald. "There were more crazies in Dallas and Denton than all of the rest of the United States," one of my sources told me. Healey said, "You had the biggest collection of wild nuts in Dallas and Denton. They really believed there was a conspiracy from within to take over the government. They really believed that the Communists we need to be afraid of are *here* and not in Moscow. Moscow took orders from here. . . ."

Jack Revill, head of the Criminal Intelligence Section of the Dallas Police Department, was busy creating a paper record of investigation in the case. He wrote that because of the rumors that President Kennedy was coming to Dallas, "the Criminal Intelligence Section had increased its efforts in attempting to gather data concerning known extremist and subversive groups in Dallas. This Section had previously been successful in infiltrating a number of these organizations, therefore the activities, capabilities, personalities and future plans of these groups were known. Members of the Criminal Intelligence Section frequently kept known members of these groups under surveillance to determine associations and movements. Some of the more active groups in Dallas are:

THE KU KLUX KLAN
INDIGNANT WHITE CITIZENS' COUNCIL
NATIONAL STATES RIGHTS PARTY
JOHN BIRCH SOCIETY
DALLAS WHITE CITIZENS' COUNCIL
OAK CLIFF WHITE CITIZENS' COUNCIL
THE GENERAL EDWIN A. WALKER GROUP
AMERICAN OPINION FORUM
DALLAS COMMITTEE FOR FULL CITIZENSHIP
YOUNG PEOPLE'S SOCIALIST LEAGUE
DALLAS CIVIL LIBERTIES UNION
TEXAS WHITE CITIZENS' COUNCIL
BLACK MUSLIMS

"The foregoing organizations are comprised of members whose political views are considered to be extreme, both right and left." Lieutenant Revill then noted that "The Criminal Intelligence Section had no information pertaining to LEE HARVEY OSWALD prior to November 22, 1963."[14]

The FBI was looking for an *organization* while hiding behind the cover story of the lone assassin. But there was no organization. First of all, many of the radical groups were virtual police operations. They were either set up to monitor extremist groups or were so rapidly infiltrated that more often than not, the majority of souls at their meetings were agents.

The FBI looked in the wrong places all over the country rather than under their nose, and the effort through the years that followed was to keep investigators out of Dallas. When independent researchers from other states came snooping around, a loose organization of researchers was established in Dallas to watch things, and if necessary, run an operation on interlopers. Soon it was necessary to center the whole massive national effort of independent researchers, now metastasizing across the landscape of America, in Dallas to control information in the case. The Dallas FBI and police worked closely with certain "researchers" there who fed them information and personal dossiers from across the country.

Edward Jay Epstein explains it thusly: "If, however, the newly appointed Warren Commission suggested that Oswald had any involvement with Soviet or Cuban intelligence, no matter how irrelevant it was to his killing of the President, then there would be no way to keep the FBI's mishandling of the investigation of Oswald before the assassination secret, and FBI incompetence would be blamed for the assassination. By an odd twist of fate, the FBI's interest lay in concealing, rather than revealing any hint of Soviet involvement."[15]

It is not too big a step for some overenthusiastic and highly patriotic military and former military types to convince themselves that a change of government by extralegal means might be for the good of the nation. It is especially true when quite a number of such superpatriots reside in one area and feed on and encourage each other's insecurity and overconfidence.

The National Debt

I proposed to Healey that the National Debt was the prize of the assassination. "That was a good way to cover up what otherwise would be a public clamboring about why we are going into debt. We're not at war! War is the distraction. We've got to win the war, so spend more. No one ever thought it would go to a trillion dollars." He said that we had started borrowing. "But they had started borrowing from the Social Security funds, and that had begun to bother some of the fiscal conservatives. It was the policy of the Treasury Department to not show the borrowings from the Social Security funds. Of course, they were wrong because the baby boomers were just coming on, and they were going to make a ton of money, but a lot of people were concerned about it."

General Walker

There were intact retired military command structures in the Dallas area dating from World War II and Korea, led by General Wainwright, General Harley West, and General Paul Harkins. Of course, General Walker was there. He was the man Kennedy had fired for preaching neo-Nazi propaganda to his troops. Some of General Douglas MacArthur's staff, sad to say, were radical rightists. President Harry Truman fired MacArthur for his actions in the Korean War, and this antagonized those blind followers of the hero of World War II who overlooked his faults. MacArthur was an authoritarian, paternalistic figure, a man on a white horse who commanded great loyalty. That loyalty extended to his organization and staff after he was gone.

Oswald was supposed to have taken a shot at Walker through the window of Walker's house. If Oswald was such a good shot on November 22, 1963, how did he miss Walker at a much closer range? Larry Schmidt, who, along with Nelson Bunker Hunt and Ed Crissie (oilman E. F. White's brother-in-law), paid for part of the black-bordered newspaper ad denouncing Kennedy the day Kennedy died, accusing Kennedy of various crimes, may have been with Oswald during the Walker shooting incident. One story has it that they weren't supposed to hit Walker, as the whole thing was staged to get sympathy for Walker.

Walker, a known homosexual[16] (he had been arrested for this offense), worked closely with Robert A. Surrey, who played bridge regularly with James Hosty,[17] the FBI agent who was Lee Harvey Oswald's case officer. Surrey distributed the "Wanted for Treason" leaflets along the parade route the day Kennedy died.[18] One story has a discussion between Walker and Surrey about his subpoena to appear before the Warren Commission as follows:

Walker: "Aren't you afraid to go up there?"

"No. I have the best attorney in the world."

"Who is that?"

"Earl Warren," Surrey replied. Surrey got the money for his handbills from H. L. Hunt, a leading financier of a number of politicians and many right-wing and conservative causes.[19]

The homosexual element provided a good means of secure communications. Another retired government employee told me, "It was a major factor in the assassination." He led me to a source in Washington who answered my question, which I asked very delicately long before the *Front Line* exposure of Hoover's true self became general public knowledge.[20] "Was J. Edgar Hoover a homosexual?"

"At the very moment that he was blackmailing people because he had found that they were gay, he was himself accused of engaging in those activities." This independently corroborated Anthony Summers' findings that Hoover was an active homosexual, in Summers' book *Official and Confidential: The Secret Life of J. Edgar Hoover.*

Another former FBI man in Baltimore told me, "I was in Washington. I knew what was going on. We all knew about Hoover." But apparently not the younger FBI agents, the hero-worshipers. They still believed he was Mr. Clean.

Because of threatened retaliation by those who are intent on preserving Hoover's and the FBI's reputation, I cannot name the sources for the above. Since the 1993 *Front Line* show (PBS) and Anthony Summers' book on Hoover establishing Hoover's homosexuality, the publication, *The Grapevine*, representing former agents have attempted to do what they can to censor the salacious story.

Bill Greer

"There had to be someone in the Secret Service who betrayed Kennedy," Healey told me. "That was the only way it could all work perfectly."

It seemed to me that man might have been the limousine's driver, Bill Greer, who turned around and looked at Kennedy more than once during all the shots, and all but stopped the car until Kennedy's head exploded. Greer laughed as he came down the steps of the Supreme Court of the United States after his interview with the Warren Commission.[21]

It is interesting that the FBI, in their interview with Greer, treated him like a suspect and took his physical description.[22]

The FBI and the CIA

I think the FBI was had in this case. So was the CIA. They were used as the fall guys for the real—supersecret—intelligence and police agencies that operated out of the Black Budget. The FBI was the one with the renegades and a director who betrayed Kennedy. The CIA had its renegades who were used, as well.

"Warren was controlled," Healey told me. "He wasn't just a dupe. They had something on him and were blackmailing him."

Ruby was trying to telegraph something to "Chief Warren" during that now famous interview with the Chief Justice of the United States and future president Gerald Ford. Ruby tried to tell Warren a number of things, and repeatedly asked to be taken to Washington, where he could speak more freely.[23] They wouldn't hear it.

Ruby clearly was a man drafted into the conspiracy who didn't want to go.

Of course, H. L. Hunt had taken over the Dallas FBI office. Having former FBI men such as Paul Rothermel and Robert Blount on his payroll gave him a line into their Dallas office. Robert Blount, who died in 1982, was closer to H. L. Hunt than any other person and had once stated "[H. L.] Hunt has just asked me to do something sinister. My conscience won't let me do it!"

"I knew whatever the Dallas Police knew," said Paul Rothermel, who left Hunt shortly after the Clay Shaw trial ended in New Orleans.

Apparently one of Rothermel's jobs was to deflect suspicion of their involvement in the assassination away from the Hunt family. Garrison had made public statements that H. L. Hunt and/or his sons were involved in the assassination.[24] Walter Cronkite, on CBS, stated that "Garrison was in New York today. Reporters were showing him around town. He was giving his latest version of the assassination of President Kennedy. He said it was done by anti-Castro Cubans, insanely patriotic oil millionaires, and a small, hard core of ultraconservative Dallas policemen who were the connecting link." Well, Garrison started out on the right track, anyway, before he pinned it on the CIA.

Harold Weisberg commented on this aspect of the Garrison case in a letter saying that his book *Agent Oswald* "will pretty well establish that federal power 'framed' Dallas as a necessity of framing history."[25] In the next sentence, Weisberg goes on to blame the "phony liberals" on the Warren Commission staff for covering up the case. (See the chapter "Treason and the Smoke Screen" for more on the Hunt/Weisberg connection.)

Rothermel discussed the chart that had his name on it and Garrison's interest in the Hunts' possible involvement in the assassination. He says that the author of the chart, William Wood (Boxley), after he was fired by Garrison, came to see a Hunt official. Wood said that one of the reasons he was interested in Nelson Bunker Hunt's involvement was that Bunker's good friend, George Owen, had said, "Everyone in Dallas knew who did it." When Garrison pushed Owen for an explanation, he said Hoover did it, meaning the FBI director. Garrison believed that the information originated with Bunker Hunt.[26] The implication is that if Bunker Hunt had Owen tell Garrison this, it was to deflect attention away from the Hunts.

Rothermel curiously reported in a December 1968 memo that "Garrison has, over the weekend, fired William Wood (also known as William Boxley), on the grounds of Boxley being a CIA agent. I am told that Boxley's theory is that H. L. Hunt was the key man in the assassination of President Kennedy, and that he has others underneath Mr. Hunt on a chart."[27]

Paul Rothermel wrote the Hunts on October 16, 1967, "I have information to the effect that Garrison is referring to either you or Bunker as the wealthy oilman in his probe."[28] In another memo a few months later, he writes, "The source of the information reports that Garrison is convinced that the assassination was carried out by General Edwin Walker with the financial support and backing of Herman and George Brown of Houston and H. L. Hunt of Dallas. He said that Garrison is a heavy drinker and lives extravagantly despite a modest salary as district attorney."[29]

Rothermel refused to be interviewed about memos he wrote and documents he reviewed, saying he could not confirm or deny their authenticity. A year after the first memo cited in the preceding paragraph, on September 17, 1968, another Hunt memo said, "Jim Garrison made the statement for the news media that Clay Shaw ought to be tried. He said if Clay Shaw were tried, Garrison would show a link of conspiracy between Shaw and oil money in the Southwest."[30]

One of the letters unearthed by Bernard Fensterwald in the HSCA's files stated, "Wood said that Garrison had on four or five occasions ordered him to come to Dallas to reassure the Hunts that Garrison was not after them. Wood said it got to be embarrassing to do this, and he questioned Garrison's motives."[31]

Boxley/Wood was afraid and said that Garrison was out to get him. "He feared for his life . . . and said that he had no friends."[32] The man was isolated, broke, and needed a job. It seems strange that he would go to the people who in some quarters were accused of assassinating Kennedy. Wood thought he would be a scapegoat for Garrison under the guise of a planted CIA man. Wood/Boxley thought "Harold Weisberg and Gary Schoener are behind his being dismissed, and thinks they have complete control of the Clay Shaw trial and Garrison."[33] This could certainly explain why the Garrison debacle was such a mess.

Of course, a delegation of big-name assassination researchers—Harold Weisberg, Bernard Fensterwald, and Vincent Salandria—went to see Jim Garrison and had Boxley/Wood fired on the grounds that he was still working for the CIA and screwing up the investigation. This seems a bad reason, since one view is that Garrison screwed it up with no help from anyone. Wood/Boxley died a broken man. Penn Jones,

Jr., with whom William Wood/Boxley had a close association, said that Mary Ferrell was the one behind the destruction of William Wood/Boxley.[34]

The Garrison affair was sown with the seeds of its own destruction by the premature charging of a suspect (Clay Shaw) with no case against him. Garrison could establish no actual linkage with the events of Dallas.

One comment by an employee of Hunt's was that "Garrison is still on the theory that the CIA was behind the assassination and claims to have now proven that the 'Welcome Mr. Kennedy' ad was an idea of the CIA because Larry Schmidt was a CIA agent."[35] The real culprit must have been laughing up his sleeve, because he knew that Nelson Bunker Hunt admitted to FBI investigators W. Harlan Brown and Edwin D. Kuykendall that he had paid for part of the ad.[36]

Later, the comment went into the record. Rothermel wrote to Hunt, "We have extended our cooperation to Garrison in his probe hoping to help guide his investigation. I think everyone would like the assassination solved, and certainly there is no member of the Hunt family or organization who has the least thing to hide. In spite of the above, there have been persistent stories to the effect that Garrison either suspects or is antagonistic toward the Hunts. We have no proof that this is the case."[37]

It is worth noting that here we have a former FBI agent with a high-ranking corporate position following the evidence in the JFK case closely who assumes that there was a conspiracy in Kennedy's murder. But in Rothermel's memos to Hunt (some appear to be for the record, or even for the purpose of self-delusion), we have the evidence of a major attempt to deflect or derail attention from suspects who can pay the bill.

The very next paragraph resorts to the kind of low blow that was so famous among dirty tricks: "It is reported that Garrison is a most vindictive left winger, that he is bisexual and a clever blackmailer. Garrison understands public opinion, and can without introducing evidence of proof, harass, intimidate, and smear whomever he wishes."

Did Garrison make all this up about Texas oilmen involvement in the assassination? What evidence did he have, and **why did Garrison shift over to the CIA as the bogeyman?** This tells us that there was something seriously wrong with Garrison that he could shift his perpetrators so easily. Or was he paid off? Was this some form of extortion?

The end of Garrison's shakedown came in 1967 in the form of one

Al Chapman, who said he was associated with Garrison. Chapman said that he had important proof that Garrison was on the right track toward solving the Kennedy assassination and "he would then ask Mr. Hunt to make a contribution to the Garrison probe fund. Chapman said that Garrison is in desperate need of the money, as most of his financial sources have dried up."[38]

Chapman had with him the photographs of FBI agent Robert Barrett picking up a bullet from the grass alongside the spot where the limousine had been at the moment of the head shot. With Barrett in the same picture were officer Foster and Deputy Sheriff Buddy Walters. Walters was later killed while he and Al Maddox attempted an arrest. Chapman offered these photographs as proof of conspiracy, that there had been a gunman near the car on the knoll.

Chapman pleaded Garrison's need to the Hunts by saying that Garrison suspected no one in the Hunt family, and had been misquoted and misunderstood in what he was saying. "I told Chapman that this was not the case, that I myself had seen Garrison in an interview and he was making statements which were highly misleading."[39] Rothermel told Chapman that it was slanderous for statements to be made alleging that a Texas multibillionaire was part of the assassination plot, since everyone associated such an identification of this nature with the Hunts, and that no member of the Hunt family had any remote connections with the Kennedy assassination.

The same memorandum says, "A reliable informant advises that Al Chapman, who is one armed and crippled in one leg, is a ne'er-do-well, an eccentric and a highly unreliable individual; that he has worked with Penn Jones, extreme liberal newspaper editor of the *Midlothian Mirror,* and now a frequent writer of articles about the assassination; that Chapman has been to the Texas Penitentiary on either forgery or burglary and that he is a member of the Ku Klux Klan, and as far as the informant knows still holds a position with the Klan in Oak Cliff."

Rothermel sheds some light in another memo that read, "I had a visit from William Wood of Austin, Texas, who said that he wanted to explain the chart which he drew, which had H. L., Hunt's and my name on it. He said that he in no way meant to infer that either H. L. Hunt or myself had anything to do with the assassination and that he was merely drawing it up to show that Andy Anderson, one of Jack Ruby's closest friends, had never been thoroughly checked and, that no matter how hard he had tried, he always got people who defended Anderson or failed to give information about him."[40]

"Wood said that he is not antagonistic toward Mr. Hunt; that Garrison had never indicated hostility toward Mr. Hunt. He did admit that

Garrison had checked out—and had him check on—various stories involving Mr. Hunt, all of which proved to be untrue. . . . He said that he was broke and needed a job. That he really wanted a job and preferred to have some one back him in writing a book, not about the assassination but about the Garrison investigation.

"Wood admitted that the James Bradley indictment was motivated by Garrison for publicity reasons rather than on fact. . . ."[41]

A memo then tells the Hunts that Wood wanted Hunt to distribute *Farewell America,* which accuses Hunt of involvement in the assassination! (You figure it out!)

Wood said he believed the Clay Shaw prosecution would fail and that "Garrison will blame him, the government of the United States, and particularly the CIA, for thwarting any successful prosecution by failure to disclose pertinent facts that Garrison has subpoenaed."[42] This is pretty much what happened.

The record notes, "It was important that Wood was nervous and may really believe that Garrison is determined to either assassinate him or completely ruin him by disclosures out of his office.

". . . We have over the years cooperated with Garrison in every way and, of course Garrison's investigators, including William Boxley, had full access to the information we provided. I am reassured by Garrison's staff that he had no intention of embarrassing Mr. Hunt, but we certainly have no control over what he or others might write."

Healey told me something I had heard from others. I had asked him if anyone knew the whole story who was alive: "There are only two people left alive that have most of the story. Nobody has the whole picture because that's not the way it was designed. It was the need-to-know factor. Probably only two people still living who can corroborate what you are seeking. Not myself."

"Who are they? Who knows what happened?"

"Lady Bird Johnson, I think, is one." He hesitated and said, "J. Walter Moore, the CIA guy in Dallas, told me he'll never talk."

"Does he know anything?"

"Yes." Moore died in 1993.

"Was Mac Wallace one of the shooters?"

"Maybe. I don't know that he was or wasn't."

"The Zapruder film could very well be a forgery," Healey said with a knowing tone in his voice. If the original never left Dallas and the forgery was done right there before *Life* and the Secret Service got their copies, that would explain a lot of things. (For more discussion, see the chapter on films in this book.)

*   *   *

Healey said, "Well, one thing I know for sure—Jack Ruby was a paid informant of the FBI. Oswald may or may not have been paid—or for the CIA—but I *know* that Ruby was an FBI source."[43] A little later in the same interview, he was asked why federal agents would bury evidence in the assassination even though they had no part in its planning or performance: "Well, when you have a CIA/FBI informant shooting the president, and an FBI informant shooting the assassin, they *have* to cover. If it ever came out, that would be the end of both of them so far as Congress was concerned."

Rothermel told me that most if not all of the information on the assassination that John Curington had, even though he ran the Hunt empire for twelve years, wasn't reliable. "Hunt didn't confide in Curington."

Hunt kept a lot of his money in a secret bank account at Hanover Bank in New York. "I don't recall any withdrawals," Robert Blount told me after describing the above bank account.

"If you want to understand what happened in this case, then you have to understand the connection of Lee Harvey Oswald and the local FBI office in Dallas." That connection was that Oswald was a FBI informer.

But the planners, in choosing Oswald, therefore ensured the cooperation of The FBI's lower echelons (none of whom knew Hoover was a conspirator) in accusing him. They were neutralized.

The Dallas Cover-Up

There was a cover-up. Evidence had to be planted, the patsy killed, and the police had to be controlled. "There are three people in Dallas, excluding certain police officers, who know more about the assassination than anyone alive. Their knowledge would be based on postassassination happenings," one of the former FBI men told me. The three men were Henry Wade, the district attorney; his assistant Bill Alexander; and Bob Denson.

Denson was a military intelligence officer in World War II and was employed by South West Security in Dallas. Denson worked as an investigator for Melvin Belli in his defense of Jack Ruby for shooting Oswald and he had worked for Henry Wade. Denson at first told me, "I have no information. I am a hunter. . . ." and hung up.

"Talk to Bill Alexander," Madeleine Brown advised me.

"Why?"

"Because he *knows* what happened."

"How do you know?"

"Because he was too close to the situation!"

Helen Denton worked in the courthouse for a good part of her life, and she believed that Alexander, whatever else he might be, was an honest man and knew a lot about the assassination. Helen continually pushed me toward Alexander, who continually closed the door in my face, not without reason. Alexander was one of the few people who wasn't about to talk to me. That was true because I had made the mistake of quoting things one of the Dallas researchers, Gary Shaw, had written about him in his book. Alexander didn't like this and told me so.

While Brown was at it, she told me that the police found a set of fingerprints on Tippit's car, and they weren't Oswald's. But how can we verify this? Officer Paul Bentley gives conflicting stories on the fingerprints, but told George O'Toole that "we do know that his [Oswald's] fingerprints were taken off the passenger side of Tippit's car."[44] Yet Sergeant W. E. Barnes (who dusted Tippit's car for prints) told the Warren Commission, "There were several smear prints. None of value . . . No legible prints were found."[45]

Another source told me that Tippit was up to his eyeballs in the assassination.

Healey told me, "Henry Wade prevented any toehold of the Mob in Dallas. He was totally honest." Healey told me that Wade was a conservative Democrat, and the most powerful man in Dallas at the time of the murder. "Or at least as important as the others" (Decker, Cabell, Bankstom, and Sterrett). Healey did not see Wade as a party to the conspiracy. "He wouldn't be a party to a conspiracy to murder the president. If there is anybody who knows what happened and might tell you about it, it might be him!"[46]

"Lew Sterrett was the county judge and knew who was blackmailing who and so on. He *congealed* everyone. He'd bring it to a head. If anyone set up the assassination, I'm sure he'd be one of the people that would have done it. Things are done by the good 'ol boy system. He was an implementer of business. Nothing could happen in Dallas that he didn't know."

Another source, Al Maddox, said, "Lew Sterrett would steal a nickel off his momma's eyes when she was just dead. If anybody was hungry and dirty enough to do it. He had every opportunity to be connected to Joe Civello [the local Mob head]. He was a slimy little bastard."[47]

And who were the police officers who knew so much? Some were dead, such as Buddy Walters, who was shot through the heart, Bill

Biggio; P. T. Dane, Lieutenant H. M. Hart; and Maurice "Monk" Baker, who was shot through the mouth. Baker lived on North Beckley Street near Oswald's rooming house. There were other deaths, such as those of Clarence Oliver and John Liggett. Too many we did not count, distracted with the "Strange Deaths" list we have always heard about.

"I don't think Butler [Lieutenant George Butler] was involved," Healey said. "He was on the outs with Curry, Fritz, and Gannaway. He was out of the loop. Right wing though he may be, he wouldn't have been involved in this." Some thought that Butler had helped Assistant Chief of Police Charles Batchelor take Ruby into the police station to kill Oswald.[48] "Nobody trusted Butler," Healey told me.[49]

Another source in Dallas told me that when former Dallas Police Lieutenant Jack Revill ran for sheriff, "one of the most interesting things in the world would be to get ahold of his financial contributors' list, because I *know* that he tapped into the people that were *squirming!*" When he said, "I *know* that he tapped into the people that were squirming," his voice warbled on the word *know* in that wonderful way people outside Texas ordinarily only see in films such as *Lonesome Dove.*

"Squirming on the assassination?"

"*Yeah!* And its's supposed to be down there in the courthouse."

"There is just so much that you could dig into, but the rabbit trails would take you a lifetime."

At the end of the plot, when John Kennedy was dead, power had passed to the Secret Team, the operational hand of The Club. From that moment on, elected government in the United States had a lot less meaning.

A keystone of the murder was faked evidence, and that included the films and photographs. Not only were the autopsy pictures and X-rays forged, but also the Zapruder and other films may have been tampered with. A reliable source told me that he doesn't think *Life* ever had the original Zapruder film. "Numerous copies were made," he told me.

The copies were distributed as follows: (1) FBI lab; (2) Dallas FBI office; (3) Washington, D.C., FBI office; (4) Henry Wade (5) Dallas Police; (6) and (7) two copies for the two couples who owned the film lab; (8) Secret Service copy; (9) Somewhere along the line, H.L. Hunt had his copy from the start. That's ten. Zapruder and, ultimately, *Life* had what they thought was the original.

Anyone who doesn't think that law enforcement would copy and keep copies of such sensational evidence is naive. The Zapruder film was obtained at once by the conspirators and forged. The large hole extending into the back of Kennedy's head was blacked out to mask this exit wound, and a large, fleshy exit wound was painted onto the film on Kennedy's face. A new "original" was struck from the fake film. It took very little time to doctor the few frames involved.

George Healey said that he *saw* pictures in Washington, D.C., of John Kennedy's body taken at Parkland before the body was taken to the autopsy in Maryland.[50] This was the fourth person who told us he or she saw these pictures, along with Joe Cody, Vicky Mayne, and another. We know they were taken at Parkland because some saw them before the body ever reached Washington. Joe Cody later denied that he saw such photographs. Somebody could have used a small spy camera (a Minox) to take them, and Diana Bowron and others never saw the pictures being taken.

Then there was the getaway of the shooters. There are repeated reports that cars were changed in Temple or Paris, Texas, and that a man recognized Mac (Malcolm) Wallace there. He is believed by Madeleine Brown and others of being one of the shooters.

They had so desperately to cover up the crime, and so many people got into the cover-up, because they sensed that to let the truth come out would reveal the true nature of our political system—that democracy and elections are a front; JFK wouldn't play ball.

Anticonstitutional sentiment was greatest in the Dallas area in 1963. It is still a factor in our national politics, but it lies hidden, like a sinister demon in our midst, manipulating and controlling our destinies, making puppets of our presidents and representatives.

"Nobody is going to shoot the president without something to gain,"[51] Healey told me. "Nobody had more to gain and more to lose than Johnson. And no one was closer to J. Edgar Hoover than Lyndon Johnson."

Madeleine Brown told me that Johnson used to say, "Well, he's a son of a bitch, but he's *our* son of a bitch!"

"I can see him now, see him lean back," Madeleine told me, "his feet up on the table, and give out with a little bullshit and then came the squeeze," she said from all of her seventy years. "He did a lot of things for a lot of people but he always expected something in return. He never did a favor without asking a favor in return."

"There was no one who hated Robert Kennedy more than Hoover," Healey told me. Robert Kennedy came to see Sheriff Bill Decker days after the assassination and demanded to know what really happened to his brother. We know that Decker believed there were gunmen in front of the car on the bridge.

Johnson and Hoover were allied to the Establishment that has been raping us, that has mortgaged the future of this nation to banks, big companies, and foreign nations, tying us all to the interest in the national debt and the imbalance in trade.

John Kennedy was a great enemy of these people because he was a fiscal conservative. The real answer to the assassination was that some people needed a new asset—the National Debt—and they helped kill him for that.

This is the ultimate legacy of the assassination: We became the world's largest debtor nation.

There is an inscription in stone on the sidewalk near Dealey Plaza. It says, "The joy and excitement of John Fitzgerald Kennedy's life belonged to all men. So did the pain and sorrow of his death. When he died on November 22, 1963, shock and agony touched human conscience throughout the world. In Dallas, Texas, there was a special sorrow. The young President died in Dallas. The death bullets were fired 200 yards west of this site. This memorial, designed by Philip Johnson, was erected by the people of Dallas. Thousands of citizens contributed support, money and effort.

"It's not a memorial to the pain and sorrow of death, but stands as a permanent tribute to the joy and excitement of one man's life.

"John Fitzgerald Kennedy's life."

Judge Lew Sterrett knew what was
coming down long before it
happened.

—Al Maddox

CHAPTER 18

THE PLOT

A combine of powerful people came together in 1963 to eliminate President Kennedy. A number of Kennedy's policy decisions precipitated the crisis. Planning had begun in the summer of 1963, and patsies, including Oswald, were set up. Things came to a head in the fall when Kennedy made the decision to leave Vietnam. His close watch over the Treasury and the National Debt gravely threatened the plans of powerful people who wanted to run up the debt and hold it as an asset, and they needed a war to get the country to borrow. His intent to remove the oil depletion allowance as a tax break was a flash point with the oilmen and got their support for the plot.

Meetings to discuss the murder of President Kennedy were first held at the Driskill Hotel in Austin and at Johnson's ranch on the Pedernales near Austin, after it was clear that H. L. Hunt, Clint Murchison, Jr., Lyndon Johnson, and J. Edgar Hoover agreed that Kennedy had to be removed. They spontaneously coalesced together in an *ad hoc committee,* but if there was initiative by one person, he was Vice President Lyndon Baines Johnson or H. L. Hunt. The director of the FBI, J. Edgar Hoover, like Stalin's henchman the director of the NKVD, Laurenti Beria, in the Soviet Union—was with Johnson every step of the way.

Naturally, with Johnson's widow still alive thirty years later, there were more than enough powerful people who had reason to continue to cover up the case in our own time. We were often looking at some of the conspirators—those left alive—and everyone carried on business as usual, as though nothing had happened. Protecting a presidential image for history is also important.

But some Texans could not escape the nagging notion that Lady Bird Johnson, the widow, was the one who pushed the conspiracy into being.

543

Lady Bird also thinks that her husband was poisoned by his Secret Service guards because they despised him.

The most prominent figures of industry and politics often gathered from across Texas and met at the Driskill. Austin was the capital and a university city, which provided cover. Dallas was more of a cowboy town at the time.

Texas had been a nation unto itself. It passed beneath six flags in its history, including that of the Confederacy. Having briefly been an independent nation, Texans have a very special and often arrogant view of themselves vis-à-vis the rest of the United States.

But the great oil barons who headquartered in Dallas and Fort Worth had other plans. H. L. Hunt and Clint Murchison, Jr., along with their right hand—the law firm of Locke, Purnell—intended to drive Dallas/Fort Worth forward into the defense business, plowing their oil and gas earnings into missiles, sophisticated computerized ordnance, helicopter gunships, and combat aircraft. The Murchisons owned Centex, the largest residential development company in the country at the time, and the huge construction company Tecon.

Fort Worth, a companion city to Dallas forty miles away, was a center of wealth and power of its own. Syd Richardson had lived in Fort Worth before he died, and CIA man David Atlee Phillips and his brothers, prominent in Forth Worth, had to have been tight with Richardson, who was widely rumored to be Clint Murchison, Jr.'s lover. Governor John Connally was a director of Syd Richardson's oil empire, and when Syd died, Connally had control of that money, which translated into great power.

These were extremely powerful people in our nation who resented John Kennedy on many scores. Part of it was the resentment of a man attractive to women who could have many women, and yet a man who was essentially moral, who tried to reign in the murderous impulses of a country with a long history of violence. Secret Service agents close to the President who knew of some of his feminine liaisons resented it, sat in judgment of him, and cooperated with the plotters to kill him.

Violence was too endemic in our society for John Kennedy to defeat it. His attempts to get under control the anti-Castro Cubans, stop the assassination plots against Castro, promote nonviolent desegregation in the South, and prosecute organized crime helped kill him.

There are certain traits that become part of certain behavior patterns. J. Edgar Hoover was homosexual, and he ruined people or blackmailed them with that accusation. The people who killed John Kennedy shared certain things in common, among them murderous impulses, lasciviousness, excess, homosexuality, greed, and corruption of the spirit and body.

In the weeks just before the assassination, the drums were beating in Dallas, working up hatred for Kennedy in speeches before the luncheon and foreign affairs clubs, as in a statement by Peter O'Donnell, Jr., rapping Kennedy's wheat sale plan to the Soviet Union: "When will we ever learn that the Communists are our sworn enemy?"[1] O'Donnell was one of Richard Nixon's close contacts in Dallas.

Planning

The first planning sessions at the Driskill provided for future meetings elsewhere, and for signals to draw one another together. Their main problem was to settle on a director, or mastermind, but that was easy enough to solve. A man skilled in intelligence and the compartmental-ization of operations was chosen. His right hand was a man who paid the bills with untraceable cash provided by Hunt and the others. Hunt's many cash outlays to radical right groups provided a cover.

The mastermind drew a chart showing how the operation would play out. He picked four gunmen, decoys, their backups, and patsies—Lee Harvey Oswald among them. They were selected on the basis of their supposed leftist backgrounds. That was a little touch that pleased the right-wing plotters.

Each person at the top had a job. Johnson's was to lure Kennedy to Dallas and, after the murder, to pick a blue-ribbon commission to inves-tigate and whitewash the crime. Hoover picked one gunman, and John-son, Hunt, and Murchison settled the rest.

Information about plots in other cities was planted to drive Kennedy toward Texas and Dallas, where the killing ground could best be con-trolled. Some key representatives of the eastern Establishment were made privy to the plot after their anti-Kennedy sentiments became known. With the New Yorkers and New Englanders it was a simple matter of money. The banks were getting into trouble from overexten-sion of real-estate loans, and they needed a way to tax the public to save their investments; hence the plan to drive up the National Debt.

The cooperation of the Easterners was needed by the Texans. Other men, such as Earl Warren, a California Republican connected to the Teamsters and perhaps other Mobsters but cloaked in the mantle of liberalness, as Lyndon Johnson was—could be counted on to cover up.

So they killed John Kennedy.

The plotters included J. Edgar Hoover, Lyndon Johnson, Clint Murchison, General Charles Cabell, Mayor Earle Cabell, and David Atlee Phillips. In Dallas, Sheriff Bill Decker, Chief of Police Curry, Assistant Chief of Police Charles Batchelor, Judge Lew Sterrett, Morris Jaffe, and Mob boss Joe Civello all cooperated. Men such as Mac Wallace and Charles Harrellson of the Texas Mafia appear to have been used.

I was able to obtain mug shots taken in other towns of Harrellson from the period when Kennedy died, and police officers positively identified him as the tall tramp arrested in the train yards just after the assassination. Al Maddox, in addition, told us that Harrellson had been picked up on a "Decker Warrant" and held for several months in 1963 in Dallas. Maddox said that he took Harrellson his mail every day at the jail.[2] There were no mug shots taken. "I saw Harrellson a bunch of times in jail."

"Was he a contract hit man?" I asked.

"Hell, yeah!" It would seem that someone in Dallas law enforcement who knew Harrellson might remember if he was brought in with the other tramps arrested in the rail yards after the assassination. Officer Roy Vaughan climbed into a gondola car to get the tramps out. Like so many other examples in formerly lawless Dallas, records of Harrellson's February 1963 incarceration were not kept. It seems reasonable that holding Harrellson on possibly trumped-up charges was either for his own protection, or to soften him up before pointing him at Kennedy.

Others were kept close, without knowing what was up, such as Richard Nixon, and then were made privy to it at Murchison's house on the night before the murder. Meanwhile, Kennedy's Secret Service detail was kept out drinking all night at the Cellar, an after-hours place connected to these wealthy gamblers and the Mob.

They had to be certain that Lee Harvey Oswald was at work the following morning. Oswald's case officer (the FBI agent who ran him) made sure that Oswald's every move was known. Oswald followed orders, went to the Texas Theatre to meet his contact after the assassination, and was picked up there by the police.

General Cabell had been fired by Kennedy in April 1962, replaced as Deputy Director of the CIA, due to what Kennedy "believed" was Cabell's poor performance during the Bay of Pigs invasion and planning. "The aftermath of General Charles Cabell's pleas of help for the Bay of Pigs and President Kennedy's 'betrayal' would soon be heard in Dallas," former Office of Naval Intelligence (ONI) man Bob Goodman writes. "For those that believe that the Bay of Pigs disaster was a main motive in the death of President Kennedy, it is only left to the imagination as to what must have raced through the minds of those that supported the invasion as the anger and humiliation must have been of the highest degree. When President Kennedy said the final 'NO' to General Cabell, he basically put an end to Cabell's 'colorful career.' This is the short story of a dedicated conservative patriotic man from Dallas,'' Goodman says.[3] Goodman, a native Dallasite, was in the ONI for five years.

General Cabell controlled events at the autopsy of John F. Kennedy. Participants were made to fabricate or ignore evidence and findings. The doctors were ordered to lie at the autopsy, to make it look like there was only one gunman, from behind.

"Judge Lew Sterrett knew what was coming down long before it happened,'' former deputy sheriff Al Maddox told officer Marco Miranda.[4] ''He was a sneaky little bastard!'' Sterrett was one of the three men, along with Sheriff Bill Decker and Mayor Earle Cabell, who ran Dallas. ''He was in the middle between those who were going to kill Kennedy, and those who had to cover it up,'' Maddox said.

Did Johnson and Hoover have the nation and the wealthy Establishment boxed in with a *fait accompli*? Not completely. Johnson was the great "consensus-builder,'' and he and his cohorts rounded up support for the plan. Those wealthy people in it from the start also gathered support on their end for a change in government. Hunt and the others had backing and contacts in New York, Los Angeles, Chicago, San Francisco, and Kansas City. Of course, only a few people could be privy to what was occurring, including those at the "party'' the night before. The game was to establish firm control within hours of the murder, put out a cover story, hide the evidence so those who might object and fight back had nothing to go on, and at the same time put out signals of what had really happened to placate those who wanted Kennedy out of the way.

In other words, at first they needed only the backing of some of the most powerful people, and there were enough from Texas to provide tight-lipped support from the Establishment.

This is the real reason Richard Nixon and John J. McCloy were in Dallas. They represented the interests of the New York banks and their owners.

The plotters had people and doctors waiting at Parkland Memorial Hospital to take care of problems. Surreptitiously, some took pictures of John Kennedy's body at Parkland. Prints were made in 1990 from two of the Parkland negatives showing the face and the back of the head to check against the pictures that were being published, and they conflicted greatly with the forged autopsy pictures from Bethesda. The 1990 prints were made at the University of Texas Medical Center, across the boulevard from Parkland Memorial Hospital.

Dallas Police officers had previously seen the Parkland photographs. So did people who developed them at the National Photo Company.

The Autopsy

The plotters had to be on the spot at the place of autopsy wherever it was going to be. They had to stay with the body to be sure it did not get out of their hands until they could get the result they needed.

They steered the body to Washington. It was necessary to control what happened, obtain the rolls of film and X-rays, and begin faking the material on the spot. I have no doubt that Humes was told what to write, namely that the throat wound was an exit wound, and to cover up the fact that the back wound did not penetrate the body. He faked the so-called exploration of this alleged through-and-through wound. The plotters did not care so much about the head wound because the head was so badly damaged that the doctors could write their report in such a way that the position and all of the facts were not too clear. The pictures give no clue as to how it really looked, and the photos are, in fact, at great variance with the autopsy report itself, not to speak of the descriptions given by numerous doctors including Humes and Boswell, in both cities.

The doctors left clues and a trail to let us know they were made to do it. They tried to tell us that they had to do it by leaving clues such as a brain weight of 1500 grams, saying they didn't know about the throat wound when they did, and saying that there was an entrance wound near the occipital protuberance when there could have been none because there was no bone there. The liver weighed far too little to support life, in addition, and this was another signal from the doctors at Bethesda.

Yes, there was a general (more than one) in the autopsy room, and admirals, too, and some of those tried that night to get the results they needed from the doctors to have just one gunman. There can be no doubt from the destruction of Humes's notes and the original autopsy report that he was acting under orders, just as Hosty was ordered to destroy Oswald's note.

It is devastatingly clear that the autopsy was deliberately botched, and that the autopsy photographs described by the House Committee as being of poor quality and inadmissible in court were botched deliberately.

*   *   *

Bell Helicopters and General Dynamics in the Dallas/Fort Worth area had a big stake in the death of Kennedy, and the oilmen had a large investment in those new defense industries in their area. They needed the Cold War.

The plotters had a dirty tricks and security specialist who knew whom to go to for gunmen, all of whom were personally known to the plotters. They would not use all Mob shooters because the plan required implicating people who could then be forced to cover up.

They also needed a compartmentalized command structure. This came ready-made in the Dallas area and they needed a lot of hands on this job, so unwitting helpers were found among the Secret Service, the Dallas Police, the FBI, and at the autopsy.

Operations

The sheriff of Dallas County, Bill Decker, was one of the most powerful men in the state and may have been part of the plot. The fact that he privately said the shots came from in front of the car was simply a smoke screen for his firsthand knowledge. Having control over men such as Harrellson, whom Decker had kept in jail earlier that year, and dishonest police officers may have been a good way to organize the shooters and their backups and to point them at Kennedy.

The chief of police of a small town near Dallas was good friends with Decker. He recalls, "Bill Decker did not believe the shots to have come from the TSBD. When asked where he believed the shots did come from, he said, 'That sewer up there on the hill' . . . Decker told him that there was no way Oswald fired those shots. When asked why that was, he replied that the shots 'Came from that damn drain up near the overpass.' "[5] Chief of Police Jesse Curry was videotaped also saying that he believed at least one shot was fired from in front.[6]

Preparing the Patsy

Oswald had to be prepared, and his CIA baby-sitter for that purpose, although perhaps unwitting of the plan, was George De Mohrenschildt. Oswald was sent to New Orleans as part of his ongoing government work. The fact that he had been in New Orleans got everyone off the track in assuming the plot came from Louisiana, unless we figure into the equation the fact that the Murchison brothers owned a third of New Orleans. Carlos Marcello knew that something was going on, through

Civello, but was probably not privy to the details of the plot or who was involved. Decker had control of Ruby and didn't need Marcello, Civello, Campisi, or Jaffe.

Murchison, a close friend of Hoover, had the power in New Orleans to direct attention away from Dallas and the FBI. So District Attorney Jim Garrison is pointed at the CIA.

The Ambush

John Kennedy was the victim of a military-style ambush involving several gunmen. Shooters were placed all around the car, though not all fired.

We know from the physical evidence that there was an ambush, with gunmen in front and behind. There had to be two gunmen firing from behind, and it is most likely that shots came from the Dal-Tex Building.

Statements of Harold Norman indicate that the rifle fired from that window of the TSBD was fired too rapidly to have been aimed properly. It was a diversion establishing the frame-up of Oswald, who was on a lower floor at the time of the assassination, for the crime.

Other shots came from in front of the limousine. Several years later, I personally observed the bullet strike on the sidewalk as coming from the manhole/storm drain on the bridge to the left front of the limousine. The storm drain was in a perfectly straight line with the bullet scar later removed by Earl Golz. This was a missed shot.

A bullet hit the President in the back and then a missile struck him in the throat from in front. This shot had to come either from the Grassy Knoll or from one of the storm drains in front of the car. Another shot or two in the fusillade hit John Connally. One miss struck the sidewalk beside the car, and another hit cement in front of James Tague, who was struck with debris.

Certainly there was someone firing from the storm drain just to the right front of the car. That had to be where the fatal head shot originated, because the trajectory of head matter went backward and to the left and not to the side as much as a shot from the Grassy Knoll. Such a shot from the Grassy Knoll would have knocked the President sideways. There may have been a diversionary gunman on the Grassy Knoll, attracting attention away from those who had more difficulty in firing unobserved, screened by men with phony Secret Service credentials who turned the crowd running up there away.

"I was standing in the middle of Elm Street from the southeast curb of Elm and Houston," Dallas police officer J. M. Smith wrote. "I heard the shots and thought they were coming from bushes of the overpass."[7] There is only one place where bushes and the overpass meet, and that is at the far western cdge of the Grassy Knoll, by the storm drain on the bridge at the juncture with the wooden fence. You can still see that and the drain today. It is not the Grassy Knoll area where we have always been told by researchers there were gunmen, allegedly seen in the vague Mooreman Polaroid photograph. Far from it.

Cover-up

The murder was covered up because Lee Harvey Oswald worked for the government. He was a paid informant of the FBI and, in fact, a provocateur for them. He had gone to the Soviet Union as an operative of the Office of Naval Intelligence.

There is a paymaster, left in place, a lawyer who pays some of the researchers. Some are paid to collect information, others to plant false information or disrupt any serious investigation. A trust fund was set up to handle disbursements.

The shooters and others were paid with property transactions. They were given leases and options that could be cashed at a later date. Cash payments were deemed too risky. Oil, gas, and uranium leases were one means of payment.

And Ruby had to die because he was talking too much. "He would have been out on the street in another month if he hadn't died. He chose to die. A doctor gave him the needle. I was one of the first ones to come out with that," Al Maddox told us.[8] "Ruby was writing too many letters." Maddox said that Dallas Police sergeant P.T. Dane was "right in the middle."

The Dal-Tex Building

Anyone in the windows of the Dal-Tex Building or on the roof of the Dal-Tex Building could chart the progress of the President's car and signal the gunmen facing the car in the two storm drains to either side of the triple overpass. The fallback area and immediate safe house for the gunmen coming out of the tunnels leading from the storm drains was Downtown Lincoln/Mercury.

The report of Secret Service agent Winston Lawson describes the advance meeting with John Connally's close friend Eugene Locke, who was a senior partner in the firm of Locke Purnell, where the planning for Kennedy's trip took place.[9] Elizabeth Forsling Harris and Jack Puterbaugh also played key roles at the planning session. "Puterbaugh was working closely with Billie Sol Estes, later convicted and sent to prison. It was Puterbaugh who made the decision to hold the luncheon in the Trade Mart 'because of the proximity to Love Field,' and it was Puterbaugh who made the decision to take the unauthorized and unnecessary detour in Dealey Plaza."[10] Neither Puterbaugh nor Betty Harris was questioned by the Warren Commission.

Harris worked for the Sol Bloom Advertising Agency and was the Dallas contact of the Washington planners for Kennedy's visit.[11] Bill Moyers, a presidential assistant, directed Mrs. Harris to publish the motorcade route.[12]

Dallas Uranium and Oil operated out of the Dal-Tex Building. Dallas Uranium and Oil had the same phone number, RI 2-8063, as Morty Freedman and Marilyn Belt.

Morty Freedman was an attorney and held a small part of Zapruder's company. Freedman evidently operated Dallas Uranium and Oil from the sixth floor in that building, level with the alleged sniper's window across the street. There is no record of Dallas Uranium and Oil among registered businesses in the state capital at Austin. It was not listed on the directory in the lobby of the Dal-Tex Building, nor was it listed at the County Records Building. It was only listed in the 1963 Yellow Pages (page 536) under "Oil Producers."

The Dal-Tex Building's businesses were primarily garment-related, such as Abraham Zapruder's Jennifer Juniors, Inc., and the Marilyn Belt Manufacturing Company.

Abraham Zapruder's son Henry Zapruder worked for the Department of Justice and knew J. Edgar Hoover. Zapruder's assistant was Jeanne De Mohrenschildt, wife of George De Mohrenschildt, who ostensibly committed suicide the day investigators from the House Assassinations Committee located him, and during the time he was being interviewed by Edward Jay Epstein. Zapruder's secretary was Lillian Rogers.[13]

Interestingly, George De Mohrenschildt worked at one time for Waldem Oil Company,[14] which was headquartered in the Dal-Tex Building. Researcher and former Office of Naval Intelligence Dallasite Bob Goodman comments on Dallas Uranium and Oil as follows: "The suggestion has been made that it might have been, pardon the expression, a 'dummy corporation,' the term suggesting that it was possibly a shield or a front for activities or operations being conducted which were not to be associated with its true owners or executives. In the search for a clandestine, well-hidden operation that had no apparent explanation for existing in the Dal-Tex Building on the date of JFK's assassination, the investigation continued.''[15]

The powerful people of Dallas are in a conspiracy to cover up the murder of John Kennedy. It is truly a conspiracy of silence, but on a massive, citywide scale, opposed only by the legion of Dallas citizens who persist in doubting, and who ask questions or who know what is going on and who look for that certain writer they can trust and talk to. And whom can you believe?

> Beware of false prophets that
> come to you in sheep's clothing,
> but inwardly they are ravening
> wolves.
>
> —Matthew 7:15

CONCLUSION

On November 22, 1963, Texas in the form of its powerful people intervened violently in the affairs of the rest of the United States. Essentially, one of our big states seized control of the nation by means of the political assassination of President John F. Kennedy. That assassination ultimately benefited the Republican Party, financial interests, and conservatism. We have paid a terrible price.

There can be no doubt that the doctors were controlled by military officers who knew how to use both persuasion and threats. Nevertheless, those doctors tried to leave us a few clues, such as the too-small liver and the overweight brain.

With the national police in control, the cover-up of the crime was assured. The office of the President was held by a man with foreknowledge of the plot. That man's widow, Lady Bird Johnson, knows the truth of what happened. She believes that her husband was poisoned by his own Secret Service detail.

Individual elements of the FBI, CIA, the Secret Service Military Intelligence, Dallas law enforcement, and organized crime were used. Almost all the men involved had a Texas background in this tight little circle, and these agencies were compelled to cover up when the situation became known to them.

The conservative Democrats in the South bolted to the Republican Party, which—along with the assassination of Robert Kennedy—assured the election of Richard Nixon to the presidency in 1968. Though perhaps unwittingly, Richard Nixon and men connected to the CIA close to him were used in the conspiracy in 1963, and that sowed the seeds of Nixon's destruction in Watergate. The Texas oilmen had always backed Nixon.

The result of this terrible murder was the enormous disorder of the

554

1960s. The Johnson administration became, by the end of his term, an illegitimate government that nobody really accepted, the destruction of faith in the word of the government, the vast cost in lives, stability, spirit, and money of the Vietnam War, the emasculation of our politics, Watergate and the resignation of President Nixon, and the bankruptcy of our Treasury. We became the world's largest debtor nation.

The spirit of this country was stricken thirty years ago, and it has never really recovered. Only new generations bring their own spirit to restore something that has been lost. Most of the rest of us haven't been right since, just as though someone we loved in our family had died. But we have to go on.

There are two concepts I would like to convey. One I have already talked about in my previous books, and that is the concept of the Secret Team, first put forward by Fletcher Prouty. This is a sort of shadow government, a group of powerful people in and out of government and the Pentagon who influence or control events.

The other concept is more vague, more like a veil, or a fog, where lines are blurred. It becomes difficult to discover the true identity of people in this case. These people are different things to different people. They live in a world of appearance.

We have been dealing with people in this case who at one and the same time may be a policeman, a gangster, a homosexual, a blackmailer of homosexuals, an entrepreneur, or a gunrunner. It's easy to be fooled by appearances. H. L. Hunt, a gambler tied up with mobsters friendly with Jack Ruby, employed anything he had, including assassins, to build his empire. He would do *anything,* and that was true of most of the big oil pirates in Texas.

You see, that is the nature of America, where even the Mob sits on the Board of Directors of the United States. It's been that way for a long time thanks to J. Edgar Hoover.

Richard Nixon was also affiliated with gangsters from the beginning of his political career.

We can have a general whose brother is a *capo* in the Mob. We can have somebody as complicated as Lyndon Johnson, who was almost all things to all people, but certainly a man who could order another to be killed.

We can have a leading researcher or "archivist" who pulls the wool over everyone's eyes for thirty painful years, convincing everyone that he or she is a critic of the Warren Commission, or simply a collector of evidence in the case, ever helpful to others, but who in fact is a radical conservative or private intelligence agent. As an example of such multifaceted personalities (and I don't intend to imply that he was part of the 1963 events) is E. Howard Hunt. He was an intellectual and a writer, and yet a CIA intelligence agent involved in murder plots. Lots of people were like that.

An entirely new splatter of attackers and third-rate apologists was launched in 1992–93, such as Robert Artwohl and Jerry Organ, who spread far and wide on computer networks and in publications blatant misstatements of facts in the medical evidence, and attempted to demolish our work on the fake X-rays with absurd and fabricated assertions that the frontal bone was in fact there. Some, including the supraorbital ridge may be, but the right forehead and right temple area is completely gone. Dr. John Lattimer, a longtime apologist for the Warren Report, and Artwohl claimed they could actually see the frontal bone, denying the validity of Lattimer's own drawings of the X-rays. They could reverse the place of missing bone in the front/back (A/P) X-ray taken alone without the lateral or side view, which shows quite clearly that a lot of the right side of the face is missing and practically no bone missing in the back of the head.

I feel that one of the signs that we are in the middle of an intelligence operation, albeit private, is that there is so much that is false in the case, and so much that is falsely said about people just trying to do the job of digging out the truth. I can see why this case has not been solved with individuals like the big-name researchers running things, obstructing real research every step of the way.

The Lies

It was claimed by the autopsy doctors that they found what appeared to be an entrance wound on pieces of bone brought in and assembled hours after the autopsy had begun, and were able to identify an entry hole near the occipital protuberance or bump on the back of the head.

The trouble is (like so much else in this case), the doctors may have made it up, because they didn't have the entry hole in the right place— the place on the head where the entry had to be to have come from the sixth-floor window of the TSBD. Now we have an X-ray and photographs that purport to show the entry hole four or five inches higher, in the cowlick of the head, where the cover-up people needed it. But it can't be there because there wasn't any bone there, as the Dallas and Bethesda doctors said.

How can we have a completed skull in the X-rays showing no bone loss in the back of the head except for a small wound of entry when that is where the large defect was?

I know the doctors were not dissembling when they found no entry hole in the cowlick area. They couldn't have found it there. So either they were lying about locating an entry hole lower on the back of the head, or they were caught in the huge lie perpetrated by the cover-up people who were fabricating the X-rays and photographs. It must have been a terrible shock for Humes and Boswell to see the alleged autopsy photographs and X-rays several years later and find themselves trapped.

Another misrepresentation was perpetrated when the doctors had to pretend they did not know there was a bullet hole in the throat. Dr. Robert Livingston had called Humes before he received the body[1] and told him that Dr. Malcolm Perry in Dallas said there was an entry hole in the throat. By pretending that he did not know that, he didn't have to examine the throat wound, and he just put it down as a tracheostomy. After the body had gone, he could write in his report the *speculation* that that was where a bullet *exited*. And surly Admiral Burkley would have told them about the neck wound when he arrived at the autopsy.

Still another clue was Dr. Humes' failure to mention in his report that "the next largest fragment [of a bullet] appeared to be at the rear of the skull at the juncture of the skull bone," as Sibert and O'Neill wrote in their report of the autopsy.[2] The two FBI men made mistakes, but they could not have made a mistake about this, and must have heard such a discussion of a large fragment.

Where on the back of the head? "At the juncture of the skull bone" could mean where sutures come together from different bones, or at the very base of the skull where it meets the neck, in the area where the original head entry wound was placed in the autopsy report. But this fragment was on the brain: Sibert and O'Neill's FBI report of November 26 says, "Two fragments of metal were removed by Dr. Humes, namely, one fragment measuring 7 x 2 millimeters, which was removed from the right side of the brain. An additional fragment of metal measuring 1 x 3 millimeters was also removed from this area. . . ." Both of these are mentioned with the same measurements in the autopsy report, and these have to be the two "missiles" mentioned on the receipt that has caused so much confusion for three decades. It is clear, therefore, that the large piece of bullet seen on the present X-rays on the outer table of the back of the skull did not exist at the autopsy.

The doctors did not report this large fragment at all. *Why?* Is it a simple omission? I hardly think so. They didn't dare report it because, even before Humes wrote his report, the fragment was being taped to pieces of bone and X-rayed by Jerrol Custer[3] so that a new, composite

X-ray of the skull could be made, moving that wound a lot higher than it was—that is, if we can believe Kennedy was in fact wounded in the back of the head.

And what about this?: "Also during the later stages of the autopsy, a piece of the skull measuring 10 x 6.5 centimeters was brought to Dr. Humes who was instructed that this had been removed from the President's skull. Immediately this section of skull was X-rayed, at which time it was determined by Dr. Humes that one corner of this section revealed minute metal particles and inspection of this same area disclosed a chipping of the top portion of this piece, both of which indicated that this had been the point of *exit* of the bullet entering the skull region. . . . The portion of the skull measuring 10 x 6.5 centimeters was maintained in the custody of Dr. Humes who stated that it also could be made available for further examination."[4] From what part of the head was this from? What do they mean by "removed"?

Adding to this mystery, Dr. Michael Baden writes, "Three skull fragments had been retrieved from the limousine, brought to Washington, X-rayed, and later vanished. The fourth, measuring about two by one and a half inches, was found a few days after the autopsy by a premed student walking his dog in Dealey Plaza. (This is the "Harper fragment," which the FBI came and got from the student). . . . It later disappeared from the National Archive[s], along with the other fragments."[5]

We know from the testimony of Clint Hill that the entire rear section of the President's head was lying in the backseat of the limousine.[6] Was it the 10 x 6.5-centimeter piece? That is a rather large piece of bone.

How could they have retained all of this bone and not buried it with the body? What we are being told is that a lot of what was buried was plaster.

I have trouble with the fact that all of this evidence, all of these bones, *plus* the brain, *plus* the interior chest photographs, *plus* the microscopic slide sections taken from the edges of the wounds, *plus* a bullet fragment removed from the brain have *disappeared* from the National Archives. And trust this institution with some of our nation's most priceless treasures? It seems to me to be a clear indication that the President's murder was political in nature when so much of the key evidence is gone.

At times the autopsy doctors have left a trail, trying to tell us in code that there is a gun at their head. Let us remove that gun and get the truth out of them now while we are all still alive.

The conspirators, operating on a high level of government, were able to flash the fake pictures at some of the Warren Commission members, and only in 1968, when the Clark Panel saw the X-rays and photographs, did the autopsy doctors discover that they had been stranded, abandoned, with an insupportable story about the wound. It is unfortunate that we don't know if the photographs and X-rays they saw in 1966 were the same pictures that the Clark Panel and the House Committee saw and which got out to the public in 1988–89.

There was another terrible lie of omission in this case, perhaps an act of treason by the President's physician, Admiral George Burkley. This man had to have known about the entry bullet hole in the throat. He was with the body all along its terrible trip to Bethesda Naval Hospital, the autopsy, and until the body was put into its coffin. Yet this man was never interviewed by the Warren Commission, never submitted any real report for the record, and never talked for the record about what he had seen or experienced that day, unless there is another secret tape in the Oral History Section of the John F. Kennedy Presidential Library. Burkley stayed on with President Johnson and never spoke out.

There is a U.S. senator who bears much of the responsibility for the cover-up of the truth in John Kennedy's murder. We know that a certain amount of the testimony before the Warren Commission was altered. Witnesses were coached. I think there is a lot more to the story of what happened with that Commission, handpicked by President Lyndon Johnson, than anyone has dared speculate. I believe that some of those on the Commission had guilty knowledge.

It bears repeating what President Kennedy's special assistant and close friend Kenneth O'Donnell wrote: ''I distinctly remember that when Johnson and I talked at the hospital there was no mention of which of the two planes he should use. Nor was there any mention that he was considering waiting for Jackie and the President's casket to be on the same plane with him before he left Dallas. Later a lawyer for the Warren Commission, Arlen Specter, pointed out to me that Johnson's testimony that I had told him to board *Air Force One* disagreed with my own testimony before the commission about our conversation at the hospital. Specter asked me, to my amazement, if I would change my testimony so that it would agree with the President's. 'Was I under oath?' I asked Specter, as, of course, I was. 'Certainly I wouldn't change anything I said under oath.''[7]

This is a devastating comment on this case, our system, and our life.

Maryland

The State of Maryland has concurrent jurisdiction in the assassination of President Kennedy. It has jurisdiction by virtue of the fact that the National Naval Medical Center at Bethesda, Maryland, is an "open" federal base. That means that there is no gate, and local and state officials can and do come on the base to investigate any crimes that might be committed on federal property.

Since it is clear that some of the forgeries of the autopsy materials were actually done at Bethesda, and since it is clear that the autopsy information involved fabricated evidence and perjury by the doctors, then it is within the power of the county district attorney and the State of Maryland's attorney general to deal with this.

There is no statute of limitations on homicide. The case is not and cannot be closed. The body was illegally stolen from Texas and brought to Maryland, which is an additional reason for jurisdiction by the county and state. The federal government never had any jurisdiction in the case.

It is the duty of the State of Maryland to take jurisdiction and initiate an investigation and action in this case, since it is clear that the State of Texas has abrogated that responsibility.

President Bill Clinton

If Clinton is a true Democrat and a constitutionalist—not just the puppet of powerful forces in this country who dictate what he says and does—he will take action in the case of the assassination of President John F. Kennedy, whose name he traded on to be elected.

I believe that the evidence is clear that there was a major domestic conspiracy benefiting President Kennedy's long-term enemies, and that it is up to the present government to deal with it. It has been covered up for thirty years, and there has to be a stop to all of this.

This nation is in agony. Its soul is stricken, its heart wounded, and its people are financially strained. But it is the psychological level that concerns me. After decades of culturation, brainwashing, and mass reprogramming, there is a frightening undercurrent. No thinking person would deny that television—a federally regulated and controlled business—has helped desensitize a large proportion of the population to human life. Teenagers seem surprised that it hurts when they get shot. The point of all the violence Americans are fed daily is to create a sense of invulnerability, and this helps prevent people from analyzing the fix they are in and taking responsibility for their lives. We live in a form of socialism where corporations and conglomerates are the real government over our lives. Few have a hope of owning their own farms and small businesses and making a go of it, and fewer and fewer can afford to own their own homes. There is less and less opportunity for diversity.

But all this did not happen naturally. We were conspired against in 1963 by those who did not trust the people with economic and democratic freedom. I fear for the future when so many values essential to the well-being of a great nation are being lost from the body politic.

Our constitutional process was subverted and circumvented by powerful interests not afraid to use the gun if necessary to dispense with traitors to their class. Five percent of the people own more than 75 percent of the wealth in this nation, and many of those powerful people have never believed in our form of government. The Founding Fathers never believed in direct elections of the President and, as we all know, the majority of the population did not have the right to vote in the beginning.

John Kennedy's mistake was in thinking that he was in control. Whenever anybody is elected to that high office, great forces come into play. Whether we wish to call it "the shadow government," as Bill Moyers does, or the Secret Team, or The Club, there are those who impress on every one of our high elected officials that the power does not lie with them but with those behind the scenes. If necessary, the President is destabilized. In a worst-case scenario, they kill him.

We all know that there is an Establishment, and at best the Establishment acts as a force for civilization and culture and a counterbalance to demagoguery. But at what point can the control of real political power and the puppets they saddle us with destroy the benefits of democracy and alienate the population? The public does not vote anymore. We have the worst voting record of any developed nation, which perhaps is what the powerful want. They don't want people participating in governing. The assassination defused the office of the President.

The process of alienation and disaffection began with the murder of John Kennedy. It is now rotting our nation as its middle class is slowly crushed and disaffected. I think it was deliberate. Our bosses don't want participatory democracy. Our hopes were dashed with Jack's murder

Highly motivated people cannot do a good, honest job in government when the people have lost faith in them and when they themselves become cynical because of the pervasive effect of corruption of the political process.

*   *   *

After all, historically, leaders are ordinarily only symbols, the visible public figureheads for the committees behind the scenes that run them. Kennedy listened to the nation itself, and died for his country.

John Kennedy made the mistake of thinking that he was President.

BIBLIOGRAPHY AND AUTHOR INDEX

Readers are urged to visit and support the **JFK Assassination Information Center** at 110 S. Market St., Dallas, TX 75202, the new quarters are at the KATY Building across the street from the JFK Memorial centopath. (214) 653-9238. Robert Johnson and Larry Howard have put up a monumental struggle to open and keep open the doors of this effort, which presents in visual terms our point of view. A movie may be viewed and books can be obtained. The Center makes a major effort to find and report to the public any new information pertaining to the case.

The Assassination Archives and Research Center (the "AARC") was founded in 1984 by Bernard Fensterwald, Jr., and Jim Lesar, two Washington attorneys who had a longstanding interest in political assassinations. Fensterwald once served as speech writer and campaigner for his Harvard classmate, John Kennedy. He was also the lawyer who represented Watergate burglar James McCord when McCord cracked the coverup through his famous letter to Judge John Sirica. Fensterwald and Lesar both represented James Earl Ray, the alleged assassin of Dr. Martin Luther King, Jr., in his attempts to get a trial. Lesar has handled most of the Freedom of Information Act litigation for those seeking records on the assassinations of President Kennedy, Senator Robert F. Kennedy, and Martin Luther King, Jr. The AARC is a unique and valuable repository of information on political assassinations and related matters, such as intelligence activities and organized crime. It is also a contact center for authors, researchers and members of the media, many of whom have donated their own manuscripts and research materials to the AARC. Fensterwald provided virtually all the financial support for the AARC until his death in April, 1991. As a result, AARC's very existence is now threatened and is urgently in need of financial support. Contributions are tax deductible and may be sent to: The AARC, 918 F St., N.W., Washington, D.C. 20004. The AARC's new president is Jim Lesar. Annual membership is $25.00, but large contributions are needed.

For new and used or hard-to-get books on this case and related matters, the following stores are recommended: The Last Hurrah Bookshop, 937

Memorial Avenue, Williamsport, PA, 17701, 717-327-9338; M & A Book Dealer, P.O. Box 2422, Waco, TX 76703; The President's Box Bookshelf, P.O. Box 1255, Washington, D.C. 20013, 703-998-7390; Cloak and Dagger Books, 9 Eastman Avenue, Bedford, NH 03102, 603-668-1629. To obtain new copies of *Farewell America,* call Al Navis at 416-781-4139— Handy Books, 1762 Avenue Road, Toronto, ONT, M5M 3Y9, Canada.

Journals:

The Investigator, devoted to assassination and allied research. Published by Gary Rowell, editor, 1529 Elizabeth, Bay City, MI 48708. A new and up-and-coming magazine. ($3.50 per issue, $20 for one year.)

Dateline: Dallas Published by the JFK Assassination Information Center, KATY Bldg., 110 S. Market St., Dallas, TX 75202. This has a nice layout, columns of text, photos, and a smooth, professional appearance. It even seems to be open to criticism of the Center's own pet stories, such as the Roscoe White and Paul Groody business. ($20 per year.)

The Third Decade, A Journal of Research On The John F. Kennedy Assassination, is published by Prof. Jerry Rose at the State University College, Fredonia, New York, 14063. At this time (1993) *The Third Decade* remains the best journal published in the field, except for the occasional amateur material which serves to disinform. ($20 for one year, $36 for two years, and $50 for three years. Single issues are $4.)

Back Channels, A Quarterly Publication of Historical & Modern Espionage, Assassination & Conspiracies, Editor: Peter Kross, Kross Publications and Research Services, P.O. Box 9, Franklin Park, NJ 00823. ($4.50 per issue.)

Honor Guard, A magazine devoted to keeping alive the case of John F. Kennedy's assassination. Published by Deanie Richards. "In general only Member's material is printed." ($15 for the first 12 issues.) P.O. Box 3724 Akron, OH 44314

Echoes of Conspiracy, 1525 Acton St., Berkeley, CA 94702 (Paul Hoch) A Journal of assassination research which publishes only occasionally.

The Continuing Inquiry (TCI), journal of assassination research, monthly. No longer published, but bound volumes are available from the JFK Assassination Information Center in Dallas. Editor: Penn Jones, Jr.

Cover-Ups:, 4620 Brandingshire Place, Fort Worth, Texas 76133 (Gary Mack) A Journal of assassination research. No longer published.

Encyclopedia: The Assassination of President John F. Kennedy: A Complete Book of Facts, by James Duffy, edited by James Waller, Thundermouth Press, 1992. This is a reference work for the beginner.

Abbreviations Used For Citations:

3 H 67: Vol 3. p 67 Appendix or Hearings of the Warren Report.

3 HSCA 422: Vol 3. p. 422 Appendix to the Report of the House Select Committee on Assassinations, or Assassinations Committee. 12 vols JFK; 13 vols King.

WR: Warren Report (*The New York Times* edition used here unless otherwise stated) Report: Report of the Assassinations Committee; also Bantam, Books, New York, 1979.

CD: Commission Document.
CE: Commission Exhibit.

Investigation of the Assassination of President John F. Kennedy, Book 7. G.P.O., U.S. House of Representatives Select Committee on Assassinations, 1976–78.

Final Report of the Select Committee to Study Governmental Operations with Respect to Intelligence Activities, U.S. Senate, 1976. Recommended reading.

Report to the President by the Commission in CIA Activities Within the United States (The "Rockefeller Commission"); also Manor Books, New York, 1976.

SICROFA: Senate Intelligence Committee Report on Foreign Assassinations, *Alleged Assassination Plots Involving Foreign Leaders.* Recommended reading.

Books:

Ashman, Charles. *The CIA-Mafia Link.* New York: Manor Books 1975.

Bishop, Jim. *The Day Kennedy Was Shot.* New York: Funk & Wagnalls 1968; New York: Bantam Books, 1969.

Blair, Joan and Clay. *The Search For JFK*. Berkley, Publishing Group, New York: 1976.

Blumenthal, Sid, with Harvey Yazigian. *Government by Gunplay: Assassination Conspiracy Theories From Dallas to Today*. New York: Signet, 1976. Recommended reading.

Bowart, William. *Operation Mind Control, Our Secret Government's War Against Its Own People*. New York: Dell, 1978. Recommended reading.

Brown, Walt. *The People v. Lee Harvey Oswald*. New York: Carroll & Graf, 1992.

Buchanan, Patrick. *Who Killed Kennedy?* New York: Putnam, 1964; London: Secker, Warburg, 1964; New York: MacFadden, 1965.

Callahan, Bob. *Who Shot JFK? A Guide to the Major Conspiracy Theories*. Simon & Schuster, 1993.

Cameron, Gail. *Rose*. New York: Berkley Publishing Corp, 1971.

Christic Institute. *Inside The Shadow Government*. Washington, D.C.: The Christic Institute, 1988.

Collier, Peter and Horowitz, David. *The Kennedys: An American Drama*. New York: Warner Books, 1985.

Crenshaw, Charles A., with J. Gary Shaw and Jens Hansen. *JFK, Conspiracy of Silence*. New York: Signet (Penguin), 1992.

Curry, Jesse. *JFK Assassination File* 1969 American Poster & Printing Co. Inc., 1600 S. Akard, Dallas, Texas 75215.

Evica, George Michael. *And We Are All Mortal*. University of Hartford, 1978; $7.95 plus $1 for postage and University of Hartford, 200 Bloomfield Ave. West Hartford, CT 06117.

Fall, Bernard B. *The Two Vietnams; A Political and Military Analysis*. New York: Praeger, 1963; revised in 1964.

Fensterwald, Bernard. *Assassination of JFK by Coincidence or Conspiracy?* New York: Zebra Books, 1977. Committee to Investigate Assassinations (C. to I.A.). Recommended reading.

Flammonde, Paris. *The Kennedy Conspiracy: An Uncommissioned Report on the Jim Garrison Investigation*. New York: Meredith, 1969.

Fonzi, Gaeton, *The Last Investigation.* Thunder's Mouth Press, 1993—about how the HSCA failed—by its only field investigator.

Ford, Gerald R., with John R. Stiles. *Portrait of the Assassin.* Simon & Schuster, 1965.

Fox, Sylvan. *The Unanswered Questions About President Kennedy's Assassination.* New York: Award Books, 1965 and 1975.

Galloway, John. *The Kennedys and Vietnam.* New York: Facts On File, Inc.

Garrison, Jim. *A Heritage of Stone.* New York: Putnam, 1970; Berkley Publishing Group, 1972. Recommended reading for all Americans.

Garrison, Jim. *On The Trail of the Assassins.* Sheridan Square Press (Institute For Media Analysis), 1988.

Goodwin, Doris Kearns. *The Fitzgeralds and The Kennedys.* New York: Simon & Schuster, 1987.

Haley, J. Evetts. *A Texan Looks at Lyndon: A Study in Illegitimate Power.* Canyon, Texas: Palo Duro Press, 1964.

Hepburn, James (pseudonym, author unknown, but thought to be French Intelligence according to former FBI agent William Turner and American sources). *Farewell America.* Vaduz, Liechtenstein: Frontiers Publishing Company 1968. (Printed in Canada and Belgium, but this is a fictitious publishing company.) Available from Al Navis, Handy Books, Toronto. Recommended reading. This very important book was written by someone with an intimate knowledge of the CIA and the United States.

Hill, Jean, and Sloan, Bill. *JFK, The Last Dissenting Witness.* Gretna, LA: Pelican, 1992.

Hinckle, Warren and Turner, William. *The Fish is Red.* New York: Harper and Row, 1981.

Hougan, Jim, *Spooks. The Haunting of America—The Private Use of Secret Agents.* New York: William. Morrow, 1978. Recommended reading. *Secret Agenda.* Random House, 1984, Ballantine pb, 1985.

Hougan, Jim. *Secret Agents.* New York: Random House (Ballantine), 1985.

Joesten, Joachim. *Oswald: Assassin or Fall Guy?* Marzani & Munsell, 1964.

Jones, Jr., Penn. *Forgive My Grief.* Vols I-IV. Rt 3, Box 356, Waxahachie, TX. 75165. Recommended reading. Most out of print now.

Kantor, Seth. *Who Was Jack Ruby?* New York: Everest, 1978.

Kennedy, Rose. *Times to Remember.* Garden City, NY: Doubleday, 1974.

Text by *The New York Times, The Kennedy Years.* New York: Viking Press, 1966.

Lincoln, Evelyn. *My 12 Years With John F. Kennedy.* New York: David McKay, 1965; Bantam, New York, 1966.

Livingstone, Harrison E. *High Treason.* Baltimore: The Conservatory Press, 1989; New York: Berkley Publishing Group, 1990.

Livingstone, Harrison E. *High Treason 2.* New York: Carroll & Graf, 1992.

Manchester, William. *The Death of a President: November 20-25, 1963.* New York: Harper & Row, 1967; Popular Library, 1968.

Marchetti, Victor & John D. Marks. *The CIA and the Cult of Intelligence.* New York: Knopf, 1974. Recommended reading.

Marks, John. *The Search For The Manchurian Candidate.* New York: Times Books, 1979. Recommended reading.

Martin, Ralph G. *A Hero For Our Time—An Intimate Study of the Kennedy Years.* New York: MacMillan, 1982; Fawcett Crest, 1983.

Meagher, Sylvia. *Accessories After the Fact: The Warren Commission; the Authorities, and the Report.* New York: Bobbs-Merrill, 1967: Vintage, 1976. Recommended reading.

Melanson, Philip H. *Spy Saga: Lee Harvey Oswald and U.S. Intelligence.* New York and London: Praeger, 1990. Praeger was a famous (and documented) CIA front, so their publication of this book is of interest in itself.

Milan, Michael. *The Squad; The U.S. Government's Secret Alliance With Organized Crime.* New York: Shapolsky Books, 1989.

Subject Index to the Warren Report and Hearings and Exhibits. New York: Scarecrow Press, 1966: Ann Arbor, Michigan University microfilms, 1971.

Miller, Tom. *The Assassination Please Almanac.* Chicago: Henry Regnery Co., 1977. A reference of sorts to people and events.

Moyers, Bill. *The Secret Government: The Constitution in Crisis.* 1988. Seven Locks Press, P.O. Box 27, Cabin John, Md. 20818. (301) 320-2130; ($9.95 plus postage and handling.)

Newman, John M., *JFK and Vietnam, Deception, Intrigue and the Struggle for Power.* New York: Warner Books, 1992.

North, Mark. *Act Of Treason: The Role of J. Edgar Hoover in the Assassination of President Kennedy.* New York: Carroll & Graf, 1991.

Noyes, Peter. *Legacy of Doubt.* New York: Pinnacle Books, 1973.

O'Donnell, Kenneth P., David F. Powers, and Joe McCarthy. *Johnny, We Hardly Knew Ye,* New York: Little Brown, 1970.

Oswald, Robert with Myrick and Barbara Land. *Lee: A Portrait of Lee Harvey Oswald.* New York: Coward-McCann, 1967.

O'Toole, George. *The Assassination Tapes: An Electronic Probe Into the Murder of John F. Kennedy and the Dallas Cover-up.* New York: Penthouse Press, 1975.

Popkin, Richard H. *The Second Oswald.* New York: Avon Books, 1966.

Prouty, L. Fletcher. *The Secret Team. The CIA and Its Allies in Control of the United States and the World.* New York: Prentice Hall, 1973. Recommended reading. A very important book.

Roffman, Howard. *Presumed Guilty.* Fairleigh Dickinson University Press, 1975; Cranbury, NJ, London, England: Associated University Presses, Inc. An important book.

Russell, Dick. *The Man Who Knew Too Much: Richard Case Nagell and the Assassination of JFK.* New York: Carroll & Graf, 1992.

Rust, William, J. and the editors of *U.S. News & World Report. Kennedy in Vietnam.* New York: Scribner's, 1985.

Salinger, Pierre. *With Kennedy.* Garden City, NY: Doubleday, 1966.

Sauvage, Leo. *The Oswald Affair: An Examination of the Contradictions of the Warren Report.* Cleveland: World Publishing Co., 1966.

Scheflin, Alan W. and Upton, Jr., Edward. *The Mind Manipulators.* London: Paddington Press Ltd., 1978. Recommended reading.

Scott, Peter Dale. *Crime and Cover-Up, the CIA, the Mafia, and the Dallas-Watergate Connection.* Berkeley, CA: Westworks, Recommended reading.

Scott, Peter Dale. *Deep Politics and the Death of JFK.* University of California Press, 1993.

Schlesinger, Arthur. *A Thousand Days: John F. Kennedy in the White House.* Boston: Houghton-Mifflin, 1965.

Schlesinger, Arthur M., Jr. *Robert Kennedy and His Times.* Boston: Houghton-Mifflin 1978; New York: Ballantine Books, 1985.

Sculz, Tad. *Compulsive Spy, The Strange Career of E. Howard Hunt.* New York: Viking, 1974.

Sorensen, Theodore C. *Kennedy.* New York: Harper & Row, 1965.

Sorensen, Theodore C. *The Kennedy Legacy.* New York: New American Library, 1970.

Summers, Anthony. *Conspiracy.* New York: McGraw Hill, 1980. Reprinted by Paragon House, 1989. (Some material added). Recommended reading.

Thomas, Ralph D. *Missing Links in the JFK Assassination Conspiracy.* Self-published. No date, but presumed to be 1992. Write to Thomas Investigative Publications, Inc., P.O. Box 33244, Austin, TX 78764. The book has no sources or index, but is an interesting work.

Thompson, Josiah. *Six Seconds in Dallas: A Microstudy of the Kennedy Assassination* (revised). New York: Berkley Publishing Corp. 1967, 1976; Bernard Geis Associates, 1967. Recommended reading; an important book.

Thornley, Kerry. *Oswald.* Chicago: New Classics House, 1965.

Turner, William & Christian, John G. *The Assassination of Robert Kennedy—A Searching Look at the Conspiracy and Cover-Up 1968-1978.* New York: Random House, 1978. Recommended reading.

Weisberg, Harold. *Whitewash.* Vols. I-IV. Write Weisberg at 7627 Old Receiver Rd., Frederick, MD., 21701; Vols. I & II, New York: Dell, 1966, 1967. Also, *Oswald in New Orleans: The Case for Conspiracy with the CIA.* Canyon Books; New York, 1967. *Post-Mortem* self-published, 1975, address above. A very crucial book on the medical evidence and cover up, but, like most of Harold's writing, very difficult for many readers to follow.

Weissman, Steve. *Big Brother and the Holding Company. The World Behind Watergate.* Palo Alto: Ramparts Press, 1974. Recommended reading.

Wilber, Charles. *Medicolegal Investigation of the President John F. Kennedy Murder.* Springfield, Illinois: Charles C. Thomas, Publisher. Very important study, but the author wrote Livingstone admitting that he missed the main point of the head wounds.

Wise, David, and Ross, Thomas B. *The Invisible Government. The CIA and U.S. Intelligence.* New York: Random House, 1964; Vintage, 1974. Recommended reading. *The Espionage Establishment,* New York: Random House, 1967; Bantam, 1968. Recommended reading.

Wofford, Harris. *Of Kennedys and Kings, Making Sense of the Sixties.* New York: Farrar, Straus, and Giroux, 1980.

Zirbel, Craig I., *The Texas Connection: The Assassination of John F. Kennedy.* TCC Publisher, 1991 (self-published) The Texas Connection Company, 7500 E. Butherus Dr., Scottsdale, AZ, 85260. Tel: (602) 443-3818. Fax: (602) 948-8206. The author maintains LBJ and others in Texas were involved in the assassination.

There are many other books on the subjects of assassination and intelligence, as well as about Kennedy, but those listed above are the most important. The appendix to the report of the Assassinations Committee is crucial to study the case, but only 20 sets were printed for libraries and the public.

Sources and Notes

Preface

1. Richard E. Sprague. "The Assassination of President John F. Kennedy: The Application of Computers to the Photographic Evidence." *Computers and Automation,* May, 1970.
2. Sylvia Meagher. *Accessories After the Fact.* New York: Vintage/Random House, 1967, p. 22.
3. Richard E. Sprague. "The Framing of Lee Harvey Oswald." *Computers and Automation* October, 1973.
4. Chris Sharrett letter to the author (October 9, 1992).
5. Letter of Christopher Sharrett to the author (September 8, 1992).
6. Downard, James Shelby. *Apocalypse Culture.* New York: Amok Press, 1987.
7. E.B. White. *Stuart Little.* New York: Harper & Row, 1945, p. 131.

Introduction

1. Dale Hawkins-Elliott, letter to the author (July 21, 1992).
2. *Journal of the American Medical Association* (May 27, 1992).
3. 7 HSCA 114–15, 246, 251, 254, 256.
4. *State of Louisiana* v. *Clay Shaw.*
5. Interview of Dr. James J. Humes with Dan Rather on CBS (June 1967) as reprinted in *JAMA* Vol. 268, No. 13 (October 7, 1992), pp. 1736–37.
6. *The Baltimore Sun*, front page (November 24 and 25, 1966). These are extensive articles.
7. "Autopsy Forum," a display conducted by the Dallas Council on Foreign Affairs (June 4, 1992).
8. Ibid.
9. 7 HSCA 228–29, 223, 218, 282; mention of the missing bone by Dr. Angel, 7 HSCA 249.
10. Allen Dulles at a Warren Commission meeting (July 9, 1964).
11. A major study of the feelings of the public prior to the 1992 elections was published in the *San Jose Mercury* (September 1992).

12. Hugh Eames. *Winner Lose All.* Little, Brown, (Boston: 1973).
13. *U.S. Naval Institute Proceedings.* See April 1991 issue, pgs. 20, 32.
14. The Naval Institute in Annapolis can make available a video of the second tape of the panel discussion (call 1-800-233-USNI), or it can be ordered from the Frederick A. Cook Society: Mary Allison Farley, Sullivan County Historical Museum, P.O. Box 247, Hurleyville, NY 12747-0247.
15. *U.S. Naval Institute Proceedings* (April 1991), p. 32. For an additional book on this affair, read Howard S. Abramson, *Hero in Disgrace* (New York: Paragon House, 1991).
16. Harold Weisberg. *Whitewash,* (1965), Introduction, p. ix.
17. Richard E. Sprague. *The Taking of America 1.2.3.,* (privately published, 1976, 1980).
18. Ibid., pp. 83–84.
19. Sprague, *The Taking of America 1.2.3.*
20. Dick Russell. *The Man Who Knew Too Much* (New York: Carroll & Graf, 1992), p. 606.
21. Conversation with Madeleine Brown, Lyndon Johnson's former mistress (June 1992).

Chapter 1

1. 7 HSCA 16–18.
2. Ibid.
3. Warren Report (1964) pp. 501–2 (Appendix 9).
4. Ibid. p. 502 (Appendix 9).
5. 7 HSCA 246.
6. Dallas Council on Foreign Affairs (June 4, 1992).
7. Discussions with Richard Tobias of Parkland Hospital (September 12 and 26, 1992). I previously noted what might be wounds in the forehead temple area but had no way to prove it.
8. 7 HSCA 312–13.
9. WR, *The New York Times* edition (1964) p. 501 (Appendix 9).
10. WR, *The New York Times* edition p. 90.
11. WR, *The New York Times* edition (1964), p. 503 (Appendix 9).
12. *Journal of the American Medical Association* (May 27, 1992).
13. Livingstone, Harrison, E. *High Treason 2* (New York: Carroll & Graf, 1992), pp. 214, 219.
14. Interview with Paul O'Connor, as described in the author's *High Treason 2* chapter.
15. WR, *The New York Times* edition (1964), p. 505.
16. 7 HSCA 15.
17. Livingstone, *High Treason 2,* p. 113.
18. Discussion with the author (October 19, 1992).
19. Additional corroboration of this is in the *JAMA* article of May 27, 1992, wherein the Dallas doctors specifically comment on the appearance of the throat wound in the picture, if we can believe the authors. I believe it, because they all said the same to me before that.

20. The author's press conference of May 29, 1992, as reported by the Associated Press and Reuters. Floyd Riebe, Jerrol Custer, and Paul O'Connor came to the press conference and denounced the autopsy materials. Their more extended comments can be found in my book *High Treason 2*.

21. 1 HSCA 500–501, 503, 514, 517, 531, 533, 561; Anthony Summers, *Conspiracy*, pp. 33, 34.

22. CE 856, CE 853; Josiah Thompson, *Six Seconds in Dallas*, pp. 151–53, with WC Exhibit photos, wrist (CE 856), Goat (CE 853).

23. WR, p. 104 *The New York Times* edition, p. 104.

24. Ibid.

25. Dr. Roger McCarthy testifying at the American Bar Association mock trial of Oswald (July 1992), San Francisco.

26. Interview of Carolyn Arnold, *Conspiracy* (1989 edition), p. 77.

27. Testimony of John Connally, 4 H 130, notes they were due at the luncheon at 12:30 P.M.

28. Testimony of Officer Marion Baker, 3 H 254; period from shots to encounter with Oswald reconstructed as seventy-four to seventy-eight seconds from time of shots.

29. Ibid; 3 H 252.

30. WR 560.

31. WR 561.

32. Testimony of J. C. Day, 4 H 260.

33. Curry, *JFK Assassination File*.

34. Ibid.

35. Harrison E. Livingstone, *High Treason*.

36. Dallas Council on Foreign Affairs "Autopsy Forum," (June 4, 1992).

37. Ibid.

38. Thompson, *Six Seconds in Dallas*, p. 161.

39. WR *The New York Times* edition (1964), p. 504 (Appendix 9).

40. John K. Lattimer, "Observations Based on a Review of the Autopsy Photographs, X-Rays, and Related Materials of the Late President John F. Kennedy," *Resident and Staff Physician* (May 1972), p. 43. Lattimer ignores the severe conflict between the placement of the large hole in the first drawing he made (the right lateral) and the next drawing he has (p. 46) of the anterior view, both made from the X-rays. This drawing is the more accurate of the two, and shows the entire right eye and front of the head missing, which is what the X-ray shows, but is entirely fraudulent. His first drawing is not according to its corresponding X-ray, and has the hole more centrally placed on the right side of the head, more toward the rear, but, of course, not far enough back.

41. 2 H 360.

Chapter 2

1. Warren Report, GPO, p. 558; *The New York Times* edition, p. 87.

2. Ibid. p. 19, 38.

3. Ibid.
4. Ibid. *The New York Times* edition p. 112.
5. O'Hara, Charles, *Fundamentals of Criminal Investigation*, Thomas Publishers, Illinois, 1972, p. 562–4.
6. Summers, *Conspiracy*, p. 36.
7. Malcolm Barour/John Langley, Sagan with Jack Anderson. "American Exposé: Who Murdered JFK?" (1988).
8. Former crime lab employee, "Rusty" Livingston reported seeing "an old palmprint" on the evening of November 22; Martin Shackelford, "Midwest Symposium on the Assassination of John F. Kennedy: A Report," *Third Decade* bonus (September 1992), p. 5.
9. "The Men Who Killed Kennedy" U. S. Version shown on A & E (1991 and 1992).
10. Paul Groody on "The Men Who Killed Kennedy" produced by Nigel Turner, shown in 1988 abroad and in the U.S. in 1991 and 1992. Groody's segment is not in the 1988 version.
11. Summers, *Conspiracy*, p. 46–7.
12. Marrs, *Crossfire*, p. 238.
13. 5 H 60; also CD 525, 20 H 1–2.
14. CE 842 (Connally fragments); CE 567 and CE 569 (Limousine fragments); 1 HSCA 562; *The Washington Post* (September 9, 1978).
15. Summers, *Conspiracy* (1989 revised edition), p. 34; 1 HSCA 196, 515, 562; 7 HSCA 199, 366 n; 1 HSCA 500–1 Guinn testimony on brain fragment, chart; p. 503: Chart comparing various fragments (related testimony 502–504); Guinn's Report (excerpts, (6) FBI nos. Q4 Q5 (CE-843). One larger fragment and one smaller fragment, reportedly recovered from President Kennedy's brain at the autopsy. (Note that CE 843 was originally three fragments, not two, and two small fragments, not one), p. 514; Chart of specimens examined, p. 517; Grouping of brain fragments with limousine fragments, p. 531, 533.
16. Livingstone, *High Treason 2*, p. 304–5; Summers, *Conspiracy*, op. cit. 38, p. 546.
17. CE 842 (wrist); 6 H 111, 2 H 382.
18. 1 HSCA 561.
19. *High Treason 2*, p. 213.
20. 7 HSCA 249
21. Warren Report, p. 60; *The New York Times* edition, p. 502.
22. Humes' testimony to the Warren Commission, 2 H 353.
23. Wecht, Cyril H. and Robert P. Smith. "The Medical Evidence In The Assassination of President John F. Kennedy," *Forensic Science*, 3 (1974) p. 117.
24. John K. Lattimer. "Observations Based on A Review of the Autopsy Photographs, X-Rays and Related Materials of the late President John F. Kennedy." *Resident and Staff Physician* (May 1972) p. 43, (I) and p. 56.
25. Ibid.

26. Interview of Francis X. O'Neill by a panel and George Michael Evica: "Questioning the Facts, Research v. Witness, the Assassination of John F. Kennedy," Team Video Productions (1992).

27. Commission on CIA Activities Within the United States. Dr. Richard Lindenberg, the Director of Neuropathology and Legal Medicine for the State of Maryland's Department of Health and Mental Hygiene. Report (May 9, 1975), p. 4, Gerald Ford Library.

28. Warren Report, *The New York Times* edition (1964) p. 502 (Appendix 9).

29. HSCA exhibits F-55 and F-66 (front) and F-52, F-53 and F-297 (side).

30. P. 46 of his article above.

31. Harold Weisberg, *Postmortem*, pp. 199–200.

32. "1968 Panel Review of Photographs, X-ray Films, Documents and Other Evidence Pertaining to the Fatal Wounding of President John F. Kennedy on Nov. 22, 1963 in Dallas, TX" *Maryland State Medical Journal* (March, 1977), p. 77. The Clark Panel Report is also reprinted in Weisberg's *Postmortem*, p. 580–595.

33. 7 HSCA 93, section 264: "This analysis is based on the fracture of the transverse process of T-1 and the air in the soft tissues, which probably resulted from the laceration of the trachea."; See also discussion before the D.C. Bar Mock Trial of Lee Harvey Oswald, Mark Flannigan and Dr. Michael Baden (June, 1992).

34. Summers, *Conspiracy* (1989), p. 34.

35. Letter from Shaun Roach to Gary Aguilar, MD (February 15, 1993).

36. Ibid.

37. Ibid.

38. Vincent DiMaio, "Gunshot Wounds: Practical Aspects of Firearms, Ballistics and Forensic Techniques," Chapter 7, (Centerfire Rifle Bullets), p. 145.

39. Ibid.

40. Ibid.

41. Ibid.

42. Ibid, p. 157.

43. Letter to Dr. Gary Aguilar (February 15, 1993).

44. Ibid.

45. Thompson, *Six Seconds in Dallas*, p. 146; Hurt, *Reasonable Doubt*, p. 74; Weisberg, *Postmortem*, p. 440, photocopy of portion of a letter from Clarence Kelley, FBI Director, regarding neutron activation analysis: "CE 834, Q4, Q5, Metal fragments from President's head"; p. 449; "Q4 and Q5, lead fragments from JFK's head (those called 'a missile' by the FBI.)"

46. Ibid. 161–4.

47. Raymond Marcus, *The Bastard Bullet*, Rendell Publications (1966).

48. Ibid.

49. 3 H 428 (March 31, 1964).

50. The D.C. Bar mock trial of the case (June, 1992).

51. CE 572, CE 853, CE 856 and CE 857.
52. CE 81 b: FBI Laboratory report PC 78243 BX dated November 23, 1963 (Hoover to Curry).
53. FBI Laboratory work sheets, part of report PC 78243 BX dated November 23, 1963, concerning Spectro tests by Gallagher. Quote is from an article, "Neutron Activation Analysis," by Emory Brown, *The Continuing Inquiry* (November, 1976).
54. Emory Brown. "Neutron Activation Analysis," *The Continuing Inquiry* (November 1976).
55. Ibid; Forensic Neutron Activation Analysis of Bullet Lead Specimens by Lukens, Schlesinger, Guinn and Hackman. Gulf Radiation Project 295 (June 30, 1970) National Technical Information Service, Springfield, VA; Comparison of Bullet Lead Specimens By Nondestructive Neutron Activity Analysis by Lukens and Guinn, American Academy of Forensic Sciences.
56. Ibid.
57. Ibid.
58. Anderson show cited above.
59. Gene Roberts' article described the first work done on the car in December, 1964, in the *Detroit Free Press* (October, 1968). Ron Ishoy, *Detroit Free Press* (January 30, 1978) said the car was rebuilt in 1964. Sandra McClure, *Detroit Free Press*, March 9, 1979; Randy Mason, *Car Exchange* (December 1983), states that the final work was finished on May 11, 1964.
60. Richard Dudman, in the *St. Louis Post Dispatch* (December 1, 1963).
61. Richard Dudman, in the *New Republic* (December 21, 1963).
62. 6 H 38 (McClelland), 6 H 42 (Baxter).
63. 7 HSCA 270.
64. *High Treason 2*, 6 H 55-6, pp. 106–7.
65. CE 392, 7 HSCA 269, 270.
66. 7 HSCA 312; NBC News; *Seventy Hours and Thirty Minutes,* New York: Random House, 1966; Meagher, *Accessory After the Fact,* p. 153.
67. 6 H 42; Dallas Autopsy Forum, June 4, 1992, in this book.
68. Richard Dudman of the *St. Louis Post-Dispatch* reported that the neck wound was a small, undamaged punctuate area which "had the appearance of the usual entrance wound of a bullet." (Dec. 1, 1963); 6 H 36–37.
69. Crenshaw, *Conspiracy of Silence*, p. 79;
70. 6 H 65, 67.
71. 6 H 143.
72. See the chapter in this book on Diana Bowron.
73. For an early compendium of this evidence, see Sylvia Meagher's *Accessory After the Fact*, pp. 150–1; 7 HSCA 270; Livingstone, *High Treason 2*, pp. 106–109, 121.
74. Letter of Dr. Robert Livingston to the author of May 2, 1992.
75. Crenshaw *Conspiracy of Silence*, p. 11; Livingstone, *High Treason 2*, p. 113.

76. *High Treason 2*, p. 255 (O'Connor).

77. Ibid., p. 113.

78. 7 HSCA 296.

79. 7 HSCA 312.

80. WR, p. 502.

81. The author's press conference (May 29, 1992). AP and Reuters wire stories of that date; Scott Hatfield, "RT Disputes X-Ray Photos in JFK Case," *Advance* (August 31, 1992), p. 7.

82. Witness v. Research Video, George Michael Evica.

83. "1968 Panel Review of Photographs, X-ray Films, Documents and Other Evidence Pertaining to the Fatal Wounding of President John F. Kennedy on November 22, 1963 in Dallas, TX," *The Maryland State Medical Journal* (March, 1977).

84. 2 H 367, on probing with fingers.

85. 16 H 980.

86. CD 7.

87. Author's interview with Jerrol Custer in *High Treason 2* (November 11, 1991), pp. 188, 206, 209–210, 221; 7 HSCA 15.

88. *The Baltimore Sun* (November 25, 1966).

89. 2 H 354 (Humes), Warren Report p. 541.

90. 2 H 354 (Humes); Author's interview with James C. Jenkins in *High Treason 2* (March 25, 1991).

91. 1 HSCA, 326–30; 7 HSCA 113–115, 246, 251, 254, 256.

92. 7 HSCA 114, 115; 246, 251, 254, 256, 261; 1 HSCA pp. 326–330 (contradicts this on p. 327); *Journal of the American Medical Association* (May 27, 1992).

93. 7 HSCA 254.

94. Dallas Council on Foreign Affairs meeting of June 4, 1992, when five of the Dallas doctors were present and subjected to Dr. Lattimer's lecture and attempted distortion of the medical evidence. See chapter in this book.

95. *High Treason 2*, p. 290 (Jenkins).

96. *High Treason 2*, pp. 580–1.

97. On fragment just above the right eye: Humes in 2 H 353; Warren Report, p. 541; *The New York Times* edition, p. 502, "The Medical Evidence in the Assassination of President John F. Kennedy," Cyril Wecht, *Forensic Science 3* (1974) pp. 117–118.

98. Wecht, Cyril and Robert P. Smith, "The Medical Evidence in the Assassination of President John F. Kennedy." Forensic Science, 3 (1974), p. 117 a diagram of the lateral skull X-ray.

99. WR, p. 505.

100. See discussion in *High Treason 2*.

101. Commission on CIA Activities Within the United States. Dr. Richard Lindenberg, the Director of Neuropathology and Legal Medicine for the State of Maryland's Department of Health and Mental Hygiene Report (May 9, 1975), p. 4. (Gerald Ford Library).

102. Clark Panel Report, p. 8, (1968).

103. 7 HSCA 6, 16–18, 46, 102, 177, 180, 193, 181–194, 311.
104. Medicolegal Investigation of the John F. Kennedy Murder, Charles G. Wilber. pp. 129, 131; Wilber letter to the author (July 25, 1991).
105. Philip R. Rezek, M.D, and Max Millard; *Autopsy Pathology,* p. 778.
106. Pittsburgh Press (November 26, 1963).
107. 2 H 348.
108. Charles G. Wilber, *Six Seconds in Dallas,* Thompson, pp. 96–97 (Appendix D); Cyril Wecht, "A Critique of President Kennedy's Autopsy," pp. 278–284.
109. As photo reproduced in Weisberg, Clark Panel Report p. 7. (1968). (See note 18.)
110. 7 HSCA 246.
111. 7 HSCA 250.
112. 6 HSCA 70, 225–8; 7 HSCA 37–71; Keeton in *The Continuing Inquiry,* "The Autopsy Photos and X-rays of President Kennedy and a Question of Authenticity."
113. 7 HSCA 46.
114. See the chapter on X-rays in this book; 7 HSCA 122, 222–3, 229.
115. Comment by doctors to Humes: 7 HSCA 249.
116. 2 H 351.
117. From Humes: 2 H 364, 372.
118. 7 HSCA, 122, 222–3, 229.
119. Dr. Norman Chase, 7 HSCA 283.
120. 7 HSCA 277.
121. *Postmortem,* Clark Panel Report, pp. 13–15.
122. Dr. John K. Lattimer, "Observations Based on A Review of the Autopsy Photographs, X-rays, and Related Materials of the Late President John F. Kennedy," *Resident and Staff Physician* (May, 1972): pp. 37 and 49.
123. Lattimer, Dr. John K., Dr. Edward B. Schlesinger and Dr. Houston Merritt, "President Kennedy's Spine Hit by First Bullet," bulletin of the New York Academy of Medicine, (1977) illustration p. 285.
124. Ibid, p. 284.
125. *High Treason,* pp. 50–2, 83, 92, 124; and *High Treason 2,* pp. 556–9.
126. *High Treason 2,* pp. 556–9.
127. 1 HSCA 327.
128. "Lattimer, Kennedy and Lincoln" *Resident and Staff Physician* (May, 1972).
129. Cyril Wecht, "Pathologist's View of JFK Autopsy: An Unsolved Case." *Modern Medicine* (November 27, 1972).
130. Discussions with the author (1992).
131. Letter of June 5, 1993.
132. FBI report of Milton L. Newsom (November 25, 1963)
133. Interview of Charles Bronson by the author (September 27, 1992).
134. 7 HSCA 246, 252
135. 2 H 353.
136. Wecht, Cyril and Robert P. Smith. "The Medical Evidence in the

Assassination of President John F. Kennedy." *Forensic Science*, (1974), p. 117.

137. Ibid.

138. Ibid.

139. Lattimer, Dr. John K., "Observations Based on A Review of the Autopsy Photographs, X-rays, and Related Materials of the Late President John F. Kennedy." *Resident and Staff Physician* (May, 1972), p. 43.

140. *Journal of the American Medical Association* (May 27, 1992).

141. Clark Panel Report, p. 10.

142. *The Dallas Morning News* (June 5, 1992).

143. 6 H 85, 88; Testimony of Dr. Michael Baden to Mark Flannigan before the Bar of the District of Columbia's Mock Trial of the case (June 17, 1992); and Dr. Robert Shaw's statements at the Dallas Autopsy Forum (June, 1992) as reported in the chapter in this book.

144. WFAA, Dallas (November 22, 1963).

145. Audrey Bell and others to the author, *High Treason 2*, and drawing p. 305.

146. Warren Report, weight of fragments, see 1 HSCA 500–1: Guinn testimony on brain fragment, chart; 503: Chart comparing various fragments (related testimony 502–4). Chart of specimens examined, p. 517.

147. Ibid; *High Treason 2*, pp. 60, 64, 102, 200, 331.

148. 6 H 159 (Malcolm Couch); Wallace Chariton et al., *Unsolved Texas Mysteries*, pp. 37–54.

149. Sylvia Meagher, *Accessories After the Fact*, pp. 9–27; Thompson, *Six Seconds in Dallas*, pp. 18–27, 252–270.

150. Warren Commission, Vol. 18, H 742; Thompson, *Six Seconds in Dallas*, p. 98.

151. Jack Brazil of Tyler, Texas, and some compatriots investigated the sewers and storm drains of Dealey Plaza and made a video of it: "JFK Update" is about the sewer in Dealey Plaza, 1992, Western Intelligence, Denver, CO. It is said that this is a right–wing disinformation group.

152. *Dallas Times Herald* (November 22, 1963).

153. 7 H 107 (Weitzman); 6 H 312 (Harkness); 7 H 535 (Smith), 19 H 524; Anthony, Summers, *Conspiracy,* p. 50; Henry Hurt, *Reasonable Doubt*, p. 120.

154. *Warren Report* p. 52; Meagher, *Accessories After the Fact*, p. 25.

155. Marrs, Ed Hoffman in *Crossfire*, p. 52, and appearing on "The Men Who Killed Kennedy," 1991; Jean Hill, *The Last Dissenting Witness*; Jean Hill and Bill Sloan; *Now It Can Be Told*; Lee Bowers (May 6, 1992 transcript).

156. Marrs, Beverly Oliver, Mary Ann Moorman in *Crossfire* pp. 36, 38; Gordon Arnold, "The Men Who Killed Kennedy," 1991.

157. For example, Charles Givens, discussed in *Accessories After The Fact*, by Sylvia Meagher, pp. 65–68; in *Presumed Guilty*, by Howard

Roffman, pp. 274–5, 287–8 (the latter, in his FBI report, contradicts the time given in his printed Warren Commission testimony. When the stenographic transcript of his testimony was released, it was found to match the time in the FBI report, and had been changed in the printed version of his testimony. The transcript is in the Warren Commission files (National Archives). A close study of other stenographic vs. printed transcripts might prove informative). Endnote by Martin Shackelford.

158. *High Treason 2*, pp. 412–416; various articles in volumes one through four of Penn Jones' *Forgive My Grief.*
159. WR, pp. 516–517. Livingstone, *High Treason.* p. 205.
160. Richard Warren Lewis and Lawrence Schiller, *The Scavengers and Critics of the Warren Report,* New York: Delacorte (1967), pp. 158–9.
161. 12 HSCA 186, 132; Sylvia Meagher, *Accessories After the Fact,* p. 234.
162. Anthony Summers, *Conspiracy,* p. 77, 108; Henry Hurt, pp. 90–1; *Dallas Morning News,* November 11, 1978.
163. WR, p. 513 (appendix on fire arms).
164. Larry Ray Harris, "Tippit Shooting Chronology," October 1992; *Kurtz, Crime of the Century,* p. 134; Hurt, pp. 144–5.
165. See Sylvia Meagher's brilliant discussion of this incident. Meagher hangs much of her case against the Warren Commission on the Odio affair. *Accessories After the Fact,* pp. 377–387.
166. Phillip Melanson in *Spy Saga,* provides a good summary on intelligence ties. There are many other comments on the subject by others.
167. Summarized in *Conspiracy* by Summers, p. 157, and notes, p. 570; Eddowes, *The Oswald File,* p. 28.
168. Ibid, p. 45; 12 HSCA 153, 171; contains DeMohrenschildt's entire manuscript on Oswald, which is very interesting. See "Three Witnesses," *New Times* (June 24, 1977).
169. Interview with Edwin Lopez (August 17, 1992).
170. Summarized in R. B. Cutler's and W. R. Morris's *Alias Oswald*; Michael Eddowes, *The Oswald File* (Appendix D), p. 211–222, Popkin, *The Two Oswalds.*
171. *High Treason 2*, p. 454; and to Larry Howard in 1990.
172. 2 H 281, Cecil McWatters notes that Oswald was the shortest man in the lineup, and the only one who came near fitting the description he gave; 3 H 310–311, Helen Markham identifies Oswald in a lineup based on "cold chills"; 2 H 260–61, William Whaley says they brought in six teenagers: "You could have picked him out without identifying him just by listening to him, because he was bawling out the policemen, telling them it wasn't right to put him in line with these teenagers . . . they were trying to railroad him and he wanted his lawyer . . . Anybody who wasn't sure could have picked out the right one just for that."; WR 625, "Oswald complained of a lineup wherein he had not been granted a request to put on a jacket" like

the other men in the lineup; Meagher, *Accessories After the Fact*, pp. 79, 256–7 259 (endnote by Martin Shackelford).

173. Marrs, *Crossfire*, p. 417; "The Men Who Killed Kennedy" (1991).
174. Billy Grammer on "The Men Who Killed Kennedy" produced by Nigel Turner, shown in 1988 abroad and in the U.S. in 1991 and 1992.
175. *Don Ray Archer* (DPD) "Investigative Report: The Men Who Killed Kennedy" A&E (November 1991).
176. Video entitled "The Kennedy Assassinations: Coincidence or Conspiracy?" (July 7, 1990).
177. Interview of Marco Miranda and Al Maddox (January 13, 1993). The author was present during the phone call.
178. Interview (June 14, 1993).
179. Second interview of Diana Bowron and the author (January 8, 1992).
180. *High Treason 2*, pp. 53–65, 67.
181. *High Treason 2*, pp. 179–180, 189; Dr. Lawrence Altman, *The New York Times* (October 6, 1992) p. C3.
182. Lattimer, "Kennedy and Lincoln," p. 220; Quotes from *Resident and Staff Physician* (May 1972) pp. 58–9.
183. *High Treason 2*, p. 152; author's interview with Boswell (October 7, 1991), see p. 199.
184. Ibid. pp. 182, 184–5 (author's interview with Dr. Karnei).
185. Ibid. p. 234 (author's interview with James Curtis Jenkins, June 16, 1991).
186. Ibid. pp. 188, 206, 209–210 (author's interviews with Jerrol Custer, November 22, 1991); 7 HSCA 15.
187. 7 HSCA 257, 2 H 361–362.
188. Interview with Kathlee Fitzgerald and the author (March 31, 1993).
189. For further information on one aspect of government record keeping, see "Federal Records, Document Removal by Agency Heads Needs Independent Oversight," General Accounting Office report to Congressional Requesters, GGD-91-117 (August 1991).
190. *Journal of the American Medical Association* (May 27, 1992).
191. James Cottone "The Exhumation and Identification of Lee Harvey Oswald," *Journal of Forensic Sciences*, pp. 1–84; "The Men Who Killed Kennedy" (1991). The statements of the undertaker, Paul Groody, have been discounted by M. Duke Lane, in his article, "DeBunking the Severed Head Myth," published by the JFK Assassination Information Center in Dallas (Summer/Fall issue of *Dateline: Dallas*, 1992).
192. Robert Blakey and Billings, Richard *The Plot To Kill The President*, p. 308, citing Seth Kantor.
193. Anthony Summers, *Conspiracy*, p. 450.
194. Ibid., p. 348.
195. 10 H 354.
196. Rusty Livingstone. *"The Third Decade."* Lecture given at the Midwest Symposium in Chicago (July 1992).

197. Ralston, *History's Verdict.*
198. Hurt, *Reasonable Doubt*, p. 411; HSCA Report p. 234; Shaw with Harris, *Cover-up*, p. 169.
199. Summers, *Conspiracy*, pp. 591–2: Hurt, *Reasonable Doubt*, 411–12.
200. The image was seen in the Dillard photograph enlargement shown by Robert Groden at the Pittsburgh Conference (1988).
201. Summers, *Conspiracy*, pp. 42–4.
202. Ibid., p. 79–80.
203. Ralston.
204. Meagher, *Accessories After The Fact*, pp. 59–62.
205. Summers, *Conspiracy*, p. 75.
206. Ibid. p. 50; Henry Hurt, *Reasonable Doubt*, p. 110.
207. Summarized in *Conspiracy*, pp. 22–30.
208. Johnny Brewer, 7 H 6.
209. Thompson, *Six Seconds in Dallas*, pp. 154–169.
210. Summers, *Conspiracy*, p. 500.
211. "The Men Who Killed Kennedy," Part Four, 1991–2.
212. 17 H 282.
213. *The Continuing Inquiry* (April, 1984); *The Third Decade* (January, 1985), p. 33.
214. Jerry D. Rose, *The Third Decade*, "They Got Their Man On Both Accounts," (March, 1988), pp. 1–8. Rose has the citations in his article reversed, so this note may apply to the following note and vice versa.
215. Rose, *The Third Decade*, "Important To Hold That Man" (May 1986), pp. 17–20. This note may apply to the preceding note and vice versa, due to the fact that Rose has his citations out of sequence.
216. Rose, *The Third Decade*, "They've Got Their Man on Both Accounts" (March 1988), p. 9–11.
217. Rose, *The Third Decade*, "We've Been Expecting You" (January, 1990), pp. 14–17.
218. Interview (January 3, 1993).
219. 11 HSCA p. 3.
220. Rose, *The Third Decade*, "Agent 179: The Making of a Dirty Rumor" (May, 1985), p. 14–19.
221. Scott Van Wynsberghe, *The Third Decade*, "Dead Suspects, Part 1" (November, 1986), pp. 10–16.
222. Melanson *The Third Decade*, "Leftist Lee At Work" (July, 1986), pp. 1–6.
223. 3 HSCA 136; Rose *The Third Decade*, "The Trip That Never Was: Oswald in Mexico" (May, 1985).
224. Author's interviews with Edwin Lopez (August 17, 1992), and Gaeton Fonzi (June 5, 1992)
225. Summers, *Conspiracy*, pp. 353–362.
226. J. Gary Shaw and Larry R. Harris, *Cover-up*, self–published, p. 203.

Chapter 3

1. Comment on manuscript (July, 1993).
2. *Journal of the American Medical Association* (May 27, 1992).
3. *Journal of the American Medical Association* (October 7, 1992).
4. Summers, *Conspiracy of Silence,* New York: Signet, 1992.
5. *High Treason 2,* (New York: Carroll & Graf, 1992), pp. 110–115.
6. *Cover-up,* Gary Shaw and Larry Harris, p. 187; Jones, *Forgive My Grief III*, p. 101; Zirbel, *The Texas Connection*, p. 18.
7. Penn Jones, Jr. *Forgive My Grief III.* p. 101. This is a second–hand story, but there is no reason to believe that it did not happen.
8. Author's interview with Dr. Phillip Earl Williams (May 10, 1992) confirmed by him to *The New York Times* (May 27th, 1992) in an article by Dr. Lawrence Altman; interview with Dr. Robert McClelland, April 29, 1992.
9. *New York Times* (May 26, 1992).
10. "JFK's Death—the Plain Truth From The Mds Who Did The Autopsy," *Journal of the American Medical Association* (May 27, 1992). Not "performed," but who "did" it. The perpetrators.
11. *Journal of the American Medical Association* (May 27, 1992).
12. "JFK's death, Part II, Dallas Mds Recall Their Memories." *Journal of the American Medical Association* (May 27, 1992), p. 2804.
13. Ibid. p. 2894.
14. Dallas Council on Foreign Affairs "Autopsy Forum" (June 4, 1992).
15. Ibid., p. 2804.
16. Ibid., p. 2804.
17. Ibid., p. 2085.
18. *JAMA* (October 7, 1992), p. 1737 and Note 16 therein; p. 1738; "Disturbing Issue of Kennedy's Secret Illness," *The New York Times*, (October 6, 1992).
19. 6 H 55–6, *High Treason 2*, pp. 106–7.
20. CE 392, 7 HSCA 269, 270.
21. 7 HSCA 312; NBC News; *Seventy Hours and Thirty Minutes* (Random House, 1966); Meagher, p. 153.
22. 6 H 42; Dallas Autopsy Forum (June 4, 1992) in this book.
23. Richard Dudman of the *St. Louis Post-Dispatch* (December 1, 1963) that the neck wound was a small, undamaged, punctuate area which "had the appearance of the usual entrance wound of a bullet."; 6 H 36–37.
24. Summers, *Conspiracy of Silence*, p. 79.
25. 6 H 65, 67.
26. 6 H 143.
27. See the chapter in this book on Diana Bowron.
28. For an early compendium of this evidence, see Sylvia Meagher's *Accessory After the Fact*, pp. 150–1; 7 HSCA 270; *High Treason 2*, pp. 106–109, 121.
29. "1968 Panel Review of Photographs, X-rays Films, Documents and

Other Evidence Pertaining to the Fatal Wounding of President John F. Kennedy, on Nov. 22, 1963 in Dallas, TX,'' *Maryland State Medical Journal* (March, 1977), p. 69.

30. *Life Magazine* (December 6, 1963); Author's interview with Malcolm Perry, (August 10, 1979); *High Treason 2*, pp. 106–7 (Jones); Author's filmed interviews with Parkland witnesses (April 6, 1991); Zirbel, *Texas Connection*, p. 16; Thompson, *Six Seconds In Dallas*, pp. 58–67; Wilber, p. 177–206.
31. *JAMA* (May 27, 1992), p. 2807.
32. 6 H 31–2, 40, 60, 80–1, 141.
33. 7 HSCA 8, CE 1126; Sibert & O'Neill FBI Report.
34. All of the quotes in this chapter are made from tape recordings provided by Kevin McCarthy.
35. Marrs on Geraldo Rivera (December 23, 1991).
36. Dr. Gary Aguilar's comment on the manuscript.
37. Dr. Joseph Riley *The Third Decade* (March, 1993), pp. 6–7.
38. JAMA article (May 27, 1992), p. 2804.
39. *High Treason 2*, p. 106–7, 298; Thompson, p. 58–67; Crenshaw, *Conspiracy of Silence*; Author's interviews, 4/6/91; *Life Magazine*, 12/6/63.
40. *High Treason 2*, pp. 304–5; *The Continuing Inquiry* (October, 1980); Summers, Op cit 38, p. 546.
41. CBS, Dan Rather (June, 1967).
42. *The Baltimore Sun* (November 11, 1966).
43. *High Treason 2*, p. 194, interview (October 2, 1990), Associated Press "JFK Autopsy Doctor Admits Sketch Error," (November 24, 1966).
44. *High Treason*, Conservatory Press (1989), pp. 188–201.
45. 7 HSCA p. 190.
46. 2 H 348.
47. 2 H 361; *High Treason 2* p, 260 (O'Connor), p. 303 (Jenkins); WC FBI Document 7 (Sibert & O'Neill); Thompson, *Six Seconds in Dallas*, (Boswell).
48. *State of Louisiana* v. *Clay Shaw*, 1968.
49. Letter from Robert Livingston, M.D. to the author (May 2, 1992).
50. Comment directly on this manuscript.
51. Letter from Robert B. Livingston, M.D. (May 2, 1992).
52. Investigation by the HSCA revealed that the brain was never placed with the body at any time. Cited elsewhere.
53. 1 HSCA 561–2; 500–1, 503, 514, 517, 531, 533, 561; Summers, *Conspiracy*, pp. 33–34.
54. 1 HSCA 562–3.
55. FBI Report signed by J. Edgar Hoover, "In the 1930's, Mussolini ordered all arms factories to manufacture the Mannlicher-Carcano rifle. Since many concerns were manufacturing the same weapon, the same serial number appears on weapons manufactured by more than one concern." (April 30, 1964).

56. "National Archives." Hearings before the House Subcommittee on Government Information (1976).
57. *State of Louisiana* v. *Clay Shaw*; Garrison, *Heritage of Stone* p. 198; Thompson, *Six Seconds in Dallas*, p. ix; Wilber, *Medicolegal Investigation of the Assassination of the President John F. Kennedy Assassination*, p. 256; *Destiny Betrayed*, James DiEugenio, Appendix A, pp. 288–309.
58. *High Treason 2*, under back wounds, and chapters on Paul O'Connor, Jerrol Custer, etc.
59. 7 HSCA 261.
60. Author's interview with Perry (August 10, 1979).
61. Author's interview with McClelland, April 6, 1991; *Boston Globe* (May 21, 1981); *Baltimore Sun*, (November 18, 1979).
62. Lundberg, G. D. *JAMA* (1987), 262: 945–6.
63. Lundberg, G. D. "RFIT and the goals of *The Journal*," *JAMA* (1982) 248: 1501.
64. *The Third Decade*, "Another Letter to *JAMA*" (March, 1993).
65. Lundberg, *JAMA* (1989) 262: 946.
66. 7 HSCA 245–6.
67. *The Third Decade* (March 1993), p. 29.
68. Military Review. Report of the three autopsy doctors after review of the autopsy photos and X-rays in January 1967. This is a public document available at the Justice Department.
69. 7 HSCA 251.
70. November 2 and December 2, 1992.
71. 7 HSCA 246, 260.
72. 7 HSCA 260.
73. 7 HSCA 249.
74. Finck, P.A. "Ballistic and forensic pathologic aspects of missile wounds." Conversion between Anglo-American and metric-system units. Military Medicine, (1965), 130: 545–569.
75. 7 HSCA 113–119.
76. 7 HSCA 254.
77. First reversal in the public hearing: 1 HSCA 323–332: *JAMA*, (1992), 268: 1681–2.
78. 7 HSCA 115.
79. *The Third Decade* supra (March, 1993), p. 31.
80. 2 H 382; 374–6.
81. *The Third Decade* (March 1993).
82. Lundberg, "The Quality of a Medical Article—Thank you to our 1990 Peer Reviewers." *JAMA* (1991) 265: 1161–2.
83. Dr. James H. Fetzer, Phd, *The Third Decade* (March, 1993), p. 35.
84. Bonar Menninger, *Mortal Error* (New York; St Martin's Press, 1992) pp. 44–45.
85. February 14, 1965.
86. 2 H 141.
87. Wecht CH, Smith RP, "The Medical Evidence in the Assassination

of President John F. Kennedy." *Forensic Science Gazette* (1973), 4:9–19.

88. Comment of Prof. William Alfred, Department of English, to the author, who consulted him on April 18, 1993, concerning Artwohl's use of the term "conspirati" and its total absence in the English language.
89. *JAMA* (1992); 268: 1681–1682.
90. *JAMA* (1992), 268:1681–1682.
91. Warren Report, *New York Times* edition, p. 502.
92. Artwohl, *JAMA*, (March 24/31, 1993) p. 1540.
93. Ibid.
94. Comment written on this manuscript by Gary Aguilar, M.D.
95. *High Treason 2*, chapter on Jerrol Custer (1992).
96. Ibid.
97. Discussion (May 3, 1993).
98. Cunningham and Fitzgerald statements were marginally noted on this manuscript.
99. *JAMA* (March 24/31, 1993), p. 1541.
100. Ibid.
101. Discussion with Kathy Cunningham (April 10, 1993).
102. Ibid, p. 1541.
103. The Autopsy Report, p. 501, *The New York Times* edition (1964).
104. Visit at the author's home (April 17, 1993).
105. 7 HSCA 249.
106. *High Treason 2*, p. 580.
107. Interview with Dr. Randolph Robertson (April 21, 1993).
108. *The New York Times* edition (1964), p. 501.
109. *High Treason*, 2, pp. 99, 199, 579–80.
110. *High Treason 2*, p. 199.
111. *High Treason and High Treason 2*.
112. Letter from Dr. Donald Siple, Chief of Radiology, Maryland General Hospital, to the author (April 16, 1993).
113. *JAMA*, p. 1541.
114. *JAMA*, p. 1542.
115. Interview with Dr. Donald Siple (April 17, 1993).
116. 2 H 141.
117. Interview with Josiah Thompson, in his book *Six Seconds in Dallas*, paperback version, Berkley Medallion, (1976), p. 133.
118. 18 H 722–784.
119. Letter of Douglas Mizzer to the author (April 19, 1993).
120. Prodigy, a nationwide bulletin board network (December 1, 1992).
121. Prodigy (December 7, 1992).
122. High Treason 2, chapters on Karnei and Boswell.
123. Letter from Douglas Mizzer to the author (April 12, 1993).
124. *JAMA* (March 23/31, 1993), p. 1543.
125. Richard Dudman in the *St. Louis Post Dispatch* (December 1, 1963).

126. Prodigy note from Robert Artwohl to David Lifton (December 2, 1992).
127. Smear of Dr. Robert Artwohl to Ron Carmichael (December 14, 1992).
128. Prodigy (December 19, 1992).
129. Post from Robert Artwohl to David Lifton (November 23, 1992).
130. Post from Robert Artwohl to "All" (December 21, 1992).
131. Robert Artwohl to Robert Wagstaff, (November 28, 1992).
132. Robert Artwohl to David Lifton (November 25, 1992).
133. Robert Artwohl to Dr. Gary Aguilar (December 14, 1992).
134. Robert Artwohl to Dr. Gary Aguilar (December 7, 1992).
135. Prodigy (December 20, 1992).
136. *JAMA* (March 23/31, 1993), p. 1542.
137. Dr. John Lattimer. "Additional Data on the shooting of President Kennedy, *Journal of the American Medical Association* (March 24/31, 1993), p. 1544.
138. Ibid, p. 1547.
139. Vincent DiMaio. *Gunshot Wounds* (New York: Elsevier Science Publishers, 1985).
140. *JAMA*, p. 1546.
141. Dr. Gary Aguilar writing in Prodigy (April 29, 1993).
147. *JAMA* (March 24/31, 1993), p. 1544.
143. Prodigy (January 29, 1993).
144. *JAMA*, p. 1544.
145. *JAMA* (March 24/31, 1993), p. 1545.
146. *JAMA*, p. 1544.
147. *JAMA* (March 24/31, 1993), p. 1545.
148. *JAMA* (March 24/31, 1993), p. 1545–6.
149. Ibid.
150. "The Ayoob Files. The JFK Assassination: A Shooter's Eye View." *The American Handgunner* (March 1993).
151. Remarks at the Chicago conference (April 3, 1993).
152. Transcript made and provided by Gary Aguilar, M.D. from his tapes.
153. *JAMA* (October 7, 1992), p. 1737.
154. Lawrence Altman, M.D., *The New York Times* (October 6, 1992).
155. *High Treason 2*, 52–68; 179.

Chapter 4

1. Reuter dispatch by Jean King (May 29, 1992).
2. *The Dallas Morning News* (May 1, 1992), p. 38 A
3. *High Treason 2*, Chapter 14, p. 283.
4. WR, (Appendix VIII), p. 483. (CE 392).
5. 7 HSCA 15
6. Autopsy Report in the Warren Report, The *New York Times* edition (1964), p. 500; *Journal of the American Medical Association* (May 27, 1992), p. 2798, ("The fatal wound was ... slightly above the occipital protuberance.")

7. *Journal of the American Medical Association* (May 27, 1992), p. 2797.
8. Associated Press (May 29, 1992).

Chapter 5

1. David Real. *The Dallas Morning News*, (June 5, 1992).
2. Interview (March 16, 1964), 2 H 375.
3. 6 HSCA 269.
4. See *High Treason 2* by the author, pp. 106–7.
5. All of the quotes in this chapter were taken from tape recordings provided by Kevin McCarthy.

Chapter 6

1. Document dated 24 January, 1993, from Diana Bowron to the author.
2. Bowron Exhibit 4, Warren Commission Exhibits.
3. Interview (January 8, 1993).
4. Bowron Exhibit 3, Warren Commission Exhibits.
5. Ibid.
6. Price Exhibit No. 12, 212 H 203–4.
7. Additional phone interview of January 8, 1993. There were several calls that day, and not all the information exchanged was contained in the same interview.
8. Telephone Interview of Diana Bowron by Harrison Livingstone (January 8, 1993).
9. Interview (March 15, 1993).
10. Interview (May 2, 1993).
11. Letter (April 25, 1993).
12. Ibid.
13. Ibid.
14. Ibid.
15. Letter (May 11, 1993).

Chapter 7

1. Summers. *Conspiracy*, p. 312.
2. Warren Report, *The New York Times* edition, p. 516.
3. Ibid.
4. WR, p. 517.
5. Ibid.
6. 7 HSCA 376.
7. Letter from Evan P. Marshall (January 19, 1990).
8. WR *New York Times*, p. 517.
9. Letter (January 19, 1990).
10. *New York Times* edition of the Warren Report, p. 513.
11. Holmes Exhibit No. 2, 20 H 174.
12. O'Toole. *The Assassination Tapes,* on Buell Wesley Frazier, p. 170; 2 H 243; Linnie Mae Randle pp. 248–251.

13. WR, p. 134.
14. Ibid. p. 118
15. CE, 773
16. WR, p. 119; CE 788, p. 120.
17. WR, 119–121
18. WR, p. 120
19. WR, 118–119.
20. XXV WC, p. 808.
21. 10 H 224, 227, 228; 23 H 727.
22. Summers, *Conspiracy*, p. 312. Alba interview with Summers (1978), and affidavit made for Ian McFarlane (December 23, 1975); *Dallas Morning News*, August 7, 1978; HSCA Report pp 193, 146.
23. CD 74, p. 262. Paul Hoch 1970.
24. Letter from the National Archives to Patricia Dumais (August 19, 1991).
25. 7 H 370.
26. Letter from the National Archives to Patricia Dumais (July 12, 1991).
27. WR, p. 518.
28. Charles E. O'Hara and Gregory O'Hara. *Fundamentals of Criminal Investigation*, Springfield, IL (Charles C. Thomas, 1956, 1970, 1973, 1980, Fifth Edition, second printing 1981), p. 771, or page 691 in earlier editions.
29. Ibid.
30. Ibid.
31. Ibid., p. 772.
32. Dallas City-County Criminal Investigation Lab # 3531 11/23/63.
33. Dallas City-County Criminal Investigation Lab # 3531 (11/23/63.
34. Supplementary offense report, 11/24/63, serial number F-85950, Dallas Police Department.
35. Patricia Dumais letter to the author (February 26, 1963).
36. Ibid.

Chapter 8

1. Memo from Jerry Hunt to Richard Baker (October 24, 1979).
2. Letter from Mark Crouch to the author concerning David Lifton's attempt to market the photographs taken from Crouch (December 12, 1992).
3. *Globe* (December 31, 1991).
4. David Lifton planted a story in *The New York Times* in 1979 through his friend Robert Blair Kaiser, saying that I was trying to *sell* the autopsy pictures. In fact, I never possessed the pictures, but was asked by Groden to try to get them out. I didn't know that Groden was asking a high price (or any price), and my plan was to print some of them to illustrate the observations of the Dallas doctors to whom I had shown the HSCA tracings. The *Times* story was retracted the next day, but permanent damage was done to my reputation, bringing

humiliation and ostracism to me. Lifton succeeded in driving the photographs underground and terrorized Groden, telling him that the FBI was coming to his door. Groden burned his pictures on the spot, retaining a roll of black and white negatives which he took of them, not having any color film in the house. These were later colorized. Nobody was interested in the startling evidence I had developed which cast into question the authenticity of the pictures. Ten long years were to pass before I could publish this in *High Treason*, at my own expense, once again falling into the clutches of Robert Groden. Lifton's scheme, though, worked. He had to drive the pictures and my evidence of forgery underground because he was planning to inflict a massive hoax on the public, known as *Best Evidence.*

5. Letter of transmittal from Burke Marshall to Lawson B. Knott, Jr., Administrator of General Services, October 29, 1966.
6. *D. Mark Katz v. National Archives and Records Administration,* Civil Action No. 92–1024 GHR, U.S. District Court for the District of Washington, D. C.
7. *Plaintiff's Memorandum of Points and Authorities in Opposition to Defendant's Motion for Summary Judgment,* D. Mark Katz v. National Archives, Civil Action No. 92–1024 GHR, U. S. District Court for the District of Columbia.
8. *United States Dep't of Justice v. Tax Analysts,* 492 U.S. 136, 144 (1989), citing *Forsham v. Harris,* 445 U.S. 169, 182 (1980).
9. *Tax Analysts,* 492 U.S. at 145.
10. *Plaintiff's Memorandum of Points and Authorities in Opposition to Defendant's Motion for Summary Judgment.* Supra.
11. Ibid., 5 U.S.C. Section 552 (b)(6).
12. Ibid. *Plaintiff's Memorandum of Points and Authorities in Opposition to Defendant's Motion for Summary Judgment.*
13. *Plaintiff's Memorandum of Points and Authorities,* etc., p. 14.
14. Ibid., p. 15.
15. 44 U.S.C Section 2201(2).
16. 5 U.S.C. Sec. 552 (a)(3).
17. *U.S. Department of Justice v. Tax Analysts,* 494 U.S. 136 (1989).
18. *Defendant's Reply Memorandum In Support of Motion to Dismiss the Complaint,* Katz v. National Archives, p. 8.
19. Ibid.
20. Ibid., p. 22.
21. Ibid., p. 23.
22. Discussion with Mark Katz (December 16, 1992).
23. *Custer in Photographs,* Yo-Mark Production Co., 1985, republished by Random House, New York, 1990.
24. *Witness to an Era: The Life and Photographs of Alexander Gardner,* New York: Viking Press, 1991.
25. Declaration of Mark Katz, *D. Mark Katz v. National Archives & Records Administration,* Civil Action No. 92-1024 GHR, February 11, 1993.

26. *The Plaintiff's Memorandum of Points and Authorities in Support of His Cross-motion For Summary Judgment and in Opposition to Defendant's Motion For Summary Judgment,* February 16, 1993, p. 4.
27. Def. S.J. at 10–12.
28. *The Plaintiff's Memorandum of Points an Authorities in Support of His Cross-motion For Summary Judgment and in Opposition to Defendant's Motion For Summary Judgment,* February 16, 1993, p. 13.
29. Ibid., p. 14.
30. Ibid.
31. Ibid., p. 17.
32. Ibid., p. 19.
33. Ibid., p. 20.
34. Ibid., p. 18.
35. Ibid., p. 20, declaration of Mark A. Crouch, Louis P. Kartsonis, and Harrison E. Livingstone.
36. Ibid., pp. 21–23.
37. Ibid., p. 24.
38. Ibid., p. 26.
39. Ibid., p. 29.
40. *Cause No. 92-10500-H, Joe H. West v. Dr. Jeffrey J. Barnard* District Court of Dallas County, Texas, 160th Judicial District.
41. Press Release, "Shaw-West" News Conference—New Evidence in JFK Case (May 11th, 1990).
42. See *High Treason 2*, pp. 534–4.
43. *The Houston Post* (February 16, 1992).
44. Robert Morrow, *Betrayal*, Regnery, Illinois, 1976.
45. *The Houston Post* (February 16, 1992).
46. Author's interview (December 5, 1992); WR, pp. 78, 80, 134–5, 143, 232.
47. *The Houston Post* (February 16, 1992).
48. Ibid.
49. Ibid.
50. 38 C.F.R. Part 1, & 1.621 (1991).
51. 7 HSCA 180 (493).
52. 92-10500-H, *Joe H. West v. Dr. Jeffrey J. Barnard*, District Court of Dallas County, Texas, 160th Judicial District.
53. Ibid., Original Answer, (September 10, 1992).
54. Mark Potok. *The Dallas Times Herald* (November 16, 1991).
55. Ibid.
56. Ibid.
57. *Dallas Morning News* (November 16, 1991).
58. *Thomas Wilson v. David Belin and G. Robert Blakey*, District Court of Dallas County, Texas, 92–13668.
59. Letter from Mr. Bradley Kizzia to the author (December 10, 1992).
60. Interview with Robert Blakey (December 11, 1992).
61. 2 HSCA 344.
62. *The Third Decade*, Van Wynsberghe, May 1992, p. 39.

63. *"Charles Crenshaw, M.D. and Gary Shaw v. Lawrence Sutherland, George Lundberg, Dennis Breo, The American Medical Association, D/B/A Journal of American Medical Association, the Dallas Morning News and David W. Belin,"* District Court of Johnson County, Texas, 18th Judicial District, No. 73–93.
64. Ibid.

Chapter 9

1. "The JFK Autopsy Pictures, The Crouch Affidavits" (1993). Not formally published as of this date, but in manuscript.
2. Crouch 1993 Affidavit, p. 3.
3. Crouch Affidavit (February 5, 1993), p. 11.
4. Ibid., p. 11.
5. *High Treason 2*, pp. 321–6.
6. David Litton, *Best Evidence* p. 703.
7. Crouch Affidavit (February 5, 1993), p. 12.
8. Sibert & O'Neill FBI report (November 26, 1963).
9. Crouch Affidavit (February 5, 1993), p. 12.
10. *Dallas Times Herald* (October 29, 1988), letter from Mark Crouch to Oliver Stone (February 27, 1991).
11. Crouch Affidavit (February 5, 1992), p. 15.
12. Ibid, p. 16.
13. Ibid, p. 17.
14. Ibid. p. 18.
15. Letter from Mark Crouch to the author (January 23, 1991).
16. Crouch Affidavit, p. 20.
17. Ibid.
18. Ibid.
19. Ibid.
20. Ibid., p. 22.
21. Ibid., p. 23.
22. Ibid., p. 25.
23. Ibid., pp. 25–26.
24. Memo from Jerry Hunt to Richard Baker, "Faking of the Autopsy Photos" (October 24, 1979).
25. Ibid., p. 26.
26. Ibid., p. 26.
27. *Dallas Times Herald* (October 29, 1988).
28. Letter of David Lifton from Mark Crouch (March 17, 1991).
29. Ibid., pp. 27–29.
30. Ibid., p. 29.
31. Ibid., pp. 28–30.
32. Ibid., p. 33.
33. Ibid., p. 34.
34. Ibid., p. 36.
35. Ibid., p. 37.

36. Ibid., p. 35.
37. Ibid., p. 38.
38. Ibid., p. 39.
39. Ibid., p. 40.
40. Ibid., p. 41.
41. Ibid., p. 42.
42. Ibid., p. 44.
43. Ibid., p. 46–47.
44. Ibid., p. 52.
45. UPI (March 29, 1990).
46. Ibid.
47. Ibid.
48. Letter from David Lifton to Gary J. Rowell (November 3, 1991).
49. Letter from Martin Shackelford (May 15, 1993) and his 1991 (ASK conference) notes, p. 25.
50. *Dallas Times Herald* (October 29, 1988).
51. Lifton. *Best Evidence*, p. 703.
52. Letter from David Lifton to Mark Crouch (April 5, 1991).
53. Letter from David Lifton to Mark Crouch (March 23, 1990).
54. Depositions of Robert Groden, *Groden v. Carroll & Graf and Harrison Livingstone* (March 15–16, 1993).
55. Letter from David Lifton to Gary Rowell (November 5, 1991).
56. Letter from David Lifton to Mark Crouch (April 5, 1991).
57. Letter from James Allgeyer, Attorney Adviser, U.S. Copyright Office to Mark Crouch, Control No. 60 114 577 C. Not dated.
38. Letter from David Lifton to Mark Crouch (April 5, 1991).
59. Letter from David Lifton to Mark Crouch (March 17, 1991).
60. Letter from David Lifton to Mark Crouch (March 17, 1991).
61. Letter from David Lifton to Mark Crouch (March 26, 1991) and other communications.
62. Letter from David Lifton to Mark Crouch (March 17, 1991).
63. Ibid.
64. Ibid.
65. Letter from David Lifton to Mark Crouch (March 17, 1991).
66. Ibid.
67. Letter from Mark Crouch (February 4, 1993).
68. Letter from Martin Shackelford to the author (April 29, 1993).
69. Letter (May 15, 1993).
70. Letter from Martin Shackelford to the author (April 29, 1993).
71. Letter from Mark Crouch to the author (August 26, 1991).
72. Crouch notes (March 5, 1991).
73. Crouch notes (March 5, 1991).
74. Ibid.
75. Discussion with Jane Downey (December 12, 1992).
76. Letter from Mark Crouch (January 23, 1991).
77. Memo from Jan Shwartz at Dwyer & Brennan, New York City (March 20, 1993).

78. Letter (May 15, 1993).
79. *Dallas Times Herald* (October 29, 1988).
80. December 31, 1991. This was also discussed in *High Treason 2* in the caption for the color photograph as well as in the chapter on the autopsy pictures.
81. *High Treason 2* (April, 1992).
82. I have unfortunately lost this letter as well as its source because of an accident (a lightening bolt) involving my computer caused it to crash.
83. Letter from Martin Shackelford to the author (November 5, 1992).
84. Martin Shackelford letter (May 15, 1993).
85. *JAMA*, March 24/31, 1993, p. 1544.
86. Prodigy (January 29, 1993).

Chapter 10

1. *High Treason*, p. 72, photo insert pp. 22–25, and elsewhere; *High Treason 2*, p. 341, and other photos in the book.
2. 7 HSCA 228–9, 223, 218, 282; mention of the missing bone by Dr. Angel, 7 HSCA 249.
3. Discussion (April 25, 1993).
4. Both Dr. Artwohl and Dr. Lattimer had articles printed in the *Journal of the American Medical Association* (March 24/31, 1993).
5. Jerry Organ, *The Third Decade*, "Insights On The X-rays" (March, 1993).
6. Dr. Robert Artwohl writing on Prodigy (November 11, 1992).
7. Dr. Robert Artwohl writing on Prodigy (November 17, 1992).
8. Cyril Wecht and Robert P. Smith, "The Medical Evidence in the Assassination of President John F. Kennedy," by *Forensic Science*, 2 (1974), p. 117.
9. *The Third Decade* (March, 1993), p. 17.
10. Letter from Dr. Donald Siple, Chief of Radiology at Maryland General Hospital, to the author (April 16, 1993).
11. *The Third Decade* (March, 1993).
12. *High Treason 2*, chapter on Jerrol Custer.
13. RT Images (August 31, 1992).
14. Associated Press, (June 1, 1992).
15. Ebersole interview with Art Smith (March 28, 1978).
16. 7 HSCA 221.
17. 7 HSCA 109.
18. Dr. John K. Lattimer, "Observations Based on A Review of the Autopsy Photographs, X-rays, and Related Materials of the Late President John F. Kennedy," by *Resident and Staff Physician* (May 1972).
19. 1 HSCA 202.
20. Ibid.
22. Jerry Organ, *The Third Decade* (March 1993), p. 17.
23. "Observations Based On A Review of the Autopsy Photographs, X-

Rays, and Related Materials of the Late President John F. Kennedy,'' Dr. John Lattimer, *Resident and Staff Physician* (May, 1972), pp. 43–46.

24. ''The Kennedy Assassination: A Case Study in the Use of Demonstrative and Forensic Evidence'' (The D.C. Bar mock trial of the case, June 17, 1992); Cyril H. Wecht and Robert P. Smith, ''The Medical Evidence in the Assassination of President John F. Kennedy,'' *Forensic Science* (1974), p. 117.

25. Fitzgerald, Kathlee, *The Third Decade*, ''What's Wrong With This Picture?'' (January/March, 1992).

26. *High Treason 2,* Chapter on Jerrol Custer; at the author's press conference with Jerrol Custer, Floyd Reibe and Paul O'Connor (May 29, 1992) Reuters and AP stories of that date; *Advance*, a radiographer's magazine (August 3, 1992).

27. *The Third Decade*, (March, 1993), p. 20.

28. *High Treason*, Afterword, (1989).

29. Ibid.

30. Ibid.

31. In 1963–4, the Parkland doctors and other witnesses testified and made records as to the position of the large defect in the posterior part of the skull and only there. They confirmed this to me in 1979 (and to others thereafter), and I published that compendium in my first book, *High Treason* (1989) as well as a compilation of the medical evidence in the appendix of this book. This evidence came under severe assault by those who would distort it for obvious reasons, and who tried to have it appear that the doctors had repudiated it. See some of their comments in the chapter on Dallas autopsy doctors forum in this book.

32. *High Treason* (1989), chapter on the head wounds.

33. Ibid., p. 20.

34. Ibid.

35. Letter from Kathy Cunningham (May 3, 1993).

Chapter 11

1. A one–paragraph discussion of the Bronson film can be found in 6 HSCA 120–1. Also see pp. 308–9.

2. 6 HSCA, Letter from C. J. Leontis, of the Aerospace Corporation, to Mr. Michael Goldsmith (11, December, 1978).

3. Ibid.

4. *The Dallas Morning News* (November 26, 1978); and the author's discussion with Earl Golz (October 10, 1992).

5. Ron Rosenbaum *Travels With Dr. Death* (New York: Penguin Books, 1991), pp. 78–79.

6. Author's interview with Charles Bronson (September 27, 1992).

7. Interviews with Steve Barber (October 10 and 30th, 1992).

8. *The Dallas Morning News* (November 26, 1978).

9. *The Rolling Stone* (April 24, 1975), p. 34. Note also the ''face'' of

the assassin on that page. Frame 413 was also slipped into my first book, *High Treason,* in the photo section following p. 232.

10. Author's interview with Charles Bronson (September 27, 1992).
11. *The Dallas Morning News* (December 20, 1978); *The Continuing Inquiry* (January, 1979).
12. Memorandum of Martin Shackelford to the author (December 10, 1992).
13. Interview (September 24, 1992).
14. Kent Biffle, *The Dallas Morning News* (November 26, 1978).
15. Memo Comment # 12 by Martin Shackelford to the author (December 10, 1992).
16. Shackelford Memo Comment # 15 to the author (December 10, 1992).
17. Letter of Robert Selzer of the Jet Propulsion Laboratory to Michael Goldsmith (December 21), HSCA 1078: 6 HSCA 120–1.
18. *The Dallas Morning News* (November 27, 1978).
19. UPI in *The Detroit Free Press* (November 30, 1978).
20. UPI and AP stories in the *Detroit Free Press* (November 27, 1978).
21. FBI Memorandum, Milton L. Newsom, 11/25/63.
22. Chris Sharrett letter to the author (October 9, 1992).
23. Interview with Madeleine Brown (January 5, 1993).
24. AP story in *The Dallas Morning News* (September 5, 1988).
25. William Turner, "How French Intelligence Wrote A Book About The Kennedy Assassination, in 'Farewell America,' " *The Rebel* (February 13, 1984.
26. Ibid.
27. *Entertainment Weekly* (January 17, 1992).
28. *The Dallas Morning News,* AP story (September 5, 1988).
29. Letter from Martin Shackelford (May 18, 1993).
30. Martin Shackelford letter to the author (October 18, 1992).
31. Letter from Elizabeth L. Hill of the National Archives to Martin Shackelford (October 14, 1992).
32. Change of Holdings Report of the National Archives (May 12, 1975) Transaction No. NN-375-222.
33. Chris Sharrett letter to the author (October 7, 1992).
34. Memo from Elizabeth Hill (May 11, 1992) and letter by same to Martin Shackelford (October 14, 1992).
35. *The Rolling Stone* (April 24, 1975).
36. Shackelford letter (May 18, 1993).
37. *Rolling Stone* (April 24, 1975), p. 34.
38. Letter from Martin Shackelford, May 18, 1993.
39. Shackelford Memo, Comment # 27 to the author (December 10, 1992).
40. Anthony Summers, *Conspiracy,* McGraw-Hill, (1980), p. 80.
41. Chris Sharrett letter to the author (October 7, 1992).
42. Chris Sharrett letter to the author (October 9, 1992).
43. Memo of Martin Shackelford to the author (September 23, 1992).
44. __ HSCA __.
45. Letter of Martin Shackelford to the author (October 18, 1992).

46. William Weston, "The Fifth Floor Sniper," *The Third Decade* (May, 1993), p. 23.
47. Letter from Todd Vaughan to Martin Shackelford (January 7, 1992).
48. Ibid.
49. Chris Sharrett letter to the author (September 8, 1992).
50. Chris Sharrett letter to the author (October 9, 1992).
51. Letter to Todd Vaughan to Martin Shackelford (January 7, 1993).
52. Letter of Martin Shackelford to the author (January 17, 1993).
53. Letter of Todd Vaughan to Martin Shackelford (January 7, 1993).
54. Martin Shackelford, "The Zapruder Film: Contents" (1992).
55. Thompson, *Six Seconds In Dallas,* p. 134.
56. Shackelford Memo, Comment # 54 to the author (December 10, 1992).
57. *The Third Decade* conference, Fredonia, NY (June, 1991).
58. Memorandum from Martin Shackelford to the author (January 18, 1993).
59. Part of this history of the Nix film is told in *J.F.K., The Book of the Film* by Oliver Stone & Zachary Sklar (New York: Applause Books, 1992), p. 496.
60. Letter of Martin Shackelford to the author (January 17, 1993).
61. Chris Sharrett letter to the author (October 9, 1992).
62. Penn Jones, Jr. *Forgive My Grief III,* pp. 36–37, 100; and *Forgive My Grief IV,* pp. 15–16, 172 for further data on Weatherford.
63. Letter (May 15, 1993).
64. *Groden v. Carroll & Graf,* Groden deposition (March 15, 1993).
65. Letter of May 15, 1993.
66. Contract of Robert Groden with L.F.P. Inc. (December 30th, 1977).

Chapter 12

1. Interview with Sheriff Jim Bowles (January 3, 1993).
2. Ibid.
3. 5 HSCA 704, 625, 629.
4. Bowles manuscript, p. 139–141; McLain, Channel 5, KXAS–TV, Ft. Worth/Dallas (1979).
5. NRC Report, p. 7; Bowles manuscript, p. 140.
6. Bowles manuscript, p. 139–140.
7. *Double Decker* (June 24, 1989). Write to Robert Cutler at Box 1465, 38 Union St., Manchester, MA 01944, or Steve Barber, 3392 State Rt. 314, Shelby, OH 44875.
8. Letter from James Barger to Robert Blakey (February 18, 1983).
9. Letter from Dr. James Barger to G. Robert Blakey (February 18, 1983).
10. Larry Darkel, aka Gary Mack, "Acoustic Analysis Confirmed: FBI Bakes Down" *The Continuing Inquiry* (April, 1981).
11. Sheriff Jim Bowles, *The Kennedy Assassination Tapes, A Rebuttal to the Acoustical Evidence.* Unpublished manuscript. No date.
12. Interview with Sheriff Jim Bowles (January 3, 1993).

13. Manuscript by Todd Vaughan, "The Acoustical Evidence in the Assassination of President John F. Kennedy," (1980), p. 11.
14. 8 HSCA 65–67; Todd Vaughan manuscript, p. 13.
15. 8 HSCA 80–94.
16. *Report,* IISCA, 638–676.
17. Todd Vaughan manuscript, p. 15.
18. 8 HSCA 71.
19. Todd Vaughan manuscript, p. 16.
20. Todd Vaughan manuscript, p. 17.
21. Todd Vaughan manuscript, p. 18.
22. *Report,* HSCA 82.
23. 5 HSCA; photos of motorcycles at Parkland; and McLain's testimony p. 633–634.
24. Todd Vaughan manuscript, through p. 26.
25. Ibid. p. 28.
26. Memorandum from Todd Vaughan to the author (November 7, 1992) and statement to the author (February 14, 1993).
27. Steve Barber, in *The Continuing Inquiry* (February, 1983).
28. The "Critics Copy" of the police recordings were those copies of the DPD recordings passed from officer Gerald Hill to Mary Ferrell, copied by her and given to other critics, and eventually passed on to the House Committee on Assassinations.
29. Barber, Steven. *The Continuing Inquiry* (February, 1983). p. 1.
30. Ibid.
31. National Research Council, "Report of the Committee on Ballistics Acoustics," National Academy Press, Washington, D.C., (1982). p. 30–1.
32. Ibid., p. 9.
33. Memorandum to the author and others from Todd Vaughan (November 7, 1992).
34. Letter from Gary Mack to the author (April 10, 1985).
35. Gary Mack in "J.D. Tippit: The 'Missing' Broadcasts." *The Continuing Inquiry* (September, 1984).
36. Interview of J. C. Bowles with the author (January 3, 1993).
37. Ibid.
38. Bowles' FBI interview (8/27/80 and 9/15/80).
39. Interview with Sheriff Jim Bowles, January 3, 1993.
40. Interview with the author (January 3, 1993).
41. Interview with the author (January 3, 1993).
42. Gary Mack, *Coverups* (September, 1984).
43. Gary Mack, *Coverups* (September, 1984).
44. 8 HSCA 32.
45. G. Robert Blakey and Richard N. Billings, *The Plot to Kill the President: Organized Crime Assassinated JFK* (New York: Times Books, 1981), p. 91–92.
46. Gary Mack in *The Continuing Inquiry* (August 1977).
47. 8 HSCA 11. "To the ear, these sounds resemble static, not gunshots."

48. 8 HSCA 65–67.
49. Letter from Gary Mack to Todd Vaughan (February 8, 1982).
50. Channel 5, KXAS, Dallas/Ft. Worth August 20, 1978; prime time news national news.
51. CBS Television Report (August 19, 1978).
52. F. Peter Model and Robert J. Groden, *JFK: The Case for Conspiracy,* Manor Books (1977 update).
53. 5 HSCA 706–718; See "No McLain, No Motorcycle, No Microphone: The Assassination Films Disprove the Assassination Tapes" by Sim Heninger, *The Third Decade* (July 1990).
54. 5 HSCA 706–718.
55. Letter from Tony Marsh to the author (March 23, 1993).
56. 5 HSCA 627–9, 705.
57. Sim Heninger, "No McLain, No Motorcycle, No Microphone: The Assassination Films Disprove the Assassination Tapes" *The Third Decade* (July, 1990). p. 15.
58. Conversation with Sheriff Jim Bowles of Dallas, January 3, 1993.
59. Ibid.
60. Gary Mack, *The Continuing Inquiry* (August, 1977).
61. Discussion with Todd Vaughan (February 14, 1993).
62. Ibid., p. 16–17.
63. 18 H 767.
64. Letter from Tony Marsh to the author (March 23, 1993).
65. 5 HSCA 706–718.
66. Independent analysis of Sim Henninger, "No McLain, No Motorcycle, and No Microphone," *The Third Decade* (July 1990), p. 14, (Dorman and Hughes, p. 15); and Todd Vaughan, photographic presentation in meeting with the author (February 14, 1993).
67. Identifies self 5 HSCA 629, 635, 640–1, 678–9, 703–21; testimony, 5 HSCA 617–41.
68. Conversation with Sheriff Jim Bowles (January 3, 1993).
69. Gary Mack in *The Continuing Inquiry* (April, 1981).
70. Gary Mack in *The Continuing Inquiry* (April, 1981).
71. Letter of Tony Marsh to the author (March 23, 1993).
72. 8 HSCA 11–12.
73. Phone conversation with Todd Vaughan (December 29, 1992).
74. 8 HSCA 15.
75. *Report of the Committee on Ballistic Acoustics,* Commission on Physical Sciences, Mathematics, and Resources, National Research Council, National Academy Press, Washington, D.C., (1982) p. 4.
76. Supra, p. 13.
77. Supra, p. 13–14.
78. Memorandum by Todd Vaughan to the author and others (November 7, 1992).
79. Letter from Dr. James Barger to G. Robert Blakey (February 18, 1983); *High Treason 2,* Harrison E. Livingstone, Appendix "E" (New York: Carroll & Graf), p. 614.

80. Ibid., p. 612.
81. Conversation with the author (December 29, 1992).
82. Associated Press (October 31, 1980).
83. *Report,* HSCA (1979), p. 65–6.
84. AP story of October 28, 1980, *The New York Times,* etc., that day.
85. Letter to Todd Vaughan (May 13, 1993).
86. Conversation with Sheriff Jim Bowles (January 3, 1993).

Chapter 13

1. "The Assassination of President John F. Kennedy: A Model for Explanation," *Computers and Automation* (December, 1971 and January, 1972).
2. Ibid.
3. Ibid.
4. Ibid.
5. Conversations on almost every (of many) occasions with Penn Jones, Jr.
6. Meeting of the American Bar Association, San Francisco (July 1992).
7. *Journal of the American Medical Association* (May 27, 1992). See the chapter in this book on this.
8. FBI report to President Johnson (November 8, 1966).
9. Ibid.
10. Letter from Harold Weisberg to Richard Waybright (January 22, 1993).
11. Letter from Harold Weisberg to the author (October 23, 1991).
12. Letter from Harold Weisberg to Hunt Oil Company (February 17, 1969).
13. Letter from the author to Harold Weisberg (November 24, 1992).
14. Letter from Harold Weisberg to the author (November 20, 1992).
15. Letter from the author to Harold Weisberg (November 24, 1992).
16. Letter from the author to Harold Weisberg (November 24, 1992).
17. Letter from Harold Weisberg to the author (November 20, 1992), p. 3.
18. William Turner, "Farewell America," *The Rebel* (February 13, 1984) Reprinted by Prevailing Winds Research, P.O. Box 23511, Santa Barbara, CA 93121.
19. Back cover of Weisberg's *Photographic Whitewash* (1967).
20. "Memorandum For the Garrison File," files of Hunt Oil Company (January 9, 1969).
21. Meeting of March 9, 1993, Dallas.
22. Bill Poulte (October 1992) and to Officer Richard Waybright (January, 1993).
23. Discussions with "The Source." See chapter by that name.
24. Discussions with Gary Shaw, Al Fisher, and Larry Howard on several occasions.
25. Interview (May 30, 1993).

26. Interview (April 23, 1993).
27. Interview (May 30, 1992).
28. Jones, Jr., *Forgive My Grief III,* p. 80; 20 H 426.
29. Ibid., p. 14.
30. Interview (October 16, 1992).
31. Interview (May 30, 1993).
32. Interview with Mary Ferrell (May 30, 1993).
33. Interview (May 30, 1993).
34. Interview (May 30, 1993).
35. Interviews (March 12, April 23, May 30, 1993).
36. Interviews (April 23 and May 30, 1993).
37. Interview (May 30, 1993).
38. J. Gary Shaw with Larry Ray Harris, *Cover-ups,* (1992), p. 90, 110.
39. Report to the author (February 6, 1993). The writer must remain anonymous for the time being.
40. Memo from Steve Jaffe to Louis Ivon and Jim Garrison (December 27, 1967).
41. Interview with Larry Howard (October 12, 1992).
42. Interview (May 30, 1993).
43. Conversation at Riskies, Dallas (October 16, 1992).
44. Discussion with Mary Ferrell (April 23, 1993).
45. Interview (May, 1993).
46. Discussion with the author at Ferrell's house (March 13, 1993); interview (May 30, 1993).
47. Interview with a former Mrs. Norman Mailer.
48. Interview with Mary Ferrell (June 15, 1990).
49. From the book jacket of *The Scavengers and Critics of the Warren Report* (New York: Delacorte Press, 1967).
50. Interview (May 30, 1993).
51. Interview with Gordon Novel (May, 1993).
52. Conversation (April 23, 1993).
53. Interview with Mary Ferrell (May 30, 1993).
54. *Congressional Record* (May 13, 1970), S 7112.
55. Interview with Linda and Dan Wells in Dallas (March 10, 1993). See also the article by Dave Perry in *The Third Decade,* "Who Speaks for Roscoe White?" (November, 1991) p. 16; "I was Mandarin . . .", *Texas Monthly,* by Gary Cartwright (December, 1990).
56. David Real, *The Dallas Morning News* (August 21, 1990).
57. *The Continuing Inquiry* (May, August, September 1979) and (January 1980).
58. J. Gary Shaw with Larry R. Harris, *Cover-Up* (1976), p. 189.
59. Conversation with Sheriff Jim Bowles of Dallas (January 3, 1993).
60. Prof. Norman Cameron, *Encyclopedia Britannica,* Yale University.
61. Roger B. Feinman, *Between the Signal and the Noise* (unpublished manuscript, 1993), pp. 7–9.
62. Lifton's witnesses appeared on KRON in 1988, and as Lifton wrote

in his letter to Crouch dated April 5, 1991, he had to start thinking long and hard about forgery as an explanation in October, 1988.

63. Letter from David Lifton to Gary J. Rowell (November 5, 1991).
64. Letters from David Lifton to Mark Crouch (March 26, 1991 and April 5, 1991).
65. Affidavit of Mark Crouch (February 5, 1993).
66. Letter from David Lifton to Mark Crouch, April 5, 1991.
67. Lifton, *Best Evidence* (1988).
68. Letter from David Lifton to Jacqueline Liebergott (December 8, 1992).
69. Lifton, *Best Evidence,* Chapter 30 and Afterword, p. 707.
70. Letter from David Lifton to Mark Crouch (April 5, 1991).
71. CBS Memorandum by Bob Richter (June 7, 1967).
72. Roger B. Feinman, *Between the Signal and the Noise* (unpublished manuscript, 1993), p. 84.
73. Letter from David Lifton to the author (April 3, 1990).
74. Letter from Dean John Adams, Harvard University, to David Lifton (April 16, 1990).
75. Roger B. Feinman, *Between the Signal and the Noise* (unpublished manuscript, 1993), p. 95.
76. Ibid., p. 120.
77. Ibid., p. 122.
78. Ibid., p. 121.
79. Ibid., pp. 188–89.
80. Ibid., p. 195.
81. Ibid., p. 197.
82. Ibid., p. 198.
83. Today's Post (Pennsylvania) on March 30, 1989, p. 25.
84. Article by Warren Patton, Montgomery Newspapers, Jenkintown, PA (March 15, 1988), p. 9.
85. Discussion of July 12th, 1977, and over the period from June 1977 through March 15, 1987.
86. Cyril Wecht and Robert P. Smith, "The Medical Evidence in the Assassination of President John F.Kennedy," *Forensic Science,* 2 (1974) 117.
87. Presentation of Tom Wilson at A.S.K. (1991).
88. Discussion with Jones Harris and Sarah McClendon (June 17, 1992).
89. Richard Warren Lewis and Lawrence Schiller, *The Scavengers and Critics of the Warren Report,* (New York: Delacorte Press, 1967).
90. Ibid.
91. *Miami Herald* (February 6, 1985).
92. Martin Shackelford on Prodigy (February 17, 1993).
93. Martin Shackelford on Prodigy (March 6, 1993).
94. Mark Lane, *Plausible Denial* (New York: Thunder's Mouth Press, NYC, 1991), p. 75–87. See chapter entitled "The Confession," for illustration of one more distortion of reality by Lane.
95. *Mother Jones* (August, 1979), p. 27.
96. Bob Katz in *Mother Jones* (August, 1979), p. 22.

97. George Lardner in *The Washington Post* (December 2, 1976).
98. See the author's *High Treason* for the story, p. 313, 316–7, and note 3 for Chapter 17.
99. CBS, "The American Assassination, Part 1" (1975); University of Northern California presentation (1988); The Ron Reagan Show (syndicated) 11/20/91; "The Assassination of JFK" (1992).

Chapter 14

1. Interview (October 18, 1992).
2. Deposition of Robert Groden, *Groden v. Carroll & Graf and Harrison E. Livingstone* (March 16, 1993).
3. *Globe* (December 31, 1991).
4. Letter to the author (June 12, 1993).
5. Interview (October 10, 1991).
6. Discussion with Christ Sharrett (1993).
7. Letter to the author (June 12, 1993).
8. Discussions with Ed Lopez, Jane Downey, Robert Blakey, Michael Goldsmith and others (1991–1992).
9. Discussion with Steve Parks, Robert Groden, and many other witnesses.
10. Letter from David S. Lifton to Robert Groden (March 23, 1990).
11. Ibid.
12. Telephone interview with Peter Model (December 7, 1992).
13. Letter from Simmie Heninger to the author (May 24, 1991).
14. David Real, *The Dallas Morning News* (August 21, 1990).

Chapter 15

1. Craig I. Zirbel, *The Texas Connection,* 1992; The Texas Connection Company, 7500 Butherus Drive, Scottsdale, AR 85260; (602) 443–3818.
2. Zirbel, *The Texas Connection,* pp. 105, 242, 253.
3. There are several chapters in *The Texas Connection* dealing with these facts.
4. Interview (August 11, 1992) and previous meetings, particularly the one on April 30, 1992.
5. I. F. Stone, (October 1966).
6. *The Texas Connection,* p. 121.
7. J. Evetts Haley, *A Texan Looks At Lyndon: A Study in Illegitimate Power* (Canyon, TX: Palo Duro Press 1964); P.O. Box 390, Canyon, TX.
8. *The Texas Connection,* p. 181.
9. Letter from Cindy McNeill to the author (August 18, 1992).
10. *The Texas Connection,* p. 185.
11. Jerry Bruno and Jeff Greenfield, *The Advance Man,* (New York: William Morrow, 1971).
12. *The Texas Connection,* pp. 218–19.

13. Ibid.
14. *The Texas Connection,* p. 225.
15. *The Texas Connection,* p. 256.
16. *The Assassination of JFK: The Jim Garrison Tapes,* Vestron, (video) 1992, statement by an FBI agent. (Blue Ridge Filmtrust—a John Barbour film).
17. Nigel Turner's video, ''The Men Who Killed Kennedy'' was shown in England in 1988, on Arts & Entertainment in the U.S. in 1991 and 1992. P. 41 of the transcript.
18. Ibid., p. 43.
19. Ibid.
20. Jones, Jr., *Forgive My Grief I–IV.* For interesting write–ups about Jones, I suggest *Citizen's Arrest, The Dissent of Penn Jones, Jr., In the Assassination of JFK,* by H. C. Nash, (Latitudes Press book, 1977), but it may be very hard to get. ''The Persistence of Memory '', by Ernest Sharpe, Jr., in *Third Coast* (October 1983).
21. *The American Experience,* ''LBJ'', PBS (date unknown).
22. *The Texas Connection,* p. 172.

Chapter 16

1. Warren Hinckle, *If You Have a Lemon, Make Lemonade,* (New York: Bantam Books, 1976), pages 268–286; and Putnam edition (1974).
2. Interview with a judge in Dallas (1972). He declines to be identified.
3. *Dallas Morning News* (October 15, 1972).
4. *Dallas Morning News* (March 31, 1987).
5. Ibid.
6. Ibid.
7. Ibid.
8. Ibid.
9. Jane Wolfe, *The Murchisons, the Rise and Fall of a Texas Dynasty,* St. Martins Press (1989), p. 369.
10. Ibid., p. 669.
11. Ibid., p. 367.
12. *The Dallas Morning News,* March 31, 1987.
13. Ibid.
14. Wolfe, *The Murchisons, the Rise and Fall of a Texas Dynasty,* St. Martin's Press (1989).
15. Ibid.
16. Ibid.
17. Ibid.
18. Interview, (May 1993).
19. Interview with Al Maddox (June 14, 1993). Maddox also said that Marcello had an interest in Buckner; Interview with Bill Poulte (June 20, 1993); Interview with Larry Howard (October 18, 1992); Interviews with sources that cannot be named at this time.
20. Wolfe, *The Murchisons, the Rise and Fall of a Texas Dynasty,* p. 411.

21. Ibid., p. 441.
22. Ibid.
23. Jones, Jr., *Forgive My Grief III,* p. 84–86.
24. Interview with Val Imm (October 29, 1992).
25. Interview with Madeleine Brown at the Anatole Grill, Dallas (October 16, 1992).
26. Interview (December, 1992).
27. Madeleine Brown interview (October 30, 1992).
28. Madeleine Brown interviews (October 16 and October 30, 1992).
29. Jones, Jr., *Forgive My Grief III,* p. 85.
30. Ibid.
31. William Turner, *Ramparts,* report on the origins of *Farewell America.* No date.
32. Tyler Abell, ed., *Drew Pearson Diaries, 1949–1959,* (New York: Holt, Rinehart and Winston, 1974), pp. 228–2229; *Assassination of JFK By Coincidence or Conspiracy?;* Bernard Fensterwald, Committee to Investigate Assassinations, (New York: Zebra Books, 1977), p. 573.
33. Ibid; and the *Texas Observer* and compiled by Michael Ewing (August 23, 1968).
34. Letter from H. M. Hart to Captain W. P. Gannaway (July 8, 1964).
35. *The Washington Post* (November 30, 1974).
36. Ibid.
37. Ibid.
38. Ibid.
39. *The New York Times* (1960. Exact date unknown.)
40. Ibid.
41. AP news story by Saul Pett in *The Dallas Morning News* (April 3, 1960).
42. Warren Report: 333; Commission Exhibit: 2270 (FBI report); Fensterwald, p. 572.
43. Ibid.
44. Commission Exhibit: 2980; Fensterwald, p. 572.
45. Ibid.
46. *Assassination of JFK: Coincidence or Conspiracy?* Committee to Investigate Assassinations, Bernard Fensterwald compiled by Michael Ewing, (New York: Zebra Books, 1977, p. 495–498).
47. CIA memorandum, (February 14, 1969) "H. L. Hunt Interest in Garrison Investigation of Kennedy Assassination"; Fensterwald, p. 574.
48. *Farewell America,* "James Hepburn" (Vaduz, Liechtenstein: Frontiers Publishing 1968), p. 251–2; Fensterwald, p. 575.
49. Interview with John Curington (September, 1992).
50. Letter from Harold Weisberg to Paul Rothermel (January 14, 1969) and mention on page two of letter to Rothermel (February 22, 1969).
51. *Farewell America,* (Vaduz, Liechtenstein: Frontiers Publishing Co., 1968) p. 185 and pp. 245–252.

52. Ibid., p. 251.
53. H. L. Hunt, "Taking a Stand," *Dallas Times Herald* (January 10, 1968).
54. Anthony Summers, *Official and Confidential: The Secret Life of J. Edgar Hoover* (New York: Putnam, 1993).
55. *Pittsburgh Post Gazette* (March 20, 1993).
56. Ray Carroll in *The Third Decade* (July 1992), p. 13.
57. Carroll, supra, p. 14.
58. Harry Hurt III, *Texas Rich: The Hunt Dynasty From the Early Oil Days Through the Silver Crash* (New York: W. W. Norton & Co., 1981), p. 264.
59. Ibid.
60. Ibid., p. 369.
61. Ibid.
62. Ibid., p. 265.
63. Zirbel, *The Texas Connection*, p. 250.
64. Ibid.
65. Ibid., p. 251; Warren Report, Bantam Ed., p. 343.
66. Ibid., pp. 234, 251; Henry Hurt, *Reasonable Doubt* (New York: Holt, Rinehart, Winston, 1986) p. 236.
67. Ibid., p. 234, 251; Hurt, *Texas Rich: The Hunt Dynasty From the Early Oil Days Through the Silver Crash*, p. 380.
68. Hurt, *Texas Rich*, p. 234.
69. Hurt, *Texas Rich*, p. 239.
70. Discussion (March 1, 1993).
71. Letter from Ray Carroll to the author (March 9, 1993).
72. Conversation with Madeleine Brown (May 2, 1993).
73. Arnold Forster and Benjamin Epstein, *Danger On The Right*, p. 134.
74. Kirkpatrick Sales, *Power Shift*, 1975, p. 101.
75. Kirkpatrick Sales, *Power Shift*, 1975, p. 105.
76. Kirkpatrick Sales, *Power Shift*, 1975, p. 105.
77. Discussion (February 10, 1993).
78. Discussion with Madeleine Brown (January 12, 1993) and with Larry Howard (January 13, 1993). The belief that Peoples had such documents is widespread in Texas.
79. Interview (September 9, 1992).
80. Interview (September 11, 1992).
81. *The National Enquirer* (June 14, 1977), p. 4.
82. *High Treason*, pp. 202–03.
83. *National Enquirer* (June 14, 1977).
84. Interview with Madeleine Brown (October 16, 1992).
85. Deed Record, Vol. 732, p. 0667, January 10, 1966, 04299: "Being lots three (3), four (4), five (5), and six (6) of block 14/21 of the City of Dallas, and lots one (1), and two (2) in block 16/39 of the City of Dallas."
86. Interview with Madeleine Brown (October 16, 1992).
87. Various discussions with Dr. Charles Crenshaw.

88. Meeting (December 10, 1993).
89. Shaw and Harris, *Cover-Up!*, 1976, p. 185.
90. Ibid.
91. I discovered in a talk with Dr. McClelland that Williams had over-
    heard the call from Johnson. This was confirmed by Dr. Altman of
    The New York Times, in his story in the Science Section (May 27,
    1992).
92. Cited in the next note.
93. Penn Jones, Jr., *Forgive My Grief III,* p. 101.
94. Interview (January 12, 1993).
95. Sheldon Inkol writing in an endnote in *The Third Decade* (September,
    1992) note 13: "J. Gary Shaw with Larry Harris, *Cover-up!*, pp.
    51–54, 90. I wrote to Oliver Stone to let him know of Jerry Ruffner's
    discovery that the Super–8 camera supposedly used by Oliver to film
    the assassination was not even available until 1969. I was amused
    to see Oliver appearing on TV with Geraldo Rivera on March 27,
    1992. She now says that she was using "an experimental camera"
    in Dealey Plaza. This is one 'witness' whom I wish really would
    disappear."
96. Harrison E. Livingstone, *High Treason;* Dick Russell, *The Man Who
    Knew Too Much,* p. 642.
97. Interview of Robert Gemberling with Mark Oakes (October 20,
    1992).
98. Interview with Stan Szerszen (November 1, 1992).
99. Letter from V. J. Brian of the Criminal Intelligence Section to Cap-
    tain W. P. Gannaway, Special Service Bureau, (April 20, 1964).
100. Letter from Lt. Jack Revill to Captain Gannaway of the Special
    Service Bureau (November 22, 1963).
101. Videotaped interview with Mark Oakes (October 20, 1992).
102. Letter from Lt. Jack Revill to Captain W. P. Gannaway, Special
    Service Bureau, Dallas Police Department (May 20, 1964).
103. Interview with Vickie Mayne (October 29, 1991).
104. Ibid.
105. Interview with Vicky Mayne (January 20, 1992).
106. Craig Zirbel, *The Texas Connection* (1991), p. 157.
107. Discussion with Larry Howard (February, 1993).
108. Zirbel, *The Texas Connection,* p. 159.
109. Ibid.
110. Zirbel, *The Texas Connection,* p. 56.
111. Pam Estes, *Billie Sol* (Abilene, Texas: Nobel Craft Books, 1983),
    p. 81.
112. Evetts Haley, *A Texan Looks At Lyndon* (Canyon, TX: Palo Duro
    Press, 1964), p. 124.
113. Associated Press and *The New York Times* stories of March 24, 1984.
114. *The Dallas Morning News* (March 24, 1984).
115. Zirbel, *The Texas Connection,* self–published, 1991, p. 156.
116. Ibid.

117. See the petitions of Harry Moore (November 14, 1962) and Williamson Petroleum Company (October 1962), case 299. U.S. District Court, the Western District of Texas, Pecos Division, El Paso.
118. J. Evetts Haley, *A Texan Looks At Lyndon,* pp. 148–9.
119. Ibid., p. 156.
120. J. Evetts Haley, *A Texan Looks At Lyndon,* pp. 151.
121. Ibid., p. 151.
122. Ibid., p. 152.
123. Ibid., p. 154.
124. Ibid., p. 155.
125. Ibid., p. 156.

Chapter 17

1. Interview (December 1, 1991).
2. Discussion (October, 1991).
3. Walter Cronkite on CBS in 1968 on Garrison's visit to New York; and memo of the Hunt Oil Company, that "I have information that Garrison is referring to either you or Bunker as the wealthy oil men in his probe." "You" is H. L. Hunt, and Bunker is his son. Another memo dated January 26, 1968, says "The source of this information (from within Garrison's office) reports that Garrison is convinced that the assassination was carried out by General Edwin Walker with the financial support and backing of Herman and George Brown of Houston and H. L. Hunt of Dallas."
4. Interview (April 6, 1991).
5. Both in interviews when he was being taken from court and in notes he wrote and smuggled out of jail.
6. Discussion (February 20, 1991).
7. Livingstone, *High Treason* (1989), 202–3.
8. Interview in Dallas (1991).
9. Interview (December 1991).
10. Interview (December 1991).
11. Interview (December 1991).
12. Letter from Patricia Dumais to the author (December 16, 1991).
13. Interview (December 1991).
14. Letter from Jack Reville to Captain W. P. Gannaway (February 5, 1964); Commission Exhibit 710.
15. Edward Jay Epstein, *Legend: The Secret World of Lee Harvey Oswald* (New York: McGraw–Hill, 1978).
16. Larry Howard (October 18, 1992).
17. Penn Jones, Jr., *Forgive my Grief 1,* p. 156; 5 H 420.
18. Penn Jones, Jr., *Forgive My Grief 1,* p. 156; Gary Shaw and Larry J. Harris, *Cover-Up,* p. 167; Warren Report 298.
19. Interview (October 1991).
20. Public Broadcasting System, "Front Line" (February 1993).
21. See photograph published in *High Treason* by the author.

22. Commission Exhibit 7, Sibert & O'Niell's report on Greer, Kellerman and Behn.
23. *High Treason,* pp. 254–6; Warren Report 5 H.
24. Earl Lively memo to H. L. Hunt and Paul Rothermel: "Subject: District Attorney Garrison's New York Remarks."
25. Letter from Harold Weisberg (February 17, 1969).
26. Hunt Oil memo about a talk with William Boxley (Wood) (February 12, 1969).
27. Memo from Paul Rothermel to the Hunts (December 16, 1968).
28. Hunt Oil memo (October 16, 1967).
29. Hunt Oil memo (January 26, 1968).
30. Hunt Oil memo (September 17, 1968).
31. Hunt Oil memo (February 12, 1969).
32. Hunt Oil memo (February 12, 1969).
33. Hunt Oil memo (February 12, 1969).
34. Numerous discussions with Penn jones and the author, Richard Waybright, Marco Miranda, etc.
35. Hunt Oil memo (August 23, 1967).
36. Hunt Oil memo (May 18, 1964).
37. Memo from Paul Rothermel to the Hunt files (January 26, 1968).
38. Hunt Oil memo (November 30, 1967).
39. Ibid.
40. Hunt Oil memo (January 29, 1969).
41. Ibid.
42. Ibid.
43. Report by William Boxley (Wood) (June 5, 1967).
44. See O'Toole, *The Assassination Tapes,* Penthouse Press, p. 161.
45. See O'Toole, *The Assassination Tapes,* Penthouse Press, p. 161.
46. Meeting (March 1993).
47. Interview with Marco Miranda and the author (June 14, 1993).
48. It is widely known in Dallas that Batchelor took Ruby in, and attorney James Niell told me this in 1976. Niell represented Roy Vaughan in his suit against Mark Lane.
49. J. Gary Shaw and Larry R. Harris, *Cover-Up,* p. 21.
50. Interview (December 1991).
51. Interview (December, 1991).

Chapter 18

1. *Dallas Morning News* (October 11, 1963).
2. Author's interview with Al Maddox (June 14, 1993) with Officer Marco Miranda, BCPD.
3. "A Colorful Career for the General" an unpublished paper by Bob Goodman (1993).
4. Interview of Marco Miranda (January 13, 1993).
5. Prodigy letter from Robert Wagstaff to Jonathan Cohen (November 21, 1992).

6. "Declassified, The Plot to Kill The President," VidAmerica video (1988).
7. Letter from J. M. Smith to Chief J. E. Curry (July 16, 1964).
8. Interview (June 14, 1993).
9. 11 HSCA 516–521.
10. Jones, Jr., *Forgive My Grief IV,* p. 51.
11. Ibid., p. 50.
12. 11 HSCA 520.
13. Todd Vaughan (April 10, 1993).
14. *Who's Who in the South & Southwest.*
15. Robert Goodman, "The Dal-Tex Building" (January 1993). Unpublished manuscript.

Conclusion

1. See the chapter on *The Journal of the American Medical Association* in this book.
2. Sibert & O'Neill FBI report (November 26, 1963).
3. Livingstone, *High Treason 2,* p. 213.
4. Sibert & O'Neill FBI report (November 26, 1963).
5. Baden, Dr. Michael M. *Unnatural Death* (New York: Random House, 1989), p. 17.
6. Livingstone, *High Treason* (Baltimore: The Conservatory Press, 1989), p. 48; 2 H 141, 124.
7. O'Donnell, Kenneth P. and David F. Powers, with Joe McCarthy. *Johnny, We Hardly Knew Ye: Memories of John Fitzgerald Kennedy* (Boston: Little, Brown & Co., 1972), p. 37.

APPENDIX A

Addendum to Chapter 10

David Mantik

Dr. David W. Mantik, of the Eisenhower Medical Center in California, a radiologist, wrote the following in his unpublished manuscript *The JFK Assassination: Cause For Doubt*:

"The number of skull radiographs in the official record is three; of these, only two are available to the public. Jerroll F. Custer, the radiology technologist at the autopsy, has reported taking at least five skull radiographs,[39] including one oblique/tangential view of the large posterior defect. Ebersole[40] also informed this author that a total of five or six views of the skull were obtained. In addition, one of the HSCA radiologists, Dr. David O. Davis, referred to other skull views that he had seen;[41] this is a particularly odd comment, especially since nothing else has ever been said about these other views. The critics naturally wonder if views showing the large posterior defect were culled out some time after the autopsy.

"The radiologists who consulted for the HSCA concluded that there was no suggestion of a shot from the front. It is strange, however, that the evidence for this conclusion was based almost exclusively on the lateral skull radiograph. The condition of the right posterior skull, based on the AP radiograph was largely ignored. There appear to be surprising findings on the AP view that warrant further investigation.[42] Were the radiologists deliberately avoiding the condition of the right occiput on the AP view? Quantitative scans of the original AP radiograph could still be done to ascertain just how much bone remains in the right occiput.[43] So far, however, access to this material has been remarkably limited and the proper studies have never been done.

"Some radiologists described an entry wound near the cowlick area, 10 cm above the EOP. However, radiologist William B. Seaman[44] observed, regarding the proposed cowlick entry on the lateral skull radiograph, that this upper point '. . . suggests entry but is not conclusive.' He also said

612

that he could *not* denote beveling of the skull at that point.[45] Despite this equivocation, Dr. Michael Baden,[46] Chairman of the HSCA Forensic Pathology Panel, altered the meaning of plain English to conclude that '... all of the radiologist consultants with whom the panel spoke with [sic] and met with [sic], all concluded that without question there is an entrance bullet hole on the upper portion of the skull. ...' Dr. Seaman was not invited to comment on this statement.

"The critics wonder where these experts would have placed this entry wound on the AP view. Based on HSCA data,[47] the entry was 1 cm above the 6.5 mm radiopaque object. At this site on the AP radiograph there is no apparent entry hole. There is instead a small transverse defect clearly narrower than the 6.5 mm object seen here. The bone fragment in this vicinity is otherwise intact. A corollary question is whether this bone fragment lies on the posterior or anterior surface of the skull. If this bone fragment lies on the anterior skull surface, then the posterior skull surface is nowhere evident, an intolerable situation for the loyalist. If the fragment is on the posterior surface, there is no evident ingress. The loyalists must therefore choose between (a) absent right occiput or (b) no visible entry site on the AP radiograph.

"Radiologists described fracture lines as radiating outward from the proposed cowlick entry site. On the AP view, however, these lines do not actually extend to the proposed entry site; they stop short of it. Dr. David O. Davis[48] was careful to choose his words: '... the linear fractures seem to more or less [sic] emanate from the embedded metallic fragment.' Unless they unequivocally extend to this 6.5 mm object they cannot represent fracture lines caused by a posterior skull bullet. On the contrary, based on the radiographs and on Boswell's diagram, several of these obvious fracture lines may lie in the inferior orbital rim and not on the posterior skull at all. The inferior orbital rim fractures were confirmed by radiologist Seaman.[49] 'Fractures were evident through the upper part of the right eye, including the top and bottom of the right orbit.' If these fractures lie on the anterior skull surface they cannot, of course, represent fracture lines emanating from the proposed cowlick entry site, and therefore, they cannot be used as evidence for a cowlick entry. The critics urge readers, especially physicians, to examine the radiographs[50] for themselves on this crucial point.

"The apparently linear, nearly horizontal 'trail' of radiopaque densities seen near the vertex on the lateral skull radiograph lies well above the proposed cowlick entry site. A spinning bullet would be expected to eject small pieces of metal at a wide range of angles and not solely in the small solid angle that is seen. In addition, the trail would be expected to be cone shaped, narrower at the beginning and wider toward the end; instead, it shows no such effect at all. Moreover, the 'trail' is obviously too high to fit with the proposed entry site. And, on the AP view the 'trail' simply vanishes, there is no 'trail' at all. The apparent trail on the lateral view is merely an optical illusion; the particles are, in fact, widely scattered in space. The AP and lateral views are so different, in fact, that some observers have wondered whether they are even spatially compatible. Dr. David

O. Davis[51] stated his own impression as follows: 'It is not possible to totally explain the metallic fragment pattern that is present from some of the metallic fragments located superiorly in the region of the parietal bone, or at least projecting on the parietal bone are [sic] actually in the scalp. The frontal view does not give much help in this regard and it is impossible to work this out completely.' Surely, if one of the HSCA's foremost experts had difficulty with the locations of these radiopaque objects, they deserve more attention.

"The imaginary trail on the lateral view lies in the superior right hemisphere, just were Humes said that ⅔ of the right cerebrum was missing. As these 'bullet fragments' appear to be suspended in midair, the critics naturally wonder what tissue is supporting them in space.

"The trail of metal debris described in the autopsy protocol is more than 10 cm inferior to that seen in the extant radiographs. This has already been discussed. It is a serious conflict all by itself.

"Humes made one more comment that is particularly striking. While looking at the radiographs with the HSCA,[52] he implied that the fragments he had previously seen (at the autopsy, presumably) were *smaller*, i.e. 'grains of sand type fragments.' To the Warren Commission,[53] also, he described them as mostly less than 1 mm in size. The extant radiographs, on the other hand, show many objects at least two or three times larger than this. That Humes commented at all on this apparent discrepancy is most peculiar. It suggests a significant difference in fragment sizes between the autopsy radiographs and the extant radiographs. Humes was never questioned further on his odd comment, nor were the other pathologists or Ebersole questioned on this point."

Chapter 10

39. Livingstone, H. E. *High Treason 2*, New York, Carroll & Graf, 1992, p. 209; Hatfield S., "RT disputes X-ray photos in JFK case," *Advance: For Radiologic Science Professionals,* 1992; 5:7.
40. Mantik, D. W., telephone conversations with John H. Ebersole, November 2 and December 2, 1992.
41. 7 HSCA 200–203.
42. Unpublished research of David Mantik.
43. Ibid.
44. 7 HSCA 212–214.
45. Ibid.
46. 7 HSCA 242.
47. 7 HSCA 205.
48. 7 HSCA 200–203.
49. 7 HSCA 212–214.
50. *Best Evidence,* Lifton, David, Carroll & Graf, 1992, Chapter 31.
51. 7 HSCA 200–203.
52. 7 HSCA 251.
53. 2 H 353.

Memorandum

SECRET

DATE   January 28, 1988

TO   Captain W. R. Rollins
    Intelligence Division

SUBJECT   Request for Assistance from Midland County
    District Attorney's Office

On December 30, 1987, Inv. J. D. Luckie, Midland County District
Attorney's Office contacted the Intelligence Division for information
on a former officer, Roscoe Anthony White. Inv. Luckie stated their
office had been contacted by White's son, Ricky Don White, who stated
he had found a diary, pictures and $200,000 in cash which his dad
had left to him and his brother. Mr. White told Inv. Luckie that
there was a possibility that his dad had been involved in the Kennedy
assasination. Mr. White alledged that his father had known Lee Harvey
Oswald and had been involved with an unknown woman who worked at
the School Book Depository. Inv. Luckie stated they were just getting
bits and pieces from the son, and that he was being very cautious
with the information. Inv. Luckie asked for assistance in varifying
the information.

Roscoe Anthony White was hired by the Dallas Police Department on
October 7, 1963. He attended recruit class #79 from December 4,
1963 to February 28, 1964. Mr. White resigned on October 7, 1965
to accept employment with Page Drugs.

On Monday, January 4, 1988, Inv. Luckie came to Dallas. Inv. Luckie,
Special Agent Kenneth Bersano of the FBI, and I, attempted to locate
a Savings and Loan described by Ricky White, which allegedly held
a safety deposit box containing $200,000.00. We were unable to
discover the location. I gave Inv. Luckie and S. A. Bersano all
the information we had on Roscoe White.

January 26, 1988, I was contacted by Inv. Luckie, who stated the
FBI had taken over the investigation. Inv. Luckie said that the
FBI had met with Ricky White, had seen the pictures and diary, and
there was nothing to what had been alleged by Mr. White. Inv. Luckie
stated he has not been in contact with Mr. White since the FBI talked
to him. Inv. Luckie stated he was able to determine that Roscoe
White and Lee Harvey Oswald were in the Marines together and both
served a tour in a Light Helicopters Unit in El Toro, California
at the same time, but does not know if they actually knew each other.
He has been unable to confirm that Roscoe White was involved with
any woman at the School Book Depository. Inv. Luckie stated that
he has been told to withdraw from the investigation and let the FBI
handle it.

SECRET

SECRET

Since we were only assisting Midland County District Attorney's Office
with their investigation, and they are now withdrawing from the
investigation; I recommend this investigation be closed pending
further requests for assistance.

Jack L. Beavers

Jack L. Beavers
Corporal/Investigator
Intelligence Division
Public Integrity Section

pdr

J.G. Tilley - CONCUR.

SECRET

Wednesday, March 17, 1993

Greetings Mr. Livingstone:

Enclosed you will find the statement concerning the dog tags. I trust it will be used to help clear my brother, Roscoe White, of any wrong doing. You gave your word that you would use the text only as I have and not alter it in any way that would cause it to have a different meaning. I had trusted others in the past and have been stung but as long as there is breath in me I must keep trying to clear his name. Few men could measure up to Rock he was loved by too many too deeply to just let this matter lie.

I have also enclosed other items for your viewing ... some of which you may already have or seen. I have taken the liberty of highlighting some of the material and providing an explanation, comment or disagreement. I don't have as much as many of the researchers but I am willing to share what I have as long as it is used to help resolve the wrong doings of Ricky White, the Matsu Corporation and the JFK Center.

It is my prayer that you and others will listen to us and inform the world of what a fraud and scam this story really is. My intentions are not to purposely hurt anyone; but to provide the facts and truths. With no evidence shown as promised and numerous holes in the story, I can only be reminded of the scriptures found in I Timothy 6:7–10 "... for the love of money is the root to all evil ..."

If you wish to discuss the contents or other matters you are welcome to contact me.

Best wishes and good luck,

Linda M. Wells
(proudly the sister of Roscoe A. White)

This statement is to the best of my memory of events—how they happened and when—in regards to the military dog tags that belonged to Roscoe "Rock" Anthony White, my brother.

Rock gave his military dog tags to our mother when he returned home from his military tour of duty in February of 1963. There were two metal tags on a long metal "365 bead" chain. (We don't know what happened to the short "52 bead" chain that is issued with the tags.) Mother kept them in an old jar with some other keepsakes of his.

Dog Tag # One

The tags remained in Mother's possession until January of 1989 when Ricky White (Rock's youngest son) and Andy Burke came to visit us in Dora, Missouri. Ricky had expressed his need to find out about his dad since Rock had died when he was so young. After visiting with Ricky and going through old keepsakes of Rock's, Mother told Ricky she would let him have one of the dog tags for a keepsake if he promised to take good care of it. He promised to keep it close to him at all times and put it on his key chain where he said it would remain. The tag was given to Ricky in the presence of myself, my husband Danny, and Andy Burke. The subject was discussed later during the visit with Mother's sister Mary Hood and my daughters Kelly and Sandy. (Ricky and Andy also borrowed several items from Mother and told us we would get them back in a couple of months. These items included several photographs, newspaper clippings, report cards, a speech he gave at his graduation, an autopsy report, and miscellaneous items. We have never received nor seen them since. We have requested their return several times and were told by Gary Bailey of the Matsu Corporation that although Ricky had presented them to the Corporation as his items, the items were of no value to them and he saw no reason that they could not be returned; however, nothing has been returned.)

Dog Tag # Two

The second tag (still on the chain in the jar) was given to me (Linda) during that same time span in January 1989, as Mother was going through a lot of old things and dividing them up. The tag remained with me until approximately June of 1990. I'm not exactly sure to the date but it was just prior to the discovery of the canister by Ricky and prior to the press conference of August 6, 1990, at the JFK Center in Dallas. At that time Ricky White, Gary Shaw (one of the partners of the JFK Center in Dallas), and Joe West (private investigator hired by the JFK Center) came to my house at 618 King Lane in Garland, Texas. They had lots of questions but were specifically interested in the dog tag and any medals of Roscoe's I might have. I handed the dog tag (still on the chain) to Ricky who then turned and handed it to Gary Shaw. At that point I left the room to put up the jar and didn't see who took possession of the tag, but my husband Danny said that Gary gave it back to Ricky and that Ricky then handed it to Joe West who asked for it, stating, "I'll take care of it." We were told that Joe West had a safe in which he was keeping materials/evidence. Ricky said that he had entrusted the JFK Center with everything he had and that Joe West was guarding it. They said they needed the tag to check on something they were working on. They assured me that the tag along with all the other things we had loaned them would be returned as soon as it was safe after the press conference. I did not give nor tell them I had Rock's medal. They would never actually show us evidence and told us bits and pieces saying the less we knew the safer we were. I was told several times I should give Joe West everything that I had of Rock's so the FBI would not take it when they came to my house as they surely would after the conference but the FBI never came. Joe West said he would lay down his life if necessary for the safekeeping of items he'd been entrusted with. They continuously told us of the grave danger that Ricky and others were in and that our children might be the subjects of kidnapping and to watch them carefully. Our family lived in constant worry of what might happen. You can only imagine what it did to our children who were now afraid to walk a few blocks to school or to even let their little brother play outside in the front yard. I have not received nor seen the tag since (although I personally believe it to be the tag shown in the picture contents of the canister in the *Texas Monthly* magazine). All articles say that they found "tags" in the canister so accordingly Ricky along with the Matsu Corporation and the JFK Center should be able to produce four tags—two from the canister and two that belonged to my mother. It's simple enough but when asked about it all I get is: "Well, I didn't really know who has the tags"; "Ah, let's see the last time I saw them one was in a bank bag and ah, well, Joe West must have the others, ah''; or "Well, I don't know where they are but I assure you I will check on this matter and get back with you." I have never had any of them contact me and the last time I spoke with Ricky was November 1991 after confronting him on this and other issues such as the diary.

In closing all I have to say is "well, Ricky White—Gary Bailey of the Matsu Corporation—and Gary Shaw and Larry Howard of the JFK Center . . . as the old saying goes it's time to —— or get off the pot! . . . give the world your undeniable proof that Roscoe Anthony White did in fact kill John F. Kennedy or anybody for that matter and I'll back off— otherwise YOU OWE MY MOTHER AND ROCK'S FAMILY AN APOLOGY TO BE SENT OUT OVER THE SAME AIR WAVES YOU DESTROYED ROCK'S UNBLEMISHED NAME/MEMORY ON. None of you will ever be able to be as much of a man as he was or to fill the shoes he wore. I wish I could be there the day each of you meet your Maker and see Rock face-to-face and answer to what you have done for the sake of money. At least our other brother, Walton will be standing by Rock's side and get to live that moment . . . just think Geneva as well as Joe West has already faced it. You've danced the dance, now it's time to pay the fiddler. I'm not perfect in my life's walk but I never destroyed someone else for my own gain. And, Tony (Jr.), what can I say to you other than if you don't stand against them you are just as guilty and stand beside them.''

There, I've spoke my peace and you have my permission to print what I've said as long as you print it word for word as I said it and in the context I said it not changing the meaning behind it.

Linda M. Wells

CITY OF DALLAS
TEXAS
POLICE DEPARTMENT

July 16, 1964

Mr. J. E. Curry
Chief of Police

SUBJECT: Statement of J. M. Smith

Sir:

On the morning of November 22, 1963, instructions were to
make detail at 8:45 a.m., which I did, and then I received
my assignment to work traffic at Elm and Houston and also
assist in the control of the crowd in that vicinity. I
was to report to my assignment no later than 10:00 a.m.

My instructions were from Captain P. W. Lawrence to hold
all the traffic up when the motorcade was approaching. I
was to assist in handling of the crowd - more specifically
to be on the lookout for anyone throwing things from the
crowd.

At approximately 11:50 a.m. there was a white male who had
an epileptic seizure on the esplanade which was between Elm
and Main Street on Houston. I went from my assignment down
to see if my assistance was needed. After the man was put
into the ambulance and sent to the hospital, I reported
back to my assignment.

I was standing in the middle of Elm Street from the southeast
curb of Elm and Houston Streets at the time of the shooting.
I heard the shots and thought they were coming from <u>bushes
of the overpass</u>.

Respectfully submitted,

J. M. Smith

J. M. Smith
Traffic Division

JMS:nw

Exhibit No. 48
*Eye witness statement of Officer J. M. Smith. This statement is similar to those of other
officers who thought the shots were coming from the direction of the underpass (For
other eye witness accounts see pages 30 and 61-62).*

THE LAW CENTER
UNIVERSITY OF SOUTHERN CALIFORNIA
UNIVERSITY PARK
LOS ANGELES 90089-0071

W. DAVID SLAWSON
TORREY H. WEBB PROFESSOR OF LAW

(213) 740-2554
FAX (213) 740-5502

December 4, 1992

Ms. Amanda Rowell
1501 Park Avenue
Bay City, MI 48708

Dear Ms. Rowell:

Yes, I listened to the tape of Lee Harvey Oswald's telephone conversations with the Soviet Embassy in Mexico City. I did not feel that the voice sounded any different from what I expected his would sound like.

In evaluating anyone's claims that the voice on the tape is sufficiently different from Oswald's to raise a reasonable doubt that it was he talking, you should keep several things in mind. One, since Oswald was killed only two days after the assassination, of course he was not around, still talking. No one, therefore, can honestly claim to have compared his voice on this tape or anyplace else with what he actually sounded like. Two, wiretaps, in the early 1960's at least, commonly did not give good sound reproductions. They were scratchy and full of static. Three, Oswald, like anyone else, presumably sounded slightly different under different circumstances, and he undoubtedly was under severe stress while he was in Mexico City. Fourth, under the circumstances he might well have been intentionally disguising his voice. We had evidence that he had been repeatedly warned by the Soviet official with whom he talked that their telephone wires were probably tapped, so that he should assume that the CIA was listening.

I am convinced that the Commission was right. Oswald alone shot and killed the President.

I have enclosed a copy of our law school magazine, which just came out. It has an article by me on this subject.

Sincerely,

W. David Slawson

WDS/mp

Enclosure

To the Editor.—Rather than quell doubts about President Kennedy's autopsy findings, I fear that Drs Humes' and Boswell's[1,2] remarks in *JAMA* will only serve to heighten the level of disbelief in their observations. Neither Humes nor Boswell addressed their critics on contradictory evidence that subsequent government investigations have consistently revealed, namely, that neither the available photographs nor the roentgenograms support Humes' and Boswell's claims regarding the entrance location of the fatal skull wound. At least three qualified groups have reviewed the roentgenographic and photographic evidence and are unanimous in claiming that Humes' and Boswell's claims in the Warren Commission Report erred in placing the fatal skull entrance wound at the base of the skull just above the hairline ("2.5 cm to the right and slightly above the external occipital protuberance" according to Humes both in the *JAMA* interview, and before that, in his Warren Commission testimony). The Clark Panel in 1968,[3] John Lattimer, MD, in 1972,[4] and the House Select Committee on Assassinations in 1978[5] all determined that the fatal entrance wound was 10 cm higher in the cowlick area at the top of the head on the basis of the available roentgenograms and the autopsy photographs.

Humes and Boswell also never reported seeing a round "large metallic fragment which on the antero-posterior film lies 25 mm to the right of the midline"[3(p11)] measuring 6.5 mm in diameter in the rear of the skull in the autopsy roentgenograms that Humes and Boswell claim to have reviewed during the autopsy.[1,2] While Humes took pains to describe all the visible bullet fragments in his Warren Commission testimony, this very large fragment was never described and, presumably, was never seen. This large fragment in the rear of the skull, however, was plainly seen and described by all subsequent groups reviewing the roentgenograms. Thus, the "incontrovertible" photographic and roentgenographic evidence appears to directly contradict sworn statements by Humes and Boswell before the Warren Commission that were repeated in their *JAMA* interview.

Humes' contradictory statements, regrettably, have occurred before. When questioned by Dr Charles Petty before the House Select Committee on Assassinations, he was asked where the skull entrance wound was. He replied, "It's below the external protuberance."

"It's below it?" Dr Petty asked incredulously.

"Right," answered Dr Humes.

"Not above it?" pressed Dr Petty.

"No. It's to the right and inferior to external occipital protuberance. And when the scalp was reflected from there, there was virtually an identical wound in the occipital bone," was Dr Humes' unequivocal reply.[6]

Inexplicably, Humes later changed his mind, stating before the House Committee, "Yes, I think that I do have a different opinion," and at that point Humes endorsed the photographic and roentgenographic placement of the wounds at least 10 cm higher at the cowlick area in the parietal bone![7] The question of the unmentioned bullet fragment seen by subsequent reviewers in the roentgenograms was not brought to Dr

Humes' attention before the House Select Committee, but the question certainly should be answered.

Neither Boswell nor Dr Pierre Finck, the other pathologist present at the autopsy, would change his mind about the location of the fatal entrance wound. They continued to claim that the entrance wound was low, 10 cm below where the House Select Committee panel and Humes then claimed it was.[8] From the interview, Humes seems to be changing his mind again to agree with Boswell and Finck that the entrance wound is low and, presumably, that the roentgenograms and photographs are wrong.

These discrepancies in evidence are far from inconsequential clinically, forensically, or evidentially. A 10-cm "error" just does not occur in a careful forensic autopsy and a 6.5-mm bullet fragment is simply not "missed" on a roentgenogram, particularly when a radiologist, John Ebersole, was present at the autopsy to review the films. If Humes and Boswell's eyewitness observations are right, that the fatal entrance wound was low in the skull and that no rear bullet fragments were visible radiographically, then the repeated claims of evidence tampering by Jerrol Custer and Floyd Riebe,[9,10] roentgenogram and photographic technicians who were present at the autopsy, are greatly strengthened. Are Humes and Boswell "open" to address these issues? Why has not Finck also come forward to defend the Warren Commission findings, and why was he unavailable for the *JAMA* interview, or even for a brief message of endorsement?

With the distrust many Warren Commission critics have of JFK's military autopsy, *JAMA* might have aided its cause by choosing a public representative other than the well-respected George Lundberg, MD, if only because of his well-known military ties. Humes or Boswell might have been more helpful if either had joined Dr Lundberg for the news conference announcing *JAMA*'s publication of the "plain truth" about JFK's autopsy.

Gary L. Aguilar, MD
University of California
San Francisco

1. Breo DL. JFK's death—the plain truth from the MDs who did the autopsy. *JAMA.* 1992;267:2794-2803.
2. Breo DL. JFK's death, part II—Dallas MDs recall their memories. *JAMA.* 1992; 267:2804-2807.
3. Clark R. *Clark Panel Report: 1968 Panel Review of Photographs, X-ray Films, Documents and Other Evidence Pertaining to the Fatal Wounding of President John F. Kennedy on November 22, 1963, in Dallas, Tex.* Washington, DC: US Government Printing Office; 1969.
4. Lattimer JK. Observations based on a review of the autopsy photographs, x-rays, and related materials of the late President John F. Kennedy. *Resident Staff Physician.* May 1972;18:33-64.
5. House Select Committee on Assassinations. Washington, DC: US Government Printing Office; 1978;7:114-115, 254-255.
6. House Select Committee on Assassinations. Washington, DC: US Government Printing Office; 1978;7:246.
7. House Select Committee on Assassinations. Washington, DC: US Government Printing Office; 1978;1:323-332.
8. Hurt H. *Reasonable Doubt.* New York, NY: Henry Holt and Company; 1985:53.
9. Livingstone HE. *High Treason II.* New York, NY: Carroll & Graf Publishers Inc; 1992:209-225, 308.
10. King J. JFK autopsy photo called phony: navy technicians charge tampering. *San Francisco Examiner.* April 29, 1992:A8.

To the Editor.—Your recent JFK autopsy report[1,2] quotes Dr Humes as saying, "In 1963, we proved at the autopsy table that President Kennedy was struck from above and behind by the fatal shot. . . ."

That is not what Humes told the House Select Committee on Assassinations in 1979.[3] When asked if the essential findings were two gunshot wounds from above and behind, he said, "I think behind is probably the most one can say from the anatomic findings."

Has Humes made new anatomic discoveries on JFK since 1979 that now permit him to assert that the shots were clearly from above? If so, will he share those findings with *JAMA*? If he was unsure of the superior location of the gunman, how could he be sure, from the anatomic data, that Oswald was on the sixth floor? Or did he conclude this from data outside the autopsy? If so, is he qualified to pass judgment on nonanatomic data?

I trust *JAMA* will permit Humes to clarify this important issue. He may wish to do so simply for the sake of his own credibility.

Patricia L. James, MD
Idyllwild, Calif

1. Breo DL. JFK's death—the plain truth from the MDs who did the autopsy. *JAMA.* 1992;267:2794-2803.
2. Breo DL. JFK's death, part II—Dallas MDs recall their memories. *JAMA.* 1992; 267:2804-2807.
3. House Select Committee on Assassinations. Washington, DC: US Government Printing Office; 1979;7:243-255.

To the Editor.—Drs Humes and Boswell,[1] in their interview with *JAMA* editor Dr George Lundberg, state that it was "perfectly obvious" that President Kennedy was shot from behind. They decry the "supreme ignorance" of the prevailing doubts about the assassination, blaming money-hungry conspiracy "buffs" for indulging in "ridiculous theories."

The essence of their statement is that the beveled appearance of the entrance and exit wounds in the President's skull provide an "irrefutable diagnostic fact" that the bullet came from the rear and above. It is curious that so much controversy would remain in the face of such an easily interpretable fact. If the reality is as they state, it would be a simple act to remove all controversy. Rather than provide supportive material, we are asked to believe them simply because they insist it is true.

As I write this letter, I am looking at one of the widely published autopsy photographs of Kennedy.[2] It shows the rear of Kennedy's skull, with the scalp removed, and a close-up of the bullet wound that Humes and Boswell report is beveled inward. In the photograph, this particular wound appears to be beveled outward, the opposite of what Drs Humes and Boswell would have us believe. A comment on the photograph points to the wound and states, "beveled outward exiting fragment." What makes the book's assertion more believable than Humes and Boswell is that the photo is provided to substantiate the claim of the author.

If Humes and Boswell really want the speculation to end, they should lobby *JAMA* to publish the actual photographs and roentgenograms that show so obviously what they want us to believe. Then the sophisticated readership of *JAMA* could help to bring this truth to the public in a convincing way.

Anthony White, MD
Boston, Mass

1. Breo DL. JFK's death—the plain truth from the MDs who did the autopsy. *JAMA*. 1992;267:2794-2803.
2. Livingstone HE. *High Treason II*. New York, NY: Carroll & Graf Publishers Inc; 1992:432.

To the Editor.—The congruent skull and scalp defect described by Dr Humes was 400% larger in area than that reported in Dallas. The Dallas wound was more occipital; Humes described a chiefly parietal wound. Contemporary sketches prepared from the two sources are remarkably different.

Mr Breo[1,2] quotes Dr M. T. "Pepper" Jenkins as retracting his 1963 viewing of the cerebellum in Dallas. In fact, Jenkins repeated this for the Warren Commission hearings. Cerebellar tissue was also seen by Drs William Kent Clark, Charles Baxter, James Carrico, Robert McClelland, and reported by Dr Malcolm Perry to the House Select Committee on Assassinations.

The entrance wound, according to Humes, was near the external occipital protuberance. The Clark panel,[3] however, located it 100 mm (sic) superior to this site, ie, near the cowlick area. This 10-cm discrepancy was also confirmed by Dr Baden before the House Select Committee on Assassinations.

In Dallas, of many physicians who stated sizes, only Carrico described the throat wound as possibly larger than 5 mm. All physicians described a fairly round, clean, smooth wound. In transcripts of his CBS interview,[4] Perry described an entrance wound three times.

Breo quotes Humes: "Two thirds of the right cerebrum was missing." In the Supplemental Autopsy Report, the brain weighed a normal 1500 g.

Humes saw no fractures in the neck. Michael Baden, MD,[5] however, described a fracture of T1. Would the "magic bullet" (Warren Commission Exhibit No. 399) emerge unscathed after fracturing T1, fracturing Connally's fifth rib, and shattering Connally's radius?

To follow Humes' bullet trajectory within the skull, the head must be extremely anteflexed, far more than seen on any of the Zapruder film frames. Placing Humes' entrance site and the angle of elevation supplied by the Warren Commission (15° 21') on Zapruder frame 313 (impact), a straight trajectory exits through the forehead; only marked deviation permits parietal exit.

Humes' statements mean that there was anterior ejection of brain tissue. Ignoring a Secret Service man, Mrs Kennedy retrieved something from the left rear of the limousine. Breo quotes Jenkins as saying that Mrs Kennedy delivered to him a large chunk of her husband's brain tissues. Police officers Hargis and Martin, to the left and rear, both report being forcibly struck by blood and brain tissue.

The Lattimer experimental model requires JFK to recoil directly toward the proposed gunman, backward and slightly to the right. In fact, multiple eyewitnesses and the Zapruder film show that the lateral movement was abruptly to the left. In this model, Humes' entrance wound requires brain tissue ejection anteriorly near the mid-sagittal plane (analogous to the neck wound). Multiple eyewitnesses confirm left posterior ejection. Furthermore, the anterior, approximately mid-sagittal brain tissue ejection predicted by Lattimer also contradicts Zapruder, which purports to show ejection near the right zygoma. Space constraints prohibit comment on this anomalous Zapruder feature.

Does Humes believe the "magic bullet" theory? To the Warren Commission he said, "I think that is most unlikely."[6] If one bullet did not strike both Kennedy and Connally, then an additional bullet is required and an additional gunman is required.

David W. Mantik, MD, PhD
Rancho Mirage, Calif

1. Breo DL. JFK's death—the plain truth from the MDs who did the autopsy. *JAMA.* 1992;267:2794-2803.
2. Breo DL. JFK's death, part II—Dallas MDs recall their memories. *JAMA.* 1992; 267:2804-2807.
3. Clark R. *Clark Panel Report: 1968 Panel Review of Photographs, X-ray Films, Documents and Other Evidence Pertaining to the Fatal Wounding of President John F. Kennedy on November 22, 1963, in Dallas, Tex.* Washington, DC: US Government Printing Office; 1969:11.
4. White House transcript 1327-C; Lyndon Johnson Library, Austin, Tex. November 22, 1963.
5. House Select Committee on Assassinations. Washington, DC: US Government Printing Office; 1979;1:199.
6. Warren Commission Hearings. Washington, DC: US Government Printing Office; 1964;2:374-376.

To the Editor.—The two articles in the May 27, 1992, issue[1,2] of *JAMA* purportedly put the matter of the John F. Kennedy assassination to rest. They do not. On the contrary, I do not recall ever having seen so many erroneous statements in so few pages. That Dr George Lundberg, the editor of THE JOURNAL, would give them the cachet of his approval and cooperation is difficult to understand.

Let me point out only a few of the glaringly erroneous assertions in Mr Breo's article:

1. He suggests that Dr Charles Crenshaw wasn't even in the room, so how could he know anything? Yet Crenshaw is identified at least five times in Volume VI of the Warren hearings as one of the attending physicians. He does have reason to know.

2. He says the autopsy provides "irrefutable evidence that President Kennedy was struck by only two bullets that came from above and behind."

Even on the face of it, the autopsy does no such thing. Drs Humes and Boswell did not follow the path of the bullet entering at the base of the neck and in no way linked this wound to the opening in the throat, which they thought was caused by the tracheotomy performed by the doctors in Dallas. Only the next morning after talking to Dr Malcolm Perry in Dallas did they hear that the tracheotomy had obscured a bullet wound. It was at that point that they presumed this must have been an exit wound. Presumption is hardly irrefutable proof. Further, they presumed too much, which leads us to point 3.

3. The doctors in Dallas have not broken a silence of 29 years. They have talked about the wounds before. In press conferences immediately after the assassination, a number said they thought the throat wound was one of entry. According to Dr McClelland's testimony in the Warren Commission hearings (Volume VI), the initial reaction of all was that it was an entry wound, while the massive wound in the back of the head was one of exit. Subsequently, some came around to saying that the throat wound could have been either entry or exit. Others held to their original judgment that it was entry. But not a single one has ever said that the wound in the throat was an exit wound! Humes and Boswell didn't examine it, so how would they know?

4. The articles note that panels of experts, basing their analyses on the autopsy photos and roentgenograms, have consistently upheld the Warren Commission report. Yes, but the two naval medical technicians who took those roentgenograms and photos have now revealed (in a press conference on May 28) that the photos and roentgenograms sent to the Warren Commission and examined by all subsequent panels were not the ones they took. They are fakes! So much for the conclusions of the panels of experts and the irrefutable nature of the evidence.

There are too many other discrepancies in Breo's articles to cover in the space available. Suffice it to say that the mystery of the Kennedy assassination is as alive as ever.

Wayne S. Smith, MD
School for Advanced International Studies
The Johns Hopkins University
Washington, DC

1. Breo DL. JFK's death—the plain truth from the MDs who did the autopsy. *JAMA.* 1992;267:2794-2803.
2. Breo DL. JFK's death, part II—Dallas MDs recall their memories. *JAMA.* 1992; 267:2804-2807.

(Reprinted from *The Journal of the American Medical Association,* October 7, 1992; Vol. 268, No. 2.)

The following is reprinted from *The Third Decade* (March 1993)

ANOTHER LETTER TO JAMA
by

Gary L. Aguilar, MD; David W. Mantik, MD, Ph.D; Patricia L. James, MD; Wayne S. Smith, Ph.D. and Anthony White, MD

INTRODUCTION Departing from the custom of the Journal of the American Medical Association (JAMA) or "prefer(ring) that the information not be released to the public ... until the article appears in print," (JAMA, 265: 400), George D. Lundberg, MD called a press conference on May 19, 1992 with important news. The forthcoming May 27, 1992 issue of JAMA would contain definitive evidence concerning the autopsy findings of John Kennedy. There was great hope that many autopsy contradictions would finally be resolved.

Published reports of Lundberg's dramatic news conference seemed to lack sufficient detail to determine if important evidentiary discrepancies that had troubled us had been clarified. We were not alone in being unsatisfied by the formal presentation that followed in JAMA. We independently undertook to write JAMA to ask questions that had remained unasked, and to probe the apparently fickle memories of the pathologists. Our letters, despite their critical nature, were commendably published in the October 7, 1992 issue of JAMA. Lundberg commented in that issue: "... We hope that our open JAMA presentations, Mr. Breo's three articles, Dr. Micozzi's Editorial, and today's letters and responses will help to calm the ardor of the honest conspiracy theorists who have simply not had access to the facts. We further hope that all those who have been fed only 'docufiction' on this matter, as if it were truth, will cease to be misled."

Upon reading Lundberg's words we had the uncomfortable feeling that somehow we had missed something. JAMA's "open presentations" consisted of Humes' personal friend, Lundberg (a former military pathologist himself) or his surrogate, Dennis Breo—and only those two—interviewing Kennedy's military autopsists. No one else asked any questions. Neither Humes, Boswell, nor Finck would come before any open press conferences to answer questions. Lundberg insisted the autopsists would answer no further questions. Most annoyingly for us, neither Humes nor Boswell answered a single of our many questions in letters selected by JAMA's own editors as being worthy of publication, and, presumably, of being answered. This is exceptionally unusual for a scientific journal as any scientist knows. Can a presentation be fairly called "open" under such, well, unusual circumstances?

On a whim one of us thought to try to find the authors of other critical letters to discuss the matter. What follows is the result of a surprisingly enthusiastic collaboration between a group of people who were total strangers before their letters appeared in JAMA:

. . . .

December 7, 1992
D. Rennie and B. Dan, Editors
JAMA, American Medical Association
515 North State Street
Chicago, Illinois 60610

Dear Sirs:

We were pleased that our letters of response to Drs. Humes and Boswell, regarding the autopsy of John Fitzgerald Kennedy, were published in JAMA.[1] We were, however, most disappointed that all questions of evidential significance were ignored by the autopsists.[2] For individuals so uniquely placed by history to now affirm that they will forever remain silent on these issues is a great disservice to the medical community, to all Americans, and to history. If the imprimatur of scientific certainty is to be granted, as requested by Drs. Humes, Boswell, Finck, and Lundberg, for their proffered information,[3] surely the ancient and valued tradition of responding honestly to letters of inquiry is required. Without this, the value of peer reviewed literature would greatly diminish.[4] As members of the medical community addressing a matter of such historic importance, most decidedly we are accountable to the wider American public. In the Kennedy assassination, most especially, an open and uninhibited scientific interchange must be permitted. Sadly, that door has now been closed, supposedly for all time. Such a total lack of response, advanced with remarkably ringing finality, can only provoke among readers the opposite of its expressed intent. Rather than trust and confidence in Humes, Boswell and JAMA, mistrust and incredulity will result.

This aura of stifling the truth was only enhanced by Humes' and Boswell's deliberate absence from Lundberg's news conference announcing JAMA's forthcoming publication of their "plain truth" portrayal of the autopsy evidence in Kennedy's murder.[5] The impression that Humes, Boswell, and Finck are unwilling to answer questions—whether from the free press, from fellow physicians (other than from former fellow military pathologist Lundberg), and other readers of JAMA—undermines the confidence the public should have for physicians, the AMA its journal and its authoritative conclusions regarding this case.[6]

As Lundberg, himself, has advised: "It is the reader's responsibility, no matter whether an investigator, a physician, a medical reporter, or any member of the public, to read all with a skeptical eye".[7] He has suggested that we ". . . sift these data, challenge the hypotheses, results, and interpretations. And, let us hear from you."[8] Yet when we sifted and challenged and wrote JAMA, Mr. Breo answered that the ". . . only cogent question raised by all the response . . ." was that Finck's interview was absent in the first JAMA report![9] Is Lundberg seriously suggesting, via his surrogate, Breo, that these guidelines are to be ignored for the peer review discussion of Kennedy's autopsy? To be sure, there remain "cogent questions" that are still unanswered despite Breo's flip dismissive.

For example, if JAMA would be, in Lundberg's words, ". . . as correct as it is humanly possible to be . . .",[10] it might have requested that the autopsists discuss their claims in reference to the extensive work of the panel of forensic pathologists of the House Select Committee on Assassinations (HSCA). Their findings contradict the claims of the autopsists regarding the location of the fatal skull wound by 10 to 12 cm![11] Furthermore, the photographs and radiographs also contradict the claims of Humes, Boswell and Finck. We cannot imagine how Lundberg and Breo could have failed to ask the autopsists such fundamental questions, or how any peer review analysis of the data in the case could have neglected them. These contradictions were the source of the greatest and unresolved medical controversies considered by the HSCA.

There can be no disputing that there are unresolved contradictions in the data on Kennedy's autopsy, which Humes, Boswell and Finck could greatly clarify. Among the many mysteries suggested by JAMA's coverage, the following areas of ambiguity could easily be clarified by the autopsy pathologists:

1) If "two thirds of the right cerebrum was missing," as Humes reported in JAMA, how could the brain in evidence weigh 1500 grams—the upper limit of normal for an intact normal brain—as the supplemental autopsy report asserts?

2) Frame 312 of the Zapruder film establishes that Kennedy's head was ante-

flexed only slightly at the instant of the fatal shot. If the autopsy exam revealed a wound of entrance "to the right and just above" the external occipital protuberance, as Humes, Boswell and Finck have claimed, [12][13] this would place the wound of entrance very near the base of the skull from a bullet arriving from above and to the right—assuming, of course, that the assassin was firing from the sixth floor of the Texas School Book Depository. How could this bullet enter near the external occipital protuberance and then exit through the skull defect shown at the vertex in the HSCA diagram, unless it were deflected by normal brain tissue? And how could it produce a large defect extending into the occiput, as reported by Humes and Finck, and as described by all Parkland medical personnel, and as seen on the anterior skull radiographs?[14]

3) Humes, Boswell and Finck were apparently charged by Kennedy's personal physician, Dr. Burkley, with locating bullet evidence linking the murder to the (by then captured) alleged assassin, Oswald.[15] While the pathologists did retrieve 2 bullet fragments measuring 7×2mm and 3×1mm, no mention is made of the largest bullet fragment discernable on the currently available radiographs, a 6.5mm diameter, round object that is unavoidably obvious on the anteroposterior radiograph. This largest fragment is seen imbedded in the outer table of the parietal bone in precisely the area examined, according to the testimony of Humes and Boswell.[16] Could a fragment so large and so easily retrievable, and so important evidentially, have been ignored by 3 pathologists? Would the radiologist who was present, Dr. Ebersole,[17] have failed to bring so important an object to the attention of the pathologists for retrieval if it had been overlooked by them? It was not mentioned by any of the pathologists in their Warren Commission testimony. In fact, after reviewing the autopsy radiographs for 5 hours on 1-26-67 all 3 autopsists signed a statement declaring that "... careful examination at the autopsy, and the photographs and X-rays (sic) taken during the autopsy, revealed no evidence of a bullet or of a major portion of a bullet in the body of the President ...".[18] This peculiarity has taken on increased significance because the technologist who took the radiographs, Jerrol Custer, claims that the current radiographs are forgeries.[19] If the current radiographs are forged and are not those studied by the 3 autopsy pathologists and radiologist the night of the autopsy, that could explain how so large and obvious a fragment might have been neither retrieved nor mentioned by the autopsists. Do Humes, Boswell and Finck recall seeing this 6.5mm round fragment in the "cowlick" area of parietal skull on radiographs examined during the autopsy, where current radiographs show such a fragment? If they did, why did they not retrieve it while exploring this precise area, given Burkley's request?[20] Why did Dr. Ebersole, the radiologist, not recall seeing this fragment when questioned about it twice (November 2 and December 2, 1992), by one of us (Dr. Mantik)?

4) On three occasions, Humes, Boswell and Finck have stated that the fatal entrance wound was near the external occipital protuberance (EOP): to the right and just above the EOP to the Warren Commission, to the right and just below the EOP to the HSCA,[21] and to the right and just above the EOP in JAMA. The available photographs and radiographs, if true representations, indicate that Humes, Boswell and Finck erred by 10 cm to 12 cm—an enormous discrepancy. That is, the photos and radiographs if authentic show the fatal entrance wound at least 10 cm above where the autopsists claim it was.[22]

In their House Select Committee testimony, Boswell, with Humes at his side, twice asserted that a fragment of bone brought late to the autopsy fit a defect in the occipital bone surrounding the fatal entrance wound.[23] In fact, Boswell stated that it was the bevelling on the inner aspect of precisely this fragment that allowed them to determine that the "inshoot" had occurred so low in the occipital bone.[24] Do the autopsy pathologists recall a defect in the occipital bone that was made whole with the arrival of a bony fragment the night of the autopsy? Significantly, no defect in the occipital bone is seen on the current lateral radiograph. The radiographs were taken before the autopsy had begun and, presumably, at a time when the defect in the occipital bone was present, according to Boswell's and Humes' testimony.[25] Were there two traumatic defects in the skull at the beginning of the autopsy, one the entrance defect in the occipital bone reconstructed with the arrival of the fragment mentioned above, and the second a large exit defect, or was there a single continuous, large "temporo-parietal-occipital" defect as described by Finck?[26] If there were two separate defects, what was the separation between them? How wide was the occipital portion of the large skull defect mentioned by Dr. Boswell?

5) The autopsy report describes ". . . a (note the singular form of the indefinite article) large irregular defect of the scalp and skull on the right involving chiefly the parietal bone but extending somewhat into the temporal and occipital regions." How can this be reconciled with the photographs which show no defect even remotely close to the occipital region? This question is very important since the photographer who took the photographs, Floyd Reibe, claims the photographs currently available are also forgeries.[27 28]

The evidence Humes, Boswell and Finck have given to JAMA, the Warren Commission and the House Select Committee on Assassinations appear to support Reibe's stunning allegations of forgery and to undermine the conclusions of the panel of forensic pathologists of the House Select Committee which accepted the photographs as valid.[29] Is that their intent? Humes himself categorically denied the legitimacy of the higher skull wound, whose existence is "proven" by the photographs and radiographs. Reviewing a photograph of the back of the skull showing a high wound of entrance before the HSCA, Humes protested, "I can assure you that as we reflected the scalp to get to this point there was no defect corresponding to this in the skull at any point. I don't know what this is (referring to the higher wound seen on the photos). It could be to me (sic) clotted blood. I don't, I just don't know what it is, but it certainly was not any wound of entrance."[30] Furthermore, the House Select Committee's panel of pathologists reported that Finck "believed strongly that the observations of the autopsy pathologist (sic) were more valid than those of individuals who might subsequently examine photographs."[31] This implies that Finck also disputed the photographic "proof" or an entrance wound high in the skull. How do the autopsists reconcile the striking discrepancy between their localization of the fatal wound and contradictory photographic evidence?

Indeed, why, in a second interview before the House Select Committee's panel of forensic pathologists, did Humes abandon his prior low location to endorse the forensic panel's 10-12 cm higher location of the fatal wound "proven" to them by the photographs and radiographs?[32] Why has he reversed himself again and decided that the lower location of the fatal wound was right after all in his JAMA interview, even though he places that wound at a different low location ("just above" the EOP) than he did in testimony before the House Select Committee (1 cm or 2 cm "below" the EOP)?[33]

6) Was the cerebellum visible through the skull defect? How is it conceivable that no one on the Warren Commission or on the HSCA even ventured to ask such a rudimentary question? Seven Parkland physicians have reported seeing cerebellum through the skull defect: Drs. Baxter, Carrico, Clark, Jenkins, McClelland, Peters and Perry.[34] In particular, Dr. Kemp Clark, the neurosurgeon, in

a *handwritten* note reported both cerebral and cerebellar tissue. Many of these physicians were asked to confirm this in their sworn testimony, and no one recanted.[35,36]

7) Why was the designation "14 cm" on Dr. Boswell's diagram in dark blue ink, while the remainder of the diagram was entirely in pencil? When was the "14 cm" notation inserted?

8) On January 27, 1964, during a Warren Commission executive session, J. Lee Rankin, while holding photographs, stated that the bullet entered *below* the shoulder blade.[37] This agrees with the accounts given by: 1) Burkley in his death certificate that the wound was to the right of the 3rd thoracic vertebra,[38] 2) the autopsy diagram of Boswell, which was signed as "verified" by Burkley,[39] 3) the eyewitness testimonies of SS agent Clint Hill, FBI agents Sibert and O'Neill,[40] 4) the verbal description given twice by the attending radiologist, Dr. Ebersole, to one of us (Dr. Mantik), and 5) the corroboration that the bullet holes in Kennedy's jacket and shirt were 5 inches below the collar, while at the moment of bullet impact photographic evidence shows that his jacket was not "riding up" and distorting the clothing evidence regarding the location of bullet entrance.[41] Was the back wound where Burkley placed it, to the right of the third thoracic vertebra, in the recollection of Humes, Boswell, and Finck?

9) Do they believe the "Single Bullet Theory"—that a single bullet caused both Kennedy's and Connally's non-fatal wounds in 7 passes through skin and muscle, pulverizing a 5 inch segment of Connally's rib, and passing through his wrist while fracturing the widest portion of the radius bone yet remaining virtually undamaged? Humes and Finck strongly disagreed with this theory in their interviews before the Warren Commission.[42 43] Yet they seem to say the opposite in JAMA. If they changed their mind, what new evidence caused them to change?

10) Humes and Finck insisted in JAMA that there was no interference in the President's autopsy. While testifying under oath in the Shaw trial, however, Finck was asked why he had not dissected the track of the bullet wound in Kennedy's back, an elemental aspect of an autopsy in a shooting. He responded, "As I recall I was told not to but I don't remember by whom." Moments later he was pressed, "But you were told not to go into the area of the neck, is that your testimony?" He answered, "From what I recall, yes, but I don't remember by whom." [44] Taking a major departure from customary autopsy protocol because one is "told not to" seems to be interference. Can the autopsists maintain this was not interference?

11) How can the current photographic collection purport to be a full complement when Humes himself reports taking great care to obtain at least one photograph of the right apical pleura, which was bruised? This photograph is absent. If an extra photograph was inserted to maintain a full complement, which one is it? Is it a posterior view of the head?

12) On Boswell's face sheet diagram the anterior to posterior length of the skull defect was labelled as 17 cm with the designation "missing." (Author David Lifton reports that Boswell told him in 1979 that the measurement was made by him using a centimeter scale.[45]) If this defect starts near the coronal suture, it necessarily must extend far into the occipital bone (which is also consistent with the autopsy report). Even the use of Humes' smaller 13 cm measurement necessarily extends the large defect into the occiput on skull models. Dr. Ebersole locates the posterior border large skull defect as 2-2.5 cm lateral to the smaller occipital entry wound (which was near the EOP). All 3 of these physicians' descriptions are in gross anatomic disagreement with the current posterior head photograph, which shows no sign whatsoever of a large skull defect. Who should be be-

lieved: the eyewitness testimony of 4 physicians (the autopsists and Ebersole), or a photograph whose authenticity has been denied by the photographer himself (Reibe)?

13) The current posterior head photographs show no large defect. Is this what the pathologists saw? It is astounding that they were not asked this question. On the one issue raised (the site of the bullet entry) their recollections were, in fact, vastly different.

14) Why was the brain not sectioned coronally? When did Humes intend to do this if not for the supplemental autopsy report? Surely by that time (December 6, 1963) he could leisurely have reviewed standard forensic pathology protocols and would have known that such sectioning was an essential component of a full report. Also given the absence of urgency in the examination of the brain, why did Humes not request an AFIP consultation for a definitive pathologic study of the brain?

15) The JAMA interview makes frequent use of phrases rarely found in scientific papers: "irrefutable proof," "foolproof," "blatantly obvious." (The authors challenge the reader to find similar terminology in any contemporary JAMA articles.) The autopsy report, however, makes liberal use of the word "presumably", even when describing such critical items as wounds. Have Humes and Boswell made new discoveries since the autopsy which increase their scientific certainty? If so, an opportunity to share such discoveries should not be missed.

16) The trail of bullet fragments reported by Humes began at the external occipital protuberance. Ebersole has confirmed that these tiny fragments did extend from the occiput toward the right forehead, which is consistent with Humes' testimony. The current lateral radiograph, however, shows them much higher near the vertex. Which version is correct?

17) The HSCA reported that the back wound had an abrasion collar at the inferior border. Did the pathologists see this? It was recognized by the HSCA that this implied a rising bullet. The HSCA also reported that Kennedy was leaning forward by only a few degrees. Did this bullet then enter him going superiorly? If so, how did it then reverse course, without striking bone (as everyone agrees), and enter Connally going downward?

18) Why does the autopsy report describe Kennedy as falling *forward* (by implication, from a rear fatal head shot) while the Zapruder film shows him violently propelled *backward*? The autopsists were also told that the lone assassin, Oswald, had been apprehended and that he had fired at the President from above and to the rear. Were the autopsists influenced in their conclusions by this information? Who told the pathologists that Kennedy fell forward with the fatal shot?

19) Why are there no photographs of the brain in the skull? Were any photographs taken before manipulations had been performed?

20) Were the skull radiographs taken before or after the brain was removed, or both? Do the extant radiographs purport to contain brain?

As a final question to Lundberg: Were outside consultants used by JAMA to analyze the data given by Humes, Boswell and Finck, JAMA's standard peer review process?[46] If so, who were they and what are their qualifications?

We hope that raising these issues will invite additional expertise to examine unsettled aspects of the autopsy and will promote additional clarification. We harbor little hope that our queries, even if fully answered, will quiet all doubters, since there seems to be an unlimited supply. We do, however, share with Lundberg an abiding faith in the peer review process. We hope that the full exercise of that process, which Lundberg has long championed, will leave physicians, the American Medical Association, its journal, and the concerned public confident that JAMA will continue to be "as correct as it is humanly possible to be".

Very truly yours,

Gary L. Aguilar, MD
David W. Mantik, MD, PhD
Wayne S. Smith, PhD
Anthony White, MD
Patricia L. James, MD

Notes

1. JAMA 1992; 268: 1681-1685.
2. JAMA 1992; 268: 1685.
3. Lundberg GD. Closing the case in JAMA on the John F. Kennedy autopsy. JAMA. 1992; 268: 1736-1738.
4. Carney, MJ, Lundberg GD. We've come a long way—thanks to peer review. JAMA. 1987; 258:87.
5. New York Times; 5-20-92, p. A-1.
6. Lundberg GD. Closing the case in JAMA on the John F. Kennedy autopsy. JAMA. 1992; 268;1736-1738.
7. Lundberg GD. Providing reliable medical information to the public-caveat lector. JAMA 1987; 262: 945-946.
8. Lundberg GD. MRFIT and the goals of The Journal. JAMA 1982; 248: 1501.
9. Breo DL. Letter "In Reply". JAMA. 1992; 268: 1684-1685.
10. Lundberg GD. JAMA 1989; 262: 946.
11. House Select Committee on Assassinations (HSCA). Washington, DC; US Government Printing Office; 1978; 7:245-265.
12. Breo DL. JFK's death-the plain truth from the MDs who did the autopsy. JAMA 1992; 267:2794-2803.
13. Breo DL. JFK's death, part III-Dr. Finck speaks out: 'two bullets, from the rear'. JAMA. 1992; 268:1748-1754.
14. HSCA. Washington, DC; US Government Printing Office; 1978; 7:260.
15. HSCA. Washington, DC; US Government Printing Office; 1978; 7:263.
16. HSCA. Washington, DC; US Government Printing Office; 1978; 7:254.
17. Breo DL. JFK's death-the plain truth from the MDs who did the autopsy. JAMA 1992; 267:2797.
18. Military Review. Report of the three autopsy doctors after review of the autopsy photos and X-rays in January 1967. A public document available at Justice Department. Referred to in: Lifton DS: Best Evidence. New York: Carroll & Graf; 1992:721. Copy available from Gary Aguilar, MD.
19. Livingstone HE. *High Treason II*. New York, New York: Carroll & Graf Publishers, Inc; 1992:209-225, 308.
20. HSCA. Washington, DC: US Government Printing Office; 1978; 7:2.
21. HSCA. Washington, DC: US Government Printing Office: 1978; 7:246.
22. Livingstone HE. *High Treason II*, New York, New York: Carroll & Graf Publishers, Inc; 1992:432-433.
23. HSCA. Washington, DC: US Government Printing Office; 1978; 7:246 & 7:260.
24. HSCA. Washington, DC: US Government Printing Office: 1978: 7: 260.
25. HSCA. Washington, DC: US Government Printing Office; 1987; 7:249.
26. Finck PA. Ballistic and forensic pathologic aspects of missile wounds. Con-

version between Anglo-American and metric-system units. Military Medicine. 1965; 130:545-569.

27. King J. JFK autopsy photo called phony: Navy technicians charge tampering. San Francisco Examiner. April 29, 1992: A8.

28. Livingstone HE. *High Treason II.* New York, Carroll & Graf 1992: 305-309.

29. HSCA. Washington, DC: US Government Printing Office; 1978; 7:113-119.

30. HSCA. Washington, DC: US Government Printing Office; 1978; 7:254.

31. HSCA. Washington, DC: US Government Printing Office; 1978; 7:115.

32. HSCA. Washington, DC: US Government Printing Office; 1978; 1:323-332.

33. Aguilar GL. Letter to the editor. JAMA. 1992; 268: 1681-1682.

34. Lifton DS. Best Evidence. New York, Carroll & Graf; 1980:321-327.

35. Report of the President's Commission on the Assassination of President John F. Kennedy (Warren Commission). Washington, DC; US Government Printing Office; 1964; vol 6:20.

36. Groden RJ, Livingstone HE. *High Treason.* New York, New York: Berkley Books; 1990:453.

37. National Archives; Record group 272, entry 1.

38. Wilber CG. Medicolegal Investigation of the President John F. Kennedy Murder. Springfield, Illinois: Charles C. Thomas; 1978:111.

39. Groden RJ, Livingstone HE. *High Treason.* New York, New York: Berkley Books; 1990:27-29.

40. Ibid, p. 94.

41. Thompson J. Six Seconds in Dallas-A Micro-Study of the Kennedy Assassination. New York, New York; Bernard Geis Associates-distributed by Random House; 1967:222-223.

42. Report of the President's Commission on the Assassination of President John F. Kennedy (Warren Commission). Washington, DC; US Government Printing Office; 1964: Vol 2:382.

43. Ibid, vol 2:376 & vol. 2:374-375.

44. Reprinted in: DiEugenio J. Destiny Betrayed. New York, Sheridan Square Press; 1992:302.

45. Lifton DS. Best Evidence. New York, Carroll & Graf; 1980:319-320.

46. Lundberg GD. The quality of a medical article—thank you to our 1990 peer reviewers. JAMA 1991; 265:1161-1162.

. . . .

Appendix H

In response to the letter reprinted above, its authors received on January 12, 1993 the following response from Rennie Drummond, MD, Deputy Editor of JAMA:

"Thank you for your letter to the editor. Since we have already given you space by publishing your views, we do not intend to publish this letter. I have sent copies to Mr. Breo and Dr. Lundberg."

A PIECE OF MY MIND: LUNDBERG, JFK AND JAMA
by
James H. Fetzer, Ph.D.*

As a professor of philosophy with an extensive background in the study of scientific reasoning, as the editor of one journal (*Minds and Machines*) and the co-editor of another (*Synthese*), and as a citizen who has been disturbed by the dissemination of incomplete and inaccurate information regarding the death of John Fitzgerald Kennedy, I was extremely disillusioned to read the articles on this subject that have been published in JAMA, including interviews with Humes and Boswell (27 May 1992) and subsequently with Finck (7 October 1992). In my opinion, these pieces should never have been published, especially in a journal as prestigious as JAMA, because they display the application of improper and unwarranted methods of investigation and procedures of inquiry that lead to unjustifiable conclusions and create the impression that the AMA has engaged in a cover-up in JFK's assassination.

I previously conveyed my concerns in this matter to a member of the Board of Trustees, William Jacott, on 24 May 1992, before the appearance of the first of these two issues of JAMA but after it had received extensive coverage in local and national news sources on the basis of a press release and other forms of publicity by Lundberg (including an interview on "Good Morning America" that week). I subsequently wrote to him to elaborate my concerns with reference to articles and editorials that had already appeared in a local newspaper, *The Duluth News-Tribune* (20 May 1992, pp. 6A and 7A), and in *The New York Times* (20 May 1992, pp. A1 and A13). On 10 June 1992, I reiterated my distress after studying that issue of the journal to reaffirm my objections to the conduct of the editor in this case.

Dr. Jacott and I subsequently discussed this matter on 8 August 1992. His response was to propose that he arrange a telephone conversation between Lundberg and me in order for me to explain my position directly to Lundberg. On 12 August 1992, Lundberg contacted me and we discussed the differences in our viewpoints. The substance of our conversation convinced me that I was correct in thinking that the articles were based upon improper methods of research and inquiry, which had led to faulty conclusions presented as facts in a biased and unjustifiable presentation in JAMA. Because the issues involved here are so important and because the editor's behavior is so blatant, I wrote a series of letters to the members of the Board of Trustees of the AMA, which outlined these concerns.

The most important problems with the preparation and presentation of these articles I raised during our discussion were the following. When I emphasized to Lundberg that the number and the source of bullets that have been fired at a target cannot be determined on the basis of the number that happen to hit the target, he explained that he had restricted his focus to the two wounds he claims the body had sustained and the question of whether JFK was killed by two bullets which had been fired from above and behind. (Even if JFK had been killed by two bullets which had been fired from above and behind, however, that would hardly establish how many shots had been fired or the identity of whomever fired them.)

When I protested that there was considerable evidence—including the testimony of Malcolm Perry—that the throat wound was a wound of entry, he insisted that it could easily have been an exit wound, as though the conclusion that JFK had been shot twice did not hang in the balance. When I alluded to the autopsy photographs and X-rays and photographs of a bullet impacted on the limousine, of another bullet being picked up from a grassy area behind the vehicle's location, and of the curbing that was hit by (as even the Warren Commission conceded) a shot that missed, he was very dismissive, suggesting that photographs and X-rays can be faked and that there is no legal chain of custody to support them.

This attitude bothers me more than any other aspect of our conversation. The problem we confront in attempting to figure out what happened in Dealey Plaza on 22 November 1963, after all, is an historical problem, not a legal one. Moreover, anyone with a serious interest in the assassination should have known that the Warren Commission was never able to establish that Oswald had either the motive, the means, or the opportunity to assassinate the President. As various authors have reported, Oswald was observed on the second floor of the Texas School Book Depository by a motorcycle officer and by a supervisor within 90 seconds of the shooting (as Lifton, *Best Evidence*, pp. 350-352, among others, has explained). But if Oswald was on the second floor having a Coke, then he could not have also been on the sixth floor shooting at JFK.

The more we talked the more apparent it became to me that he was operating on the basis of what might be called the principle of selection and elimination, selecting the evidence that agreed with a predetermined conclusion and eliminating the rest. This approach violates a basic principle of scientific reasoning, which is known as *the requirement of total evidence*. According to the total evidence requirement, scientific conclusions must be based upon all of the relevant evidence that is available, where evidence is relevant when its truth or falsity makes a difference to the truth or falsity of the conclusion. In the case of JFK's assassination, any evidence about the number of shots fired obviously qualifies as relevant.

Violations of the requirement of total evidence are commonly committed by politicians, advertisers, and lawyers, who are typically called upon to present a biased case in support of a predetermined point of view. (We do not expect a used car dealer, for example, to tell us what is wrong with a vehicle, even though some states require "full disclosure.") In courts of law, the requirement is satisfied by having the prosecution and the defense present their cases for the guilt or for the innocence of the accused, where the jury must sort out how the evidence presented fits together in arriving at a conclusion. The interests of both sides are reflected in various ways, including the right to cross-examine the testimony of witnesses.

Insofar as the articles in *JAMA* were based upon unsworn testimony from persons such as Humes and Boswell, whose reputations could irredeemably suffer from any admissions of evidence at variance with their previous testimony and who were not subject to cross-examination, I was struck by Lundberg's reliance upon a double-standard. Evidence that upheld the Warren Commission's findings was included (even in cases where it could properly qualify as no more than "hearsay"), while evidence that undermined those findings was excluded (even in cases where it properly qualified as relevant photographic evidence that has gone unchallenged).

Indeed, it is striking how blatantly these articles are biased in favor of the recollections of Humes and Boswell, as though there were no other or more reliable evidence available. Photographs and X-rays might provide more accurate and dependable information than fallible and limited memories, especially nearly thirty years after the event. Yet none of the autopsy photographs or X-rays appear here, much less any photographs or diagrams of Dealey Plaza. No mention is made of the "missile" Humes turned over to FBI agents at the autopsy (see Groden and Livingstone's *High Treason*, for example) nor of the wounds sustained by John Connally, even though they make it difficult to believe only three shots were fired.

One of the *JAMA* articles, of course, was devoted to interviews with Parkland physicians who had attended JFK in Dallas. Like its companion piece, no citations or references were given in support of any quotations or assertions, as though they should be taken for granted at face value. Much of this piece was devoted to discrediting the published testimony of Charles Crenshaw, who has maintained that JFK's fatal wound hit him just above the right temple (from the right front rather than above and behind). His views have been elaborated in his book, *JFK: Conspiracy of Silence*, and indeed he was interviewed following Lundberg's interview on "Good Morning America," during the very same television broadcast.

One need not believe every claim that Crenshaw has made concerning this case to be struck by certain facts. On the page following page 586 of Lifton's *Best Evidence*, for example, a photograph identified as "Photo 28" shows then White House Press Secretary Malcolm Kilduff pointing to his right temple in answering a question at Parkland Hospital as to where the bullet that struck JFK hit his head. And several autopsy photographs in Livingstone's *High Treason 2* (found between pages 432 and 433) show a peculiar "bat wing" configuration that conceals the President's cranium at the same location Crenshaw reports having observed a wound of entrance. These facts suggest that his testimony should not be so readily dismissed.

The tone in which these articles are written, moreover, ought to give pause to anyone who imagines that they are objective reports of the testimony of these physicians. From its first sentence to its last, these stories are clearly intended to present the case in support of the predetermined conclusion that the Warren Commission's "findings" were correct. Indeed, the language in which it is written seems to be altogether antithetical to a scientific or medical journal. Instead of qualified characterizations of the evidence and the conclusions that it might render "probable" or perhaps make "likely," many definitive declarations are advanced in a case where it should be painfully apparent that conclusive findings are not available. Thus, consider the second paragraph found on page 2794 of *JAMA*:

"The *scientific evidence* they documented during their autopsy provides *irrefutable proof* that President Kennedy was struck by only two bullets that came from above and behind from a high-velocity weapon that caused the fatal wounds. This *autopsy proof*, combined with the bullet and rifle evidence found at the scene of the crime, and the subsequent detailed documentation of a six-month investigation involving the enormous resources of the local, state, and federal law enforcement agencies, *proves* the 1964 Warren Commission conclusion that Kennedy was killed by a lone assassin, Lee Harvey Oswald." (Italics added for emphasis)

This passage, which reads like a promotion for the Warren Commission, not only grossly exaggerates the kind of evidential support that is possible here but ignores the controversial character of the Commission's most important conjectures, including, for example, the single-bullet theory. (See below) This emphasis upon "scientific evidence," "irrefutable proof," and so forth ought to be taken as a sign that what is being presented here consists of opinions masquerading as facts. If we know anything about this case at all, it is that "irrefutable proofs" are out of the question. I cannot imagine, moreover, how anyone could take seriously the suggestion that the Warren Commission had "proven" that Oswald killed Kennedy, given everything that is known about the case today. Lundberg's own bias is evident when he extends his personal endorsement on page 2803. His attitude, like those Humes and Dennis Breo express in the last few paragraphs on this page, is that any other evidence simply does not matter.

A less partisan and more objective article on the same subject can be found in a recent issue of *U.S. News and World Report* (17 August 1992, pp.28-42). It should come as no surprise that a piece of this kind, which focuses on the fashion in which the Warren Commission staff conducted its analysis (by interviewing Gerald Ford and numerous members of the staff) would also support their previous "findings." More interesting to consider are its reports that Warren viewed the task of the commission to be establishing that JFK was killed by Lee Harvey Oswald, that the staff itself was composed almost entirely of lawyers rather than of investigators, and that its members were chosen by reliance upon the standard "old boy network."

These considerations provide a partial explanation for how it could be the case that the staff itself tended to function less in an investigative role (which was left almost exclusively to the FBI) and more in a prosecutorial role. As those of us familiar with the television series, "Law and Order," are no doubt aware, lawyers in the role of prosecuting attorneys seldom conduct investigations of their own but instead are trained to present evidence that tends to establish the guilt of the accused, where that "guilt" itself is a matter about which they have predetermined conclusion. Thus, the staff was well-positioned to "build a case" against Oswald, which was in effect the task to which they had been assigned by Warren and by LBJ.

Even more instructive than these aspects of the operation of the staff are the accompanying photographs. On page 31, for example, is a familiar photograph alleged to be Oswald wearing a holstered revolver and holding his rifle and a communist newspaper, which was used to convict him in the eyes of ordinary citizens. The accompanying discussion conveniently omits the evidence that this picture was one of several that appear to have been faked. (See, for example, the discussion and accompanying copies of three different photos of this type in Groden and Livingstone's *High Treason*.) Even more important than this widely-disputed photograph are those of the staff reconstructing the scene of the crime that appear on pages 38-39.

In this case, of course, what we find are three photographs of a vehicle, one of which is described as being the young Arlen Specter "demonstrating the single-bullet theory." There are several fascinating features of these photographs. One is that this demonstration shows the back wound below Specter's hand by about six inches, thereby illustrating how extremely implausible it is to suppose that a bullet which entered there could possibly have exited through JFK's throat. Indeed, in view of the exact alignment of Specter's hand in relation to the pointer in his hand, which is intended to display the path that a single-bullet would have been required to take if the single-bullet theory were true, this photograph refutes that theory.

Even more striking is the use of a Cadillac for the purpose of reconstruction. JFK, of course, was riding in a Lincoln Continental when he was killed. You do not have to be an expert to recognize the difference between these cars, which include the relative locations of the seats and distance between them. Thus, the single-bullet theory, which is the crucial element that ties together the assassination scenario advanced by the Warren Commission, was not only not based on a reconstruction that used the actual vehicle in which JFK was riding when he was killed but was instead actually based on analysis with a vehicle of an entirely different make. This invalidates any conclusions that were drawn by means of the "reconstruction" which these photographs record. They cannot establish the single-bullet theory.

The precise location of the wound in JFK's back, of course, has proven difficult to identify. On page 37, for example, two diagrams that were used by the Warren Commission are presented, which characterize it as a *neck* wound. This appears to be indispensable to the single-bullet theory, since otherwise it seems inexplicable how a bullet fired in a downward direction should have exited from the center of his throat at just the level of his tie. The photograph on pages 38-39, however, identifies its location by means of a circular mark (which is evident in this photograph) as a *back* wound, although the single-bullet theory requires that it has to have hit his neck.

The autopsy photographs that appear in Livingstone's *High Treason 2* (between pages 432 and 433) display two possible wounds, one of which is considerably higher than the other, but both of which are clearly back wounds and not neck wounds. The higher of the two, which Livingstone reports witnesses have said was merely a blood clot, appears to provide such factual basis as there may be for the single-bullet theory. At least, the circular mark locating the back wound in the photo in *U.S. News And World Report* corresponds to this position and not the much lower location of the second wound. Neither location fits the single-bullet theory, however, and there is no other evidence of any other wound to the neck.

The use of the wrong kind of vehicle to reconstruct "the crime of the century" appears to defy credulity, yet the evidence is categorical. The misdescription of the back wound as a neck wound likewise seems to be beyond belief, yet the diagrams leave no doubt. There can be different kinds of "smoking guns", and these appear to be smoking guns that discredit the Warren Commission's findings. Other kinds of "smoking guns" can be found in the testimony of persons who claim to have participated in the assassination, such as Charles Harrelson and Chauncey Holt, whose interview with *Newsweek* (23 December 1991, p. 54) invites further investigation. Yet if the Warren Commission's findings are in doubt, so are the articles in JAMA.

Were this matter of any lesser importance, I would not impose upon you to consider these issues further. Before closing, moreover, I ought to express my appreciation to William Jacott for hearing me out and to George Lundberg for talking with me. Lundberg, I might add, expressed his agreement that many aspects of the autopsy had gone wrong, from moving the body from Dallas to the choice of autopsy surgeons. He even invited me to submit a Letter to the Editor for consideration for publication in JAMA. My choice of this alternative approach instead reflects my dissatisfaction not just with the contents of the articles that were published in this journal but with his dereliction of duty in allowing their appearance.

For reasons such as these and others conveyed in my correspondence with the AMA Trustees, I believe the editor of JAMA has abused his position by the publication and promotion of these articles on the assassination of JFK. I believe that his conduct has been unprofessional and improper. I therefore suggest that his behavior in this case be subjected to a formal review. In my view, the AMA could make an important contribution by clarifying the attitude of the association about the conduct of its journal editor. Whether or not all of the facts in this case will ever be brought to light, it would be unfortunate for the AMA to be even remotely associated with a cover-up in the assassination of President John Fitzgerald Kennedy.

. . . .

°Since JAMA is supposed to be a "peer review" journal, I asked myself what the referees of the articles that appeared in the 27 May 1992 issue should have noted. I would expect comments such as these in any competent referee report, which strongly hints that they were never subjected to review:

p. 2794, left-hand column: the middle paragraph provides an unsupported summary of the Warren Commission's disputed findings as though they had not been repeatedly challenged; moreover, it asserts conclusions regarding the shooter, etc., which go far beyond the medical evidence.

p. 2796, center column: how can a "blatantly obvious" wound create so much controversy? Where is appropriate supporting photographic evidence? If the head was not thoroughly examined, how could he be sure there were no other wounds? What do *photographs of the physicians* prove?

p. 2797, left-hand column: Surely Crenshaw never made the absurd suggestion attributed to him here. More important, if the wound really was a large exit wound of the kind the autopsy photographs display, why would a tracheostomy be performed in the first place? Would it be necessary? Would it not be vital to staunch the flow of blood into the throat, etc.?

p. 2799, right-hand column: how could tracking the neck wound have been "criminal"? How could a proper autopsy be completed in its absence?

p. 2800, center column: to conduct a proper autopsy, the clothes were necessary, so how could a proper autopsy be conducted without them?

p. 2800, right-hand column: if the wounds could not be adequately described in words, why were the photographs not provided? Drawings, like memories, can be distorted; there might be many sets of photographs.

p. 2800, right-hand column: repeatedly this author begs the question by asserting that views at variance with those of the Warren Commission are "crazy conspiracy theories coming out of the woodwork". Begging the question in this blatant fashion does nothing to establish the truth.

p. 2801, right-hand column to p. 2803, left-hand column: are these medical personnel experts on the Garrison investigation and on the movie "JFK"? Here and elsewhere, recollections are used to "establish" facts going far beyond what the doctors could reasonably be assumed to know; yet in other cases, what the doctors could reasonably be assumed to know (such as an Army Lt. Colonel knowing the difference between generals and staff, in the case of Finck, on p. 2802) is forcefully brushed aside. Why are the opinions of Jack Valenti, George Will, Anthony Stone and Paul Galloway quoted in this piece in JAMA? Are they witnesses too?

p. 2804, right-hand column: why not simply show the photos themselves? Here and throughout, why is so much opinion masquerading as fact?

p. 2805, middle column: what did his throat look like *before the incision*?

Summary: there is a disproportionate percentage of opinion and quotation provided in lieu of evidence. The complete absence of documentation undermines the purpose that these "reports" were allegedly intended to fulfill. It reads more like tabloid journalism than scholarly research.

*University of Minnesota, Duluth, MN 55812

JFK's Assassination:
Conpiracy, Forensic Science, and Common Sense

by James H. Fetzer, Ph.D.

Fallacy #1: first paragraph, left hand column, p. 1540:

Artwohl: "correspondence to THE JOURNAL indicates many physicians are still sympathetic to a key proconspiracy tenet regarding the Kennedy assassination: that the autopsy physicians conspired with the military, the Central Intelligence Agency (CIA), the Federal Bureau of Investigation (FBI), the Secret Service, and other agencies of government to disguise and suppress medical evidence that would show President Kennedy was publicly executed in Dealey Plaza on November 22, 1963, by multiple gunmen."

This is an example of *the straw man* fallacy, which creates an artificially inflated version of a position in order to destroy it and thereby claim to have discredited readily available but more defensible versions thereof. Notice, for example, that JFK could have been killed by multiple gunmen without a conspiracy involving the autopsy physicians; that the autopsy physicians could have been unwitting pawns; that the entire military and CIA and FBI or whatever need not have been involved for there to have been a conspiracy; etc. A conspiracy does not require mass mettings, pep rallies in Washington Stadium or anything of the like to exist and succeed.

Consider a parallel argument concerning the Iran-Contra affair: Reagan would have had to consult with his cabinet, the White House, the Central Intelligence Agency (CIA), the State Department and numerous ambassadors, etc. Everyone in Washington would have had to know. So the Iran-Contra affair could never have taken place. Or that legal segregation, for example, should be opposed because it means blacks will be moving into your neighborhood, they will be living next door, dating your daughter, fathering your grandchildren. Or that gay rights means that gays are going to be able to rent rooms in your home, seduce your sons, embarrass your wives and friends, throw naked parties in the backyard, on and on.

Fallacy #2: second paragraph, left hand column, p. 1543:

Artwohl: "To simulate the neck wound, they fired through 14-cm-thick gelatin blocks or animal muscle."

This is a case of *fabricating evidence*. What *neck* wound? We know of an injury to the throat, which Malcolm Perry originally described as a small wound of entrance. We know of one or more possible back wounds, which do not align properly to have been the entry wound for an exit wound at the location of the throat wound. So what wound is Artwohl discussing?

This can also be described as a case of *begging the question* by taking for granted something that is disputed and not in evidence. In the form of a question, this occurs in the form of a *leading question*. When the issue is whether Bentz murdered Klutz, the prosecutor might ask a hostile witness, "Mr. Bentz, what made you think your plan would work?" Of course, there are *drawings* of a neck wound that were used during the Warren inquiry, but the existence of a corresponding neck wound is another thing entirely.

Fallacy #3: third paragraph, left hand column, p. 1543:

Artwohl: "To investigate the head wound, his group fired at gelatin-filled skulls from a distance of 270 feet, approximately the distance from the Texas School Book Depository to President Kennedy's head at the time of the fatal shot. . . . Olivier, a scientist, used his realm of expertise and he formed a reasonable conclusion: Oswald's rifle and ammunition were capable of inflicting both of President Kennedy's wounds."

Several fallacies are going on here at once. Notice the presumption that JFK was hit by only two bullets ("both of [his] wounds"), which obviously *begs the question*, since there is conflicting evidence of a back wound, a throat wound, and possibly two head wounds, not to mention evidence of other missiles that appear to have been fired at the President. Moreover, no indication is given of whether the rifle used (described as "Lee Harvey Oswald's gun") was in the same condition in which it was originally said to have been found (with a misaligned sight, etc.). Nor is there mention of any other experiments conducted by firing from other locations, such as the grassy knoll, the Dal-Tex Building, or the Criminal Courts Building. This is another case of *special pleading* by considering only evidence favorable to your own pre-determined point of view and ignoring the rest.

Notice especially that the only question addressed is whether or not it is *possible* to inflict such wounds with a rifle of that kind. Even if it were possible, that hardly shows that it *happened* or even that its occurrence is *probable*. If Oswald was on the second floor having a Coke, for example, then he could not have been on the sixth floor firing at Kennedy. If the foliage on a Texas oak would have obscured the vision of anyone who fired at the motorcade at the time of the first shot, it is silly to suppose it was fired from that location. Nancy Sinatra *could* have inflicted the damage described *if* she had been there shooting at JFK. The question is not whether a reworked Mannlicher-Carcano could possibly have done the damage—incidentally, precisely which wounds are being accounted for here: the imaginary neck wound? Some specific head wound?—but the actual cause of the actual wounds that the President actually sustained.

Fallacy #4: fourth paragraph, left hand column, p. 1543:

Artwohl: "One must also remember that what might seem unusual or even impossible to the inexperienced may be quite common to the expert. The relatively small amount of deformation of the so-called pristine bullet is a rally cry for the conspirati. However, *forensic pathologists with extensive gunshot* wound experience do not find this unusual."

This is a nice example of the *appeal to authority.* There are two kinds of *appeals to authority,* however, only *one of which is fallacious.* The fallacious appeal occurs *when someone who is an authority in one area is cited as an authority in another.* The non-fallacious appeal occurs if someone *who is an authority in an area* is cited in relation to that area. *Citing Einstein on religion,* for example, *might be fallacious,* but citing *Einstein on physics is not.* In this case, the author is identified with a "Department of Emergency Medicine," but is not otherwise described. Moreover, "forensic pathologists with extensive gunshot experience" who do *not find this [lack of deformation]* "unusual" are uncited except *for an "oral communication" from a* V. G. M. DiMaio. But the case of JFK and the magic bullet is hardly a normal case, and no evidence is cited that establishes that the slightly-deformed bullet under consideration could reasonably have been supposed to have caused all the damage it has to have caused if the magic bullet theory is true. *The question once again is not merely one of possibility but of probability or of actual fact. Observe that the evidence cited is essentially anecdotal ("story telling") instead of comparative studies under controlled experimental conditions.*

Since this concluding section of his paper is entitled, "Forensic Science and Common Sense," it is intriguing *that here he is appealing to expert opinion to correct common sense, which might indeed find the idea that so much damage could be done with so little deformation improbable or impossible.* If common sense and expert opinion conflict, then one might cite whichever "evidence" strengthens your cause. This appears to be a *methodological inconsistency* that functions as a case of *special pleading.*

It may be appropriate to observe that *Lattimer commits a different kind of fallacy in* describing the same bullet *as "deformed and decidedly not pristine"* in Figure 4 on p. 1546, for example. What is going on here is a tacit shift in the *comparison class* that determines *the meaning of the* description of the bullet as "pristine." The bullet shown in Figure 4 may be *"deformed" in relation to bullets in mint condition,* but it is *surely "pristine" in relation to the deformed slugs that typically result from inflicting the kind of damage this* one is supposed to have inflicted. *Using language that is ambiguous* in this fashion is *to commit the fallacy of equivocation.*

Fallacy #5: first paragraph, middle column, p. 1543:

Artwohl: "The autopsy findings and all photographic and available assassination films support the fact that there were two shots from the rear."

Blatant *question begging.* This claim is highly disputed on many grounds and cannot possibly qualify as a "fact" if it is untrue. *Fabricating evidence.*

Fallacy #6: first paragraph, middle column, p. 1543:

Artwohl: "Although the preponderance of nonmedical evidence indicates that Lee Harvey Oswald acted alone as a maladjusted individual killing President Kennedy with a Mannlicher-Carcano rifle, it *cannot totally disprove* his acting with (or being duped by) *a small private group of conspirators in a plot to assassinate President Kennedy.*"

Question begging in the first instance, but *curiously concessionary and disingenuous in the second.* The "nonmedical evidence" to which he refers is no doubt the Warren Commission Report, which was never able to establish that Oswald had either the motive, the means, or the opportunity to assassinate the President. So this part is clearly begging the question. To admit that Oswald might have "acted with . . . a small private group of conspirators in a plot to assassinate President Kennedy," however, is remarkable in several ways. Why would the group have to be *small*? Moreover, how small is "small"? If we add one more member to a small group is it still small? Why couldn't it be *fairly large*? And why does it have to be *private*: to imply that it is not "public"? Do assassins normally conspire in public? A small group plotting together would still be a *conspiracy.* So what he is apparently trying to subtly convey is that "public officials" (of the government) could not possibly have been involved. But how could he possibly know? This is more purely gratuitous begging the question.

Fallacy #7: second paragraph, middle column, p. 1543:

Artwohl: ". . . there are large problems with logic and common sense with the government-led or government-involved conspiracy theories."

Straw man. No one suggests that the government as such was involved, which would invite the question, "If so, which branch?" Individuals who happened to be government officials may have been involved in a conspiracy without it being either government led or government involved. Logic and common sense require that all of the evidence be considered.

Fallacy #8: second paragraph, middle column, p. 1543:

Artwohl: "If the Secret Service, the FBI, the CIA, and other agencies with close access to the President wanted to dispose of him, they could have availed themselves of a number of covert means of dispatch. It is difficult to believe a government-led team of President's assassins came up with the following complex plan. First, take several years setting up Lee Harvey Oswald. Then, get him a job in the Texas School Book Depository so he could be in position to kill the President and meticulously plant evidence with which to frame him. For the central piece of evidence, obtain a cheap mail-order rifle with an inexpensive sight. (Apparently no one thought to spend a few more dollars and get a more credible rifle.) Arrange to have the President fired upon from several different directions using at least three teams of marksmen. (Why would it take several teams of marksmen, not one, not two, but, by conspirati count, three to six volleys of gunfire to hit a slow-moving target at close range with the fatal head shot?) After the President is hit with multiple bullets from multiple directions, the military and numerous government agencies, beginning right at Parkland Hospital, move quickly to conceal multiple bullet holes from civilian physicians (or coerce them all into silence), whisk away bullets, alter the President's body, forge roentgenograms and photographs, and alter every home movie and photograph of the assassination to conceal the true nature of the injuries and the number of accomplices involved."

Absolutely vintage *straw man*. Notice, for example, that conspiracy scenarios do not require involvement by "the military" or "government agencies," numerous or not, but only by enough people in the right places at the right times. Depending on who wanted JFK dead—there are quite a few candidates, from LBJ and J. Edgar Hoover to Charles Cabell and other associates in the CIA, including anti-Castro Cubans and the mob—it may have been more fitting to assassinate him in public, especially by having a convenient patsy to throw off public suspicion, than to remove him by covert means, which would inevitably create questions and motivate inquiries that might have been inconvenient. Moreover, a public execution sends signals of many kinds about who really controls power in the USA. Artwohl betrays a remarkable lack of imagination about the possibilities of conspiracies of different kinds, where there could have been a number of alternative assassination scenarios, with other "patsies" waiting in the wings if the Dealey Plaza scenario had not played itself out. Moreover, it would have been essential to have the means to make sure the President was killed. Triangulated fire provides a standard method of ambush, especially in the case of a moving target, which can be difficult to hit under the best of conditions. (Is Artwohl familiar with the problems involved in hitting relatively small moving targets from 100 yards or so? Here I think his lack of knowledge betrays him. Having several teams would be virtually indispensable to guaranteeing the success of the kill.) Moreover, the problem with the rifle may well have been that easy access to quality weapons by buying them on any corner store in

Dallas would not leave a paper trail to implicate Oswald. Not all the photographic evidence needed to be dealt with—only the most important. Some photographs were not picked up at the scene of the crime, which is one of a number of reasons the case has remained alive. And if Artwohl really wants to understand the behavior of the physicians at Parkland, for example, he ought to pick up a copy of Charles Crenshaw's *Conspiracy of Silence*. This exaggerated caricature of assassination theories may look impressive on the surface, but resorting to such arguments betrays the superficiality of his position.

Fallacy #9: third paragraph, middle column, p. 1543:

Artwohl: "The most astonishing feature of this plan is that the plotters would have to have been confident in advance they would be able to recover every bullet, find every witness, control the movements of hundreds of witnesses, and destroy every photograph and home movie that had incriminating evidence and leave behind those that did not."

Another *straw man*. It is not the case that every bullet had to be found, every witness intimidated or killed, or every photograph or home movie with incriminating evidence be distorted or destroyed. But the more the better. The key is having a story that diverts attention from the actual motives of those who were behind the assassination on to a patsy, preferably one far removed (even apparently of the opposite political persuasion) from those of the conspirators. Artwohl appears to be ignorant of the vast literature on this subject, from *Six Seconds in Dallas* to *Farewell America* to *The Fish is Red* to *Best Evidence* to *High Treason* to *High Treason 2* to *Act of Treason* and many other works that provide substantial evidence of conspiracy and cover up in the assassination of John Kennedy. He mentions a few works, including *Conspiracy* and *Crossfire,* but merely to lampoon them. His understanding of this case appears to be shallow.

Fallacy #10: fourth paragraph to end, middle and last column, p. 1543:

Artwohl: "In the illogical world of the Kennedy assassination conspiracy and its associated booming entertainment industry, any fact or finding that contradicts the popular Rube Goldberg scenario is dismissed as disinformation. Any contrary document or photograph is judged to be a government forgery. Any person or group who questions the conspirati's erroneous or unsubstantiated claims is denounced as a coconspirator or dupe. . . . Even **JAMA**, its editor, and the American Medical Association have been added to the proconspiracy list of accessories after the fact. As the years pass, one thing becomes abundantly clear: for the conspirati, it is conspiracy above all else, including forensic science, and common sense."

Ad hominem (abusing the man). Saving the best for last, Artwohl goes out in a blaze of criticism, which impugns the motives of everyone who ever doubted the account found in the Warren Commission Report. The inadequacies of this position are enormous, since a scientific analysis of any phenomenon must be based upon serious consideration of all of the available evidence. If **JAMA**, its editor, and the American Medical Association are now candidates for being accessories after the fact, it may be because the editor of **JAMA** appears to have abused his position by repeatedly publishing articles that display the application of improper and unwarranted methods of investigation and procedures of inquiry that lead to false or unjustified conclusions and create the impression that the AMA has engaged in a cover-up in the assassination of JFK.

UNITED STATES DISTRICT COURT
FOR THE DISTRICT OF COLUMBIA

D. MARK KATZ,

    Plaintiff,

    v.

NATIONAL ARCHIVES & RECORDS
   ADMINISTRATION,

    Defendant.

Civil Action No.
92-1024 GHR

DECLARATION OF HARRISON E. LIVINGSTONE

I, Harrison E. Livingstone, hereby declare as follows:

1. I am a 1970 graduate of Harvard University and the author of four published novels. I have been researching and writing about the assassination of President John F. Kennedy since 1963. I am an author of <u>High Treason</u>, (Conservatory Press, March 1989), which was a national bestseller for the winters of 1990-91 and 1991-92, and I am the author of <u>High Treason 2</u>, (Carroll & Graf Publishers, Inc., New York 1992), which was a national bestseller in the Spring of 1992.

2. I have spent almost thirty years researching and writing on the assassination. In my informed opinion, most of the autopsy photographic and radiographic materials ("photographs") of the late President Kennedy are already in the public domain. Indeed, they have been published world wide.

3. In 1979, life-like tracings from some of the photographs, purportedly taken during the autopsy, were published by the House of Representatives in the public hearings of the House Select

Committee on Assassinations.   Photographic reproductions of the autopsy x-rays were also published at the same time.

4. Actual photographs of the President's body were published in a reprint of Best Evidence, by David Lifton, (Carroll and Graf, New York, 1988), and by me in High Treason.   These photographs were widely marketed by Robert Groden, who obtained a set of copies from the National Archives, and color reproductions were published in the Globe (a supermarket tabloid), Details, a magazine which printed an autopsy photograph within a cartoon format, in many newspapers throughout the world marketed by Gamma Liaison, through an agreement with Robert Groden, and in stories by Ronald Laytner who writes for the Robert Maxwell newspaper group. Numerous other books, including reprints of Cover-Up: The Governmental Conspiracy to Conceal the Facts About the Public Execution of John Kennedy, by Gary J. Shaw, and Conspiracy, by Anthony Summers, (New York: McGraw-Hill) published some of the autopsy photographs. I included a more complete collection of the autopsy photographs in High Treason 2.

5. Photographs purportedly taken during the autopsy have been reprinted in many foreign newspapers and magazines such as The Mirror, Bild, Sunday Mail, Bilderna. See, e.g., Exhibits A, B, C, & D attached.

6.   The photographs of the autopsy have been shown on broadcasts to mass television audiences, sometimes worldwide, on "KRON" in San Francisco, "Geraldo," Montel Williams, "The Men Who Killed Kennedy," "NOVA," and other shows. Many of these programs

2

have also been distributed to the public on video cassettes.

7. Oliver Stone's blockbuster movie "JFK," which was seen by millions of people in the cinema, or on videocassette, contained autopsy photographs and the actual recreation of Kennedy's body at autopsy. See Exhibit E attached (depicting frames from the movie).

8. It is my professional opinion that there is a tremendous benefit to be gained from the public disclosure of the records at issue in this case. It is of key importance to experts on the assassination to be able to do careful and unhurried studies of the actual prints of the photographs and copies of the x-rays in the National Archives.

9. Worldwide publication of the autopsy photographs has given rise to an active controversy over their authenticity and the accuracy of the conclusions reached by the Warren Commission regarding the assassination. Numerous witnesses who saw the body have come forward and have stated that the published photographs differ from their recollections. Researchers and analysts have also identified a number of respects in which the photographs are technically inaccurate or inconsistent with findings made in various government investigations.

10. A few illustrative examples of these discrepancies include:

    a. I have concluded that the tracings of photographs released by the House Assassination Committee, and the actual photos themselves, reveal that the medical evidence has been tampered with or forged because they

3

depict wounds which are not mentioned in the autopsy report, wounds that had moved as much as four inches, and no wounds at all where there should have been wounds. For example, Jacqueline Kennedy, who I interviewed through her staff, and Tom Joyce, aide and friend to the Kennedy brothers who was familiar with the wounds, have indicated that the photograph of the head published by the House Select Committee is false.

b.   Leading medical witnesses in a 1992 article in The Journal of The American Medical Association ("JAMA") made statements that seriously contradict the available photographs and x-rays. For example, Dr. James J. Humes and Dr. J. Thornton Boswell, the autopsy doctors, severely questioned some of what the pictures show. Moreover, a number of medical personnel at the hospital where the President was taken immediately after the assassination, Parkland Memorial Hospital in Dallas, have denounced the tracings and photographs at one time or another. These witnesses include: Drs. Ronald Coy Jones, Kemp Clark, Fouad Bashour, Charles Baxter, Robert McClelland, Marion Jenkins, Jackie Hunt, Richard Dulaney Adolphe Giesecke, Paul Peters, Gene Akin, Malcolm Perry, Charles Crenshaw, James Carrico, and David Stewart, as well as nurses Diana Bowron, Margaret Henchcliffe, Doris Nelson, Audrey Bell, Patricia (Hutton) Gustafson, and Ambulance Attendant Aubrey Rike. Moreover, the autopsy assistants Floyd Riebe, the medical photographer, and Jerrol Custer, the x-ray technician, who took the photographs and x-rays, insist that these are not the photographs and x-rays that they took. See Exhibit F attached.

c. The testimony of lay witnesses, including mortuary attendants, and the President of Gawler's in Washington, Joseph Hagen, have said that the pictures -- tracings and photos -- do not show the wounds they saw.

11. In my professional opinion, it is simply impossible to ignore the testimony of all the leading medical witnesses, as well as the autopsy doctors themselves, who have repeatedly found fault with the pictures. Various assassination scholars, including myself, have raised serious questions about the authenticity of the publicly available autopsy materials. It is of significant public interest to the assassination research community that the public be allowed access to the x-rays and photographs at the National Archives to address the persistent questions concerning the credibility of the government's conclusions concerning the assassination.

12. The autopsy x-rays and photographs constitute the primary scientific proof of the Warren Commission's theory of the medical evidence. The release of these records will shed light on the government's conduct and how this evidence bears on the conclusions reflected in the government-commissioned Report and in the subsequent study by the House Select Committee on Assassinations.

More precisely, the medical evidence at issue in this suit and in the possession of the National Archives will demonstrate whether the Warren Commission and House Select Committee properly performed its mandate or whether it overlooked significant evidence and reached erroneous conclusions.

13. Access to the records will enable researchers to compare those autopsy records at the National Archives to those already widely disseminated in the public domain, and, accordingly, will inform the current debate in the research community over the wildly differing assessments of the publicly available documents. Thus, access will enable the research community to determine the validity of the conclusions now based on the available materials, as well as the authenticity of the records held by the National Archives.

Pursuant to 28 U.S.C. § 1746 and Local Rule 106(g), I declare under penalty of perjury that the foregoing is true and correct.

Executed this _10_ day of February, 1993.

_____

Harrison E. Livingstone

UNITED STATES DISTRICT COURT
FOR THE DISTRICT OF COLUMBIA

D. MARK KATZ,   )
)
     Plaintiff,   )
)
     v.   )   Civil Action No.
)   92-1024 GHR
NATIONAL ARCHIVES & RECORDS   )
     ADMINISTRATION,   )
)
     Defendant.   )
)
)

DECLARATION OF LOUIS P. KARTSONIS, M.D.

I, Louis P. Kartsonis, M.D., hereby declare as follows:

1. I am a board-certified ophthalmologist in private practice in San Diego. I have published three articles on the assassination of the late President John F. Kennedy.

2. In 1979, I requested permission to view the autopsy materials (the x-rays and optical photographs) requested by the plaintiff in this case. I submit this declaration in support of plaintiff's request for access to those records.

3. I have a scholarly interest in the assassination of President Kennedy. I sought to review the autopsy records based in part on the fact that David Belin, assistant counsel to the Warren Commission and a defender of its report, has acknowledged that the Commission's decision not to examine the post-mortem materials was an error. It is my belief that that decision caused much of the doubt and suspicion that persists concerning the Warren Commission's conclusions regarding the assassination.

4. On November 23, 1979, I examined the post-mortem x-rays

and optical photographs of the late President. Thus, I am among the few individuals who has had access to the records, but who was not associated with a government-commissioned request to review them.

5. On the basis of my examination of the materials, it is my belief, as a physician and assassination scholar, that all materials related to the autopsy of John F. Kennedy should be made public.

6. Release of the x-rays taken during the autopsy would not, in my opinion, result in any invasion of personal privacy. As with most x-rays, these x-rays are clinical in nature; they only reveal the osseous structure of their subject, and not the actual skin and musculature. I have examined the x-rays at issue in this case and they reveal nothing that could lead to the invasion of privacy of the Kennedy family.

7. While release of the optical photographs taken during an autopsy might constitute an invasion of privacy under other circumstances, this would not be true in this case. Both the x-rays and optical photographs at issue in this case have been widely examined and widely published. In fact, some of the optical photographs and x-rays have already been published in at least three books, Best Evidence, High Treason, and High Treason 2. Two of these books made national best-seller lists. In addition, the National Broadcasting Company and the Public Broadcasting Service have shown post-mortem photographs of President Kennedy on national telecasts.

8.   Three decades after the assassination, the right of the
American people to examine materials related to the death of their
President outweighs any interest in preventing the disclosure of
those records.

Pursuant to 28 U.S.C. § 1746 and Local Rule 106(g), I declare
under penalty of perjury that the foregoing is true and correct.

Executed this 11ᵗʰ day of February, 1993.

Louis Kartsonis

Louis P. Kartsonis, M.D.

3

```
                                    )
D. MARK KATZ,                       )
                                    )
     Plaintiff,                     )
                                    )
     v.                             )         Civil Action No.
                                    )         92-1024 GHR
NATIONAL ARCHIVES & RECORDS         )
   ADMINISTRATION,                  )
                                    )
     Defendant.                     )
                                    )
                                    )
```

DECLARATION OF DAVID W. MANTIK, B.S., M.S., Ph.D, M.D.

I, David W. Mantik, B.S., M.S., Ph.D., M.D., hereby declare as follows:

1. I am a board-certified radiologist, and the Director of Radiation Oncology at Eisenhower Memorial Hospital, in Rancho Mirage, California. Since 1980, I have been an Assistant Professor of Radiation Science at the School of Medicine, Loma Linda University, Loma Linda California. I am an active member of a number of professional associations dedicated to the study of radiology and oncology. I am also the author or co-author of numerous scholarly publications in my fields.

2. In the Spring of 1992, I became interested in the assassination of President John F. Kennedy and I began examining some of the available medical data. I learned that reproductions of the Kennedy autopsy x-rays, which are found in popular books, show, on close examination, the presence of many small metallic fragments. It is common in my specialty to use a three dimensional

1

reconstruction based on Anterior/Posterior (AP) and lateral radiographs to identify the precise location of such small metallic objects in each of the three dimensions. In this technique, the spatial coordinates from a number of different photographs are entered into a computer, which is used to localize in three dimensional space the location of each of the objects identified.

3. I was astonished to learn that this type of examination has never been done for the x-rays of the late President Kennedy. My background in physics (Ph.D) and radiology make me almost uniquely suited to this task, and I believe that such a reconstruction would bear heavily on both the authenticity of the x-rays. It may also provide new information concerning the direction of the bullet while in transit through the skull.

4. On August 20, 1992, I wrote to the National Archives to obtain access to the autopsy records, the optical photographs and x-rays at issue in this case, as well as other exhibits presented during the hearings of the House Select Committee on Assassinations. The Committee reported on the existence of three skull x-rays, two laterals and one AP. The Committee published reproductions of one lateral and one AP of these x-rays, but did not publish one of the lateral x-rays. The Committee also published two computer-enhanced reproductions of the published x-rays. A comparison of the two lateral x-rays would be most useful in my own research and might also offer evidence on the authenticity of the x-rays. If such a comparison has ever been made at any time by anyone, it is nowhere reported in the public

record. This comparison needs to be done and it is one of the main reasons that I have asked for access to the x-rays.

5. By letter dated September 3, 1992, I was told that the x-rays and other photographs were "donated to the National Archives by the Kennedy family by an agreement dated October 29, 1966" and that the "agreement limits access to such materials" to persons authorized by the federal government and to recognized experts in the field of pathology or related areas of science whose applications are approved by Burke Marshall, the Kennedy family representative. See Exhibit A attached.

6. Nevertheless, the Archives was willing to sell me reproductions of autopsy records, including photographs of some of the x-rays listed in the deed of gift. By letter dated September 10, 1992, Robert W. Coren ("Coren"), Chief of the Archival Programs Branch of the Center for Legislative Archives at the National Archives, stated that several public exhibits of the Select Committee on Assassinations, including black and white photographs of x-rays, drawings, diagrams, other photographs, and textual documents reproduced in the printed hearing are available for purchase from the Archives. See Exhibit B attached. In a letter dated October 2, Mr. Coren explained that the Archives also sells frames of the Zapruder film, and allows individuals to view the originals at the National Archives. See Exhibit C attached.

7. The Kennedy assassination materials that the Archives offers for sale include 8 x 10 photographs of x-rays of President Kennedy that were reproduced in the published hearings of the

3

Committee's investigation. According to Mr. Coren's September 10, letter, four these published photographs are photographs of x-rays listed in the deed of gift; two are reproductions of original x-rays, and two are computer enhanced reproductions of the original x-rays. See Exhibit B.

8. I have obtained from the National Archives 8" x 12" black and white photographs of one of the lateral and the AP x-ray, as well as the computer-enhanced versions of these x-rays. I have also obtained 3" x 4" negatives of these x-rays. See Exhibits D, E, F & G attached. I have concluded that these photographs of the x-rays must be third, and probably even fourth generation copies of the original. I have reviewed this issue with our medical photographers at Eisenhower Hospital and with pertinent individuals at the National Archives, including the photography lab at the National Archives. All parties concur that the copies which are available to the public must be at least third or fourth generation copies.

9. This lack of access to the original records or second generation copies is a severe limitation when one is attempting high resolution precise work of the type that is required for three dimensional reconstruction as I have described above. I have begun analyzing the optical densities of the skull x-rays based on the 3" x 4" negatives. I have also performed my own experiments starting with x-rays and proceeding through four generations of photographs. From this exercise, it is abundantly clear that significant information is lost in going from the original x-ray to a fourth

4

generation copy. An accurate reconstruction and analysis cannot be performed without access to the originals or superior copies of hte originals.

10. Even though I have obtained from the Archives copies of reproductions and computer-enhanced reproductions of original x-rays borrowed from the Archives, and then published in the House Select Committee Report, in a letter dated December 3, 1992, Mr. Coren stated that the deed of gift also applies to any copies of the autopsy materials that were provided to the House Select Committee on Assassinations. See Exhibit H. Access to the original x-ray films must be obtained through Mr. Marshall.

11. In a letter dated September 11, 1992, I wrote to Mr. Burke Marshall at the Yale Law School, by certified mail, to explain my interest in conducting a three-dimensional reconstruction of metallic objects, or bone, from the autopsy x-rays at issue in this case. I indicated that I wanted him to permit me to proceed with the proposed reconstruction and that I would be in Washington, D.C. in October of 1992. See Exhibit I attached. Although I received a return receipt, to date, I have not heard from Mr. Marshall concerning my request. See Exhibit J attached.

12. X-rays in general are of a clinical nature; they show only the images of the skeletal structure. Based on my professional examination of publicly available reproductions of the autopsy x-rays, I conclude that the x-rays at issue here would not personally invade the privacy of the family.

5

13. It is my professional opinion that the public debate surrounding the assassination would benefit from access to the x-rays. I believe that information on the x-rays may show where shots came from and thereby help to resolve some of the issues concerning the conspiracy theories.

Pursuant to 28 U.S.C. § 1746 and Local Rule 106(g), I declare under penalty of perjury that the foregoing is true and correct.

Executed this 12th day of February, 1993.

Dr. David W. Mantik
_____
Dr. David W. Mantik

APPENDIX J

ENCYCLOPEDIA OF MEDICAL EVENTS AND
WITNESSES TESTIMONY
by Harrison E. Livingstone and Kathlee Link Fitzgerald

ANDREWS AIR FORCE BASE

At 5:00 P.M., Capt. Patton informed the Military District of Washington (MDW) that the "President's remains will arrive AAFB (Andrews Air Force Base) 18:05 hrs."(b)

At "approximately 5:55 P.M. agents were advised through the Hyattsville Resident Agency that the Bureau had instructed that the agents accompany the body to the National Naval Medical Center, Bethesda Maryland."(h)

At about 6:00 P.M. O'Neill received word that J. Edgar Hoover said he and Sibert were to get the evidence recovered from the body.(f)

At 5:58 P.M. the plane landed at Andrews (b, WR 59, 2H102). This touchdown time is also confirmed by Marie Fehmer in her notes written while aboard Air Force One on Nov. 22, 1963. The plane taxied to a stop at 6:05 P.M. (c, f)

Immediately upon landing, Samuel Bird, the officer in charge of the joint service casket team, reported to Gen. McHugh who informed Bird that the Secret Service would remove the casket from the aircraft. (d) Prior to 5:30 P.M., a call had been placed from the presidential plane (AF1) regarding the instructions that "Secret Service agents aboard the aircraft would remove the President's casket." (d) Bird reports that upon "seeing that the casket was being poorly handled, I had two (2) men remain in place on the truck (the lift that had been wheeled to the rear exit door of AF1). We assisted General McHugh and the agents until they had the casket out of the aircraft." (d)

A second casket team had been positioned on the ground at the left side of the lift, and as this team moved forward to secure the casket, the casket team "was disrupted by a host of agents moving forward pushing the team out of the way. The agents then placed the casket in an awaiting Navy ambulance." (d) This incident is also outlined in the MDW "After Action Report" which states that "A joint service casket bearer and security detail met the remains of the late President Kennedy at Andrews Air Force Base at 221805 Nov. 22, 1963 but were prevented from removing the remains from the aircraft. The detail assisted the Secret Service in transferring the remains to an ambulance for movement to U.S. Naval Medical Center, Bethesda, Maryland." (c)

FROM ANDREWS TO BETHESDA

The Navy ambulance left with the body at approximately 6:15 P.M.–6:20 P.M for Bethesda Naval Hospital. Roy Kellerman, the chief of the Secret Service detail who accompanied President Kennedy, testified to the Warren Commission, "By the time it took us to take the body from the plane into the ambulance, and a couple of carloads of staff people who followed us, we may have spent fifteen minutes there. And in driving from Andrews to the U.S. Naval Hospital, I would' judge, a good 45 minutes." (2H102–3)

Francis X. O'Neill, the FBI man present at the autopsy, said that he "had the plane in my eye view every single moment from the time it pulled in front of me on the tarmac, there, where the headquarters was, until the body was taken out. So any possibility of somebody taking the body out on the other side is as far as Lifton is concerned, is ridiculous." (a: May 20, 1991)

The record is quite clear that Bethesda Naval Hospital was the destination of the ambulance carrying the body of President Kennedy. At 4:00 P.M., Paul Miller called General Wehle and informed him that the late President would go "to the Naval Medical Center for autopsy." (e) At 5:00 P.M., Capt. Patton informed MDW headquarters that the "remains" were to be taken from Andrews Air Force Base to Bethesda. (b) At 5:30, "General Clifton radioed by phone General Mock at 17:30 that President Kennedy will be taken directly to Bethesda [sic] Naval Hospital." (e)

David Lifton, initiator of the "body-was-secretly-taken-off-Air-Force-One-and-taken-to-Walter-Reed-for-body-alteration-to-disguise-the-wounds" theory, admitted on the Nov. 19, 1991, "Ron Reagan Show" that "I personally today, in 1991, don't think they went to Walter Reed . . . But the fact that they're talking Walter Reed, and about a ramp on the starboard side of the plane, and one of them says on the radio, we're going to bring the First Lady off by that route." The First Lady, at the time of those radio transmissions from Air Force One was Lady Bird Johnson, and Kennedy's body was not secretly taken to Walter Reed Hospital, as is reinforced by the statements of O'Neill.

O'Neill was asked if the body was taken to Malcolm Grow Hospital on Andrews Air Force Base. "That had nothing to do with this particular thing. The body was never taken there. I was in the second car in the motorcade. There were no stops anywhere, no stops at Walter Reed—it went straight all the way through to Bethesda."

"It was always in your sight?"

"Of course." (a: May 20, 1991)

Accompanying O'Neill in the same car in the motorcade from Andrews to Bethesda were Pam Turnure (the widow's assistant), FBI Agent Sibert, and the White House valet. O'Neill gave the route of the ambulance from Andrews to Bethesda, as well as the information that he had been in the service and knew well some of the men at Andrews: The Provost Marshal in charge of security, the legal officer of the base, and so on, with whom he had been at school or in the service. (a: Nov. 20, 1991) O'Neill and Sibert were attached to Andrews Air Force Base (f) and reported to the Baltimore office of the FBI. (a: Nov. 20, 1991)

"Questioning the Facts: Research v. Witness," an extensive two-and-a-half-hour long interview was conducted in 1992 with O'Neill and George Michael Evica, made by Jack Gambardella, Team Video Productions. In it, O'Neill made the following observations: That the trip from Bethesda took about 35 to 45 minutes. He said that they didn't go at break–neck speed, but not too slowly either. He reiterated that the ambulance bearing the casket from Andrews to Bethesda "never left my sight." (f)

It was a 45-minute trip from Andrews Air Force Base to Bethesda. (WR 59; Kenneth O'Donnell, 2 H 455, 2 H 102–3; and (i), p. 391)

BETHESDA TIME OF ARRIVAL

The sun set at 4:48 P.M. on Nov. 22, 1963. This meant that it would be dark on that damp and partly cloudy night by 5:30 P.M. or so. Air Force 1 did not touch down until 5:58 P.M. The ambulance would not have arrived at Bethesda until about 7:00 P.M. There is no absolute, clear record stating a unified time for the exact moment of arrival of the ambulance.

Testimony before the Warren Commission has the ambulance coming in at about 6:55, 7:00, or 7:05 P.M.

6:50 P.M. an Army escort officer's report states that he had been ordered by the Provost Marshall's office to "proceed to Bethesda Naval Hospital, Bethesda, Maryland, and rendezvous with the CG, MDW." This order was given at approximately 5:45–5:50 P.M. "I arrived at the Naval Hospital at approximately 18:50 hours. The remains of the deceased President arrived at the same time." (g)

6:55 P.M: the Warren Commission testimony of Clint Hill (18 H 744) and Landis (18 H 757) cite Mrs. Kennedy as leaving the ambulance in front of Bethesda at 6:55 P.M.

7:00 P.M.: Kellerman testified to the Warren Commission that the distance from "Andrews to the U.S. Naval Hospital, I would judge, [is] a good 45 minutes. So there is 7 o'clock. We went immediately over, without too much delay on the outside of the hospital, into the morgue." (2 H 102–3)

6:55 to 7:15 P.M. Francis X. O'Neill recalls that the car in which he was riding from Andrews to Bethesda pulled up right behind the ambulance in front of Bethesda. Roy Kellerman got out. McHugh, Larry O'Brien, and Ken O'Donnell were there at the front of Bethesda talking for 10–12 minutes. O'Neill got out of his car and asked them what the hold up was. They told him that they did not know where to go, and no one had instructed them where to go. Because O'Neill was familiar with the layout of the hospital, he knew where the morgue was and how to get there. O'Neill had the ambulance follow him to the rear dock outside the morgue. "It [the ambulance] came right with us. Right there. No extra buts. In view all the time." (f)

Air Force One landed at Andrews Air Force Base at 5:58 P.M. (Roy Kellerman, 2 H 102; WR 59) The casket, Mrs. Kennedy and Robert Kennedy were in the ambulance and left by approximately 6:15 P.M. The trip took no more than 45 minutes. (Kenneth O'Donnell, 2 H 455; WR 59) There was a few minutes' delay before the body was taken around back, but it should have actually been at the morgue dock at between 7:05 P.M. at the earliest to about 7:17 P.M. at the latest.

There sometimes appears that half an hour is missing after the alleged arrival, and that half–hour is crucial because of what has been alleged regarding what may or may not have happened off the record at Bethesda. Kellerman and the Warren Commission has the body arriving at 7:00, but the House Committee (7 HSCA 8) and Humes (2 H 349) has it come in 35 minutes later. Why is there a thirty–minute discrepancy? This cannot be explained as a simple mistake. Two different investigations have two different answers, without explanation. An explanation may be as simple as, in times of crisis and great stress, which definitely applies to the murder of a President, exact times are not the paramount issue and are not given a lot of attention by most individuals. Also the perception of the passing of time under such circumstances may seem very slow or very fast to different individuals. Therefore, when a witness places an event in a particular time slot, it is important to go to records of exact time notations, place the event recalled by the witness within those time slots, and determine if the recorded time and the witness' time is the same or to what degree they vary. In the Kellerman/Humes example, Kellerman's 7:00 P.M. arrival at Bethesda was an estimate predicated on the approximate time he thought he left Andrews and the trip from Andrews to Bethesda taking "I would judge, a good 45 minutes." The record shows he could be off on the 7:00 P.M. time by plus or minus five minutes. Kellerman got out at the front of Bethesda, presumably walked through the hospital in order to reappear coming out of the rear of the hospital at the morgue dock (f), helped unload the casket from the ambulance there, and helped take that casket to the autopsy room. These events can be placed in time by other witnesses and the records to have occurred in a general time slot of at the earliest 7:07 P.M. to about 7:20 P.M. at the latest. Kellerman merely states: "We went immediately over, *without too much delay* on the outside of the hospital, into the morgue." In considering the Humes statement that the body arrived at the autopsy room at 7:35 P.M., it is not clear how he determined that time. Did he look at his watch? If so, how accurate was his watch? Or was he also approximating the time predicted on his perception of the passage of time?

ARRIVAL AT THE MORGUE DOCK

7:07 to 7:18 P.M.: O'Neill reports that as he and the ambulance pulled up to dock outside the morgue, Kellerman was walking out of the rear entrance where they were. "The four of us (Kellerman, Sibert, O'Neill, and Greer) opened the back of the ambulance and the four of us took the casket out . . . They moved out a stretcher or cart and the President was placed on that. There was also an Honor Guard coming out and we, meaning all of us, pushed that particular dolly with the President's body on it into the—up the little ramp and through the doors" and into the autopsy room. O'Neill insisted that it was a "ceremonial casket," and "not a shipping casket." (f)

O'Neill affirmed his statement prior to the 1992 video that "Kellerman, Greer, and myself took the casket out of the ambulance . . . We were met by the Honor Guard." (a: May 5, 1991)

O'Neill was unable to answer the questions concerning the arrival time differentials, if any in fact exist. (f)

James Metzler was alone with Paul preparing the autopsy room. He went out on the platform to receive the coffin. (a: June 1, 1991)

James Metzler remembers that a dress military team was there in the back of a pickup truck. (a: May 27, 1991) He also recalls that the ambulance "was unloaded by men in dress military uniforms" (a: May 27, 1991), and that they were "from all the Services." (a: Sept. 28, 1991) He recalled men in Army uniforms, a sailor, and men in other service uniforms. He also stated that an old admiral with gray hair and a moustache wanted to help. This had to be the Honor Guard with Kellerman, Greer, O'Neill, and Sibert. Metzler held the door open and stated that he saw the casket go into the autopsy room. (a: June 1, 1991) This makes Metzler a direct chain-of-possession witness of the casket from the ambulance to the autopsy room.

Metzler had previously stated "It was not yet completely dark outside. What struck me when I saw the videos of the plane landing and the coffin being removed was that it was dark outside, and when we received the body, it was not yet dark." (a: May 27, 1991, repeated at the recording with Mark Crouch on June 1, 1991.) This cannot be possible unless the body was not on Air Force 1 and came earlier, as has been charged. However, there may not have been enough time for the body to get from Dallas according to any body-theft scenario in time to be in Maryland before 5:30 P.M. or so, when it would be dark. That is 4:30 Dallas time, and the body did not leave Parkland until 2:14 P.M. The body either had to be stolen sometime earlier from Parkland, or taken off the plane before it left Dallas. In order to give either of these two scenarios any credibility, the body would probably have had to go on a supersonic plane, and that is highly unlikely. Body theft is not necessary to prove that the evidence could be manipulated and tampered with in such a way so as to cover up the real evidence. According to Metzler, the body (we would have to surmise because of the light in the sky) arrived at the hospital before 5:30 P.M.

Metzler has since stated that he might be wrong about it still being daylight when the coffin arrived. (a: Sept. 1991) It is likely that it was still light when he was alerted that Kennedy was expected to arrive at Bethesda, and that it was still light when he began waiting for that arrival. However, it is NOT likely, by the majority of accounts, that it was still daylight when the late President did, indeed, arrive.

Roy Kellerman stated: "We went immediately over, without too much delay on the outside of the hospital, into the morgue." (2 H 102–3)

Bishop writes that "The body was driven to a rear entrance. It was taken out of the ambulance and placed in an empty and well-lighted corridor. There it reposed. McHugh stood by it and wondered what had happened. Kellerman and Greer stood looking around. No one spoke. No one appeared. They waited." (j: p. 338)

Bishop, a writer and a non-witness, is the only one to report a pause in the hall located between the door to the dock and the autopsy room. This does not mean that a momentary pause did or did not occur. It just has not been stated as occurring by the actual witnesses.

ARRIVAL AT THE AUTOPSY ROOM

7:00 P.M.: Jerrol Custer says that the body had to have come about seven. But he says that he was then asked to leave the morgue with Reed and that he was brought back sometime after 8 P.M. and found that they had already made the Y incision. (a: Sept. 23, 1991) The record indicates that the Y incision was done either after 8:00 P.M. or 8:15 P.M. If he is right, there is an enormous amount of lying going on by the doctors.

However, Custer has made conflicting statements regarding the time of the arrival of the body. Custer has repeatedly said that he had already taken some of his X-rays and was taking a set of films up to be developed when he encountered Mrs. Kennedy and her entourage in the Rotunda. He places the real arrival of the body at least a half hour before she came. (a: Sept. 23, 1991) The record reflects Mrs. Kennedy arriving at Bethesda between 6:50 P.M.–7:05 P.M. According to Custer's statement, this would mean, that the body arrived between 6:20 P.M.–6:35 P.M. Custer's sighting of Mrs. Kennedy after he had already taken X-rays of her husband's body is completely contradicted by his statements that he did not take those X-rays for about an hour after the body came. (a: Sept. 23, 1991) This would place Mrs. Kennedy arriving at the front of Bethesda at 7:20 P.M.–7:35 P.M., and that did not happen. Custer also told Warren Patton (Dec. 2, 1988) that he started taking X-rays at 6:45 P.M. which, according to his other statements, would place the body arriving around 5:45 P.M., and Mrs. Kennedy's arrival at 6:15 P.M. at the earliest. Again, this is not consistent with the record.

Paul O'Connor said he heard two helicopters. "The morgue was full of people. We were all in there. There were two helicopters and one landed out in the rear someplace, and I think it was in the Officer's Club parking lot. Yeah, and as soon as that happened, it was about oh, 3 or 4 minutes later that the door burst open and in came the casket and we started. (a: Apr. 19, 1990)

7:00–7:14 P.M.: At 7:00 P.M., "Sgt. Humphrey, CG's Driver, checked into the office and advised that they were still at Bethesda." (e) Humphrey had been waiting for General Wehle to arrive there at the back of Bethesda. "At about 19:14 (7:14 P.M.) hours the CG arrived with his aide." (g)

7:30 P.M.: "At 19:30, General Wehle called his office . . ." (c) It is not logical to assume that Wehle would be making calls until AFTER the casket had been delivered to the autopsy room.

7:35 P.M.: "19:35: Sgt. Farland called and stated CG, DMW (Wehle) is on his way from Naval Medical Center to Hq, DMW." (b) It is logical to assume that Wehle would not have left Bethesda before his casket team had helped deliver the casket to the autopsy room.

7:35P.M.: Dr. Humes told the WC that "The President's body came at 25 minutes before 8." (2 H 349) He also told the House Committee that the body "arrived about 7:35, 7:40 in the evening." (7 HSCA 324)

8:00 P.M.: Dr. John Ebersole said that the body came in at 8 P.M. (*Philadelphia Inquirer,* March 10, 1978). Paul O'Connor also originally had said it had come in at 8 P.M. This would seem impossible because the plane landed at 5:58 P.M. and the body would have had to arrive at the hospital at around 7 P.M. Unless it stopped somewhere, which is unlikely and contrary to the existing records and witness testimony. Paul O'Connor was absolutely certain that he logged the body in at 8 P.M., with the number A 63 272. O'Connor told Lifton it was about 8 P.M.: O'Connor insisted that the casket arrived at 8:00 P.M. on the dot, and that he had entered that information in the autopsy log. O'Connor also told the HSCA it came in at 8 P.M. (7 HSCA p. 15)

However, on about June 10, 1991, Paul began to express doubt about the 8 P.M. idea. (a) He realized he did not really know for sure, and that he thought he was wrong. It could be that he merely entered the room then, looked at the clock and logged in the body. Or it may be the time that, after the preliminary examination, X-rays, and photographs, the autopsy began. O'Connor may not have been there when the casket actually arrived in the autopsy room and did not arrive until the body was placed on the autopsy table. This is evidenced in the following statements: 1. Only two men carried the casket into the autopsy room. (a: April 20, 1990) This is incorrect and is very contrary to many other confirmed witness accounts; 2. The body was nude with a sheet wrapped around the head. (a: April 20, 1990; May 9, 1990) At no time does he mention any sheet other than around the head. The relevant omission here in O'Connor's statements is the sheet that was wrapped around the body and removed to reveal the nude body; 3. O'Connor's recollections of who removed the body from the casket is, for the most part, inaccurate; and

4. O'Connor first stated that he was not there when the body was removed from the coffin (a: April 20, 1990), and then said nineteen days later that he was there for the removal. (a: May 9, 1990)

Metzler does not recall Paul O'Connor being there when he came back in with the casket from the dock area, though by then the room had filled with people and Paul may have been in the background. Metzler held the door open. (a: June 1, 1991)

O'Connor does state that: "The photographs were taken before the actual autopsy began. Yes, the scalp was retracted so that the wound would be seen. After the autopsy began, there were *no photos* taken." (Letter from O'Connor to Livingstone, June 11, 1990)

Quoting from a radiographers' magazine article about Edward F. Reed: "Reed was in the morgue when the President's casket arrived. 'I was asked to assist in carrying it. There were three gentlemen on one side of the casket and two on my side, and it started to slip out of my hands because it weighted 600–700 pounds. I said to a five-star admiral standing there 'Admiral, can you help me with this?', and he ran over and grabbed it. Later I realized that I had been telling a five-star admiral to help me and he had been saying 'Yes, sir. Yes, sir' to me.' " (*RT Images,* Nov. 21, 1988).

According to Metzler, Boswell was present when the coffin came into the autopsy room. (a: June 1, 1991)

Stringer said that he was there when the body arrived and he helped remove it from the casket. (a: Apr. 29, 1990)

Rudnicki said, "I remember the casket being wheeled in." He remembers that it was the bronze casket. (a: Oct. 14, 1990)

Jenkins was in the morgue. (a: May 24, 1991). But Jenkins did not get a close look at the casket.

WHERE WAS THE COFFIN PUT DOWN?

Jim Metzler: "The casket went into the autopsy room" (a: June 1, 1991) and "I saw them put the coffin down on the floor of the autopsy room by the door. It was not put down in the cold room." (a: May 27, 1991) He helped remove the body from that coffin, put it on the table, and take off the sheet.

Paul O'Connor: "The coffin was put down beside the table in the autopsy room." (a: April 19, 1990; May 26, 1991)

Edward F. Reed states: "We laid the casket on the floor." (*RT Images,* Nov. 21, 1988) Reed does not clearly say it was in the morgue, but he was in the morgue when the casket arrived and he helped carry it in and set it down.

Francis O'Neill states that it was put in the autopsy room but did not specify exactly where. (a: May 5, 1991)

WHEN THE AUTOPSY STARTED

The start of the autopsy may generally be construed as when the examination begins, not the making of the Y incision. However, some may consider the autopsy as actually beginning only after the preliminary examinations have been completed. This difference in meaning could account for the various stated times concerning the start of the autopsy.

7:00 P.M. to 8:00 P.M.: Jan Rudnicki said that the autopsy began "at 7 or 8 P.M." (a: Oct. 14, 1990)

7:30 P.M.: Roy Kellerman testified that "The Navy people had their staff in readiness right then. There wasn't anybody to call. They were all there. So at the latest, 7:30, they began to work on the autopsy." (2H102–3)

8:00 to 8:15 P.M.: Dr. Humes told the Warren Commission that "the autopsy began at approximately 8 P.M. that evening." (2 H 349) and after some preliminary examinations, about 8 or 8:15." (7 HSCA 324)

8:05 P.M.–8:20 P.M.: after the casket was unloaded, Custer and the other X-ray techs were asked to leave. They waited elsewhere about three–quarters of an hour and when they came back, *Custer says the Y incision had been made.* (a: Sept. 23, 1991) This would be about 7:30 P.M. according to Custer's recollection of when the body arrived at around 6:30 P.M. This, of course, does not add up and conflicts with all other suppositions that the X-rays and photographs were first taken and then the head was examined. But there is no clear–cut documentation that the Y incision was in fact made *after* the above would have been normally done and may very well have been made beforehand. An autopsy may be thought of as beginning when they first begin examining a body, not when the first cut is made. Custer has also stated that the body arrived about 7 P.M. Allowing for time to remove and unwrap the body, Custer's statement that he arrived back in the autopsy room about 45 minutes later would place him there at about 8:05 P.M. However, using the body arrival time span of 7:17 P.M. to 7:35 P.M., Custer would have re-entered the room at approximately between 8:05 P.M. and 8:20 P.M. Humes stated that the first incision was made at approximately 8 P.M. or 8:15 P.M. (7 HSCA 11; 2 H 349)

It has been suggested that just as in a court where people go up to the judge's desk to have a private word off the record, or when a committee ducks into executive session or "in camera," there is always a lot off the record. The Warren Commission operated that way, with many private talks with witnesses before they went on the record, and the record clearly reflects often enough changes in direction and statement by a witness after Specter, Belin or Liebeler had a word with them.

What we apparently have at the autopsy is a lot that happened before things went on the record at 8 or 8:15 P.M.

What has been postulated is the possibility of two different autopsies and two different bodies, unless these men are each planting some piece of conflicting information to cloud the record. It's hard not to believe much of what they say, and so wonder if there is some major deception in this hall of mirrors that is being missed, such as two autopsies. But the most likely explanation is the fact that a lot seems to have happened while off the record, and that may include tampering to remove bullets, although the procedure may not necessarily have been performed by the autopsy doctors. It seems, though, that the doctors would have had to have known if something was done at Bethesda to remove bullets.

If what Custer says about the Y incision having been done before he began his X-rays, is correct, then it is clear evidence that there was some extensive examination of the body surgery before the autopsy actually officially began.

HSCA said Humes made the first incision at approximately 8:15. (7 HSCA 11) The Sibert and O'Neill FBI autopsy report says the same thing. (h) This means that prior to whatever incision that was, the photos and X-rays were made, and then the examination of the head began and was concluded. That gives approximately 40 minutes to one hour to do all of the above, which is reasonable.

10:30 P.M.: Lifton says that Ebersole told him that "we actually started the autopsy formally about ten-thirty at night." Both Lifton and Ebersole seem quite mixed up on a number of things at the autopsy.

FBI Report: Although many names of those in attention during the autopsy do not appear, this report does give some time frames to when some people were there: 1) At the beginning: Holloway [sic, this should be Galloway], Burkley, Humes, Stoner [sic, this should be Stover], Stringer, Ebersole, Reibe, Boswell, Rudnicki, O'Connor, Jenkins, Custer, Reed, and Metzler; 2) Came in during autopsy: Finck, Gregg Cross, David Osborne, and Gen. Wehle; 3) Came in towards the end of autopsy: AMC Chester Boyers; and 4) At the end of the autopsy: "personnel from Gawlers" John Van Hausen, Stroble, Tom Robinson, and Joe Hagen. Noted as "also present" but without a time reference were McHugh and Dr. George Bakeman. (h)

O'Neill stated that Mrs. Kennedy wanted only a partial autopsy, but the four Secret Service and FBI agents (Kellerman, Greer, Sibert, and O'Neill) wanted a full autopsy. "Galloway asked us if we would like that [a full autopsy], and we said 'yes' and he [Galloway] was the one who ordered a full autopsy." (f)

REMOVAL OF BODY FROM CASKET and UNWRAPPING THE BODY

O'Connor said he thought that the following people helped remove the body from the casket: Humes, Boswell, Finck, Jenkins, and maybe Custer. (a: May 18, 1991) Boswell did assist with the removal, but Jenkins and Custer did not. Finck may not have arrived in time to help with the removal of the body from the casket, and then everyone waited for Finck's arrival, which the testimony seems to indicate.

O'Connor also states that neither O'Neill nor Sibert helped remove the body from the coffin. (a: May 26, 1991) O'Neill, however, has stated that he did help remove the body from the casket. (f) Jenkins has stated that he did not help unload the casket, but he thought O'Connor had. However, O'Connor did not help remove the body from the casket. Stringer helped take the body out and put it on the table. (a: Apr. 29, 1990; May 11, 1990)

Edward Reed helped carry in the casket and remove the body from the casket in the morgue. (*RT Image,* Nov. 21, 1988)

Jan Gail Rudnicki helped place the body on the table ("I remember the casket being wheeled in"), the removal of the body from that casket, and placing the body on the table. (a: Oct. 14, 1990)

Metzler was present when the casket was opened, and helped remove the body from the coffin, put it on the table, and take off the sheet. He saw the head unwrapped. Then he was asked to leave. (a: May 5, 1991)

Dr. John H. Ebersole said to Art Smith that he helped remove the body from the casket. (July, 1978, *The Continuing Inquiry*)

Dr. Thornton Boswell helped.

Paul O'Connor helped unwrap the head. (a: Apr. 20, 1990; May 9, 1990)

Jim Jenkins helped unwrap the head. (a: Oct. 8, 1990)

Dr. James Humes unwrapped the head.

Jerrol Custer saw the body come out of the casket but did not help with the removal of the body from the casket. (a: Oct. 23, 1991)

Admiral Osborne witnessed the removal of the body from the casket. (7 HSCA graph 84–5)

Jerrol Custer and Jim Metzler say that they and Reed were asked to leave as soon as the body was unwrapped.

THE BODY BAG

There is a semantic confusion over what is meant by body bag. To some, it refers to an especially manufactured "crash bag" which is designed to contain a body. Few former police officers such as Paul O'Connor would call a crash bag a body bag, which usually refers to any materials used to wrap up and contain a body.

O'Connor has often said that the body bag he saw was made of a rubberized material. Manchester writes in regards to the events at Parkland Hospital in Dallas, "Motioning to Orderly David Sanders, Oneal directed him to line the inside of the coffin with a sheet of plastic. Nurse Doris Nelson and Diana Bowron swooped around wrapping the body in a second plastic sheet. Then the undertaker asked Doris to bring him a huge rubber sheath and a batch of rubber bags. Placing the sheath over Sanders' plastic lining, he carefully cut the bags to size, enveloping the President's head in them one by one until he had made certain that there would be seven protective layers of rubber and two of plastic between the damaged scalp and the green satin. All this took twenty minutes." (i, p. 294)

Nurse Diana Bowron told Livingstone that "A clear plastic sheet was placed in the bottom of the coffin, which may have been a mattress cover. The body was wrapped in—at the most—two sheets plus the one around the head. All the sheets were white and none had zips. There was no 'body bag.' " (*Killing The Truth*)

General Wehle, who may be assumed to be Manchester's source, described how "Two naval officers had sliced away Vernon Oneal's rubber and plastic envelopes. . . ." (i, p. 400)

Edward F. Reed states: "We laid the casket on the floor" (*RT Images,* Nov. 21, 1988) and "opened it up and there's President Kennedy laying there, in the nude, in a plastic bag with no flags draped over him." Reed does not state that this was or was not a body bag, merely what appeared to him to be a plastic bag. This material had to be somewhat transparent because of Reed's statement that he had observed that the body was nude. This possibly could have been the plastic material mentioned by Manchester. Reed also is not explicit here as to any other wrappings like sheets or the sequence of events in which he observed that the President was nude.

O'Neill: "We opened the casket . . . The body was wrapped in a sheet, after they had taken off this plastic type material that was wrapped around him." (f)

WITNESSES WHO REPORT SEEING A BODY BAG

Paul O'Connor: O'Connor said he saw a body bag. (a: Apr. 19, 1990; 7 HSCA 15, graph 85; David Lifton, *Best Evidence,* p. 599) "I can't be wrong about the body bag" (a: May 18, 1991) He also said that he told Lifton about it before Lifton could mention it. (a: May 18, 1991) "The casket was opened and inside was a slate gray, rubber body bag with a zipper that ran from the head all the way down to the toes . . . We unzipped the body bag and inside was the body of the President." (*The Men Who Killed Kennedy,* BBC, Oct. 25, 1988)

Jim Jenkins: "I can't say it was or was not in a body bag." (a: Apr. 6, 1991)

Jerrol Custer: Custer said that there was a shipping casket in the morgue, but he had no knowledge of the President's body being in it. He said that there was a body of an officer there, in a body bag and in a shipping casket. (a: Oct. 8, 1990)

However, at a later time, Custer said the President was in a body bag. (a: Sept. 23, 1991; and on film Nov. 22, 1991) "They brought the body out, and that's when I saw the body bag." "Not a mattress cover?" "It was a body bag." "He was inside of it?" "Right." "Zipped in?" "Right." (a: Sept. 23, 1991)

Riebe reported that he thought the President was in a body bag. (a: Apr. 1, 1991; Apr. 5, 1991)

Capt. John Stover: "I think there was a body bag . . . I think I remember seeing a body bag peeled off." Stover is not definite in his remembrance and the interviewer who recorded this statement says: "On a number of points, Captain Stover's memory was very fuzzy . . ." (Lifton, *Best Evidence,* Carroll & Graf, 1988, p. 630)

WITNESSES WHO REPORT THERE WAS NO BODY BAG

Stringer, who helped take the body out of the casket and put it on the table, states that there was no body bag. (a: Apr. 29, 1990; May 11, 1990)

Metzler said: "There was no body bag. Definitely not a body bag." (a: May 27, 1991)

O'Neill said definitely no body bag. (f)

THE WRAPPINGS: TOWELS

Jenkins is the only person who recalls that the head was wrapped in small hand towels *underneath* the sheet. The body did not leave Parkland like that.

Jenkins said that the head was wrapped in two bath towels and inside that, barber towels, all within the sheet. (a: Apr. 6, 1991)

Custer has firmly stated that: "There were no towels around his head. There were sheets."

"Entirely sheets?"

"Yeah."

"No terry cloth towels inside the sheet?"

"I don't remember seeing any of that."

"There was a sheet around the outside which every one remembers, and that's how . . ."

"Yeah, I remember seeing that." (a: Apr. 4, 1991)

Metzler also reports there were no towels. (a: May 27, 1991) Diana Bowron states there were no towels around the head when the body left Parkland in Dallas (interview with the author, 1993; and in *Killing The Truth*.)

SHEETS

Aubrey Rike (Oneal Funeral Home, Dallas): "They told us to go into the trauma room and prepare the President to be moved. He had his head wrapped in sheets . . . We wrapped him in one of the sheets and placed him in the casket." (*The Men Who Killed Kennedy*, BBC TV documentary, Oct. 25, 1988)

Diana Bowron (Parkland): "Miss Henchcliffe and myself prepared the body by removing the remaining clothes . . . and covered him with a sheet." (6 WC 134–9)

Custer remembers the head being wrapped in sheets. (a: Apr. 28, 1991)

Paul O'Connor, "And I removed the sheet and we got on with it." (a: Apr. 19, 1990) "We put the body on the table. He was nude, no clothes on. He had a white sheet, a bloody white sheet on, wrapped around his face and head." (*The Men Who Killed Kennedy*, BBC, Dec. 25, 1988)

Metzler stated that he assisted in removing sheets from the body after it was placed on the table. (a: May 27, 1991)

"I am definite about seeing Kennedy's body inside the coffin which was carried into the morgue. His head was wrapped in a sheet which was very bloody. A separate sheet covered his body. I helped to remove Kennedy's body from the coffin and lay it on the autopsy table." (Letter from Metzler to Livingstone, June 18, 1991)

O'Neill: "We opened the casket and we assisted in taking the President's body out . . . The body was wrapped in a sheet, after they had taken off this plastic–type material that was wrapped around him.'' O'Neill stated that there were two sheets: "one wrapped around the body . . . one wrapped around the head.'' (f)

FBI Report: the body "was wrapped in a sheet and the head area contained additional wrapping . . . clothes had been removed.'' (h)

A BULLET OR FRAGMENT IN WRAPPINGS OF THE BODY

Jerrol Custer has said: "When we lifted him up, a bullet dropped from the shoulder area down to the trunk area . . . A piece of metal fragment fell out of his back when we picked up the body to place a film under his head. An autopsy pathologist picked it up with forceps and put it in a glass of formaldehyde.'' (a: Oct. 8, 1990)

In another interview conducted with Custer, Custer stated that the fragment which fell from the posterior area of the President when they moved him early after the body arrived, was a whole bullet and not a fragment; it was, however, damaged as though it had struck bone.

"When we lifted the body out to put a plate under it, the fragment fell out.'' He said it could have come "From anyone of those regions,'' referring to the back of the head or the back itself. "A misshapen bullet.'' "Not a half of a bullet, not a fragment?'' "It was like a bullet. It was misshapen as if it had hit bone and flattened partially out . . . It was fairly sized.'' (Meaning it was not small, like a .22.) (a: Oct. 29, 1990)

He said he clearly recognized this bullet the next day when Ebersole had him hold that and other fragments up against pieces of skull bone to make X-rays. (a: Oct. 29, 1990)

Custer: "Custer said that, on the day after the shooting, he was instructed to take X-rays of 'a bullet fragment taped to a skull. I was told by Dr. Ebersole that was for a bust (of Kennedy) . . . I did that the next day in the main department in one of the small rooms with a portable on a stretcher.' '' Custer also stated here that the X-ray log where he logged in the X-rays has subsequently disappeared. (Scott Hatfield, *RT,* "RT Disputes X-ray Photos in JFK Case,'' Aug. 31, 1992)

Custer: "Custer recalls lifting Kennedy's body to place films on the day of the shooting. 'A bullet fell out of the upper torso of the back,' he said.'' (Scott Hatfield, *RT,* "RT Disputes X-ray Photos in JFK Case,'' Aug. 31, 1992)

James Curtis Jenkins remembered very clearly that a bullet had rolled out of the sheets from the back area.

Officer Osborne at one time said a whole bullet fell out of the wrappings. Of course, the House Committee got Osborne to appear to retract this. However, many of these "retractions" were anything but.

O'Connor felt that Captain Osborne is (concerning his statement that a bullet had rolled out of the wrappings, which he later retracted to the HSCA) "absolutely crazy. Number one, when we got the body he was completely nude, uh, (chuckle) there was just no way that could happen. Not in that morgue it didn't.'' However, O'Connor must have changed his mind about this because he is quoted as saying: ''The bullet from the (back) wound fell out when the body was lifted from the coffin to the examining table at Bethesda.'' (AP article dated June 1, 1992)

Rudnicki: ''I remember them making a comment, and there seemed to be some controversy about looking for a shell fragment, and one was missing, and looking through the sheets. It fell out, or something of that nature.''

He was asked if he remembered anything about Admiral Osborne's comment that a whole bullet had fallen out of the sheets or from the back area when they moved him.

''Yeah, that may very well be. I may not have been in the room during that time, but I remember some conversations concerning that . . . I assume it was a bullet.'' (a: Oct. 14, 1990)

O'Neill denies that a bullet rolled out of the President's wrappings. (a: May 20, 1991) On another occasion, O'Neill stated that he not only doesn't remember anything like that occurring but that it wasn't ever discussed during the autopsy. (f)

ARRIVAL OF FINCK

The record seems to indicate that there was a wait for Doctor Finck to come, and photos and X-rays were taken.

The FBI report says Finck arrived after the autopsy was in progress. (h)

Rebentisch says that he was detailed to wait out back for Finck, who would arrive in a green Karmann Ghia. Finck came, presented identification, and Rebentisch led him to the autopsy room.

''Then the Army captain came to me—I was already out there—and he told me there was a ballistics expert coming here by the name of Lt. Col. Pierre Finck. That rang a bell with me because we have a bar here in Grand Rapids by the name of McFinck's. But he told me to wait for a green Karmann Ghia with Dr. Finck. He'll be in civilian clothes. I was to check his identification and bring him immediately to the autopsy room.''

''What was Finck dressed in?''

''Civilian clothes. They had already started the autopsy. Finck drove up and I asked him for his identification and he showed it to me and I led him in.'' (a: May 27, 1991)

PRESENCE OF RIGOR MORTIS

Paul O'Connor: ''Rigor had not set in'' when the body first arrived in the autopsy room. (a: May 18, 1991)

Dr. Karnei: ''Rigor was setting in by the time they were trying to probe the back wound.'' (a: Aug. 26, 1991)

APPEARANCE OF THE FACE

Dr. Robert McClelland (Parkland): "The face was intact, very swollen . . ." (*The Men Who Killed Kennedy,* BBC-TV documentary; Oct. 25, 1988)

Diana Bowron told Livingstone, "There was no damage to the front of his face, only the gaping wound in the back of his head, and the entry wound in his throat. When we prepared the body for the coffin, we washed the face and closed the eyes: there was no damage to the face, there was no flap of scalp on the right, neither was there a laceration pointing toward the right eyebrow from the scalp. (*Killing the Truth*)

In *Killing The Truth*, the following exchange takes place between Diana Bowron and the author:

DB: There was no damage to the front of the face, it looked like a face, let's put it that way. When he left us, his eyes were closed, which they weren't in these photographs.

HL: His eyes were closed, not open?

DB: Yes.

HL: Do you think that any part of his face—like the right eye and the right forehead above it—did that sag in or was there any bone missing in that area? Did his face look so perfectly normal? Did you feel his face?

DB: Um, . . .

HL: You washed his face?

DB: I can't remember whether I washed it or Margaret washed it. I know I washed his hair.

HL: Well, you would have noticed if a large piece of bone— see, the X-rays, if you look at the X-rays in my book, they show the whole right front of the face is gone from the eye area. And the lateral view X-ray is not the same as the AP view. There's a lot more bone missing in the lateral view. But most of the—most of them have the whole right eye area, from the top of the orbit at least, plus the forehead and the temporal bone is gone.

DB: No, no. I mean, I would have noticed something like that. You know, to say his face looked like a dead body's face. You know, there was no injury to the face.

HL: Yeah.

DB: It was just to his—the back of his head. And the one in his, in his throat. But and by then it was the tracheotomy opening. But his face itself, no.

HL: OK. One more question about that. Do you remember any laceration across the scalp from front to back where it comes on to the forehead, where the scalp would have been lacerated and it goes straight back from that area. Picture the right eyebrow. A laceration about a half an inch into his forehead, and then going straight back, where the scalp was torn. Do you remember anything like that?

DB: No.

Dr. Humes told *JAMA* (May, 1992) that the face was "intact" and "normal" when he unwrapped the head.

John Thomas Stringer, the photographer present: "There's no way that the face was gone because you knew who it was. Looking at him from the front, you'd never know anything was wrong." (a: Apr. 29, 1990; May 11, 1990)

Jan Gail Rudnicki: when asked "How did the face appear to you?" He replied, "Normal. It looked perfectly normal, if you didn't look at the back of the head." (a: Oct. 14, 1990)

Jim Jenkins: does not recall any damage to the face (a: Oct. 8, 1990)

O'Neill said there was no damage to the face. (a: May 20, 1991)

Ebersole: "I remember definitely seeing an intact forehead." (Interview of Ebersole by Art Smith, Mar. 28, 1978)

Custer: ". . . photos show the entire face intact and unmarked. 'That's how I remember it,' Custer said." (AP New York, 6/1/92)

Dr. Thornton Boswell: was adamant that there was no wound to the face (except for small fracture through the floor of the right orbit, and another small fracture) (Interview of Boswell by Richard Waybright 10/2/90)

Tom Robinson of Gawlers funeral home: "The face was perfect and undamaged, except for a small laceration about a half inch into the forehead, which I covered up."

When asked if any of the frontal bone or bone behind any part of the face, forehead or front top of the head underlying the scalp was damaged, he responded, "It may have been fractured—and I couldn't see that—but it was perfectly intact. I don't think any of it had been removed or replaced before we got it. The face was perfect. It would have fallen in without the frontal bone." (a: Aug. 17, 1991)

Joe Hagen of Gawlers: The face was undamaged except for a small laceration extending about a half inch into the forehead towards the right eyebrow. This can be seen in the right profile picture. (Interview of Joe Hagen by Harrison Livingstone and Kathlee Fitzgerald, 8/15/91)

The same observation was made by Dr. Robert Karnei: "They [Gawlers] did a real good job. There was a sort of a laceration that extended beyond the hairline in front. They did a tremendous job of fixing that up."

"You mean on the forehead?"

"Yeah. So that was really—they did a great job that night. You could hardly tell where that laceration was."

"Was it a sort of V-shaped triangle pointing at the right eye, about half an inch into the forehead?"

"Yeah, something like that . . . You know, it just extended beyond the hairline. It wasn't very far. A half-inch sounds about right. It was just beyond the hairline. They sutured it and covered it with a wax, I guess—is what they use. It was great, I mean, you couldn't tell where it was, unless you knew what was there." (a: Aug. 26, 1991)

All three (Jenkins, Hagen, and Karnei) state that the frontal bone beneath it was undamaged.

All witnesses have stated that the face was basically perfect except Jerrol Custer who said it sagged somewhat due to the scalp being loose elsewhere on the head.

Custer: "The scalp was so loose from the base of the skull in the occipital region to the front, it drooped. His face was deformed. Instead of how the face normally looked—it seemed like his face was squished. It seemed like someone had taken a clay image of his face and pushed it together. The whole skin part—the scalp and the front part of the face seemed like everything had drooped forward.

"This is lying on his back, right?"

"Right. There was no continuity to the face part at all. He did not look like he looks in the photographs taken at the autopsy. The photos look like a normal body lying there."

"That isn't the way it looked to you?"

"No. Absolutely not!"

"Could the face in the picture be false somehow?"

"It's hard to say." (a: Oct. 29, 1990)

CONDITION OF FRONTAL BONE

Tom Robinson: "Perfectly intact." (a: Aug. 17, 1991)

Dr. Robert Karnei: "The only hole I remember (in the forehead) . . . was that laceration, but I don't remember any other hole being there." (a: Aug. 27, 1991)

Joe Hagen: ". . . the face had not fallen in. I know very well the frontal bone was intact . . . I do not remember any extensive damage to the frontal bone." (Interview of Joe Hagen by Harrison Livingstone and Kathlee Fitzgerald, 8/15/91)

Ebersole: "I remember definitely seeing an intact forehead." (Interview of Ebersole by Art Smith 3/28/78)

Custer: "To my recollection, there was no frontal damage at all." (AP New York, 6/1/92)

Reed: The only eyewitness to mention any damage at all to the frontal bone (*RT Image,* Nov. 21, 1988)

The Clark Panel stated the results of their analysis of the autopsy X-rays to be: #2 skull left lateral shows "(fragments moving P–A stop) just anterior to the region of the coronal suture (and end in front just) below the badly fragmented frontal and parietal bones . . ." ("1968

Panel Review of Photographs, X-rays Films, Documents and Other Evidence Pertaining to the Fatal Wounding of President John F. Kennedy on November 22, 1963'' aka the Clark Panel)

Clark Panel: "The only conclusion reached by the Panel from study of this series (X-rays) was that there was no existing bullet defect in the supraorbital region of the skull." In discussing the alleged high rear entry wound in the head, it concluded: "The photographs do not disclose where this bullet emerged from the head, although those showing (the inside of the cranium with the brain removed) indicate that it did not emerge from the supraorbital region." ("1968 Panel Review of Photographs, X-rays Films, Documents and Other Evidence Pertaining to the Fatal Wounding of President John F. Kennedy on November 22, 1963'' aka the Clark Panel)

THE RIGHT EYE

The right eye as it appeared at Parkland in Dallas was described as being "divergent" by Dr. Charles Crenshaw (a: Sept. 21, 1991) and Audrey Bell. (a: Sept. 22, 1991) Otherwise the eye and the whole area was undamaged.

Ebersole: "In the front, there was a slight bruise above the right eye." (Ebersole interview by Art Smith, 3/28/78)

O'Connor said that the right eye was slightly popped out due to the fractured orbit beneath it, and gave them some trouble when they were preparing the body for possible viewing after the autopsy. He noted that the left eye was not as open as the right eye. (a: May 18, 1990)

Custer: "On his eyes—I never forgot his eyes—the right eye seemed to protrude a lot further than the left eye. It had a dead, cloudy stare." (a: Sept. 29, 1990)

Jenkins: "They had some problems keeping the right eye closed after they [Gawlers] were doing the cosmetics." (a: Sept. 8, 1990)

APPEARANCE OF THE HEAD and SCALP

The following compilation can be found in Chapter 2 of *High Treason* (Parkland Hospital):

Dr. Adolphe Giesecke told Livingstone (1979) that the back of the head was missing when L. showed him a copy of the official autopsy picture of the back of the head. "Was this blown out here?" "Yes, it was missing." Dr. Giesecke later wrote co-author Livingstone: "In doing so (pulling down the flap), the underlying bony defect is obscured," (Letter to the author, April 1, 1981; JFK Library) making clear that the large hole was still there.

Dr. Robert McClelland told the Warren Commission that he stood at the head of the table in the Emergency Room in "such a position that I could very closely examine the head wound, and I noted that the right posterior portion of the skull had been extremely blasted. It had been shattered, apparently, by the force of the shot so that the parietal bone was protruded up through the scalp and seemed to be fractured along its right posterior half, as well as some of the occipital bone being fractured in its lateral half, and this sprung open the bones that I mentioned in such a way that you could actually look down into the skull cavity itself and see that probably a third or so, at least, of the brain tissue, posterior cerebral tissue and some of the cerebellar tissue, had been blasted out." (6 H 33) Dr. McClelland went on to say that the bullet went "out the rear of the skull." (17 H 33, 36)

Some time later, Dr. McClelland approved a drawing showing the large gaping hole in the back of the head, which was then used in the book by Josiah Thompson (*Six Seconds in Dallas*).

Nurse Patricia (Hutton) Gustafson told the Warren Commission that there was a "... massive opening in the back of the head." (21 H 216) She had gone out to the limousine and helped wheel President Kennedy to the Emergency Room. She was asked to put a pressure bandage on the head wound. "I tried to do so but there was really nothing to put a pressure bandage on. It was too massive. So he told me just to leave it be." She said the large wound was at "the back of the head." "Definitely in the back?" she was asked. "Yes." She strongly rejects the official picture. This testimony was taken by Ben Bradlee, Jr. of the *Boston Globe*. (June 21, 1981)

Dr. Ronald Coy Jones was the chief resident in surgery at Parkland in 1963. He told the Warren Commission of "what appeared to be an exit wound in the posterior portion of the skull." He told Arlen Specter, "There was a large defect in the back side of the head as the President lay on the cart with what appeared to be some brain hanging out of this wound with multiple pieces of skull noted next with the brain and with a tremendous amount of clot and blood." (6 H 56, 6 H 53) Note that he states that the large hole in the back of the head was an exit wound.

Nurse Doris Nelson was the supervisor of the Emergency Room at the time of the tragedy. She assisted in treating the President, and helped prepare his body to be placed in the coffin. Nurse Nelson drew a picture of the head wound, mostly in the parietal area, but well towards the rear of the head. Her drawing conflicts strongly with the official autopsy photograph. When she saw that picture she said immediately "It's not true ... There wasn't even hair back there. It was blown away. All that area (on the back of the head) was blown out." (*Boston Globe,* June 21, 1981)

Dr. Paul Peters was an assistant professor when he assisted at the death of the President. Dr. Peters told reporters that the large defect was in both the occipital and parietal area of the head. When shown the official picture, he stated: "I don't think it's consistent with what I saw." (*Boston Globe,* June 21, 1981) He said of the McClelland drawing, "It's not too far off. It's a large wound, and that's what we saw at the time."

Livingstone first showed the official picture to Dr. Peters in 1979, along with the sketch approved by Dr. McClelland. He returned them, marking with an X the sketch of the large exit wound in the back of the head as being accurate, and rejected the official picture. He wrote that: "There was a large hole in the back of the head through which one could see the brain." He reconfirmed this in long phone conversations, and in talks with fellow researcher Gary Mack, Ben Bradlee of the *Globe,* and others. Dr. Peters told the Warren Commission, "We saw the wound of entry in the throat and noted the large occipital wound, and it is a known fact that high velocity missiles often have a small wound of entrance and a large wound of exit." (6 H 71; 17 H 31)

Dr. Gene Akin was an anesthesiologist at Parkland. He told the Warren Commission that "the back of the right occipital-parietal portion of [Kennedy's] head was shattered, with brain substance extruding." (6 H 65) "I assume that the right occipital parietal region [right rear] was the exit." (24 H 212) Akin reaffirmed this to the *Globe* team and basically did not accept the official picture. On seeing the sketch, he said, "Well in my judgment at the time, what I saw was more parietal. But on the basis of this sketch, if this is what Bob McClelland saw, then it's more occipital." (*Boston Globe,* June 21, 1981) Akin further said that Dr. Kemp Clark saw the entry wound in the temple.

Dr. Fouad Bashour, an associate professor of medicine in cardiology, was the subject of an article in the *Texas State Journal of Medicine* in January, 1964, along with some of the other doctors present in the Emergency Room. Livingstone interviewed Dr. Bashour in 1979 in his office in the presence of his secretary, Lee, and others. He was most insistent that the official picture was not representative of the wounds, and he continually laid his hand both on the back of Livingstone's head and his own to show where the large hole was. "Why do they cover it up?" he repeated numerous times. "This is not the way it was!" he kept repeating, shaking his head no. (TCI/October, 1980)

On the same day in 1979, Livingstone interviewed Dr. Charles Baxter in a lengthy taped conversation. He had told the Warren Commission that there was a "large gaping wound in the back of the skull." (6 H 40–1) He told Livingstone that without question, the back of the head was blown away: "It was a large gaping wound in the occipital area." (TCI/October 1980; author's tape—JFK Library) He did think it might have been a tangential wound of some kind. But he could not have been more clear when he rejected the official picture. When the *Globe* interviewed him later, he again did not fully support the picture. (*Boston Globe* summary and tape, chart of 1–10)

Margaret Hood, whose name was Henchcliffe at the time, had been an Emergency Room nurse for twelve years when the President was brought in. She helped wheel him in and helped prepare the body for the coffin. Interviewed by reporters in 1981, she drew a picture of the large wound on a model of a skull. She sketched a gaping hole in the occipital region which extended only slightly into the parietal area, thereby rejecting out of hand the official picture. (*Boston Globe* summary) She also insisted the President had an "entry" wound in his throat.

Livingstone taped an interview with Dr. Marion Jenkins in 1979 in the presence of 13 witnesses. Dr. Jenkins stared at the official picture for a long time and then said: "No, not like that. Not like that. No. You want to know what it really looked like?" (TCI/October, 1980; author's tape—JFK Library) It was Dr. Jenkins who picked up the head of the President to show Dr. Dulany that the back of it was completely gone.

Dr. Jenkins had told the Warren Commission, "There was a great laceration of the right side of the head . . . (temporal and occipital) even to the extent that the cerebellum had protruded from the wound. I would interpret it (as) being a wound of exit." (17 H 15; 6 H 48; 6 H 246; WR 492) In 1979, when shown the official photograph, he told Livingstone: "Well, that picture doesn't look like it from the back." Jenkins continually demonstrated on his head and Livingstone's where the large exit wound was, in the rear and slightly to the side, covering the cowlick area where it would certainly show in the autopsy photograph. "You could tell at this point with your fingers that it was scored out, that the edges were blasted out." He emphasized the word "out" twice. He continually beat on the back of the author's head with the palm of his hand to demonstrate where the large hole was.

The House Assassinations Committee interviewed Dr. Jenkins in November 1977. He told the investigator that he "was the only one who knew the extent of the head wound." "His location was customary for an anesthesiologist. He was positioned at the head of the table, so that he had one of the closest views of the head wound. Regarding the head wound, Dr. Jenkins said that only one segment of bone was blown out—it was a segment of occipital or temporal bone. He noted that a portion of the (lower rear brain) cerebellum was hanging out from a hole in the right-rear of the head.'' (7 HSCA 286–7) They did not show him the autopsy photographs.

Dr. Malcolm Perry, a general surgeon, performed the tracheostomy on the President when he was brought into the emergency room. He appeared twice before the Warren Commission and described ''a large wound of the right posterior parietal area in the head exposing lacerated brain,'' (3 H 372; 17 H 4) and ''a large avulsive wound of the right occipital parietal area in which both scalp and portions of skull were absent, and there was severe laceration of underlying brain tissue. . . .'' (6 H 11)

The Assassinations Committee interviewed Dr. Perry in 1978, but did not show him the autopsy photographs. Perry told the interviewer that he had looked at the head wound and that it ''was located in the 'occipital parietal' region of the skull and that the right posterior aspect of the skull was missing.'' (7 HSCA 295) It does not make sense that Dr. Perry and the only other two Parkland doctors (Jenkins and Carrico) the Committee interviewed would have somehow changed their observation that the back of the head was missing for the *Boston Globe*. In addition, the testimony of Dr. Perry to the Warren Commission, and his extensive first-hand experience with the wounds, makes any later retraction attributed to him not credible.

Dr. Carrico told the Warren Commission: ''The wound that I saw was a large gaping wound, located in the right occipito–parietal area. I would estimate it to be about 5 to 7 cm. in size, more or less circular, with avulsions of the calvarium and scalp tissue. As I stated before, I believe there was shredded macerated cerebral and cerebellar tissues both in the wounds and on the fragments of the skull attached to the dura.'' (6 H 3)

When interviewed in January 1978 by the House Assassinations Committee, Dr. Carrico repeated the same thing. ''The other wound was a fairly large wound in the parietal, occipital area. One could see blood and brains, both cerebellum and cerebrum fragments in that wound. . . . The head wound was a much larger wound than the neck wound. It was five by seven centimeters, something like that, 2½ by 3 inches, ragged, had blood and hair all around it, located in the part of the parietal occipital region . . . above and posterior to the ear, almost from the crown of the head,'' (7 HSCA 278) that is, just where the small entry wound shows in the alleged autopsy photograph. It would have been impossible for this to be true without showing on the photograph.

Dr. Jackie Hunt, like Dr. Bashour, was not interviewed by *The Globe,* but Livingstone showed her the picture in 1979 and she instantly denounced it. She did not see the back of the head because she was standing directly over the President, but she insisted that the back part of the head was blown out and rejected the official picture. "That's the way it was described to me," she said, saying that the back of the head was gone. (TCI/October, 1980; author's tape—JFK Library) Had the large defect been anywhere else, she would have seen it and described it. Dr. Akin said that if you looked directly down on Kennedy, you could not see the large hole. (*Boston Globe,* tape of Akin) Therefore, Dr. Hunt's testimony is significant.

Dr. Hunt responded to Livingstone's question: "So, the exit wound would be in the occipital-parietal area?" "Yeah, uh-huh. It would be somewhere on the right posterior part of it. . . ." She pointed to the sketch from *Six Seconds In Dallas*: "That's the way it was described to me." "I went around this way and got the equipment connected and started—but I saw the man's face like so, and I never—the exit wound was on the other side—and what was back there, I don't know. That is the way it was described to me," she said, pointing to the sketch showing the large hole in the back of the head. "I did not see that. I did not see this part of his head. That would have been here," she said, and put the palm of her hand on the back of Livingstone's head. She did this before Livingstone showed her the sketch from Thompson. (TCI/October, 1980; Author's tape—JFK Library)

The Secret Service agents who were in the limousine when it arrived at Parkland, in the trauma room, and in the autopsy room at Bethesda, testified, beginning with Clint Hill: "The right rear portion of his head was missing. It was lying in the rear seat of the car. His brain was exposed. There was blood and bits of brain all over the entire rear portion of the car. Mrs. Kennedy was completely covered with blood. There was so much blood you could not tell if there had been any other wound or not, except for the one large gaping wound in the right rear portion of the head." (2 H 141)

The driver of the limousine, William Greer, said: "His head was all shot, this whole part was all a matter of blood like he had been hit." (2 H 124) The examiner asked Greer if the part of the head that was gone was "the top and right rear of the head?"

"Yes, sir; it looked like that was all blown off."

Secret Service agent, Roy Kellerman, was shown a picture of a head, indicating the rear portion: "Yes." "More to the right side of the head?"

"Right. This was removed."

"When you say, 'This was removed,' what do you mean by this?"

"The skull part was removed."

"All right." Representative—later President—Gerald Ford asked him, "Above the ear and back?"

"To the left of the ear, sir, and a little high; yes. About right here."

"When you say 'removed,' by that do you mean that it was absent when you saw him, or taken off by the doctor?"

"It was absent when I saw him."

"Fine. Proceed."

"Entry into this man's head was right below that wound, right here," Kellerman said. "Indicating the bottom of the hairline immediately to the right of the rear about the lower third of the ear?"

"Right. But it was in the hairline, sir."

"In his hairline?"

"Yes, sir."

"Near the end of his hairline?"

"Yes, sir."

"What was the size of that aperture?"

"The little finger," this indicating the diameter of the little finger.

"Right."

"Now, what was the position of that opening with respect to the portion of the skull which you have described as being removed or absent?"

"Well, I am going to have to describe it similar to this. Let's say part of your skull is removed here; this is below."

"You have described a distance of approximately an inch and a half, 2 inches, below."

"That is correct; about that, sir," Kellerman said. (2 H 81)

ADDITIONAL DATA ON THE HEAD WOUND:

In a 1993 interview with the author, Diana Bowron responded to Livingston, as follows:

HL: So, in this massive hole, was there a flap of scalp there, or was scalp actually gone?

DB: It was gone. Gone. There was nothing there. Just a big gaping hole.

HL: We're talking about scalp first, and then bone, right?

DB: Yeah. There might have been little lumps of scalp, but most of the bone over the hole, there was no bone there.

HL: Was there any part of the flap of scalp over that big defect in the bone missing?

DB: What I'm saying is that the hole where the bone had gone, perhaps the skin was a little bit smaller, if you know what I mean, but only fractionally, just over the edge ...

HL: So the scalp was blown out too?

DB: Yes.

Bowron made it clear that there was no bone or scalp missing from the top of the head. (*Killing The Truth*)

Dr. Kemp Clark (Parkland): "... said in Dallas today that a bullet did much massive damage at the right rear of the President's head ... A missile had (come or gone) out the back of his head, causing extensive lacerations and loss of brain tissue." ("No Report of Autopsy Given on Kennedy," AP, Nov. 26, 1963)

The autopsy report states that: "There is a large irregular defect of the scalp and skull on the right involving chiefly the parietal bone but extending somewhat into the temporal and occipital regions. In this region there is an actual absence of scalp and bone producing a defect which measures approximately 13 cm. in greatest diameter." This is basically the identical position where the defect was seen in Dallas and can be seen in a few frames of some copies of the Zapruder film.

Rudnicki: "It was a big hole."

"Was the scalp missing on the back of the head?"

"Yes."

"Not just shredded, but gone?"

"As far as I could tell, it was *gone* (his emphasis). I couldn't see any gray matter in there, you know. There was some hair hanging over it. There wasn't a big hole type thing, but there wasn't any scalp there, either. It was a lasting impression, as I recall. ... from the ear back the scalp was either gone or definitely destroyed in that area. I don't know whether it was implosion or explosion. I can't recall that. Not being an expert in forensic medicine or anything, it would look more like it was an exit than an entrance." He was asked if there was any scalp left in the right rear of the head behind the ear, and he said no, "That was gone ... With the recent pictures that were shown on television I recall the frontal area missing in the X-rays rather than the back area."

"What did the top of the head look like? Was there a large hole in the top of the head?"

"No, not that I recall." But he said that he did not get a good look at it. Then he clarified something by saying that when he said that the right rear quadrant of the head was missing, "that could extend to the top of the head."

He did not recall any entry wound in the back of the head. (a: Oct. 14, 1990)

John Thomas Stringer: "The top of the head was not gone." When reminded that Dr. Boswell had written on the autopsy face sheet that the top of the head was missing, Stringer said, "Well, certainly the hair and all (on the top of the head) was intact from what I remember, it was the back of the head that was gone." (a: April 29, 1990, May 11, 1990)

O'Connor: "See the scalp covered it up so you couldn't tell, tell how bad the wound was until he pulled the scalp off. . . . they could have never showed him to anybody, there was too much scalp gone up there, but it was just all macerated, it was just torn in little shreds."

"The scalp in the back?"

"Yeah, the whole, wound area was all to shreds. Uh, pieces of brain kept falling out of the scalp, it was a mess." (a: Apr. 19, 1990)

"You see that one picture? The close-up shows the cowlick?"

"Yes."

Paul: "Supposedly there's supposed to be a hole in there."

"Yeah."

"That's a bunch of shit too."

"There wasn't any hole there?"

"No," Paul said. "That's painted in." (a: Apr. 19, 1990)

Francis O'Neill: When asked if there was a hole in the back of the head, "Don't say a hole. It was the whole massive right side of the head. Tremendous." (a: May 20, 1991)

James Curtis Jenkins: "Everything from just above the right ear back was fragmented. It was broken up but it was being held together by the scalp."

"Was there an area of actual absence of scalp and bone?"

"Yeah, there was. There was an area along the midline just above the occipital area.

"In the occipital area?"

"Yeah, right at the occipital area. It was higher. One of the things I don't understand is that this would not have been low enough to have gotten into the cerebellum."

Jenkins does not remember the kind of damage to the cerebellum that was described in Dallas, but only to the rest of the brain on the right side.

When asked about the X-rays showing the right upper front of the face apparently missing, he said: "I'm sure that's not the case." This put him in line with Dr. Boswell and all the other witnesses from the autopsy who have talked about it.

He was also asked if he had seen any damage to the left temple area. In Dallas, the death certificate said that the President had died "from a gunshot wound to the left temple." Jenkins said that neither he nor anyone else at the autopsy to the best of his knowledge had seen any such gunshot wound in that area.

"I might have gone along with *right* temple," he said. There was some discoloration of the skull cavity with the tissue area being gray and there was some speculation that it might be lead.

"There might have been an entry wound there?"

"Yeah. And the opening and *the way the bone was damaged behind the head would have definitely been a type of exit wound.* The reason I have said this is I saw this before in other wounds and it was very striking." (a: Oct. 8, 1990)

In response to questions as to whether or not there was enough intact scalp on the back of the head to cover up the large hole described by all witnesses, Jenkins said no.

"There was a hole in all of it [the scalp and the bone]. There was a hole in the occipital-parietal area. I had seen a wound similar to that before . . . I just never could understand how they came up with the conclusions that they did." (a: Mar. 25, 1991)

Custer: "There was a flap of scalp in the back of the head but it was badly shredded. As I have said, it would not make a picture like the one we now have, which shows the scalp so intact . . . Every time you moved the head, the whole scalp moved forward. It was all loose . . . I'm a big man, and I have big hands. I was asked to make fists with both hands and put them in the head, and a medical corpsman (Floyd Albert Riebe) took a picture. So it has to be a big hole." (a: Dec. 29, 1990)

Metzler: (speaking of the large rear defect) "It came downward toward the neck. Torn apart rather than cut with a surgeon's knife. It was a pretty long cut, at least three inches. Not quite . . ." (a: May 27, 1991)

Dr. Humes told the WC that it was more to the right side of the head. (2 WCH 351) ". . . and a large roughly 13 cm. diameter defect in the right lateral vertex of the skull. . . . there was a defect in the scalp and some scalp tissue was not available. However, the scalp was intact completely past this defect. In other words, this wound in the right posterior region was in a portion of scalp which had remained intact." (2 WCH 352)

SMALL HOLE IN TEMPLE

Tom Robinson: "There was one very small hole in the temple area, in the hairline. I used wax in it, and that is all that I had to do. I just put a little wax in it."

"What side was it on?"

"I can't remember for sure, but I think it was on the right side." (a: Aug. 17, 1991)

Jenkins was asked if he had seen any damage to the left temple area. In Dallas, the death certificate said that the President had died "from a gunshot wound to the left temple." Jenkins said that neither he nor anyone else at the autopsy to the best of his knowledge had seen any such gunshot wound in that area.

"I might have gone along with *right* temple," he said. Just above the right ear there was some discoloration of the skull cavity with the tissue area being gray and there was some speculation that it might be lead.

"There might have been an entry wound there?"

"Yeah. And the opening and *the way the bone was damaged behind the head would have definitely been a type of exit wound.* The reason I have said this is I saw this before in other wounds and it was very striking." (a: Oct. 8, 1990)

Jenkins also stated that there was some gray discoloration of the skull and skin in the right temple area that possibly could have been caused by lead. (a: May 24, 1991)

O'Neill saw no entry hole in the right or left temple. (a: May 20, 1991)

O'Connor does not remember seeing a hole in the right temple. (a: May 9, 1990)

X-RAYS

Two men, Reed and Custer, claimed to have taken X-rays, as well as the acting chief of radiology, John Ebersole. It might seem possible that each did, in fact, do so, but at different times perhaps without the other knowing it. They have certainly been fighting about who took them ever since.

Custer denies that Reed or Ebersole took any of the X-rays: "Ebersole . . . involved himself only in film interpretation."; "Edward Reed was a first year student. There is no way in God's creation he would get involved in such an important situation like that." (Scott Hatfield, *RT*, "RT Disputes X-ray Photos in JFK Case," Aug. 31, 1992)

Reed: "Around 4 P.M., we were called into the office again and told that there was a good possibility that we would be doing the autopsy on President Kennedy anytime between 4 and 6 . . . I took a GE 225 portable unit down to the morgue in case we needed it and went off to the mess hall for dinner. There were four of us on duty: the supervisor, and three junior technologists. I was selected to take the X-rays because I had previous training at Annapolis. I knew the portable unit and the supervisor never took X-rays even though he was a supervisor in X-ray . . . I was selected because with my past experience, I was the only one really qualified to do the job." (*RT Image,* Nov. 21, 1988)

O'Connor wrote that "all X-rays were taken on the autopsy table with a portable X-ray machine." (Letter from O'Connor to Livingstone, June 11, 1990) Ebersole also confirmed "We were using a portable machine." (Interview of Ebersole by Art Smith, 3/28/78)

6:45 P.M.: Custer told Warren Patton that he started taking X-rays at about 6:45. (Interview of 12/2/88) See references to Custer in the section called ARRIVAL AT THE AUTOPSY ROOM for time discrepancies.

O'Neill described the X-rays being taken. He could do this because, although he was asked to leave the autopsy room, he stood observing every move in the autopsy room during that time through the window which looked into the room. (f)

Rudnicki also said that the room was cleared when X-rays were taken. (a: Oct. 14, 1990)

It took six minutes to develop each film. (Reed, *RT Image,* Nov. 21,

1980) Custer stated that each X-ray had to be developed separately. (a: Oct. 29, 1990)

Reed said that he used a "2 × 4 mm piece of scrap metal taped to the side of the skull for magnification purposes." (*RT Image*, Nov. 21, 1988)

8 to 9:30 P.M.: Ebersole stated ". . . the first group of X-rays had to be taken roughly some time between 8 and 9:30 . . . taken prior to the (Y) incision." (Interview of Ebersole by Art Smith, 3/28/78)

8:30 P.M.: Dr. John H. Ebersole said that he attended the autopsy from about 8 P.M. and took X-rays at 8:30 P.M. (to Art Smith, *The Continuing Inquiry* July 1978)

Ebersole: "Approximately half (of the X-rays) were taken before the incision was made . . . probably took no more than 20 minutes. And the taking of them up to the 4th floor and having them processed, probably another 20 minutes. All in all, probably it was about 35–40 minutes for the first group, and probably the same time for the second group." (Interview of Ebersole by Art Smith, 3/28/78)

Ebersole: "After some of the organs had been removed—the lungs (. . . and the intestines) had been removed . . . we took a *second series of X-rays* at the request of one of either the FBI or Secret Service men." This would appear, from Ebersole's statements regarding the back wound, to be at the time of the examination of the back wound. "Once again, we saw no bullet." (Interview of Ebersole by Art Smith, 3/28/78)

12:30 A.M. to 1:00 A.M.: Ebersole: "No further X-rays were taken until 12:30, one o'clock in the morning when, from Dallas, three pieces of skull bone arrived . . . I X-rayed those . . . a bullet had been found in a blanket (in Dallas) and . . . sent up at approximately the same time as the three pieces of skull were being X-rayed." (Interview of Ebersole by Art Smith, 3/28/78)

1:00 A.M.: Ebersole also said he took X-rays at 1 A.M. (*Continuing Inquiry,* July 1978)

Ebersole: "The only (skull) fragments I have knowledge of arrived around 1:00 in the morning . . . (the largest one was) 2 × 3 inches . . . the other two were smaller. Significantly smaller." He also stated that he never saw any skull fragment as large as the "Harper fragment." (Interview of Ebersole by Art Smith, 3/28/78)

On questioning of Secret Service agent, Gerald Behn, who was in charge of the White House detail regarding the "section of the President's skull which was brought to the National Navy Medical Center at Bethesda, Maryland after the autopsy was in progress, he advised that this section, which was measured by the doctors performing the autopsy as being 10 × 6.5 centimeters, was found in the Presidential car on the floor between the front and rear seats." (FBI Report file # BA 89–30, Washington, D.C. by James Sibert and Francis O'Neill, 11/29/63)

Humes reports that there were three skull fragments; however, O'Neill reports that he remembers only one skull fragment. (f)

Custer: "Custer said that, on the day after the shooting, he was instructed to take X-rays of 'a bullet fragment taped to a skull. I was told by Dr. Ebersole that it was for a bust (of Kennedy) ... I did that the next day in the main department in one of the small rooms with a portable on a stretcher." Custer also stated here that the X-ray log where he logged in the X-rays has subsequently disappeared. (Scott Hatfield, RT, "RT Disputes X-ray Photos in JFK Case," Aug. 31, 1992)

Ebersole: "Roughly within a month of the autopsy, I was called by Capt. James Young who was on the White House medical staff, and asked if I could, from the skull X-rays, furnish life measurements ... so I went down to the White House annex and saw the skull films ... and provided Dr. Young with those measurements for whatever reason, I don't know. I was told they were for a sculptor. They had to be corrected because, you know, an X-ray distorts. So I had to take and make up the same set-up I used to take the autopsy films, from that determine a correction factor that was duly given to them." (Interview of Ebersole by Art Smith, 3/28/78) It is interesting to note that the X-ray films were in multiple hands.

O'Neill said that "to the best of my knowledge, the X-rays were developed right in the room there. Developed on the spot. We were right there. They did not have to leave the room." (a: May 20, 1991) O'Neill's own FBI report, however, states that the X-rays "were developed and *returned* (emphasis added) to the autopsy room." (h)

Ebersole stated "And the taking of them up to the 4th floor and having them processed ... I was not in the room at all times. I had to leave at times to process X-rays. There would be intervals of 15, 20 minutes, I think." (Interview of Ebersole by Art Smith, 3/28/78)

Dr. Humes: "In further evaluating the head wound, I will refer back to the X-rays which we had previously prepared. These had disclosed to us multiple minute fragments of radio-opaque material traversing a line from the wound in the occiput to just above the right eye, with a rather sizable fragment visible by X-ray just above the right eye." (2 WC 353)

FBI Report: "X-rays of the brain area which were developed and returned to the autopsy room disclosed a path of a missile which appeared to enter the back of the skull and the path of disintegrating fragments could be observed along the right side of the head. The largest section of this missile as portrayed by X-ray appeared to be behind the right frontal sinus. The next largest fragment appeared to be at the rear of the skull at the juncture of the skull bone ... approximately 40 particles of disintegrated bullet and smudges indicated that the projectile had fragmentized while passing through the skull region." (h)

Ebersole (head of the radiology team at the autopsy): "I personally did not testify at the Warren Commission." When he was asked why he thought that was, he responded, "Frankly, I don't think the X-rays were that important. Remember why they were taken. They were taken because, at the time, there was a bullet not yet identified—a wound of entrance, I shall say, and no apparent wound of exit, and we were not taking X-rays to get the fine detail that we might, in retrospect, want ... We were taking them to look for a metallic slug ... and to us at Bethesda, no obvious wound of exit." (Interview of Ebersole by Art Smith, 3/28/78)

FBI Report: All the developed X-rays and all the developed photographic film was turned over to Secret Service agent Roy Kellerman at the end of the autopsy. (h) It states that there were *eleven* X-rays. (h) The complete X-ray inventory lists 14 X-rays. This figure included 3 X-rays of the skull fragments.

FBI Report: "Mr. Behn advised that the undeveloped photographs and X-rays made during the course of the autopsy conducted at the National Naval Medical Center, Bethesda, Maryland, are in the custody of Mr. Bob Bouck, Protective Research Section, United States Secret Service." (FBI File # BA 89–30 by James Sibert and Francis O'Neill, Washington, DC, 11/29/63)

Clark Panel: The results of their analysis of the autopsy X-rays was listed as follows: #1 AP skull "has been damaged in two small regions . . . (by) the heat of a spotlight, . . . [fragment] embedded in the outer table of the skull . . . lies 25 mm to right of midline, . . . (adjacent to hole on internal surface) localized elevation of soft tissue (plus bone fragments)"; #2 skull left lateral has "a pair of converging pencil lines . . . drawn on the film, . . . [fragments moving P–A stop] just anterior to the region of the coronal suture (and end in front just) below the badly fragmented frontal and parietal bones . . . (covering a) 45 mm long- 8 mm wide area . . . [which] overlies part of the coronal suture, . . . [elliptical scalp wound near midline and high above hairline] position . . . corresponds to hole . . . [the hole] measures 8 mm in diameter on outer skull and as much as 20 mm on interior surface . . . [the head wound was located] approximately 100 mm above the occipital protuberance . . . bone of the lower edge is depressed, . . . fragment as seen . . . is round and measures 6.5 mm in diameter."; #7 AP thoracolumbar showed no bullets or fragments; #8 right thorax, shoulder shows no fracture of the scapula, clavicles, ribs or cervical and thoracic vertebrae; #9 AP chest showed that just right of the cervical spine "above apex of the right lung . . . several small metallic fragments"; #10 AP left thorax, shoulder; (#8 and #9 were used to visualize the "neck" shot/wound); #11 AP thoracolumbar showed no bullets or fragments. ("1968 Panel Review of Photographs, X-rays Films, Documents and Other Evidence Pertaining to the Fatal Wounding of President John F. Kennedy on November 22, 1963"—aka the Clark Panel)

Clark Panel: "The only conclusion reached by the Panel from study of this series (X-rays) was that there was no existing bullet defect in the supraorbital region of the skull." ("1968 Panel Review of Photographs, X-rays Films, Documents and Other Evidence Pertaining to the Fatal Wounding of President John F. Kennedy on November 22, 1963," aka the Clark Panel)

AUTHENTICITY OF THE X-RAYS

1972: Dr. John Lattimer traced the X-ray in the National Archives showing that the frontal bone in the upper right skull region was completely gone. He published his drawings in *Resident and Staff Physician* (May

1972, pp. 43, 46) showing that the lateral film was almost coordinated with the A/P view showing the frontal bone to be entirely missing in the right forehead and back to the suture with the parietal bone, down to and including part of the orbit, with no right frontal sinus. (See APPEARANCE OF HEAD and LOCATION OF LARGE DEFECT)

1978: Dr. G. M. McDonnel (Aerospace Corp) was asked to interpret the X-rays on March 8, 1978. "These radiographs were unenhanced. My preliminary interpretation follows: 1) A nearly complete loss of structure of the right frontal and parietal bone." (7 HSCA 221)

Dr. Donald Siple (Chief Radiologist at Maryland General Hospital): the "so called temporal thinning refers to the fact that the temporal area of the skull is thinner (usually) than the other areas, i.e., occipital, parietal, and therefore appears less dense, or more grey than the dense, compact bone which appears white (dense). On a normal skull X-ray, this so called temporal thinning is a gradual change, with a long transitional zone, rather than an abrupt transition from a compact bone to black (i.e., air). Secondly, the cortex remains intact on all normal skull views.

"On the lateral view of President Kennedy's skull, the temporal bone near the skull base appears beveled as if a chisel had been applied, but not normal thinning, which is gradual. Finally, more than one view (s) (i.e., AP and Lateral) are used to localize abnormalities. A large defect in front on lateral view has to be in front on AP view, either right, left, or midline—not shine through from occipital defects." (Letter from Siple to Livingstone, April 16, 1993)

Dr. Humes: "How can X-rays be doctored? And why?" ("Doctor Who Performed JFK Autopsy Calls Conspiracy Theory 'Nonsense.' " May 19, 1992)

John Ebersole, remarking on the depiction of the large head wound in the X-rays said, "To me, it seems too much forward. It'd be back further." (Interview of Ebersole by Art Smith, 3/28/78)

Jerrol Custer said at Livingstone's press conference on May 29, 1992, in New York that the X-rays the government claims are of Kennedy are not, and that these were not what they took. He said they are fake. (Reuters and Associated Press, May 30, 1992)

Custer: "The right side of the skull on the X-rays . . . do not match the right side of the skull in the pictures (autopsy photographs). Not only that, but I remember the skull not being damaged in that area. It was all further back." He further stated that the X-ray photos do not resemble the radiographs he actually took. "The X-rays are not the ones I took." (Scott Hatfield, RT, "RT Disputes X-ray Photos in JFK Case," Aug. 31, 1992)

O'Connor: "See this X-ray picture in here? That's wrong. . . . there's an X-ray picture, lateral of the head X-ray. See, there's no exit deficit from the rear of the head. You're darn right that's not his X-ray . . . Now the anterior-posterior X-ray is not right either because that's part of the frontal area. Now there was a fracture down through there, but it wasn't missing. Okay, because I can see a fracture into the right orbit." (a: April 19, 1990)

In another interview he explains that the X-ray does not show the large defect in the back of the head.

Jenkins: When asked about the X-rays showing the right upper front of the face apparently missing, he said, "I'm sure that's not the case." This put him in line with Dr. Boswell and the other witnesses from the autopsy who have talked about it. (a: Oct. 8, 1990)

Custer: "Custer said that, on the day after the shooting, he was instructed to take X-rays of 'a bullet fragment taped to a skull.' I was told by Dr. Ebersole that it was for a bust (of Kennedy) . . . I did that the next day in the main department in one of the small rooms with a portable on a stretcher." Custer also stated here that the X-ray log where he logged in the X-rays has subsequently disappeared. (Scott Hatfield, *RT*, "RT Disputes X-ray Photos in JFK Case," 8/31/92)

Ebersole: "Roughly within a month of the autopsy, I was called by Capt. James Young who was on the White House medical staff, and asked if I could, from the skull X-rays, furnish life measurements . . . so I went down to the White House annex and saw the skull films . . . and provided Dr. Young with those measurements for whatever reason, I don't know. I was told they were for a sculptor. They had to be corrected because, you know, an X-ray distorts. So I had to take and make up the same set-up I used to take the autopsy films, from that determine a correction factor that was duly given to them." (Interview of Ebersole by Art Smith, 3/28/78) It is interesting to note that the X-ray films were in multiple hands.

DOCUMENTATION THAT THE RIGHT FRONTAL BONE IS MISSING IN X-RAYS

Dr. Fred J. Hodges, who examined the X-rays for the Rockefeller Commission on April 18, 1975 (President Gerald Ford Library), said: "The X-rays . . . are diagnostic of a gunshot wound. . . . producing a small hole of entry largely obscured on the X-ray by the more extensive havoc caused in the brain and anterior skull represented by extensive fractures, missing bone, disrupted soft tissues and gas within the cranial cavity. . . . finally a bursting forward of bony fragments and brain tissue in the frontal region, apparently adjacent to the coronal suture within the right frontal bone. The main portion of the bullet had thus left the skull." (p. 3)

Dr. John Lattimer traced the X-ray in the National Archives in 1972 showing that the frontal bone in the upper right skull region was completely gone. He published his drawings in *Resident and Staff Physician* (May 1972, pp. 43 and 46) showing that the lateral film was almost coordinated with the A/P view showing the frontal bone to be entirely missing in the right forehead and back to the suture with the parietal bone, down to and including part of the orbit, with no right frontal sinus.

Dr. Cyril Wecht: "The exit point of the bullet or its larger fragments cannot be determined because of the large loss of skull bone in the right parietal and frontal regions." (*Forensic Science,* 1974, p. 117)

Dr. G. M. McDonnel (Aerospace Corp, asked to interpret the X-rays March 8, 1978): "These radiographs were unenhanced. My preliminary interpretation follows: 1) A nearly complete loss of structure of the right frontal and parietal bone." (7 HSCA 221)

McDonnel wrote on August 4, 1978: "The findings and interpretation of the skull films are: nearly complete loss of right parietal bone, the upper portion of the right temporal bone, and a portion of the posterior aspect of the right frontal bone." (7 HSCA 218)

There seems to be a serious conflict with the X-rays shown to Dr. Davis which appears to show no bone in the back of the head, and nothing about the X-ray which was made public or interpreted by Dr. McDonnel. (7 HSCA 223)

Dr. Lawrence Angel: "It's really hard to be sure, square this with the X-ray which shows so much bone lost in this right frontal area." (Interview of Drs. Humes and Boswell with the panel of doctors for the House Associations Committee, HSCA, p. 249) Dr. Angel: "In order to approximate the position of two major loose fragments, it is necessary to define the gap seen in X-rays (especially #1 and 2) and photographs (especially #44 transparency and photograph) of the head and skull of JFK now kept at the National Archives. This gap where bone is missing along the top and right side of the skull vault extends from just behind obelion (area of the parietal foramina) forward almost to the frontal bosses anteriorly. From the radiopaque lump behind obelion which with cracks appears to mark the bullet entry the left margin of the gap goes forward just to the right of the sagittal suture to a region of major fracture just behind vertex where the margin moves about 1 cm to the left of the midline. From here the margin extends diagonally forward to the left to a curved area about 5 cm. above the left orbit and about 5 cm. from the midline. The anterior edges of the gap crosses to the right, stepping down about the midline to a level 5 cm. above the nasion and then sloping down to an area where there is an almost semicircular lacuna about 35 mm. above the midline of the right orbit. . . . From a level about 4 cm. above the frontomalar angle, the bone margin extends backward on the right side, with another V-shaped crack in front of the coronal suture. Behind this point the whole antero-inferior quarter of the right parietal lies loose. Its upper border was about 5 cm. above the squamous suture, but in X-ray #2 it appears shifted downward about 1 cm. From the point where it met the posterior half of the right parietal a big crack extends back and down, and the posterior boundary of the gap goes backward and upward to the starting point just to the right of obelion." (7 HSCA 228)

"X-rays, 4, 5 and 6 show a large piece of skull vault, clearly frontal bone with an apparent jagged line indicating coronal suture, about 7 to 8 cm. long. . . . This large fragment appears to be the upper part of the frontal bone, extending more on the right than on the left, and leaving spaces both in front and to the right. . . . The two big loose fragments of skull vault, from upper frontal and parietal areas, more on the right than on the left side, do not articulate with each other and leave three appreciable gaps unfilled." (7 HSCA 230)

FRAGMENT BEHIND EYE

FBI Autopsy Report: "The largest section of this missile as portrayed by X-ray appeared to be behind the right frontal sinus. The next largest fragment appeared to be at the rear of the skull at the juncture of the skull bone." (h)

Dr. Humes: ". . . a rather sizable fragment visible by X-ray just above the right eye . . . this one which was seen to be above and very slightly behind the right orbit." (2 H 353) If there was no bone there according to the X-rays and little brain matter in this area, what held the fragment in place?

PHOTOGRAPHS

Custer: ". . . a medical corpsman (Floyd Albert Riebe) took a picture . . . Someone else was taking photos in civvies." Custer was probably referring to John Thomas Stringer, Jr., the medical photographer, who was a civilian, but there are indications that some other civilian was there taking pictures. (a: Oct. 29, 1990)

O'Connor: "Riebe took the photographs with Stringer's direction." (Letter from O'Connor to Livingstone, June 11, 1990) O'Connor later reaffirmed that Riebe took them (a: May 18, 1991)

Riebe said he "used a flash in a room that was already brightly lit." (AP, New York, June 1, 1992)

Riebe used 35 mm (a: April 6, 1991) and 4 × 5 (a: April 1, 1991)

Stringer: He stated that he used two light sources with one on each side of the camera, both on stands. The camera was mounted on a tripod. Also he said he used the same camera for black/white and color, using pan film, and just switching the holders. This could explain why some of the black/white and color photographs seem to be identical. (a: Jan. 20, 1992)

O'Connor wrote that there were no photographs of the brain taken. "There was no brain to photograph." (Letter from O'Connor to Livingstone, June 11, 1990)

Humes stated that: "We also prepared photographs of the brain from several aspects to depict the extent of these injuries." (2 WCH 355)

Clark Panel: In listing the materials this panel examined, their report states the following photographs: "(3) brain from above, (4) brain from below . . ." ("1968 Panel Review of Photographs, X-rays Films, Documents and Other Evidence Pertaining to the Fatal Wounding of President John F. Kennedy on November 22, 1963")

O'Connor: "The photographs were taken before the actual autopsy began. Yes, the scalp was retracted so that the wound would be seen. After the autopsy began, there were *no photos* taken." (Letter from O'Connor to Livingstone, June 11, 1990)

Ebersole: "There were probably some (photographs) taken before the X-rays. I am sure there were some taken after, while the body was still intact." (Interview of Ebersole by Art Smith, 3/28/78)

Dennis David: "I'm sure there were others in the gallery who were not on the FBI's list." This is also a direct reference to Pitzer and the motion picture film David says Pitzer took during the autopsy not being listed. (a: June 4, 1991)

Joe Hagen (Gawlers funeral home): "There were quite a few people in that amphitheater looking on . . . I know there were a lot of pictures taken . . . from the amphitheater, taken apparently of his body." When asked if photos were taken while the men from Gawlers were doing their work, Hagen replied. "Not a lot . . . before we were asked to get on with it, there were extensive pictures taken to the best of my knowledge . . . I think they were taking pictures during the whole process (the autopsy), not just before . . . pretty well all during it." (Interview of Joe Hagan by Harrison Livingstone and Kathlee Fitzgerald, 8/15/91)

Riebe claimed that the lower hole seen in the autopsy photo of the back was the wound. Others claim what looks like a wound in the shoulder is it.

FBI Report: All the developed X-rays and all the undeveloped photographic film was turned over to Secret Service agent, Roy Kellerman. The inventory of these photos given was "twenty-two 4 × 5 color . . . eighteen 4 × 5 black and white . . . 1 roll of 120 film containing 5 exposures." (h)

FBI Report: "Mr. Behn advised that the undeveloped photographs and X-rays made during the course of the autopsy conducted at the National Naval Medical Center, Bethesda, Maryland, are in the custody of Mr. Bob Bouck, Protective Research Section, United States Secret Service." (FBI File # BA 89-30 by James Sibert and Francis O'Neill, Washington, DC, Nov. 29, 1963)

Dr. Charles Wilber: "The outrageous procedures of photo-taking at autopsy with no development of the negatives or transparencies, as may be, and then shuttling them off to Secret Service personnel or to Admiral Burkley can never be justified. In my view these were criminal acts: Secret Service is assigned to protect the President, not to interfere with handling of a corpse . . . Admiral Burkley was not a member of the autopsy team; his function in this instance seems to have been official obfuscator and 'Sanitizer' of factual materials." (Letter from Wilber to Livingstone, July 25, 1991)

Clark Panel: In listing the materials this panel examined, their report states the following photographs: 52 black/white and color photographs and transparencies: 10 head viewed from above; 9 head viewed from right and above that show part of the face, neck, shoulder, and upper chest; 7 neck and head from the left; 4 back of the head; 4 cranial cavity with brain removed from front and above; 3 brain from above; 4 brain from below. Their report states that it had negatives for the black/white and color prints except for 7 black/white negatives of the brain had no prints accompanying them. The panel stated that photos #19-25 which seem to be the same as photos #46–52.

In discussing the alleged high rear entry wound in the head, the Clark Panel concluded that "the photographs do not disclose where this bullet emerged from the head, although those showing [the inside of the cranium with the brain removed] indicate that it did not emerge from the supraorbital region." ("1968 Panel Review of Photographs, X-rays Films, Documents and Other Evidence Pertaining to the Fatal Wounding of President John F. Kennedy on November 22, 1963," aka the Clark Panel)

AUTHENTICITY of the AUTOPSY PHOTOGRAPHS

Dr. Robert Artwohl stated that "the pictures in *High Treason 2* and in *Best Evidence* are undoubtedly the autopsy photos. They match the Dox tracings, (which came out before any of the photos were published in these books). They match the conversations between Humes, Boswell, and the HSCA forensics panel. I believe one or two of the Dallas doctors HAVE stated the published photos are the same, and even Humes and Boswell said as much in their October 7, 1992 letter in *JAMA*. We continue to believe that no useful purpose would be served by widespread publication of the very unsightly head wounds and we lament the fact that this has already, to some extent, occurred." (Prodigy, 1/29/93) If the pictures were not what is in the Archives, the autopsy doctors doctors would have said so at that moment in their letter to *JAMA*.

In addition, Dr. Wecht confirmed that the photos Livingstone had published in his books were precisely what he had seen in the National Archives. So did Dr. Dulany, Dr. McClelland, Dr. Peters and Dr. Jenkins from Parkland.

Noone has questioned that the photos which were published are the same as those in the National Archives as of 1993.

Dr. Cyril Wecht: "No question . . . that the 'Stare-of-Death' photo and others are fudged." (JFK Assassination Midwest Symposium, Chicago, Ill. June 1992. Video tape #8)

Repeated statements by Drs. Humes and Boswell call into question these pictures. Their statements in 1978 to the HSCA and in 1992 to *JAMA* asserting that the entry wound was at or near the occipital protuberance show that both the X-rays and the photos cannot be authentic.

I was the first person to show representations of the autopsy photographs to the Dallas witnesses. They drew a unanimous voice from all that the picture depicting the back of the head did not show the large defect as it was and that there was no such flap of scalp as is apparently present. The results were published in *High Treason,* chapter 2. *The Boston Globe* working on this issue as a result of my efforts basically corroborated my findings, although the interpretation of their raw data is arguable. The weight of the evidence shows that the pictures cannot be accurate. My comment on the *Globe*'s findings can be found on pages 41-46 of *High Treason*.

Among the doctors who told Livingstone that the pictures of the back of the head were inaccurate or completely wrong were Dr. Robert McClelland, Dr. Ronald Coy Jones, Dr. Richard Dulany, Dr. Jackie Hunt, Dr. Charles Crenshaw (*High Treason 2*) Dr. Marion Jenkins, Dr. Adolphe Giesecke, Dr. Paul Peters, Dr. Gene Akin, Dr. Fouad Bashour, Dr. Charles

Baxter, Dr. Robert Grossman, Dr. Robert Frederick Karnei (at the autopsy, *High Treason* 2). The *Boston Globe* corroborated me on most of these doctors, but claimed that four doctors agreed with the photo, all of whom were on the record as denouncing the pictures. The *Globe*'s raw data has always been in my possession, and I placed copies of them in the JFK Library in Boston. It seems clear that for the purpose of seeking "balance," the *Globe* distorted their own findings. The *Globe*'s chart shows that twelve doctors and nurses disagreed with the photos to one degree or another. That makes their result three to one in favor of forgery. (See section headed *"The Globe's Report,"* pp. 41-46 of *High Treason*)

Dr. Malcolm Perry told *Baltimore Sun* reporters in 1979 that the picture did not show the back of the head as he saw it. Although I had no interview, Dr. Kemp Clark passed a verbal message to me in his outer office that the picture of the back of the head was inaccurate.

Nurses Doris Nelson, Patricia Hutton (and to the *Globe*), and Margaret Henchcliffe told Livingstone that the back-of-the-head pictures could not be of Kennedy. Nurse Diana Bowron sent Livingstone a drawing of the head wound (reproduced herein), captioned "This is where I remember the wound." She returned a copy of an autopsy photograph of the President's back with the comment "THIS IS NOT THE BACK I SAW" written in capital letters. With reference to the photograph captioned "The Back" (F5), "I only saw one wound, and not the number of wounds in the photograph: I do not think that the photo (F5) is of the President. I have marked for you on the photostat that you sent me where I think the entry wound was. . . . I washed his hair. This is what I was going to write to you about all these autopsy photographs with all the blood clots and everything on the back." (Diana Bowron interview, (1993):

HL: Is there anything peculiar about those pictures?
DB: Very peculiar, very peculiar.
HL: Well, I think they're fake as hell.
DB: Definitely. Definitely. On those pages that you told me, there's three together, top of the F6 and F7, and something that—all are fake completely because I washed all the clots out of his hair before I wrapped it up.

The alleged entry wound in the cowlick depicted in the autopsy photographs is four inches higher in the photos than where it was reported to be at the autopsy. (1 HSCA 326-330, 7 HSCA 246, 251, 254, 256)

O'Connor: "The photographs were taken before the actual autopsy began. Yes, the scalp was retracted so that the wound would be seen. After the autopsy began, there were *no photos* taken." (Letter from O'Connor to Livingstone, June 11, 1990)

Custer: "There was a flap of scalp in the back of the head but it was badly shredded. As I have said, it would not make a picture like the one we now have, which shows the scalp so intact." (a: Oct. 29, 1990)

Floyd Riebe, the Navy photographer, said at Livingstone's press conference on May 29, 1992, in New York that the photographs the government claims are of Kennedy are not, and that these were not what they took. He said they are fake, and pointed out problems with them. (Reuters and Associated Press, May 20, 1992)

Jim Metzler who was there when the head was unwrapped denied, when shown the pictures showing the open flap on the right side, that it could be there. (a: May 27, 1991)

When asked if the scalp that he saw on the very back of the head going down to the hairline would have been whole enough to pull together to make the back of the head picture the way it appears, O'Connor said, "No. It was macerated . . . See, that's the thing. See this one picture where it shows the doctors hand in there, lifting the scalp?"

"Yeah."

Paul: That's a bunch of shit."

"That he wasn't pulling the flap over it?"

"No. I don't know that." (while laughing)

"Did you see that Cronkite show, *Nova*?"

"Yeah."

"And so you're saying that was bullshit?"

"That's a bunch of bullshit!"

"True."

"You see that one picture? The close-up shows the cowlick?"

"Yes."

Paul: "Supposedly, there's supposed to be a hole in there."

"Yeah."

"That's a bunch of shit too."

"There wasn't any hole there?"

"No," Paul said. "That's painted in. It's a touched-up fake job. Well, as a matter of fact that all, that scalp is touched up because it was all shredded."

Paul then pointed out that in a second view of the back of the head, "Okay, you look at it real close, so you can see the cowlick too."

"Uh, and it's undamaged."

"Uh-huh. Right." Paul said. "That's a bunch of shit."

"So, in your opinion, that picture's a forgery," I ask.

"Yes. Yeah."

"And they couldn't have reconstructed the head to make it?"

"No." (a: Apr. 19, 1993)

O'Connor: "When I first saw the pictures of the President's body's so-called wounds, what really struck me was that, especially the head wounds, they show a nice little, neat, round bullet hole in the back of his head. Well, actually, what I saw was the whole side of his head blown off. I don't know where those things came from, but they're totally wrong, every one of them." (*The Men Who Killed Kennedy*, BBC, Oct. 25, 1988)

O'Connor: "I have a set of photographs with me right now, and uh, I know that there is one, two, three good forgeries in there." He said that the back-of-the-head picture was one of them, but then said that the pictures showing the right side of the head were others. "You've got the one picture showing him on the table and I've never seen this picture before (referring the The-Stare-of-Death photo)." When asked about the back-of-the-head photos, "Yeah, yeah. This is, this is wrong too," O'Connor said.

"Which one?"

"The rear of the head, this is composite forged photography masking a large defect in the very back of the head." (a: Apr. 19, 1990)

There could not have been any reconstruction of the scalp to make the back-of-the-head pictures because the scalp was not totally reconstructed. Part was left open because it was on the pillow and noone would see that scalp was missing. (a: Tom Robinson, August 17, 1991) There was no pre-existing flap because all the last witnesses to the body's final preparation have said that there was not enough scalp to cover over the back of the head.

Reibe: "Reibe ... said he too believes that the autopsy photographs, showing the back of Kennedy's head to be intact, are forgeries ... 'retouched to conceal a large exit wound from the bullet entering from the front.' " Reibe also noted objects in the room that appear in the photographs, like the wooden table, that did not exist at Bethesda: "We had no such structure ... All we had was white tile and stainless steel." (Scott Hatfield, *RT,* "RT Disputes X-ray Photos in JFK Case," Aug. 31, 1992)

Reibe: "The pictures I've seen *resemble* the pictures that I'd taken. That's all I can say. The quality of (these) prints is very poor. I'd have been in deep trouble if I'd turned in work like this." Reibe "also contended they (the photographs) were doctored because they show Kennedy lying on what appears to be a wooden table, with a dark background and odd shadows. "We had no such structure ... and he said he used a flash in a room that was already brightly lit." (AP, New York, 6/1/92)

Paul O'Connor was asked if anyone could have torn open the throat more than it was so that it looks something like the large gash we now see in the photograph. In other words, making it look like an exit wound, or trying to find a bullet. He wrote simply, "no." O'Connor feels that the throat wound in the pictures is retouched. (Letter from O'Connor to Livingstone, June 3, 1990)

Dr. McClelland said the throat wound (tracheostomy incision) in the picture was the same as what he saw. (*Nova,* PBS, 1988)

The edges of the throat wound in the picture may be retouched so as to make it look jagged and enlarged, like an exit wound. But we can see the round diameter of where a bullet entered, and it is a clean hole, not at all what an exit wound would leave.

SIZE OF THE LARGE DEFECT

Dr. Robert McClelland (Parkland): "My most vivid impression of the entire agitated scene was that his head had been almost destroyed ... Almost a fifth or perhaps even a quarter of the right back part of the head in this area had been blasted out ... It would be a jagged wound that involved the half of the right side of the back of the head. My initial impression was that it probably was an exit wound, so it was a very large wound." (*The Men Who Killed Kennedy,* BBC, 10/25/88)

Dr. Paul Peters (Parkland): "I could see that he had a large about 7 cm. opening in the right occipital parietal area. A considerable portion of the brain was missing there, and the occipital cortex, the back portion of the brain, was lying down near the opening of the wound." (*The Men Who Killed Kennedy,* BBC, 10/25/88)

Audrey Bell (Parkland) stated that it was large enough for the brain to be slipped out if someone knew what they were doing (a: Sept. 22, 1991)

Dr. Karnei of Bethesda: "As I said, the hole in the skull was not big enough for someone to have gotten in there and taken the brain out at the time" the body arrived at Bethesda. He also stated that most of the missing bone was in the back of the head. (a: Aug. 27, 1991)

Secret Service agent, Gerald Behn, who was in charge of the White House detail, was questioned about the "section of the President's skull which was brought to the National Navy Medical Center at Bethesda, Maryland after the autopsy was in progress. He advised that this section, which was measured by the doctors performing the autopsy as being 10 × 6.5 centimeters, was found in the Presidential car on the floor between the front and the rear seats." (FBI Report file # BA 89–30 Washington, DC by James Sibert and Francis O'Neill, 11/29/63)

Ebersole: "The only [skull] fragments I have knowledge of arrived around 1:00 in the morning ... [the largest one was] 2 × 3 inches ... the other two were smaller. Significantly smaller." He also stated that he never saw any skull fragment as large as the "Harper fragment." (Interview of Ebersole by Art Smith, 3/28/78)

O'Connor again said that he told David Lifton they couldn't have surgically removed the brain. "The hole wasn't big enough to remove half a brain. It would have been torn all to pieces." (a: Apr. 19, 1990)

O'Connor: "If you had seen the size of the hole. That's the reason I know he's been shot twice in the head. It took me a long time to finally realize that, hey, this guy's got hit by somebody else because one bullet just can't do this! It was after I left there that I went to Vietnam and I saw a bunch of stuff over there, really. And nothing there could really duplicate the massiveness of this wound.... Looked like somebody planted a small bomb in his head and it blew off ... Now that was another strange thing too. Like I said, no definition showing a, any entry or exit at all. It was like a bomb went off in his head." (a: Apr. 19, 1990)

Joe Hagen: "There was extensive damage to the President's head, most of it back up in here (indicating with his hand the rearward right side and the back) ... We had to replace just all of that area with plaster of Paris due to the extent of the wounds that were there ... If it hadn't have been that big, we wouldn't have had to use plaster of Paris, see ... Quite a bit of bone was lacking ... We had no problems in here (indicating the area of the coronal suture) ... Back up in here (again gestures back of head), his head would have been down in the pillow and, if I remember correctly, we had taken a little out of the pillow where his head would fit down in the pillow." (Interview of Hagen by Harrison Livingstone and Kathlee Fitzgerald, 8/15/91)

When asked if there was a hole in the back of the head Francis O'Neill said, "Don't say a hole. It was the whole massive right side of the head. Tremendous." (a: May 20, 1991)

Edward Reed (the X-ray technician): "When I saw Kennedy. . . . he had a large, gaping wound about the size of my fist in his right carotidal, temple and frontal areas." (*RT Image,* Nov. 21, 1988) Custer somewhat backed up Reed's description, saying that the large defect extended that far forward, but not into the forehead or eye region. (a: Sept. 23, 1991)

Custer: "The large defect extended clear to the flap on the right side of the head just in front of the ear. The scalp held the head together, but bone had fallen in beneath the scalp or was missing between what Dr. Robert Grossman had seen as two holes. Therefore, the description of Dr. Humes before the Warren Commission, indicating that it came all the way along the right side of the head from the occiput would appear to be accurate, and included the parietal and frontal bones. But the major part of the frontal bone itself and the forehead on the right was undamaged."

LOCATION OF THE LARGE HEAD WOUND

See last paragraph above, and refer to the previously quoted passage in the autopsy report placing the wound in the right parietal area, somewhat into the occipital and temporal areas which appears to be identical to the wound seen at Parkland.

Dr. Robert McClelland (Parkland): "It would be a jagged wound that involved the half of the right side of the back of the head." (*The Men Who Killed Kennedy,* BBC, 10/25/88)

Dr. Paul Peters (Parkland): "I could see that he had a large about 7 cm. opening in the right occipital parietal area." (*The Men Who Killed Kennedy,* BBC, 10/25/88)

Dr. Pepper Jenkins (Parkland): "When I tilted the head back to put the neck in a better position for the tracheostomy, I put my thumb first in the hole in the back of the occiput where the bullet had entered. And then while doing that and adjusting the head, I found what I later decided was the other wound: a wound of entrance. I didn't know what it was then because I was watching too much what was going on in the front." (*Killing the Truth;* Dallas Autopsy Doctors Forum, June 1992)

Dr. Kemp Clark (Parkland): ". . . said in Dallas today that a bullet did such massive damage at the right rear of the President's head . . . A missile had (gone) out the back of his head . . ." (AP "No Report of Autopsy Given on Kennedy," 11-26-63) The Warren Commission said that Clark "most closely observed the head wound, described a large gaping wound in the right rear part of the head . . ." (WR 68.) Clark wrote that there was "a large wound in the right occiput extending into the parietal region." (CE 392; 8 H and WR 516) In another report, he said that the large hole was "in the occipital region of the skull. . . . There was a large wound in the right occipital-parietal region . . . There was a considerable loss of scalp and bone tissue." (CE 392 ibid) He told the Warren Commission that he "examined the wound in the back of the President's head. This was a large, gaping wound in the right posterior part, with cerebral and cerebellar tissue being damaged and exposed." (6 H 20)

Dr. Robert G. Grossman told the *Boston Globe* that he had noted a large, separate wound located squarely in the occiput. Grossman also noted a smaller defect over the right ear. (*Globe*, June 21, 1981; and the *Globe*'s notes in the JFK Library, placed there by Livingstone.)

Nurse Bowron testified to the Warren Commission that "He was moribund. He was lying across Mrs. Kennedy's knee and there seemed to be blood everywhere. When I went around to the other side of the car, I saw the condition of his head . . . the back of his head . . . it was very bad . . . I just saw one large hole." (6 H 136)

Jim Metzler: The wound was above or behind the ear, but not to the top of the head, and there was no flap as we see it now in the pictures on the right side in front of the ear. Metzler helped carry the body to the table and stood on the right side as the head was unwrapped. "It looked like somebody cut it open with a can opener. It was a jagged cut. It was slightly above and maybe slightly behind the right ear . . . It came downward toward the neck. Torn apart rather than cut with a surgeon's knife. It was a pretty long cut, at least three inches. Not quite . . ." When shown the pictures showing the open flap on the right side, he denied that it could be there. (a: May 27, 1991)

Metzler never saw the whole back of the head. Metzler was told to leave by Boswell after the head was unwrapped, saying they had enough help. (a: June 6, 1991)

Dr. Robert Karnei stated the large defect was in the very back of the head and not in the front of the head or the right side or the top. "Most of the brain that was missing was in the back of the head."

"The brain? And how about the bone? Same place?"

"Yeah. Most of the bone that was missing was destroyed in the back of the head."

Karnei does not remember a wound on the top of the head. "I don't remember that. I could almost say that there was none." (a: Aug. 27, 1991)

In response to questions as to whether or not there was enough intact scalp on the back of the head to cover up the large hole described by all witnesses, Jenkins said no.

"There was a hole in all of it [the scalp and the bone]. There was a hole in the occipital-parietal area. I had seen a wound similar to that before . . . I just never could understand how they came up with the conclusions that they did." He also stated that the wound went from above the ear to the back of the head. (a: Mar. 25, 1991)

O'Neill: "There was a massive wound in the right rear of the head." (f)

Ebersole: ". . . if you drew the head in quadrants, looking down at it from above, the wound occupied the, sort of, the rear quarter of the right side . . . I don't want to give you the impression it was way up front by any means." (Interview of Ebersole by Art Smith, 3-28-78)

Joe Hagen: "There was extensive damage to the President's head, most of it back up in here (indicating with his hand the rearward right side of the back) . . . We had to replace just all of that area with plaster of Paris due to the extent of the wounds that were there . . . If it hadn't have been that big, we wouldn't have had to use plaster of Paris, see . . . Quite a bit of bone was lacking . . . We had no problems in here (indicating the area of the coronal suture) . . . Back up in here (again gestures back of head), his head would have been down in the pillow and, if I remember correctly, we had taken a little out of the pillow where his head would fit down in the pillow." (Interview of Hagen by Harrison Livingstone and Kathlee Fitzgerald, 8/15/91)

O'Connor: "Well, actually, what I saw was the whole side of his head blown off." (*The Men Who Killed Kennedy,* BBC, 10/25/88)

The placement of this very large hole is precise for each set of witnesses and most oppose the photographic evidence. Taken together with the pattern of movement with the other wounds, there is something very wrong in this placement of this wound. People in Dallas who saw it, including Mrs. Kennedy, did not make a mistake about it being in the back of the head. We see it in the front of the head in the pictures and X-rays. Humes' autopsy report described the head wound as extending into the occiput, which is far back and down on the back of the head. Dr. Humes told the WC that it was more to the right side of the head. (2 WCH 351) ". . . and a large, roughly 13 cm.-diameter defect in the right lateral vertex of the skull. . . . there was a defect in the scalp and some scalp tissue was not available. However, the scalp was intact completely past this defect. In other words, this wound in the right posterior region was in a portion of scalp which had remained intact." (2 WCH 352) This last statement runs counter to other witnesses. Others described the large hole and the absence of scalp as being in the back of the head. The photographs and Boswell's drawing, on the other hand, show an entirely different and *third* placement of the pictures: the large defect is on the very top of the head. The X-rays and Zapruder film show an entirely different and *fourth* placement for the wound: The right front of the head, blowing out that part of the face.

Dennis David: "My impression from Pitzer's film was that it was a frontal entry/rear exit wound." (a: June 4, 1991)

REAR HEAD ENTRANCE HOLE

The autopsy report placed the entry hole: "Situated in the posterior scalp approximately 2.5 cm. laterally to the right and slightly above the external occipital protuberance is a lacerated wound measuring 15 × 6 mm. In the underlying bone is a corresponding wound through the skull which exhibits beveling of the margins of the bone when viewed from the inner aspect of the skull.'' This is about four inches below where it is in the X-rays and photographs. The House Committee commented: ''The panel continued to be concerned about the persistent disparity between its findings and those of the autopsy pathologists and the rigid tenacity with which the prosecutors maintained that the entrance wound was at or near the external occipital protuberance.'' (7 HSCA 308) See transcript of Humes and Boswell in 7 HSCA.

The Clark Panel stated their results of their analysis of the autopsy X-rays to be: #1 AP skull'' (fragment) embedded in the outer table of the skull ... lies 25mm to right of midline, ... (adjacent to hole on internal surface) localized elevation of soft tissue (plus bone fragments)''; #2 skull left lateral has ''(fragments moving P-A stop) just anterior to the region of the coronal suture (and end in front just) below the badly fragmented frontal and parietal bones ... (covering a) 45mm long- 8mm wide area ... (which overlies part of the coronal suture, ... (elliptical scalp wound near midline and high above hairline) position ... corresponds to hole ... (the hole) measures 8mm in diameter on outer skull and as much as 20mm on interior surface ... (the head wound was located) approximately 100mm above the occipital protuberance ... bone of the lower edge is depressed, ... fragment as seen ... is round and measures 6.5mm in diameter.'' (''1968 Panel Review of Photographs, X-rays Films, Documents and Other Evidence Pertaining to the Fatal Wounding of President John F. Kennedy on November 22, 1963,'' aka the Clark Panel)

Based on the extant autopsy X-rays, Dr. Michael Baden states ''. . . this is an X-ray of the President, the back, the facial part. The entrance wound is in the upper back cowlick area —small hole, just typical for a high powered rifle —and it exits above the right ear. And the extrusion that's seen on the Zapruder film —there's some blood and tissue coming out of the exit wound.'' When Baden was asked why the Parkland doctors who were experienced in gunshot wounds say there was a large exit wound in the rear of the head, Baden replied, ''They didn't shave his head . . . What they were looking at was blood matted to the back of his head.'' (*Today*, NBC-TV, 2/3/92)

The alleged rear head entry hole depicted in the autopsy photos is four inches higher than the entry hole described at the autopsy. (1 HSCA 326-30, 7 HSCA 246, 251, 254, 256)

Jim Jenkins said that he did not see the entrance wound described in the autopsy report and by the Bethesda doctors in their testimony. He didn't altogether believe that it was there. (a: July 14, 1991) ''And the opening and *the way the bone was damaged behind the head would have definitely been a type of exit wound.* The reason I have said this is I saw this before in other wounds and it was very striking.'' (a: Oct. 8, 1990)

Rudnicki: ''It was a big hole . . . As far as I could tell, it [the scalp] was *gone* (his emphasis) . . . I don't know whether it was implosion or explosion. I can't recall that. Not being an expert in forensic medicine or anything, it would look more like it was an exit than an entrance." He did not recall any entry wound in the back of the head. (a: Oct. 14, 1990)

O'Connor: "You see that one picture? The close-up shows the cowlick? Supposedly there's supposed to be a hole in there . . . That's a bunch of shit too."

"There wasn't any hole there?"

"No," Paul said. (a: Apr. 19, 1990)

BRAIN and THE APPEARANCE OF THE BRAIN

Dr. Adolphe Giesecke told Livingstone (1979) that they lifted up the head and "shined a flashlight in the cranial vault there, and noticed a large amount of brain missing."

Dr. Crenshaw (Parkland): "Then I noticed that the entire right hemisphere of his brain was missing, beginning at his hairline, and extending all the way behind his right ear." (Dr. Charles Crenshaw, *Conspiracy of Silence,* p. 79)

Dr. Robert McClelland (Parkland): "Almost a fifth or perhaps even a quarter of the right back part of the head in this area had been blasted out along with probably most of the brain tissue in that area . . . I would estimate that about 20% to 25% of the entire brain was missing." (*The Men Who Killed Kennedy,* BBC, 10-25-88)

Dr. Paul Peters (Parkland): "I could see that he had a large about 7 cm. opening in the right occipital parietal area. A considerable portion of the brain was missing there, and the occipital cortex, the back portion of the brain, was lying down near the opening of the wound." (*The Men Who Killed Kennedy,* BBC, 10/25/88)

Dr. Kemp Clark (Parkland): ". . . said in Dallas today that a bullet did such massive damage at the right rear of the President's head . . . A missile had (come or gone) out the back of his head, causing extensive lacerations and loss of brain tissue." (AP, "No Report of Autopsy Given on Kennedy," 11-26-63)

Nurse Diana Bowron told Livingstone, "There was *very* little brain left. I had my hands inside of his head, trying to clean it up so there wouldn't be more of a mess in the coffin. I put cloth inside, and then removed it. The brain was almost gone. . . . There wasn't a normal brain at all. There was a lot of it on the seat. There was very little brain left. Very little. . . . far less than fifty percent on the right. A lot of the left side was gone, too. . . . Most of the right side was gone." (1993)

Audrey Bell (Parkland) saw that almost a third of it was missing in the back. (a: Sept. 22, 1991)

O'Neill: "That brain was spewed all over the backs of the two agents (Kellerman, Greer) in the car with him, in the car itself." (f)

O'Neill: There was only a "portion of the brain in the cranium . . . not a total brain. It was a pretty mish-mash of total pulp. I saw them take out what remained in the area there." (f)

Jenkins: "... right at the occipital area. It was higher. One of the things I don't understand is that this would not have been low enough to have gotten into the cerebellum." Jenkins does not remember the kind of damage to the cerebellum that was described in Dallas, but only to the rest of the brain on the right side. (a: Oct. 8, 1990)

Karnei: "The injury that he (Kennedy) had caused a lot of damage throughout the brain. He basically was brain dead. There is no way that that brain would have ever functioned from what I could see at the autopsy table. A lot of it was missing, and the part that was there was all ragged." (a: Aug. 27, 1991)

Dr. Robert Karnei: "Most of the brain that was missing was in the back part of the head. . . . Now, how much of the temporal, parietal, and occipital lobes could have fallen out superior to the membrane that is there— between the top part of the brain and the cerebellum, I'm not sure whether that could have fallen out when they opened the scalp and take out the brain or not. The brain that I saw was markedly hemorrhagic. I did see it when it was out of there. . . . Nobody got to it in Parkland, I can tell you that. The opening in the scalp was not big enough to go ahead and take the brain out." (a: Aug. 27, 1991)

O'Connor claims Kennedy "didn't have any brains left." (*Best Evidence,* 1980, p. 601) "Did you have to go through the medical procedure to remove the brain?"

"No, sir. There wasn't anything to remove." (p. 602)

"The cranium was empty." ". . . there was no brain on the body, near the body, or in the casket, or anything that I know of. They might have weighed pieces of matter, but they—I don't know how they come up with a brain." (p. 603) He has since qualified or retracted them. For example, "And there was no brain in the head when it came in?"

O'Connor: "What struck me was that when we removed the sheets I looked down, I said, 'My God, he didn't have any brains left' literally . . . There was no brain to be removed at all." (*The Men Who Killed Kennedy,* BBC, 10/25/88)

O'Connor speaking of the brain said, "Well, maybe a handful. Macerated tissue." (a: Apr. 19, 1990)

O'Connor wrote that there were no photographs of the brain taken. "There was no brain to photograph." (Letter from O'Connor to Livingstone, June 11, 1990)

Humes stated that "We also prepared photographs of the brain from several aspects to depict the extent of these injuries." (2 WCH 355)

Clark Panel: In listing the materials this panel examined, Their report lists the following photographs: "(3) brain from above, (4) brain from below . . ." ("1968 Panel Review of Photographs, X-rays Films, Documents and Other Evidence Pertaining to the Fatal Wounding of President John F. Kennedy on November 22, 1963," aka the Clark Panel)

Custer: "The whole thing makes me wonder: Was the body tampered with before the autopsy? There definitely was no brain."

"But, there had to be some brain left?!"

"There definitely was no brain—I was able to put my whole two hands inside the skull cavity. I even made the comment, 'My God, what is the sense of taking films of the head?'

"I saw tissue—surrounding tissue on the skull itself.

"But Jenkins has a very clear memory of taking the brain and infusing it and putting it in a jar of formaldehyde."

"Well, I don't know. I can't honestly say I saw much brain. If there was anything in there, it had to be very small . . . You have to remember that that night it was total mass confusion. There were too many people in that autopsy room working on that body that shouldn't have been there." (a: Oct. 29, 1990)

Dr. Charles Wilber comments that the Supplemental Autopsy Report says that "there was a 'superficial' laceration of the basilar aspect of the left temporal lobe; sample for micro was taken. Reported as same as all of the brain micro-sections." (Letter from Wilber to Livingstone July 25, 1991) These should not be the same.

Jenkins said that most of the brain was left. (a: May 19, 1991) Jenkins said that the brain stem was severed and it was not necessary to remove the brain in the normal fashion. (a: May 24, 1991)

O'Neill said they had to surgically remove the brain. (a: May 20, 1991)

Rudnicki remembers the brain being removed (Oct. 14, 1990)

Dr. Humes told Specter and the Warren Commission: "When we reflected the scalp away from the badly damaged skull, and removed some of these loosened portions of skull bone, we were able to see this large defect in the right cerebral hemisphere. It corresponded roughly in size with the greatest diameter of the defect in the scalp measuring some 13 cm. . . . We noted that clearly visible in the large skull defect and exuding from it was lacerated brain tissue which, on close inspection proved to represent the major portion of the right cerebral hemisphere." (2 WCH 355)

"Following the formalin fixation, Dr. Boswell, Dr. Finck and I convened to examine the brain in this state." (This probably happened a week later, as it takes time to fix) "We also prepared photographs of the brain from several aspects to depict the extent of these injuries. We found that the right cerebral hemisphere was markedly disrupted. There was a longitudinal laceration of the right hemisphere which was para-sagittal in position. By the sagittal plane, as you may know, is a plane in the midline which would divide the brain into right and left halves". . . . (See top of 2 WCH p. 356 for description of location) "The margins of this laceration at all points were jagged and irregular, with additional lacerations extending in varying directions. . . ."

O'Neill: "I do know that there was a portion of the brain, and I know it was placed in a jar." (f)

Dr. Cyril Wecht: "If the brain was not sectioned, then there could be no visualization of its interior. It's as if it never existed . . . It could have been the height of a sinister conspiratorial activity in the post assassination cover-up in this case to make sure that the brain was not examined." (*The Men Who Killed Kennedy*, BBC, 10-25-88)

There was an examination of the autopsy photographs and X-rays in 1975 by a group of doctors for the "Rockefeller Commission," which was the Commission on CIA Activities Within the United States. Dr. Richard Lindenberg, the Director of Neuropathology and Legal Medicine for the State of Maryland's Department of Health and Mental Hygiene, was one of those who entered the Archives to study the material. With respect to the brain, he wrote, "Instead of leaving a distinct wound canal through the brain, the bullet produced a severe injury in the right cerebral hemisphere commencing in the posterior parietal region near the border of the occipital lobe, becoming larger anteriorly. Cortex and much of the white matter of the anterior parietal lobe and central convolutions *and the entire frontal lobe are missing.* [Italics added.] Walls and floor of the large defect, essentially formed by deep white matter, show no hemorrhage and no unusual defects except anteriorly and laterally where a small, parallelogram-shaped opening exposes the anterior portion of the sylvian fissure in which two branches of the middle cerebral artery can be seen. This defect was noticed by the 1968 Review Panel and by Wecht (1972), but not identified. Still present are orbital, temporal and occipital lobes, the operculum, and most convolutions which faced the falx. Deprived of support by white matter, the latter lean over towards the defect. Except for small superficial and non-hemorrhagic lacerations opposite fractured bones of the base, the convolutions of these preserved portions of the hemisphere show no defects. The corpus callosum seen between the hemispheres is grossly intact. Some fresh subarachnoid hemorrhage is present in the open, anterior sylvian fissure.

"The entire left cerebral hemisphere is preserved except for superficial non-hemorrhagic lacerations of some convolutions opposite fractured bones. At the convexity the convolutions are somewhat flat. The leptomeninges are transparent and intact. Over the lateral aspect of the frontal and temporo-parietal areas there is local, fresh, thin subarachnoid hemorrhage over intact convolutions. Also, the convolutions of the medial aspect of the hemisphere, which faced the flax, are fully preserved.

"At the base of the brain there are small defects in the tuber cinereum and non-hemorrhagic tears in both peduncles of the midbrain. These alterations are probably postmortem artifacts. There is no subarachnoid hemorrhage. The brainstem and the cerebellum show no signs of injury." (Commission on CIA Activities Within the United States. Dr. Richard Lindenberg, the Director of Neuropathology and Legal Medicine for the State of Maryland's Department of Health and Mental Hygiene, Report, May 9, 1975, p. 4, Gerald Ford Library.) With regard to this latter, one wonders about the stories that the cerebellum was out of the head in Dallas. Clearly, this was not the same brain.

In addition, one cannot have the frontal lobe missing, as he says, and still have bullet fragments seen in it on an X-ray of the skull which has no bone in that area either.

The photographs of the base of the canal cut in the brain by the bullet on the right side, show a "gray-brown, rectangular structure measuring approximately 13 × 20 mm.'' on the right side. (Clark Panel Report, 1968, p. 8.) It would seem to be some sort of growth or other foreign material. There is no corresponding object in the X-rays in that position. It was first noticed by the Clark Panel years after the autopsy. Why then? Because it was unlikely that this structure, along with the big fragment on the outer table of the skull in the back, was on the X-rays seen during the autopsy.

The alleged brain is missing from the Archives. Robert Tannenbaum, former chief counsel to the HSCA, reported at the 1993 Chicago Conference that Frank Mankiewicz told him that Robert Kennedy placed the brain in the casket with JFK when the body was reinterred.

BRAIN WEIGHT

The brain's weight was recorded at the time of the supplemental report and not at the time of the autopsy two weeks earlier, at 1500 grams. This is roughly the exact weight of a normal male brain (some authorities say the average weight of a male brain is 1380 grams (see *High Treason 2* for references), in spite of the fact that at least one-fourth to one-third of it was described as missing.

BRAIN STEM

Jenkins is the only person to say that the stem maybe had been neatly severed before they got the body. Jenkins said that the brain stem was severed and it was not necessary to remove the brain in the normal fashion.

O'Neill said they had to surgically remove the brain. (a: May 20, 1991) O'Neill confirmed that ''there was no cutting'' of the brain stem as would normally be the case, after the autopsy began. The brain was simply removed. This may, at first, seem contradictory, however this full quote clarifies his statements: ''I saw them take out what remained [of the brain] in the area there . . . no cutting of the main thing (indicates with his hand the upper back of the neck) which I understand is normally done.'' (f)

Dr. Robert Karnei was asked ''Did he [Humes] mention to you whether or not it [the brain] fell out without his having to cut the brain stem?''

''Uh, I don't remember his having said that. Normally, the cut is made through the medulla oblongata, in order to get the brain stem and that part out of it.''

''Is the medulla what we would normally call the brain stem?''

''Yeah.''

''So, they had to cut that or could the bullet have torn it loose?''

''Ah, the bullet would not have torn that loose. That was down deep in the brain. At the base of the brain.'' (a: Aug. 27, 1991)

Dr. Wilber: ''It is interesting that a sample of tissue, for microscopic examination, was taken from the 'line of transection of the spinal cord.' No report was given on the microscopic reading of that tissue.'' (Letter from Wilber to Livingstone, July 25, 1991)

Dr. Humes stated that "We also prepared photographs of the brain from several aspects to depict the extent of these injuries." (2 WCH 355)

PREVIOUS TAMPERING WITH BRAIN

Audrey Bell said that the brain would have dehydrated and that the hole in the back of the head was large enough for it to slip through if somebody "knew what they were doing." (a: Sept. 22, 1991) She saw that almost a third of it was missing in the back.

Jenkins is the only witness to indicate that there had been a pre-examination of the brain and that it had been removed from the head somewhere, then replaced.

Dr. Robert Karnei: "Nobody got to it at Parkland, I can tell you that. The opening in the scalp was not big enough to go ahead and take the brain out . . . Most of the brain that was missing was in the back part of the head." (a: Aug. 27, 1991)

Paul O'Connor has said the same thing as Karnei. "The hole wasn't big enough even to remove half a brain. It would have been torn all to pieces." (a: Apr. 19, 1990) This is backed up deductively because they had to make cuts in the scalp and skull at the autopsy in order to get the brain out, which is described by Jenkins himself.

THE BULLET TRACK IN THE HEAD

Dr. Humes: "In further evaluating the head wound, I will refer back to the X-rays which we had previously prepared. These had disclosed to us multiple minute fragments of radio-opaque material transversing a line from the wound in the occiput to just above the right eye, with a rather sizable fragment visible by X-ray just above the right eye." (2 WC 353)

SURGERY TO SKULL OR BRAIN

FBI Report: ". . . It was ascertained that the President's clothing had been removed and it was also apparent that a tracheotomy had been performed as well as surgery of the head area, namely, in the top of the skull."(h)

O'Neill, who had written the FBI autopsy report, said he had no idea what "surgery to the head area" meant, and was simply reporting what he heard. "I don't know what that means. You'll have to ask Dr. Humes. He's the one who said it." (f)

"In an affidavit to the Committee, Sibert acknowledged that the statement that head surgery was performed was determined 'not to be correct following detailed inspection.' (See affidavit of James Sibert, October 24, 1978, JFK document 012806)" (7HSCA 19 (62))

James Curtis Jenkins stated several instances of surgery to the head, including a neatly severed brain stem, and what he thought were two or three small cuts along the scalp, fracture and suture lines, which might have been made to remove the brain before the autopsy began. (a: May 29, 1991)

O'Connor: when asked, "Now on the surgery to the top of the head, remember, uh . . ."

"I don't understand that."

"Yeah."

"I don't know. See, these guys that say that kind of stuff were, well, I don't think that, were they doctors that said that at all?" (a: Apr. 19, 1990)

O'Connor: when asked, "And there was no brain in the head when it came in?"

"Well, maybe a handful. Macerated tissue."

"But your impression was that someone had removed the brain?"

"No, I thought had his brains blown out, really." (a: Apr. 19, 1990)

O'Connor: "And I removed the sheet and we got on with it."

"So you couldn't tell from that whether or not there had been any kind of tampering or surgery or anything?"

"No." (4-19-90)

Nova, a PBS television show with Walter Cronkite in 1988, pointed to the temple area as possibly what was meant by surgery to the head area, even though the FBI report (h) referred to the top of the head. Interestingly, the skull X-rays, according to radiologist Dr. Siple show evidence of surgery in exactly that area, where the bone was cut away.

In addition, the skull X-rays may show evidence of nippers having cut away the skull from just left of the center line of the forehead above the eyes according to Dr. Siple. (a: May 1993)

SPINAL CORD

O'Connor said that his spinal cord "did not look all that well." (a: Sept. 23, 1991)

Doctor Robert Karnei: The spinal cord was not removed. He was quite strong about this. (Aug. 27, 1991)

Jim Jenkins: said that later the spinal cord was removed separately—use of Stryker saw but both sides of the vertebral column. Jenkins saw Dr. Boswell remove the spinal cord (a: June 6, 1991) Jenkins thinks the brain stem was severed before it arrived at the autopsy because when they removed it from the head, the spinal cord did not come with it. He also said during the same interview that he did not recall removing the spinal cord and that he would have removed it (a: May 29, 1991)

However, approximately 90% of the time the spinal cord will separate from the brain when the brain is removed.

ADRENALS

Jim Jenkins: "We did a full scale autopsy on JFK. We tested for everything. We examined the testes (they were sectioned), the adrenals, etc. There were sections of the heart and other organs taken." (June 16, 1991)

Dr. Karnei: "'There were no adrenals.'" (a: Aug. 27, 1991) They are not mentioned in the pathologists' autopsy report. This was corroborated by Dr. Boswell and Dr. Karnei to *The New York Times (October 6, 1992) and to JAMA* (October 7, 1992, p. 1737).

Dr. John Lattimer (viewed autopsy material in Archives, 1972) said the adrenals were not calcified (John K. Lattimer, "Observations Based on a Review of the Autopsy Photographs, X-Rays, and Related Materials of the Late President John F. Kennedy," *Resident and Staff Physician Medical Times*, May 1972)

THROAT WOUND

Dallas witnesses who saw the throat wound repeat to this day that there was a small wound of entry in the front of the throat.

Dr. Perry (who saw it first and who made a tracheostomy incision through it) stated three times during the press conference that followed the death of the President that there was an entry wound in the throat. (WFAA-TV, 11-22-63) He would not state this after Specter talked to him for the Warren Commission, though he did not retract it. The transcript of the press conference is in the LBJ Library in Austin.

Dr. McClelland (Parkland) told reporter Richard Dudman of the *St. Louis Post-Dispatch* (Dec 1, 1963), that the neck wound was a small, undamaged punctuate area which "had the appearance of the usual entrance wound of a bullet."(6 H 36-37)

Dr. Ronald Coy Jones (Parkland): "A small hole in anterior midline of neck thought to be a bullet entrance wound. (Jones, Dr. Ronald, Exhibit 1, written report of Nov. 22, 1963) Jones had stated in his report of Nov. 22 that the wound in the anterior neck was an entrance wound because it was very small and relatively clean-cut, as would be seen in entry rather than exit. (6 H 55–6) Dr. Jones stated that it was emphatically a wound of entrance to Harrison E. Livingstone which was filmed by Al Fisher. (*High Treason 2*, pp. 106-7)

Dr. Charles Carrico (Parkland): "A small penetrating wound" (CE 392, written report of Nov. 22, 1963.)

Perry, Baxter and Clark did not suggest in their written reports whether the wound was produced by the entrance or the exit of a bullet. (CE 392)

The testimony of the Dallas doctors in March 1964 as expressed to Arlen Specter of the Warren Commission is paraphrased here by Meagher (see Meagher, pp. 150–151):

Dr. Clark did not see the anterior neck wound (G H 22). Dr. McClelland did not see the original neck wound, though he helped perform the tracheostomy. McClelland said that he and the other doctors discussed the wounds afterwards and they concluded that the throat wound was an entry wound. (6 H 33, 35.) If McClelland said this is what they decided, then that is the way it was. He is the most honorable man on the earth.

Dr. Charles Baxter said it was more like an entrance wound than an exit wound and was not jagged (so it was not from a high velocity weapon). (6

H 42) On June 4th, 1992, Baxter spoke at some length about this wound again, at the forum of Dallas doctors: "Looking at that hole, one would have to—and my immediate thought was that this was an entry wound because it was *so small*. The hole was only the size of a pencil eraser, about two or two and a half millimeters across, and air was bubbling out of it, and a little blood. . . . We went right through it. You'd obviously would go through where the hole was if you are going to try to control what the hole is doing. It happened to be at exactly the level that we do tracheostomy. That much incision is just the size that you have to have to get down to get the muscles spread to get the tracheostomy tube in. So there is nothing about that that is not routine."

Dr. Marion Jenkins did not mention the wound in his written report, but he told Specter that he thought it was an exit wound because it was not a clean wound (a clearly demarcated, round, punctuate wound). It may be that Jenkins did not see it, as he has a history of sometimes saying things he later contradicts (6 H 48, 51)

Dr. Gene Akin said the wound was a slightly punctate hole: ". . . this must have been an entrance wound. . . ." (6 H 65, 67)

Dr. Paul Peters: "We speculated as to whether he had been shot once or twice, because we saw the wound of entry in the throat and noted the large occipital wound. . . ." But he then explained that he had *not* seen the throat wound before the tracheotomy. (6 H 71)

Nurse Margaret Henchliffe: "She saw a small hole in the middle of the President's neck, about as big as the end of her little finger. It looked like an entrance bullet hole to her. She had never seen an exit wound that looked like that. It was small and not jagged like most exit wounds." (6 H 143)

Nurse Diana Bowron: ". . . and the entry wound in his throat."

HL: OK. And what did that look like?

DB: Well, that looked like an entry wound.

The following made comments since 1964:

Dr. Charles Crenshaw: In his book, *Conspiracy of Silence*, p. 79: "I also identified a small opening about the diameter of a pencil at the midline of his throat to be an entry bullet hole. There was no doubt in my mind about that wound. I had seen dozens of them in the emergency room. At that point, I knew that he had been shot at least twice."

Dr. Kemp Clark had originally been quoted by CBS, NBC, and the BBC, *The New York Times* and *L'Express*, all of which quoted him as saying that the bullet had entered Kennedy's neck from in front and entered the chest. (6 H 21-30) He tried to get out of this by saying that they had quoted him "incompletely and inaccurately." (Meagher)

NBC reporters said that Perry said that "A bullet struck him in front as he faced the assailant." (NBC News, *Seventy Hours and Thirty Minutes*, Random House, 1966; Meagher, p. 153)

AP article of 11-26-63 entitled "No Report of Autopsy Given on Kennedy" quotes Clark as saying he was unable to tell if the bullet that caused the head wound also caused the throat wound but "there could have been two bullets."

JFK Dallas Death Certificate (11-22-63): "Multiple gunshot wounds of the head and neck." The only part of the neck examined in Dallas was the front of the throat.

Clark Panel: At and above the tracheostomy is the "upper half of the circumference of a circular cutaneous wound ... characteristic ... of the exit wound of a bullet ... lower half of this circular wound is obscured ... center of this circular wound is situated approximately 9 cm. below the transverse fold in the skin of the neck." The conclusion of the Ciark Panel was that the bullet that made the throat wound travelled downward and to the left. ("1968 Panel Review of Photographs, X-rays Films, Documents and Other Evidence Pertaining to the Fatal Wounding of President John F. Kennedy on November 22, 1963," aka the Clark Panel)

APPEARANCE OF THROAT TRACHEOSTOMY WOUND

Dr. McClelland: the throat wound (trach incision) in the picture was the same as what he saw. (*Nova*, PBS, 1988) A group of the Dallas doctors were quoted in the May, 1992 *JAMA* article as saying that the throat wound as depicted in the photographs was of the right appearance. It is simply retouched, in the author's opinion, to look jagged and like a large wound of exit. No medical witness from Dallas, with the possible exception of Dr. Charles Crenshaw, has questioned the appearance of the wound in the photos. (*High Treason 2*, p.113).

Dr. Humes: tracheostomy was "some 7 or 8 cm. in length." (2 WC 361)

Ebersole: "There was a transverse wound across the lower neck in the front ... I would say slightly below the Adam's apple. This was, appeared to be ... a transverse surgical wound." (Interview of Ebersole by Art Smith, 3/28/78)

O' Neill: "the throat wound was a surgical incision." He did not imply that it was or could be anything else. (a: May 20, 1991)

Paul O'Connor was asked if anyone could have torn open the throat more than it was so that it looks something like the large gash we now see in the photograph. In other words, making it look like an exit wound, or trying to find a bullet. He wrote simply, "no." (Letter from O'Connor to Livingstone, June 30, 1990)

O'Connor feels that the throat wound in the pictures is retouched.

Jim Metzler did not see the throat wound. (a: May 27, 1991)

JFK Dallas Death Certificate (11-22-63): "Multiple gunshot wounds of the head and neck." The only part of the neck examined in Dallas was the front of the throat. Admiral Burkley was in the trauma room at Parkland with JFK and brought the Dallas Death Certificate to Bethesda with him on Nov. 22, 1963. Therefore, Burkley knew about the bullet wound in the front of the throat and did not convey that information to the medical staff at Bethesda. The pathologists did not know about the gunshot wound to the throat, and assumed the throat wound was merely a tracheostomy on the night of the autopsy.

A newspaper article quotes O'Connor as saying ". . . neither pathologist was aware that Kennedy had been hit in the throat as well as from the rear." (AP, 6-1-92)

SUTURES TO THE THROAT

Ebersole said the throat had been sutured. (*Philadelphia Inquirer*, March 10, 1978) No other witness has mentioned sutures to the throat.

Ebersole: "There was a transverse wound across the lower neck in the front . . . This was, appeared to be, a transverse surgically sutured, transverse surgical wound." (Interview of Ebersole by Art Smith, 3/28/78)

O'Connor said that there might have been but that he did not remember any sutures to the throat. (Letter from O'Connor to Livingstone, 6-11-91)

Rudnicki said there were no sutures. (a: Oct. 14, 1990)

Custer said there were no sutures. (a: Oct. 29, 1990)

BACK WOUND

Diana Bowron turned over the body and washed it at Parkland Hospital in Dallas. She examined the back wound and described it as an entry wound. She states that the photograph of Kennedy's back is not his back. (*Killing the Truth*)

Reed said, "They wanted an AP and lateral neck. Then when I lifted him up to put a plate underneath his back for an AP chest, I found right between the scapula and thoracic column a large, inch-and-a-half wound that looked like an exit wound." (*RT Image*, 11-21-88) This wound seems to correspond to the big hole seen about seven inches down on the back in the photograph.

O'Neill stated that the back wound did not penetrate the chest, describing the probing exactly as had Jenkins and Finck. (a: May 20, 1991) "They used a surgical probe and it just went in so far. In fact, there was a question as to how could it go in and not come out. And Jim Sibert went out and called the FBI Laboratories and asked if there was such a thing as an ice bullet. When he came back in, we just learned that they had found a bullet on a stretcher in Dallas. That explained it."

"As far as you could see, it did not penetrate into the chest?"

"As far as I could see, it did not penetrate." (a: May 20, 1991)

O'Neill reaffirmed that the back wound was located in the upper right back, just below the shoulder. "Sibert was the first to notice it." Humes probed the wound with his finger and said that "there is no point of exit, absolutely no point of exit for this." O'Neill further stated that, because there was no wound of exit for the back entrance wound, Humes assumed that the stretcher bullet (aka "The Magic Bullet," CE 399) worked its way out of the back. (f)

O'Connor said, "The doctors probed the hole in Kennedy's back to a depth of about 2 inches, but found no exit wound." (AP article, 6-1-92)

Ebersole: ". . . there is a very definite wound of entrance . . . to the right of the midline. . . . At this point, there was . . . no obvious wound of exit . . . At that point . . . took X-rays." (Interview of Ebersole by Art Smith, 3-28-78)

Ebersole stated that the back wound was not at the base of the neck. (Interview of Ebersole by Dr. David Mantik, 11-2-92 and 12-2-92) The bullet entered to the right of the 4th thoracic vertebra. Dr. Gary Aguilar said, "Burkley said [the back entrance wound] to the right of the 3rd [vertebra]. Either way, both of the physician-eyewitness accounts contradict the photos and the WC conclusions regarding a single bullet being able to do the work. Ebersole was consistent about his identifying the location to the right of the 4th vertebra . . . Boswell's face sheets show it there also." (Prodigy, 12-4-92)

Ebersole: He places the time of the back probing as "Humes first probed it [the back wound] after he made his [Y] incision." (Interview of Ebersole by Art Smith, 3/28/78)

Riebe claimed that the lower hole seen in the autopsy photo of the back was the wound. Others claim what looks like a wound in the shoulder is it.

Humes: The wound started out six inches down the President's back and it was gradually moved up to the shoulder, about three inches below the shoulder, and then to the neck. First, it was a wound of "the upper right posterior thorax," according to Humes in his autopsy report, but by the time he talked to the Warren Commission, it became a neck wound. There is something of a difference.

The back wound was not proven at the autopsy to have come out the throat. (Testimony of Doctor Pierre Finck, trial of Clay Shaw; *Heritage of Stone*, Jim Garrison, Putnam, 1970; *Six Seconds in Dallas*, Josiah Thompson, Berkley, 1976, p. ix; *Cover-Up*, Gary Shaw and Larry Harris, pp. 195–7; *Medicolegal Investigation of the of the President John F. Kennedy Murder*, Dr. Charles Wilber, Charles Thomas & Sons, p. 256)

Roy Kellerman (the Secret Service man in the front seat of the President's limousine) testified that "A Colonel Finck—during the examination of the President, from the hole that was in his shoulder, and with a probe, and we were standing right alongside of him, he is probing inside the shoulder with his instrument and I said, 'Colonel, where did it go?' He said 'There are no lanes for an outlet of this entry in this man's shoulder.' " (2 H 93)

And did Kellerman really say it was in the "shoulder," or did someone change his testimony? This is asked because some of the other men said they saw the bullet hole in Kennedy six inches down on Kennedy's back. "I saw an opening in the back, about 6 inches below the neckline to the right-hand side of the spinal column." (2 H 143) There is no possible way that six inches down on the back, which coincides with the holes in Kennedy's shirt and coat, could be confused with the image seen two or three inches from the shoulder line in the autopsy photograph. Maybe its just a clot.

FBI Report "During the later stages of this autopsy, Dr. Humes located an opening which appeared to be a bullet hole which was below the shoulders and two inches to the right of the middle line of the spinal column. This opening was probed by Dr. Humes with the finger, at which time it was determined that the trajectory of the missile entering at this point had entered at a downward position of 45 to 60 degrees. Further probing determined that the distance travelled by this missile was a short distance inasmuch as the end of the opening could be felt with the finger.

"Inasmuch as no complete bullet of any size could be located in the brain area and likewise no bullet could be located in the back or any other area of the body as determined by total body X-rays and *inspection revealing there was no point of exit*, [emphasis added] the individuals performing the autopsy were at a loss to explain why they could find no bullets." (FBI Report of November 26, 1963, File No. 89-30-31)

Dr. Humes, testifying to the Warren Commission, talked about the back and throat wound. He said "we examined carefully the bony structures in this vicinity as well as the X-rays, to see if there was any evidence of fracture or of deposition of metallic fragments in the depths of this wound, and we saw no such evidence, that is no fracture of the bones of the shoulder girdle, or of the vertical column, and no metallic fragments were detectable by X-ray examination." (2 WCH 361)

Clark Panel on *NECK REGION*: "Several small metallic fragments are present in this region." ("1968 Panel Review of Photographs, X-rays Films, Documents and Other Evidence Pertaining to the Fatal Wounding of President John F. Kennedy on November 22, 1963," aka the Clark Panel).

Clark Panel: Their examination of the X-rays provided to them showed: #8 rt thorax, shoulder shows no fracture of the scapula, clavicles, ribs or cervical and thoracic vertebrae; #9 AP chest showed that just right of the cervical spine "above apex of the right lung ... several small metallic fragments"; #10 AP left thorax, shoulder, #8, and #9 were used to visualize the "neck" shot/wound. ("1968 Panel Review of Photographs, X-rays Films, Documents and Other Evidence Pertaining to the Fatal Wounding of President John F. Kennedy on November 22, 1963," aka the Clark Panel)

In referencing the location of the back wound with the bullet holes in Kennedy's clothing, the Clark Panel described the back of the suit coat (CE 393) hole as 15 mm. long vertically and "located 5 cm. to the right of the midline in the back of the coat ... 12 cm. below the upper edge of the coat collar." They also described the shirt (CE 394) as having a hole 10 mm. long vertically "corresponding to the one described in the coat, is located 2.5 cm." to the right of the middle of the shirt and 14 cm. from the top of the collar." ("1968 Panel Review of Photographs, X-rays Films, Documents and Other Evidence Pertaining to the Fatal

Wounding of President John F. Kennedy on November 22, 1963," aka the Clark Panel)

Clark Panel: "elliptical penetrating wound of the skin of the *back* (emphasis added) located approximately 15 cm. medial to the right of the acromial process, 5 cm. lateral to the mid-dorsal line and 14 cm. below the right mastoid process . . . has characteristics of the entrance wound . . . marginal abrasion measures approximately 7 mm. in width by 10 mm. in length . . . "This panel concluded that the bullet that made this wound travelled downward and to the left. ("1968 Panel Review of Photographs, X-rays Films, Documents and Other Evidence Pertaining to the Fatal Wounding of President John F. Kennedy on November 22, 1963," aka the Clark Panel)

Dr. John Lattimer (urologist who viewed the autopsy materials at the National Archives): Using the autopsy photos, he stated the back wound was located 5 cm. below "the transverse double fold in the skin at the junction of the neck and the back" He also reinforced this by stating that the wound was located "just below the junction of neck and back." (John K. Lattimer, "Observations Based on a Review of the Autopsy Photographs, X-Rays, and Related Materials of the Late President John F. Kennedy," *Resident and Staff Physician Medical Times*, May 1972)

Dr. Cyril Wecht (forensic pathologist who viewed the autopsy material at the Archives; member of the HSCA forensic panel): Using the autopsy photos, he located the back wound to be 5.7 cm. below the lowest crease in the neck and 4-4.5 cm from the midline of the back. (Cyril H. Wecht and Robert P. Smith, "The Medical Evidence in the Assassination of President John F. Kennedy," *Forensic Science* 3, 1974)

PASSAGE OF THE BULLET FROM FRONT TO BACK THROUGH THE BODY

The Warren Report says "further exploration" had disproved the theory of the surgeons who had determined that the bullet had passed between two large strap muscles and bruised them without leaving any channel. (Epstein, *Inquest*, p. 58)

Meagher notes that none of the four non-medical witnesses at the autopsy, Greer, Kellerman, Sibert and O'Neill heard anything about the bullet passing through the body: "The claim that further exploration had caused the autopsy surgeons to abandon the first assumption that the bullet had penetrated a short distance and dropped out is without the slightest corroboration from the four non-medical witnesses." (p. 145, see 2 H 127)

Dr. Milton Helpern, former Medical Examiner of New York insisted that it is impossible for a bullet to pass through a human body under such circumstances without leaving a discernible path. (Epstein, *Inquest*, p. 58; Meagher note p. 145.)

Humes, with reference to the bullet that he admits may have passed through Kennedy, could not be the same one they say went through Connally. "I think that extremely unlikely. The reports (again, Exhibit 392 from Parkland) tell of an entrance wound on the lower mid-thigh of the Governor, and X-rays taken there are described as showing metallic fragments in the bone, which apparently by this report were not removed and are still present in Governor Connally's thigh. I can't conceive of where they came from this missile.'' (2 WCH 376) The Warren Commission claimed that a bullet that struck Kennedy in the back of the ''neck'' and came out the front of his throat to strike Governor Connally. This is the ''magic bullet theory.''

Ebersole stated that the back wound was not at the base of the neck. (Interview of Ebersole by Dr. David Mantik, 11-2-92 and 12-2-92) The bullet entered to the right of the 4th thoracic vertebra. Dr. Gary Aguilar said, ''Burkley said [the back entrance wound] to the right of the 3rd [vertebra]. Either way, both of the physician eyewitness accounts contradict the photos and the WC conclusions regarding a single bullet being able to do the work. Ebersole was consistent about his identifying the location to the right of the 4th vertebra ... Boswell's face sheets show it there also.'' (Prodigy, 12-4-92)

SCALPEL CUTS IN UPPER CHEST

Dr. Charles Carrico (Parkland) wrote that there were no air leaks noted after insertion of chest tubes. (Doctors' Notes, Parkland Hospital, 11-22-63)

O'Connor was asked ''Did the doctors probe the knife cuts in the chest? ''No.,'' ''Did they know what penetrated the chest?'' ''No.'' (Drainage tubes were inserted there at Parkland.) ''No probing of these cuts were made. There were two small incisions above each breast nipple—what they were for, I'll never know—these were superficial cuts and did not penetrate the pleura—as for chest tubes, I never saw these incisions—which does not say they were not there. I was at the head of the body during the autopsy and could not see what transpired in the body cavity except to notice blood in the upper right intercostal muscles.'' (a: June 11, 1990)

FRAGMENTS OR BULLETS

Dr. Kemp Clark (Parkland): states Clark as saying that no bullets were removed while the body was at Parkland, and that he was unable to tell if the bullet that caused the head wound also caused the throat wound but ''there could have been two bullets.'' (AP article, ''No Report of Autopsy Given on Kennedy,'' 11-26-63)

Ebersole: ''We did take those X-rays ... [and] did not find a bullet. We could see metal fragments, of course, in the skull.'' (Interview of Ebersole by Art Smith, 3/28/78)

Regarding the back wound, O'Neill stated that ''Humes probed the wound with his finger and said 'there is no point of exit, absolutely no point of exit for this.' '' O'Neill further stated that, because there was no wound of exit for the back entrance wound, Humes assumed that the stretcher bullet (aka "The Magic Bullet," CE 399) worked its way out of the back. (f)

Ebersole: "After some of the organs had been removed, the lungs (. . . and the intestines) had been removed . . . we took a *second series of X-rays* at the request of one of either the FBI or Secret Service man." This would appear, from Ebersole's statements regarding the back wound, to be at the time of the examination of the back wound. "Once again, we saw no bullet." (Interview of Ebersole by Art Smith, 3/28/78)

Ebersole: "No further X-rays were taken until 12:30, one o'clock in the morning when, from Dallas, three pieces of skull bone arrived . . . I X-rayed those . . . A bullet had been found in a blanket [in Dallas] and . . . sent up at approximately the same time as the three pieces of skull were being X-rayed." (Interview of Ebersole by Art Smith, 3/28/78).

Former FBI agent, Francis O'Neill stated that they found 2-3 very small fragments in the head. (a: May 20, 1991).

FBI Report: "X-rays of the brain area which were developed and returned to the autopsy room disclosed a path of a missile which appeared to enter the back of the skull and the path of disintegrating fragments could be observed along the right side of the head. The largest section of this missile as portrayed by X-ray appeared to be behind the right frontal sinus. The next largest fragment appeared to be at the rear of the skull at the juncture of the skull bone . . . approximately 40 particles of disintegrated bullet and smudges indicated that the projectile had fragmentized while passing through the skull region." (h)

This report also states that the size of the removed fragments to be 7 × 2 millimeters from the right side of brain, and 1 × 3 millimeters also from the right side of the brain. (h)

O'Neill stated that 2 fragments were removed during the autopsy "from in back of the sinus and in back of the whole head cavity here (gestures from top of cheeks to above the eye)." (f)

Dr. Humes: "In further evaluating the head wound, I will refer back to the X-rays which we had previously prepared. These had disclosed to us multiple minute fragments of radio-opaque material transversing a line from the wound in the occiput to just above the right eye, with a rather sizable fragment visible by X-ray just above the right eye." (2 WC 353)

Dr. Guinn testified to HSCA that the brain fragments he used for his tests were NOT the same fragments used for testing by the FBI in 1964 for the Warren Commission. "The particular little pieces they analyzed, I could just as well have analyzed over again, but the pieces that were brought out of the Archives—which reportedly, according to Mr. Gear, were the only bullet-lead fragments from the case still present in the Archives—did not include any of the specific little pieces that the FBI analyzed. Presumably, those are still in existence somewhere, I am sure nobody threw them out, but where they are, I have no idea." (1 HSCA 561).

A photograph of Warren Commission Exhibit 843 shows "three lead-like fragments removed from President Kennedy's brain during the autopsy." (7 HSCA 392) The Clark Panel report states that it examined "CE 843 (3 lead fragments)." Dr. Guinn's report states "(6) FBI nos. Q4, Q5 (CE-843). One larger fragment and one smaller fragment, reportedly recovered from President Kennedy's brain during autopsy." (1 HSCA 514) It is important to note that CE 843 originally had three fragments in 1964 and the same exhibit had only two fragments during HSCA. The missing fragment is a small fragment because CE 843 originally had two small fragments, not one.

O'Neill thought that a fragment from the head shot came out of his throat, nicking his tie. When told that "the photos and films show he was hit in the throat long before the head shot. He is holding his throat." "Sure. So what?" (a: May 20, 1991)

Clark Panel on *NECK REGION*: "Several small metallic fragments are present in this region." This was when the Clark Panel examined the films and X-rays in 1968.

Clark Panel stated their results of their analysis of the autopsy X-rays to be: #1 AP skull" [fragment] embedded in the outer table of the skull ... lies 25 mm. to right of midline, ... [adjacent to hole on internal surface] localized elevation of soft tissue [plus bone fragments]"; #2 skull left lateral has "(fragments moving P-A stop) just anterior to the region of the coronal suture (and end in front just) below the badly fragmented frontal and parietal bones ... [covering a] 45 mm. long 8 mm. wide area ... [which overlies part of the coronal suture, ... (elliptical scalp wound near midline and high above hairline) position ... corresponds to hole ... (the hole) measures 8mm in diameter on outer skull and as much as 20 mm. on interior surface ... (the head wound was located) approximately 100 mm. above the occiptal protuberance ... bone of the lower edge is depressed, ... fragment as seen ... is round and measures 6.5 mm. in diameter"; #7 AP thoracolumbar showed no bullets or fragments; #8 rt thorax, shoulder shows no fracture of the scapula, clavicles, ribs or cervical and thoracic vertebrae; #9 AP chest showed that just right of the cervical spine "above apex of the right lung ... several small metallic fragments"; #10 AP left thorax, shoulder, #8, and #9 were used to visualize the "neck" shot/wound; #11 AP thoracolumbar showed no bullets or fragments. ("1968 Panel Review of Photographs, X-rays Films, Documents and Other Evidence Pertaining to the Fatal Wounding of President John F. Kennedy on November 22, 1963," aka the Clark Panel)

FBI Report: "Inasmuch as no complete bullet of any size could be located in the brain area and likewise no bullet could be located in the back or any other area of the body as determined by total body X-rays and *inspection revealing there was no point of exit*, (emphasis added) the individuals performing the autopsy were at a loss to explain why they could find no bullets." (FBI Report of November 26, 1963, File No. 89-30-31)

Dr. Humes: regarding the back wound, "we examined carefully the bony structures in this vicinity as well as the X-rays, to see if there was any evidence of fracture or of deposition of metallic fragments in the depths of this wound, and we saw no such evidence, that is no fracture of the bones of the shoulder girdle, or of the vertical column, and no metallic fragments were detectable by X-ray examination.'' (2 WCH 361)

Reed: "We still didn't find any large fragments—only small fragments, but we could see the trace of the fragments and the line of them projecting upwards and downward. They couldn't figure out if it was a bullet from the top that went down or from the front that went up because the bones were outward which means that he would have been shot from the front. . . . Humes couldn't find the bullets. I X-rayed his whole body and we only had fragments. He didn't have anything larger than 4 or 5 mm. long.'' (*RT Image*, Nov 21, 1988)

O'Neill denies that there was a bullet which rolled out of the President's wrappings. (a: May 20, 1991)

O'Connor feels that Captain Osborne is (concerning his statement that a bullet had rolled out of the wrappings, which he later retracted to the HSCA) "absolutely crazy. Number one, when we got the body he was completely nude, uh, (chuckle) there was just no way that could happen. Not in that morgue it didn't.'' However, O'Connor contradicted himself later when he is quoted as saying, "The bullet from the (back) wound fell out when the body was lifted from the coffin to the examining table at Bethesda.'' (AP-New York, 6-1-92)

O'Connor was asked about a 1966 *Washington Post* article saying that a bullet had been found at the autopsy. "Not a bullet but a bullet fragment probably was found. As I stated to you earlier, after the chest cavity was eviscerated, I noticed blood in the upper right intercostal muscles indicating trauma in that area.'' (a: June 11, 1990)

FBI Report: Because the autopsy participants couldn't figure out why there were no bullets in the body, "a call was made . . . to Firearms Section of the FBI Laboratory. SA Charles L. Killion advised that the Laboratory had received through Secret Service Agent Richard Johnson a bullet which had reportedly been found on a stretcher in the emergency room of Parkland . . . and that this bullet consisted of a copper alloy full jacket . . . The two metal fragments removed from the brain area were hand-carried by SAs Sibert and O'Neill to the FBI Laboratory immediately following the autopsy and were turned over to SA Kurt Frazier.'' (h)

Custer: "Custer said that, on the day after the shooting, he was instructed to take X-rays of 'a bullet fragment taped to a skull.' I was told by Dr. Ebersole that it was for a bust (of Kennedy) . . . I did that the next day in the main department in one of the small rooms with a portable on a stretcher.'' Custer also stated here that the X-ray log where he logged in the X-rays has subsequently disappeared. (Scott Hatfield, *RT*, "RT Disputes X-ray Photos in JFK Case'', 8-31-92)

END OF AUTOPSY

O'Neill stated that right before the end of the autopsy between 11:00 P.M.–12:00 A.M., General Wehle came in with the mahogany casket supplied by Gawlers. (f)

Humes: "The examination was concluded at 11 o'clock on the night of November 22." (2 H 374)

Reed: Ebersole came in after midnight to take more X-rays. (Reed in *RT Image*, and Gil Dulaney in the *Lancaster Intelligencer-Journal*)

FBI Report: "The two metal fragments removed from the brain area were hand carried by SAs Sibert and O'Neill to the FBI Laboratory immediately following the autopsy and were turned over to SA Kurt Frazier." All the developed x-rays and all the undeveloped photographic film was turned over to Secret Service agent Roy Kellerman. (h)

The FBI Report stated that the skull fragment "measuring 10 × 6.5 centimeters was maintained in the custody of Dr. Humes who stated that it also could be made available for further examination." (h)

PREPARING THE BODY FOR BURIAL

Joe Hagen: "I had some guy screaming at us the whole time . . . some Air Force major . . . There was a lot of interference with the autopsy, I understand." (Interview of Hagen by Harrison Livingstone and Kathlee Fitzgerald, 8/15/91)

The professionals from Gawlers Funeral Home arrived while "they were proceeding with the post mortem . . . the head, I think the thoracic cavities and all, had been opened . . . Our hearse took the (mahogany) casket out to the Naval Hospital late that evening . . . we dressed him and rolled the casket right in and put him in it." (Interview of Joe Hagen by Harrison Livingstone and Kathlee Fitzgerald, 8/15/91)

Joe Hagen: "There was extensive damage to the President's head, most of it back up in here (indicating with his hand the rearward right side and the back) . . . We had to replace just all of that area with plaster of paris due to the extent of the wounds that were there . . . If it hadn't of been that big, we wouldn't have had to use plaster of paris, see . . . Quite a bit of bone was lacking . . . We had no problems in here (indicating the area of the coronal suture) . . . Back up in here (again gestures back of head), his head would have been down in the pillow and, if I remember correctly, we had taken a little out of the pillow where his head would fit down in the pillow." (Interview of Joe Hagen by Harrison Livingstone and Kathlee Fitzgerald, 8/15/91)

O'Connor stated that he helped dress the body before it was placed in the casket. "Also, I was the last person to actually touch Kennedy when I placed a black rosary in his hand." (Letter from O'Connor to Livingstone)

Joe Hagen of Gawlers Funeral Home: stated that *he* put the rosary in Kennedy's hand. (Interview of Joe Hagen by Harrison Livingstone and

Kathlee Fitzgerald 8-15-91) Also Hagen in Manchester doing same. (i: p. 433)

O'Connor wrote that "When the embalmers reconstructed the throat wound they used an adhesive to close the wound plus different compounds to seal the wound and erase the wound area." (letter from O'Connor to Livingstone, June 11, 1991)

There could not have been any reconstruction of the scalp to make the back-of-head pictures because the scalp was not totally reconstructed. Part was left open because it was on the pillow and noone would see that scalp was missing. (Tom Robinson, a: August 8, 1991) There was no pre-existing flap of scalp in the rear of the head because all the last witnesses to the body's final preparation have said that there was not enough scalp to cover the back of the head.

Paul O'Connor was asked if there had been any reconstructions made in order to take photos, or "that no pictures were taken during the embalming and preparation of the body for burial." This last is most important. The issue is whether there were reconstructions of the head and that pictures of the back of the head then made, or whether these are simply forgeries?"

"The only reconstructions made was after the autopsy was finished—we filled the cranium with plaster of Paris. The wound area was put together along with the brown rubber sheet, which covered an area about 3" × 3". The hair was then washed and brushed back over the wound area—that way the body was able to be shown to the Kennedy family in the White House." (a: June 11, 1990)

10:30 P.M.: "(Item 32) AT 22:30 Maj. O'Malley called and informed Maj. Pearson that the cortege would leave Bethesda Naval Center at approximately 01:00 hrs for the White House . . . Mrs. Kennedy to ride with cortege." (b)

11:45 P.M.: "(Item 33) 2345 Maj. O'Malley called in . . . Procession to leave Bethesda approximately 03:00 hrs and go directly to White House." (b)

3:55 A.M.: "At 03:55 Nov. 23, 63 (11/23/63, 3:55 A.M.), the details transferred the remains to the White House." (c)

4:00 A.M.: "The body bearers were released after the remains arrived at the White House at 04:00 Saturday, 23 November 1963." ("Breakdown of Daily Navy Participation" Navy Report: L.H. Frost, Commandant, Potomac River to Commanding General, MDW HQ, 12/20/63)

4:30 A.M.: ". . . the details transferred the remains to the White House, arriving at 0430 Nov. 23, 63 (11/23/63, 4:30 A.M.)." (c)

RECORDED OBSERVATIONS

Francis X. O'Neill: "We recorded our own observations and we recorded what they were saying. If we had questions, we asked them. Then we wrote the answers down." (a: May 20, 1991)

HISTOLOGICAL WORK

The histological work was done at Bethesda, not downtown, according to Dr. Joseph Brierre.

ACTIONS OF SECRET SERVICE

FBI Report: All the developed X-rays and all the undeveloped photographic film was turned over to Secret Service agent Roy Kellerman. (h)

"Mr. Behn advised that the undeveloped photographs and X-rays made during the course of the autopsy conducted at the National Naval Medical Center, Bethesda, Maryland, are in the custody of Mr. Bob Bouck, Protective Research Section, United States Secret Service." (FBI File # BA 89-30 by James Sibert and Francis O'Neill, Washington, DC, 11-29-63)

Dr. Karnei: "All I know is that they confiscated everything that night. And then they set a Secret Service man beside the tissue processor all night long. The next day when they put the tissues in to be processed for the histological sections, they had a Secret Service man beside the tissue processor, and when they took the sections, when they put the trimmings on the block, they confiscated all those trimmings. They didn't let anything go." (a: Aug. 27, 1991)

Dr. Charles Wilber: "The outrageous procedures of photo-taking at autopsy with no development of the negatives or transparencies, as may be, and then shuttling them off to Secret Service personnel or to Admiral Burkley can never be justified. In my view these were criminal acts: Secret Service is assigned to protect the President, not to interfere with handling of a corpse ... Admiral Burkley was not a member of the autopsy team; his function in this instance seems to have been official obfuscator and 'Sanitizer' of factual materials." (letter from Wilber to Livingstone, July 25, 1991)

FBI Report: Secret Service agent Gerald Behn, who was in charge of the White House detail, was questioned regarding the "section of the President's skull which was brought to the National Navy Medical Center at Bethesda, Maryland after the autopsy was in progress. He advised that this section, which was measured by the doctors performing the autopsy as being 10×6.5 centimeters, was found in the Presidential car on the floor between the front and the rear seats." (FBI Report file #BA 89-30 Washington, DC by James Sibert and Francis O'Neill, 11-29-63)

STATEMENTS THAT HAVE CAUSED CONFUSION REGARDING THE ACTUAL EVENTS AT BETHESDA NAVAL HOSPITAL NOVEMBER 22, 1963

LUNCH BREAKS OR ABSENCE FROM AUTOPSY ROOM

In order to evaluate and/or validate the witnesses' statements, it is important to determine if they were in a certain place at the time an event occurred. This helps in determining if their statements are from eyewitness observance or hearsay.

O'Connor did say he took a break in the cafeteria. Also "I left the morgue one time to get a rubber sheet to place in the cranium—5 minutes at the most. As to using the bathroom—we had them in the morgue." (a: June 11, 1990) This reference would appear to be towards the end of the autopsy or during the burial preparation period with the men from Gawlers.

"I *was* there all of the time. The only time I was away from the table was probably five or ten minutes when I was told to get a sandwich. But I did not leave the room." (October 8, 1990)

Jenkins said that he and Paul were told to go to the morgue at 3:30-4 p.m. Jenkins was not allowed to leave the morgue, but he said "Paul (**O'Connor**) was a kind of courier. He always had an escort, and was in and out of the morgue." (a: May 24, 1991)

O'Connor insisted that the casket arrived at 8:00 P.M. on the dot, and that he had entered that information in the autopsy log. O'Connor also told the HSCA it came in at 8pm (7 HSCA p.15.) However, on about June 10, 1991, Paul began to express doubt about the 8pm idea. (a) He realized he did not really know for sure, and that he thought he was wrong. It could be that he merely entered the room then and looked at the clock, and logged in the body. Or it may be the time that, after the preliminary examination, X-rays and photographs, the autopsy began. O'Connor may not have been there when the casket actually arrived in the autopsy room and did not arrive until the body was placed on the autopsy table. This is evidenced in statements: 1. Only two men carried the casket into the autopsy room. (a: Apr. 20, 1990) This is incorrect and is very contrary to many other confirmed witness accounts; 2. The body was nude with a sheet wrapped around the head. (a: Apr. 20, 1990; May 9, 1990) At no time does he mention any sheet other than around the head. The relevant omission here in O'Connor's statements is the sheet that was wrapped around the body and removed to reveal the nude body; 3. O'Connor said he thought that the following people helped removed the body from the casket: Humes, Boswell, Finck, Jenkins, and maybe Custer. (a: May 18, 1991) Boswell did assist with the removal, but Jenkins and Custer did not. Finck may not have arrived in time to help with the removal of the body from the casket if the body was removed from the casket, and then everyone waited for Finck's arrival, which the testimony seems to indicate. (a: May 18, 1991) O'Connor also states that neither O'Neill nor Sibert helped remove the body from the coffin. (a: May 26, 1991) **O'Neill**, however, has stated that he did help remove the body from the casket. (f) Jenkins has stated that he did not help unload the casket, but he thought O'Connor had. However, O'Connor did not help remove the body from the casket. Stringer helped take the body out and put it on the table. (a: Apr. 29, 1990; May 11, 1990) Edward Reed helped carry in the casket and remove the body from the casket in the morgue. (*RT Image*, Nov. 21, 1988) **Metzler** was present when the casket was opened, and helped remove the body from the coffin, put it on the table, and take off the sheet. He saw the head unwrapped. (a: May 27, 1991) Dr. John H. Ebersole said that he helped remove the body from the casket (to Art Smith, July, 1978, *The Continuing Inquiry*). Dr. Thornton Boswell helped; 4. O'Connor first stated that he was not there when the body was removed from the coffin (a: Apr. 20, 1990), and then said nineteen days later that he was there for the removal. (a: May 9, 1990) If, indeed, O'Connor was not there for the arrival of the casket in the autopsy room, and did not arrive at the autopsy room himself until the body was already on the autopsy table, then his remembrance of Kennedy's body arriving in a body bag and a shipping casket like the casket used by the military is definitely in question.

Metzler does not recall Paul **O'Connor** being there when he came back in with the casket from the dock area, though by then the room had filled with people and Paul may have been in the background. Metzler held the door open for the "bronze" casket. (a: June 1, 1991)

Jenkins was not allowed to leave the room after about 3:30 P.M., except once when Captain Stover told him to eat his lunch. He was only gone a few moments. (a: Mar. 25, 1991)

Metzler never saw the whole back of the head. Metzler was told to leave by Boswell after the head was unwrapped, saying they had enough help. (a: June 1, 1991)

During X-ray sessions, most persons must were asked to leave to autopsy room.

About 7:45 P.M. at the earliest to 8:30 P.M. at the latest, Jerrol **Custer** says that he was then asked to leave the morgue with **Reed** and that he was brought back sometime after 8 P.M. and found that they had already made the Y incision. (a: Sept. 23, 1991) The record states that the Y incision was done either at 8:00 P.M. or 8:15 P.M.

Ebersole stated "And the taking of them up to the 4th floor and having them processed . . . I was not in the room at all times. I had to leave at times to process X-rays. There would be intervals of 15, 20 minutes, I think." (Interview of Ebersole by Art Smith, 3/28/78) Ebersole would have left after the first set of X-rays, returned around 8:30 P.M. or a little before, which is the time he states X-rays were taken.

O'Neill: "They used a surgical probe and it just went in so far. In fact, there was a question as to how could it go in and not come out. And Jim **Sibert** went out and called the FBI Laboratories and asked if there was such a thing as an ice bullet. When he came back in, we just learned that they had found a bullet on a stretcher in Dallas." (a: May 20, 1991) The back probe was executed towards the latter part of the autopsy.

DEAD BABY

O'Connor knew about the dead baby. There was an outbreak of spinal meningitis at Patuxant River Naval Air Station, he said, and several babies died. (a: May 9, 1990)

Frank O'Neill also saw the dead baby. (a: May 20, 1991)

"Two Navy corpsmen passed, rolling a litter. Nothing appeared to be on it, except a small lump wrapped in sheeting." Lt. Bird asked what it was and was told by one of the men that it was a dead baby. (Manchester, p. 399.)

TIME OF FIRST HEARING ABOUT BODY ARRIVAL

2:00 P.M.: Edward F. Reed said that they were alerted at 2 P.M. that LBJ had had a heart attack and that he might be coming to Bethesda. (*RT IMAGE*, 11/21/88)

3:30-4:00 P.M.: Jenkins said that he and Paul were told to go to the morgue at 3:30-4 p.m. Jenkins was not allowed to leave the morgue. "Paul was a kind of courier. He always had an escort, and was in and out of the morgue." (a: May 24, 91)

4:00 P.M.: Reed: "Around 4 P.M. we were called into the office again and told that there was a good possibility that we would be doing the autopsy on President Kennedy anytime between 4 and 6 . . . I took a GE 225 portable unit down to the morgue in case we needed it and went off to the mess hall for dinner. There were four of us on duty, the supervisor, and three junior technologists." (*RT Image*, Nov. 21, 1988)

4:00 or 5:00 P.M.: Rebentisch said it was 4 or 5 o'clock and they were told to go in back and wait. It was still light when he went out back to wait. "Oh, yes!" he answered to the question if it was light. He doesn't know how long he waited, but Rebentisch said the casket came in 20 minutes (at least) before the Kennedy party. (a: May 27, 1991) He said his duty officer got about six of the men from the barracks when he learned the body was coming in at 5 o'clock or so. An Army captain was in charge of them. He was in charge of the color guard. (a: May 17, 1991)

4:30 P.M.: Rebentisch: "It was about 4:30 when our chief petty officer came to me and about five other petty officers and told us to go to the back of the hospital." (UPI story of January 25, 1981, *Miami Herald*; see also AP story of January 24, 1981, in the Ft. Worth *Star Telegram*),

Metzler was alone with Paul preparing the autopsy room. He went out on the platform to receive the coffin and does not recall Paul being there when he came back in with it, though by then the room had filled with people, and Paul may have been in the background. Metzler held the door open. Boswell was present when the coffin came in. He never saw the whole back of the head. Metzler was told to leave by Boswell then, saying they had enough help. (a: June 1, 1991)

ARRIVAL BY HELICOPTER:

There were several helicopter arrivals and departures at Andrews, and the honor guard from Walter Reed was flown to Bethesda by helicopter. (i: p. 390) They got into a pick up truck and went to look for the casket.

"Captain Canada had been advised that Kennedy would arrive by helicopter. He had placed an honor guard at the helipad; two helicopters arrived, but they carried the Andrews Air Force Base honor guard, which wanted to be on hand at Bethesda when the body arrived. Both honor guards were standing at attention at the pads." (j: p. 337)

INITIAL CONFUSION ABOUT BODY BEING FLOWN TO BETHESDA:

4:00 P.M.: "At 16:00 hours Paul Miller called General Wehle and informed him of the following: a.) President would arrive at Andrews at 18:00 hours (6 P.M.). b.) He will be choppered from there (Andrews) to the Naval Medical Center for autopsy." (e)

4:25 P.M. "At 16:25, General Wehle spoke to Admiral Frost, Commandant, PRNC. Remains arrival, chopper, and joint detail."(e)

4:34 P.M. "16:34 hours: General Wehle spoke with Colonel Lemon, Chief of Staff to General Brooke Allen, HQ! Cmd, USAF. Subject: Arrival of remains, chopper, joint details, etc." (e)

5:00 P.M.: Capt Patton (Special Events Officer, DMW who was at Andrews Air Force Base at 5 P.M.) informed DMW HQ that the "President's remains will arrive AAFB 18:05 hrs . . . Remains will be airlifted to Navy Medical Center in Bethesda. Vehicle escorts required: 1) Navy Medical Center to Gawlers Funeral Home to White House front entrance." (b)

5:10 P.M.: "At 17:10 Paul Miller called CG and informed: a. No change on tonight. Chopper is being laid on by White House Executive Flight Detachment for trip to Andrews . . . f. White House requests that General Wehle be responsible for contacting Admiral Galloway (of Bethesda) . . . re: request to lay security cordon around the heliport. The lights in the area would be turned on just before time for the chopper . . . Major Rutherford to take care of this detail." (e)

5:15 P.M.: "General Wehle departed this headquarters at 17:15 en route to Andrews AF Base." (e) He was flying there by helicopter.

5:30 P.M.-5:45 P.M.: Samuel Bird (Officer in Charge, Joint Service Casket Team): ". . . prior to the aircraft's (Air Force 1) landing, I formed two (2) joint service teams . . ." One team was to go up on the lift to help remove casket from plane to lift, and one team to remove the casket from the lift after it had been lowered to the ground "and place it *either in an ambulance or helicopter* (emphasis added)." This shows that the plan to helicopter the remains to Bethesda were changing at this point in time, or had been changed and word was just reaching Bird about this time. (d)

CONFUSION AT BETHESDA

5:10 P.M.: "At 1710 Paul Miller called CG and informed: . . . (f.) White House requests that General Wehle be responsible for contacting Admiral Galloway (of Bethesda) . . . re: request to lay security cordon around the heliport. The lights in the area would be turned on just before time for the chopper . . . Major Rutherford to take care of this detail." (e)

5:30 P.M.: "At 1730 hours, Major Rutherford notified Admiral Galloway's office, advising them to provide a security cordon around the heliport at the Bethesda Naval Center, expecting arrival of remains at approximately 1830 (6:30 P.M.), and to turn the lights on just prior to the arrival of the remains." (e)

The plans Rutherford was transmitting to Galloway at this time were those given to Rutherford 20 minutes prior (5:10).

5:30-5:45 P.M.: Samuel Bird (Officer in Charge, Joint Service Casket Team): "... prior to the aircraft's (Air Force 1) landing, I formed two (2) joint service teams ..." One team to go up on the lift to help remove casket from plane to lift, and one team to remove the casket from the lift after it had been lowered to the ground "and place it *either in an ambulance or helicopter* (emphasis added)." This shows that the plan to helicopter the remains to Bethesda were changing at this point in time, or had been changed and word was just reaching Bird at Andrews about this time. (d)

6:30 P.M.: Previous time set for remains arrival when remains were being helicoptered to Bethesda from Andrews. (Plans were changed prior to 5:45 P.M. to the remains arriving by ambulance.)

7:00-7:14 P.M.: At 7:00 P.M., "Sgt Humphrey, CG's Driver, checked into the office and advised that they were still at Bethesda." (e)

"The details (Honor Guard and Security that was at Andrews) was airlifted (by helicopter) to Bethesda for the reception of the remains at the U.S. Naval Medical Center ..." (c)

"At about 19:14 (7:14 P.M.) hours the CG arrived with his aide." (g)

"The detail transferred the remains to the Medical Center and remained as security during the autopsy and preparation period." (c)

Commander L.H. Frost: "From Andrews, one body bearer flew to the National Naval Medical Center by helicopter and one went by ambulance." (Navy Report: Frost to Commanding General, DMW HQ "Breakdown of Daily Navy Participation," 12/20/63)

Custer: Custer was told by the security chief at the Naval Hospital that the President's body was arriving by helicopter from Walter Reed and would land as close as possible to the Naval Hospital, where it would be brought the rest of the way by ambulance. (a: Oct. 8, 1990).

Dennis David: When asked about Kennedy's body possibly arriving by helicopter, he replied, "I don't think so. It was after that, they, someone said they thought there was a helicopter that landed back in either the ... or back in that area, but I saw one that landed up on the helipad.... landed shortly before Mrs. Kennedy's entourage came in and all this was *after* we had off-loaded that black hearse."

Dennis David believes that the casket he saw brought in at the morgue dock before Jackie arrived was a shipping casket and that Kennedy's body had arrived. He was on the second floor of the rotunda and saw the helicopter arrive. He says he thinks (but does not know) the bronze casket was empty. Boswell told him that JFK was in a shipping casket. (a: Dec. 17, 1991)

THE CASKET CONFUSION

Capt. John Stover "referred to the casket in which the body arrived as a 'transport coffin'. When I asked him whether he meant 'shipping casket', he said it 'could be,' but that he did not remember." (Lifton, *Best Evidence,* interview of April 1980, Carroll & Graf, 1988, p. 630) This is another example of twisted language.

Jim Jenkins: "There were no shipping caskets around there." (a: May 5, 1991)

Jenkins was in the morgue. (a: May 24, 1991). But Jenkins did not get a close look at the casket that contained Kennedy's body.

O'Neill insisted that it was a "ceremonial casket," and "not a shipping casket ... Nor was there ever a shipping casket in that autopsy room during the period of time I was there which was the entire evening." (f)

Stringer helped take the body out and put it on the table. He states that there was no shipping casket. (a: Apr. 29, 1990)

Jan Gail Rudnicki helped place the body on the table. He does not recall the shipping casket, but only the ornate bronze casket. His testimony seems accurate in all other respects. "I remember the casket being wheeled in." (a: Oct. 14, 1990)

Custer said that there was a shipping casket in the morgue, but he had no knowledge of the President's body being in it. He said that there was a body of an officer there, in a body bag and in a shipping casket. (a: Oct. 8, 1990)

THE BRONZE CASKET

Bronze (plated?) Elgin Britannia, Unit #26 Handley Regular solid bronze full top with double inner panels—twin sealing feature—no glass—amber Brit. finish, made by the Texas Coffin Company was listed at $3995. It remained at Gawlers in Washington until March 19, 1964, when it was picked up by Mr. Lewis M. Robeson, Chief Security Agent for the National Archives. Joe Hagen helped load it in the truck.

But Oneal was apparently asking $13,495 and according to a receipt alleged to be from the National Funeral Registry, was paid that amount. But the receipt does not show who wrote it or what company. There seems to be some dispute about the price. The U.S. government actually paid $13,495. Ten thousand dollars was added on to the price by someone, or to the payment. Oneal had wanted more, according to the *Washington Post* (Feb. 27, 1965), more than the $3,495 which was the public price. He went to Washington to get it, and there he met with the former Mayor of Dallas when JFK died, Earle Cabell, who had gone to the House of Representatives. Cabell made the arrangements for him to be paid.

The casket was referred to in the Dallas evidence by some at the hospital as a "bronze-colored plastic casket" (Warren Report, *NY Times* edition, p. 483; CE 392, and Price Exhibit No. 2, 21 H 162). The undertaker is going to try to get all he can, and certainly there is a double-entry book-keeping going on here.

COLOR OF THE "BRONZE" DALLAS CASKET

Aubrey Rike (Oneal Funeral Home, Dallas): "They told us to go into the trauma room and prepare the President to be moved ... It was an expensive bronze-colored type, it was a bronze casket. One of the most expensive we had in stock." It is important to note that the color was "bronze," and not that the casket was made of bronze metal. Also a judgement of the quality of the casket can not be made based on it being one of the most expensive Oneal "had in stock." (*The Men Who Killed Kennedy*, BBC-TV Documentary, 10-25-88)

Jim Metzler said it was a lightish brown, or pinkish grey, or dark brown. (a: June 1, 1991). He is not really sure of the color but feels it was the casket from Dallas. (Letter from Metzler to Livingstone, June 18, 1991)

Jim Jenkins said he originally told both Livingstone and Lifton that it was brown, but he is not really sure he ever saw it.

Francis O'Neill described the casket as "brownish in type." (f)

WHO SAW THE "BRONZE" CASKET AND WHEN

Aubrey Rike (Oneal Funeral Home, Dallas): "They told us to go into the trauma room and prepare the President to be moved ... It was an expensive bronze colored type, it was a bronze casket. One of the most expensive we had in stock ... It has a white satin lining inside the casket. We wrapped him in one of the sheets and placed him in the casket." It is important to note that the color was "bronze" and not that the casket was made of the metal bronze. Also a judgement of the quality of the casket can not be made based on it being one of the most expensive Oneal "had in stock." (*The Men Who Killed Kennedy*, BBC-TV documentary, 10-25-88)

Jim Metzler had originally stated that the body also did not come in the bronze casket, but it was in a cheap coffin, which he conceded might also be called a shipping casket. (a: June 1, 1991) Dr. Clark in Dallas had called it "plastic."

Jim Metzler at one time said: "I know it was not a shipping casket. But it was a cheap coffin, and I don't think it was the bronze coffin from Dallas." What color was it? "Dark brown." "Are you sure?" "I'm not really sure. It was a lighter brown or pinkish gray." But then Metzler wrote Harrison Livingstone on June 18, 1991: "You asked me whether the coffin I saw was an expensive or cheap one. Unfortunately, I'm not familiar with the different varieties of coffins and their prices. I'm not even sure of the color of the coffin. My first impression is that the color was dark brown, but I'm not sure because I also think that it could have been a grayish color. As many times as I thought about it, I still can't be sure of the color." Metzler rented a video just before writing this letter, which showed the coffin being unloaded from Air Force 1, and viewed it "at least a dozen times. My gut feeling is that the coffin in this video, which came from Dallas, Texas, is the coffin that I saw brought into the Bethesda Hospital morgue.

"Even though I am not sure, I have a feeling that this is the coffin which contained Kennedy's body. Also, the description from the funeral director's assistant as to how he wrapped Kennedy's head in a sheet and placed another sheet on his body is how I remember seeing Kennedy's body arrive in the Bethesda morgue."

Metzler held the door open, and stated that he saw the casket go into the autopsy room. (a: June 1, 1991)

Metzler has also reinforced to another interviewer that "it was dark brown, I believe it had handles on the side of it. It would be something that you'd see at a viewing ... It's not a rubber bag or a metal box." (Lifton, *Best Evidence,* interview of Nov. 1979, Carroll & Graf, 1988, p. 631-2)

O'Neill insisted that it was a "ceremonial casket. It was not known as a shipping casket ... (It was) brownish in type, handles on the side." (f)

Everyone recalls it coming in from the loading dock behind the hospital just by the door of the autopsy room.

THE SHIPPING CASKET

COLOR OF THE "Shipping" Casket

O'Connor: "It was slate gray." "It was the big, grey, sleek grey, cheap casket."
Rebentisch: "grey"
Riebe: grey
Dennis David: No stated color

WHO SAW THE "SHIPPING" CASKET AND WHEN

Dennis David: "I was there with the casket when it was off-loaded." "I didn't lift the body or anything ... I don't remember the exact time ... That was the shipping casket ... It was a typical shipping casket. Just like the ones we used to ship men back from Vietnam." (a: June 6, 1991)

Dennis David believes that the casket he saw brought in was a shipping casket and that it contained Kennedy's body before Jackie arrived. He was on the second floor of the rotunda and saw the helicopter arrive with a shipping casket. He said it was offloaded from a helicopter and taken over to the back door in a hearse. He says he thinks (but does not know) the bronze casket was empty.

Says that Boswell told him that JFK was in a shipping casket. (a: Dec. 17, 1991)

Rebentisch said "We were out there an awful long time" from the time he heard ("4 or 5 o'clock") that the body was coming. It was dark when it came. "It was still light when we went out there."

AP story of Jan 24, 1981, says that Rebentisch said that the coffin came in through a rear freight entrance 30 to 40 minutes before the bronze coffin arrived.

Jenkins did not get a close look at the casket, as he was in the morgue. (a: May 14, 1991)

Metzler was alone with Paul preparing the autopsy room. He went out on the platform to receive the coffin and does not recall Paul being there when he came back in with the "bronze" casket. (a: June 1, 1991)

O'Connor: "I was fortunate enough to work in a funeral home as a teenager, so I had my wits still in hand. I noticed things there that people never noticed at all. Just like, uh, the type of casket he came in. It wasn't the casket that went on Air Force 1." (a: Apr. 19, 1990)

"The body was in the shipping casket. When I say shipping casket, I use that figuratively because any casket can be a shipping casket. This is a kind of casket that was very cheap, and that isn't ornate. And, uh, the casket that went on Air Force 1 was, had gothic corners, it was very ornate ... It was the big, grey, sleek grey, cheap casket." (a: Apr. 19, 1990)

"... Six or seven men carrying this casket in and set it in the floor next to the table, the autopsy table. As I remember, this casket was the type of casket that was a cheap shipping casket. What I mean by a shipping casket is that it's not a very ornamental casket; it's not very expensive or it's a very plain casket." (*The Men Who Killed Kennedy*, BBC-TV, 10-25-88)

Donald Rebentisch, a Petty Officer studying dental and medical equipment repair at the hospital at the time: "It was a typical Navy gray shipping coffin. Just exactly as we expected. I helped take it out of the hearse. But then somebody else came and took it upstairs ... We put it on a gurney and wheeled it in." (UPI story of Jan. 25, 1981 in the *Miami Herald*; see also AP story of Jan. 24, 1981 in the Ft. Worth *Star Telegram*) "It was bout 4:30 when our chief petty officer came to me and about five other petty officers and told us to go to the back of the hospital. I'm talking about the loading ramps where they used to bring in supplies ... He told all of us that we were going to be there and we were going to bring the President's casket into the mortuary. We were told not to leave our posts. The chief said we got all the ghouls and reporters and the TV and everybody at the front of the hospital. He said there would be an empty casket in the ambulance. He said the President's body would really come in the back. We took the casket out ... and pushed it down a long, illuminated hall. Now this is a service area, not the main part of the hospital."

Rebentisch did not see the body. "There was no bronze ceremonial casket come in the back door when I was there ... it was a grey metal aluminum-type shipping casket. That I remember." (a: May 27, 1991)

Rebentisch said the casket came in 20 minutes (at least) before the Kennedy party. Said his duty officer got about six of the men from the barracks when he learned the body was coming in at 5 o'clock or so. An Army captain was in charge of them. He was in charge of the color guard.

AP story of Jan. 24, 1981, says that Rebentisch said that the coffin came in through a rear freight entrance 30 to 40 minutes before the bronze coffin arrived.

Floyd Riebe: "It was a shipping casket." (a: Apr. 2, 1991)

O'Connor never saw the bronze casket. (a: Apr. 19, 1990)

O'Connor: In response to the question, "Now you don't think that there's any way that you could have made a mistake about the shipping casket?" he replied, "Absolutely not. I swear on my grave. . . . And Dennis David remembers the exact same casket. See, I thought I was the only person that ever saw the difference."

"Yeah."

"See, the reason I know what it was, was because I used to work in a funeral home when I was 14 years old. And one of my jobs was to clean off caskets all of the time."

"Yeah."

"And put people in them and that sort of thing."

"Right."

"And I said 'that was just a grey shipping casket,' and I went to a funeral director here in town and we talked. He's been in the business for four years. And he says, 'Yes, I remember the same casket you're talking about, if you're talking about the ornate casket that Aubrey Rike put him in, and when we got it. You're talking about a Mercedes and a Chevrolet, okay?' "

"That's how you grade caskets, that's how they work. I knew exactly what it looked like." (a 5-9-90)

THE "SHIPPING CASKET" STORY

A document discovered by Patrick Boyles surfaced, which originated at Gawlers Funeral Home in Washington, and was passed around at the 1992 Dallas A.S.K. conference. The document had a handwritten notation on it which read "Body removed from metal shipping casket at USNH at Bethesda." Joe Hagan, the president of Gawlers, wrote this himself. (Interview with Kathlee Fitzgerald and the author, March 31, 1993.) Hagan explained that the confusion is over semantics. He told me that the use of the term "casket" cannot be confused with what bodies are normally shipped in, such as a Zigler case, an air tray, a combination casket, or a "shipping *container*" which he said is what the military normally ships a body in. He stated that it would always be called a "container" in that case, and is not considered a casket, nor would it be called a casket.

Hagan went on to say that "The only reason we used that phrase was to identify the casket as a casket and as metal." He said that noone at Gawlers saw the body come out of any casket, nor was anyone from the funeral home there when the body arrived, but came much later, so they had no knowledge of it. He wrote the notation about a shipping casket because this is what he was told the body came in from Dallas. He said that noone would have called it a casket if it had been a shipping container or anything else, and that a casket is only called a casket if it is for viewing. (See Medical Encyclopedia Appendix for witnesses and events regarding the shipping casket.)

THE BLACK HEARSE

THE ARRIVAL OF THE SHIPPING CASKET

Dennis David: "I called the dental school and the medical school barracks" for help to receive the casket. He was Chief of the Day.

4:00 or 5:00 P.M.: Rebentisch said it was 4 or 5 o'clock and they were told to go in back and wait. It was still light when he went out back to wait. "Oh, yes!" he answered to the question if it was light.

4:30 P.M.: Rebentisch: "It was about 4:30 when our chief petty officer came to me and about five other petty officers and told us to go to the back of the hospital." (UPI story of Jan. 25, 1981 in the *Miami Herald*, see also AP story of January 24, 1981 in the Ft. Worth *Star Telegram*)

After 5:30 P.M. Rebentisch said, "We were out there an awful long time" from the time he heard ("4 or 5 o'clock") that the body was coming. It was dark when it came. That would have been after 5:30 P.M. "It was still light when we went out there." (a: May 27, 1991)

6:10 P.M.-6:45 P.M. Rebentisch doesn't know how long he waited but Rebentisch said the casket came in 20 minutes (at least) before the Kennedy party. (a: May 27, 1991)

AP story of Jan. 24, 1981, says that Rebentisch said that the coffin came in through a rear freight entrance 30 to 40 minutes before the bronze coffin arrived. The statements regarding the arrival of Mrs. Kennedy and her party is between 6:50 P.M. and 7:05 P.M. Given Rebentisch's times of 20 to 40 minutes prior to this, the black hearse would have arrived between 6:10 P.M at the earliest, and 6:45 P.M at the latest.

Dennis David said a helicopter had landed ". . . shortly before Mrs. Kennedy's entourage came in and all this was *after* we had off-loaded that black hearse." (a: June 4, 1991) Mrs. Kennedy's arrival time, according to the record and witness statements was between 6:50 P.M and 7:05 P.M.

Donald Rebentisch saw a 1958 black Chevy hearse. (a: May 27, 1991)

Dennis David: "It came in a black ambulance. I called it a hearse, yeah."

WHO WAS WITH THE BLACK HEARSE?

On the hearse drivers, Dennis David said: "They wore slacks and short sleeve O. R. (Operating Room) tops or smocks. Waist-like pullover tops. Just two guys. In back were five, six or seven guys in suits and ties . . . I never touched it. I never left the passageway door." (a: June 4, 1991)

Dennis David: ". . . shortly before Mrs. Kennedy's entourage came in and all this was after we had off-loaded that black hearse."

"You are absolutely certain in your own mind that you already had the body?"

"Oh, no question about it." (a: June 4, 1991)

Donald Rebentisch saw a 1958 black Chevy hearse. He helped unload the casket. He said two other cars came in with the hearse. No lights on. No uniformed military men with the three vehicles. "I assumed they were all Secret Service. First it backed in, and then turned around and drove straight in. The men went down the ramp. There was a lot of pushing and shoving all over to try and get a hold of that casket, and so I just stepped back, and then from there, if I remember right, they had some sort of a wheeled gurney. They put it on that gurney and wheeled it up the stairs and I never seen it again." (a: May 27, 1991)

"There were no civilians with that hearse?" "Oh, there were all kinds. I assumed they were Secret Service. There were two other cars that came in with it. They were four-door cars. They all came in with no lights on. There was no escort with them. I didn't see anybody in uniform." (a: May 27, 1991)

Dennis David: "No, no, no. It was not a color guard. I received a call to get a detail to off-load the ambulance. I called the dental school and the medical school barracks." He was Chief of the Day, the senior enlisted man. He later retired as a Lt. Commander. This was the "Air Force major."

Rebentisch remembers the color guard captain, and said he died a week later from the strain.

Dennis David: "I was there with the casket when it was off-loaded." "I didn't lift the body or anything ... I don't remember the exact time." "Was that the shipping casket or the bronze coffin" "That was the shipping casket." "It was a typical shipping casket. Just like the ones we used to ship men back from Vietnam." (a: June 4, 1991)

CASKETS SET DOWN IN THE COOLER ROOM

Custer said the casket was put down in the anteroom and removed from the casket there. (a: Nov. 22, 1991) He said it went directly into the autopsy room. (a: Sept. 9, 1991)

4:00 P.M.: Reed said, "Around 4 P.M. we were called into the office again and told that there was a good possibility that we would be doing the autopsy on President Kennedy anytime between 4 and 6 ... I took a GE 225 portable unit down to the morgue in case we needed it and went off to the mess hall for dinner. There were four of us on duty, the supervisor, and three junior technologists." (Rt. Image, Nov. 21, 1988)

Jenkins: "All that happened in the anteroom where the cold boxes are." Jenkins says it was put down in the cooler room and taken out of the casket there and came in on a gurney. "When the body came into the morgue, it came in on a stretcher wrapped in sheets. There was a casket already in there when this one came in." (a: Mar. 25, 1991)

"He (Kennedy) was taken out of the casket in the atrium before we went into the morgue. As you came into the morgue there was a little room that had the cold boxes. He was in that and logged and tagged with a toe tag there. But he was taken out of that and brought in on a gurney all wrapped in sheets. The body bag was already open. We put him on the table and we were *told not to take the towels off his head.* We did unwrap him and we did the body work. (a: Oct. 8, 1990)

When the President's body came in, Jim Jenkins did not help take it out of the casket. He saw it come into the morgue on the gurney wrapped in sheets. "It came out of the casket in the cold room. Paul was in the (cold) anteroom." Jenkins says Paul *did* help take it out of the casket, (a: May24, 1991) but Jenkins did not get a close look at the casket, as he was in the morgue.

Another time, O'Connor said that Jenkins was wrong about it being set down in the cooler room. He said the FBI men were wrong about this too.

PRESENCE OF THE BODY OF AN OFFICER AND THE SHIPPING CASKET

AIR FORCE MAJOR

Jim Jenkins is the primary source saying that there was another casket in the cold room with the body of an Air Force major. He was not permitted to log it in, which he thought was out of order.

3:30 P.M.- on: Jenkins was not allowed to leave the room, except once when Captain Stover told him to eat his lunch. He was only gone a few moments. (a: Mar. 25, 1991)

Jenkins said, "I remember a nice casket coming in. We were told that we had an Army or Air Force major for burial the next day, which is kind of unusual. We were told not to worry about logging him in, and that was extremely unusual." (a: Oct. 8, 1990)

3:30 P.M. or later: Jenkins was asked, "Was the body in the casket?"

"Yes. *It wasn't taken out of the casket* and put in a cold box. It sat on a pop-up cart in the cold room, not in a cold box and *that's where it remained.*"

He said it had to be after 3:30, "when the other kid went off duty. I remember it coming in. It was Paul's and my job to log it in, but they wouldn't let us log it in." Jim said that he did not actually see the body in the casket, as it was not opened. (a: May 24, 1991)

Jim said that along with them was a First Class (E-6) hospital corpsman as the duty corpsman that night. "He was First Class and he was one of the few First Class in that position. He was an instructor in the School of Laboratory Sciences, and worked in special chemistry. He was in *there the early part of that night.* He was there when the major came in. He told me not to log the body in. Said he had been told not to log it in."

He said that the casket the Air Force major's body was in was a "nice casket," rosewood or red mahogany. It was not a *cheap casket.* It had brass fixtures.'' During another interview, he said it was mahogany, with ornate brass fixtures. "It was a beaut." (a: May 24, 1991)

"He came in at least an hour before. Maybe more." But the casket of the alleged officer came in after they had started to prepare for the President's autopsy. "It was not there when we came on."

"It was not there when you came on?"

"No. When a body came into the morgue, we had to log it in, Paul and me." (a: June 16, 1991)

Speaking again about being stopped from logging the body of the Air Force officer in, Jenkins said, "It was highly irregular. The military was real emphatic about that. Everybody had to be logged in. I mean, you got a body, it had to be tagged immediately. It had to be logged. They didn't ever. They said don't worry about logging him in."

"Did you see the body in that casket?"

"No, I did not."

"I can definitely tell you that there was an ornate type casket already in the laboratory when the President came in."

"How about the bronze casket?"

"That type, whatever it was. It was already there." He was in the morgue and "the doors were open and I could see them come into the cold room." He saw the ornate casket and asked about it. He was told it was the Air Force major. "Do we need to log him into the morgue log?"

"No," he was told. "They said it was too late to take him to Arlington that afternoon. They'd take him over in the morning." (a: May 29, 1991)

SHIPPING CASKET BODY

Dennis David believes that the casket he saw brought in was a shipping casket and that it had Kennedy's body before Jackie arrived. He was on the second floor of the rotunda and saw the helicopter arrive with a shipping casket. Said it was offloaded from a helicopter and taken over to the back door in a hearse. (a: May 29, 1991)

Jenkins believed that the major came in a shipping casket. "In a body bag wrapped in sheets and towels. The coffin was there at the same time as Kennedy. They had apparently put him with Kennedy in that coffin. But all of that was done in the atrium there." (a 10-8-90)

6:17-6:35 P.M. or earlier: When asked about the other body that was received that afternoon, November 22, 1963, Jenkins had previously said that he was told it was the body of an Air Force major. "It came in earlier in the evening, after I arrived from classes. It came in about the time we first went to the morgue. I'm sure it was at least an hour before JFK came in. Maybe quite a bit more." (a: Oct. 8, 1990)

Rudnicki had a vague recollection of a pick-up of the remains of someone else just before Kennedy's body arrived. (a: Oct. 14, 1990)

Custer said that there was a shipping casket in the morgue, but he had no knowledge of the President's body being in it. He said that there was a body of an officer there, in a body bag and in a shipping casket. (a: 10-8-90: repeated on Sept. 23, 1991) Custer: "There was another casket there. It was closed." "With an officer in it?" "Yes." "Was he in a cold box?" "Not that I can see." (a: Sept. 23, 1991)

SEEING JACKIE

Rudnicki: "There seems to be some controversy as to when Jackie actually arrived at the hospital. I remember seeing her—I peeked my head out—the entourage coming down the corridor. I remember looking out and I remember seeing her, and for some reason he (Lifton) seems to think she wasn't even there at the time I supposedly saw her. So I don't understand that one. I don't see these people every day, so I'm sure it wasn't something that happened previously."

He said that he thought the body of the President had not been there when he first saw her coming down the corridor. "She preceded it in?"

"That's correct." Lifton did not mention Rudnicki's testimony to him in his book.

Jerrol Custer insists that he was on the way to go upstairs to develop the second or third set of X-rays when Jackie came in the front door in her bloodstained dress. Many people, among whom were many photographers and reporters were at the front door.

7:00 pm: Jerrol Custer says that the body had to have come about seven. But he says that he was then asked to leave the morgue with Reed, and that he was brought back sometime after 8 P.M. and found that they had already made the Y incision. (a: Sept. 23, 1991) The record indicates that the Y incision was done either after 8:00 P.M. or 8:15 P.M. If he is right, there is an enormous amount of lying going on by the doctors.

However, Custer has made conflicting statements regarding the time of the arrival of the body. Custer has repeatedly said that he had already taken some of his X-rays and was taking a set of films up to be developed when he encountered the entrance of Mrs. Kennedy and her entourage in the Rotunda. He places the real arrival of the body at least a half-hour before she came. (a: Sept. 23, 1991) The record reflects Mrs. Kennedy arriving at Bethesda between 6:50 P.M.-7:05 pm. This would mean, according to Custer's statement, that the body arrived between 6:20 P.M and 6:35 pm. Custer's sighting of Mrs. Kennedy after he had already taken X-rays of her husband's body is completely contradicted by his statements that he did not take those X-rays for about an hour after the body came. (a: Sept. 23, 1991) This would place Mrs. Kennedy arriving at the front of Bethesda at 7:20 pm-7:35 pm. and that did not happen. Custer also told Warren Patton (12-2-88) that he started taking X-rays at 6:45 P.M. which, according to his other statements, would place the body arriving around 5:45 pm, and Mrs. Kennedy arriving at 6:15 P.M. at the earliest. Again, this is not consistent with the record of her arrival.

Dennis David believes that the casket he saw brought in was a shipping casket and that it contained Kennedy's body before Jackie arrived. He was on the second floor of the rotunda and saw the helicopter arrive with a shipping casket. He said it was off-loaded from a helicopter and taken over to the back door in a hearse. He thinks (but does not know) the bronze casket was empty.

He also says that Boswell told him that JFK was in a shipping casket. (a: Dec. 17, 1991)

Dennis David wrote Joanne Braun: "As to my observations of Mrs. Kennedy, I watched her enter through the main doors, cross the lobby (rotunda) and enter the elevators directly beneath me. Several dignitaries, including Secretary McNamara, followed Mrs. Kennedy by a few feet. I do remember watching the elevator indicator to know that it went directly to the VIP suite on the 17th floor." (Letter from David to Braun, Sept. 1991)

O'Connor was asked direct questions about whether or not he thought he had the body before Jackie arrived, and he skated around it. This is probably because he honestly could not know that, other than the rumor or what he had been told by others that she came after the body did. He just doesn't answer. (a: Apr. 19, 1990) After all, he thinks the body did not get there until 8 P.M.

Rebentisch said the casket came in 20 minutes (at least) before the Kennedy party. (a: May 27, 1991) Said his duty officer got about six of the men from the barracks when he learned the body was coming in at 5 o'clock or so. An Army captain was in charge of them. He was in charge of the color guard. "We were just thrown off by that. They were going to draw the ghouls to Wisconsin Avenue. Everything was not organized real well. After the casket came in, I thought we could leave, and I went up to the front of the hospital to my normal duty station. He said that later, he was standing in the rotunda when Mrs. Kennedy and her party came in. "We were just flabbergasted. My duty officer said, 'Hey Red, you aren't supposed to be here.' 'Well, damn it, the body is already in.' 'You have to stay in the back until that Army captain releases you.' Then there was a lot of talk about the autopsy. They were all throwing up from the autopsy, and what not. Kennedy was very popular with the military." (a: May 27, 1991)

KEY TO SOURCES

a = Witness interviews conducted by Harrison Livingstone.

b = Daily Staff Journal/Duty Officer's Log, Military District of Washington headquarters, November 22, 1963.

c = "After Action Report—President John F. Kennedy's Funeral," Report to Commanding General, MDW, Washington.

d = "Memorandum for the Record," Samuel Bird to Commanding General, MDW, November 27, 1963.

e = "After Action Report/Summary," Gen. Wehle's Office, MDW, November 22, 1963.

f = "Questioning the Facts: Research v. Witness," Francis X O'Neill, Team Video Productions, 1992 (video).

g = "I. Alert and Initial Action" concerning the events of November 22, 1963, by Escort Officer to the Commanding General.

h = "Autopsy of the Body of President John F. Kennedy," FBI Autopsy Report File #89–30 by Agents James W. Sibert & Francis X. O'Neill, Bethesda Field Office, 11/26/63.

i = Manchester, William, *Death of a President,* Harper & Row, 1967.

j = Bishop, Jim, *The Day Kennedy Was Shot,* Funk & Wagnalls, New York, 1968.

H = Hearings of the WC (Warren Commission).

HSCA = House Select Committee on Assassinations.

WR = Warren Report

INDEX